STUDIES IN THE THEORY OF

INTERNATIONAL TRADE

Also Published in

Reprints of Economic Classics

BY JACOB VINER

DUMPING [1923]
GUIDE TO JOHN RAE'S LIFE OF ADAM SMITH [1965]

STUDIES
IN THE THEORY OF
INTERNATIONAL TRADE

BY

JACOB VINER

Professor of Economics, University of Chicago

AUGUSTUS M. KELLEY • PUBLISHERS

CLIFTON 1975

First Edition 1937

(New York: Harper & Brothers, Publishers, 1937)

Reprinted 1965 and 1975 by

Augustus M. Kelley Publishers

Clifton New Jersey 07012

By arrangement with Jacob Viner

Library of Congress Cataloged.
The original printing of this title as follows:

Viner, Jacob, 1892–
   Studies in the theory of international trade. New York,
A. M. Kelley, 1965.

   xv, 650 p. illus. 21 cm. (Reprints of economic classics)

   "Original edition 1937."
   Bibliography : p. 602–631.

   1. Commerce. 2. Commercial policy. 3. Economics.   I. Title.
II. Title : International trade.

[HF1007]   382.01   65–20928/CD

ISBN 0–678–00122–7

To
F. W. TAUSSIG,
Teacher and Friend

Contents

Preface

In this book I first endeavor to trace, in a series of studies of the contemporary source-material, the evolution of the modern "orthodox" theory of international trade, from its beginnings in the revolt against English mercantilism in the seventeenth and eighteenth centuries, through the English currency and tariff controversies of the nineteenth century, to its present-day form. I then proceed to a detailed examination of current controversies in the technical literature centering about important propositions of the classical and neo-classical economists relating to the theory of the mechanism of international trade and the theory of gain from trade. The annual flow of literature in this field has become so great in the last few years, and the claims on my time and energy from other unfortunately unavoidable activities of a quite divergent sort have been so heavy, that the completion of this book and the rendering of full justice to the recent literature have proved to be incompatible objectives. I hereby present my sincere apologies to the substantial number of economists who have in recent years made valuable contributions to the theory of international trade which are here either wholly neglected or treated more summarily than they deserve.

This book is not presented as a rival to, or substitute for, the excellent textbooks on the theory of international trade which are at last available. The main contributions of a good textbook are usually its contribution to general synthesis of doctrine, its illustrative material, and its restatement in compact, simplified, and systematic form of materials familiar to scholars. My objectives have been, rather, to resurrect forgotten or overlooked material worthy of resurrection, to trace the origin and development of the doctrines which were later to become familiar, and to examine the claims to acceptance of familiar doctrine. Since, until recent years, it was at first almost solely English writers, and later almost solely English and American writers, who were responsible for the development of the theory along the classical lines, there is but little reference to writings by Continental economists antedating the War. While my main objective in writing this book

xiii

was that it should prove a useful supplement, for both teachers and students, to the textbooks on the theory of international trade, I hope that the extensive discussion of early monetary theories will make it of interest also to students of monetary and banking theory.

Acknowledgments are due to the University of Chicago Press and to the editors and publishers of *Weltwirtschaftliches Archiv* for their kind permission to include in this book the material which appeared in my articles "English theories of foreign trade before Adam Smith," *Journal of Political Economy,* XXXVIII (1930), 249-310, 404-57, and "The doctrine of comparative costs," *Weltwirtschaftliches Archiv,* XXXVI (1932, II), 356-414. Both articles, however, and especially the latter, have been substantially revised, recast, and extended, in the process of incorporation in this book.

My heaviest intellectual indebtedness is to Professor F. W. Taussig, who first aroused my interest in the field of international trade as long ago as 1914, who has done much by his writings and oral discussion to sustain it since and to set the mold for my thinking, and to whose teachings I have remained faithful in my imperfect fashion. As a gesture of gratitude in this connection, I have taken the liberty of dedicating the book to him. To Professor Bertil Ohlin's persistent refusal willingly to accept the same mold for his thinking in this field, and to his consequent persistent refusal to agree with me, I am also greatly indebted, for it has forced me repeatedly to think problems through more thoroughly than I would otherwise have done, and to revise—and perhaps even upon occasion to abandon—doctrines to which I was disposed to cling as long as it was still possible to do so without violating the intellectual decencies. I am greatly indebted also to a long line of able and sceptical students, who have pointed out my errors to me in the hope, not always realized, that I would find ways of correcting them. I am especially indebted to the following students, past and present, who have at one time or another accepted the responsibility of assisting me in checking my references, in meeting the physical burden of using libraries, and in keeping my errors of fact and analysis within the accustomed limits of tolerance: Leroy D. Stinebower, Michael L. Hoffman, Virginius F. Coe, Henry J. Wadleigh, Lily M. David, Benjamin F. Brooks, Arthur I. Bloomfield. The charts were drawn for me by Y. K. Wong, who has once more been patient with my mathematical ineptitude while refusing to make concessions to it. My thanks are due also to the Social Science Research Committee of the University of Chicago, who provided the funds which enabled me to recruit the aid of these students and also furnished the typing facilities.

JACOB VINER.

STUDIES IN THE THEORY OF

INTERNATIONAL TRADE

Chapter I

ENGLISH THEORIES OF FOREIGN TRADE, BEFORE ADAM SMITH: I

All antient or scarce Pieces may justly be esteem'd curious and valuable, either on account of their own intrinsick Perfection, or out of respect to the great Names which they go under or purely on account of their relation to the Times and nice Conjectures in which they were compos'd: and tho mean and inconsiderable in the stile and manner of writing, in comparison with some modern Composures, may yet deserve to be perpetuated and transmitted to Posterity, if they manifestly discover the Seeds and Principles from which the greatest Events, and perhaps Revolutions in Church and State, have taken their rise. These Characters, singly or all together, have been our Rule in the present Collection.—The Phenix: or, A Revival of Scarce and Valuable Pieces No where to be found but in the Closets of the Curious, II (1708), preface, iii-iv.

1. INTRODUCTION

A study of the theories of foreign trade before Adam Smith must of necessity consist of an examination of the mercantilist doctrines with respect to foreign trade and of the contemporary criticisms thereof. It is a common impression that they have already been sufficiently studied, but the economic historians and the economists of the German historical school have been almost alone in studying the mercantilists, and they have generally been more interested in the facts than in the ideas of the mercantilist period, have often based sweeping generalizations as to the character of mercantilist doctrine on what they found in a handful of the mercantilist writings, have displayed neither interest in, nor acquaintance with, modern economic theorizing with respect to monetary and trade process, and have almost without exception shown a tendency to defend the mercantilist doctrines by reasoning itself of decidedly mercantilist flavor. The severe critics of mercantilist doctrine have generally been economic theorists of the

English classical-school tradition, and they have usually relied on Adam Smith's account plus the vague mass of nineteenth-century tradition for their information as to the contents of mercantilist doctrine.

The present study, is therefore, primarily an inventory of the English ideas, good and bad, with respect to trade prevalent before Adam Smith, classified and examined in the light of modern monetary and trade theory. Its aim is rather to discover and explain the divergencies of doctrine than to formulate inclusive and simple formulas descriptive of mercantilist doctrine *en masse*, formulas which are almost necessarily half-truths at best or empty. It is based on a careful study of such of the actual economic literature of the period as was available to me, and its findings will be supported by as much of the evidence derived from that literature, in the form of quotations and references, as space limitations permit.

No attempt will be made to compare in detail the results of this investigation with the findings of other modern commentators on English mercantilism, but those who are sufficiently interested to make such comparisons for themselves will find, I believe, that the differences as to fact and interpretation are numerous and of some importance, and that new information is presented on a number of points.[1] To keep the study within manageable proportions, the doctrines of the period with respect to the fisheries,

---

[1] A. Dubois, *Précis de l'histoire des doctrines économiques,* 1903, and Br. Suviranta, *Theory of the balance of trade in England,* 1923, were helpful, although I cannot accept many of the latter writer's interpretations and appraisals. Except for a few special studies to which reference is made at appropriate points no other secondary studies were of much help to me. E. Lipson, *Economic history of England* (3 vols., 1929-1931, and especially vol. III [1931], Ch. IV, "The mercantile system"), appeared after this study had been published in its original form. It contains a great mass of valuable material and relates the doctrines to the historical conditions much more completely and authoritatively than I could do. Lipson in the main presents a defense of the mercantilist doctrines against their modern critics, although more moderately than is usual for economic historians. To me most of his defense appears insubstantial, or unsubstantiated by the evidence, or irrelevant, and I have not felt obliged to modify my appraisal because of what he has written. It seems to me especially that he relies too strongly on citations from a few contemporary critics of the prevailing views, such as Davenant, Barbon and North, and from writers after 1690, as evidence of what was prevailing doctrine from say 1550 to 1750. E. Heckscher has recently published in Swedish a two-volume account of the mercantilist doctrines on the Continent as well as in England (*Merkantilismen,* Stockholm, 1931, 2 vols.) whose English translation (*Mercantilism,* 1935, 2 vols.) became available too late to permit of my profiting extensively from it in the revision of my orig-

population, and colonies will be ignored even when they are closely related to the general foreign-trade theories.

II. "MERCANTILISM" AND "BULLIONISM"

In the English economic literature prior to Adam Smith, the most pervasive and the most emphasized doctrine is the importance of having an excess of exports over imports. To this doctrine and the trade regulations which it inspired, Adam Smith, following the usage of some of the Physiocrats,[1] gave the name of the "commercial" or "mercantile" system, which later became, with the aid of the Germans, the now familiar "mercantilism."[2] Many writers, however, assign "mercantilism" only to the period after about 1620, and distinguish with varying degrees of emphasis between the "bullionist" doctrines of the earlier period and the "balance-of-trade" doctrines of the later period. The grounds most commonly given for distinguishing between the two periods are as follows: (1) that, before 1620, stress was put on the importance of a favorable balance in each transaction of each merchant, whereas in the later period the emphasis was on the aggregate or national balance of trade; (2) that, before 1620, concern about the state of the individual balances was due to anxiety that the country's stock of bullion be *not reduced*, whereas in the later period there was anxiety that it be *increased*; (3) that, before 1620, the chief economic objective of trade policy was to protect the national currency against exchange depreciation, whereas after 1620 this was a minor objective, if a matter of concern at all; (4) that, in the early period, the means advocated and employed to carry out the objectives of the prevailing trade

---

inal study. It is a work of the highest quality on both the historical and the theoretical sides, and I am happy to find that where we are dealing with the same topics there is no substantial conflict of interpretation or appraisal. I have reviewed Heckscher's book in *The economic history review*, VI (1935), 99-101.

[1] Cf. Oncken, article on Quesnay, *Handwörterbuch der Staatswissenschaft*, 2d ed., 1901, VI, 280.

[2] If Adam Smith intended the name to be used as a contrast to the physiocratic system, he had considerable justification. Just as the physiocrats claimed that agriculture alone (or extractive industry alone) was productive, so many of the English mercantilists claimed that foreign trade was the only source of wealth, and many of them, while not taking so extreme a position, arranged activities in the order of their contribution to the wealth of the country with foreign trade in the first rank.

policy were close regulation of the transactions of particular individuals in the exchange market and in coin and bullion, while in the later period the policy recommended and put into practice was to seek the objective of a greater stock of bullion indirectly by means of regulation of trade rather than directly through restrictions on exchange transactions and on the export of coin and bullion.

The actual course of official policy seems to give no strong support to this chronological contrast between the bullionist and the balance-of-trade doctrines. In the earlier period, it is true, regulation of the foreign trade and exchange transactions of the merchants had been stricter and more detailed than it subsequently became. But the outstanding changes in legislation and in administrative practice extended over a long period, and all of any importance occurred long before 1620 or did not occur until long after. The institution of the Staple, which served as an instrument of regulation of individual transactions, finally expired with the loss of Calais in 1558, although it had already been moribund. The Statutes of Employment, requiring foreign merchants to pay for the English commodities which they bought, in part at least, in coin or bullion, had become inoperative long before the end of the sixteenth century. The Royal Exchanger, with his control over exchange transactions, went out of existence practically, if not legally, when Burleigh, in the reign of Elizabeth, refrained from exercising his prerogative of nominating the holder of the office, although Charles I attempted unsuccessfully to revive the institution as late as 1628. The restrictions on the export of coin and bullion had been relaxed during the reign of Elizabeth. They were more strictly enforced, as far as gold was concerned, in the reign of James I, in accordance with a proclamation of 1603, but even stricter regulations were laid down by Charles I in 1628, and it was not until 1663 that gold and silver bullion and *foreign* coin could be freely exported, and not until 1819 that *English* coin or bullion derived therefrom could be legally exported. In other words, the "bullionist" regulations were either repealed or had become obsolete long before 1620, or persisted and even were strengthened long after 1620. Prohibitions and customs duties on imports and exports imposed for trade regulative purposes originated centuries before 1620, and although the customs system was revised during the reign of

James I, and again by Walpole in the 1720's, in order that it might more effectively serve the purpose of procuring a favorable balance of trade, it continued until late in the nineteenth century to be a medley of provisions of miscellaneous character serving in unascertainable proportions the largely contradictory purposes of fiscal needs, trade regulation, special privileges to favored individuals or groups, and foreign diplomacy.

If, however, the dividing line be set at about 1560, instead of about 1620, the contrast may be made with respect to actual trade regulation that such devices as the Staple, the Royal Exchanger, and the Statutes of Employment had been important in the first period, and were repealed or permitted to become inoperative in the later stage. For the earlier period also, it can be said that there was much more concern about the menace to the national stock of bullion from the operations of brokers and merchants in paper exchange than there was in the later period, and on this question 1620 serves fairly well as the approximate date at which doctrinal controversy cleared away many of the older illusions about the consequences of unregulated exchange transactions. No attempt will be made here to examine the bullionist reasoning with respect to the exchanges, of which an excellent summary has been given by Tawney.[3] In the controversy over the exchanges at the beginning of the seventeenth century, the new views which were expounded chiefly by Misselden and Mun won a definitive victory over the old views as presented by Malynes and Milles, and in the later literature a spokesman for the older views is only rarely to be encountered. Perhaps for the first time, a matter of economic policy was made the occasion for a war of tracts, and the tracts seem, moreover, to have exerted an immediate and traceable influence on government policy. But commentators who have not explored the earlier literature nor examined carefully the later literature have applied to the entire contents of these tracts what was true only, if at all, of their arguments with respect to paper exchanges, and have attributed to Misselden and Mun priority with respect to doctrines which were already old and established and to Malynes and Milles final utterance of doctrines which still had a long life to live.

---

[3] In his Introduction to his reprint of Thomas Wilson, *A discourse upon usury* [1572], 1925, pp. 60-86; 134-69. Cf. also E. R. A. Seligman, article on the Bullionists, *Encyclopaedia of social sciences,* III (1930), 60-64.

III. THE BALANCE-OF-TRADE DOCTRINE

The Concept and Its Application.[1]—The most pervasive feature of the English mercantilist literature was the doctrine that it was vitally important for England that it should have an excess of exports over imports, usually because that was for a country with no gold or silver mines the only way to increase its stock of the precious metals. The doctrine is of early origin, and some of the mercantilists, in the earlier period when it was still customary to scatter miscellaneous tags of classical wisdom through one's discourse, succeeded in finding Latin quotations which seemed to expound it. It was clearly enough stated as far back as 1381 by Richard Leicester, a mint official, in answer to an official inquiry as to the cause of, and remedy for, the supposed drain of gold out of England:

> First, as to this that no gold or silver comes into England, but that which is in England is carried beyond the sea, I maintain that it is because the land spends too much in merchandise, as in grocery, mercery and peltry, or wines, red, white and sweet, and also in exchanges made to the Court of Rome in divers ways. Wherefore the remedy seems to me to be that each merchant bringing merchandise into England take out of the commodities of the land as much as his merchandise aforesaid shall amount to; and that none carry gold or silver beyond the sea, as it is ordained by statute. . . . And so me-seems that the money that is in England will remain, and great quantity of money and bullion will come from the parts beyond the sea.[2]

---

[1] Cf. also Jacob Viner, article, "Balance of trade," *Encyclopaedia of the social sciences*, II (1930), 399-406; F. W. Fetter, "The term 'favorable balance of trade,'" *Quarterly journal of economics*, XLIX (1935), 621-30.

[2] Bland, Brown, and Tawney, *English economic history, select documents*, 1914, pp. 219-20. The concept here clearly implied of a *national* balance ("the *land* spends too much in merchandise") and the emphasis on *increase*, and not merely on prevention of reduction, of England's stock of money, support the contention made above that there has been exaggeration of the differences in doctrine between the so-called "bullionist" and "mercantilist" periods. Other officials, Aylesbury and Cranten, at the same time offered the same explanation of the loss of bullion. For Aylesbury, see *ibid.*, p. 222. For Cranten, see the original source, *Rotuli parliamentorum* [1381], III (1767), 127: "Quant a primr̄ article: Ne soit pluis despendu deinz le Roialme des Marchandies estraunges en value q̄ les Marchandies de la cresceance du Roialme issant hors de mesme le Roialme ne sont en value."

The following citations from sixteenth-century sources show that the doctrine was current throughout that century:

The whole wealth of the realm is for all our rich commodities to get out of all other realms therefor ready money; and after the money is brought in to the whole realm, so shall all people in the realm be made rich therewith.[3]

But it is an infallible argument that if we send yearly into beyond the seas one hundred thousand pounds worth of wares more than we receive yearly again, then must there needs be brought into this realm for the said hundred thousand pounds worth of wares so much in value either of gold or silver. . . . The only means to cause much bullion to be brought out of other realms unto the king's mints is to provide that a great quantity of our wares may be carried yearly into beyond the seas and less quantity of their wares be brought hither again.[4]

. . . for if England would spend less of foreign commodities, than the same [i.e., English] commodities will pay for, then the remain must of necessity be returned of silver or gold; but if otherwise, then it will fare in England in short time, as it doth with a man of great yearly living that spendeth more yearly than his own revenue and spendeth of the stock besides.[5]

If we keep within us much of our commodities, [because of heavy duty on wool exports] we must spare many other things that we have now from beyond the seas; for we must always take heed that we buy no more of strangers than we sell them; for so we should impoverish ourselves and enrich them.[6]

And another [object of policy] is that the things which we carry out do surmount in price the things which we bring in; else shall we soon make a poor land and a poor people.[7]

---

[3] [Clement Armstrong?] "A treatise concerning the staple and the commodities of this realme" [ms. *ca.* 1530], first printed in Reinhold Pauli, *Drei volkswirthschaftliche Denkschriften aus der Zeit Heinrichs VIII von England*, 1878, p. 32. Cf. also "Clement Armestrong's sermons and declaracions agaynst popish ceremonies" [ms. *ca.* 1530], *ibid.*, pp. 46-47; "How to reforme the realme in settyng them to worke and to restore tillage" [ms. *ca.* 1535], *ibid.*, pp. 60 ff., 76.

[4] "Polices to reduce this realme of Englande unto a prosperous wealthe and estate" [ms., 1549], Tawney and Power, *Tudor economic documents*, III (1924), 318, 321. This collection will henceforth be cited as *T.E.D.*

[5] "Considerations for the restraynte of transportinge gould out of the realme" [reign of Elizabeth], printed in Georg Schanz, *Englische Handelspolitik gegen Ende des Mittelalters*, 1881, II, 649.

[6] [John Hales] *A discourse of the common weal of this realm of England* [written, *ca.* 1550, first printed, 1581], Elizabeth Lamond ed., 1893, pp. 62-63.

[7] "A discourse of corporations" [*ca.* 1587], *T.E.D.*, III, 267. For additional statements of the balance-of-trade doctrine during the sixteenth century, see:

Although the concept of a national balance of trade was already common in the sixteenth century, the exact term itself seems to have first been coined in 1615, when it almost immediately passed into common usage.[8] In that year two customs officials, Wolstenholme and Cranfield, were instructed to compute the exports and imports for the two preceding years, in order to ascertain the effect on foreign trade of "Alderman Cockayne's Project" restricting the export of undyed or undressed woolens. The results of their computations are still extant in manuscript, indorsed as follows: "A computation of all merchandises exported and imported into England one year by Mr. Wolstenholme 21 May 1615" and "Sir Lionell Cranfield his balance of trade 21 May 1615."[9] In the next year, Sir Francis Bacon, who was acquainted in his official capacity with these computations, in his "Advice to Sir George Villiers" wrote as follows:

This realm is much enriched, of late years, by the trade of merchandise which the English drive in foreign parts; and, if it be wisely managed, it must of necessity very much increase the wealth thereof; care being taken, that the exportation exceed in value the importation; for then the balance of trade must of necessity be returned in coin or bullion.[10]

The first appearance in print of the phrase appears to have been in the title and text of a pamphlet by Misselden published in 1623, *The Circle of Commerce, or the Ballance of Trade*. It is to be found *ad nauseam* in the subsequent literature. The term was, of course, borrowed from the current terminology of bookkeep-

---

William Cholmeley, "The request and suite of a true-hearted Englishman" [ms., 1553], *The Camden miscellany*, II (1853), 11-12; "Memorandum prepared for the royal commission on the exchanges" [1564], *ibid.*, III, 353; "Memorandum by Cecil on the export trade in cloth and wool" [1564?], *ibid.*, II, 451; "D'Ewes' journal" (for 1593) [1693], *ibid.*, II, 242; "An apologie of the cittie of London," in John Stow, *A survey of London*, C. L. Kingsford ed., 1908, II, 210.

[8] I owe some of the following references to the excellent account by W. H. Price, "The origin of the phrase 'balance of trade,'" *Quarterly journal of economics*, XX (1905), 157 ff.

[9] Astrid Friis, *Alderman Cockayne's project and the cloth trade*, 1927, p. 207, and W. H. Price, *loc. cit.* There were no value statistics of imports and exports at that time, but the customs rates on all goods were 5 per cent of the official values of the goods. The balance was computed, therefore, by multiplying the customs revenues by twenty.

[10] *Works*, 1852, II, 385. (The essay was written in 1616, but first published in 1661.)

ing, into which the word "balance" had apparently been incorporated from the Italian about 1600. Prior to 1615, such terms as "overplus,"[11] "remayne,"[12] "overvallue"[13] were used to signify the excess of exports over imports, or vice versa, and Malynes,[14] in 1601, and Cotton in 1609,[15] used the term "overballancing" for the same purpose. A memorandum of 1564 spoke of exports sufficient "to answer the foreign commodities" to mean exports adequate to balance the imports,[16] and John Stow in 1598 used "overplus" and "countervail" for the two meanings of "balance."[17] Nothing was invented or discovered in 1615 except the precise term "balance of trade." There is no evidence that when in that year attempts were made to compute the actual balance any person regarded it as the application of a novel idea. Misselden, in 1623, did write of "this balance of trade, an excellent and politic invention, to shew us the difference of weight in the commerce of one kingdom with another,"[18] but what he regarded as novel was not the notion of a balance but its actual measurement in the absence of periodic trade statistics such as those with which we are now familiar. Malynes did criticize Misselden's balance-of-trade argument, but not because the notion of a balance between exports and imports was unfamiliar or objectionable to him, for he had himself stressed the concept years before. What Malynes was criticizing was the overemphasis which Misselden was giving to the mere computation of the actual balance, since "the conceited balance of trade proposed by Misselden, can be but a trial and discovery of the overbalancing of trade, without that it can

---

[11] "Polices to reduce this realme" [1549], *T.E.D.*, III, 324.

[12] "Considerations for the restraynte of transportinge goulde" [time of Elizabeth], Schanz, *op. cit.*, II, 649.

[13] "Memorandum prepared for the royal commission on the exchanges" [1564], *T.E.D.*, III, 353.

[14] Gerard Malynes, *A treatise of the canker of England's commonwealth* [1601], *T.E.D.*, III, 386.

[15] Sir Robert Cotton, "The manner and meanes" [1609], in *Cottoni Posthuma*, 1672, p. 196.

[16] "Memorandum by Cecil on the export trade in cloth and wool," *T.E.D.*, II, 45.

[17] "Apologie of the cittie of London" [1598], in Stow, *A survey of London*, Kingsford ed., 1908, II, 210.

[18] *The circle of commerce*, 1623, p. 117. Misselden cites from an alleged manuscript an attempt made during the reign of Edward III to estimate the English balance of trade.—*Ibid.*, p. 118.

produce any other benefit to the commonwealth,"[19] and in any case, was likely to be highly inaccurate.[20]

The term "favorable balance of trade" now so common, and so commonly attributed to the mercantilists, seems first to have been used in 1767 by Sir James Steuart,[21] although the phrase "balance in our favor" had been used by Cary[22] in 1695, Pollexfen in 1697,[23] and Mackworth[24] in about 1720, and corresponding terms were used by many other writers.[25]

General and Partial Balances.—There is no historical basis for the distinction which some writers have tried to make between a balance-of-individual-bargains stage and a chronologically later general balance-of-trade stage in the evolution of mercantilist doctrine. Richard Jones coined the phrase "balance-of-bargain" in order to distinguish between means and not ends: "To effect their purposes, they [i.e., the early politicians] adopted a very complicated system, which we may call the *balance-of-bargain system*; and which, though its object was precisely the same with that of the balanace-of-trade system long subsequently established, yet sought to attain that object by very different means."[26] An influx of bullion resulting from an excess of exports over imports was the common objective both of the earlier and of the later period. To the extent that the methods advocated or actually applied to attain this end differed, it is more accurate to say that the early bullionist regulations dealt directly with the transactions in coin and bullion and foreign exchange, whereas the later cus-

---

[19] *The center of the circle of commerce*, 1623, pp. 68-69.

[20] *Ibid.*, pp. 58-59.

[21] *An inquiry into the principles of political œconomy*, 1767, II, 422: "when one nation is growing richer, others must be growing poorer; this is an example of a favorable balance of trade." Cf. also *ibid.*, II. 425-26. Steuart also used the terms "passive" and "active" for import and export surpluses, respectively. (*Ibid.*, II, 207.)

[22] John Cary, *An essay on the state of England in relation to its trade*, 1695, pp. 131-32; *ibid.*, *An essay on the coyn and credit of England*, 1696, p. 20.

[23] [John Pollexfen] *A discourse of trade, coyn, and paper credit*, 1697, p. 40.

[24] Sir Humphrey Mackworth, *A proposal for payment of the publick debts*, 2d ed., *ca.* 1720, p. 9.

[25] F. W. Fetter nevertheless considers it an anachronism to attribute the use of the terms "favorable" or "unfavorable" to the mercantilists. "The term 'favorable balance of trade,'" *Quarterly journal of economics*, XLIX (1935), 629.

[26] "Primitive political economy of England" [1847], in *Literary remains*, Whewell ed., 1859, p. 295.

toms regulations sought the same results indirectly by regulating the commodity imports and exports. No trace is to be found in the early literature of anything even approaching a theory of the importance of the individual balances except as items in a clearly conceived national balance and it is only as inference from the character of the bullionist regulations that the prevalence of the notion that such a theory was once expounded can be explained.

In some of the modern literature on mercantilism there is to be found an exposition of the evolution of the balance-of-trade doctrine in terms of *three* chronological stages: first, the individual bargain; then an intermediate stage in which the notion of the balance of trade with particular countries, but not the total balance of trade, had been grasped; and, finally, the emergence of the concept of the national or aggregate balance. This is all the product of vivid imagination. In the seventeenth and eighteenth centuries there was much controversy about the state of the balances with particular countries, but always with reference to their bearing on the aggregate balance. In the seventeenth century the state of the balance in the East India trade was the principal object of controversy in this connection; in the eighteenth century it was the balance with France which gave rise to most misgiving. The East Indian balance was indisputably "unfavorable," and the East India Company was attacked on this ground. Its spokesmen tried to meet the attack by the contention that, although the balance was immediately unfavorable, the East India trade had indirect effects, such as the reexport at a profit of commodities imported from India and the substitution of imports from India for imports to greater value from other countries, which made its net result, direct and indirect, a favorable instead of an unfavorable contribution to the total national balance.[27] It

---

[27] The argument was made by many who were not personally interested in the fortunes of the East India Company, and was accepted, in theory, by the critics of the company. The following citations are only to spokesmen for the company: Thomas Mun, *A discourse of trade, from England unto the East Indies* [1621], Facsimile Text Society reprint, 1930, pp. 9 ff.; *ibid., England's treasure by forraign trade* [first published 1664, written about 1630], Ashley ed., 1895, pp. 19 ff.; [Sir Thomas Papillon] *A treatise concerning the East-India trade being a most profitable trade to the kingdom* [1677], 1696 reprint, pp. 12 ff.; [Sir Josiah Child] *A treatise wherein is demonstrated that the East-India trade is the most national of all foreign trades,* 1681, pp. 6 ff.; [Child] *A discourse about trade,* 1690, p. 142; Charles Davenant, *An essay on the East-India trade* [1696], in *Works,* Charles Whitworth ed., I, 97; *Some considerations on the nature*

would be difficult to demonstrate such a theory to determined
critics, even if it were in accord with the facts, and when this
method of argument failed to be effective, the defenders of the
company, while still conceding in the abstract that any trade was
harmful if it did not contribute, directly or indirectly, to a favorable balance for the country, resorted to questioning the possibility of applying the test with sufficient accuracy to warrant the
condemnation of any trade.[28] When this argument also failed to
subdue criticism, the defenders of the company were finally driven
to questioning and even to explicitly rejecting the validity of the
balance-of-trade test, however qualified, as a measure of the value
of trade.[29] But none of the writers on either side of the controversy claimed that the particular balance of trade was to be
judged except in terms of its contribution to the total balance,

---

and importance of the East-India trade, 1728, pp. 30 ff. As representative instances of the acceptance of the argument by critics of the company who denied, however, that the company could meet the test even if indirect effects
were taken into consideration, there may be cited: [William Petyt?] *Britannia
languens* [1680], McCulloch ed., *Early English tracts on commerce,* 1856, pp.
342 ff.; [John Pollexfen] *England and East-India inconsistent in their manufactures,* 1697, p. 52.

[28] Cf. Charles Davenant, *Discourses on publick revenues* [1698], in *Works,*
I, 388: "It is hard to trace all the circuits of trade, to find its hidden recesses,
to discover its original springs and motions, and to shew what mutual dependence all traffics have one upon the other. And yet, whoever will categorically
pronounce that we get or lose by any business, must know all this, and besides,
have a very deep insight into many other things." Cf. Sir Leslie Stephen, *History of English thought in the eighteenth century,* 3d ed., 1902, II, 294, with
reference to Davenant's position: "Merchants easily assumed their own balances to be a sufficient test of the national prosperity, but when the theories
thus framed were applied to limit their own dealings and to prevent them from
importing the most advantageous articles of commerce, they naturally found
more or less ingenious modes of meeting the awkward inference. It was better, they admitted, to import gold than silk; but by some dexterous manipulation it must be shown that the importation of silk would enable them to get
more gold."

[29] Cf. Nicholas Barbon, *A discourse concerning coining the new money lighter,*
1696, p. 36: "And yet there is nothing so difficult, as to find out the balance of trade in any nation; or to know whether there ever was, or can be
such a thing as the making up the balance of trade betwixt one nation and
another; or to prove, if it could be found out, that there is anything got or
lost by the balance." *Ibid.,* p. 40: "But if there could be an account taken of
the balance of trade, I can't see where the advantage of it could be. For the
reason that's given for it, that the overplus is paid in bullion, and the nation
grows so much the richer, because the balance is made up in bullion, is altogether a mistake: for gold and silver are but commodities; and one sort of
commodity is as good as another, so it be of the same value."

to the Midas fable I have found in the lit...
is in a work sharply critical of the mercantili...
although unobjectionable definitions of weal...
they are usually offered by moderate or sk...
icisms of the prevailing views. "Riches," "w...
ambiguous meanings in the seventeenth and...
s. They meant money, jewels, and other esp...
modities at one moment, and all goods useful t...
pment. Very often this shift of meaning occ...
its of a single paragraph or even sentence, and...
ing, and obtaining what plausibility it has...
the meaning given to terms constitutes a larg...
ercantilist argument, and especially of the bal...
ine.

ntilists did not have in mind the possibility t...
make investments abroad or may borrow...
here is no mercantilist writer who explains his d...
ble balance of trade as a desire that his cou...
capital abroad rather than borrow abroad...
s disregarded, the one difference between an ex...
n import surplus is that there is a net exchang...
ney in the first case, and of money for good...
se. It is impossible, therefore, to understand s...
antilist arguments as that foreign trade was the...
nal wealth, that a country can gain from for...
it results in a favorable balance payable in bull...
t surplus is both the proof and the measure of g...
nd that an import surplus is both the proof and...
ational loss,[5] unless they believed, momentarily

octrine are, of course, mutually contradictory, and reflect
modern times of the confusion from which the original
...

essay on money & bullion, 1718, p. 15.
only mercantilist I have found who even cites the desira
abroad as *one* of the reasons for desiring a favorable balan
ly incidentally and obscurely.—*Principles of political œcono*
". : . a balance may be extremely favorable without augme
the precious metals . . . by constituting all other nati
"

ents must be carefully distinguished from the milder forms,
t foreign trade will be *more* profitable if it produces an exp
t does not, or that foreign trade is the *best* source of weal
ove does not necessarily apply to the milder forms, which
o other objections. See *infra*, pp. 22 ff.

and there was certainly none who argued about particular balances without first having conceived of the notion of a total balance. On this question there was no conflict of doctrine, but only disagreement as to the facts and as to the possibility of ascertaining them.

Constituent Items in the Balance.—The mercantilists have sometimes been charged with failure to see that the international balance does not consist only of commodity exports and imports,[30] and many suppose that the "invisible items" are a recent discovery. But most of the important writers of the seventeenth and eighteenth centuries took care to point out that allowance must be made for non-commodity items in explaining the net balance payable in bullion. Reference to an "invisible" item is to be found as far back as 1381, when both Aylesbury and Lincoln explained the drain of gold as due partly to remittances to Rome.[31] An early writer argued that if foreign merchants were required to come to England to buy English cloth instead of being permitted to buy it abroad, their living expenses in England would be an item in England's favor.[32] Misselden, in 1623, mentioned the profits from the fisheries, reexport trade, and freight earnings as items to be added to the commodity statistics in computing the balance.[33] Malynes,[34] in the same year, pointed out that interest payments on foreign loans should be included in the balance. Robinson,[35] in 1641, included diplomatic expenditures abroad, travelers' expenses, and freight charges. Mun, writing in about the year 1630, listed almost all the items which would be included today: freight earnings, military expenditures abroad, marine insurance payments, gains from fisheries, losses at sea of outward and inward shipments of goods, Catholic remittances to Rome, travelers' expenses, gifts, and the excess over their living expenses in the country for which the balance is being computed of payments to foreigners for exchange commissions, interest, and life and com-

[30] Cf., for example, C. F. Bastable, *The theory of international trade*, 4th ed., 1903, p. 73; Paul Leroy-Beaulieu, *Traité théorique et pratique d'économie politique*, 2d ed., 1896, IV, 175.

[31] Bland, Brown, and Tawney, *English economic history*, pp. 221, 222.

[32] [Clement Armstrong] "How to reform the realme" [*ca.* 1535], Pauli ed., *op. cit.*, p. 67.

[33] *The circle of commerce*, 1623, p. 124.

[34] *The center of the circle of commerce*, 1623, p. 59.

[35] Henry Robinson, *England's safety; in trades encrease*, 1641, pp. 50 ff.

modity insurance.[36] Child,[37] in 1690, added absentee incomes and losses from bad debts. Hugh Chamberlain, in 1606, listed, in addition to commodity trade, the earnings of migratory labor abroad, tourist expenditures ("what foreign travellers spend here to see the country"), diplomatic and military expenditures abroad, and other items.[38]

The mercantilists were most interested in the "balance of payments" in its strict sense of a net balance of immediate obligations payable in specie, and the specie flows inward or outward resulting from the balance of payments were their primary concern. Payments on account of shipping freights or interest payments on foreign indebtedness were therefore recognized as having, value for value, the same significance as payments for commodity imports. But it was long before separate terms were coined to distinguish between the commodity balance of trade and the total balance of payments, and the writers of the period ordinarily used the term "balance of trade" to mean at one time one of these balances, at another time the other. John Pollexfen,[39] however, referred to the "balance of accompts" as meaning the total balance inclusive of both commodity and non-commodity items, and Justice[40] and Harris[41] later used the same term in the same sense. Steuart spoke of "the whole mass of reciprocal payments" and their "balance,"[42] and at one point used the actual phrase, "balance of payments," in its modern sense: "We must always carefully avoid confounding the grand balance of payments with the balance between importation and exportation, which I consider as the balance of trade."[13] Arthur Young in 1772 used the phrase "temporal balance of remittance" to signify

[36] *Englands treasure by forraign trade* [1664], Ashley ed., 1895, p. 11, and chap. xx.

[37] *A discourse about trade*, 1690, pp. 138, 140.

[38] Dr. Hugh Chamberlain, *A collection of some papers writ upon several occasions*, 1696, pp. 2-3.

[39] *A discourse of trade, coyn, and paper credits*, 1697, p. 40. Pollexfen also spoke of "debts and credits" in connection with international transactions of all sorts.—*Ibid.*, pp. 4, 10.

[40] A. J. [Alexander Justice] *A general treatise of monies and exchanges*, 1707, p. 74.

[41] [Joseph Harris] *An essay upon money and coins*, part I (1757), 119.

[42] *An inquiry into the principles of political œconomy*, 1767, II, 316.

[43] *Ibid.*, II, 453, note.

the immediate balance
debtedness" seems not
century. Adam Smith, h
he referred to the "stat

iv. Reasons

The Mercantilist
wanted an export surp
bullion and because the
silver mines a favorab
available to procure bull
tion of the mercantilist
on which their belief in
tion of the precious met
of the mercantilists is
the sole constituents o
made this charge a cent
tilist doctrines, and he
for mercantilism, of in
trines.[1] On behalf of the
of the identity of wealt
incredible that able mer
been familiar, should b
to passages in writings
wealth, or else deny tha
ure" had the same mea

[44] [Arthur Young] *Politica Empire*, 1772, p. 534.

[45] *Wealth of nations* [1776

[1] Cf. A. Oncken, *Geschicht* Cunningham, "Adam Smith *sammte Staatswissenschaft,*

[2] An amusing conflict of Some defend the balance-of ground that the mercantilists and that when they spoke of result of a favorable balance, the mercantilists against the what they wanted was an ir of money. How a favorable total amount of capital or wealth are not the same thin

only referenc
prior to 1760
trines,[3] and,
to be found,
writers as cri
"treasure" ha
eenth centurie
precious comn
at another m
within the lim
soning involv
such shifts in
tion of the m
of-trade doctr

The merca
country may
abroad, and th
for a favora
should expor
indebtedness
surplus and a
goods for m
the second ca
common merc
path to natio
trade only if
that an expor
from trade, a
measure of i

of mercantilist
persistence into
cantilists suffere

[3] [Jocelyn] *A*

[4] Steuart is th
ity of investmen
and he does so o
1767, II, 425-26
ing the mass
debtors to it, . .

[5] These argum
for example, tha
surplus than if
What is said ab
open, however,

least, that all goods other than money were worthless, or were of value only as they served as means of securing money. If it be replied that the mercantilists meant by "wealth," "treasure," "riches," "gain," "loss," "poverty," "prosperity," "profit," etc., only money or absence of money, their arguments generally become merely laborious tautologies, and it becomes a mystery: (a) why they should have thought it necessary to present so earnestly and at such great length arguments reducing to the assertion that the only way for a country without gold or silver mines to get more bullion is to obtain it from abroad in return for goods, and (b) what terms they used when they were thinking of what we mean today when we speak of riches, wealth, gain, prosperity.

Statements involving either the attribution of value to the precious metals alone, or else the use of all the terminology now associated with the notion of wealth to mean merely money, abound in the mercantilist literature, and only a few heretics were never guilty of the confusion, real or terminological, between mere money and wealth. There follow some representative passages, taken from the writings of prominent mercantilists, which cannot, I feel certain, be absolved from the charge that they reveal confusion between quantity of money, on the one hand, and degree of wealth, riches, prosperity, gain, profit, poverty, loss, on the other. It would be easy to multiply the number of such citations.

. . . the wealth of the realm cannot decrease but three manner of ways, which is by the transportation of ready money or bullion out of the same; by selling our home commodities too good cheap; or by buying the foreign commodities too dear, wherein chiefly consisteth the aforesaid overbalancing. . . .[6]

If the native commodities exported do weigh down and exceed in value the foreign commodities imported, it is a rule that never fails, that then the Kingdom grows rich, and prospers in estate and stock; because the overplus thereof must needs come in, in treasure.[7]

The ordinary means therefore to increase our wealth and treasure is by foreign trade, wherein we must ever observe this rule: to sell more to strangers yearly than we consume of theirs in value.[8]

---

[6] Malynes, *A treatise of the canker* [1601], *T.E.D.*, III, 387.

[7] E. Misselden, *The circle of commerce*, 1623, p. 117.

[8] Mun, *England's treasure* [1664], Ashley ed., p. 7.

. . . the only way to be rich, is to have plenty of that commodity to vent, that is of greatest value abroad. . . .[9]

Foreign trade is the only means to enrich this Kingdom . . . Where the consumption of things imported, does exceed in value the things exported, the loss will be as the excess is.[10]

For exportation is gain, but all commodities imported is loss, but ready silver or such commodities, that being carried out again bring in silver from other nations.[11]

. . . gold and silver is the only or most useful treasure of a nation . . . nothing but bullion imported, can make amends for bullion exported.[12]

If we export any value of our manufactures for the consumption of a foreign nation, and import thence no goods at all for our own consumption, it is certain the whole price of our own manufactures exported must be paid to us in money, and that all the money paid to us is our clear gain.[13]

. . . to take the right way of judging of the increase or decrease of the riches of the nation by the trade we drive with foreigners, is to examine whether we receive money from them, or send them ours; . . .[14]

Mr. Deslandes says his country has a balance in trade of 7,000,000 *l.* sterling per annum; which, if true, is infinitely more than Britain can pretend to: It will follow from hence, that the French must be much richer than the English; . . .[15]

The general measures of the trade of Europe at present are gold and silver, which, though they are sometimes commodities, yet are the ultimate objects of trade; and the more or less of these metals a nation retains, it is denominated rich or poor. . . . Therefore, if the exports of Britain exceed its imports, foreigners must pay us

[9] Samuel Fortrey, *Englands interest and improvement* [1663], Hollander ed., 1907, p. 29.

[10] Roger Coke, *A discourse of trade,* 1670, pp. 4, 6.

[11] Carew Reynel, *The true English interest,* 1679, p. 10.

[12] [John Pollexfen] *England and East-India inconsistent in their manufactures,* 1697, pp. 18-19. *A vindication of some assertions relating to coin and trade,* 1699, undoubtedly also the work of Pollexfen, is an elaborate defense of Pollexfen's argument cited above against Davenant's attack on it in his *Discourse of Publick Revenues* [1698]. Pollexfen's argument is also effectively criticized in [Gardner] *Some reflections on a pamphlet, intituled, England and East India inconsistent in their manufactures,* 1696, pp. 6-7. (This tract, in spite of the date (1696) on its title page, cannot have been written before 1697.)

[13] *The British merchant* [1713/4], 3d ed., 1748, I, 28.

[14] Joshua Gee, *The trade and navigation of Great-Britain considered* [1729], 1767 ed., p. 205.

[15] W. Horsley, *A treatise on maritime affairs,* 1744, p. 37.

the balance in treasure, and the nation grow rich. But if the imports of Britain exceed its exports, we must pay foreigners the balance in treasure, and the nation grow poor.[16]

Adam Smith, however, did exaggerate the extent of the dependence of the mercantilist case on the absolute identification of money and wealth, inasmuch as he failed to make clear that there were some mercantilists who were never guilty of such identification and few mercantilists who were never guiltless of it. Certainly, few writers of any prominence relied solely on this identification in arguing for the desirability of the indefinite accumulation of bullion, even though few failed to fall back on it to ease the course of their argument at critical points and to give it an axiomatic appearance both to themselves and to their readers.

To most of the *moderate* mercantilists the distinction between money and wealth was clear enough, if not always at least in moments of enlightenment and when recognition of the distinction would not hamper them and might even help them to make the point at issue at the moment. Thomas More had already, in 1516, tried to destroy the current illusions about the importance of gold and silver and in his ideal commonwealth they were to be relegated to use in the hire of foreign mercenaries and in the making of vessels serving lowly and unromantic purposes indeed, in order to free the Utopians from the tendency to exaggerate their importance: "And these metals, which other nations do as grievously and sorrowfully forego, as in a manner their own lives, if they should altogether at once be taken from the Utopians, no man there would think that he had lost the worth of one farthing."[17] The following quotation from another sixteenth-century writer illustrates the use of the word "treasure" to signify more than merely the precious metals:

> But he that hath treasure, gold, silver, house and land,
> He shall be obeyed as lord with young and old, . . .[18]

There follow some quotations from writers who had a broad concept of wealth and who used to signify wealth the same terms

---

[16] [Matthew Decker] *An essay on the causes of the decline of the foreign trade* [1744], 1756, pp. 1-2.

[17] *Utopia* [1516], A. W. Reed ed., 1929, p. 78.

[18] Roger Bieston, *The bayte and snayre of fortune* [*ca.* 1550], 1894 reprint, p. 21.

which we now use but which the apologists claim then had a different and narrower meaning. It is to be noted, however, that the authors cited were all critics of at least the more extreme monetary doctrines of the mercantilists.

. . . all men do know, that the riches or sufficiency of every kingdom, state, or commonwealth, consisteth in the possession of those things, which are needful for a civil life.[19]

It is true that usually the measure of stock and riches is accounted by money; but that is rather in imagination than reality. . . . The stock or riches of the kingdom doth not only consist in our money, but also in our commodities and ships for trade, and in our ships for war, and magazines furnished with all necessary materials.[20]

By riches, is meant all such things as are of great value. By value, is to be understood the price of things; that is, what anything is worth to be sold. . . .[21]

It is a very hard thing to define what may be truly called the riches of a people. . . . We esteem that to be treasure, which for the use of man has been converted from gold and silver into buildings and improvements of the country; as also other things convertible into those metals, as the fruits of the earth, manufactures, or foreign commodities and stock of shipping. We hold to be riches, what tends to make a people safe at home and considerable abroad, as do fleets and naval stores. We shall yet go farther, and say that maritime knowledge, improvement in all kind of arts, and advancing in military skill, as also wisdom, power and alliances, are to be put into the scale when we weigh the strength and value of a nation.[22]

We commonly count money and bullion riches, whereas they are not riches in themselves, but the instruments and conveyances of them. . . . The riches therefore of a man consist in the abundance of those things that are in themselves useful to our delight or sustenance. . . . The riches of a nation consist in the plenty of those commodities which are most useful in human life, whose air is healthy, whose soil is fruitful, whose people are diligent and ingenious, and busied in manufactures, whose ports are open and free for commerce with the nations about it. This nation is rich, tho' it has not in it an ounce of gold and silver. . . .[23]

The abuse or indefinite use of words, has in no one article of

---

[19] Mun, *A discourse of trade from England* [1621], 1930 reprint, p. 49.

[20] Papillon, *A treatise concerning the East India trade* [1677], 1696 reprint, p. 4.

[21] Barbon, *A discourse concerning coining the new money lighter*, 1696, p. 2.

[22] Davenant, *Discourses on the publick revenues* [1698], *Works*, I, 381.

[23] [Jocelyn] *An essay on money & bullion*, 1718, p. 11.

human reasoning caused greater confusion in ideas, than the calling wealth or riches by the name of money:—Riches, in respect to a nation, are the universal plenty of all necessaries, as food, raiment, houses, and furniture, provision for war, etc. Money, as gold or silver coin, are properly the medium of exchange, but by its quantity may become, and is an article of commerce itself; yet, where it most abounds, as in Portugal, it makes but a small proportion of the riches of that country, though the country itself is extremely poor. And nothing is so erroneous, as to judge of the riches of a country by the quantity of gold and silver in it.[24]

Similar passages can occasionally be found in the works of even the extreme mercantilists, but if they are examined in their context it will generally be found that they justify including other things than gold and silver as wealth only because gold and silver can be obtained in exchange for them;[25] or defend the inclusion of other things on less than parity with the precious metals, on the ground that it cannot with certainty be assumed that these other things can and will be sold abroad in exchange for bullion.[26]

Identification of wealth with the precious metals, whether explicitly or as a tacit assumption underlying their reasoning, is to be regarded, however, as an extreme phase of mercantilist doctrine, prominent in the literature, and contributing largely, no doubt, to its hold on public opinion, but resorted to somewhat

---

[24] [Robert Wallace] *A view of the internal policy of Great Britain*, 1764, p. 2. Similar definitions of wealth are to be found in: Gardner, *Some reflections*, 1696, pp. 6-7; Petty, *Political Arithmetick* [1690], *The economic writings of Sir William Petty*, C. H. Hull ed., 1899, I, 259; *ibid., The political anatomy of Ireland* [1691], *Economic writings*, I, 192; Bernard Mandeville, *Fable of the bees* [1714], F. B. Kaye ed., 1924, I, 197, 301. (See also Mandeville's own index, *ibid.*, I, 376, under "Nations: What the wealth of all nations consists in"); Berkeley, *The querist* [1735-37], in *Works*, Fraser ed., 1871, III, 357, 402; John Bellers, *An essay for imploying the poor to profit*, 1723, p. 6; [Robert Wallace] *Characteristics of the present political state of Great Britain*, 1758, pp. 113 ff.

[25] E.g., Lewes Roberts, *The treasure of traffike* [1641], McCulloch ed., *A select collection of early English tracts on commerce*, pp. 60-65; John Cary, *An essay on the state of England in relation to its trade*, 1695, p. 10; Erasmus Philips, *An appeal to common sense*, 1720, p. 18; *ibid., The state of the nation*, 1725, p. 37; John London, *Some considerations on the importance of the woollen manufactures*, 1740, preface: "It requires no deep knowledge in trade to comprehend, that the riches of a nation must arise from the labor of its inhabitants in working up such goods as it can vend to other nations for specie."

[26] E.g., Thomas Manley, *Usury at six per cent. examined*, 1669, p. 8; [William Petyt] *Britannia languens* [1680], McCulloch ed., *Early English tracts on commerce*, pp. 455-56.

apologetically by its faint-hearted adherents, and not present at all, and even expressly repudiated, in the writings of a few of the most enlightened mercantilists, whose enlightenment, however, tended to take the form of an abandonment of some of the central propositions of mercantilism. Some of the apparent identification may have been purely terminological, although it must be repeated that the ambiguity of terminology was closely associated, as both cause and effect, with genuine confusion of thought. Much more important in the writings of the abler mercantilists than the absolute identification of wealth with gold and silver was the attribution to the precious metals of functions of such supreme importance to the nation's welfare as to make it seem proper to attach to them a value to the commonwealth superior to that of other commodities of equal exchange value. These functions, of which different ones or combinations were stressed by different writers, were to serve as state treasure, as private stores of wealth, as capital, and as a circulating medium. In the following sections, the mercantilist theories with respect to these functions of the precious metals will be examined.

State Treasure as an Emergency Reserve.—The mercantilist argument for the importance of accumulating precious metals which is logically most easily defended is that resting on the value to the state of having a financial reserve on hand in liquid form immediately available in case of emergency. When monetary transactions had become the normal state of affairs, but before public borrowing could be relied upon as a quick and dependable source of funds, and before taxation had become a regular source of revenue quickly responsive to changed fiscal needs, there was much to be said for the accumulation of a state treasure consisting of a stock of the precious metals. This was a common practice in the medieval period, and it has had survivals into modern times, notably in Prussia. It is an important element in present-day monetary policy. The maintenance intact of a state treasure required, however, the exercise by the monarch of a certain degree of restraint in his expenditures, and the profligacy of Henry VIII resulted in the dissipation of the treasure which he had inherited from his predecessor, and the disappearance of the institution as a phase of English state finance. Later monarchs, without exception, relied upon borrowing and special taxation to finance their wars. Even if a state treasure were maintained, moreover, it would call, not for an indefinite accumulation of the precious metals, but only for an amount sufficient for the probable needs. The requirements for the upbuilding of a state treasure could not logically have served, therefore, as a sufficient basis for the mercantilist insistence upon the urgent need of an indefinite augmentation of the national stock of the precious metals. No state treasure, moreover, was in existence or projected during the seventeenth century, and even the most loyal adherent of the Stuarts could have had no great confidence in their ability to restrain themselves from encroaching for current purposes upon any state treasure which they might inherit or have bestowed upon them. In fact there is little mention of state treasure in the mercantilist literature, and its use as an argument for the importance of a favorable balance of trade is extremely rare. The common impression that it played an important part in English mercantilist doctrine has no historical basis.

Even the few references to state treasure which do occur in the literature of the period are not enthusiastic in tone. Sir Thomas More refers to state treasure only to urge the need of subjecting it to a maximum limit, to keep the king from becoming avaricious, and so that "his people should not lack money, wherewith to maintain their daily occupying and chaffer."[27] Another early sixteenth-century writer also recommends that the king should limit his accumulation of treasure in due proportion to the amount of gold and silver that was in the country or could be procured from abroad in return for English commodities, as otherwise there would be scarcity of money for the people and impairment of their capacity to produce.[28] Mun discusses the desirability of a state treasure more fully than any other mercantilist writer. He defends the institution against unnamed critics, but seems to urge it more as an inducement to frugality on the part of princes in dealing with their ordinary revenues in times of plenty than as an emergency reserve deliberately built up by special exactions or taxes. He advises, very much along the same lines as the sixteenth-century writers referred to above, that the prince should not add to his treasure annually, in the form of gold and silver, more than the amount of the year's excess of exports over imports,

---

[27] *Utopia* [2d ed., 1556], A. W. Reed ed., 1929, p. 44.

[28] "How to reform the realme" [*ca.* 1535], in Pauli, *Drei volkswirthschaftliche Denkschriften,* p. 61.

even if his revenues exceed his expenditures by more than that amount, since otherwise he would draw into the treasure all the money needed for trade and industry. He states that it is not necessary, or even desirable, for all the state reserve to be accumulated in the form of a stock of the precious metals, for it can better and more profitably be used to build ships of war, to store up grain against periods of dearth, and to accumulate war supplies, or lent to citizens for productive use. He writes:

> ... although treasure is said to be the sinews of the war, yet this is so because it doth provide, unite and move the power of men, victuals, and munition where and when the cause doth require; but if these things be wanting in due time, what shall we then do with our money?[29]

Except for minor references to state treasure,[30] the only other discussions of it that I have found in the literature of the period are by John Houghton and Henry Home. Houghton, in the course of a plea that Parliament vote Charles II whatever funds he should ask for, deals with the possible objection that the king might hoard the money. He argues that such a hoard would lend prestige and power to the king in his dealings with foreign countries. He claims that Henry VII was the only English king who accumulated a great hoard, and that no ill resulted to the country in that case. He argues that by making money dear in England, hoarding would lead to the import of further supplies of bullion from abroad. But he concedes that hoarding would be the worst use to which the king could put his revenue, except expenditure on sinful purposes.[31] Home supports the maintenance of a state treasure, but contingent upon the existence of wise and good government: "In the hands of a rapacious ministry, the greatest treasure would not be long-lived: under the management of a British ministry, it would vanish in the twinkling of an eye; and do more mischief by augmenting money in circulation above what is salutary, than formerly it did good by confining it within moderate bounds." His chief reason for supporting a state treas-

---

[29] *England's treasure by forraign trade* [1664], Ashley ed., chaps. xvii, xviii.

[30] [John Hales] *A discourse of the common weal* [1581], Elizabeth Lamond ed., p. 113; Petty, *A treatise of taxes* [1662], *Economic writings*, I, 36; [Henry Lloyd] *An essay on the theory of money*, 1771, p. 14 (where it is condemned as hoarding and therefore injurious to industry and trade).

[31] John Houghton, *A collection of letters*, 1681-83, II, 115.

ure, moreover, would have seemed paradoxical to the ordinary mercantilist. Its virtue was that it could absorb a redundancy of currency, which otherwise would get into circulation, raise prices, and thus hamper trade. Where there was no redundancy of currency, the accumulation of treasure, he held, would be prejudicial to commerce. Its availability as a reserve in emergencies was apparently a minor factor to him.[32]

There are other passages in the mercantilist literature which may have state treasure in mind, even though they do not explicitly refer to it. Such perhaps are the frequent references to money as the "sinews of war," and especially to its importance in diplomacy and in conducting war in foreign territory with mercenary troops. But money procured through current taxation or borrowing would serve as well, and the emphasis may therefore be intended to be rather on the importance of plenty of gold and silver within the country than specifically in the state treasure.[33] Many of these passages, moreover, seem to identify money with the things which money can buy, and financial power with the size of the stock of the precious metals.[34]

---

[32] Henry Home, Lord Kames, *Sketches of the history of man,* 1774, I, 82 ff.

[33] Such is explicitly the argument in "Polices to reduce this realme" [1549], *T.E.D.,* III, 324; [J. Briscoe] *A discourse of money,* 1696, pp. 27-29; and Henry Home, *loc. cit.*

[34] As representative passages, the following may be cited:

. . . it is his [the king of Spain's] Indian gold that endangereth and disturbeth all the nations of Europe; it purchaseth intelligence, creepeth into counsels, and setteth bound loyalty at liberty in the greatest monarchies of Europe.—Sir Walter Raleigh, *A Voyage for the discovery of Guiana* [1596], in *Works,* 1751, II, 149.

[Restriction of the export of bullion] concerns the safety and well-being of the army, the keeping of treasure within the nation; for they and the army are like a ship at sea, which must be well-provided with anchors and cables, and victuals; money is to them all this, nay, everything.—Thomas Violet, *Mysteries and secrets of trade and mint-affairs,* 1653, p. 35.

. . . since the wealth of the Indies came to be discovered and dispersed more and more, wars are managed by much treasure and little fighting, and therefore with little hazard to the richer nation.—William Petyt, *Britannia languens* [1680], in McCulloch ed., *Early English tracts on commerce,* p. 293.

For, since the introduction of the new artillery of powder guns, &c., and the discovery of the wealth of the Indies, &c., war is become rather an expense of money than men, and success attends those that can most and longest spend money: whence it is that princes' armies in Europe are become more proportionable to their purses than to the number of their people; so that it uncontrollably follows that a foreign trade managed to the best advantage will make our nation so strong and rich, that we may command the

The Precious Metals as a Store of Wealth.—The really important bases of the mercantilist belief in the desirability of the indefinite accumulation of the precious metals still remain to be dealt with. They divide the mercantilist writers into two fairly distinct groups, holding different and, to a large extent, conflicting views as to the important functions of the precious metals. The first group attached great significance to the precious metals because they held saving or the accumulation of wealth as the chief objective of economic activity and, failing to understand the nature of the process of productive investment, believed that the only, or the most practicable, form in which wealth could be accumulated was in an increase in the national stock of the precious metals.

The disparagement of consumption and the exaltation of frugality and thrift were common doctrines of the period, not wholly dependent upon economic reasoning but deriving much of their vitality from moral and religious principles and class prejudices. The Puritans disapproved of luxury and regarded thrift and saving as one of the major virtues on moral and theological, as well as on economic, grounds. The landed gentry, on the other hand, were typically not Puritans themselves either in their religion or in their mode of life, but they tended to regard extravagance and expensive display as the exclusive prerogatives of the hereditary aristocracy, and thrift and frugality as the appropriate virtues of the middle and lower classes. Eulogy of frugality and thrift and condemnation of luxury are common throughout the mercantilist literature, and only a few instances need be cited. Sir William Temple praises the Dutch and, following a custom which seems already to have become established at the beginning of the seventeenth century and to have persisted until late in the eighteenth, sets them up as a model to be followed by the English in economic matters, because, among other virtues, "they furnish infinite luxury, which they never practice, and traffic in pleasures, which they never taste."[35] Petty stresses saving above all other means of acquiring wealth:

But above all the particulars hitherto considered, that of superlu-

---

trade of the world, the riches of it, and consequently the world itself. . . . —
James Whiston, *A discourse of the decay of trade*, 1693, pp. 2-3.

[35] *Observations upon the United Provinces of the Netherlands* [1668], *Works*, 1754, I, 131.

cration ought chiefly to be taken in; for if a prince have never so many subjects, and his country be never so good, yet if either through sloth, or extravagant expenses, or oppression and injustice, whatever is gained shall be spent as fast as gotten, that state must be accounted poor; . . .[36]

The emphasis on saving is shown also by the frequent exclusion of consumable goods, or goods destined for consumption instead of for accumulation, from "riches," the latter term being confined to saved or accumulated goods. The following passages are representative of such verbal usage:

The two great principles of riches are land and labor; . . . whatever they [i.e., the people] save of the effects of their labor, over and above their consumption, is called riches. . . .[37]

And this increase of wages is the greatest tax on the nation, though the receiver is made no richer, only sprucer and lazier.[38]

. . . By what is consumed at home, one loseth only what another gets, and the nation in general is not at all the richer; . . .[39]

The notion that saving consisted of the piling-up of valuable goods led naturally to an identification of saved wealth or "riches" with stored-up goods of a special kind suitable for accumulation and not capable of, or destined for, current consumption. Commodities of high value and of great durability and not liable to loss of value through change of fashion would be specially suitable as the constituent items of stored-up wealth. The exaltation of saving led in turn to the attachment of superior importance to such commodities than to more perishable commodities and those destined for current consumption. The precious metals met these tests of suitability as stores of wealth better than any other commodities. Here is an important element in the explanation of the

---

[36] *Political Arithmetick* [1690], *Economic writings,* I, 254. The etymological affinity of "superlucration," which means, of course, saving, to the piling-up of money, has bearing on the argument which I make here that for many of the mercantilists that was what saving meant. The etymological relationships between the terms connected with saving and those signifying money are much closer in French than in English. See Charles Rist, "*Quelques définitions de l'épargne,*" *Revue d'économie politique,* XXXV (1921), 734 ff.

[37] [Thomas Sheridan] *A discourse on the rise and power of parliaments* [1677], reprint by Saxe Bannister, in *Some revelations in Irish history,* 1870, pp. 182-83.

[38] Richard Lawrence, *The interest of Ireland in its trade and wealth stated,* 1682, Part I, p. 28.

[39] Davenant, "An essay on the East-India trade" [1696], *Works,* I, 102.

importance attributed to gold and silver by the mercantilists. There follow a few quotations, illustrating the attachment of superior importance to the precious metals than to other commodities because of their greater suitability as stores of wealth:

Also they [i.e., foreign merchants] bear the gold out of this land
And soak the thrift away out of our hand;
As the waffore sucketh honey from the bee,
So minceth our commodity.[40]

. . . gold and silver are . . . the most necessary and lasting instruments to procure all things that are, or shall be found useful, or any ways serviceable to mankind, being portable and durable, when most other goods are burthensome, subject to perish and decay. . . . Silver and gold being preferable to house and land, and the only instruments that have increased and improved trade.[41]

The great and ultimate effect of trade is not wealth at large, but particularly abundance of silver, gold, and jewels, which are not perishable, nor so mutable as other commodities, but are wealth at all times, and all places: whereas abundance of wine, corn, fowls, flesh, etc., are riches but *hic & nunc,* so as the raising of such commodities, and the following of such trade, which does store the country with gold, silver, jewels, etc., is profitable before others.[42]

All other commodities end with the consumer, but money still lives, and the more hands it runs through the better; so that in a sense the use doth not destroy it, as it doth other commodities, but leaves it as it were immortal.[43]

Gold and silver, for many reasons, are the fittest metals hitherto known for hoarding: they are durable; convertible without damage into any form; of great value in proportion to their bulk; and being

[40] *The libelle of Englyshe polyce* [ms. 1436] Sir George Warner ed., 1926, p. 21. "Waffore" = predatory wasp; "minceth our commodity" = diminishes our resources. This passage is cited here as apparently an instance of the identification of thrift with the accumulation of the precious metals.

[41] Thomas Houghton, *The alteration of the coyn, with a feasible method to do it,* 1695, pp. 5, 15.

[42] Petty, *Political arithmetick* [1690], in *Economic writings,* I, 259-60. In a recently published Petty manuscript, accumulation of gold, silver, and precious stones is stated to be the best mode of saving, because they are durable and are not dependent on time and place for their value, but are "morally speaking perpetual and universal wealth."—*The Petty papers,* Marquis of Lansdowne ed., 1927, I, 214.

[43] Hugh Chamberlain, *A collection of some papers,* 1696, p. 9. The store of wealth and the circulation functions of money are here brought into combination. Chamberlain remarked that money was more than tenfold as important as other commodities, presumably of the same exchange value. (*Ibid.*)

the money of the world, they are the readiest exchange for all things, and what most readily and surely command all kinds of services.[44]

As gold is a treasure, because it decays not in keeping . . . no other metals are a treasure, because they either decay in keeping, or are in too great plenty.[45]

If the only possible or practicable means of saving is by the accumulation of a hoard of the precious metals, it becomes obvious that the accumulated wealth of a country is limited to its stock of the precious metals and can increase only through an increase in the latter. If that country is without gold or silver mines, it can therefore add to its saved wealth only through a favorable balance of trade payable in bullion. Reasoning such as this explains—and exposes—the balance-of-trade theories of an important and numerous group of the English mercantilist writers. There follow several representative passages in which the ideas of riches as saved wealth, of saving as the piling-up of the precious metals, and therefore of a favorable balance of trade as necessary for an increase of riches, are stated or clearly implied:

. . . no trades carried on by the exportation of [our] own products and manufactures, or those from our plantations, though what brought back in return be all perishable commodities, can diminish our riches, for all such goods of ours (unless some objection be made as to tin and lead) would have perished by time, if had been kept here; but a great distinction ought to be made, between trades carried on by the exportation of our products, and trades carried on by the exportation of our bullion, to purchase perishable commodities, because in such case we exchange what is durable, and most useful, for what cannot long do us any service.[46]

That silks, woolen goods, wines, etc., may be esteemed riches between man and man, because may be converted into gold and silver, yet do not deserve to be esteemed the riches of the nation, till by exportation to foreign countries are converted into gold and silver, and that brought hither, because are subject to corruption, and in a short course of years will consume to nothing, and then of no value.[47]

Now it falls out in the natural course of things, that whilst men

---

[44] Joseph Harris, *An essay upon money and coins,* Part I (1757), 99.

[45] *An inquiry concerning the trade, commerce, and policy of Jamaica,* 1759, pp. 2-3.

[46] [Pollexfen] *England and East-India inconsistent in their manufactures,* 1697, p. 49.

[47] *Ibid.,* p. 7.

are employed in searching after the necessaries of life, they find riches: for the earth is grateful, and repays their labor, not only with enough, but with abundance; and out of the plenty of these materials, plenty of things are formed to supply the wants of mankind. Now the more of these things any nation has, the more comfortably the people live; and whatever they have of them more than they consume, the surplus is the riches of that nation, I mean, the intrinsic riches of it. This surplus is sent to other nations . . . and is there exchanged or sold; and this is the trade of a nation. If the nation, to which it is sent, cannot give goods in exchange to the same value, they must pay for the remainder in money, which is the balance of trade; and the nation that hath that balance in their favor, must increase in wealth; for this is the only way to bring money into any nation, that has no natural fund of it in mines in its own bowels; and the only way to keep it in any nation that has.[48]

The doctrine of thrift also led to emphasis on the importance of a favorable balance of trade through another chain of reasoning. Throughout the mercantilist period, the imports into England consisted largely of expensive luxuries and conveniences which contributed more to the pleasures and comforts of life than to the dull but virtuous process of enrichment through thrift. Also if Englishmen were sparing in their consumption of even domestic goods, there would result, it was claimed, either unemployment or the piling-up of unsold and perishable commodities, unless the surplus stocks of domestic goods were exported abroad. Small imports and large exports were therefore a necessary adjunct of thrift and enrichment. These views were widely prevalent, and they are sufficiently illustrated by passages cited in other connections.

Protests against the importation of "apes and peacocks," "toys and baubles" recur throughout the mercantilist period and were already common in the sixteenth century. Thus Starkey makes one of the participants in his dialogue reproach as "ill-occupied" "all such merchants which . . . bring in . . . vain trifles and conceits, only for the foolish pastime and pleasure of man," although his adversary does say something in defense of the joys of life.[49]

---

[48] [William Hay] *Remarks on the laws relating to the poor* [1735], 2d (?) ed., 1751, pp. 20, 21.

[49] Thomas Starkey, *England in the reign of King Henry the Eighth* [ms. ca. 1538], Early English Text Society print, 1871. pp. 80, 81. Cf. also "Memorandum

Money as Invested Capital.—With only a few exceptions, the mercantilists either identified or failed clearly to distinguish between money, on the one hand, and capital or "stock" employed by its owner or lent out at interest, on the other. They always wrote of direct employment of capital and of loans at interest in monetary terms, and as a rule they showed no signs that they had penetrated in their analysis beneath the monetary surface. Verbally, at least, they identified money with capital; much of their argument can be explained only if they regarded money and capital as identical in fact as well as in name. This is most clearly brought out in the important doctrines of the period: that interest was paid for the use of money, that the rate of interest depended on the quantity of money, and that high interest rates were proof of the scarcity of money, doctrines which were questioned by very few writers before Hume.[50] Several passages illustrating the common confusion of money with capital follow:

That by the plenty of money [resulting from raising the nominal value of English coin and thus keeping it from being exported] the price of usury may of course decrease and the price of lands be improved.[51]

It is an infallible sign that money abounds, and is plentiful, when the interest thereof is low, for interest or forbearance is the price of money. . . .[52]

Now, I think, the natural interest of money is raised two ways: first, when the money of a country is but little, in proportion to the debts of the inhabitants, one amongst another. . . . Secondly, that, which constantly raises the natural interest of money, is, when money is little, in proportion to the trade of a country. For in trade everybody calls for money, according as he wants it, and this disproportion is always felt. For, if Englishmen owed in all but one million, and there were a million of money in England, the money would be well enough proportioned to the debts: but, if two millions were necessary to carry on the trade, there would be a million wanting, and the price of money would be raised, as it is of any other com-

---

. . . on the exchanges" [1564], *T.E.D.*, III, 353; "Memorandum by Cecil on the export trade in cloth and wool" [1564?], *T.E.D.*, II, 45.

[50] See *infra*, p. 89.

[51] John Gilbert, a mint official, in 1625, quoted by W. A. Shaw, *Select tracts . . . illustrative of English monetary history*, 1896, p. 7.

[52] [William Paterson] *A brief account of the intended Bank of England* [1694], reprinted in Saxe Bannister, *The writings of William Paterson*, 2d ed., 1859, III, 85.

modity in a market, where the merchandise will not serve half the customers, and there are two buyers for one seller.[53]

This confusion of money with capital contributed directly to the attachment of great importance to the size of the national stock of money, and indirectly to emphasis on the importance of a favorable balance of trade as the only way in which that stock could be increased.

The Analogy from Personal Finance.—All the variants of the mercantilist doctrine which rest on an identification of money with wealth, or with accumulated and stored wealth, or with loanable capital, found support for their position in a superficially plausible analogy with personal finance which with unimportant modifications recurs repeatedly in the mercantilist literature from the earliest to the latest writers, and is frequently supported by citations from classical writers. Two early statements of the analogy follow:

. . . we must always take heed that we buy no more of strangers than we sell them; (for so we should empoverish ourselves and enrich them). For he were no good husband that hath no other yearly revenues but of husbandry to live on, that will buy more in the market than he selleth again.[54]

The ordinary means therefore to increase our wealth and treasure is by foreign trade, wherein we must ever observe this rule; to sell more to strangers yearly than we consume of theirs in value. . . . By this order duly kept in our trading, we may rest assured that the kingdom shall be enriched yearly two hundred thousand pounds, which must be brought to us in so much treasure; because that part of our stock which is not returned to us in wares must necessarily be brought home in treasure.

For in this case it cometh to pass in the stock of a kingdom, as in the estate of a private man; who is supposed to have one thousand pounds yearly revenue and two thousand pounds of ready money in

---

[53] John Locke, *Some considerations* [1691], in *Works*, 1823 ed., V. 9-10.

For additional statements to the same effect, see: *Interest of money mistaken*, 1668, pp. 14, 18; John Asgill, on *Several assertions proved* [1696], Hollander ed., 1906, pp. 29 ff.; [J. Briscoe] *A discourse of money*, 1696, p. 21; James Hodges, *The present state of England, as to coin and publick charges*, 1697, p. 18; William Wood, *A survey of trade*, 1718, p. 335; *A letter to the . . . Commissioners of Trade and Plantations, wherein the grand concern of trade is asserted*, 1747, pp. 76, 86.

[54] [Hales] *A discourse of the common weal* [1581], Elizabeth Lamond ed., p. 63.

his chest. If such a man through excess shall spend one thousand five hundred pounds per annum, all his ready money will be gone in four years; and in the like time his said money will be doubled if he take a frugal course to spend but five hundred pounds per annum, which rule never faileth likewise in the Commonwealth. . . .[55]

There was little contemporary criticism of this analogy, obvious though its shortcomings seem to be both as an analogy and as an interpretation of personal finance. Papillon pointed out that it was foolish for a person managing a farm to buy less than he sells in order to accumulate a stock of *money*.[56] Barbon tried to meet it by the argument that although the "stock" of a person is finite, and therefore exhaustible, that of a country is infinite, and "what is infinite can neither receive addition by parsimony nor suffer diminution by prodigality."[57] Mandeville conceded that frugality or "saving" was the most certain method to increase an estate, but he denied, on "make-work" grounds, that this also held true for a nation.[58] Hume pointed out, on quantity theory of money grounds, that while an individual would be richer if he had more money, the same would not hold for a country.[59]

More Money in Order to Have Higher Prices.—In the modern literature on mercantilism, the desire of the mercantilists for more money is sometimes explained as largely due to a prevailing desire for higher prices, and the apologists find economic justification for such a desire in the circumstances which they

---

[55] Thomas Mun, *England's treasure by forraign trade* [1664], Ashley ed., pp. 7-8. For additional instances of the use of this analogy, see "Considerations for the restraynte of transportinge gould out of the realme" [ms. reign of Elizabeth], in Schanz, *op. cit.*, II, 649; "Debate in House of Commons on subsidies" [1593], *T.E.D.*, II, 242; Misselden, *Free trade*, 2d ed., 1622, pp. 12-13; *ibid.*, *The circle of commerce*, 1623, p. 130; Samuel Lamb, *Seasonal observations* [1659], in *Somers' tracts*, 2d ed., VI, 465; Temple, *Observations upon the United Provinces* [1668], in *Works*, I, 130; Locke, *Some considerations* [1691], in *Works*, V, 19 ff., 72; Davenant, *An essay upon ways and means* [1695], in *Works*, I, 13; [S. Clement] *A discourse of the general notions of money, trade and exchanges*, 1695, p. 11; Pollexfen, *A discourse of trade, coyn, and paper credit*, 1697, pp. 80 ff.; Steuart, *Principles of political œconomy*, 1767, I, 421.

[56] Papillon, *A treatise concerning the East India trade* [1677], 1696 ed., p. 4.

[57] *A discourse of trade* [1690], Hollander ed., p. 11. Cf. also, by the same author, *A discourse concerning coining the new money lighter*, 1696, pp. 47-48.

[58] *The fable of the bees* [1714], Kaye ed., I, 182.

[59] *Political discourses* [1752], in *Essays, moral, political, and literary*, 1875 ed., I, 337.

allege then prevailed, for example, the necessity for increase in the national stock of money if the period of transition from a barter to a money economy were not to be accompanied by the evils of falling prices. But even in the literature of the early seventeenth century, barter is already referred to as a system characteristic of a primitive economy from which England had long since emerged. From early in the sixteenth century to late in the eighteenth, the general trend of English commodity prices was decidedly upward rather than downward, although the economic historians do seem to be agreed that there were intervals of some length during which prices were falling. But throughout the period the complaints of scarcity of money were unintermittent. I can find in any case very few mercantilists who wanted higher prices and wanted more money as a means of obtaining a higher price level. For such to have been the case, recognition of the dependence of prices on the quantity of money would have been necessary, and many mercantilists showed no trace of such recognition, while others denied the existence of any such relationship between the quantity of money and the price level.[60] Some mercantilists, moreover, who shared in the general desire for more money, complained of high prices and wanted lower instead of higher prices. To them high prices were an evil which they did not associate with the quantity of money, or which they thought could be remedied by more money, or which created a need for more money if trade was to be carried on and the poor were to be able to buy the necessaries of life. Two typical complaints that prices were too high, made by writers who nevertheless were anxious that England have a favorable balance of trade in order that bullion should flow in, are cited below:

. . . the high price of all things is not only the greatest matter that the people grudge at; and one of the principal occasions of poverty and famine; but also the chiefest cause that the king's majesty cannot without expense of wonderful great sums of money maintain his wars against his enemies. . . . [61]

. . . cheap wares do increase trade, and dear wares do not only cause their less consumption, but also decline the merchant's trade, impoverish the Kingdom of treasure, lessen his Majesty's customs

---

[60] See *infra,* pp. 40 ff.

[61] "Polices to reduce this realme of Englande" [1549], *T.E.D.,* III, 315.

and imposts, and abate the manufactures and employments of the
poor in shipping, clothing, and the like. . . .[62]

There were very few *price* inflationists among the English mercantilists, and even the advocates of paper money did not want
higher prices. Many mercantilists claimed that if their projects
were adopted land values would rise, but such claims were made
in order to win the support or weaken the opposition of the landed
classes to their proposals. In any case, they were usually based on
the argument that more money meant lower interest rates, and
lower interest rates meant higher land values, or on the argument
that more money meant more trade and therefore a readier sale
for agricultural products, or more production and therefore
greater exports, and rarely made specific reference to higher commodity prices. Some mercantilists argued, on what would now
be called "terms-of-trade" considerations, that it was desirable that
export prices should be high and import prices low.[63] But one of
these writers said that it did not matter what domestic prices
were,[64] and others argued that even with respect to exports low

---

[62] *Decay of Trade. A treatise against the abating of interest*, 1641, p. 9.
For further references to high prices as an evil, see "How to reforme the
realme" [*ca.* 1535], in Pauli, *op. cit.*, p. 64; Henry Brinklow, *The complaynt
of Roderyck Mors* [ms. *ca.* 1542], Early English Text Society, 1874, pp. 49-
50; Thomas Wilson, *A discourse upon usury* [1572], Tawney ed., pp. 258, 284,
312, 356; Thomas Milles, *The customers replie*, 1604, p. 13; Malynes, *The
center of the circle of commerce*, 1623, preface; Mun, *England's treasure by
forraign trade* [1664], Ashley ed., p. 24; A. V[ickaris], *An essay for regulating
of the coyn*, 1696, pp. 23-24; *An essay towards carrying on the present war
against France* [*ca.* 1697], in *The Harleian miscellany*, X (1810), 380; Vanderlint, *Money answers all things* [1734], Hollander ed., 1914, pp. 16, 95; Steuart,
Principles of political œconomy, 1767, I, 423.
Rice Vaughan, in *A discourse of coin and coinage*, 1675, pp. 68 ff. and chap.
xi, concedes that prices had risen in England, but wants more money nevertheless, because the quantity of money had not increased in as great a proportion
as prices and the rise in prices had therefore caused scarcity of money. Vanderlint (*op. cit.*, pp. 15 ff.), who complained about scarcity of money, spoke of
an increase in the supply of money or a lowering of prices as alternative remedies.
[63] E.g., Malynes, *A treatise of the canker* [1601], *T.E.D.*, III, 389; Locke,
Some considerations [1691], *Works*, 10th ed., V. 50; Thomas Houghton, *The
alteration of the coyn*, 1695, p. 44.
[64] Fortrey, *Englands interest and improvement* [1663], Hollander ed., 1907,
p. 29: ". . . for what the price of any thing is amongst our selves, whether
dear or cheap it matters not; for as we pay, so we receive, and the country
is nothing damnified by it; but the art is when we deal with strangers, to sell
dear and to buy cheap; and this will increase our wealth."

prices were desirable if, or because, high prices would mean a small volume of sales.[65] I have found very few mercantilist writers who unambiguously expressed a desire for higher prices in general,[66] although there were probably many mercantilists who would not have regarded higher prices as an evil if accompanied by at least an equal increase in money, stocks or incomes. Such seems to have been Misselden's position in his answer to the possible objection, against his proposal to raise the denomination of English coin, that it would result in an increase in commodity prices :

And for the dearness of things, which the raising of money bringeth with it, that will be abundantly recompensed unto all in the plenty of money, and quickening of trade in every man's hand. And that which is equal to all, when he that buys dear shall sell dear, cannot be said to be injurious unto any. And it is much better for the kingdom, to have things dear with plenty of money, whereby men may live in their several callings, than to have things cheap with want of money, which now makes every man complain.[67]

More Money in Circulation Means More Trade.—Many of the mercantilists, some of whom also used the arguments already discussed, wanted more money because they regarded money, not merely as a passive medium of exchange, but as a force acting through its circulation from hand to hand as an active stimulus to trade. An increased amount of money in circulation, they believed, meant (or caused) an increased volume

---

[65] E.g., Robinson, *Englands safety; in trades encrease*, 1641, pp. 55-56; Samuel Lamb, *Seasonal observations* [1659], in *Somers' tracts*, 2d ed., VI, 464; [John Browne] *An essay on trade in general*, 1728, p. 31; [Mildmay] *The laws and policy of England relating to trade*, 1765, p. 62.

[66] [Petyt] *Britannia languens* [1680], McCulloch ed., pp. 283, 290; Thomas Houghton, *The alteration of the coyn*, 1695, p. 43; Browne, *An essay on trade in general*, 1728, p. 18; Robert Wallace, *Characteristics of the present political state of Great Britain*, 1758, p. 35; Arthur Young, *Political Arithmetic*, 1774, pp. 55 ff.

[67] *Free trade*, 1622, pp. 106-07. Misselden advocated that landlords and creditors should be protected from loss by a provision that contracts made before the raising of the currency should be paid at the value of the money current when the contracts were made. (*Ibid.*) Thomas Manley (*Usury at six per cent.*, 1669, p. 67) borrows some of the above, without acknowledgment. Heckscher (*Mercantilism*, 1935, II, 224 ff.) finds a much wider prevalence of the desire for higher prices among the English mercantilists than I have found. The specific evidence which he presents is not sufficient to convince me that I am wrong, but does weaken my conviction that I am right.

of trade, and since men would produce only what they could sell a quickening of trade meant an increase of production and therefore a wealthier country. Here, it should be noted, money is valued as an instrument or stimulus of trade rather than for its own sake. The writers who stressed "circulation" as the valuable service of money often shifted, however, from the concept of money circulating as a medium of exchange to money passing from the hands of a lender to those of a borrower, and rarely distinguished clearly between them. The underlying reasoning is often presented in the form of analogies, especially with the circulation of the blood, which William Harvey had discovered not long before.[68]

Stress on the importance of an abundance of money in circulation if trade was to flourish is already to be found in very early writers.[69] The most elaborate expositions of the "circulation" argument were made by William Potter[70] and John Law.[71] Potter's argument seems to reduce to this: The wealth of a country is equal to the value of the goods of all sorts therein, money being valuable only as it serves to bring about the production of more goods.[72] The more money men have, the more they spend and the

---

[68] "By the means of which measures [i.e., the reduction, by "concoction" of all commodities which are not immediately consumed, to money], all commodities, moveable and immoveable, are made to accompany a man, to all places of his resort, within and without the place of his ordinary residence; and the same passeth from man to man, within the commonwealth; and goes round about, nourishing (as it passeth) every part thereof; in so much as this concoction is as it were the sanguification of the commonwealth; for natural blood is in like manner made of the fruits of the earth; and circulating, nourisheth by the way, every member of the body of man."—Thomas Hobbes, *Leviathan* [1651], Everyman's Library ed., p. 133.

"And as money is the sinew of war, so doth it appear to be the life of trade, all commodities being valued by it, and in both as useful in the body politic as blood in the veins of the body natural, dispersing itself, and giving life and motion to every part thereof. . . ." (Samuel Lamb, *Seasonal Observations* [1659], in *Somers' tracts,* 2d ed., VI, 463.)

Cf. also Bernardo Davanzati, *A discourse upon coins* [1588], translated by John Toland, 1696, pp. 18-19; *Omnia comesta a bello,* 1667, p. 11; R. Haines, *England's weal and prosperity proposed,* 1681, p. 12; *Taxes no charge,* 1690, p. 11; Berkeley, *The querist* [1735-37], in *Works,* Fraser ed., 1871, III, 395.

[69] Cf. Sir Thomas More, *Utopia* [1516], A. W. Reed ed., 1929, p. 44.

[70] *The key of wealth,* 1650.

[71] *Money and trade considered* [1705], 1750.

[72] Cf. Berkeley, *The querist, Works,* III, 395: "Whether the public is not more benefited by a shilling that circulates than a pound that lies dead?"; John Smith, *Chronicon rusticum-commerciale, or memoirs of wool,* 1747, I, 414:

faster they spend it. If men acquire more money and spend it as fast as they receive it, the sales of merchants and manufacturers will increase proportionately. If they sell five times as much in money value, they will produce five times as much, and even more, in physical quantities, since they can afford to charge lower prices on the greater volume of sales.[73]

> . . . in reference to a commonwealth, or any society of men, the greater quantity there is amongst them, of money, credit, or that which is taken by them for commodities, the more commodity they sell, that is, the greater is their trade. For whatsoever is taken amongst men for commodity, though it were ten times more than now it is, yet if it be one way or other laid out by each man, as fast as he receives it, it must needs come to pass, that (resting nowhere) it doth occasion a quickness in the revolution of commodity from hand to hand, that is trade, proportionable to the greatness of its quantity.[74]

John Law's argument is essentially the same, although stated more conservatively.[75] The most enthusiastic advocates of the circulation argument, Potter and Law included, were advocates of paper money. But if paper money were accepted as of equal value to metallic money, the great reason for desiring a favorable balance of trade, that it results in an inflow of bullion, should lose its force. Such in fact was the case with some of them, as the following extracts show:

> . . . for whether a nation have any silver amongst them or no, yet if they can trade as well without it, what need they care? for their estates in vendible commodities (and consequently their credit) is of as real value as if it were in money.[76]

Whatsoever quantity of credit shall be raised in this office, will be as good, and of as much use, as if there were so much money

---

"And money itself is not properly riches, i.e., it is not serviceable to a community, but as it is circulated."

[73] *Key of wealth*, pp. 1-20.

[74] *Ibid.*, p. 7. Potter later makes his proposition even stronger: increase money and "both trading and riches will increase amongst them, much more than proportionable to such increase of money, and that without increasing the price of commodity, as I shall prove in place convenient" (*ibid.*, p. 10, incorrectly paged 6). This, he explains, is due to the fact that when men have little money they tend to keep it, but when they have much, they make it "revolve" much more rapidly (*ibid.*, p. 11).

[75] *Money and trade considered* [1705], 1750, pp. 20 ff.

[76] William Potter, *Key of wealth*, p. 69.

in specie added to the present stock of the nation . . . 'tis more prudent and advantageous to a nation, to have the common standard or medium of their trade within their power, and to arise from their native product, than to be at the mercy of a foreign prince for his gold and silver, which he may at pleasure behold. . . . Credit can neither be hoarded up, nor transported to the nation's disadvantage; which consequently frees us from the care and necessity of making laws to prevent exportation of bullion or coin, being always able to command a credit of our own, . . . as useful, and as much as shall be necessary.[77]

The only necessity of a foreign trade for England is because we make a foreign commodity (gold and silver) the standard of all ours, and the only medium of commerce, which (as long as it continues so) if we want, all trades must cease; but if we can find out another and safer medium of exchange (as this credit) appropriated to the place where we live and not subject to such obstruction as the other, why should we not readily embrace it?[78]

And if the proprietors of the bank can circulate their fundation of twelve hundred thousand pounds, without having more than two or three hundred thousand pounds lying dead at one time with another, this bank will be in effect, as nine hundred thousand pounds, or a million of fresh money, brought into the nation. . . .[79]

Whether in any one year half a million is brought into a commercial country by trade, or issued out by banks, in notes, upon good security, it will serve for the same purposes.[80]

Some advocates of paper money made little or no reference to the balance of trade or to trade policy in their tracts. This freedom from the prevailing obsession with the state of the balance of trade may have been due to a loss of interest in a policy of securing laboriously through the complicated regulation of trade the increase of money which could be secured more quickly, with greater certainty, and with less effort, by means of the printing press. But some of the advocates of paper money displayed loyalty to the current belief in the importance of a favorable balance of

---

[77] *Englands interest or the great benefit to trade by banks or offices of credit,* 1682, pp. 1-2.

[78] *Several objections sometimes made against the office of credit, fully answered, ca.* 1682, p. 9.

[79] [William Paterson] *A brief account of the intended bank of England* [1694], Bannister ed., *The writings of William Paterson,* III, 85.

[80] Robert Wallace, *Characteristics of the present political state of Great Britain,* 1758, p. 37. Wallace, however, relapses at times into concern about the state of the national stock of bullion.

trade, either because of blind acceptance of traditional doctrine, or on the basis of the store of wealth argument or the analogy from personal finance that one should buy less than one sells, and these writers claimed that an increase of paper money would not drive bullion out of the country, but on the contrary would make the balance of trade more favorable through its beneficial effect on production and trade.[81]

The Quantity Theory of Money.—Those mercantilists who sought an increase in the supply of money because they wanted more circulation or more invested capital clearly wanted genuine physical increases in trade or capital and not merely nominal increases in terms of a depreciated monetary unit. Their doctrines, therefore, would seem to come into sharp conflict with any theory of the value of money which makes it vary inversely with its quantity, whether proportionately or not.[82] Only for those mercantilists who wanted an increase of money for use as hoards or stores of wealth would acceptance of a quantity theory of money involve no problem of reconciliation. Many of the mercantilist writers gave no evidence of recognition of the dependence of the value of money upon its quantity. A few of them, in fact, wanted more money as a cure for the evils resulting from high prices. But, although Locke is sometimes credited with the first clear English formulation of the quantity theory, many of the mercantilists, from the beginning of the seventeenth century on, did present, in one connection or another, some simple version of the quantity

---

[81] E.g., Samuel Lamb, *Seasonal observations* [1659], *Somers' tracts,* 2d ed., VI, 455; Edward Forde, *Experimented proposals* [1666], in *The Harleian miscellany,* VII, 343; M. Lewis, *Proposals to the King and Parliament, or a large model of a bank,* 1678, p. 20; Richard Lawrence, *The interest of Ireland,* 1682, Part II, p. 11; *An essay towards carrying on the present war against France* [*ca.* 1697], in *The Harleian miscellany,* X, 380; *Proposals for restoring credit: for making the Bank of England more useful and profitable,* 1721, p. 17; Robert Wallace, *Characteristics of the present political state of Great Britain,* 1758, p. 30. See also pp. 44-45, *infra,* with respect to the views of Potter and Law.

A number of writers, however, disapproved of paper money, on the ground that it made the balance of trade unfavorable and drove metallic money out of the country; e.g., Vanderlint, *Money answers all things* [1734], Hollander ed., p. 15; Patrick Murray (Lord Elibank), *Essays, I. on the public debt, II. on paper-money, banking, &c., III. on frugality,* 1755, pp. 20-25; and surprisingly enough, David Hume, *Political discourses* [1752], in *Essays, moral, political, and literary,* 1875 ed., I, 311, 337 ff.

[82] See also the discussion of the theory of the "self-regulating mechanism," pp. 74 ff., *infra.*

theory,[83] although in most cases they failed to incorporate it as an integral part of their foreign-trade doctrine and failed also to show any concern about its consistency with the rest of their doctrine. There follow quotations from writings antedating Locke by some forty to ninety years which present some form of quantity theory of the value of money:

. . . plenty of money maketh generally things dear, and scarcity of money maketh likewise generally things good cheap. Whereas things particularly are also dear or good cheap according to plenty or scarcity of the things themselves, or the use of them.[84]

. . . even as plenty of money maketh things dear, and scarcity of money maketh things good cheap: even so plenty or scarcity of commodities maketh the price thereof to rise and fall according to their use more or less.[85]

It is a common saying, that plenty or scarcity of money makes all things dear or good or cheap. . . .[86]

Gold and silver . . . in the intrinsic . . . are commodities, valuing each other according to the plenty or scarcity; and so all other commodities by them; and that is the sole power of trade.[87]

. . . money through want or plenty raises or diminishes the price of all things. . . .[88]

. . . in those countries where monies are scarce, there the lands and native wares are cheap, so likewise where money doth abound, there the lands and wares are dear; . . .[89]

---

[83] J. W. Angell, *The theory of international prices*, 1926, pp. 13, 15, 18, etc., denies specifically to Malynes and Mun, and generally to all the English mercantilists before Locke (1691) possession of any form of the quantity theory. A. E. Monroe, *Monetary theory before Adam Smith*, 1923, gives the same impression. For purposes of the theory of international trade, differences in the mode of formulation of the quantity theory have as a rule little qualitative significance, but as is shown in the text, several variants of the quantity theory were presented by English writers prior to Locke.

[84] Malynes, *A treatise of the canker* [1601], *T.E.D.*, III, 387.

[85] Malynes, *The center of the circle of commerce*, 1623, p. 14.

[86] Mun, *England's treasure* [1664—written about 1630], Ashley ed., p. 28. See also p. 24.

[87] Sir Robert Cotton, "A speech touching the alteration of coyne" [1626], in *Cottoni posthuma*, 1672, p. 303.

[88] Henry Robinson, *Englands safety; in trades encrease*, 1641, p. 60. If interpreted literally, this appears to be the quantity theory reversed, but the context shows it is not intended to be so interpreted.

[89] *Decay of trade*, 1641, p. 2. See also, *A discourse . . . for the enlargement and freedome of trade*, 1645, p. 23. For the period after 1650 the following may be cited, in addition to the writers discussed in the text: Ralph Maddison, *Great Britains remembrancer* [1640], 1655, p. 7; [William Paterson] *A brief*

Several mercantilists faced squarely the apparent conflict between the quantity theory of money and their doctrines and attempted to meet the issue either by arguing that they could be reconciled or by denying the truth of the quantity theory.[90] Apparently the first of these was William Potter, who has not received the attention which he deserves in this connection.[91] Potter, as has been shown,[92] claimed that an increase of money *in circulation* would result in an even more than proportionate increase in trade and production, or in goods in circulation. In order to refute it, he states a quantity theory of money in its simplest one-sided form:

> If then, in opposition to what is thus undertaken to be proved, it should be objected, that an increase of money would occasion an increase in the price of commodities, proportionable to such increase of money, (that is, if the money were twice as much, commodity would be twice as dear) consequently (going never the further in commodity by the increase thereof) would not occasion any increase in the sale of commodity: therefore not any increase of trade; and yet (by causing the price of commodities to rise) incur an inconvenience, contrary to what is before affirmed.[93]

His answer is elaborate and not always intelligible. He assumes the basis of the theory of money he is attacking to be that an increase of money increases prices by increasing the (physical?) volume of sales (by increasing the demand for commodities?).

---

account of the intended Bank of England [1694], in Bannister ed., *Writings of William Paterson*, III, 85; John Briscoe, *A discourse of money*, 1696, pp. 47-58: $\left(\dfrac{\text{stock of money}}{\text{number of persons}} = \text{rate of money wages} = \text{prices} \times \text{average real income} \right)$; Vanderlint, *Money answers all things* [1734], Hollander ed., pp. 13, 44; [Erasmus Philips] *The state of the nation in respect to her commerce*, 1725, pp. 40 ff. After Hume (1752) the quantity theory was a commonplace.

[90] Cf., however, Angell, *op. cit.*, p. 211: "In England no effort was ever made to reconcile the two conflicting doctrines."

[91] Neither Dubois, *Précis de l'histoire des doctrines économiques*, 1903, I, 258 ff., who of all the commentators on mercantilism deals most acutely with the difficulties created for the doctrine by the development of the quantity theory of money, nor Angell (*op. cit.*) who follows Dubois, mentions Potter. Dubois attaches great importance in this connection to Law and Verri, who were anticipated on the points relevant here by Potter.

[92] *Supra*, pp. 37-38.

[93] *Key of wealth*, 1650, p. 13.

He replies that if, when money is doubled, the prices of commodities are also doubled, there will be no increase in the (physical?) amount of sales. The theory therefore involves a contradiction.[94] He then attempts to meet it by another line of reasoning. Quick trade permits of a small profit, and therefore a lower price. Quick sales enable artisans and others to produce more quickly, and if they sell more they can afford to charge a lower price. The increase in the amount of commodities resulting from the stimulus to trade of an increase in money, instead of raising prices, will therefore lower them. Prices will rise only if the increase in commodities is proportionately less than the increase in money, which is not likely to be the case. But even if prices should rise somewhat, it is better to have an abundance of comforts, though dear, than a smaller amount thereof, though never so cheap.[95]

Another advocate of paper money, John Asgill, denied the truth of the quantity theory of money on different and exceedingly slender grounds: an increase in money would lower the rate of interest and therefore raise land values, but not the prices of commodities in general, because "the price of corn and cattle don't rise and fall with the interest of money."[96] John Law attacked it, partly by arguments closely resembling those of Potter, partly on reasoning peculiarly his own. The stimulus to trade and industry resulting from an increase in money would result in an increase in commodities. Because money would be easier to borrow, merchants would be able to increase the extent of their operations and to sell at lower rates of profit, and therefore the value of the money would not fall, i.e., prices would not rise.[97] Money falls in value only when given to a people in greater quantity than there is demand for; if the money is issued only as there is demand for it, its value will not depreciate, "the

---

[94] *Ibid.*, p. 13. Cf. also p. 15.

[95] *Ibid.*, pp. 17-20.

[96] *Several assertions proved* [1696] Hollander ed., p. 20. This is, of course, an unusually clear instance of the confusion between loanable capital and money.

[97] *Money and trade considered* [1705] (Glasgow, 1750), pp. 141-42. Cf. also, *Englands interest or the great benefit to trade by banks*, 1682, p. 7: if a bank were established, "All sorts of wares will be afforded at cheaper rates, without prejudice to those that make and sell them, because trading will be greater and quicker."

quantity and demand increasing and decreasing together."[98] Law concedes that if the quantity of money in any particular country "should increase beyond the proportion that country bears to Europe," prices would rise there, but the rise of prices would spread elsewhere, so that the value of money would become the same, or about the same, everywhere. The country which had acquired the increase of money would profit greatly thereby, "for that country would have the whole benefit of the greater quantity, and only bear a share of the lesser value, according to the proportion its money had to the money of Europe."[99] What would make the prices rise elsewhere, he does not explain.

Another writer, James Hodges, who complained of scarcity of money, wanted plate called in and coined and the monetary value of the English standard coin raised as a remedy for this scarcity. He claimed that these measures would result in higher prices *only after they resulted in an increase in the number of coins in circulation*. The effect on prices would therefore be gradual, and meanwhile there would be a stimulus to trade. After a short time the value of the coin could be gradually lowered, and the surplus bullion returned to be made into plate again if its owners so desired. His argument is interesting as an anticipation of Hume's doctrine that *rising* prices are a stimulus to trade, and for its endeavor to find a method of obtaining this stimulus without involving a permanent increase in the price level. The difficulty with the scheme, granting its logic, is, of course, that the period of stimulus would be followed by a period of at least corresponding depression.[100]

Both Potter and Law claimed that an increase of (paper) money would make the balance of trade more favorable and would lead to an inflow of bullion. Potter argued that the beneficial effects of an increased quantity of money would enable

---

[98] John Law, *op. cit.*, pp. 166-73, 221. This argument is an anticipation of the doctrine of the nineteenth-century "banking school," which applied it, however, only to convertible, and denied its applicability to inconvertible paper money.

[99] *Ibid.*, pp. 142-43. Law's reasoning is reproduced at length and largely verbatim, without any acknowledgment, by Sir Humphrey Mackworth, *A proposal for payment of the publick debts*, 2d ed. (*ca.* 1720), pp. 9-16. The quantity theory is also attacked, in an obscure and ineffective way, by B-I-M.D. [William Temple of Trowbridge], *A vindication of commerce and the arts* [1758], McCulloch ed., *Select collection of scarce and valuable tracts on commerce*, 1859, pp. 517 ff.

[100] *The present state of England*, 1697, pp. 27 ff., 122 ff., 230 ff., 333.

England to outsell other countries, for "the greater trade of one country hath a capacity of undermining and eating out the lesser trade of other countries."[101] For reasons not explained, unless it be the fall in English prices alleged to result from an increase in the quantity of money, both foreign and English commodities would fall in price in England, but not abroad Exports would therefore be paid for with bullion (and presumably imports would be paid for with English commodity exports), and the bullion could be coined into English money without loss. But with unusual consistency Potter admits that when paper money or credit is available as a substitute, metallic money would be of little importance to England.[102] Law showed more concern than did Potter about the state of the balance of trade, but he also claimed that an increased amount of money through the issue of paper money would make the balance favorable: "Most people think scarcity of money is only the consequence of a balance due; but 'tis the cause as well as the consequence, and the effectual way to bring the balance to our side, is to add to the money."[103] More money, by employing more people, would make a surplus of goods available for export, and if sufficient money was issued production would reach a level at which more would be exported than imported. Conversely, if the amount of money was reduced, some of the laborers would be rendered idle, the domestic output would shrink, exports would fall, and an unfavorable balance would result.[104] These results of a change in the quantity of money he would apparently expect not to be transitory but to persist as long as the new quantity of money persisted.

The Mercantilists on Hoards and Plate.—Because the mercantilists differed among themselves as to the character of the benefit which resulted from an increase in the amount of bullion in a country, they also differed in their attitudes toward the miser, the collector of gold or silver plate, the usurer, and the spendthrift. Those mercantilists for whom the chief virtue in an increased supply of bullion lay in its stimulus to circulation condemned private hoards as an evil, and also regarded other prac-

[101] *Key of wealth*, p. 12.

[102] *Ibid.*, pp. 68 ff.

[103] *Money and trade considered* [1705], 1750, p. 217.

[104] *Ibid.*, pp. 23-24. Sir Humphrey Mackworth plagiarized Law here as elsewhere.—*A proposal for payment of the publick debts, ca.* 1720, p. 9.

tices which kept bullion from circulating as money, such as its use in the manufacture of plate, as objectionable.[105] Vaughan condemned hoarding and the use of plate as contributing factors to the scarcity of money, and recommended sumptuary legislation to check the melting of money and its manufacture into plate.[106] An anonymous writer criticized the Established church on the ground that it hoarded riches which should circulate, so that "the money that before ran current in trading, is dammed up in their coffers."[107] Another pamphlet, written as an answer to this one, condemned the excess of silver plate for the same reason, but claimed that there was no occasion for alarm about hoarding, as there was not much of it, and urged in the defense of the church that it could be charged with responsibility for the prevailing scarcity of money only if the clerics kept "banks of money dead by them," which was not the case. Complaint against the usurer as a hoarder of money was likewise without basis, since "his money walks, though upon other legs, either serving the tradesman or the gentleman, for preparing commodities to export, or to buy what is imported for his expenses."[108] Manley found fault with the miser, because "money locked up in the miser's coffers is like dung in a heap, it does no good, but being dispersed, and orderly disposed abroad, enricheth the land."[109] An anonymous writer wanted misers' hoards taxed, in order to draw some of their money into circulation, especially in time of war when trade was slack. "I know no difference," he wrote, "betwixt bringing treasure out of an iron chest by a good law, and

---

[105] Cf. *A discourse of the nature, use and advantages of trade,* 1693, p. 20:

It may likewise be considered, whether the advancement of trade is not greatly prevented by the unaccountable humor of having so much plate in every family, which if turned into coin would infinitely promote the general trade, but while it remains in plate is of no more public benefit than if it were buried in the bowels of the earth, while so many other manufactures are neglected that would otherwise be employed to supply the use and ornament of plate.

[106] Rice Vaughan, *A discourse of coin and coinage,* 1675, p. 66.

[107] *Omnia comesta a bello,* 1667, p. 10.

[108] *Et à dracone: Or, some reflections upon a discourse called Omnia à belo comesta,* 1668, pp. 5 ff. Cf. *Taxes no charge,* 1690, pp. 13 ff.

[109] Thomas Manley, *Usury at six per cent. examined,* 1669, p. 53. Manley borrowed the analogy from Francis Bacon: "Money is like muck, not good except it be spread."—"Of seditions and troubles" [1625], in *Works,* 1852, I, 23. But the context shows that Bacon meant more equal distribution of wealth and not monetary circulation.

plowing the seas by long and dangerous voyages" in order to secure bullion through foreign trade.[110] One of Locke's objections to the reduction of the interest rate by law was that it would result in men keeping their money "dead" by them, instead of lending it, with resultant loss to trade.[111] Petty expressed a preference for money over plate, because it served trade better,[112] as did also Hugh Chamberlain: "Money is living riches, plate but dead; that being capable of turning and improving trade, when this is not."[113]

Hodges's scheme for a forced three-year surrender of plate in return for "raised" money, with prohibition of ownership of plate in the interval, in order for a time to secure relief from the prevailing scarcity of money, and to obtain the stimulus to trade of slowly rising prices, has already been referred to.[114] Another writer urged a similar scheme for raising money 5 per cent, in order to draw hoards of the old, and therefore undervalued, coins into circulation.[115] One writer made the same sort of contrast between hoarded and circulating credit which other writers confined to hoarded and circulating money, hoarded credit being the exchequer bills which, because of the high rate of interest they carried, were held instead of being used as money: ". . . in the frequent passing of credit from hand to hand, consists its great usefulness in trade; for when either money or credit is hoarded up, it may more properly be said to stagnate, than to circulate."[116] Postlethwayt, in a curious argument, claimed that lending of money at interest involved hoarding and therefore on circulation grounds was to be condemned. If some money is hoarded, the volume of trade will fall. In order to bring the hoarded money back into trade, those in great need of it will offer interest ("profit") for its loan. The result will be that other moneyed men, instead of "circulating their money" in trade, will "lock it up," while awaiting the opportunity to lend it, preferring to get their income by usury instead of by trade. Eventually the

[110] *Taxes no charge*, 1690, p. 17.

[111] *Some considerations* [1691], *Works*, 1623 ed., V, 12.

[112] *Political arithmetick* [1690], *Economic writings*, I, 243.

[113] *A collection of some papers*, 1696, p. 4.

[114] *Supra*, p. 44.

[115] *The circumstances of Scotland consider'd*, 1705, p. 25.

[116] *The vindication and advancement of our national constitution and credit*, 1710, p. 84.

money so withdrawn from trade would be lent and would thus return to trade, but bearing an interest charge which would act as a restraint on trade.[117]

Some writers objected, on similar grounds, to the establishment of banks, holding that they monopolized money, and kept it from circulating. Child, for example, maintained that "principally this seeming scarcity of money proceeds from the trade of bankering, which obstructs circulation."[118] Strangely enough, considering his views on the effect of lending at interest on monetary circulation referred to above, Postlethwayt made the most effective rejoinder to this argument which I have found:

> It may be here requisite to take notice of that erroneous notion entertained by some, that banks and bankers engross the money, hoard it up, and hinder its circulation in trade; but, if such will consider this matter in its true light, they will easily be convinced, that the money lodged in banks, and in the hands of bankers, is the most constantly employed of any; for, though the specie should lie still till called for, yet the notes given out for its value, are continually circulating; whereby is done abundantly more service to trade, than if the same lay dormant in private hands; and yet the necessities of the depositors are effectually answered.[119]

Once hoarding and the use of coin or bullion in the making of plate were attacked, there were few to come to their defense, and the use of gold and silver in the making of thread or in gilding met with almost general condemnation. Mun, however, opposed restrictions on the melting-down of coin into plate on the ground that gold and silver were more apt to be carried out of the kingdom in payment of purchases of foreign goods if in

---

[117] Malachy Postlethwayt, *Great-Britain's true system*, 1757, pp. 337-42.

[118] *A discourse about trade*, 1690, author's preface. Cf. also: *Reasons offer'd against the continuance of the Bank*, 1707; *A short view of the apparent dangers and mischiefs from the Bank of England*, 1707, p. 12; *Some queries, humbly offer'd . . . relating to the Bank of England*, 1707, p. 1; *An enquiry into the melancholy circumstances of Great Britain* (n.d., ca. 1730), p. 36.

[119] *The universal dictionary of trade and commerce*, 4th ed. 1774, Art. "Banking." What some of the critics of the Bank really had in mind was the danger that a great bank controlling a substantial proportion of the available loan funds would be able to exercise a monopolistic control over credit, to charge excessive interest rates, and to discriminate between borrowers. Cf. *Remarks upon the Bank of England, with regard more especially to our trade and government*, 1705; *A short view of the apparent dangers*, 1707, pp. 10 ff.

the form of coin than if kept in the form of plate,[120] and Misselden before him, while conceding that too much plate in the kingdom would cause scarcity of money, nevertheless held that it was better to have bullion kept in the form of plate than to turn it into coin and thus turn it out of the kingdom because of the undervaluation of coin which he alleged then prevailed in England.[121] A sixteenth-century writer condoned the use of bullion for plate, because it resulted in the formation of a sort of secondary national reserve for emergencies, upon which the king, in case of a great war, could draw "without any grouching of the Commons."[122] The same argument is to be found occasionally in the later literature, and is made by Briscoe to serve as a defense of private hoards. Hoarded treasure, bullion and coin, is part of the "capital stock of national treasure" and can be drawn upon in a national emergency. Private hoarding is as good as having treasure stored by the king.[123]

Toward the end of the seventeenth century there appeared a new doctrine of the existence of a "due proportion" between money and goods, and therefore of the possibility of excess of money as far as trade needs were concerned. The quantity theory of money also tended to lead to the conclusion that an increase in the amount of money by increasing prices would reduce exports and thus eventually be lost to the country. Writers who on "due proportions of money to trade" or on quantity-theory grounds conceded that there was under any given set of circumstances a maximum amount of money which could be kept in circulation, and who still attached special importance to the precious metals, were likely to approve of turning the money into plate or of its hoarding as a means either of stimulating the further import of bullion or of checking an outflow. It was doubtless such reasoning which led John Houghton to the conclusion that "if the King should hoard up much money, it would for the present make it dearer, that dearness would make it be brought in more plentifully, and that would make it more plentiful than it was before."[124] Petty wrote: "For there may be as well too much money

---

[120] *England's treasure* [1664], Ashley ed., p. 28.

[121] *Free trade,* 2d ed., 1622, p. 11.

[122] "Policies to reduce this realme" [1549], *T.E.D.,* III, 323-24.

[123] J. Briscoe, *A discourse of money,* 1696, pp. 27-29. Cf. also Henry Robinson, *Englands safety; in trades encrease,* 1641, p. 9.

[124] *A collection of letters,* 1681-83, II, 115.

in a country, as too little. I mean, as to the best advantage of its trade; only the remedy is very easy, it may be soon turned into the magnificence of gold and silver vessels."[125]

On similar grounds another writer would tolerate the increased use of plate if there was more money than was necessary to carry on trade and "defray the expense of living,"[126] and Vanderlint, who accepted the quantity theory and wanted low prices but at the same time wanted a favorable balance of trade payable in specie, recommended as a means of attaining these apparently conflicting objectives that the private hoarding of gold and silver and their use in plate, and even in gold and silver cloth and gilding, be encouraged. He cited with approval the practice of the East Indians of hoarding the silver they receive, with the result that prices remained low there, exports continued to exceed imports, and the balance was paid in still more silver.[127] Harris presents a similar solution of the same dilemma. If the inflow of bullion resulting from a favorable balance of trade is kept:

as a dead stock, either by turning it into plate or by any other method, so as to prevent its getting into trade as money; it may continue to go on increasing in more bullion, which in this case will be a real increase of wealth. . . . Let an increased stock of bullion get out again into trade, and it will soon turn the balance the other way.[128]

But gold and silver can be best stored up in the form of plate:

But people in general will not hoard up cash; all like to display their wealth, and to lay out their superfluities in some costly things. There seems then no method so effectual for the securing of a dead stock of treasure in any country, as the encouraging the use of plate, by making it fashionable, preferable to more brittle or more perishable commodities. Plate would be a national resource in case of emergency, and not the less so, because the precious metals had not as yet received the shape of coins.[129]

Hume in 1752 claimed that state hoarding was the only expedient by which a country could raise its supply of the precious metals above the equilibrium level, but commented that this was

[125] *The political anatomy of Ireland* [1691], *Economic writings,* I, 193.
[126] *The circumstances of Scotland consider'd,* 1705, p. 9.
[127] *Money answers all things* [1734], Hollander ed., pp. 94 ff.
[128] Joseph Harris, *An essay upon money and coins,* Part I (1757), 89.
[129] *Ibid.,* pp. 99-100.

"a practice which we should all exclaim against as destructive, namely, the gathering of large sums into a public treasure, locking them up, and absolutely preventing their circulation."[130]

Henry Home accepted so whole-heartedly the lesson of the quantity theory of money that he looked upon an export surplus alike with an import surplus as dangerous to the country. The latter meant an outward drain of money, with a consequent fall of prices and stoppage of industry. The former meant an influx of specie, extravagance, rise in prices, and finally a fall in exports, rise in imports, an unfavorable balance again, and a recurrence of the drain of specie. What was to be desired was an even balance. Therefore, "let the registers of foreign mints be carefully watched, in order that our current coin may not exceed that of our industrious neighbors." But it was not the quantity of gold and silver in a country that determined the price level, but the quantity of money in circulation. Still retaining some traces of the mercantilist attachment for the precious metals, he therefore advocated the conversion of money into plate and even, under favorable circumstances, the formation of a state treasure.[131]

v. Employment and the Balance of Trade

The mercantilist arguments for a favorable balance of trade so far considered all rest upon the desirability of more bullion. But there was one mercantilist argument which was not dependent upon the attachment of superior economic importance to the precious metals than to other commodities of equal exchange value, namely the "employment" argument. Exports were the product of English labor whereas imports, especially if they consisted of finished products and of commodities competitive with home products, displaced English labor. The greater the exports, and the smaller the imports, the greater, therefore, was the employment of English labor. This argument was not, as is sometimes supposed, of late seventeenth-century origin. It is to be found in the very earliest mercantilist writings,[1] and it persists

---

[130] *Political discourses* [1752], in *Essays, moral, political, and literary*, 1875, I, 340.

[131] *Sketches of the history of man*, 1774, I, 82. See also Postlethwayt, *Great-Britain's true system*, 1757, p. 357.

[1] E.g. [Starkey], *England in the reign of King Henry the Eighth* [*ca.* 1538], 1871 reprint, p. 94; "How the comen people may be set to worke" [*ca.* 1530],

without break throughout the literature of the seventeenth and eighteenth centuries. It is not even clear that it was more emphasized in the eighteenth- than in the seventeenth-century mercantilist literature, and it could even be argued that the sixteenth-century writers stressed it most of all. Of all the mercantilist reasoning, it withstood criticism most successfully, and persisted into the nineteenth and twentieth centuries as an important element in the protectionist doctrine.

The stress on employment led to an appraisal of exports not merely in terms of their value, or of their value relative to imports, but in terms of the amount of labor they represented. Exports of manufactured articles were rated more highly than exports to the same value of raw materials, because the former embodied a larger proportion of labor. The stress on employment sometimes took the form of measuring the gain from trade by the exports alone, and in a few cases the argument even went to the extreme of recommending production of goods simply to employ labor, even though the product of their labor were burnt upon their completion.[2] In the case of a few later writers, the employment argument gave rise to a new balance-of-trade concept, in which the amounts weighed against each other were not the values respectively of the exports and the imports, but the respective amounts of labor or employment they represented, i.e., the "balance of labor" or the "balance of employment." Barbon seems to have been the first to come close to this concept. The measure of benefit from different exports is the amount of employment they had given to English labor, and, similarly, the measure of benefit from imports is the amount of employment to which they will give rise in their further manufacture. His employment test leads him at times to liberal conclusions. Imports of

---

Pauli ed., *Drei volkswirthschaftliche Denkschriften,* p. 56; "How to reforme the realme" [*ca.* 1535], *ibid.,* p. 76; "Polices to reduce this realme of England" [1549], *T.E.D.,* III, 333; [John Hales] *A discourse of the common weal* [1581], Elizabeth Lamond ed., pp. 63 ff.; Malynes, *Treatise of the canker* [1601], *T.E.D.,* III, 399; Misselden, *The circle of commerce,* 1623, p. 35. Mun is one of the few early writers who dealt with trade matters extensively who makes no use of the employment argument. Reliance upon Mun as adequately representative of the earlier literature may have been responsible for the conclusion that the argument first appeared in the later period.

[2] Petty, *Treatise of taxes* [1662], in *Economic writings,* Hull ed., I, 60; [Sheridan] *A discourse on the rise and power of parliaments* [1677], Bannister ed., p. 200; *Taxes no charge,* 1690, p. 16.

raw silk are more profitable than imports of gold and silver, because more hands are employed in the manufacture of the first than in working the latter. If woolen goods are exported for Westphalian bacon and then the import of the latter is prohibited, England would lose even if the consumption of English bacon increased, because woolen cloth employs more hands in its production than does bacon.[3]

Tucker stated the argument somewhat differently. The balance of trade for country A is the excess of the number of laborers working up manufactures for country B in A as compared to the number of laborers working up manufactures for A in B:

> . . . when two countries are exchanging their produce or manufactures with each other, that nation which has the greatest number employed in this reciprocal trade, is said to receive a balance from the other; because the price of the overplus labor must be paid in gold and silver. . . . This is the clearest and justest method of determining the balance between nation and nation: for though a difference in the value of the respective commodities may make some difference in the sum actually paid to balance accounts, yet the general principle, that labor (not money) is the riches of a people, will always prove, that the advantage is on the side of that nation which has most hands employed in labor.[4]

A closely similar doctrine is presented also by Harris, Steuart, and Arthur Young:

> . . . a nation that pays ultimately upon its trade a balance in bullion, is a loser of so much of its dead stock; and a loser also, if its exports maintained fewer of its own inhabitants, than its imports did of those foreign nations.[5]

In all trade two things are to be considered in the commodity sold. The first is the matter; the second is the labor employed to render this matter useful. The matter exported from a country is what the country loses; the price of the labor exported is what it

---

[3] Nicholas Barbon, *A discourse of trade* [1690], Hollander reprint, pp. 23, 37; *ibid.*, *A discourse concerning coining the new money lighter*, 1696, pp. 50-51.

[4] Josiah Tucker, *A brief essay on the advantages and disadvantages which respectively attend France and Great Britain, with regard to trade* [3d ed. 1753], McCulloch ed., *Select collection of . . . tracts on commerce*, p. 315. This passage first appeared in the third edition. See also Tucker, *Reflections on the expediency of a law for the naturalization of foreign protestants*, 1751, Part II, p. 21.

[5] [Joseph Harris] *An essay upon money and coins*, Part I (1757), 89. See also p. 24.

gains. If the value of the matter imported be greater than the value of what is exported the country gains. If a greater value of labor be imported, than exported, the country loses. Why? Because in the first case, strangers must have paid, *in matter,* the surplus of labor exported; and in the second case, because the country must have paid to strangers, *in matter,* the surplus of labor imported. It is therefore a general maxim, to discourage the importation of work, and to encourage the exportation of it.[6]

A balance in our favor is a proof that foreigners take more products and fabrics from us than we do from them, which is an advantage of the highest consequence, because it suggests at least a strong probability that they employ more of our poor than we do of theirs.[7]

These writers apparently would compare the amount of English labor embodied in the exports with the amount of foreign labor represented by the imports in computing the English "balance of labor." On this basis, a given trade balance measured in money would have to be regarded as more favorable the lower the prices at which English exports were sold and the lower the wages earned by English labor engaged in their production, although it is not evident that these writers saw this implication of their doctrine. The objective they had in mind, to the exclusion of other considerations, was employment of English labor, and in the case of Young the assumption is fairly clear that the labor engaged in the production of exported goods would in the absence of such exports remain idle. He states that "whatever is paid to other countries in bullion, as a balance upon the year's trade, is just so much loss to any nation that has unemployed poor or unpurchased commodities," but he concedes to Hume that the loss of the bullion is important only as it is a sign "that we do not export a due quantity of products and labor."[8]

---

[6] Sir James Steuart, *Principles of political œconomy,* 1767, II, 336. (Italics in original text.)

[7] Arthur Young, *Political essays concerning the present state of the British Empire,* 1772, p. 538.

[8] *Ibid.,* p. 533. Although they both stress employment, this "balance-of-labor" argument differs from the earlier argument that an excess of the *value* of exports over the *value* of imports results in an inflow of bullion, which increases trade and therefore employment. (Cf. Malynes, *Treatise of the canker* [1601], *T.E.D.,* III, 399: "the more ready money . . . that our merchants should make their return by, . . . the more employment would they make upon our home commodities, advancing the price thereof, which price would augment the quantity by setting more people on work; . . .") In the balance-of-labor doctrine

The balance-of-labor doctrine is of course absurd and probably even more absurd than the earlier and at the time still dominant balance-of-trade doctrine. It nevertheless can be regarded as a stage of some importance in the evolution toward more sensible doctrine. In the first case, any criticism of or substitution for the dominant balance-of-trade doctrine helped to promote the disintegration of the mercantilist errors, and thus was a service even if it proposed an even less satisfactory alternative doctrine, provided the criticism survived and the proposed substitute did not survive. Secondly, the balance-of-labor doctrine reversed the roles of employment and foreign trade as compared to the conventional balance-of-trade doctrine. In conventional mercantilism increased population, increased employment, improvement in the arts, in roads, canals, in the energy and skill of labor, were all welcomed because they would make possible increased production of goods for export or in lieu of imports from abroad, and would thus promote a favorable balance of trade. In the balance-of-labor doctrine the end was employment, and the favorable balance was the means, and even if its exponents did not themselves see clearly that income and consumption were in turn the rational ends of employment, and of economic activity in general, they at least made it easy for Adam Smith and later writers to take the next step and thus to bring about a revolutionary change in the orientation of economic thought.

One student of English mercantilism, E. A. Johnson, noting the indisputable—and undisputed—fact that the mercantilists approved of a large working population, hard work on the part of laborers, the progress of skill in the application of labor, improvements in transportation and industry, and so forth, has concluded that serious injustice has been done to them by accounts such as presumably the present one of their doctrines:

All of which should prove that the ultimate concern of the mercantilists was the creation of effective factors of production. Not ten per cent of English mercantilist literature is devoted to the ill-fated doctrine of the balance of trade. [Let anyone who doubts this assertion turn through the pages of the English mercantilist literature and be convinced!] Their ardent passion for productive efficiency is shown by their advocacy of improvement of lands, mines and fish-

---

it is the direct effect of the exports on employment which is stressed, and not the indirect effect consequent upon the inflow or outflow of specie.

eries, and by their encouragement of inland communication and canal building. Industry was to be encouraged, idleness to be repressed. . . .[9]

But evidence that the mercantilists desired efficient production, be it piled up mountain high, of itself proves nothing as to their "ultimate concern." They may have desired, and did desire, increased production, because they thought that it would promote a favorable balance of trade, even though they also desired it for other reasons. Such quantitative propositions have an unearned air of precision, but on the basis of my turning of the pages of English mercantilist literature I venture the conclusion that not ten per cent of it was free from concern, expressed or clearly implied, in the state of the balance of trade and in the means whereby it could be improved.

The labor doctrines of the English mercantilists need not be examined at length here, since they have been ably dealt with by other writers.[10] On only one point, it seems to me, is critical comment on their exposition called for. The mercantilists, as they point out, were led by their obsession with the balance of trade and also, perhaps, by unconscious class sympathies, to deal with questions affecting labor as if laborers were a set of somewhat troublesome tools rather than human beings whose own comfort and happiness were a proper and primary object of concern for statesmen. The dominant doctrine, in consequence, advocated low wages, as a means of stimulating the worker to greater effort and of increasing England's competitive strength in foreign trade by lowering the money costs of English products. Sir James Steuart was merely expressing in blunter fashion than was common the position implicit in much of the mercantilist treatment of the labor question when he stated that "the lowest classes of a people, in a country of trade, must be restrained to their physical-necessary."[11] But Furniss and Gregory fail to do full

---

[9] "The mercantilist concept of 'art' and 'ingenious labour,'" *Economic History*, II (1931), 251-52. The sentence placed here in brackets is a footnote in the original text.

[10] E. S. Furniss, *The position of the laborer in a system of nationalism*, 1920; T. E. Gregory, "The economics of employment in England, 1660-1713," *Economica*, I (1921), 37-51.

[11] *An inquiry into the principles of political œconomy*, 1767, I, 502. Cf. *ibid.*: "It is therefore a principle, to encourage competition universally until it has had

justice to the size and importance of the dissenting group, who on grounds either of economic analysis or humanitarian sentiment opposed the dominant doctrine that low wages were desirable. Such important writers as Cary, Coke, Davenant, and Defoe belonged to this group, and in the latter part of the eighteenth century the growth of humanitarianism operated to give even stronger challenge to the prevailing views.[12] Representative of the opposition on humanitarian grounds was the complaint of an anonymous writer: "it is a great pity the laboring poor have not better encouragement, the cries of those unskillful men, who made a clamor of labor being too high, is a doctrine propagated more by theory than practice."[13] Hume conceded that high wages resulted in some disadvantage in foreign trade, but insisted that "as foreign trade is not the most material circumstance, it is not to be put in competition with the happiness of so many millions."[14] Since Hume was an enlightened critic of mercantilism, this is not of great significance, but Wallace, who was a mercantilist, agreed with Hume's doctrine, as "a maxim . . . suitable to a humane disposition. Agreeably to such a benevolent sentiment, we ought to extend our notions of trade, and consider not only how much money it gains to a nation, but how far it is conducive to the happiness of the people."[15]

---

the effect to reduce people of industry to the physical-necessary, and to prevent it ever from bringing them lower. . . ."

[12] Cf. the citations in Lujo Brentano, *Hours and wages in relation to production* (translated from the German), 1894, pp. 2-5, to which many additions should be made.

[13] *An enquiry into the melancholy circumstances of Great Britain*, ca. 1730, pp. 19-20.

[14] *Political discourses* [1752], in *Essays, moral, political and literary*, 1875 ed., I, 297.

[15] [Robert Wallace] *Characteristics of the present political state of Great Britain*, 1758, p. 46.

Chapter II

ENGLISH THEORIES OF FOREIGN TRADE,
BEFORE ADAM SMITH: II

*He shewed me a very excellent argument to prove, that our **importing**
lesse [gold?] than we export, do not impoverish the kingdom, according to the received opinion: which, though it be a paradox, and that
I do not remember the argument, yet methought there was a great
deal in what he said.*—Samuel Pepys, *Memoirs*, February 29, 1663/4.

I. Legislative Proposals of Mercantilists

Introductory.—The mercantilist writers were often critics of
the prevailing legislation, and they cannot be understood unless
this is constantly borne in mind. The actual body of statutes and
proclamations in force at any one time was always an uncoordi-
nated accumulation of measures adopted at various periods and
for various reasons, and was far from conforming to any self-
coherent set of ideas or principles with respect to trade policy.
Of these laws and proclamations there were always a number
which were non-enforced or were only spasmodically enforced,
either because their legal status was questionable or because
change of circumstances or of official or public opinion made
their strict enforcement inconvenient or impossible. There were
others which were flagrantly violated, sometimes in spite of efforts to enforce them, sometimes with the connivance of corrupt
or unsympathetic officials.

The laws and proclamations were not all, as some modern
admirers of the virtues of mercantilism would have us believe,
the outcome of a noble zeal for a strong and glorious nation,
directed against the selfishness of the profit-seeking merchant,
but were the product of conflicting interests of varying degrees of
respectability. Each group, economic, social, or religious, pressed
constantly for legislation in conformity with its special interest.

The fiscal needs of the crown were always an important and generally a determining influence on the course of trade legislation. Diplomatic considerations also played their part in influencing legislation, as did the desire of the crown to award special privileges, *con amore,* to its favorites, or to sell them, or to be bribed into giving them, to the highest bidders. After the Revolution the crown's authority in matters of trade regulation was largely shorn away, and factional jealousies and party rivalries replaced the vagaries of monarchical whim as a controlling factor in trade policy.

The mercantilist literature, on the other hand, consisted in the main of writings by or on behalf of "merchants" or businessmen, who had the usual capacity for identifying their own with the national welfare. Disinterested exposition of trade doctrine was by no means totally absent from the mercantilist literature, and in the eighteenth century many of the tracts were written to serve party rather than self. But the great bulk of the mercantilist literature consisted of tracts which were partly or wholly, frankly or ·disguisedly, special pleas for special economic interests. Freedom for themselves, restrictions for others, such was the essence of the usual program of legislation of the mercantilist tracts of merchant authorship.

There follows a survey of the specific legislative proposals of the mercantilist writers with respect to the regulation of foreign trade proper. A complete survey would require consideration also of their recommendations for dealing with the fisheries, the colonial trade, the interest rate, and poor relief, as well as with the monopolies and the internal regulation of manufacture, for all of these subjects were approached more or less in terms of their bearing on the balance of trade. Space limitations, however, prevent such extension of this essay as would be necessary to deal with these even sketchily, and in any case the mercantilist doctrines with respect to most of these topics have been ably and comprehensively dealt with in their special literatures and in Heckscher's masterly treatise. Sufficient has already been said to make clear the relationship to mercantilist trade doctrine of proposals for restricting hoarding or the conversion of bullion into plate, for prohibiting or subjecting to heavy taxation use of the precious metals for making thread or cloth or for gilding, and for increasing the monetary circulation through the introduction of paper money, to make unnecessary further discussion of such proposals.

Bullionist Proposals.—Following the common usage, the term "bullionist" will be applied to the measures intended to promote the mercantilist objectives through direct regulation of transactions in the exchanges and in the precious metals. Even prior to 1600 opinion in support of the policy of controlling specie movements indirectly through control of trade, instead of directly by regulation of exchange and specie transactions, seems already to have been fairly common. As early as 1381, Aylesbury said that the way to prevent a drain of specie was to prevent more merchandise from coming into England than was exported from it.[1] An anonymous writer in 1549 stated that regulation of trade so as to bring about a surplus of exports over imports was the *only* means of securing an influx of bullion.[2] An official memorandum of 1559, justifying the restoration of the currency to its former metallic content, denied the efficacy of raising the nominal value of the standard coin as a means of preventing its export.[3] In the sixteenth-century manuscripts discovered by Pauli there are to be found both bullionist and non-bullionist proposals. Revival of the staples and enforcement of the Statutes of Employment are recommended. The acceptance by English sellers of wool of exchange in lieu of specie in payment for their wool should be prohibited. English coin should be overvalued in exchange for foreign coin, so as to attract foreign gold and silver. But imports of unnecessary foreign goods are to be restrained.[4] Hales had made one of the participants in his dialogue urge that some English commodity be made salable to foreigners only in exchange for specie in whole or in part, but in the course of the discussion heavy export duties on wool, the prohibition of the export of unwrought goods, and either prohibition of import of competitive

---

[1] Bland, Brown, and Tawney, *English economic history, select documents,* 1914, p. 222.

[2] "Polices to reduce this realme of Englande" [1549], *T.E.D.,* III, 321: "The only means to cause much bullion to be brought out of other realms unto the king's mints is to provide that a great quantity of our wares may be carried yearly into beyond the seas and less quantity of their wares be brought hither again. . . ."

[3] "Memorandum on the reasons moving Queen Elizabeth to reform the coinage" [1559], *T.E.D.,* II, 195. Cf. also [John Hales] *A discourse of the common weal* [1581], Elizabeth Lamond, ed., p. 79.

[4] Pauli, *Drei volkswirthschaftliche Denkschriften,* pp. 12, 32, 56, 64, 66, 71, 76.

foreign goods or duties high enough to make them more costly than similar domestic goods, are recommended.[5]

Bullionist proposals, on the other hand, are still to be encountered in the seventeenth century. Malynes advocated the revival of the Royal Exchanger, with a monopoly over exchange transactions, the maintenance of the mint par by royal proclamation as the actual rate of exchange, and prohibition of the export of bullion.[6] Revival of the official regulation of exchange rates was urged also by Milles,[7] Maddison,[8] and Robinson;[9] and Rowe, following Malynes, suggested that exchange rates be fixed by treaty with foreign governments.[10] Mun in his first book[11] (though not in his second),[12] Rowe,[13] and Violet[14] wanted enforcement of the old Statutes of Employment. Many writers until late in the seventeenth century urged the enforcement of the prohibitions of the export of coin and bullion, or after 1663, when the export of bullion and of foreign coin was legalized, their revival.[15] But with the exception of a minor lapse by

---

[5] *A discourse of the common weal,* pp. 66, 87-88.

[6] *A treatise of the canker* [1601], *T.E.D.,* III, 398 ff.; *The center of the circle of commerce,* 1623, pp. 70 ff., 121 ff.

[7] *The customers replie,* 1604, *passim.*

[8] *Great Britains remembrancer* [1640], 1655, pp. 16 ff.

[9] *Certain proposals in order to the peoples freedome,* 1652, p. 14.

[10] Sir Thomas Rowe, *The cause of the decay of coin and trade in this land* [1641], *Harleian miscellany,* 1809 ed., IV, 457.

[11] *A discourse of trade, from England unto the East-Indies* [1621], 1930 reprint, p. 54.

[12] In *England's treasure by forraign trade,* chaps. VIII-XIV, Mun presents a detailed and able criticism of the whole gamut of bullionist devices, including the Statutes of Employment.

[13] *Op. cit.* p. 458.

[14] *An humble declaration . . . touching the transportation of gold and silver,* 1643, p. 27 (advocates revival of 14 Ed. III, c. 21, requiring exporters to bring into England a proportion of their receipts in gold); *A true discoverie to the commons of England, how they have been cheated of almost all the gold and silver coin of this nation* [1651], 1653 reprint, p. 83 (advocates revival of 3 Hy. VII, c. 8, one of the Statutes of Employment proper, applying to merchant-strangers and requiring them to employ the money they receive through the sale of foreign goods in the purchase of English merchandise). Cf. the article on Violet in Palgrave's *Dictionary of political economy.*

[15] E.g., Violet, *An humble declaration . . .,* 1643, pp. 30 ff.; *ibid., A true discoverie . . .,* 1653, *passim; ibid., Mysteries and secrets . . .,* 1653, pp. 35, 39, etc.; *Et à dracone,* 1668, p. 4; [Petyt] *Britannia Languens* [1680], in McCulloch ed., *Early English tracts on commerce,* pp. 307 ff.; Hodges, *The present state of England, as to coin and publick charges,* 1697, p. 105; [Pollexfen] *England and East-India inconsistent in their manufactures,* 1697, p. 48.

Steuart,[16] there does not appear to have been any support of any of the bullionist devices among the prominent eighteenth-century writers.

Prohibitions vs. Duties.—The principal non-bullionist measures proposed by the mercantilists as means to secure a favorable balance of trade consisted of : restraints on the importation of foreign goods, especially manufactured goods and luxuries; encouragements to the export of English manufactured products; restraints on the export of raw materials; encouragements to the reexport trade; and restrictions on English industries which interfered with other industries or with trades which, on mercantilist or other grounds, were regarded as of greater importance.

Imports could be restricted either by the imposition of duties or by absolute prohibitions. Both methods were used and advocated, and many writers revealed no clear preference as between them. But they were more different in appearance than in fact. When writers asked for duties rather than prohibitions, they often wanted duties high enough to be prohibitive of import, or nearly so. When the government imposed prohibitions rather than duties, it often granted to particular trading companies or individuals special licenses to import. Many of the prohibitions were undoubtedly established primarily to obtain revenue by the sale of licenses to import rather than to promote a favorable balance of trade.[17] Some writers expressed a preference for import duties rather than prohibitions without stating their reasons, but probably because duties seemed less severe.[18] Other writers recom-

---

[16] *Principles of political œconomy* 1767, II, 329: "But when the balance turns against them in the regular course of business, not from a temporary cause, then he [i.e., 'the statesman'] may lay restraints upon the exportation of specie, as a concomitant restriction, together with others, in order to diminish the general mass of importations, and thereby to set the balance even." Cf. also [George Blewitt] *An enquiry whether a general practice of virtue tends to the wealth or poverty of a people?* 1725, p. 60.

[17] Cf. Thomas Violet, *Mysteries and secrets,* 1653, pp. 8-9: "But there are governments which are for the private advantage of a few men, procuring prohibition of importation of several commodities but only by particular men, and exportation of our native commodities, but only by particular men, and only for some ports, and at some seasons of the year." Violet is not objecting here to the restrictions, but to the special exemptions therefrom.

[18] E.g., Petty, *Treatise of taxes* [1662], *Economic Writings,* Hull ed., I, 60. Petty recommended that the duties be high enough to make foreign finished commodities dearer than competing domestic commodities, and if the imports much exceeded the exports he would support absolute prohibitions.

mended moderate duties rather than high duties or prohibitions, because the latter were too severe and would lead to fraud, whereas duties could be enforced and would at least produce revenue.[19] But other writers objected to the sacrifice of trade interests to fiscal considerations,[20] while Steuart suggested that prohibitions could be more effectively enforced than duties if the latter would have to be high.[21]

Some writers advised that restrictions on imports should not be carried too far, lest they excite foreign retaliation against English exports.[22] Other writers replied, however, that there was little or no danger of foreign retaliation. England exported necessaries and imported "toys," and therefore had nothing to fear.[23] Other countries already restricted the imports of things they could produce themselves; other things must be got somewhere, and they would hurt themselves if they refused to buy them where they could best be got. Most-favored-nation clauses in commercial treaties, moreover, prevented them from discriminating against England in their trade regulations.[24] "No wise nation takes from another what they can be without; and what they cannot be without, they must take, prohibit what you please."[25]

---

[19] E.g., "Polices to reduce this realme of Englande" [1549], *T.E.D.*, III, 332; Fortrey, *Englands interest and improvement* [1663], Hollander ed., p. 28; [Sheridan] *A discourse on the rise and power of parliaments* [1677], Bannister ed., pp. 210-11; Barbon, *A discourse of trade* [1690], Hollander ed., p. 37; Arthur Dobbs, *An essay on the trade and improvement of Ireland*, 1729, p. 30.

[20] See *infra*, p. 69.

[21] *Principles of political œconomy*, 1767, I, 338.

[22] E.g., Robinson, *Englands safety; in trades encrease*, 1641, p. 9; Barbon, *A discourse of trade* [1690], Hollander ed., p. 37.

[23] [Hales] *A discourse of the common weal* [1581], Elizabeth Lamond ed., p. 67; anon., *The present state of Ireland consider'd*, 1730, p. 29 (the reference here is to Ireland, however, and not England).

[24] [David Bindon] *A letter from a merchant who has left off trade*, 1738, p. 47. Mildmay, in another connection, claimed that countries carried out their obligations under most-favored-nation treaties only when it suited their convenience. (*The laws and policy of England*, 1765, p. 78.)

[25] "On the neglect of trade and manufactures," *Scots magazine*, II. (1740), 476. Cf. also [Simon Clement] *The interest of England, as it stands with relation to the trade of Ireland, considered*, 1698, pp. 13-14: "And though this caution [i.e., the danger of foreign retaliation] hath been often urged in discourses of trade, yet I never knew one instance of any nations being piqued at another to such a degree as to break off their commerce; though I have known several instances of such occasions given. Some prevailing regard, either to the benefit of the customs, the profit of the merchants, or the like, is always had; so that governments seem to be steered by this principle, that if they cannot vend in

One argument made repeatedly by the opponents of the French treaty of 1713 in support of treating Portuguese wines more favorably than French wines was that the balance of trade was more favorable with Portugal than with France, and that lighter duties should be imposed on the imports of the former, either because retaliation would therefore be more injurious to England in the case of Portugal,[26] or because Portugal's capacity to buy English goods would be reduced if England did not take her wine.[27]

Those who urged restraints on the exportation of raw materials—especially wool—almost invariably advocated prohibitions, probably because on mercantilist grounds a stronger case could be made for shutting-off access of foreigners to English raw materials than for completely shutting-out foreign imports, with the resultant danger of foreign retaliation, loss of shipping traffic, and so forth. It was always assumed by advocates of export prohibitions on raw materials that if foreigners could not take them unmanufactured they would be forced to buy them in manufactured form, so that trade would gain instead of lose thereby.[28] Tucker, consistently with his balance-of-labor doctrine, recommended that taxes on exports should vary inversely with their completeness of manufacture, even to the extent of absolute prohibitions of export for raw materials, while the taxes on imports should vary directly with their completeness of manufacture.[29]

There were few criticisms of the absolute prohibition of export of raw materials, and especially wool, and these came chiefly from spokesmen for the agricultural interest.[30] But the objection was sometimes made that the Continental weavers were not as de-

---

trade as much as they would, they will yet continue to sell what they can, and acquiesce with the shopkeeper's rule, that custom is no inheritance; if they lose one chapman, they get another. . . ."

[26] E.g., *The British merchant* [1713], 3d ed., 1748, II, 3.

[27] E.g., Joseph Massie, *Ways and means for raising the extraordinary supplies,* 1757, p. 27 (cited from Br. Suviranta, *Theory of the balance of trade in England,* 1923, p. 30, note 1).

[28] The export of wool was first prohibited in 1647. Other commodities whose export was prohibited were fuller's earth, pipe clay, hides, lead, and knitting machinery.

[29] *Instructions for travellers,* 1757, pp. 38-39.

[30] Cf., *Reasons for a limited exportation of wool,* 1677, p. 4; Davenant, *An essay on the East-India trade* [1697], *Works,* I, 98 ff.; and John Smith, *Chronicon rusticum-commerciale,* 1747, *passim.*

pendent on English wool as the advocates of the prohibition claimed, and that the prohibition would not be effective, therefore, in preventing the development of a continental wool industry. Sheridan also recommended "vast" duties on the export of raw material, especially wool, with additional duties when attempt was made to export without paying the tax, in preference to the absolute prohibition then in force, infraction of which was a felony punishable by death. If the penalty for violation were a fine, instead of death, many would turn informers "who now out of tenderness of men's lives forbear the discovering this injurious practice."[31] Petty asked whether when English clothiers could not sell all the woolens that were already produced, it would not be better to lessen sheep-raising and transfer the labor to tillage. If additional corn was not needed, and there were no idle hands and more wool than could be worked up, it would be proper to permit the export of wool. But if the advantages of the Dutch in making woolens exceeded those of the English by only a little, so that it would be easy to turn the scale in favor of English woolens, he favored the prohibition of export of wool.[32] Brewster opposed the prohibition of the export of wool on the ground that England had an oversupply of it.[33] Henry Home urged that the export of wool should be made subject to a moderate duty instead of to an outright prohibition. The French had alternative sources of supply, and absolute prohibitions stimulated smuggling. Freedom to export would result in an increased output of wool, and therefore in lower prices to English woolen manufacturers. The export could be prohibited at times of high prices, and thus difficulties created for the foreign rivals of English woolen manufacturers at critical times when the raw material was scarce. The revenue from export taxes on wool could be used to pay an export bounty on wool cloth.[34] In general, Home favored the restriction of the export of raw materials only when free export

---

[31] *A discourse on the rise and power of parliaments* [1677], Bannister ed., pp. 198-99.

[32] *Treatise of taxes* [1662], *Economic Writings,* Hull ed., I, 59. Cf. also similarly moderate views with respect to leather, but a much more extreme attitude with respect to the export of wool, John Cary, *An essay on the state of England, in relation to its trade,* 1695, pp. 21, 37-40.

[33] *New essays,* 1702, p. 9.

[34] *Sketches of the history of man,* 1774, I, 494 ff.

would not lead to increased output and therefore to a lower price for English manufacturers.[35]

Discriminatory Treatment of Domestic Industries.—The argument for international specialization in industries is, of course, the central point in free-trade doctrine. There were some instances, however, of writers who were so anxious that England specialize in some particular industry or industries that they proceeded to the length of a sort of inverted protectionism, and proposed that other domestic industries which competed with the ones they regarded as of special importance to England should be suppressed or limited. As early as 1564 Cecil suggested that it would be good for England to make and export less cloth, so that corn should not have to be imported, because clothmakers were harder to govern than farmers, and because so many were employed in making cloth that labor had become scarce for other occupations.[36] One writer would have suppressed stagecoaches, because they led to less drinking in inns, fewer privately-owned horses, and other similarly objectionable consequences.[37] An anonymous writer in 1691 opposed any attempt to set up a linen industry in England, because it would interfere with the woolen industry by causing an increase in spinning wages.[38] Another writer argued that:

> . . . the woolen and silk manufacturers of this kingdom being the staple of our trade, and the most considerable and essential part of our wealth, . . . it is therefore the common interest of the whole kingdom to discourage every other manufacture, whether foreign or assumed [i.e., domestic?] so far as those manufactures are ruinous to and inconsistent with the prosperity of the said British manufactures of wool and silk.[39]

---

[35] *Ibid.*, I, 493. Home apparently failed to see that increased production for export would not, of itself, lead to lower *English* prices.

[36] "Memorandum by Cecil on the export trade in cloth and wool" [1564?], *T.E.D.*, II, 45 ff.

[37] *The ancient trades decayed, repaired again,* 1678, pp. 26-27.

[38] *The linen and woollen manufactory discoursed* . . . [1691], in John Smith, *Chronicon rusticum-commerciale,* I, 383-88.

[39] *A brief state of the question between the printed and painted callicoes, and the woollen and silk manufacture,* 2d ed. 1719, introduction, p. 4. This pamphlet was directed against the calico industry. In answer to it, Asgill replied that neither silks nor calicoes were "staple commodities," that calicoes competed with silks rather than with woolens, and that there was therefore as strong a case for restriction of the silk as of the calico industry.—Asgill, *A brief answer to a brief state of the question,* 1719.

Defoe approved of encouraging all manufactures that could be set up in England, but "with this one exception only, namely, that they do not interfere with, and tend to the prejudice of the woolen manufacture, which is the main and essential manufacture of England."[40] Arthur Young argued that because agriculture was more valuable to England than manufactures, no encouragement should be given to the increase of manufactures until England was completely cultivated, "it being proved that, until such cultivation is complete, the generality of them [i.e., manufactures] are a prejudice to the state, in that circumstance of not being employed about the most important concern of it."[41]

Those who presented such arguments were usually, of course, special advocates of some particular industry rather than disinterested students of the general welfare, but it is of interest that they should have thought it possible to appeal to the public by such reasoning. There was, in fact, some actual legislation based on the principle of discouraging industries which interfered with other industries regarded as of superior importance. Defoe cited the prohibition of the cultivation of tobacco on the ground that it would use land useful for raising wool,[42] and alleged (apparently without basis in fact) that the mining of inland coal was not permitted in certain localities because it would injure the shipping trade, as examples of actual measures based on this principle. From 1699 to 1720 a series of acts was passed prohibiting covering buttons with wool, or with silk or mohair imported from other countries than Turkey, in order to promote the English silk industry and the trade with Turkey, with which country the balance of trade was favorable. Further examination of the trade legislation would no doubt reveal additional measures involving the deliberate discouragement of one English industry in order to benefit another.

---

[40] [Daniel Defoe] *An humble proposal to the people of England* [1729], *The novels and miscellaneous works*, 1841 ed., XVIII, 50.

[41] [Arthur Young] *The farmer's letters to the people of England*, 2d ed., 1768, p. 42.

[42] Cf. *An act prohibiting the planting of tobacco in England, 1652*: "Whereas divers great quantities of tobacco have been of late years and now are planted in divers parts of this nation, tending to the decay of husbandry and tillage, the prejudice and hindrance of the English Plantations abroad, and of the trading, commerce, navigation, and shipping of this nation. . . . Be it enacted and ordained that no person or persons whatsoever . . . plant, set, grow, make, or cure any tobacco in any field, place or places within this nation. . . ."

The Reexport Trade.—To foster the reexport or entrepôt trade, and to win the carrying trade away from the Dutch without opening the domestic market to foreign goods, free ports, drawbacks, and bonded warehouses were generally approved by even the extreme mercantilists,[43] but some writers approved of the prevailing restriction of drawbacks of import duties to commodities which could not be conveniently manufactured at home.[44]

A more important and radical proposal, however, was that all import and export duties be abolished, and that there be substituted, both for fiscal and for trade regulatory purposes, internal excises on the consumption of foreign manufactured products. This would free the merchants engaged in reexport trade from the inconveniences and expense of the drawback system, and thus enable them to compete more effectively with their foreign rivals.[45]

---

[43] Mun, *England's treasure by forraign trade* [1668], Ashley ed., p. 16, advocated specially favorable customs treatment of the reexport trade. The establishment of free ports was specifically recommended by B. W., *Free ports*, 1652 (not available for examination) ; Maddison, *Great Britains remembrancer* [1640], 1655, pp. 37 ff. ; Violet, *Mysteries and secrets*, 1653, pp. 22 ff. ; [Sheridan] *A discourse on the rise and power of parliaments* [1677], Bannister ed., p. 214; [Petyt] *Britannia languens* [1680], McCulloch ed., *Early English tracts on commerce*, p. 359 ; Gee, *The trade and navigation of Great Britain considered* [1729], 1767, pp. 180 ff. Petty apparently opposed free ports, because they would facilitate evasion of duties on imports for consumption—*A treatise of taxes* [1662], in *Economic Writings*, Hull ed., I, 61. Some steps toward the establishment of a drawback and bonded-warehouse system were taken in the seventeenth century (e.g., 16 Car. I, cs. 25, 29, 31 ; 14 Car. II, cs. 11, 25, 27) and further extensions were introduced in the eighteenth century, but England has never had any free ports.

[44] E.g. Mildmay, *The laws and policy of England*, 1765, p. 70.

[45] E.g. [Petyt], *Britannia languens* [1680], McCulloch ed., *Early English tracts on commerce*, pp. 317, 497; Davenant, *Reports to the commissioners* [1712/13], *Works*, V, 379; Dobbs, *An essay on the trade and improvement of Ireland*, 1729, Part II, pp. 30, 31 : "Since all duties inwards, besides being disadvantageous to trade, are found to lie at last upon the consumer ; and the landed interest, the rich and luxurious pay the greatest part ; the prudentest and best method of raising taxes, and least expensive in trading countries that have many ports to guard, and of securing the payment of the duties, and preventing the frauds in running them clandestinely, would be to take off all port duties and place the taxes upon land, moveables and inland excises. . . . Where the intention is to discourage the importation of foreign goods prejudicial to the public, there to put high licenses and excises upon them in the retailers' or consumers' hands ; and if they are entirely prohibited, then to lay the penalty upon the consumer or wherever found." Cf. also John Collins, *A plea for the bringing in of Irish cattel*, 1680, p. 21, where the Dutch use of excises not levied until the goods were sold for consumption is credited with being "the prime cause of the greatness of the Dutch trade, wealth, and power at sea."

It would at the same time get rid of the customs duties imposed on English goods for fiscal reasons and inconsistently with mercantilist doctrine.[46] Walpole was sympathetic to such a policy, and under his administration the customs system was overhauled in the direction of freeing imports of raw materials from duty and abolishing export taxes except on commodities such as lead, tin, and leather, with respect to which it was supposed that the dependence on English supplies would force the foreigner to bear the tax. On several foreign commodities, also, import duties were replaced by excises on domestic consumption. In 1733, Walpole proposed to move farther in the same direction by substituting internal excises for the import duties on tobacco and wine. In support of his proposal, he pointed out that it would leave the reexport trade in those commodities wholly free from taxation and from the inconveniences and expense of the drawback system.[47] The proposal has not appeared objectionable to later commentators, but Walpole's political opponents, appealing to the traditional connection of excises with the exercise of arbitrary power by the government against the people, and stressing the inconveniences which would result if, as alleged, acceptance of this limited excise would quickly lead to its wide extension, succeeded in arousing violent opposition to the measure, and in forcing its abandonment.

Export Bounties.[48]—In 1673, an export bounty was granted on corn. It remained in effect, however, only for some five

---

[46] The mercantilists complained repeatedly against the duties laid on English exports for fiscal reasons, and Misselden, in 1623, cited the Dutch as a model to follow in this respect because in Holland "their own commodities [were] eased of charge, the foreign imposed."—*The circle of commerce,* p. 135. Cf. also Robinson, *Englands safety; in trades encrease,* 1641, pp. 8-9; Violet, *Mysteries and secrets,* 1653, p. 14; Reynel, *The true English interest,* 1679, pp. 10-11: "No customs, or very small, should be paid for exportation of our own manufactures. It were better to advance the king's revenue any other way than by gaining custom on our own commodities, which hinders exportation, or to encourage foreign commodities that we can make here, to advance the customs"; Mildmay, *The laws and policy of England,* 1765, p. 73: "It must give us the utmost concern to find several duties at our ports imposed to satisfy rather the public exigency of our government, than to regulate the interest of our foreign commerce."

[47] [Robert Walpole] *A letter from a member of parliament to his friends in the country, concerning the duties on wine and tobacco,* 1733, pp. 21 ff.

[48] On the history of the export bounties on corn, see D. G. Barnes, *A history of the English corn laws, from 1660-1846,* 1930. See also Jacob Viner's review of this book, *Journal of political economy,* XXXVIII (1930), 710-12.

years, but a new bounty was established by the famous corn law of 1689, and continued in effect, except for temporary suspensions, until 1814. Later, other export bounties were granted on linen and silk manufactures, sailcloth, beef, salt pork, and other commodities, and these were not repealed until the nineteenth century.

Until the second half of the eighteenth century the export bounties do not appear to have aroused much comment, favorable or unfavorable, in the contemporary literature, perhaps because the circumstances were then such that they had little practical importance. After 1750, however, there was considerable opposition to the corn bounties, especially in periods of short harvests, and the poorer classes repeatedly engaged in violent rioting in protest.

In so far as the export bounties stimulated the production and export of the bounty-fed commodities, the mercantilist would of course be predisposed to favor them, and on these simple grounds John Houghton defended the first corn bounty,[49] and later writers,[50] not all of whom were frank partisans of the agricultural interest, defended the later bounties. Henry Home supported the export bounty on corn both on these grounds and on the grounds that it had hurt French agriculture and therefore weakened France in case of war. In the same spirit he recommended a bounty on exports of manufactures to the colonies, "which by underselling them in their own markets, would quash every attempt to rivalship."[51]

The corn bounties were attacked on the grounds that by making corn dearer in England they resulted in a raising of wages and in the general cost of living, and thus impaired the capacity of the English to compete with other countries in non-subsidized

---

[49] *A collection of letters,* 1681-83, II, 182.

[50] E.g., Gee, *The trade and navigation of Great Britain considered* [1729], 1767 ed., p. 245; [Charles Smith] *Three tracts on the corn trade and corn laws,* 2d ed., 1766, *passim;* [Mildmay] *The laws and policy of England,* 1765, pp. 56 ff.; [Arthur Young] *The farmer's letters,* 2d ed., 1768, pp. 44 ff., and *Political arithmetic,* 1774, pp. 29 ff. Cf. also *The manufacturer's plea for the bounty on corn at exportation,* 1754, p. 6: "It cannot, I think, be denied that the real proceeds of every quarter of corn, I mean so many at least as the exporter would be disabled from carrying to market without the aid of this bounty, add to the public at least the exceeds of this bounty." Also, *ibid.,* p. 8.

[51] *Sketches of the history of man,* 1774, I, 491 ff.

commodities, and especially manufactures.[52] But some of the supporters of the corn bounties denied that they had in fact made the price of corn higher in England or lower abroad than it would otherwise have been.[53]

Infant Industry Protection.—Modern writers usually credit Alexander Hamilton or Friedrich List, or even John Stuart Mill, with the first presentation of the "infant industry" argument for protection to young industries. It is of much earlier origin, however, and is closely related both in principle and in its history to the monopoly privileges granted to trading companies opening up new and hazardous trades and to inventions (the "patents of monopoly"). A complaint of 1645, that the circumstances which originally justified the grant of trading monopolies were no longer present, reveals the probable origin of the infant industry argument for bounties or import duties:

Those immunities which were granted in the infancy of trade, to incite people to the increase and improvement of it, are not so proper for these times, when the trade is come to that height of perfection, and that the mystery of it is so well known. . . .[54]

Some early presentations of the argument for temporary protection or bounties to "infant industries" follow:

And that the linen and iron manufactures may be so encouraged here by a public law, as that we may draw these trades solely to us, which now foreign nations receive the benefit of, there ought in the first place to be a tax or custom at least of four shillings in the pound put on all linen yarn, threads, tapes, and twines for cordage that shall be imported into England, and three shillings in the pound upon all linen cloths under four shillings the ell; and this law to continue and be for seven years. And by virtue of this tax or imposition, there will be such advantage given to the linen manufac-

---

[52] Cf. Brewster, *New essays on trade*, 1702, p. 54; Dobbs, *An essay on the trade and improvement of Ireland*, 1729, Part II, p. 64; Decker, *An essay on the causes of the decline of the foreign trade* [1744], 1756, pp. 65 ff.; [Josiah Tucker] *The causes of the dearness of provisions assigned*, 1766, p. 24, and *Considerations on the policy, commerce and circumstances of the kingdom*, 1771, p. 124.

[53] Malachy Postlethwayt, *The universal dictionary of trade and commerce*, 4th ed., 1774, Art. "Corn," gives a good statement of the arguments used on both sides.

[54] *A discourse . . . for the enlargement and freedome of trade*, 1645, p. 22.

ture in its infancy, that thereby it will take deep rooting and get a good foundation on a sudden. . . .[55]

[I am] fully convinced . . . that all wise nations are so fond of encouraging manufactures in their infancy, that they not only burden foreign manufactures of the like kind with high impositions, but often totally condemn and prohibit the consumption of them. . . .[56]

Upon the whole, premiums are only to be given to encourage manufactures or other improvements in their infancy, to usher them into the world, and to give an encouragement to begin a commerce abroad; and if after their improvement they can't push their own way, by being wrought so cheap as to sell at par with others of the same kind, it is in vain to force it.[57]

I have now, I think, shewn, Sir, that the linen manufacture . . . is but in its infancy in Britain and Ireland; that therefore it is impossible for our people to sell so cheap, or to meet with such a ready sale even here at home, as those who have had this manufacture long established among them, and that for this reason, we cannot propose to make any great or quick progress in this manufacture, without some public encouragement.[58]

. . . it must be ridiculous to say to an infant manufacture, or while it is in its progress toward maturity, you have no occasion for any public encouragement, because as soon as you can make the quantities and qualities wanted, and sell them as cheap as those who have been long in possession of the manufacture, you will certainly find a vent for all you can make.[59]

All manufactures in their infancy require not only care, but considerable expense, to nurse them up to a state of strength and vigor. The original undertakers and proprietors are seldom able to lay down at once the necessary sums; but are obliged to take time, struggle with difficulties, and enlarge their bottoms by degrees.[60]

---

[55] Andrew Yarranton, *England's improvement by sea and land* [1677], as cited by Patrick Dove, "Account of Andrew Yarranton," appended to his *The elements of political science*, 1854, pp. 450-51.

[56] William Wood, *A survey of trade*, 1718, pp. 224-25.

[57] Arthur Dobbs, *An essay on the trade and improvement of Ireland*, 1729, Part II, p. 65. See also *ibid.*, pp. 62 ff.

[58] David Bindon, *A letter from a merchant who has left off trade*, 1738, p. 24.

[59] *Ibid.*, p. 60.

[60] "On the neglect of trade and manufacture," *Scots magazine*, II (1740), 477. The infant-industry argument is to be found also in Steuart, *Principles of political œconomy*, 1767, I, 302 ff., 381, and in Josiah Tucker, *Instructions for travellers*, 1757, p. 33. Adam Smith deals with the argument somewhat over-critically (*Wealth of nations*, Cannan ed., I, 422 ff.).

Mercantilism and Protectionism.—It is not easy to make a sharp distinction between mercantilism as commercial policy and the modern doctrine of protection, for they differ more in their distribution of emphasis than in their actual content. The modern protectionist urges the importance of restricting the imports of foreign goods of a kind which can be produced at home in order that domestic production and employment may be fostered. He does not stress as much as did the mercantilist, and he may refrain from discussing, and may even reject, the balance-of-trade doctrine. Except in its more popular manifestations, modern protectionism does not lay special stress on the desirability of increasing or maintaining the national stock of bullion. But most of the arguments commonly used by modern protectionists were already current in the mercantilist period. Even during the seventeenth century, and frequently during the eighteenth century, tracts were written which made no reference to the balance of trade or to monetary considerations, and dealt only with the desirability of protecting domestic industries in order to increase employment and production.[61] Usually, however, the balance-of-trade argument was invoked to reinforce the employment-production argument for import restrictions. Few writers, apparently, saw any possibility of conflict between these arguments. But the "balance-of-employment" argument, when it asserts that the "balance of work" is a better test than the balance of trade of whether trade is beneficial or not, can be interpreted as a plea for the greater importance of the protectionist than the monetary phases of mercantilist doctrine, and one author condemned the East India Company because it brought in silks to be consumed in England in place of English silks and woolens even if its activities did result in more gold coming into England than it took out.[62] There are no important differences, also, between the legislative devices of the mercantilist and those of modern protectionism. The chief differences appear to be that: absolute prohibitions of import are less common, and commercial treaties and tariff bargaining relatively more important, now than then; export prohibitions have almost completely disappeared; rates of duty are generally much

---

[61] The first use of the term "protection" in the modern sense that I have noticed is in Asgill's *A brief answer to a brief state of the question*, 1719, pp. 10 ff.

[62] A. N., *England's advocate, Europe's monitor*, 1699, p. 20.

higher now than then (although a contrary impression is prevalent) ; and there has been a substitution for some of the old arguments of new or partially new ones of comparable intellectual quality.

II. THE COLLAPSE OF MERCANTILIST DOCTRINE

The Self-regulating Mechanism of Specie Distribution.[1]— After Hume and Smith had written, mercantilism was definitely on the defensive and was wholly or largely rejected by the leading English economists. That their victory was as great as it was, was due largely, of course, to the force of their reasoning and the brilliance of their exposition, but it was due also in large part to the fact that, even before they wrote, mercantilism as a body of economic doctrine had already been disintegrating because of dissension within the ranks of its adherents and attacks by earlier critics. An important element in its collapse, especially in its monetary phases, was the development of the theory of the self-regulating mechanism of international specie distribution. The most influential formulation of this theory in England[2] prior to the nineteenth century was by Hume. But its most important constituent elements had been stated long before Hume, and several earlier writers had brought them together much as he did.

Stated briefly, the theory is that a country with a metallic currency will automatically get the amount of bullion it needs to maintain its prices at such a level relative to the prices prevailing abroad as to maintain an even balance between its exports and imports. Should more money than this happen to come into that country, its prices would rise relatively to those of other countries; its exports, consequently, would fall, and its imports increase; the resultant adverse balance of payments would have to be met in specie; and the excess of money would thus be drained

---

[1] On this section cf. Angell, *The theory of international prices,* 1926, chap. ii.

[2] In Richard Cantillon, *Essai sur la nature du commerce en général,* written *ca.* 1730, but not published until 1755, the self-regulating mechanism is clearly and ably expounded. See especially pp. 159-99 in the 1931 reprint, edited by Henry Higgs. Although material from Cantillon's manuscript had been used by French and English writers before its publication, I have found no evidence that any part of his exposition of the self-regulating mechanism appeared in print before 1752, or that Hume was influenced, directly or indirectly, by Cantillon.

off. If, on the other hand, a country's monetary supply should happen to fall below the amount necessary to maintain equilibrium, its prices would fall relative to those abroad, exports would rise and imports fall, and the resultant favorable balance of payments would bring in an amount of specie from abroad sufficient to restore equilibrium. For its formulation and its use as a basis for repudiation of certain of the monetary phases of mercantilist doctrine, five stages had to be achieved:

1. Recognition that net international balances of payments must be paid in specie.
2. Recognition that the quantity of money is a determinant of the level of prices.
3. Recognition that the volume of exports and the volume of imports depend on the relative levels of prices at home and abroad.
4. Integration of the three preceding propositions into a coherent theory of a self-regulating international distribution of the money metal.
5. Realization that this theory destroyed the basis for the traditional concern about the adequacy of the amount of money in circulation in a country, at least as a long-run matter.

The first proposition was an important element in the mercantilist doctrine, and was universally accepted. A quantity theory of the value of money, as has already been shown, was held by many of the mercantilists, and there were few who rejected it once they became aware of it. There remains to be examined only the progress made toward attainment of the last three stages. Vague statements suggestive of the existence of a self-regulating mechanism of specie distribution but not specific as to its character will be disregarded.[3]

Recognition that low prices were conducive to large exports and high prices to large imports was fairly common even in the early mercantilist literature, but I have not been able to find any gen-

---

[3] One very early instance may be quoted: "But I say confidently you need not fear this penury or scarceness of money; the intercourse of things being so established throughout the whole world, that there is a perpetual circulation of all that can be necessary to mankind. Thus your commodities will ever find out money."—Sir Thomas More in the House of Commons, 1523, cited in White Kennet, *A complete history of England,* 1706, II, 55. Cf. also the quotation from John Houghton (1681), p. 49, *supra.*

eralized statement setting forth the dependence of the trade balance on the comparative level of prices until the end of the seventeenth century. Malynes at one point approached surprisingly close to a grasp of the self-regulating mechanism, especially if one considers his general obtuseness and obscurantism. He argues that if the manipulations of exchange dealers forced English currency below its mint par, coin would be exported, home prices would consequently fall, and foreign commodities would rise in price because of the increase of money abroad.[4] Had he proceeded to consider the effect of these price changes on the balance of trade and on the flow of specie, he would have presented a complete formulation of a full cycle of the self-regulating mechanism. He proceeded, instead, to denunciation of the exchangers. Except for the development of the quantity theory of money, I can find no real traces of further progress in this connection until the last decade of the seventeenth century.[5]

Locke is sometimes credited, wrongly I believe, with having come close to a satisfactory statement of the self-regulating mechanism, although he did make some advance in that direction. He states that a country in commercial relations with, and using the same metal for currency as, the rest of the world requires under given circumstances a certain (presumably minimum) amount of money if a certain volume of trade is to be carried on at all, or is to be carried on without loss:

That in a country, that hath open commerce with the rest of the world, and uses money, made of the same materials with their neighbors, any quantity of that money will not serve to drive any quantity of trade; but there must be a certain proportion between their money and trade. The reason whereof is this, because to keep your trade going without loss, your commodities amongst you must keep an equal, or at least near the price of the same species of commodities in the neighboring countries; which they cannot do, if your money be far less than in other countries: for then either your commodities must be sold very cheap, or a great part of your trade must

---

[4] *A treatise of the canker* [1601], *T.E.D.*, III, 392-93.

[5] A passage cited by Angell (*Theory of international prices*, p. 14) as quoted by Malynes in 1622 from an unidentified contemporary author, does appear to state with adequate clearness the dependence of specie movements on the relative value of money at home and abroad, and the dependence of the value of money on its quantity. But the quotation is from the unenlightened Edward Misselden (*Free trade*, 2d ed., 1622, p. 104) who by a low value of money means a high mint price of bullion rather than low purchasing power over commodities.

stand still, there not being money enough in the country to pay for them (in their shifting of hands) at that high price, which the plenty, and consequently low value of money, makes them at in another country. . . .[6]

He proceeds to illustrate by imagining that England loses half its money, other things there and elsewhere remaining unaltered. Either half the trade, employment, etc., would cease, or prices, wages, rents would be cut in half. If the latter should result, domestic commodities would be sold abroad cheap and foreign commodities would be bought dear, to the loss of the country,[7] and labor might emigrate to where wages were high. Eventually, because of the relatively high foreign prices, foreign goods would become scarce (i.e., imports would fall?). He says nothing as to the *necessary* as distinguished from the *possible* and the *desirable* relations between prices at home and abroad, and he gives not even a hint that the departure from the initial and desirable situation will breed its own correctives, through its influence on price levels, commodity balances, and specie flows.[8] All that Locke had of the elements of the self-regulating mechanism was the quantity theory of money, with even here the defect that at the critical point he failed to make use of it and implied instead that a serious maladjustment between prices and the quantity of money was as likely to be corrected, presumably permanently, by a consequent change in the volume of trade as by a change in prices.

In dealing with the factors determining the exchange rates, Locke was much more penetrating. He explains the exchange rate between two countries as due to: (1) "the overbalance of the trade," which, the context shows, means the balance of payments

---

[6] *Some considerations of the lowering of interest* [1691], *Works*, 1823 ed., V, 49.

[7] In modern terminology, the "terms of trade" would be less favorable. *Ibid.*, pp. 49-50.

[8] Angell (*op. cit.*, pp. 19-20) gives a much more favorable interpretation of Locke, and credits him with "the first outline that I have discovered of a theory of international prices." But he does so only by reading in effect "what will be" where Locke outlines what is desirable but will not necessarily be realized. He appears to find Locke inconsistent, because he did not think "that money, despite its distribution in a definite proportion to trade, keeps a uniform value throughout the world" and quotes, to reveal the inconsistency, a passage which shows clearly what I here contend, namely, that Locke did not believe that money is actually distributed in a definite proportion to trade: "Money . . . is of most worth in that country *where there is the least money in proportion to its trade*."—Locke, *op. cit.*, p. 50, italics mine.

resulting from *past* transactions; and (2) the relative plenty of money (identified with liquid capital) which affects inversely the opportunities for profitable investment of surplus funds, and therefore determines to what country they will flow. He states fairly clearly the limits beyond which exchange rates cannot move without leading to specie flows.[9]

North, in 1691, presented a concise formulation of an automatic and self-regulating mechanism, which provides a country with the "determinate sum of specific money" required for carrying on the trade of the nation.[10] It is not, however, the mechanism described in the modern theory, and is not, explicitly at least, an explanation of the *international* distribution of money.[11] The mechanism which he presents consists of an automatic ebb and flow of money into and out of circulation according to the unexplained specific requirements of trade. When because of troubled conditions money is hoarded, the mints coin more bullion, whose source is not explained. When peace returns, money comes out of the hoards, the mints cease to coin bullion, and the excess of money is melted down "either to supply the home trades or for transportation abroad. Thus the buckets work alternately; when money is scarce, bullion is coined; when bullion is scarce, money

---

[9] *Ibid.,* pp. 50-51. Locke explains both (1) the specie-import point (mint par minus insurance between Holland and England minus additional cost of shipment because of an assumed penalty on the exportation of bullion from Holland) and (2) the point at which an English merchant having funds in one country will decide to transfer them to another, which will be determined by the relative opportunities for profitable use in the two countries, the cost of transmission, and the risk connected with investment in a foreign country.

Angell (*op. cit.,* p. 21) finds the first clear statement of the specie-point mechanism in Clement (1696). The specie points must be clear to merchants as soon as they actually engage in bullion and exchange transactions, and Gresham gives an adequate statement of the specie-import point in 1558. Cf. J. W. Burgon, *The life and times of Sir Thomas Gresham,* 1839, I, 485. Cf. also Petty, *Treatise of taxes* [1662], *Economic writings,* Hull ed., I, 48: "As for the natural measures of exchange, I say, that in times of peace, the greatest exchange can be but the labor of carrying the money in specie, but where are hazards [and] emergent uses for money more in one place than another, etc., or opinions of these true or false, the exchange will be governed by them." Cf. also, *ibid., The political anatomy of Ireland* [1691], in *Economic writings,* Hull ed., I, 185-86: "Exchange can never be naturally more than the land and water-carriage of money between the two kingdoms, and the insurance of the same upon the way, if the money be alike in both places."

[10] *Discourses upon trade* [1691], Hollander ed., pp. 35-36.

[11] Cf. Angell (*op. cit.,* p. 17) for a slightly more favorable interpretation.

is melted." He fails to relate this process either to price movements or to movements in the balance of trade.

Samuel Pratt, in 1696, urged that funds be voted to the king to meet the expenses of his Continental armies and denied that the consequent remittances to the Continent would drain England of its silver by an argument which not only corrects the "sinews-of-war" emphasis on money but, in spite of its compactness, is a satisfactory statement of the self-regulating mechanism if, as seems to me reasonable, "cheapness of silver" may be interpreted as meaning high commodity prices :[12]

Which uncoined silver will for the most part find its way back again, because the carrying over so much every year will glut that place to which 'tis carried so that silver will become cheap there, and they must disgorge at the best market; which England, in all probability, will be. And the effect of that overbalance which foreigners must, as cases now stand, get by us, cannot be carried out of the nation but in other commodities besides silver.[13]

William Wood supposes that by accident forty-odd millions of public money were to be found in specie under the ruins of Whitehall, and were paid out to the public creditors, and proceeds to trace the consequences. Interest would fall; either the added bullion would be hoarded or converted into plate, or else prices and wages would rise and exports consequently fall. If the free export of money were not permitted, England, since it now had smaller exports and high prices, would therefore now be worse off instead of better, with the implication that if it were permitted money would be exported in consequence of an unfavorable balance of payments. From which he concludes that a favorable balance of trade is the only way to keep bullion at home.[14]

In 1720, there appeared a remarkable essay of some thirty-odd pages by one Isaac Gervaise, apparently his only publication, in which there is presented an elaborate and closely-reasoned exposition of the nature of international equilibrium and of the self-

---

[12] Heckscher regards this as too favorable an interpretation, on the ground that Pratt was referring to the cheapness of silver solely in terms of other coins, not of commodities in general. (*Mercantilism,* 1935, II, 251, note.)

[13] [Samuel Pratt] *The regulating silver coin, made practicable and easie,* 1696, p. 103. See also *ibid.,* p. 104. Cf. also Hugh Chamberlain, *A collection of some papers,* 1696, p. 13: "when more can be got by our English commodities than by money, none will export money."

[14] *A survey of trade,* 1718, pp. 335 ff.

regulating mechanism whereby specie obtained its "natural" or proper international distribution.[15] In spite of the peculiarities of terminology and the occasional obscurities of exposition by which it is marred, the essay marks a great advance over earlier doctrine in this field. The brilliance of its contents, and its complete oversight by other scholars, due presumably to its rarity, warrant its being dealt with in some detail.

Gervaise starts out with the proposition that gold and silver, which he calls "the grand real measure or denominator of the real value of all things," tend to be distributed internationally in proportion to population, on the ground that only labor (i.e., the product of labor) can attract specie. He proceeds immediately to qualify this proposition in a manner which indicates that he believes that it is in proportion to national value productivity or real income, and to population only as that is an index of real income, that specie tends to be distributed:

> Whenever I mention the quantity of inhabitants, I always suppose that regard which ought to be had to the situation and disposition of the different countries of the world; the same quantity of inhabitants not producing the same effect in all countries, according as their dispositions differ. . . .[16]

If a country should for a time have more than its proportion of specie, this would break the balance between consumption and production. Consumption would exceed production, the excess being met by increased imports or decreased exports. An unfavorable balance of payments would result, which would continue until the proper proportion was restored:

> When a nation has attracted a greater proportion of the grand denominator of the world than its proper share, and the cause of that attraction ceases, that nation cannot retain the overplus of its proper proportion of the grand denominator, because in that case the proportion of poor and rich of that nation [i.e., of producers and consumers] is broken; that is to say, the number of rich is too great, in proportion to the poor, so as that nation cannot furnish unto the

---

[15] Isaac Gervaise, *The system or theory of the trade of the world,* 1720. Gervaise was of French Huguenot birth, and was taken by his parents to Ireland as a child, upon the revocation of the Edict of Nantes. He became an Anglican clergyman and a friend of Bishop Berkeley. Cf. A. C. Fraser, *Life and letters of George Berkeley, D.D.,* 1871, 259, note.

[16] *Op. cit.,* pp. 3-4. Cf. also pp. 24-25, where it is made clear that this is a correct interpretation of his reasoning.

world that share of labor which is proportioned to that part of the grand denominator it possesses: in which case all the labor of the poor will not balance the expense of the rich. So that there enters in that nation more labor than goes out of it, to balance its want of poor: and as the end of trade is the attracting gold and silver, all that difference of labor is paid in gold and silver, until the denominator be lessened, in proportion to other nations; which also, and at the same time, proportions the number of poor to that of rich.[17]

Gervaise then proceeds to consider the effects of "credit," or "that time which is allowed in trade." "As all men one with the other are equally subject to the same passions," the "denominators," or currencies, of all the countries are increased in amount by credit in equal proportions: "Credit increases the denominator, and adds unto all things an increase of denomination of value proportioned to the increase of the denominator by credit," i.e., prices rise in proportion to the increase in currency through credit.[18] If a country should, however, add to its currency by credit in more than due proportion, that increase of credit will act on that nation as if it had drawn an equal sum from a gold or silver mine. It will retain only its proportion of the increase; "so that the rest thereof will in time be drawn off by the labor of other nations, in gold or silver." The mechanism whereby this will be brought about is explained as follows: the increase in the holdings of currency will lead the holders to increase their consumption of goods; less goods will therefore be available for export; the adverse trade balance will be met by an export of specie. The reverse happens when a country decreases the amount of credit below its due proportion; by a corresponding process gold and silver will be drawn from abroad until its "denominator," including "credit," has recovered its proper proportion to that of other countries.[19] Gervaise concedes, however, another temporary possibility: an even balance may be maintained in the foreign trade even though there is increased consumption at home through the surrender (whether for domestic consumption or for export is not indicated) of the nation's "store or capital of exportable labor," by which Gervaise apparently means that the normal stocks of materials and finished goods may be allowed to

[17] *Ibid.*, p. 5.
[18] *Ibid.*, pp. 7-8.
[19] Pp. 8-9, 12.

run down. But once the available specie and stores of goods had been exhausted, credit would have to be contracted until the "denominator" was again in due proportion.[20]

A relative excess of the "denominator," or of currency, on the part of a particular country results, through its effect on the trade balance, in a decline in the foreign exchange value of its currency. If its excess of currency is great, so that coin becomes scarce and the exchange value of its currency is low, foreigners having claims for payment against that country in terms of its currency try to reduce their losses by accepting payment in goods and disposing of them abroad for specie. But this results in a rise in the wages of its labor and therefore also (by implication) in the prices of its commodities in terms of that country's currency, and the foreign creditors find that wages and prices abroad are relatively lower, and must therefore dispose of these commodities at a loss. They therefore "cease to credit this nation, by importing into it no more labor than they are sure to export out of it." In the meanwhile, foreign manufacturers find that because of the reduced value on the foreign exchanges of the currency of the country which has expanded its currency they can afford to pay a high price in its own currency for that country's materials, until the prices of those materials rise more than sufficiently to offset the discount on the exchanges. At this point, where he seems to be well embarked upon an explanation of the manner in which equilibrium is established between a country with a depreciated "credit" currency and a metallic standard outside world, Gervaise unfortunately stops short.[21]

This summary of Gervaise's analysis, which does not do full justice to it, should nevertheless be sufficient to indicate how striking an advance he had made toward a satisfactory exposition of international equilibrium. Although Hume's exposition was superior in its freedom from obsolete terminology and much clearer in its exposition, not until the nineteenth century was there to be a match for the comprehensiveness of Gervaise's account, with its specific provision for the necessity, under equilibrium, of balance between a country's exports and its imports and between its production and its consumption, and with its description of the role of wage rates and exchange rates in the mecha-

---

[20] *Ibid.*, p. 13.
[21] *Ibid.*, pp. 15-17.

nism whereby a disturbed equilibrium is restored.[22] Gervaise, in fact, in approaching the problem from the income rather than from the price angle, proceeded in a manner which many recent writers have found more to their liking than that adopted by Hume and predominantly followed by the classical school, and in this sense was more "modern" than his successors of a century or so later.

Prior, in 1730, expounds one-half of the self-regulating mechanism unobjectionably. After pointing out that the East India trade draws silver from Europe, and thereby creates a scarcity of it in Europe, apparently in relation to both gold and commodities, he says:

> And if so much treasure shall flow for any considerable time in the same channel, it may put an end to that trade: for such large remittances in silver must in time make this metal plenty in those parts, and as its quantity increases, its value will lessen; so that by degrees silver may come to bear the same proportion to gold in the East Indies as it does in Europe, and their commodities will rise in proportion.[23]

Jacob Vanderlint, in 1734, states the mechanism well, although his exposition of it is so scattered through his book that it is not possible to quote a compact statement of it. In the following passage, he comes closest to a unified exposition of the mechanism:

> But no inconvenience can arise by an unrestrained trade, but very great advantage; since if the cash of the nation be decreased by it, which prohibitions are designed to prevent, those nations that get the cash will certainly find every thing advance in price, as the cash increases among them. And if we, who part with the money, make our plenty great enough to make labor sufficiently cheap, which is always constituted of the price of victuals and drink, our manufactures, and everything else, will soon become so moderate as to turn the balance of trade in our favor, and thereby fetch the money back again.[24]

Vanderlint does not approve of this automatic mechanism when

---

[22] He also later (pp. 32-34) qualifies his conclusions with respect to the proportions in which specie can be distributed in the case where there is international lending or tribute.

[23] [Thomas Prior] *Observations on coin in general*, 1730, p. 13.

[24] *Money answers all things* [1734], Hollander ed., pp. 48-49.

it operates to raise prices, and advocates the encouragement of the use of gold and silver in the arts as a means of preventing a rise of prices when the balance of trade is favorable.[25]

When Hume published his *Political Discourses*, in 1752, therefore, all the essential elements of the theory of the self-regulating mechanism were already available in previous literature, and several fairly satisfactory attempts to bring them together into a coherent theory had been made. Hume, however, stated the theory with a degree of clarity, ability of exposition, emphasis on its importance, and consistent incorporation with the remainder of his economic views, which most of these earlier writers did not even distantly approach.[26] Since his account of the mechanism is reexamined in a later chapter, attention need be called here only to some particular phases of his analysis. He includes in the general mechanism as an additional equilibrating factor the influence of variations in the exchange rates on commodity trade,[27] a point which apparently no one had hitherto brought directly into an exposition of the larger mechanism of adjustment. He remarks that the mechanism is not peculiar to international trade, but also operates internally between the districts of a single country.[28] He does not quite follow out the consequences of his analysis to what later exponents of it regard as its logical significance for long-run policy, namely, lack of concern about the quantity of money in a country; for without stating the qualifications which would possibly justify his position, he disapproves of paper money which is not merely a certificate of deposit of an equivalent amount of metallic money, because it drives hard money out of the country;[29] he concedes that for wars conducted on foreign soil, and in negotiations with foreign nations, a country derives benefit from an abundance of metallic money at home;[30] and he concedes

---

[25] *Ibid.*, pp. 93-95. See *supra*, p. 50.

[26] *Political discourses* [1752], in *Essays, moral, political, and literary*, 1875 ed., I, 330 ff.

[27] *Ibid.*, p. 333, note.

[28] *Ibid.*, I, 334-35.

[29] *Ibid.*, I, 337 ff.; I, 311 ff. Cf., however, *ibid.*, I, 339 ff.

[30] *Ibid.*, I, 337. Adam Smith found fault with Hume for having "gone a little into the notion that public opulence consists in money," presumably with these passages in mind.—*Lectures on justice, police, revenue, and arms* (given about 1763), Cannan ed., 1896, p. 197. To Hume's objection to paper money that it drove out bullion, Henry Lloyd replied that "money cannot go out of

that an increasing amount of money acts as a stimulus to industry.[31]

After Hume, the self-regulating mechanism was much more frequently and more clearly stated than before. Patrick Murray (Lord Elibank) disapproves of paper money because, on quantity-theory grounds, it results in a rise of prices, a check to exports, and consequent depression, but:

These inconveniencies, when arising from a plenty of real money, are fully compensated by the riches which occasioned them, and the above stagnation of trade will last no longer than other states continue to undersell us, which cannot be very long; for the trade of any state will be an inlet to riches, and money will flow in upon it till that state be likewise full, and its entrance be stopped by the same repletion; from that state it will go to another, and so on, till it becomes on a perfect level and equality throughout the whole.[32]

Harris presents an excellent statement of the self-regulating mechanism.[33] Like Vanderlint, however, Harris is too much of a mercantilist to accept with equanimity the consequences of the mechanism when it results in an outward drain of money, and recommends hoarding and conversion of bullion into plate as means of withdrawing bullion from circulation when otherwise an outward drain would ensue.[34] A good statement of the mechanism, in this case free from any mercantilist qualification, is to be found also in Whatley.[35]

---

a kingdom without receiving an equivalent, which is either consumed at home, or resold with advantage." *An essay on the theory of money*, 1771, p. 16.

[31] In this, as in some of his other economic essays, Hume was apparently replying to arguments in Montesquieu's *L'esprit des lois* which he could not accept. Hume had already stated the doctrine of the self-regulating mechanism in much the same terms in a letter to Montesquieu, April 10, 1749, cited in J. Y. T. Greig, *The letters of David Hume*, 1932, I, 136-37. In a letter of Nov. 1, 1750, to James Oswald, who had apparently already seen a manuscript of the essay and had raised objections against its thesis, Hume made a concession along the Potter-John Law lines: "I agree with you, that the increase of money, if not too sudden, naturally increases people and industry, and by that means may retain itself; but if it do not produce such an increase, nothing will retain it except hoarding." (*Ibid.*, I, 143.)

[32] *Essays*, I. on the public debt; II. on paper-money, banking, &c., 1755, p. 21.

[33] *An essay upon money and coins*, Part I (1757), 90-93. Harris does not mention Hume, but in his preface he states that the main part of his essay had been written many years before.

[34] *Ibid.*, Part I, pp. 99, 100.

[35] [George Whatley] *Principles of Trade*, 2d ed., 1774, note, pp. 15-16. Benjamin Franklin helped in the preparation of this book, and the notes, which

Vanderlint, Wood, and Harris, as has been shown, accepted the automatic regulation of the amount of money *in circulation*, but still retained the mercantilist preoccupation with the amount of bullion in the country, as did Hume also to some extent. A few mercantilists after Hume tried to find a basis for rejecting the automatic mechanism, but with meager results. Wallace replies to Hume that if the amount of paper money increases, trade will increase. Making an unconscious substitution of "export trade" for "trade," he concludes: "And, as they don't take paper in payment from foreign nations, if they are gainers by trade, they must receive the balance in silver and gold."[36] Steuart rejects the quantity theory of money, on the ground that prices depend on the demand for, and supply of, commodities, and not on the quantity of specie. He tries half-heartedly to meet Hume's exposition of the self-regulating mechanism by stressing the transitory effects, with reference to hoarding and the volume of production, of the sudden change posited by Hume in the quantity of money. The removal of four-fifths of the money in circulation would annihilate both industry and the industrious. If as a result of the lower prices (all of ?) the stock of English goods were to be exported, it would mean the starvation of the English people.[37] If the quantity of money increases, on the other hand, hoarding will prevent this increase from acting on prices. In any case "reason and experience" refute the quantity theory.[38] At one point he suggests a self-regulating mechanism, whereby money goes into hoards when in excess and comes out when there is scarcity, essentially like North's except that Steuart explains the movement of specie into and out of hoards as governed by the possibility of lending it at interest:

While there is found a sufficient quantity of money for carrying

---

are generally superior to the text, have especially been attributed to him. See Jared Sparks, *The works of Benjamin Franklin*, 1840, X, 148.

An interesting and able discussion of the effect on exchange rates and specie flows of the credit operations of banks is to be found in "Considerations relating to the late order of the two banks," *Scots magazine*, XXIV (1762), 39-41, 89-94. Its general argument is that the existing adverse exchange on London was due to temporary circumstances and should be corrected by borrowing in London rather than by contraction of bank credit in Scotland.

[36] [Robert Wallace] *Characteristics of the present political state of Great Britain*, 1758, pp. 31-32.

[37] *Principles of political œconomy*, 1767, I, 405 ff., 515-16.

[38] *Ibid.*, I, 422.

on reciprocal alienations, those money gatherers will not be able to employ their stagnated wealth within the nation; but so soon as this gathering has had the effect of diminishing the specie below the proportion found necessary to carry on the circulation, it will begin to be lent out, and so it will return to circulate for a time, until by the operation of the same causes it will fall back again into its former repositories.[39]

Tucker, in the course of an attempt to refute Hume's argument, follows Hume's ambiguous terminology too closely, and in consequence shifts unconsciously from a discussion of the effects on trade of more money to the effects of more wealth, and proceeds to a discussion of whether a rich country can compete successfully with a poor one,[40] and Hume, in an unsatisfactory reply, himself follows this shift in issues.[41]

One of the mysteries of the history of economic thought is that Adam Smith, although he was intimately acquainted with Hume and with his writings, should have made no reference in the *Wealth of Nations* to the self-regulating mechanism in terms of price levels and trade balances, and should have been content with an exposition of the international distribution of specie in the already obsolete terms of the requirement by each country, without specific reference to its relative price level, of a definite amount of money to circulate trade. When a country has more money than it needs to circulate its trade, the "channels of circulation" will overflow, and the surplus money will be sent abroad "to seek that profitable employment which it cannot find at home."[42] What adds to the mystery is that Smith had in his earlier *Lectures* presented approvingly a good summary of Hume's analysis.[43]

Scarcity of Money.—It was the constant complaint of the mercantilists that England was suffering from "scarcity of money," and the main objective of the mercantilist proposals, at least during the earlier period, was to relieve this scarcity. Many modern writers accept these complaints at their face value, and cite dubious historical facts as the cause of this scarcity, without

---

[39] *Ibid.*, II, 115.

[40] *Four tracts on political and commercial subjects,* 2d ed., 1774, pp. 34 ff.

[41] In a letter of March 4, 1758, to Lord Kames: *The letters of David Hume,* J. Y. T. Greig ed., 1932, I, 143 ff.

[42] *Wealth of nations* [1776], Cannan ed., II, 277.

[43] *Lectures on justice, police, revenue and arms* [given about 1763], Cannan ed., 1896, p. 197.

either investigating what those who complained meant by "scarcity of money" or analyzing the notion for themselves. The mercantilists who voiced such complaints rarely made clear precisely what they had in mind. But where the context reveals what they were thinking of, they meant by scarcity of money some one or some combination of the following things: men not having enough "money" to buy the things they wanted—i.e., general poverty; merchants not being able to sell their goods in adequate volume—i.e., "slack trade"; merchants not having, or not being able to borrow at moderate rates of interest, enough "money" adequately to finance their operations—i.e., shortage of capital; high interest rates—i.e., scarcity of capital; money of some denominations scarce relative to other denominations—i.e., either a mismanaged currency, or the ordinary condition of a bimetallic currency whenever the market ratios of gold and silver diverge from the mint ratios; low prices; prices too high for the existing supply of money—an impossibility as a continuing phenomenon.

Even contemporary writers saw that these complaints rested on confused or inadequate economic analysis and heaped ridicule upon them. More criticized the notion of scarcity of money as early as 1523;[44] Starkey makes one of the participants in his dialogue deal disrespectfully with it; and Mun and Child, among others, refused to take it seriously:

Lupset: "For, as touching wool and lead, tin, iron, silver and gold, yea, and all things necessary for the life of man, in the abundance whereof standeth very true·riches, I think our country may be compared with any other."

Pole: ". . . All with one voice cry they lack money, . . . and it is nothing like that all should complain without a cause."

Lupset: ". . . Men so esteem riches and money, that if they had thereof never so great abundance and plenty, yet they would complain. . . ."[45]

And first concerning the evil or want of silver, I think it hath been, and is a general disease of all nations, and so will continue until the end of the world; for poor and rich complain they never have enough; but it seemeth the malady is grown mortal here with us, and therefore it cries out for remedy. Well, I hope it is but im-

---

[44] See *supra*, p. 75.

[45] Thomas Starkey, *England in the reign of King Henry the Eighth* [*ca.* 1538], 1871, pp. 88-90.

agination maketh us sick, when all our parts be sound and strong . . .[46]

. . . money seems to vulgar observers most plentiful when there is least occasion for it; and on the contrary, more scarce, as the occasions for the employment thereof are more numerous and advantageous; . . . from the same reason it is, that a high rate of usury makes money seem scarce. . . .[47]

I can say in truth, upon my own memory, that men did complain as much of the scarcity of money ever since I knew the world as they do now; nay, the very same persons that now complain of this, and commend that time.[48]

The common confusion between money and what could be bought with money or was valued in terms of money, which was usually the explanation of complaints of scarcity of money, was pointed out by North[49] and by the author of *Considerations on the East-India Trade.*[50] At least two writers before Hume explained the process of saving, to show that it need not consist merely of the piling-up of a stock of actual money.[51] As has al-

---

[46] T[homas] M[un], *A discourse of trade, from England unto the East-Indies* [1621], 1930 reprint, p. 46.

[47] Josiah Child, *Discourse about trade*, 1690, p. 152.

[48] *Ibid.,* preface. See also North, *Discourses upon trade* [1691], Hollander ed., p. 36; Harris, *An essay upon money and coins,* Part I (1757), 93-94. Another writer, in 1710, said that explanation of the decline in trade as due to scarcity of money was "a vulgar error," and that the real cause was not a decrease in its quantity but a decrease in its circulation owing to unfavorable prospects. (*A vindication of the faults on both sides* [1710] in *Somers' tracts,* 2d ed., XIII (1815), 6-7.)

[49] North, *op. cit.,* pp. 24 ff.

[50] *Early English tracts on commerce* [1701], McCulloch ed., p. 558.

[51] Barbon, *A discourse of trade* [1690], Hollander ed., p. 20; Joseph Massie, *An essay on the governing causes of the natural rate of interest* [1750], Hollander ed., 1912, *passim;* Hume, *Political discourses* [1752], in *Essays moral, political, and literary,* 1875, I, 320 ff. Cf. also Davenant, *Discourses on publick revenues* [1698], *Works,* II, 106.
The following quotation illustrates an intermediate stage in the evolution of the theory of the formation of capital, where recognition of the possibility of accumulation through productive investment has come but without leading to the complete abandonment of the notion of saving as consisting of the piling-up of the precious metals:

> The primary design, and proper end of silver and gold, is treasure, and 'tis from thence that they acquire their universal value and esteem, so that men will part with all other commodities in exchange for them, with this view, that besides that they will enable them to purchase whatsoever they stand in need of, what they can save to lay up will always be ready to serve their future occasions. 'Tis true that men soon found out ways of

ready been shown, arguments for the need of more money for the building-up of a state treasure had become wholly academic after Henry VIII squandered his inheritance, and played little part in later mercantilist discussion. The advocates of paper money and of credit banking helped to undermine the prestige of the precious metals, especially when they claimed that credit and paper money could perform all the functions of metallic money. These considerations, combined with the development of the doctrine of an automatic regulation of monetary supplies, left the monetary doctrines of the mercantilists in a sad state of disrepair, and prepared the way for their definitive exposure by Hume and Smith.

Thrift.[52]—The prevailing glorification of thrift and the acceptance of the accumulation of wealth as the end of production operated in a twofold way to strengthen the hold of the mercantilist doctrines on public opinion. On the one hand, identification of the saving process with the accumulation of the precious metals made acquisition of a greater supply of them the positive side of thrift. The stress on frugality, on the other hand, helped to create a prejudice against imports, which then consisted largely of luxuries. But the force of these considerations was weakened by counter-arguments justifying consumption of luxuries, either for their own sake, on the ground that the end of economic activity was neither production, nor the accumulation of wealth, but consumption, or enjoyment of the good things of life;[53] or as a

---

improving and increasing their treasure by purchasing lands, lending at interest, and employing it in trade, but how oft soever these ways of cultivation are iterated, still the acquiring of treasure is proposed as the ultimate end. (*A vindication of the faults on both sides. . . .* [1710] in *Somers' Tracts*, 2d ed., 1815, XIII, 5-6.)

Locke had argued that it was only the existence of money which created any incentive for the accumulation of physical capital, since without the possibility of exchanging physical goods for something not perishable and which could be hoarded men would have no motive to acquire possession of land, cattle, etc., in greater amount than they could themselves consume its product. (*Two treatises of civil government* [1690], in *Works*, 1823 ed., V, 365-66.)

[52] Cf., on this section, E. A. J. Johnson, "Unemployment and consumption: the mercantilist view," *Quarterly journal of economics*, XLVI (1932), 708-19.

[53] E.g. [Starkey], *England in the reign of King Henry the Eighth* [ca. 1538], 1878, p. 81; Potter, *Key of wealth*, 1650, p. 17: "To have a plentiful share of outward comforts, though dear, is an advantage above that of enjoying a less proportion thereof, though never so cheap, as much every whit as the end is more excellent than that means, which without such end serveth to no purpose at all"; Barbon, *A discourse of trade* [1690], Hollander ed., p. 22; Jocelyn, *An essay on money & bullion*, 1718, pp. 17-18: the East India Company, in

stimulus to productive activity, whether because free spending quickens trade and circulation,[54] or because the prospect of enjoyment is an incentive to labor and to risk-taking.[55]

Laissez-Faire and Free Trade.—The antecedents of Smith's laissez-faire and free-trade views are probably rightly to be sought mainly in the philosophic literature, and perhaps also in the writings of the physiocrats, rather than in the earlier English economic literature. Hume, no doubt, was an important influence on Adam Smith. But Hume was primarily a philosopher, rather than an economist, and although he must have helped Smith to develop

---

return for bullion, brings in commodities "both to adorn and entertain our ladies. Are not these riches? . . . The produce of the East-Indies enriches Europe . . . more than all the bullion, which comes from the West"; *Some considerations on the nature and importance of the East-India trade*, 1728, p. 71: "Providence in its infinite goodness designed to make life as easy and as pleasurable to mankind as possible, and gave us reason to find out arts, and to make them subservient to our delight and happiness"; Lindsay, *The interest of Scotland considered*, 1733, p. 63; Vanderlint, *Money answers all things* [1734], Hollander ed., p. 134: "For trade terminates ultimately in the consumption of things, to which end alone trade is carried on." Cf. Thomas Fuller, *The holy state, and the profane state* [1642], Nicholas ed., 1841, p. 109: "God is not so hard a Master, but that He alloweth His servants sauce (besides hunger) to eat with their meat." Cf., however, Steuart, *Principles of political œconomy*, 1767, I, 25: "The duty and business of man is not to feed; he is fed in order to do his duty, and to become useful."

[54] E.g., Houghton, *Collection of letters*, 1681-83, I, 52; Barbon, *A discourse of trade* [1690], Hollander ed., p. 32; Child, *A discourse about trade*, 1690, pp. 72 ff.; *Taxes no charge*, 1690, pp. 11 ff.; Vanderlint, *Money answers all things* [1734], Hollander ed., p. 29. Sir William Temple claimed that the argument that extravagance was advantageous was erroneous, even when the spending was confined to domestic goods, because it reduced the amount of goods available for export, and cited the frugality of the Dutch as a model for the English to follow.—*Observations upon the United Provinces of the Netherlands* [1668], *Works*, 1754, I, 132. But Davenant, *Discourses on publick revenues* [1698], *Works*, I, 390-91, and Mandeville, *Fable of the bees* [1714], Kaye ed., I, 186, later claimed that the Dutch were frugal through necessity rather than choice.

[55] North, *Discourses upon trade* [1691], Hollander ed., p. 27; Davenant, *loc. cit.*; Mandeville, *loc. cit.*; Vanderlint, *loc. cit.*; "Impartial essay concerning the nature and use of specie and paper-credit in any country," *Scots magazine*, XXIV (1762), 134; Harris, *An essay upon money and coins*, Part I (1757), 30: "The word *luxury* hath usually annexed to it a kind of opprobrious idea; but so far as it encourages the arts, whets the inventions of men, and finds employments for more of our own people, its influence is benign, and beneficial to the whole society." Cf. also B-I-, M.D. [William Temple of Trowbridge], *A vindication of commerce and the arts* [1758], in McCulloch ed., *Scarce and valuable tracts on commerce*, 1859, pp. 551 ff. Arthur Young, *Political arithmetic*, 1774, pp. 46 ff., defends luxury, because it creates a market for agricultural goods.

his free-trade views, he remained a moderate protectionist himself. But if Adam Smith had carefully surveyed the earlier English economic literature, including, however, tracts apparently always obscure and already scarce by his time, he would have been able to find very nearly all the materials which he actually used in his attack on the protectionist aspects of the mercantilist doctrine. He would, however, have found them scattered, often imbedded in crudely mercantilist analysis, and often consisting only of stray and vague anticipations of later doctrine of whose full significance their authors showed little or no awareness. Caution is necessary lest more be read into such passages than was really intended by their authors, and there has been great exaggeration of the extent to which free-trade views already prevailed in the English literature before Adam Smith. North, Paterson, the author of *Considerations on the East-India trade* (1701), Isaac Gervaise, and Whatley are the only writers prior to Adam Smith whom I have found who seem really to have been free traders.[56] But certain elements of doctrine tending to lead to free-trade views were fairly widely prevalent before the publication of the *Wealth of Nations*. Some of these have already been discussed, for the mercantilist doctrines with respect to the importance of money and of a favorable balance of trade were inconsistent with the principles upon which a free-trade argument could be based, and their refutation was a necessary preliminary to successful formulation of a free-trade doctrine. The formulation of the quantity theory of money and the criticisms and qualifications of the balance-of-trade doctrine prepared the way, therefore, for the emergence of a comprehensive free-trade doctrine. There were other ideas, more immediately related to Adam Smith's argument for free trade, which had attained some degree of currency before he wrote.

There was general agreement that the profit motive was the controlling factor in economic behavior, especially of merchants: "No man in England never seeketh for no common weal, but all and every for his single weal";[57] "For merchants travail for gain

---

[56] Perhaps also Jocelyn, who would lay "as few taxes and prohibitions as possibly can be upon any export or import in trade." (*An essay on money & bullion,* 1718, p. 30.)

[57] [Clement Armstrong] *A treatise concerning the staple* [*ca.* 1530], in Pauli, *op. cit.,* p. 42.

and when gain ceaseth they travail no more";[58] "Every man will sell his wares at the highest price he may";[59] "And where it is said that he is a merchant, and that he ought to have the sea open and free for him, and that trades of merchants and merchandise are necessary to export the surplus of our commodities, and then to import other necessaries, and so is favorably to be respected, as to that it is well known that the end of every private merchant is not the common good, but his particular profit, which is only the means which induceth him to trade and traffic";[60] "Every man almost is taken with the attention to profit. Love doth much, but money doth all";[61] "Men in trade, more especially than the rest of mankind, are bound by their interest; gain is the end of commerce";[62] "I am afraid there are but few men in any country who will prefer the public good to their private interest, when they happen to be inconsistent with one another."[63]

The concept of the "economic man," instead of being, as is often alleged, an invention of the nineteenth-century classical school, was an important element in the mercantilist doctrine. Between the attitudes of the two schools toward the "economic man," if the extreme positions of both may be taken for purposes of contrast, there was this important difference, however, that the classical economists argued that men in pursuing their selfish interests were at the same time, by a providential harmony of interests, either rendering the best service of which they were capable to the common good or at least rendering better service than if their activities were closely regulated by government, whereas the mercantilists deplored the selfishness of the merchant and insisted that to prevent it from ruining the nation it was necessary to subject it to rigorous control. When Malynes made the title of one of his tracts read *The center of the circle of commerce, or, a refutation of a treatise, intituled the circle of commerce*, he did so in order to emphasize his thesis that "gain" was

---

[58] John Hales, "On the unwisdom of a new imposition on cloth" [1559], *T.E.D.*, II, 224.

[59] "Polices to reduce this realme . . ." [1549], *T.E.D.*, III, 317.

[60] Fleming, J., "The case of impositions" [1606], in Howell ed., *A complete collection of state trials*, II (1809), 390.

[61] Robert Keale, *The trade's increase* [1615], in *Harleian miscellany*, III (1809), 307.

[62] [Defoe?] *An essay upon loans*, 1710, p. 14.

[63] David Bindon, *A letter from a merchant who has left off trade*, 1738, p. 12.

the "center" or objective of those engaged in economic activities, and that the only way to prevent merchants from bringing ruin to the commonwealth by their selfish pursuit of gain was to eliminate by restrictions or penalties the profitability to individuals of certain types of transactions which were opposed to the common interest.[64] In extreme cases this attitude tended to lead to wholesale denunciation of the merchant,[65] and the belief that merchants were governed only by self-interest underlay the fundamental mercantilist doctrine of the need for state regulation of commerce. As Fortrey put it, "the public profits should be in a single power to direct, whose interest is only the benefit of the whole," i.e., the statesman.[66]

There was nobody to deny that merchants were governed only or predominantly by self-interest, but some spokesmen for the merchants replied that so were the other classes, and asked the old question: *quis custodiet custodes?* or warned that those who counseled interference by government with the operations of merchants, especially if they were merchants themselves, probably had some private ax to grind. There follow a few citations illustrating these points of view:

And in general all those who are lazy, and do not, or are not active enough, and cannot look out, to vent the product of their estates, or to trade with it themselves, would have all traders forced by laws, to bring home to them sufficient prices, whether they gain or lose by it.[67]

There is hardly a commerce, but the dealers in it will affirm, we

---

[64] See pp. 51, 139, of this tract.

[65] Cf. the scathing indictment of the merchant by James I, in the course of an exposition of the duties of a monarch:

The merchants think the whole commonweal ordained for making them up; and accounting it their lawful gain and trade, to enrich themselves upon the loss of all the rest of the people, they transport from us things necessary, bringing back sometimes unnecessary things, and at other times nothing at all. They buy for us the worst wares, and sell them at the dearest prices; and albeit the victuals fall or rise of their prices according to the abundance or scantiness thereof, yet the prices of their wares ever rise, but never fall, being as constant in that their evil custom as if it were a settled law for them. They are also the special cause of the corruption of the coin, transporting all our own, and bringing in foreign, upon what price they please to set on it. . . . (*Basilikon doron*, in *The workes of . . . James*, 1616, p. 163.)

[66] *Englands interest and improvement* [1663], Hollander ed., p. 13.

[67] North, *Discourses upon trade* [1691], Hollander ed., p. 12.

lose by all the rest; and yet it is evident that in time of peace the kingdom gets by trade in general.[68]

. . . most of the laws that have been made relating to trade, since the Act of Navigation, may be presumed were calculated rather for particular interests than public good; more to advance some tradesmen than the trade of the nation.[69]

. . . only to manage a little conceit or selfish intrigue, to encourage and procure a monopoly, exclusion, pre-emption, and restraints or prohibitions; . . . to restrain, prohibit, and disjoin, not [only] the industry of His Majesty's subjects with other nations, but even with and respect to one another. They will find that all these and many more pretended encouragements are so far from the things they are called, that they are not only intrigues to make private advantage from the ruin of the public, and arise from the mistaken notions and conceits of unthinking men, who neither have temper nor allow themselves time or opportunity to consider things as they are,—but only take them as they seem to be,—a sort of presumptuous meddlers, who are continually apt to confound effects with causes, and causes with effects,—and not to measure the trade, or improvement of house, family, or country, and even that of the universe, by the nature and extent of the thing, but only by their own narrow and mistaken and mean conceptions thereof. . . .[70]

Most of the statutes . . . for regulating, directing, or restraining of trade have, we think, been either political blunders, or jobs obtained by artful men, for private advantage, under pretense of public good.[71]

Conflicting counsel was offered as to how to solve this familiar dilemma of public administration, namely, how to regulate in the public interest the selfish activities of individuals while averting the danger lest the regulations themselves be the product of advice or pressure from interested groups. The problem was made to appear even more serious by the general agreement among merchants of all shades of opinion that politicians and landed gentlemen were not competent to regulate trade on the basis of their own judgment. To the solution offered by some that the states-

---

[68] Davenant, *Discourses on publick revenues* [1698], *Works*, I, 146.

[69] Pollexfen, *A discourse of trade, coyn, and paper credit*, 1697, p. 149.

[70] William Paterson, "A proposal to plant a colony in Darien" [ms. 1701], in Bannister ed., *The writings of William Paterson*, I, 133-34.

[71] [George Whatley] *Principles of trade*, 2d ed., 1774, p. 33, note.

man should take the advice of the merchant,[72] others replied that the merchant was a bad councilor because he always had private interests to serve. Child advised that neither merchants, shop-keepers, nor manufacturers should be accepted as guides until they had become rich, retired from trade, and "by the purchase of lands, become of the same common interest with most of their countrymen."[73] But this was an argument to suit the occasion of the moment, and intended to discredit particular types of proposals by merchants which did not fit in with his own commercial ambitions. Child had no high opinion of the sort of regulation of trade which would result from the unaided wisdom of the land-owner. To a subordinate in the East India Company, who had objected against certain instructions that they seemed to be in violation of the law, Child is reported to have replied:

that he expected his orders were to be his rules, and not the laws of England, which were a heap of nonsense, compiled by a few ignor-ant country gentlemen, who hardly knew how to make laws for the good government of their own private families, much less for the regulating of companies and foreign commerce.[74]

The general effect of this common discrediting of all advice except such as emanated from one's self must have been to weaken confidence in the possibility of obtaining sound and disinterested advice as to the regulation of trade from any source.

Tending further to weaken confidence in the possibility of the beneficial regulation of trade by government was the frequently repeated argument that such regulation went counter to human nature, and could not succeed as against the power of the profit motive.[75] Some representative instances follow:

---

[72] E.g., Lewes Roberts, *Treasure of traffike* [1641], McCulloch ed., *Early English tracts on commerce*, p. 58: "So when a country is properly seated for traffic, and the sovereign willing by foreign commerce to enrich his kingdom, the merchant's advice is questionless best able to propagate the same."

[73] Cited by John Smith, *Chronicon rusticum-commerciale*, 1747, preface, I, v.

[74] Cited by McCulloch, *A dictionary . . . of commerce*, American ed., 1845, I, 620, on the authority of Hamilton's *New account of the East Indies*, I, 232.

[75] As early as 1550, Sir John Mason had objected to an ordinance limiting the price of cheese and butter, on the ground that it was attempting the impos-sible: "Nature will have her course, *etiam si furca expellatur;* and never shall you drive her to consent that a penny-worth of new shall be sold for a farthing."—*T.E.D.*, II, 188.

. . . the trade of the world will not be forced, but will find or make its own way free to all appearance of profit. . . .[76]

. . . if the matter in England, is so prepared for an abatement of interest, that it can not be long obstructed, as he [i.e., "I.C.," the author of an unnamed contemporary tract—probably Josiah Child] saith it is, we need no law for stating it, for nature will have its course with us, as well as in other countries, and he cannot instance, in any country, where by a law, interest is set under 6 per cent and nature is best let alone unforced.[77]

To pretend after this, that parties shall govern mankind against their gain, is to philosophize wisely upon what may be, and what would be politic to bring to pass; but what no man can say was ever put in practice to any perfection; or can be so by the common principles that govern mankind in the world. . . . That tradesmen should cease to seek gain and usurers to love large interests; that men that have gain'd money should leave off desiring to get more; and that zeal to a party should prevail over zeal to their families; that men should forfeit their interest for their humor, and serve their politics at the price of their interest. . . . *No, no,* it is not to be done; the stream of desire after gain runs too strong in mankind, to bring any thing of that kind to perfection in this age. The thing is so impracticable in its nature, that it seems a token of great ignorance in the humor of the age to suggest it; and a man would be tempted to think those people that do suggest it, do not themselves believe what they say about it.[78]

There is nothing weaker, than pretending to offer particular rules how a country may thrive by foreign traffic. Trade must be suffered to take its own course, and will find its own channel.[79]

. . . unless our own manufactures are as good of their kinds, and as low in their prices as the same goods of other nations are, they will not sell either abroad or at home. Trade cannot be forced, but manufacture may be improved.[80]

---

[76] "Advice of His Majesty's Council of Trade, concerning the exportation of gold and silver . . ." [1660], in McCulloch ed., *Tracts on money,* pp. 148-49. The argument is made here to support a recommendation that the exportation of bullion and foreign coin be permitted without restriction.

[77] *Interest of money mistaken,* 1668, p. 10.

[78] [Defoe] *An essay upon loans,* 1710, pp. 15-17. This is in answer to a threat that if the government did not revise its policy the moneyed interests would, on party grounds, refuse to lend to it.

[79] Davenant, *Report to the commissioners for stating the publick accounts* [1712], *Works,* V, 452.

[80] Lindsay, *The interest of Scotland considered,* 1733, preface, p. iii.

The objections so far considered against government regulation, in the public interest, of the selfish activities of the merchant rested on the incompetence of the regulators, or the unavailability of unbiased advisers, or the inability of government to cope with the strength of the profit motive.[81] A few writers, however, anticipated Adam Smith more or less clearly in formulating his fundamental principle that man in pursuing his own ends was at the same time usually serving the general good, and that unregulated trade was therefore desirable, not merely because it was the lesser of two evils, but because it was positively the servant of the public welfare.[82] The idea of the natural harmony of interests appears already to be present in the following passage from Misselden:

And is it not lawful for merchants to seek their Privatum Commodum in the exercise of their calling? Is not gain the end of trade? Is not the public involved in the private, and the private in the public? What else makes a common wealth, but the private-wealth, if I may say so, of the members thereof in the exercise of commerce amongst themselves, and with foreign nations?[83]

---

[81] Cf. Vanderlint, *Money answers all things* [1734], Hollander ed., p. 58: ". . . I am entirely for preventing the importation of all foreign commodities, as much as possible; but not by acts of parliament, which never can do any good to trade; but by raising such goods ourselves, so cheap as to make it impossible for other nations to find their account in bringing them to us. . . ."

[82] Few traces are to be found in the literature of the period of the intermediate doctrine, which concedes that self-interest is a powerful force for good, and should not be reviled or crushed, but maintains that it is also capable of doing harm to the commonwealth, and therefore needs to be watched and regulated. It is perhaps implied in the arguments of some of the moderate mercantilists, and may be what Petty had in mind in the following passage: "We must consider in general, that as wiser physicians tamper not excessively with their patients, rather observing and complying with the motions of nature than contradicting it with vehement administrations of their own, so in politics and economics the same must be used, for *Naturam expellas furcâ licet usque recurrit*." (*Treatise of taxes* [1662], *Economic writings*, I, 60.) Tucker gives expression to it at one point, although elsewhere he expounds contradictory doctrine. In his *Elements of commerce*, 1755, he asserts that self-love is an important stimulus. "Consequently, the main point to be aimed at, is neither to extinguish nor enfeeble self-love, but to give it such a direction, that it may promote the public interest by pursuing its own" (p. 7). But the only clear and elaborate exposition of this intermediate position I have found is in [Nathaniel Forster] *An enquiry into the causes of the present high price of provisions*, 1767, pp. 17-22. The relevant passages are too long for quotation, but they deserve the attention of those interested in the history of the laissez-faire idea.

[83] *The circle of commerce*, 1623, p. 17.

North states it clearly: "That there can be no trade unprofitable to the public; for if any prove so, men leave it off; and wherever the traders thrive, the public, of which they are a part, thrives also."[84] It is implied in a tract attributed to Child: ". . . trade is a free agent, and must not be limited or bounded; if it be so in any nation, it will never prosper."[85] Davenant subscribed to it, although not wholly unqualifiedly:

Trade is in its nature free, finds its own channel and best directeth its own course; and all laws to give it rules and directions, and to limit and circumscribe it, may serve the particular ends of private men, but are seldom advantageous to the public.[86]

More important, in preparing the way for Adam Smith, was Mandeville's more elaborate reasoning in support of individualism and laissez faire, resting on his famous argument that "private vices" such as "avarice" and luxury were "public benefits."[87] In Hume's economic writings the laissez-faire doctrine is to be found only by implication if at all. Tucker, although in the field of foreign trade policy he continued to be a protectionist of a somewhat extreme type, at one point vigorously asserted the identity of private and public interests and drew laissez-faire conclusions therefrom:

For let the legislature but take care not to make bad laws, and then as to good ones, they will make themselves: that is, the self-love and self-interest of each individual will prompt him to seek such ways of gain, trades, and occupations of life, as by serving himself, will promote the public welfare at the same time. The only thing necessary to be done by positive institutions is, to enforce the observance of voluntary contracts by legal penalties speedily levied. . . .

Indeed, it must be acknowledged with gratitude and pleasure that the legislature of late years hath enacted many excellent laws which

---

[84] *Discourses upon trade* [1691], Hollander ed., p. 13. Cf. also *ibid.*, p. 37: ". . . no people ever yet grew rich by policies; but it is peace, industry, and freedom that brings trade and wealth, and nothing else."

[85] *The humble answer of the Governor . . . of the East-India Company* [1692] in *Somers' tracts*, 2d ed., X, 622. Child is here objecting to a proposal, directed against himself, to limit the amount of stock in the company which could be held by any one person.

[86] *An essay on the East-India trade* [1697], *Works*, I, 98. Cf. also *ibid.*, p. 104: "Wisdom is most commonly in the wrong, when it pretends to direct nature."

[87] *Fable of the bees, passim.* Mandeville deliberately stated his conclusions in such manner as to make them offensive to moralists, but Smith accepted them in substance while finding a more palatable form for their expression.

have promoted commerce, increased industry, and extended manufactures . . . but then the laws in question are such, whose true ex-
cellence consists rather in the repeal of absurd and bad laws formerly
made, than in any particular positions or maxims of commerce.[88]

But shortly before the publication of the *Wealth of Nations*,
Whatley, obviously under physiocratic influence, made a specific
plea for laissez faire on the basis, in part, of the existence of an
identity of interest between the individual traders and the state:

Now, though it is hardly to be expected, as above hinted, that
princes should allow of a general free trade or intercourse, because
they seldom know their own true interest. . . .[89]

Perhaps, in general, it would be better if government meddled no
farther with trade, than to protect it, and let it take its course. . . .
It were therefore to be wished, that commerce were as free between
all the nations of the world, as it is between the several counties of
England: so would all, by mutual communication, obtain more enjoyments.[90]

In the ancient Greek and Roman classics is to be found the
doctrine that differences in natural conditions in different countries made trade between these countries mutually profitable. The
early Christian philosophers took over this doctrine and gave it a
theological flavor. God had endowed different regions with limited
but varied products in order to give mankind an incentive to
trade, so that through a world economy they would become united
in a world society, and as children of one God they would learn
to love each other.[91] This was apparently common doctrine among
the English theological writers of the sixteenth century and later.[92]
This doctrine was taken over to some extent by the lay writers

---

[88] *Instructions for travellers*, 1757, pp. 31-32.

[89] *Principles of trade*, 2d ed., 1774, p. 10.

[90] *Ibid.*, note, pp. 33-34. This note may have been a contribution by Benjamin
Franklin. It mentions with approval the demand reputed to have been made
of Colbert by the French merchants, "*Laissez nous faire* (Let us alone)"—
perhaps the first appearance of the term in the English literature.

[91] Cf. Heinrich Dietzel, *Weltwirtschaft und Volkswirthschaft*, 1900, p. 6.

[92] [Cf. Clement Armstrong] *A treatise concerning the staple* [*ca.* 1530], in
Pauli, *op. cit.*, p. 25: "So as all special gift of rich commodities that God first
gave unto the earth in every realm to one realm, that another hath not, to
the intent, that every realm should be able to live of God's gift, one to be help
to another to be an occasion one to live by another." Cf. also R. H. Tawney,
"Religious thought on social and economic questions in the sixteenth and seventeenth centuries," *Journal of political economy*, XXXI (1923), 478.

on commercial matters, but they managed ingeniously to adapt the intent of Providence to their own particular views. Extreme mercantilists, who in general were pleading for new or added restrictions on trade, used the doctrine either to justify the restriction of certain products to Englishmen, on the ground that Providence had assigned them to this country, or appealed to the doctrine in support of that branch or type of trade which they wished to have fostered, while conveniently forgetting the doctrine when attacking other branches or types of trades. William Cholmeley at first states the doctrine fairly, bringing out clearly its implication that a tolerant attitude toward imports and raw material exports was proper:

> But when I considered how the unsearchable purpose of God hath, by the lack of necessary commodities, driven all the nations of the earth to seek one upon another, and thereby to be knit together in amity and love, I thought, that as this realm lacketh (and that naturally) things necessarily required to the perfecting of our commodities, it might also be a thing natural to the English nation, to be so imperfect of wit that we could never be able to attain to the knowledge of true and perfect workmanship, because God would drive us thereby to suffer other nations to have a commodity by making our commodities [im?]perfect?[93]

Since his main concern, however, was that English wool should be exported only in the form of finished cloth, instead of as raw wool or as undyed cloth, he found a means of reconciling his theology and his patriotism. It would be ingratitude to God to attribute to him the intention of withholding from Englishmen "the aptness of wytt" to become perfect workmen in the weaving and dyeing of cloth, and their failure to do so was not because God intended England to supply foreign weavers and dyers with the necessary wool, but because the English craftsmen were selfish and indolent: "we being beastly minded, and seeking to gain much by doing little, every man seeking his own private commodity, without regard of the weal public, do not diligently apply our good wits to the searching out of good knowledge, but to the inventing of subtle deceit (wherein we excel all other nations),

---

[93] William Cholmeley, *The request and suite of a true-hearted Englishman* [ms. 1553], W. J. Thoms, editor, *Camden miscellany*, II (1853), 1.

to our private advancement, but the decay of the public weal of our country."[94]

Misselden similarly expounded the benevolent attitude of God toward trade between nations, in the course of a defense of the trading activities of the Merchant Adventurers, of which he was an employed official, but did not let it trouble him in his advocacy of stringent restrictions on branches of trade in which the Merchant Adventurers were not directly concerned.[95] Another writer derived from the doctrine the lesson that Providence had assigned wool-raising and the woolen industry to England, and therefore that England should concentrate her efforts on it,[96] and several later writers did call upon it for support of their more liberal views with respect to freedom of trade as against the more extreme mercantilists, much as did Adam Smith in his two famous references to the "invisible hand."

For it is not the having all things of our own growth on the one hand, and the saving of our money on the other, can make us rich; neither can our increase and plenty in some sense be said to be our wealth, if we have not a suitable vend and consumption thereof; besides, nature hath otherwise provided, and so furnished each particular part of the world with something which the rest want, whereby to preserve a friendship and commerce together.[97]

The various products of different soils and countries is an indication that Providence intended they should be helpful to each other, and mutually supply the necessities of one another.[98]

By the wise appointment of divine Providence, a mutual intercourse and commerce amongst men is both conducive and necessary to their well being. Every man stands in need of the aid of others; and every country may reap advantages by exchanging some of its

---

[94] *Ibid.*, p. 2.

[95] Edward Misselden, *Free trade*, 2d ed., 1622, pp. 25-26. Misselden cites from Aristotle and Seneca in this connection.

[96] *The linen and woollen manufactory discoursed* . . . [1691], in John Smith, Chronicon rusticum-commerciale, I, 384:

Divine Providence, that appoints to every nation and country a particular portion, seems to allot that to England, which was the first acceptable sacrifice to his Omnipotency, that of the flock. . . . Now to decline this, and set up another manufacture, looks like an extravagant mechanic, who by his improvidence hath lost his own art, and thinks to retrieve his misfortune by taking up that of another man's. This is condemned in particular persons, and to be feared in a community.

[97] *A treatise of wool and cattel*, 1677, p. 3.

[98] Davenant, *An essay on the East-India trade* [1697], in *Works*, I, 104.

superfluous products, natural or artificial, for those which it wants of foreign growth.[99]

In a remarkable passage, Henry Home gives credit to Providence for the self-regulating mechanism of international specie flows, as the means by which it is provided that commerce shall be mutually profitable:

It appears the intention of Providence that all nations should benefit by commerce as by sunshine; and it is so ordered, that an unequal balance is prejudicial to the gainers as well as to the losers; the latter are immediate sufferers; but not less so ultimately are the former. This is one remarkable instance, among many, of providential wisdom in conducting human affairs, independent of the will of man, and frequently against his will. The commercial balance held by the hand of Providence is never permitted to preponderate much to one side; and every nation partakes, or may partake, of all the comforts of life. Engrossing is bad policy; and men are prompted, both by interest and duty, to second the plan of Providence, and to preserve, as near as possible, equality in the balance of trade.[100]

International Division of Labor.—A few writers prior to Adam Smith stated or approached closely some of the specific economic arguments for unrestricted trade which were later to serve as the core of the free-trade doctrine of Adam Smith and the English classical school. John Houghton, in 1677, in a tract of free-trade flavor, argued that the same sort of reasoning should be applied to foreign as to domestic trade, since both alike consisted of a mutual exchange of goods, presumably to mutual advantage.[101] Barbon claimed that a reduction of imports as a result of prohibitions would cut off an equivalent amount of exports.[102] Davenant made explicitly a point vital to the free-trade

---

[99] Harris, *An essay upon money and coins,* Part I (1757), 14. Cf. also Charles Molloy, *A treatise of affairs maritime, and of commerce* [1676], 9th ed., 1769, I, preface, p. iv.

[100] *Sketches of the history of man,* 1774, I, 81-82.

[101] John Houghton, *England's great happiness* [1677], in McCulloch ed., *Early English tracts on commerce,* p. 261. In his *A collection of letters,* 1681-83, I, 60, Houghton claims its authorship, quotes from it, adds to it, and argues along identical lines on a number of points. Houghton adheres to the monetary phases of the mercantilist doctrine, however, and elsewhere expounds doctrine inconsistent with free-trade reasoning.

[102] *A discourse of trade,* 1690, p. 35. Barbon proceeds, however, to argue that the production of the exports would not necessarily be displaced by the production of domestic goods, since the latter might not satisfy the buyers, who would consequently not spend their money. Barbon in any case was far from

doctrine, but which the nineteenth-century economists often assumed implicitly, namely, that labor had adequate occupational mobility. He claimed that if domestic labor is displaced as a consequence of imports of foreign commodities "these hands can shift from one work to another, without any great prejudice to themselves, or the public."[103]

Several writers presented arguments in support of the international division of labor, and it requires only mildly generous interpretation to justify the conclusion that they approached more closely than did Adam Smith the high point of free-trade reasoning, the statement of the benefit of regional specialization in terms of *comparative* advantage. Davenant maintained that the artificially stimulated production of goods for which neither the soil nor the general bent of the people were adapted is never wise, and that the silk and linen industries were suitable only for countries where wages were low. "It is the prudence of a state to see that this industry, and stock, be not diverted from things profitable to the whole, and turned upon objects unprofitable, and perhaps dangerous to the public."[104] The unknown author of *Considerations on the East-India Trade* (1701), who has been rightly praised by a number of modern writers, reveals almost no trace of the mercantilist or protectionist fallacies. He meets all objections against the export of bullion or the import of foreign commodities by regarding trade as a voluntary exchange of considerations. If bullion is voluntarily exchanged for Indian manufactures, it must be because the latter are of more value. "To exchange bullion for cloth is to exchange the less for the greater value." Cheap imports, he asserts, are the valid objective of foreign trade. He even draws an analogy between foreign trade and labor-saving devices. The fact that Indian wares can be gotten through trade with less expenditure of labor than their production at home would require means that labor is saved and made available for other purposes:

---

being a free trader. Mandeville, *Fable of the bees* [1714], Kaye ed., I, iii, also claimed that reducing imports involved a reduction of exports as well.

[103] *Essay on the East-India trade* [1697], *Works*, I, 95.

[104] *Ibid.*, I, 105-10. Cf. also, Gardner, *Some reflections on a pamphlet, intituled, England and East India inconsistent in their manufactures*, 1696, pp. 9 ff., for ideas closely resembling those of Davenant, and in part also those of the author of *Considerations on the East-India trade*.

If nine cannot produce above three bushels of wheat in England, if by equal labor they might procure nine bushels from another country, to employ these in agriculture at home, is to employ nine to do no more work than might be done as well by three; . . . is the loss of six bushels of wheat; is therefore the loss of so much value.[105]

Isaac Gervaise claimed that for each country, according to the "disposition" or productive capacities of its people and their geographical situation, there was a "natural" apportionment among different industries of its productive resources. If consumption demands were such that with this "natural" apportionment of production some commodities would not be produced in adequate quantities to satisfy the demand, it was best to meet such deficiencies of production by permitting free importation of such commodities from abroad:

Taxes on imports being no more than a degree of prohibition, and prohibition only forcing those manufactures to extend themselves beyond their natural proportions, to the prejudice of those which are, according to the disposition of the country, natural beyond the entire demand of the inhabitants; which lessens or hinders their exportation, in proportion to the prejudice they receive by the increase of those manufactures which are but in part natural, and whereof the importation is prohibited.

This considered, we may conclude, that trade is never in a better condition than when it's natural and free; the forcing it either by laws or taxes being always dangerous: because though the intended benefit or advantage be perceived, it is difficult to perceive its countercoup, whichever is at least in full proportion to the intended benefit: nature not yielding at once, sharpens those countercoups, and commonly causes a greater evil than the intended benefit can balance. Moreover, trade being a tacit and natural agreement to give or furnish a proportion of certain denominations of labor, to be drawn back in like proportion in such other denominations as best suits necessity or fancy, man naturally seeks, and finds, the most easy

---

[105] In McCulloch ed., *Early English tracts on commerce,* pp. 556-59, 578-85. (Citation from p. 583.) The original tract is extremely rare, and does not appear to have exerted any influence on contemporary writers. Halkett and Laing attribute its authorship to Dudley North, and they have been followed by a number of economists. This seems, however, clearly to be a mistake. North died in 1691, whereas this tract was not published until 1701. Chapter iii of the tract discusses the effects of the competition of the *two* companies then privileged to trade with India, which definitely locates its time of writing as not earlier than 1698.

and natural means of attaining his ends, and cannot be diverted from those means but by force and against his will.[106]

Similar reasoning was presented by Patrick Lindsay. Scotland should discourage rather than encourage industries, such as woolens, which would interfere with the progress of the only "staple," linen. These other industries had no chance of success in Scotland, and it was better to buy their products from abroad than to attempt to make them at home:

We may then reasonably suppose, on the lowest computation, that we can buy . . . those woolen goods 10 and 15 per cent cheaper in England, than we can make them at home; and if we can make linen cloth, and sell it in England from 5 to 10 per cent profit, and purchase, in exchange for it, woolen goods 10 and 15 per cent cheaper than we can make them at home, then are we gainers by this trade from 15 to 20 per cent, and of consequence, so many hands as are employed in the woolen, who might be employed in the linen, just so much does the country lose by their labor.[107]

A few writers were in the rather paradoxical position of adhering to crudely mercantilistic doctrines with respect to the balance of trade, the superiority of exports over imports, or the importance of money, while advocating complete or very nearly complete free trade. Houghton[108] and Vanderlint[109] appear to belong to this group, and also Decker, who advocated free trade as a means of procuring a more favorable balance of trade.[110] Roger Coke was an out-and-out mercantilist in his general analysis, but he nevertheless disapproved of monopolies, the Navigation acts, the restriction of import of cattle from Scotland, and the restric-

---

[106] *The system or theory of the trade of the world,* 1720, pp. 22-23.

[107] *The interest of Scotland considered,* 1733, pp. 111-12. Cf. also for similar reasoning, Vanderlint, *Money answers all things* [1734], Hollander ed., pp. 96-98; anon., *Reflections and considerations occasioned by the petition . . . for taking off the drawback on foreign linens, &c.,* 1738, p. 26; Nicholas Magens, *Farther explanations of some particular subjects,* 1756, p. 6.

[108] *England's great happiness,* 1677; *Collection of letters,* 1681-83.

[109] See *supra,* pp. 83-84, 98.

[110] But Decker, after advocating the removal of all restrictions on trade except the Navigation acts, in somewhat of an anticlimax, concedes that if duties were taken off some sort of regulation would be necessary for some goods, lest they interfere with home manufactures.—*Serious considerations on the several high duties,* 3d ed., 1744, p. 31. Massie pointed out the inconsistency between Decker's general argument for free trade and this concession to protection.— Joseph Massie, *The proposal, commonly called Sir Matthew Decker's scheme, for one general tax upon houses, laid open,* 1757, p. 3.

tions on the Irish trade, and did not give explicit support to any trade restrictions in any of his writings that were available for examination.[111] There were other writers who adhered to the mercantilist doctrines without revealing their attitude toward trade regulation.

A constant note in the writings of the merchants was the insistence upon the usefulness to the community of trade and the dignity and social value of the trader, and in the eighteenth century it appears to have become common for others than the traders themselves to accept them at their own valuation.[112] Very often "trade" is not more definitely specified, but no doubt most of the writers who argued for the value of trade meant foreign trade, or even only export trade. But in the general glorification of trade, some of the tracts made no reference to the quantity of money, the balance of trade, or other phases of the mercantilist doctrines. In some cases there was explicit inclusion of imports on a parity with exports as deserving of encouragement, and support of low customs, without explicit discrimination between export and import duties, as a means of fostering trade.[113] The general tendency of such discussion must have been to weaken faith in legislative restriction of trade, and to prepare the way for the acceptance of free-trade views on explicitly stated economic grounds, although on the other side it is to be said that the chief advocates of particular restrictions were merchants.[114]

---

[111] *A discourse of trade,* 1670; *A treatise wherein is demonstrated, that the Church and State of England, are in equal danger with the trade of it,* 1671; *Reflections upon the East-Indy and Royal African companies,* 1695; *A treatise concerning the regulation of the coyn of England,* 1696.

[112] See, e.g., the eulogy of the merchant in Lillo's play, *The London merchant,* 2d ed., 1731, Act I, scene i, and Act III, scene i.

[113] Cf., e.g., John Smith, *Advertisements for the inexperienced planters of New England* [1631], in *Works,* Edward Arber ed., 1884, pp. 961-62; anon., *A discourse concerning the East-India trade* [ca. 1692], in *Somers' tracts,* 2d ed., X, 642: "The more goods are exported and imported, . . . the nation in general will have the advantage, though the traders may not . . . "; William Wood, *A letter . . . shewing the justice of a more equal and impartial assessment on land,* 1717, p. 19; anon., *Considerations occasioned by the bill for enabling the South-Sea Company to increase their capital stock,* 1720, p. 14: "Whether upon the whole, if more of our own product and manufactures are exported, and of foreign commodities imported, more of our ships and seamen, our manufactures and people of all trades will not be employed; consequently, if the customs and excises will not be greatly advanced?"

[114] A spokesman for the agricultural interests objected that in this general glorification of trade the interests of the farmer were being overlooked, and

Free-trade doctrine, however, continued to be a rank heresy, and there were probably some who subscribed to it but who did not dare to expose their peculiar views in print. Violet relates with horror that some men in high positions held such views:

. . . some men are of an opinion, that they would have trade free, to import all commodities, and export all without any restraint, not for leather, fuller's earth, corn, wool, ammunition, gold and silver, horses, and all other things that are staff and stay of this nation. I would not write it, but I have it affirmed by men of great quality, that this is the opinion of some men that are in place and power.[115]

I believe I have succeeded in showing that all the important elements in Adam Smith's free-trade doctrine had been presented prior to the *Wealth of Nations*. These were often, however, to be found only in isolated passages not wholly consistent with the views expounded in the surrounding text. There is little evidence that these early expositions had much influence on public opinion in the mass, or even on Hume and Smith. Hume himself discarded the monetary and balance-of-trade doctrines of his time while adhering to protectionism,[116] and Adam Smith both in his *Lectures* and in the *Wealth of Nations* relapsed at times into rather crude versions of the mercantilist monetary and balance-of-trade doctrines, as well as into protectionism.[117] In so far as

that even petty domestic traders were including their own trades as entitled to the special consideration which was being claimed for "trade": "The notion of encouraging trade has of late years prevailed very much, and very rightly where we speak of foreign trade; and the first promoters of the notion meant no others, but from thence we are descended to all trade, domestic as well as foreign, and the cry of it is so common, even amongst the vulgar, that I have heard my landlord, who keeps a petty ale-house in a country village, harangue it with great eloquence; and with a grave air complain, that trade was not sufficiently encouraged, when he meant the trade of ale-draping and smoking-tobacco."—*Some thoughts on the interest of money in general* (ca. 1720), pp. 65-66.

[115] *Mysteries and secrets,* 1653, p. 24.

[116] Cf. *Political discourses* [1752], in *Essays moral, political, and literary,* 1875 ed., I, 343-44: "All taxes, however, upon foreign commodities, are not to be regarded as prejudicial or useless, but those only which are founded on the jealousy above-mentioned. A tax on German linen encourages home manufactures, and thereby multiplies our people and industry. A tax on brandy increases the sale of rum, and supports our southern colonies."

[117] Cf. e.g., *Lectures,* p. 209: "If I purchase a thousand pounds' worth of French wines, and drink them all when they come home, the country is two thousand pounds poorer, because both the goods and money are gone; if I spend a thousand pounds' worth of goods at home upon myself the country is only deprived of one thousand pounds, as the money still remains; but in main-

Hume and Smith did not develop their foreign-trade doctrines for themselves, it seems likely that their chief indebtedness was to the philosophers, rather than to the earlier English economic literature. In the literature before Hume there is scarcely any discussion of the anticipations of free-trade doctrine examined in the foregoing, even for purposes of refutation,[118] and most of the controversy is between exponents of rival schemes of regulation, or between extreme and moderate mercantilists, rather than between mercantilists and free traders.

In many respects, indeed, as the mercantilist argument became more elaborate and involved, it became more objectionable from the point of view of modern doctrine, and, except with reference to the bullionist doctrines, a strong argument could be presented in defense of the thesis that the mass of ordinary tracts on trade of the first half of the eighteenth century showed a more extreme and confused adherence to the fallacies of mercantilism than did the writings of the sixteenth and early seventeenth centuries. The simplicity and brevity of the early analysis at least resulted in fallacies of comparable simplicity, but the later writers were able to assemble a greater variety of fallacies into an elaborate system of confused and self-contradictory argument. In so far as trade theory was concerned, such progress as occurred was due almost solely to a small group of capable writers, able to analyze economic problems more acutely and logically than their predecessors, but not able to make a marked impression upon their contemporaries or even to attract their attention. Even Hume made few converts in England, and his influence on the physiocrats was more apparent than on the English writers of his own generation. On legislation, it is not evident that the critics of mercantilism had much influence, and it could be seriously argued that, with the exception of the disappearance of the bullionist regulations,

---

taining an army in a distant war it is the same thing whether we pay them in goods or money, because the consumption is the same at any rate." For the history of a late American version of this fallacy, see F. W. Taussig, "Abraham Lincoln on the tariff: a myth," in *Free trade, the tariff and reciprocity,* 1920, pp. 34-47. For an earlier English version, see Richard Haines, *The prevention of poverty,* 1674, p. 11.

[118] The only exceptions of any importance that I have noticed are [David Bindon] *A letter from a merchant who has left off trade,* 1738, pp. 31-32, where a number of presumably current arguments against restrictions on imports are stated and controverted, and Gee, *The trade and navigation of Great Britain considered* [1729], 1767 ed., pp. 183 ff.

the general course of foreign-trade legislation from 1600 to *after* Adam Smith was, without important exception, away from, rather than toward, conformity with the doctrines of the critics of mercantilism.

III. SOME MODERN INTERPRETATIONS OF ENGLISH MERCANTILISM

There has been a marked tendency in recent years, more especially perhaps on the part of German economists and of economic historians, toward a more favorable appraisal of English mercantilist doctrine than has prevailed among the economic theorists of the English classical tradition. Much of this tendency can be explained away as due to participation in the interventionist, protectionist, or aggressively nationalistic sentiments of the mercantilist writers, to misconceptions of what the economic doctrines of the English mercantilists really were, or to absence of knowledge of, or interest in, the grounds for rejecting the mercantilist doctrines afforded by modern monetary and trade theory. To those apologists who defend the mercantilist doctrines on the ground either that they were not what their critics allege them to have been, or that the theoretical objections of the critics can be successfully refuted, the foregoing presentation of the mercantilist reasoning must suffice as an answer.

The modern apologies for mercantilism, however, are also supported by several arguments which do not clash directly with the propositions of modern trade and monetary theory, and these arguments are entitled to more respectful treatment. The economic historians, for instance, seem to derive from their valid doctrine, that if sufficient information were available the prevalence in any period of particular theories could be *explained* in the light of the circumstances then prevailing, the curious corollary that they can also be *justified* by appeal to these special circumstances. There are some obvious obstacles to acceptance of this point of view. It would lead to the conclusion that no age, except apparently the present one, is capable of serious doctrinal error. It overlooks the fact that one of the historical circumstances which has been undergoing an evolution has been the capacity for economic analysis. More specifically, to be invoked successfully in defense of mercantilist doctrine it needs to be supported by demonstration that the typical behavior of merchants, the nature of the gains or losses from trade, the nature of the monetary processes, and the economic significance of territorial division of labor have changed sufficiently since 1550, or 1650, or 1750, to make what was sound reasoning for these earlier periods unsound for the present-day world.

It has been claimed also for the mercantilists that they were presenting short-run doctrines and proposals, whereas their later critics had only long-run considerations in mind. It must be conceded that some of the mercantilist doctrine would not be quite so absurd if appraised from the short-run point of view. But I have found no evidence that the mercantilists intended their analysis and proposals to be regarded as holding true for the short run only, and there is abundant evidence that they were ordinarily not aware of any distinction between what was desirable monetary or trade practice, to meet a temporary situation, on the one hand, and as permanent policy, on the other.

It has been argued also, in answer to the criticisms of mercantilist doctrine by economic theorists, that the primary objective of mercantilist policy was not economic prosperity but national unity and power. In dealing with this interpretation of mercantilism, it is important to distinguish between the official and the unofficial expositions of the doctrine, between the actual policies and the reasoning by which they were supported, and between Continental and English mercantilism. In each case, it is only the latter with which this essay is concerned. Government policy, no doubt, was never governed solely by economic considerations, but for the unofficial writers this was a subject for complaint rather than for approval. Even in the unofficial literature, however, political and religious considerations were mingled with the economic to a degree without parallel in modern economic literature. But in England a strong and centralized government and an aggressive national spirit had been established long before the appearance of an important mercantilist literature, and whatever may have been the situation on the Continent the primary emphasis of the English mercantilist writers was on the means by which England's wealth could be augmented. Many writers, it is true, urged in support of the measures which they advocated that they would not only contribute to England's prosperity but would also promote her prestige and power, injure her rivals, and protect her national faith against its enemies, internal and external. But the appeal to political and religious considerations seems often to have been intended to win the support of the less commercial-minded official and landed classes for the proposals of the "merchants" or businessmen, and seems only rarely to have expressed what was really the primary concern of their authors. Especially important as a safeguard against applying erroneously to the English mercantilist literature generalizations which may be true of the Continental writers, it should be borne in mind that English mercantilist doctrine was the product of merchants to an extent without parallel on the Continent. On economic matters even the landed classes in England found their ablest spokesmen in merchants such as Child and North. And the merchants were typically impatient of official policy when it failed to place primary emphasis on the economic aspects of the matters with which it dealt, and especially when it appeared to subordinate economic to political or religious considerations.

Even if it be granted, however, that the principal objective of the English mercantilist writers was a great and powerful England rather than a prosperous England, it does not follow that appraisal of their reasoning on strictly economic grounds is unwarranted or irrelevant. It would be difficult to find convincing evidence that any of the prominent mercantilists regarded power and prosperity as generally conflicting and inharmonious objectives of national policy. On the contrary, it was a matter of general agreement among them that for England the only certain path to national power and glory was through promotion of trade and increase of wealth. Child's formula, which was often quoted approvingly, expresses accurately the mercantilist position: "Foreign trade produces riches, riches power, power preserves our trade and religion."[1] After the Revolution, in fact, trade and wealth seem to have become almost an obsession of the mercantile classes, and the emphasis which they placed on the economic phases of national policy was, if anything, excessive. I suspect that the "trade wars" of the seventeenth and eighteenth centuries were such more in the imagination of the mercantile writers than

---

[1] Cf. also, James Whiston, *A discourse of the decay of trade*, 1693, p. 3:
Neither will the pursuing these proposals, augment the nation's wealth and power only, but that wealth and power will also preserve our trade and religion, they mutually working for the preservation of each other. . . .

in the intent of the governing classes who embarked upon them, and that just as the merchants appealed to non-economic considerations to make their proposals attractive to the landed classes, so the government appealed to the cupidity of the merchants to win their support for wars embarked upon for dynastic or political reasons.[2] Even the official classes in England, however, were probably more trade-minded, and probably gave greater weight to economic considerations, than the corresponding classes on the Continent. Such, at least, appears to have been the opinion of eighteenth-century Continental observers.[3]

Not only is there little evidence that the mercantilist writers were prepared to sacrifice national economic to political interests, but a good deal of the mercantilist literature can be plausibly explained as special pleading for limited economic interests. The

---

[2] A striking instance is the following passage from a tract which is clearly the product of a writer not familiar with, nor really interested in, commercial matters, but who sensed the need for an appeal to economic considerations if his plea for the continuance of the war with France then under way was to have weight with its readers: "To proceed now to the second head I proposed, namely, that this war has produced great and lasting advantages to the people over and above liberty, and a security of our properties. The advantages I propound to speak to shall be confined to the article of wealth, as being that which most generally affects; for to talk to the common people of the great honor our nation will gain by a happy issue of this war, is to speak to little purpose."—*The taxes not grievous and therefore not a reason for an unsafe peace,* 1712, p. 15. The views of the mercantilists as to the efficacy of war as an instrument to procure economic advantages would be an interesting topic for investigation. It would be wrong to attribute to them without exception the view that trade wars, even if successfully prosecuted, promoted the national wealth, and some of them anticipated the modern argument that even a victorious war costs more than it returns in economic benefits. Others, however, looked upon trade wars as so essential to commercial prosperity that the Turkey Company tried to exclude a Quaker from its councils in 1759 as professing opinions hostile to the waging of such vars. See G. B. Hertz, *The old colonial system,* 1905, p. 10.

[3] Cf. Montesquieu, *De l'esprit des lois* [1748], Bk. xx, chap. vii: "D'autres nations ont fait céder des intérêts du commerce à des intérêts politiques: celle-ci [i.e., England] a toujours fait céder ses intérêts politiques aux intérêts de son commerce."—*Œuvres complètes,* Paris, 1877, IV, 371.

Cf. also Quesnay, "Remarques sur l'opinion de l'auteur de l'esprit des lois concernant les colonies" [*Journal de l'agriculture,* January, 1766], in Oncken ed., *Œuvres de . . . F. Quesnay,* 1888, p. 429: ". . . en Angleterre . . . où les lois du commerce maritime ne se prêtent point aux lois de la politique; où les intérêts de la glèbe et de l'État sont subordonnés aux intérêts des négociants; où le commerce des productions de l'agriculture, la propriété du territoire et l'État même ne sont regardés que comme des accessoires de la métropole, et la métropole comme formée de négociants."

most ardent advocates in the seventeenth century of the revival
or enforcement of the bullionist restrictions had a personal interest of one sort or another in these regulations. Malynes is
said to have had expectations of getting a remunerative contract
in connection with the currency if the office of the Royal Exchanger were revived. Milles was a customs official among whose
duties would be the enforcement of any bullionist regulations.
Violet had been a "searcher" and informer in connection with
the regulations prohibiting the export of bullion, and his appeals
for stricter enforcement were accompanied by pleas that he again
be employed to discover violations of the regulations.[4] Wheeler
was secretary and Misselden an important member of the Merchant Adventurers, and their tracts were written in defense of
their exchange transactions against the attacks of Milles and
Malynes. The East India Company, in its charter of 1600, was
granted the right to export a limited amount of bullion, and in
its early as in its later operations bullion constituted the bulk of
its exports from England. This led to attacks on the company of
which Robert Keales' *The Trades Increase* (1615) was typical.
Digges, a member of the company, wrote his *Defence of Trade*
(1615) as a reply to Keales, and Mun, an officer of the company,
wrote his tracts and presented a "remonstrance" to the government primarily to ward off hostile measures against the company.
Throughout the history of the company its officers and employees
were publishing tracts in its defense which were important contributions to the literature of mercantilism. Toward the end of
the seventeenth century, when attacks on the company turned
mostly on its monopolistic character, its imports of East Indian
silks and calicoes to the alleged injury of English industry, and
its unfavorable balance of trade, Child and Papillon, officers of
the company and with much of their private fortunes invested
therein, wrote in its defense. Much of the mercantilist literature
from 1670 on, written in opposition to the company, was the
work of rival merchants who wanted to participate in the East
India trade or of persons connected in some way with the domestic textile industries which were feeling the effects of East Indian

---

[4] Violet had himself been convicted of, and punished for, violation of the
laws against the export of bullion, and one of his arguments in support of his
reinstatement was that "an old deer-stealer is the best keeper of a park."—
A true discoverie to the commons of England [1651], 1653, p. 79.

competition. Tracts were written by factors in the woolen industry urging or supporting the prohibition of the export of wool and were answered by spokesmen for agricultural interests. John Houghton, Charles Smith, Arthur Young, and many others wrote in support of the bounties on the export of corn with an evident agrarian bias. The literature on taxation consisted in large part of tracts written by traders who wanted the main burden of taxation to rest on land, or by landed men who wanted it to rest on trade. There were contemporary charges that some of those who were urging the legal limitation of the rate of interest were rich merchants who had ample funds to finance their own activities and hoped that the reduction of the rate of interest by law would make it impossible for their poorer competitors to borrow the funds necessary for the conduct of their affairs. Pleas for special interests, whether open or disguised, constituted the bulk of the mercantilist literature. The disinterested patriot or philosopher played a minor part in the development of mercantilist doctrine.[5]

After the Revolution, when control of commercial policy had definitely passed from the crown to Parliament, commercial affairs became the football of party politics, and factional rivalries and conflicting economic interests were likely to be involved in any important issue of commercial policy in a complex way. If I may venture to take the controversy waged around the commercial clauses of the Treaty of Utrecht (1713) as an illustrative instance, the situation seems to have been somewhat as follows:[6] From the early decades of the seventeenth century, the trade between England and France had been greatly restricted by both countries, either by discriminatory duties of prohibitive severity or by absolute embargoes. When in 1713 a Tory government concluded peace with France, it proposed also to reestablish open trade with France. The Tories represented the landed classes and

---

[5] This interpretation of the literature of the period as consisting mainly of briefs for special interests is intended to apply to the writings of the moderate as well as of the extreme mercantilists. Child, in fact, presents one of the most glaring instances of special pleading. See Sven Helander, "Sir Josiah Child," *Weltwirtschaftliches Archiv,* XIX (1923), 233-49, and for closely similar exposure of Child by contemporaries, *A discourse concerning the East-India trade* [ca. 1692], in Somers' tracts, 2d ed., X, 634-47; *The interest of England considered: in an essay upon wooll,* 1694.

[6] Cf. the excellent account in Jehan Maintrieu, *Le traité d'Utrecht et les polémiques du commerce anglais,* 1909.

the Anglicans, and also received the support of the surviving Catholics as being less hostile to them than the Whigs. The Whigs in the unreformed Parliament of the time were also predominantly members of the landed gentry, but in order to secure a popular footing they had sought the support of the nonconformist or Low Church yeomen by adopting a policy of tolerance to dissenters and extreme opposition to Catholics, of the moneyed classes by their support of the Bank of England, and of the independent merchants and the manufacturers by opposition to the monopoly companies and by support of extreme mercantilism. The Tories, on the other hand, came to terms with the East India Company, whereby in return for support of the endeavors of the company to preserve its monopoly privileges and to be allowed to import East Indian cloth, the latter gave financial support to the crown through loans, and to its defenders in Parliament through private bribes.

On the specific issue of the resumption of trade relations with France, the Tories were favorable and the Whigs opposed. In so far as it was not a matter merely of factional rivalry, this alignment seems to have followed economic interests fairly closely, although other considerations were also important. Support for the resumption of freer trade appears to have been confined to the landed classes and to have been due mainly to three considerations: a greater trade with France would mean greater custom revenues to the crown, of which they were at the time the supporters; it would mean cheaper claret and silks; and, as a minor factor, it would be a check to the growing power of the trading classes, who were objectionable as "upstarts" and as Whigs, as enemies of the landed interest, and as exponents of a trade policy which made the cost of luxurious living higher for the country gentleman. The Whigs opposed the commercial treaty in part to embarrass the crown, in part because they were traditionally hostile to France as the leading Catholic monarchy.[7] They were supported by the independent "merchants"[8] and by

---

[7] By the Whigs, willingness to trade with France was accepted as proof of hostility to trade. Cf. the interesting pamphlet, *Torism and trade can never agree* (ca. 1713), which accused the Tories of having always been hostile to trade, and attacked *Mercator* as being anti-trade, because it supported open trade with France.

[8] " 'Merchants' in the eighteenth century meant business men, and the term was as wide as 'trade' is even now; bankers and manufacturers were included

the domestic manufacturers of liquors and cloth. The Whigs succeeded in stirring up violent opposition to ratification of the commercial treaty. In the controversies at the end of the seventeenth century, when the Tories supported both the continuance of monopoly control by the East India Company of the trade with East India and the limitation of the restrictions and duties on East Indian cloth to modest proportions, they had found in the ranks of the company itself and elsewhere able advocates, including such men as Child, North, Davenant, and Barbon. In the controversy about the Treaty of Utrecht, however, the level of argument on both sides was low. Daniel Defoe was allegedly hired by the Tories to defend the treaty in a periodical, *Mercator,* established for the purpose, and the Whigs replied in another periodical, the *British Merchant,* to which the principal contributors were prominent merchants with extreme mercantilist views. Defoe was too much of a believer in the mercantilist doctrines himself to be able effectively to meet criticism of the treaty on mercantilist grounds, and as far as public opinion was concerned the *British Merchant* had much the best of the argument. Whether or not the battle in the periodicals and tracts had much to do with the outcome, the commercial treaty failed of ratification in Parliament by a narrow margin of votes, and its defeat tended to strengthen the hold of mercantilist doctrine on the English merchant classes, and to sharpen the conflict of interest and opinion between the landed classes and the trading and industrial classes.[9]

While non-economic considerations unquestionably played an important part in this controversy, no one, as far as I could discover, conceded that these considerations clashed with the economic ones. On the basis of modern theory, the Tories had the stronger economic case. But the country gentlemen who constituted that party had no effective reply to mercantilist doctrine, and at this critical stage were without competent aid from the ranks of other classes. The ignorance and inarticulateness of the

---

in it." L. B. Namier, *The structure of politics at the accession of George III,* 1929, I, 61, note.

[9] It is of interest that the French government, on sober second thought of the mercantilist variety, had also lost its zeal for the treaty, and felt relieved when the English Parliament rejected it. See E. Levasseur, "Les traités de commerce entre la France et l'Angleterre sous l'ancien régime," *Revue d'économie politique,* XV (1901), 971.

English landed classes made them impotent in 1713 to prevent their victimization by a mercantilist policy which they vaguely sensed to be hostile to their interest, although they were in overwhelming control of Parliament. Over a century later, when the change in the status of English agriculture had made them the beneficiaries instead of the victims of mercantilism, their failure to produce spokesmen able to cope with the orators of the merchant class was a factor in their failure, in a Parliament in which they were still in the majority, to prevent the spectacular overthrow of mercantilism. Anyone who attempts an interpretation of the evolution of English trade theory solely in terms of objective historical circumstances faces the task of reconciling his account with the part played by the evolution of capacity for economic analysis. Objective fact played its part. But if the Tories had had the services of North and Barbon in 1713, they might have dealt a fatal blow to mercantilism then by showing that what was in their private interest was also in the national interest. And if Peel had been less public-spirited and intelligent in 1846, or if there had been among the back-bench squires men able to cope in debate with Cobden and Bright, the reign of mercantilism in England might not have had its 1846 to 1916 intermission.

Chapter III

THE BULLIONIST CONTROVERSIES:
I. THE INFLATION PHASE

What must we for a standard own,
By which the price of things are known?
'Twas thought, time past, by men of sense,
'Twas guineas, shillings, pounds and pence;
The Bank has said, and says so still
'Tis nothing but a paper bill;
'Tis in Sir Francis Burdett's head
The standard is a loaf of bread,
Whilst Adam Smith did always say,
It was the labor of a day.

—("William Pitt," The bullion debate; a serio-comic satiric poem, 1811, p. 7.)

I. THE PARTICIPANTS IN THE CONTROVERSY

The suspension of specie payments by the Bank of England in 1797, and the currency, exchange, and price phenomena which followed it, gave rise to a controversial literature of great extent and, on the whole, of surprisingly high quality. Until the resumption of specie payments was approaching, the general trend of prices and of prosperity was upward; but resumption was followed by a long and trying period of falling prices and of economic distress. The change in circumstances led to a marked difference in the distribution of emphasis on the issues involved, and, in a number of instances, to a sharp reversal of doctrinal position by participants in the controversies of both periods. It will be convenient, therefore, to deal separately with the literature of the earlier and the later periods, which can be distinguished as the inflation and deflation periods, respectively.

Of all the older controversies in the field of international trade theory, the inflation phase of the bullionist[1] controversy has prob-

---

[1] The participants were distinguished as bullionists or anti-bullionists according as they accepted or rejected the appearance of a premium on bullion as a demonstration of depreciation of bank notes and mismanagement of the currency.

ably been most fully and competently canvassed by modern writers.[2] But there is still room for a resurvey of the controversy.

The contemporary literature of the bullionist controversy is of great importance for the history of the theory of international trade in its monetary aspects. The germs at least of most of the current monetary theories are to be found in it. It embodies the first detailed analysis of the relationships between currency phenomena and international balances, exchange rates, and price levels, under both metallic and inconvertible paper currencies. Foreign exchange theory is carried substantially forward, and the theory of the mechanism of adjustment of international balances is advanced substantially beyond the stage at which it was left by Hume. There are also discussions of a truly pioneer character of the functions of a central bank in a complex credit economy with respect to the maintenance of international monetary equilibrium and of internal business stability.

The contemporary participants in the controversy arrayed themselves fairly sharply in two opposing groups: the "bullionists" or "anti-Restrictionists" on the one hand, who criticized the course of monetary events, and the "anti-bullionists" on the other hand, who defended the government and the Bank of England against the attacks of the bullionists. But as will be seen, there were important divergences of opinion within each group. The essential doctrines of the bullionists were expressed by a small group of writers, of whom Boyd,[3] King,[4] Thornton,[5] Wheatley,[6]

There is, of course, no relationship between the "bullionists" of this period and the sixteenth century "bullionists" whose doctrines were examined in chap. I.

[2] N. S. Silberling, "Financial and monetary policy of Great Britain during the Napoleonic wars," *Quarterly journal of economics,* XXXVIII (1924), 214-33; 397-439; *ibid.,* "British prices and business cycles, 1779-1850," *Review of economic statistics,* prel. vol. V, suppl. 2 (1923), 219-62; R. G. Hawtrey, *Currency and credit,* 3d ed., 1928, chap. xviii: J. H. Hollander, "The development of the theory of money from Adam Smith to David Ricardo," *Quarterly journal of economics,* XXV (1911), 429-70; J. W. Angell, *The theory of international prices,* 1926, pp. 40-79, 477-503; E. Cannan, *The paper pound of 1797-1821,* 1919; H. S. Foxwell, preface to A. Andréadès, *History of the Bank of England,* 2d ed., 1924.

[3] Walter Boyd, *A Letter to . . . Pitt,* 1801; 2d ed., with additions, 1801. The edition of 1811, often referred to as the second edition, is merely a reprint of the first, and lacks the important additions made in the true second edition.

[4] Lord King, *Thoughts on the effects of the Bank restrictions* [1st ed., 1803], 2d ed., 1804.

[5] Henry Thornton, *An enquiry into the nature and effects of the paper credit of Great Britain,* 1802.

[6] John Wheatley, *Remarks on currency and commerce,* 1803.

and Horner,[7] were most important, during the first period, 1801 to 1803, of marked premium on bullion and fall in the exchanges. Similar phenomena, even more marked in degree, in connection with the Bank of Ireland gave rise to a parliamentary inquiry[8] and to the bullionist publications of John Leslie Foster,[9] Henry Parnell,[10] and Lord Lauderdale.[11] The reappearance from 1809 on of a high premium on gold and a substantial fall in the exchanges gave rise to a flood of tracts and pamphlets, of which the most important on the bullionist side, in addition to the Report of the Bullion Committee of 1810, were the contributions of Ricardo, his first appearance in print as an economist,[12] T. R. Malthus,[13] Robert Mushet,[14] and William Huskisson.[15]

The most effective statements of the anti-bullionist position were in speeches in Parliament by Nicholas Vansittart[16] and George Rose,[17] and in tracts by Henry Boase,[18] Bosanquet,[19] Coutts Trotter,[20] and J. C. Herries.[21]

---

[7] Francis Horner, review of Thornton, *Edinburgh review*, I (1802), 172-201; review of Lord King, *ibid.*, II (1803), 402-21; review of Wheatley, *ibid.*, III (1803), 231-52.

[8] *Report . . . from the Committee on the circulating paper, the specie, and the current coin of Ireland* [1804], 1826 reprint.

[9] *An essay on the principle of commercial exchanges,* 1804.

[10] *Observations upon the state of currency in Ireland,* 1804.

[11] *Thoughts on the alarming state of the circulation,* 1805.

[12] Three letters to the *Morning Chronicle,* August-November, 1809, reprinted by Hollander as *Three letters on the price of gold,* 1903; *High price of bullion, a proof of the depreciation of bank notes* [1st ed., 1810], 4th ed. with appendix [1811], reprinted in J. R. McCulloch ed., *The works of David Ricardo,* 1852; *Reply to Mr. Bosanquet's practical observations* [1811], reprinted in *Works;* and three additional letters to the *Morning Chronicle,* September, 1810, reprinted by Hollander, in *Minor papers on the currency question 1809-1823 by David Ricardo,* 1932.

[13] "Depreciation of paper currency," *Edinburgh review,* XVII (1811); "Review of the controversy respecting the high price of bullion," *ibid.,* XVIII (1811).

[14] *An inquiry into the effects produced on the national currency . . . by the Bank restriction bill,* 3d ed., 1811.

[15] *The question concerning the depreciation of our currency stated and examined,* 1810.

[16] *Substance of two speeches,* 1811.

[17] *Substance of speech . . . on the report of the bullion committee,* 1811.

[18] *A letter . . . in defence of the conduct of the directors,* 1804.

[19] *Practical observations on the report of the bullion committee,* 2d ed., 1810.

[20] *The principles of currency and exchanges, applied to the report,* 2d ed., 1810.

[21] *A review of the controversy respecting the high price of bullion,* 1811.

Ricardo made but few additions to the analysis of his predecessors,[22] and, as will be shown later, on some important points he committed errors from which some of the earlier supporters of the bullionist position had been free. But the comprehensiveness and the force and skill of his exposition and the assurance and rigor of his reasoning made him at once the leading expositor of the bullionist position. It was largely through Ricardo's writings, moreover, that the bullionist doctrines exercised their influence on the subsequent century of monetary controversy. Special attention is given, therefore, to Ricardo's position in the following account of the bullionist controversy.

II. The Factual Background

An excellent statistical compilation of the significant banking, price, and exchange rate data relating to the suspension of cash payments, presented in both tabular and graphical form, is to be found in Silberling's essays, and much of this material is reproduced by Angell. Silberling has computed and compiled some of the important series from original data not hitherto available in print or available only in raw shape. There need be presented here, therefore, only the minimum amount of information as to the nature of the currency and banking system of the time and the course of monetary events essential for an understanding of the theoretical issues raised in the course of the controversy.

From the outbreak of the war with France in 1793, the Bank of England had been under a strain mainly because of the great demands for advances made upon it by the government, which it had resisted, but unsuccessfully. Early in 1797, a general panic, induced apparently by rumors of a French landing on English soil, and accentuated by failures and suspensions on the part of the country banks, led to a general clamor for gold. On February 25, 1797, there were only £1,272,000 of specie and bullion in the Bank, as compared to ordinary reserves of £5,000,000, or over. On February 26, 1797, the government, at the request of the Bank, issued an Order in Council prohibiting specie redemption of its notes by the Bank. By an Act of May 3, 1797, the restriction of cash payments was validated and continued in effect.

---

[22] This is also the conclusion of Hollander: *op. cit., Quarterly journal of economics*, XXV (1911), 469.

subject to minor qualifications, until June 24, 1797, and by a succession of later acts the suspension of specie payments was enforced until after the end of the war. With the factors responsible for the suspension of specie payments in 1797, we need not here concern ourselves.[1] The suspension of specie payments was quickly followed by an inward flow of bullion, recovery of the Bank from its strained condition, and general restoration of confidence, and it was not until toward the end of 1799 that the exchange on Hamburg fell substantially below the pre-Restriction par and a premium was quoted on bullion over paper. From 1804 to 1808 the exchanges were again at or near parity, and paper was at no or a small discount in relation to bullion. But from 1809 to the end of the war there again prevailed low sterling exchanges and substantial premiums of bullion over paper.[2]

England, prior to the Restriction, although legally on a bimetallic basis, had for some time been in effect on a gold standard basis, since the mint ratio of silver to gold was such as generally to undervalue silver and thus keep it out of circulation. The metallic currency consisted of guinea pieces ($= 21$ shillings) and multiples and subdivisions thereof, and of silver coins from the crown ($= 5$ shillings) down. Of the silver coins, only the underweight coins remained in circulation. Except for coins surviving from ancient issues, the sovereign ($= 20$ shillings) was only a money of account. English coin could not legally be melted down unless underweight, and was not legally exportable, and gold bullion was exportable only subject to oath that it had not been obtained by melting down English coin. The metallic currency was supplemented by Bank of England notes in denominations of £5 or over, redeemable in specie upon demand, and by country bank notes, also in denominations of £5 or over, payable upon demand in specie or in Bank of England notes. London bankers had in 1793 voluntarily ceased to issue their own notes. Outside of the London area the Bank of England notes circulated freely only in Lancashire, where the local banks did not issue notes but where bills of exchange of small denominations were extensively employed as a medium of exchange. Bank deposits subject to check were also in existence, and constituted a part of what would

---

[1] A good account is given by R. G. Hawtrey, *Currency and credit,* 3d ed., 1928, pp. 320-32.
[2] See table I, p. 144, *infra.*

today be regarded as the circulating medium, although this was not yet widely recognized. Checks payable to order had only recently come into common use even in London and only for large payments. The private or non-governmental deposits at the Bank of England were small in amount throughout the Restriction period, and for the years after 1806, for which alone their precise amounts are known, they reached a yearly average of £2,000,000 in only one year.[3] In the provinces also deposits seem to have been relatively unimportant, and to have been drawn upon mainly for cash, but the available evidence on this point is conflicting.[4]

iii. Premium on Bullion as Evidence of Excess Issue: The Bullionist Position

The central issue of the controversy was made to turn on the question of whether the paper pound was depreciated, the bullionists insisting that it was depreciated, and most—though not all—of the anti-bullionists denying this. The answer to such a question obviously depends on how "depreciation" is defined, and the controversy suffered from a constant tendency to degenerate into merely terminological issues. As one bullionist writer caustically remarked: "Whether reduction of prices [of paper in gold] be depreciation or not, or equivalent to it, is a verbal question very fit to be argued in 'Change Alley.' "[1] But always present,

---

[3] *Report from the Committee of secrecy on the Bank of England charter*, 1832, appendix No. 32, p. 41.

[4] Vincent Stuckey, a country banker, testified in 1819 that in his bank the deposits were about one-third in amount of the note issues, although this proportion fluctuated. (*Report from the [Commons] Committee on the expediency of the Bank resuming cash payments*, 1819, p. 245.) James Pennington, writing as late as 1861, stated that "The deposits with country bankers are generally converted into notes or coin, or into a bill upon London, before ultimate payment is accomplished." ("Letter from Mr. Pennington on the London banking system," in John Cazenove, *Supplement to thoughts on a few subjects of political economy*, 1861, p. 50, note.) Cf., however, the statement of another writer, for which I can find no independent confirmation:

"A country bank was a kind of clearing-house, where, without any actual interchange of notes or money, the greater part of all payments between man and man was effectuated by mere transfers in the books of their bankers. . . . It was merely the smaller payments for wages and weekly bills which required notes." Samuel Turner, *Considerations upon the agriculture, commerce and manufactures of the British Empire*, 1822, pp. 54-55.

[1] Sir Philip Francis, *Reflections on the abundance of paper in circulation*, 2d

even when not clearly brought into the foreground of the discussion, were genuine and important issues of fact and policy.

For the bullionists the paper currency was depreciated if issued to excess, and many of the anti-bullionists also accepted this quantitative criterion of depreciation, or at least did not explicitly reject it. Defining depreciated currency as a currency issued to excess might seem merely to substitute one term of doubtful meaning for another. But the question, What is the proper amount of currency a country should have? is an important one. To this question, as Hollander points out,[2] Adam Smith had given no answer beyond saying vaguely that it was determined by "effectual demand,"[3] and the participants in the bullionist controversy were the first seriously to tackle it. The bullionists argued, or more often simply asserted, that a circulation exceeding in amount what, under otherwise like conditions, could have been maintained under a metallic standard, was in excess. There was little express objection to this criterion of a properly-regulated currency during the inflation phase, and serious discussion of its adequacy came only with the deflation phase of the controversy.

During the inflation phase the main issue in controversy was as to the proper method of determining the existence of excess of issue. The chief test of excess issue used by the bullionists was the existence of a premium on bullion over paper currency, although since they held that the level of prices was determined by the amount of currency and that the amount of premium of bullion over paper and the amount of discount of sterling exchange from the metallic parities were closely related, they also held that a relative rise of prices in England as compared to abroad and a fall in the sterling exchanges below parity were evidence of depreciation. The bullionist position was well expressed by Boyd: "The premium on bullion, the low rate of exchange, and the high prices of commodities in general, [are] . . . symptoms and effects of the superabundance of paper."[4]

---

ed., 1810, p. 10. Cf. also, for a similar view, Mathias Attwood, *A letter to Lord Archibald Hamilton, on alterations in the value of money,* 1823, p. 8.

[2] *Op. cit., Quarterly journal of economics,* XXV, 436-37.

[3] *Wealth of nations,* Cannan ed., I, 402.

[4] *Letter to Pitt,* 2d ed., 1801, preface, p. xxxi. Ricardo, by exception, sometimes put it more strongly, and referred to the existence of a premium on bullion as not merely evidence, but as *proof* of the existence of depreciation

Their conclusions rested on the following reasoning: the rate of exchange between two currencies depended solely or mainly on their relative purchasing power over identical transportable commodities in the two countries; on quantity theory of money grounds, prices in the two countries depended on the quantities of money circulating therein; the price of bullion in paper currency was governed by the exchange rates with metallic standard currencies; therefore, if the exchanges were below metallic parity, and if there was a premium on bullion over paper, this was evidence that prices were higher in England, and the quantity of currency in circulation greater, than would have been possible under the metallic standard prevailing prior to suspension of convertibility.[5]

While Wheatley and Ricardo held that the relative rise of the prices of particular commodities in England, as compared to the prices of the same commodities in foreign countries having metallic standard currencies, would be proportional to the degree of excess of the English currency, they did not suggest that the existence of excess issue could in practice be tested by such price comparisons.[6] The notion of an index number was still in its infancy. Evelyn had published his crude index number of English prices for the preceding two centuries in 1798, and Wheatley had commented on it in laudatory terms.[7] But no current index number yet existed for England, and there was but little information as to the prices prevailing in other countries. To Ricardo, moreover, it seemed an absurd notion that the trend of prices in

and excess issue. Cf. the title of his tract, *The high price of bullion, a proof of the depreciation of bank notes.*

[5] This reasoning bears a superficial relationship to Cassel's so-called purchasing-power parity theory, but as will be explained subsequently (see pp. 382 ff., *infra*), Ricardo's stress on the *particular prices* of *identical transportable commodities* makes this part of his reasoning a truism if transportation costs and tariffs are abstracted from, whereas Cassel's doctrine, even if it be restricted, as Cassel does not restrict it, to internationally traded commodities only, instead of being a truism, is untrue. Cassel's doctrine, moreover, makes qualifications for the effect of foreign remittances which Wheatley and Ricardo expressly refused to make, and which they would have regarded—mistakenly—as fatal to their whole position if made.

[6] Francis Horner, however, did suggest that the relative prices in England and abroad could be used as a test of the existence of depreciation of the English currency. See his review of Thornton's *Paper credit, Edinburgh review,* I (1802), 201.

[7] *Remarks on currency and commerce,* 1803, chap. vi.

general, or of the general purchasing power of money, could be measured. Since prices fluctuated even under a metallic standard, he conceded that their fluctuations under an inconvertible currency could not be attributed solely to changes in the degree of excess of the currency. The only test from English prices alone of the existence of depreciation which he could consistently have accepted, therefore, would have been a comparison of the prices prevailing under inconvertibility with the prices which would have prevailed under convertibility, other conditions remaining the same, and in his treatment of arguments from price data Ricardo always adhered to this position.[8] But Ricardo held that since the premium on bullion measured the degree of excess of the currency,[9] it measured also the degree in which prices at any time, say 1810, during the suspension of cash payments were higher, not than they had been in 1797, but than they would have been in 1810 if the currency were in 1810 at the amount which could then have been maintained in circulation under a metallic standard. Ricardo, however, put much stress on the question of the extent of the depreciation, as providing an answer to the question of how great a reduction in the currency would be needed to end the depreciation.

IV. QUALIFICATIONS CONCEDED BY THE BULLIONISTS

The bullionists were prepared to make several qualifications to this reasoning and therefore to concede that the existence of a premium on bullion over paper, or of a discount of sterling exchange from metallic parity, was not an absolute proof of excess issue, and was strong presumptive evidence of excess issue only

[8] As did also at least one anti-bullionist. Cf. *The substance of a speech by Castlereagh in the House of Commons, July 15, 1811,* 1811, p. 15: "With the exception of the precious metals, bank notes have the same powers of purchasing all other commodities, which they would have had at this day, if no necessity for shutting up the guineas in the Bank, or for sending gold abroad in unusual quantities, had ever occurred. . . . Such I wish to be understood . . . is the sense, in which I deny that bank notes are now depreciated."

[9] Most of the bullionists did not seriously concern themselves with the problem of how to measure the *extent* of depreciation but were content when they had demonstrated its existence. Cf. King, *Thoughts on the effects of the Bank restrictions,* 2d ed., 1804, p. 40, note: "nor will the most careful reference to the two tests of the price of bullion and the state of the exchanges enable us to ascertain in what *precise* degree a currency is depreciated; though the general fact of a depreciation may be proved beyond dispute." (Italics in original.)

if it was substantial and prevailed for a considerable period of time.

There was first the question as to whether the price of gold or the price of silver bullion should be taken as the test. Since the bullionist comparison was always with the amount of circulation possible under the metallic standard prevailing in 1797, and since it was generally, though not universally, agreed that England had then been in fact on a gold standard basis, the bullionists preferred to use the price of gold as their test. There were fairly substantial variations in the relative prices of gold and silver on the English market, and therefore also in the extent of the premiums over paper which they respectively commanded. But as during this period a substantial premium on the one was always accompanied by a substantial premium on the other, it did not matter for practical purposes which was taken as the test of the *existence* of excess currency, although it would have mattered if what were in question was the *degree* of excess.

Secondly, when the bullionists used the exchange rates as an alternative or supplementary test of the existence of depreciation, they conceded that since even under a metallic standard the exchanges could fall below the mint parity to the limit of the cost of shipping bullion, a fall in the exchanges which did not go beyond this limit was not proof that there was excess of currency under inconvertibility.[1] Moreover, whereas England had been on a gold standard basis prior to the Restriction, Hamburg, Amsterdam, and Paris, the most important quotation points for the exchanges during the Restriction, were on a silver standard basis. Ricardo and other bullionists pointed out that since the relative values of gold and silver were not constant, the exchange parties between gold and silver currencies also were not constant, and that in computing the deviation of, say, the London-Hamburg exchange from parity it was necessary to make allowance for any alteration in the relative market values of the two metals. But the general trend of the price of silver as compared to gold was downward during the later stage of the controversy, and

---

[1] Ricardo, it is true, maintained that the foreign exchanges could fall under the mint parities even under a fully convertible currency only if the currency was "redundant" (i.e., was in excess of what could circulate consistently with the maintenance of the exchanges at mint parity), but he apparently meant by "excess" of currency under inconvertibility only the extra excess over and above that "redundancy" which was possible under convertibility.

Ricardo pointed out that comparisons of the trend of the Hamburg exchange during the Restriction period which used the prevailing rate before the Restriction as the base therefore underestimated the extent of the real fall in the exchange value of English paper currency in terms of gold bullion abroad.[2]

Thirdly, even before 1797, English gold coin, or bullion derived therefrom, was not legally exportable, and at a time when the exchanges were against England exportable bullion would command a premium over its mint price in coin or in paper. Ricardo and other bullionists insisted, however, that the prohibition of export of English coin or bullion could not be successfully enforced and that a small premium would in practice suffice to compensate for the risks involved in melting and false swearing, or in smuggling English bullion out of the country. They conceded that a premium on gold not exceeding this risk-premium was not necessarily indicative of excess. Bullion also could command a premium over coin and paper even under convertibility if the coinage was generally underweight as compared to its nominal standard, and for this also the bullionists were willing to make allowances. But the gold coinage was in good condition in 1797, and only a minor allowance was called for on this account.[3] The bullionists tended to agree that 5 per cent premium on gold was ample allowance for both these factors, and it seems that in the years prior to 1797 the premium on gold at no time exceeded this except in isolated and special transactions.[4]

Fourthly, the bullionists recognized that the substitution in England of paper for gold and the export of the displaced gold would tend to result in a rise of prices in other countries in terms of gold, and that England could share in this rise of prices, and could therefore circulate a greater quantity of currency than before, other things remaining the same, without suffering a

---

[2] *Reply to Mr. Bosanquet's observations, Works,* pp. 321-22.

[3] According to Mushet, a mint test of the weight of the gold coin still in circulation, made in 1807, showed on the average slightly under 1.5 per cent of underweight. (*An inquiry into the effects produced on the national currency . . . by the Bank restriction bill,* 3d ed., 1811, p. 30.) Since the lighter coins would tend to remain longest in circulation, this would indicate that little allowance on this account would be called for prior to 1797.

[4] The Bullion Committee estimated the maximum premium on gold bullion over paper and coin which could prevail before 1797 at about 5½ per cent. *Report,* pp. 14-15.

premium on gold or fall in the exchanges.[5] They did not attach any importance to this factor, however, presumably on the ground that any such release of gold would be negligible in comparison to the world supply.[6] Since to the extent that this consideration had weight it would tend to make the bullionists' tests of excess as they defined it too generous rather than too exacting, the anti-bullionists also made no use of it, although it became an important element in the controversy of the deflation period.

v. Possible Objections to the Bullionist Position

In addition to the qualifications which the bullionists themselves made to their argument that the existence of a premium on bullion over paper, or a fall of the exchanges below the metallic parity, was a demonstration of the existence of excess issue as compared to what could have been maintained in circulation under convertibility, there were other valid qualifications which they either deliberately abstracted from or overlooked.

Throughout the controversy, currency was generally taken to mean metallic money and bank notes, bank deposits either being overlooked or else held not to be currency. It would, of course, be possible for bank notes to depreciate even if drastically reduced in volume if at the same time deposits were increased in relatively even greater degree. But unless there was reason to suppose that mere departure from convertibility would result in a change in the relative importance of currency proper and bank deposits, the failure to give consideration to the latter would be of no significance for the main theoretical issue in controversy.

Similarly, a currency might depreciate because of an increase in its velocity of circulation, its amount meanwhile remaining constant or even falling. This was generally recognized at the time, but it was tacitly assumed, then and later, not that velocity remained constant—for it was known that it was subject to variation with the state of business confidence, with improvements in the means of communication, and with the development of clear-

---

[5] Cf. Wheatley, *Remarks on currency and commerce,* 1803, p. 187; Ricardo, *High price of bullion, Works,* p. 266, note.

[6] Cf. James Mill, Review of Thomas Smith's *Essay on the theory of money and exchange,* 1807, in *Edinburgh review,* XIII (1808), 54. But while James Mill was critical of the Restriction, at this stage he accepted many of the anti-bullionist arguments, and cannot be considered as an unqualified bullionist.

inghouse and other arrangements for "economizing currency,"[1] but that velocity would not be altered merely by the suspension of convertibility. If changes in velocity due to changing degrees of confidence in the future of the currency be disregarded, this assumption could not be expected to be a source of serious error. Under convertibility the actually circulating medium, if deposits and bills of exchange be disregarded, was partly coin, partly paper; under inconvertibility it was wholly paper. It is conceivable that individuals would tend to hold smaller cash balances in proportion to the volume of their transactions if the currency was paper than if it was coin. Holding of paper involved risk of loss through fire, or through failure of the issuers. Paper money could be shipped from one point to another more promptly, more safely, and if in small quantities more economically, than could specie, for paper money could be sent by post, whereas specie remittances required private couriers, who had to be convoyed because of the danger of robbery on the highways. This would tend to lead to the holding on the average of larger cash balances relative to volume of transactions if the currency were specie than if it were paper.[2] But it seems doubtful that this could have been an important factor.

On both *a priori* and empirical grounds, however, velocity should be expected to rise as the volume of means of payments and the price level was rising, and thus measurement of the percentage of excess of currency from the percentage of discount of paper in terms of gold would tend to exaggerate the degree of excess during rising prices and to underestimate it during falling prices.

A more serious qualification to the validity of the bullionist position lies in the fact that under inconvertibility speculative anticipations of depreciation or appreciation of the currency would affect the willingness of individuals to hold the currency and would thus influence its velocity of circulation and its value in

---

[1] Cf. the *Bullion Report*, pp. 63-64.

[2] Cf. Walter Hall, *A view of our late and of our future currency*, 1819, p. 70: It is now discovered, that the activity of the circulation multiplies its actual amount, and that it is a point of more importance to ascertain the velocity of the motion than the size of the wheel; but it is probable that this also depends, in some degree, on the nature of the currency, and that were specie again to form the medium here, a larger amount of it would be required for the same operations than of the paper which it replaced.

relation to gold, to foreign currencies, and to commodities, independently of the effects of variations in its quantity. In modern times, as we now know only too well, such speculative factors can dominate for an appreciable length of time the metallic or exchange value of an inconvertible paper currency. There is every reason to believe that such speculative factors were also operative in some degree during the period of the bullionist controversy.

Both the bullionists and the anti-bullionists were aware of the possibility that speculative factors were influencing the value of the paper pound. Neither side, however, openly charged—or conceded—that such factors were an actual influence in lowering the value of the paper pound. It may be that neither side was altogether frank in dealing with this question, which under the circumstances prevailing was a delicate one. The anti-bullionists could not maintain as they did that the management of the currency was beyond criticism and at the same time admit that there was sufficient lack of confidence in its immediate future to lead to flights from the currency to hoarded bullion, to commodities, or to foreign currencies. The bullionists, on the other hand, may have feared that if they made such a charge they would lay themselves open to attack on the ground that they were attempting to bring the national currency into "discredit" at a time of national emergency, and therefore may have refrained from saying all that they believed, although I have not found any evidence of this. In any case, the bullionists, whether from discretion or from conviction, took pains to concede that the paper currency was not "discredited."

Silberling and Angell misread into the bullionist writings in general the positive charge that the depreciation of the paper pound in relation to bullion was in part at least a "qualitative" depreciation, and they find something absurd in such a charge. Silberling claims to find in Ricardo's writings the doctrine, which he clearly regards as a strange one, that the "fall" in paper money was due to "a mere inherent debasement in quality" of the paper currency rather than to its issue to excess. He concedes that "debasement" could readily be translated into "excess," if by excess is meant the amount exceeding the quantity at which the price of gold in paper would be at its mint par.[3] But Ricardo

[3] "Financial and Monetary Policy of Great Britain," *Quarterly journal of economics,* XXXVIII, 425, 436.

repeatedly and uniformly insisted that he meant just this by excess.

Angell follows Silberling in finding among the bullionists adherence to the notion of a *qualitative* depreciation of the currency, and in treating it as an absurd notion, but his interpretation of the bullionist position in this connection is different from Silberling's. Angell claims that Boyd, Ricardo, and other bullionists held that an excess of currency led first to "a positive degradation of the standard" and that this degradation in turn led to a rise in prices, "the degradation thus being a distinct and 'intermediate' step between the increase in currency and the rise in prices."[4] Angell gives no specific references to Ricardo, but he refers to the following passage in Boyd:

> He would say, that not only the currency of the country had been changed from a *certain* to an *uncertain* standard, but that the quantity of it, in all probability, had been greatly augmented by the issuing of paper, without the obligation of paying it on demand, and that thus the prices of all objects of exchangeable value necessarily feel the influence of a *positive* degradation of the standard, and of a *probable* augmentation of the quantity of money in the country, any one of them amply sufficient to discount for a considerable rise, but both united, adequate to still greater effects than any that had already been produced.[5]

Boyd here clearly assigns to "degradation" a distinct influence on prices over and above that resulting from any increase in the quantity of the currency. But there is no trace here of the time-sequence imputed to him by Angell. The context shows that the word "positive" which qualifies "degradation" is to be understood to mean "certain," as contrasted to the "probable" increase of the amount of the currency. At the time Boyd wrote no report had been made as to the issues of the Bank since the Restriction, and increase in such issue could be only a matter of inference from circumstantial evidence. The question remains, what did Boyd mean by "degradation"? No light is afforded by the context, but a reasonable explanation which makes his position in-

---

[4] *Theory of international prices,* pp. 45, 59, 60. Angell comments that "an understanding of this chain of reasoning is important because it provides the only satisfactory key to the contradictory pronouncements upon monetary theory of the later writers, even those of Ricardo." (*Ibid.,* p. 45.)

[5] Walter Boyd, *A letter to Pitt,* 1st ed., 1801, pp. 64-65. (Italics in original.)

telligible is made possible by reference to a doctrine of other contemporary writers. Henry Thornton in 1797 had argued that the quantity of notes which it was proper at any time to issue depended much "on the state of the public mind, that is, on the disposition of persons to detain them." Thus an impairment of the general credit "while Bank notes sustain their credit" would make possible, and desirable, an increase of the issue of notes without any impairment of their value.[6] In 1802 he repeated this argument and supported it by reference to the effect of confidence in the paper money on the velocity of its circulation and on the size of the cash balances generally held by individuals.[7] He pointed out, moreover, that while paper was falling in value, foreigners generally would expect "that the paper, which is falling in value, will, in better times, only cease to fall, or, if it rises, will experience only an immaterial rise, and this expectation serves of course to accelerate its fall."[8] Thus the suspension of cash payments could conceivably result in a premium of bullion over paper even if no increase in the issue of paper had occurred. But Thornton denied that the loss of confidence in the English currency which could bring this about had occurred.

Lord King and George Woods expressed similar views:

But when the obligation to pay in coin ceases, the currency no longer retains this determinate value, but is in danger of being depreciated from two different causes; viz., by want of confidence on the part of the public, and an undue increase of the quantity of notes. . . . Though the persons who have the regulation of a currency not payable on demand should confine their issues within the most just and reasonable limits; yet if their credit or solvency is doubted, it is impossible that their notes can circulate at the full nominal value.[9]

Whether the depreciation of bank notes be owing to excess of issue or to the ticklish foundation upon which their present validity is built, the ever-varying standard of public opinion, the fact itself . . . [i.e., of depreciation of paper in terms of bullion] is undeniable. . . . If it be alleged that the issues of the Bank, compared

---

[6] *Report of the Lords Committee*, 1797, pp. 72-73.

[7] *Paper credit*, 1802, pp. 65-67.

[8] *Ibid.*, p. 65.

[9] King, *Thoughts on the effects of the Bank Restrictions*, 2d ed., 1804, pp. 5-6. King also conceded that no loss of confidence in the English currency had as yet occurred. *Ibid.*, p. 24.

with the wants of the public, are not greater now than formerly, I answer, that this reasoning may imply a decreased confidence in the Bank of England, but that it does not throw the smallest light upon the question of depreciation.[10]

Ricardo likewise disclaimed any belief that in 1810 lack of confidence in the paper pound was a factor in its depreciation: "I am not aware of any causes but excess, or a want of confidence in the issues of the paper (which I am sure does not now exist), which could produce such effects as we have for a considerable time witnessed."[11]

The bullionists on this point were in error. Their error, however, lay not, as Silberling and Angell claim, in attributing some of the depreciation of the paper pound to loss of confidence in it, but in their refusal to do so, although this refusal may have been due to prudential considerations. For as Horner and Ricardo later acknowledged,[12] some of the sharp fluctuations in the premium on gold could not be adequately explained as due to corresponding fluctuations in the quantity of paper money, and could be adequately explained only with reference to changes in anticipations as to the future of the paper pound, resulting in changes in willingness of Englishmen to hold cash balances in paper and of foreigners to hold securities payable in sterling.

The bullionist position is open to one further correction, but one of probably minor practical importance. Under a metallic standard, if due to foreign remittances or abnormally heavy grain imports there occurs a temporary rise in the relative demand for

---

[10] George Woods, *Observations on the present price of bullion,* 1811, p. 46. (Cf. also p. 184, *infra.*) For other instances of similar recognition of the possible contribution of speculative factors, or "discredit," to the discount on paper, see Henry Parnell, *Observations upon the state of the currency in Ireland,* 1804, p. 55; *Bullion Report,* 1810, pp. 22, 39; David Buchanan, *Observations on the subjects treated of in Dr. Smith's . . . The wealth of nations,* 1814, p. 88: "The value of a paper currency will . . . vary from its standard, by reason either of discredit or of excess. Where the security is defective, the value will fluctuate with the risk of ultimate loss, which may at length be such as entirely to stop its circulation. . . ." These writers also refrained from making the positive charge that the paper currency was "discredited" in this sense. Cf. also Wheatley, *Theory of money,* I (1807), 97: "It is to the aggregate quantity of the currency of a country that we are to look, and not to the state and quality of its coin, for the real cause of the fluctuation in the market price of its money."

[11] *Reply to Mr. Bosanquet's observations, Works,* p. 363.

[12] See *infra,* pp. 201-02.

foreign bills, an export of specie will tend to occur, which will operate both to lower the amount of the domestic circulation and directly to increase the supply of foreign bills by the amount for which the exported specie itself can be exchanged. Under an inconvertible currency which has been on a depreciated basis for some time, so that all the bullion has already either been exported or passed into more or less permanent hoards, there will be no specie export to constitute a direct equilibrating element in the international balance of indebtedness. With the same volume of foreign remittances to be made, a greater contraction of the currency, therefore, will be necessary under inconvertibility than under a metallic standard if the exchanges are to be kept from falling by more than the cost of shipping gold, and conversely, a fall of the exchanges by more than the cost of shipping gold will not be absolute proof that the currency has been contracted in less degree than would have been necessary if the standard were metallic.

VI. THE ANTI-BULLIONIST POSITION

By no means all of the anti-bullionists were willing to accept as the criterion under all circumstances of the proper amount of currency that amount which could circulate under a metallic standard, and to concede, therefore, that if it could be shown that the circulation was actually greater than could be maintained under a metallic standard the currency would thereby have been demonstrated to be in excess. But criticism of the bullionist position based on rejection of the metallic standard as the best criterion for regulation of the currency became much more widespread and important during the deflation period than it had been during the period of rising prices, and it will be convenient therefore to postpone an examination of such criticism.

The anti-bullionists often attempted to show from statistics as to Bank of England note issues either that the issues had not increased or that there was no relation in time or degree between the fluctuations in issue and the fluctuations in the premium on bullion or the exchanges. But Ricardo was able to show that even if the data were as alleged—as they often were not—they did not refute his argument. He was claiming not that the currency had been increased during the Restriction, but that it existed in an amount greater than could have been maintained at that time, other things remaining the same, if convertibility had been maintained. Whether the amount of actual issue in say 1810 was greater or less than in 1797 was beside the point if it was greater than could have been maintained under convertibility in 1810:

I do most unequivocally admit, that whilst the high price of bullion and the low exchanges continue, . . . it would to me be no proof of our currency not being depreciated if there were only 5 millions of bank notes in circulation [as compared to about 10 millions in 1797 and 23 millions in 1810]. When we speak, therefore, of an excess of bank notes, we mean that portion of the amount of the issues of the Bank, which can now circulate, but could not, if the currency were of its bullion value.[1]

Some of the anti-bullionists contended that to prove depreciation it was necessary to prove that gold *coin* commanded a premium over paper, since bullion was only a commodity and its price therefore of no special significance.[2] Since it was unlawful to melt or export English coin, and since persons buying such coin at a premium would come under suspicion of intent to violate the law, it is not surprising that there were no open dealings in gold coin at a premium over paper.[3] What happened was that the full-weight coin quietly but rapidly passed out of circulation and was either exported on government account or went into hoards or into the melting pot for industrial use or for illegal export abroad. As Ricardo pointed out, if the law against melting and export had been repealed, gold coin and gold bullion would have commanded the same premium over paper money;[4] on the other hand, if the law against melting and export could have been fully enforced, exportable bullion would have commanded the same premium over coin and paper money.[5]

---

[1] *Reply to Mr. Bosanquet's observations, Works*, pp. 349-50.

[2] Cf. Henry Boase, *A letter . . . in defence of the conduct of the directors*, 1804, pp. 22-23; *Substance of two speeches made by the Right Hon. N. Vansittart*, 1811, p. 15; *The Speech of Randle Jackson, Esq., . . . respecting the report of the Bullion Committee*, 1810, pp. 9 ff.

[3] Even non-exportable bullion commanded a premium over paper and there was open trade in underweight guineas, which could legally be melted down for internal use, at a premium over paper and even over full-weight guineas. See the evidence of S. T. Binns and of W. Merle, bullion merchants, before the Bullion Committee, *Report, Minutes of evidence*, pp. 18, 40.

[4] *High price of bullion, Works*, p. 280.

[5] *Ibid.*, p. 265.

VII. THE BALANCE OF PAYMENTS ARGUMENT

The anti-bullionists, however, had a more serious objection to raise against the acceptance of the premium on bullion over paper as a proof of excess currency. It was agreed on both sides that under an inconvertible as under a convertible standard the price of bullion was governed by the foreign exchanges. Both sides were also agreed that under convertibility the exchanges could not ordinarily fall below the gold export point, since below that point, representing by its distance from mint parity of the two currencies the cost of transmitting bullion, it would be more profitable to ship bullion than to buy foreign bills. The anti-bullionists argued, however, that under inconvertibility this limit to the fall in the exchanges did not exist; that the exchanges and the premium on bullion would be governed solely by the state of the balance of international payments;[1] and that in a period when heavy military remittances and extraordinary importations of grain because of deficient English harvests had to be made, there was no definable limit beyond which the exchanges could not fall or the premium on bullion rise without demonstrating that the currency was in excess.

In their treatment of this crucial issue, the bullionists were divided into two groups, offering different answers. One of these groups consisted of only two men, Wheatley and Ricardo.[2] To

---

[1] Cf. Boase, *A letter*, 1804, pp. 22-23: "the rate of exchange is governed by the balance of exchange operations, and (great political convulsions apart) by no other principle whatever. . . ."

[2] There was, therefore, substantial justification for the comment of William Blake, with reference to this doctrine of Wheatley and Ricardo, that "the opinions of these gentlemen are peculiar to themselves." (*Observations on the effects produced by the expenditure of government*, 1823, p. 26.) Cf., however, the following from the *Minutes of evidence* of the Committee on the Irish circulation, 1804, p. 22, cited with apparent approval by Lauderdale (*Thoughts on the alarming state of the circulation*, 1805, p. 20, note):

From August, 1801, to the present time, no remittances of consequence have . . . been made to London in specie. Bank [of Ireland] notes, however, have never ceased, whether the specie was coming into Ireland or going out of it, whether the exchange was under par or above par, whether the balance of debt was favorable or unfavorable, to be depreciated; and the depreciation appears to have been higher when the balance of debt was more favorable, and lower when it was less so; and, upon the whole, it is evident, that the depreciation has not been influenced by the balance of debt.

the argument that foreign remittances would under inconvertibility operate to depress the exchanges, Wheatley and Ricardo both
replied that foreign remittances would have no effect on the exchanges whether under convertibility or inconvertibility; in both
cases, they maintained, the demands of England and the rest of
the world for each other's products would so adjust themselves
automatically to the remittances that they would be transferred
in goods without changes either in relative prices or in exchange
rates. If under inconvertibility, therefore, there appeared a depreciation of sterling exchange, this was evidence of excess issue of
currency. Ricardo later made some minor concessions to his
critics,[3] but Wheatley adhered rigidly to this doctrine to the end.[4]
The other bullionists took an intermediate position. They conceded that foreign remittances would affect the exchange rates,
and conceded also, though without adequately explaining why,
that while such remittances were under way a premium on bullion
and exchanges below parity were not proof that the amount of
currency in circulation was in excess of what could be maintained
under a metallic standard currency. They confined themselves to
the argument that a continued and substantial premium of gold
over paper, and fall of the exchanges below parity, established
strong presumptions that the currency was in excess of what could
be maintained under a metallic standard. The Bullion Report, for
instance, cited the persistence of a high premium on gold and low
foreign exchanges "for a considerable time" as the evidence pointing to the existence of excess currency.[5]

It is arguable that the above account exaggerates the difference
between Ricardo and the other bullionists, although the publications of the latter and Ricardo's correspondence show that they
were conscious of their existence and were unable to reach a
mutually satisfactory reconciliation. Ricardo could very rarely
interest himself in the immediate and transitory phases of an economic process sufficiently to trace it in detail through its successive
stages, and he frequently confined his analysis to the end results,
either passing over without mention or even denying the existence

---

[3] See *infra*, pp. 140-41.

[4] Cf. *Remarks on currency and commerce*, 1803, pp. 52-57; *An essay on the theory of money and principles of commerce*, I (1807), 64-71; II (1822), 134-35; *Report on the reports of the Bank committees*, 1819, pp. 20-21.

[5] *Bullion Report*, p. 45.

of the intermediate stages. Ricardo, moreover, tended to omit at times explicit mention of qualifications whose validity he was prepared to acknowledge, if he regarded these qualifications as of minor importance or if he had already in some other connection conceded them. The result of these two habits was a rigor and a precision in his formulation which perhaps gave added force to his exposition when he was dealing with the general public, but which enabled more sophisticated critics to expose him to rebuttal often more damaging in appearance than in fact. These characteristics of Ricardo's methods of thought are now familiar to economists, and Ricardo was to some extent conscious of them himself.[6] They are well illustrated by the following passages from Ricardo, of which the first appears to involve an absolute denial of the existence of intermediate stages in the process of international adjustment to a currency disturbance, while the second recognizes their existence but reveals that his interest lay wholly in what occurs after they have fully worked themselves out:

> To me . . . it appears perfectly clear, that a reduction of bank notes would lower the price of bullion and improve the exchange, without in the least disturbing the regularity of our present exports and imports. . . . Our transactions with foreigners would be precisely the same. . . .[7]

> I am not disposed to contend that the issues of one day, or of one month, can produce any effect on the foreign exchanges; it may possibly require a period of more permanent duration; an interval is absolutely necessary before such effects would follow. This is never considered by those who oppose the principles of the Committee. They conclude that those principles are defective, because their operation is not immediately perceived.[8]

After a time Ricardo gave way somewhat to the pressure of dissent from his views not only by the anti-bullionists but by the bulk·of the bullionists. In response to criticism by Malthus, he conceded that when remittances were under way the currency in the remitting country would be in excess unless it were reduced

---

[6] Cf. Ricardo to Malthus, Jan. 24, 1817, in *Letters of Ricardo to Malthus*, 1887, p. 127.

[7] *Reply to Mr. Bosanquet's practical observations, Works*, p. 360.

[8] *Ibid., Works*, p. 364. He here concedes, with the Bullion Committee, that "a considerable time" may be necessary for the effects fully to show themselves, but remarks that "we should once have thought a year a *considerable time*, when speaking of a discount on bank notes." *Ibid.*, p. 363, note. (Italics in original.)

in the proportion which the commodity export surplus constituted of the total stock of goods in that country, which still implied that the remittances could be effected under a convertible standard, or without depreciation of the currency under an inconvertible standard, without involving a relative fall in the level of prices in the remitting country.[9] He later introduced into his exposition qualifying words and phrases of a kind not to be found in his first writings and which brought him closer to the position of the other bullionists.[10]

The bullionists other than Wheatley and Ricardo conceded that extraordinary remittances would affect the exchanges adversely, but insisted, as against either the express denial of or the failure to give consideration to this factor by the anti-bullionists, that the quantity of note issues, through its effect on commodity prices, and thus on the trade balance, was an additional factor determining the exchange value of the English currency, and ordinarily would be the dominant factor.[11] Perhaps the best brief statement of the moderate bullionist position was the following by Malthus:

The real state of the case seems to be, that though the effects of a redundancy of currency upon the exchange are sure, they are slow, compared with the effects of those mercantile transactions not

---

[9] *High price of bullion,* appendix to 4th ed., *Works,* p. 293.

[10] Cf. especially his testimony before the Parliamentary Committees of 1819:

Q. Assuming that the balance of payments should be against this country, must the payment not necessarily be made either in specie or in bullion?

A. (Ricardo) It appears to me, that the balance of payments is *frequently* the effect of the situation of our currency, and not the cause. (*Report from the* [*Commons*] *Committee,* 1819, p. 141. Italics mine.)

Q. Can you therefore conclude, from the degree to which the exchange is at any moment against any country, that the whole percentage of that unfavorable exchange is owing to the amount of its circulating medium?

A. (Ricardo) A part may be owing to other causes. (*Report of* [*Lords*] *Committee on resumption of cash payments,* 1819, p. 200.)

[11] Cf. Thornton, *The paper credit of Great Britain,* 1802, pp. 277-78:

It thus appears, that "the coming and going of gold" does not (as Mr. Locke expresses it, . . .) "depend wholly on the balance of trade." It depends on the quantity of circulating medium issued; or it depends, as I will allow, on the balance of trade, if that balance is admitted to depend on the quantity of circulating medium issued.

Silberling takes Hawtrey to task for characterizing the anti-bullionist position in this connection as erroneous. "Financial and monetary policy of Great Britain," *loc. cit.,* p. 434, note. His statement that the extraordinary remittances were a "hitherto virtually ignored element in Great Britain's balance of indebtedness during the period involved" (*Ibid.,* p. 226) is without basis, since their significance was a matter of endless debate, then and later.

connected with the question of currency; and, while the former of these causes is proceeding in its operations with a steady and generally uniform pace, the more rapid movements of the latter are opposing, aggravating or modifying these operations in various ways, and producing all those complex, and seemingly inconsistent, appearances, which are to be found in the computed exchange.[12]

Wheatley and Ricardo, it appears to me, were clearly wrong in their denial that extraordinary remittances would operate to depress the value of the English currency on the exchanges and in their insistence that in the absence of currency changes the demands of England and the rest of the world for each other's products would necessarily so immediately and completely adjust themselves to extraordinary remittances as to result under both a metallic and an inconvertible paper standard in the maintenance of equilibrium in the balance of payments without the aid of specie movements, changes in the relative level of prices in the two areas, or movements of the exchange rates. The theoretical grounds for holding these views to be erroneous are presented at length in a later chapter.[13] Silberling and Angell, moreover, have shown, in the case of Silberling by a comparison of the English foreign remittances with the price of silver in English paper currency, and in the case of Angell by a comparison of the premium on silver and the Hamburg exchange, that there was a close correlation between these remittances and the status of the English currency. These comparisons are reproduced in table I and chart I. Adequate data do not exist to permit a tabulation of the international balance of payments of Great Britain for the period, or even of its trade balance. In the absence of such data, it is reasonable to assume that the extraordinary remittances are a fair presumptive index of the degree of pressure operating to force upwards the foreign exchanges and the price of silver in terms of English paper currency. The correlation shown is in fact closer than could reasonably have been expected, given the partial character of the data made use of for the purpose of the comparison, and I know of no equally striking results from similar comparisons for other countries or periods. Whether by design or by accident the English paper currency remained at or near parity with silver and with foreign metallic currencies in the years in

---

[12] "Depreciation of the currency," *Edinburgh review*, XVII (1811), 360.
[13] See chap. vii, *infra*.

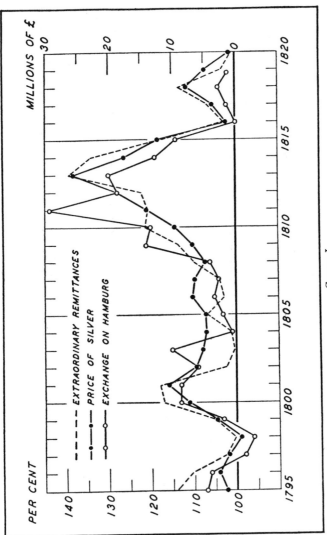

CHART I

TABLE I (data of Chart I)

EXTRAORDINARY REMITTANCES, PRICE OF SILVER, AND HAMBURG EXCHANGE,
1795–1820

Year	Extraordinary remittances[a] (In Millions of Pounds)	Price of silver[b] (Par = 100)	Exchange on Hamburg[c] 36s. banco = 100
1795	9.4	102.4	107
1796	7.0	104.2	106
1797	1.6	101.7	98
1798	0.3	99.0	96
1799	3.4	105.1	103
1800	11.3	111.2	113
1801	12.0	115.9	113
1802	1.5	109.5	109
1803	0.3	107.8	105
1804	0.7	107.0	101
1805	4.5	107.1	103
1806	1.8	110.0	105
1807	2.6	109.7	104
1808	6.6	107.2	106
1809	9.1	110.2	121
1810	14.1	114.4	120
1811	13.8	121.1	144
1812	14.8	128.0	128
1813	26.3	138.2	130
1814	23.1	126.4	119
1815	11.9	118.4	114
1816	2.9	102.3	100
1817	4.4	105.4	102
1818	8.9	111.6	105
1819	2.2	107.2	102
1820	0.7	101.5	. . .

[a] Silberling, "Financial and monetary policy of Great Britain," *Quarterly journal of economics* XXXVIII (1924), 227. (Government remittances to Continent plus value of grain imports into Great Britain in excess of £2,000,000.)

[b] *Ibid.* (Spanish silver dollars.)

[c] Hawtrey, *Currency and credit*, 3d ed., 1928, p. 335, and *Reports by the Lords Committee . . . [on] the expediency of the resumption of cash payments*, 1819, p. 330.

which no, or small, foreign remittances had to be made, and departed from parity in roughly corresponding degree in the years in which heavy foreign remittances were necessary.[14]

[14] Similar results were obtained by similar methods by an anonymous contemporary writer. From a chart presenting the foreign expenditures of the government, the amounts paid for imported grain, and the rates of the exchange on Hamburg, this writer derived the following conclusions:

The exchanges are affected by two great principles of political economy, namely, by the foreign expenditure, and by the amount paid for grain

Ricardo could, however, have conceded to his opponents the point that extraordinary remittances tend to depress the exchanges without surrendering his main contention that actual depreciation of the exchanges was evidence of greater issue of currency than could be maintained in circulation under a metallic standard. Extraordinary remittances tend to depress the exchanges alike under a metallic and under a paper standard, but under a metallic standard this depreciation is prevented from going beyond the gold export point by contraction of the currency. If speculative factors be abstracted from, or if it be assumed that their mode of degree of operation is not affected by extraordinary remittances, then such remittances, *if accompanied by equal contractions of the currency of the remitting country in the two cases,* should not result in appreciably greater[15] depreciation of the exchange under a paper than under a metallic standard. It was primarily because under the paper standard the English currency was not contracted as it would necessarily have been contracted under a metallic standard that the foreign remittances resulted in such marked depreciation of the paper pound on the exchanges.

If Wheatley and Ricardo erred in their exposition of the relation under inconvertible currency between the exchange rates and the state of the balance of payments, the anti-bullionists erred more grievously. The anti-bullionists insisted rightly that under inconvertibility the exchanges were immediately determined solely by the demand for and supply of foreign bills, but failed to see that this was equally true of a metallic standard and that a very important factor determining the relative demand for and supply

---

imported. When, therefore, the importation of grain, and the foreign expenditure have been great, the exchange has become unfavorable, and the latter has, vice versa, increased nearly in the same ratio as the two former have diminished. In the accompanying table it will be seen, that each protruding line of demarcation, specifying the variation of the exchange, has, with very trifling exceptions, a corresponding sinus in the two lines which designate the increase or diminution of the foreign expenditure and the amount paid for imported grain.—"Two tables . . . illustrative of the speeches of the . . . Earl of Liverpool and the . . . Chancellor of the Exchequer," in *Pamphleteer,* XV (1819), 286.

[15] Under a metallic currency the contraction of the currency takes the form, in part, of an actual export of specie, and this specie exercises a direct liquidating effect on foreign obligations which is absent in the case of a paper standard currency. To this extent, a greater currency contraction will be necessary under a paper than under a metallic standard to prevent exchange depreciation when foreign remittances of a given amount are to be made. See pp. 135-36, *supra.*

of foreign bills was the relative level of prices in the two countries, which in turn was determined largely by the relative amounts of currency. Many of the anti-bullionists, moreover, must have thought that in some way a fall in the foreign exchanges made possible the payment of foreign remittances without the need of a commodity export surplus. No other explanation is available of their repeated insistence that throughout the period of low exchanges England either had an unfavorable balance of payments on trade account, or else had a balance insufficiently favorable to offset the military expenditure abroad. As Ricardo pointed out, in reply to reasoning of this sort by Bosanquet, this left it a mystery how the military expenditures abroad were actually met, since specie was not available.[16]

Not all the anti-bullionists, however, were confused on this point. One of them stated very compactly and clearly the possibilities under such circumstances:

[Under a depreciated paper currency] it would be literally impossible that the balance of payments should be any longer against us, because we could have no means of paying an unfavorable balance. Our receipts from, and payments to, foreign nations must therefore be reduced to an equality (or the balance must be turned in our favor) either by an increase of our exports of merchandise, a diminution of our imports and of the foreign expenditure of government, or by some . . . international transfers of capital. . . .[17]

Another anti-bullionist, Herries, explained that foreign remittances could exceed the export surplus for a time if the balance was met by borrowing abroad, and, writing no doubt from first-hand knowledge, since he had been engaged in the task of making the remittances for the government, said: "This is, probably, the case, with respect to our drafts from abroad at this time:—we are borrowing money to carry on our foreign expenditure, at a high rate of interest."[18]

There are passages in Silberling's critique of the bullionists which seem to indicate that Silberling also subscribes to the notion that the fall in the exchange value of a remitting country's cur-

---

[16] *Reply to Mr. Bosanquet's observations, Works,* pp. 334-35.

[17] John Hill, *An inquiry into the causes of the present high price of gold bullion in England,* 1810, pp. 8-9.

[18] J. C. Herries, *A review of the controversy respecting the high price of bullion,* 1811, pp. 43-44.

rency can operate to supply it with foreign funds with which to meet its foreign liabilities in some other way than by stimulating its exports and restricting its imports.[19] Silberling cannot consistently fall back on the argument that a decline in the exchanges under inconvertible currency would lead to a debt-liquidating shipment of bullion, for he and Angell have characterized this as one of the erroneous doctrines of the bullionists, and especially of Ricardo. As I have elsewhere shown,[20] Ricardo distinguished carefully between an inconvertible paper currency depreciated in terms of bullion and one not so depreciated—a distinction which Silberling and Angell fail to make—and denied the possibility of bullion shipments as a part of the regular mechanism of adjustment of international balances in the case of the former. Curiously enough, both Silberling and Angell place some emphasis on bullion shipments as part of the explanation of the phenomena of the Restriction period, and tacitly, and probably wrongly, assuming that the Bank of England's gold losses were mainly to the government, that when the Bank sold gold it ordinarily did not charge the market price, and that most or all of the gold exported while the Restriction was in effect came from the Bank's holdings instead of from private stocks, cite these bullion shipments as an item in the meritorious record of the Bank of England during the period of suspension of cash payments.[21]

The notion that even under *depreciated* inconvertible paper exchange fluctuations will give rise to bullion movements as an ordinary everyday occurrence is not as absurd on *a priori* grounds as Silberling and Angell regard it for *any* inconvertible currency.

[19] Cf. "Financial and monetary policy of Great Britain," *Quarterly journal of economics,* XXXVIII, p. 229, note: "We may conclude, however, that the adverse balance of military payments of itself caused no important readjustments in the volume of foreign commerce which might have compensated the rise of the exchange rates against England"; *Ibid.,* pp. 433-34: "In the absence of data, the Committee resorted to hypothesis: if the foreign payments of the State had created marked deviations from exchange parities, this could be only a very temporary matter, since foreigners, attracted by low prices of sterling, would forthwith begin to buy British commodities and thus immediately expand British exports, with the result of readjusting the balance of payments. It happened that many erstwhile foreign buyers had other preoccupations at the moment."

[20] "Angell's theory of international prices," *Journal of political economy,* XXXIV (1926), pp. 603-06.

[21] Silberling, "Financial and monetary policy," *Quarterly journal of economics,* XXXVIII, 226; Angell, *Theory of international prices,* p. 478.

While there is no internal demand for bullion for monetary purposes at a market price in excess of the mint price, there still remains an internal demand for industrial use, for hoarding, and for speculative purposes. A rise in the paper premium on bullion resulting from a fall in the exchanges will operate to induce some of the holders of bullion to offer it for sale for export. There is considerable evidence, both for the Restriction period in England and for other past and present cases of countries with depreciated paper currencies, that, where legal restrictions do not prevent, bullion moves fairly freely into and out of such countries in response to changes in its paper price.[22] It is quite conceivable that the net export of bullion from England during the suspension period was even greater than it would have been if the metallic standard had been retained, and that the absence of the direct debt-liquidating effect of bullion shipments cannot therefore be invoked as even a partial explanation of the depreciation of the paper currency.

VIII. THE POSSIBILITY OF EXCESS ISSUE BY BANKS

There were among the anti-bullionists some crude inflationists for whom no amount of currency could be too great. Most of the anti-bullionists, however, recognized that there were limits beyond which it was not desirable to go in the issue of currency. What these limits were, they failed to specify, except in terms of the "needs of business." They claimed that as long as currency was issued only by banks, and was issued by them only in the discount of genuine and sound short-term commercial paper, it could not be issued in excess of the needs of business, since no one would borrow at interest funds which he did not need. If currency should perchance be issued to excess, it would rapidly return to the banks either in liquidation of bank loans or, under convertibility, for redemption in specie.[1] To this doctrine the directors of

---

[22] Cf. on this point, the excellent analysis of the Argentine experience in J. H. Williams, *Argentine international trade under inconvertible paper money, 1880-1900*, 1920.

[1] Cf. e.g., Bosanquet, *Practical observations*, 2d ed., 1810, pp. 49-64; John Hill, *An inquiry into the causes of the present high price of gold bullion*, 1810, p. 36; Coutts Trotter, *The principles of currency and exchanges*, 2d ed., 1810, pp. 10 ff. In view of his subsequent prominence as an advocate of the "currency principle," it is of interest that Torrens at this period should have subscribed to the doctrine that it was impossible to issue even inconvertible paper money

the Bank of England and prominent members of the Cabinet also subscribed, and the authority of Adam Smith was appealed to in support thereof.[2]

The bullionists explicitly denied the validity of this doctrine, at least for an inconvertible currency. Thornton in 1797 had objected against the usury laws that they limited the Bank of England to a rate at which "there might be a much greater disposition to borrow of the Bank . . . than it might become the Bank to comply with,"[3] and in 1802 he pointed out that the extent to which the charge of interest acted as a check on the demand for discounts depended on the rate of interest which was charged; the Bank of England was prevented by the usury laws from charging more than 5 per cent, and if the prevailing rate of commercial profit were higher than that, the demand for loans would be greater than the Bank should meet.[4] Lord King put it more strongly: when the market rate of interest exceeds the bank rate, the demand for discounts "may be carried to any assignable extent,"[5] and in this somewhat extreme form it was repeated by other bullionists.[6] In a speech in the House of Commons on May 7, 1811, Henry Thornton expounded with great ability, and with interesting references to the experience of other central banks, the mode of operation of the rate of interest as a regulator of the volume of note issue. He pointed out that even John Law's

to excess if it were issued only upon discount of good mercantile bills. (R. Torrens, *An essay on money and paper currency*, 1812, p. 127.) James Mill also subscribed to this doctrine: see his review of Thomas Smith's, *Essay on the theory of money*, 1807, *Edinburgh review*, XIII (1808), 57-60.

[2] Cf. *Wealth of nations*, Cannan ed., II, 287.

[3] *Report of the Lords Committee*, 1797, p. 83.

[4] *The paper credit of Great Britain*, 1802, pp. 287-90.

[5] *Thoughts on the effects of the Bank Restrictions*, 2d ed., 1804, p. 22.

[6] E.g., J. L. Foster, *Essay on the principle of commercial exchanges*, 1804, p. 113; *Report of the Bullion Committee*, 1810, pp. 56-57; Dugald Stewart, in a memorandum to Lord Lauderdale, 1811, first published in his *Collected Works*, 1855, VIII, 444; McCulloch, review of Ricardo's *Proposal for an economical and secure currency, Edinburgh review*, XXXI (1818), 62.

The Bank of Ireland was compelled by law to discount at one per cent below the legal maximum rate of interest. Lauderdale in 1805 commented that: "By the restriction, . . . , unattended with the repeal of the clause compelling discount below the legal interest, the Bank [of Ireland] was obviously exposed to all the ardor of solicitation which must naturally attend the practice of discounting at an inferior rate of interest, whilst the check on the extent to which the indulgence might be carried was completely annihilated." (*Thoughts on the alarming state of the circulation*, 1805, pp. 23-24.)

bank had issued only on loans at interest, and that it was Law's error that "he considered security as every thing and quantity as nothing" and failed to see the significance of the rate at which he offered to lend.[7] Thornton argued, moreover, that during a period of rising prices the real rate of interest was less than the apparent rate; while businessmen did not generally perceive this, they did realize that borrowing at such times was usually profitable, and therefore increased their demands for loans if the bank rate did not rise.[8]

Ricardo agreed with the other bullionists that the "needs of commerce" for currency could not be quantitatively defined, and that through a resultant change in prices commerce could absorb whatever amount was issued.[9] But he ordinarily denied any relationship between the rate of interest and the quantity of money, and presumably also between the rate of interest and the demand for loans: "Whilst the Bank is willing to lend, borrowers will always exist, so that there can be no limit to their overissues, but that which I have just mentioned," i.e., convertibility.[10] In a speech in Parliament he expressly denied that the rate of interest was a check to the amount of issues: "For . . . what the directors thought a check, namely, the rate of interest on money, was no check at all to the amount of issues, as Adam Smith, Mr. Hume, and others had satisfactorily proved."[11] Here once more Ricardo was applying long-run considerations to a short-run problem. But in his *Principles* we find Ricardo at one point expounding the same views as the other leading bullionists:

The applications to the Bank for money, then, depend on the comparison between the rate of profits that may be made by the employment of it, and the rate at which they are willing to lend it. If they charge less than the market rate of interest, there is no amount of money which they might not lend,—if they charge more

---

[7] *Substance of two speeches of Henry Thornton, Esq. on the Bullion Report,* 1811, pp. 19-37.

[8] *Ibid.,* pp. 20 ff. This contains the essence of Irving Fisher's theory of the influence of changing price levels on interest rates. Cf. his *Appreciation and interest, Publications of the American Economic Association,* XI (1896, No. 4).

[9] Cf. *Reply to Mr. Bosanquet's practical observations, Works,* p. 341.

[10] *Three letters on the price of gold* [1809], p. 11.

[11] Hansard, *Parliamentary debates, 1st series,* XL (May 24, 1819), 744. The doctrine of Hume and Smith to which he refers is apparently their denial that there is a close connection between the volume of money and the rate of interest (see *supra,* p. 89), a doctrine requiring qualification for the short run.

than that rate, none but spendthrifts and prodigals would be found to borrow of them. We accordingly find, that when the market rate of interest exceeds the rate of 5 per cent at which the Bank uniformly lends, the discount office is besieged with applications for money; and, on the contrary, when the market rate is even temporarily under 5 per cent, the clerks of that office have no employment.[12]

To the denial by the bullionists that the charge of interest on loans was a sufficient guarantee, irrespective of the rate charged, against overissue, the anti-bullionists apparently never attempted to reply.[13] In evidence before the Bullion Committee, Bank of England officials had emphatically denied that the security against overissue by the Bank would be reduced if the discount rate were to be lowered from 5 to 4 or even to 3 per cent. No person, they insisted, would pay interest for a loan which he did not need, whatever the rate, unless it were for the purpose of employing it in speculation, "and provided the conduct of the Bank is regulated as it now is, no accommodation would be given to a person of that description."[14]

That the quantity of bank loans demanded is dependent on the rate of discount is now universally accepted by economists and need not be further argued. On the question whether or not the rate of 5 per cent uniformly charged by the Bank of England during the Restriction was lower than the market rate, there is,

[12] *Principles of political economy and taxation,* 3d ed. [1821], in *Works,* p. 220. This passage is unchanged from the first edition, 1817.
Earlier in the same paragraph Ricardo had argued that the market rate of interest was determined, not by the Bank rate of discount, but by the rate of profits which could be made by the employment of capital, which was totally independent of the quantity or of the value of money. "Whether a bank lent one million, ten million, or a hundred millions, they would not *permanently* alter the market rate of interest; they would alter only the value of the money which they thus issued." (Italics not in original.)

[13] Cf., however, W. T. Comber, *A view of the nature and operation of bank currency,* 1817, p. 16: "These advances [of the Bank of England] did not depend, as many suppose, on the caprice of the Bank, but were regulated by the amount of cash payments on transactions, which would afford a profit to the borrower after paying an interest of five per cent to the Bank."

[14] *Report of the Bullion Committee,* 1810, *Minutes of evidence,* p. 129. Cf. also the testimony of Dorrien, Governor of the Bank, in 1819: "The demand for discount always proceeds from the wants of the public, and if the bank were to discount at a lower rate of interest than five per cent, in my opinion there would be no greater application than if it were to discount at the present rate." *Report of [Commons] Committee,* 1819, p. 145.

however, a conflict of opinion. The usury laws would operate to prevent any overt charge of more than 5 per cent, and the uniform 5 per cent rate which is often said to have prevailed during the Restriction period[15] may have been only nominally that. There is contemporary evidence that bankers found means of evading the restrictions of the usury laws. In 1818, the Committee on the usury laws stated in its Report that there had been "of late years . . . [a] constant excess of the market rate of interest above the rate limited by law."[16] Thornton notes that borrowers from private banks had to maintain running cash with them, and borrowers in the money market had to pay a commission in addition to formal interest, and that by these means the effective market rate was often raised above the 5 per cent level.[17] Another writer relates that long credits were customary in London and a greater discount was granted for prompt payment than the legal interest for the time would amount to.[18]

More convincing evidence that the 5 per cent rate was not of

[15] Cf. Thomas Tooke, *A history of prices,* I (1838), 159: ". . . the market rate of interest for bills of the description which were alone discountable at the Bank ["good mercantile bills, not exceeding sixty-one days' date"], did not materially, or for any length of time together, exceed the rate of five per cent per annum."

Silberling, "British prices and business cycles," *Review of economic statistics,* preliminary volume V (1923), supplement 2, p. 241: "The Usury Laws fixed the maximum rate of interest and discount at five per cent, and contemporary literature indicates that this rate was, at least from 1790 to 1822, the prevailing and unvarying rate of discount throughout the country. Instead of varying their rates, the banks either granted or refused loans."

In evidence given in 1857 before a Parliamentary Committee, John Twells, a member of a London banking firm who had operated as a banker in London since 1801, stated that 5 per cent was the only rate charged by bankers during the Restriction and that no one ever thought of any other rate. (*Evidence of John Twells . . . before the select committee,* 1857, pp. 13-15.)

[16] *Report from the select committee on the usury laws,* 1818, p. 3. Cf. also Ricardo, *On protection to agriculture* [1822], *Works,* p. 474: "During the last war the market rate of interest for money was, for years together, fluctuating between 7 and 10 per cent; yet the Bank never lent at a rate above 5 per cent."

[17] *Substance of two speeches,* 1811, p. 20.

[18] David Prentice, *Thoughts on the repeal of the Bank restriction law,* 1811, p. 14. A later writer states that: "During the war it was very customary to make loans which were to be repaid by the transfer of a sum of stock, instead of money. This was done to secure to the capitalist the market rate of interest, which was then higher than he could have legally reserved in the deed." (James Maclaren, *The effect of a small fall in the value of gold upon money,* 1853, p. 12.)

itself always an effective barrier to indefinite expansion of loans by the banks is to be found in the fact that the directors of the Bank of England, although they professed that they discounted freely at the rate of 5 per cent all bills falling within the admissible categories for discount,[19] in reply to questioning admitted that they had customary maxima of accommodation for each individual customer and occasionally applied other limitations to the amount discounted.[20]

Even if it were conceded that the Bank rate was never lower than the market rate of discount for the same classes of loans, it might still be low enough to permit or even to foster a wild inflation, if the Bank rate was low absolutely, and if it was the Bank rate which determined the market rate. On important classes of loans the Bank of England was a direct competitor with other lending agencies, and it was certainly important enough as a lending agency to exercise at least an important influence on the market rate. Also, by lowering its credit standards, or offering its credit to a wider range of applicants for commercial loans, it could actively promote currency expansion without lowering its interest rate below the hitherto prevailing level. It may be accepted, therefore, that the 5 per cent rate was not necessarily an adequate check to the volume of bank credit extended to commercial borrowers.

The powers of the Bank of England to expand its note issues, moreover, were not confined to its commercial discount activities. The Bank could also, and did, get its notes into circulation by advances to the government, by purchases of exchequer bills and public stocks in the open market, and by advances to investors in new issues of government stocks. Since even many of the anti-bullionists conceded that there was no automatic check to excess issue where the issues were made in connection with loans to the government, there should have been no occasion for extended controversy as to the existence of a possibility of excess issue.[21]

---

[19] *Report of Bullion Committee*, 1810, p. 26.

[20] *Ibid.*, pp. 22, 24; *Minutes of evidence*, p. 89. Cf. also Thornton, *Paper credit*, 1802, pp. 179, 294; A. W. Acworth, *Financial reconstruction in England, 1815-1822*, 1925, p. 146.

[21] There was some discussion as to the comparative susceptibilities to excess of issue through commercial discount and through loans to government. Some writers contended that there was no difference between the two, but most writers agreed that the latter was more susceptible to excess. Mathias Attwood pre-

IX. Responsibility for the Excess Issue: Bank of
England vs. Country Banks

Since bank notes were issued both by the Bank of England and
the country banks, responsibility for any excess issue of paper
currency could lay with either or with both. With the exception of
Wheatley, who held the country banks largely responsible,[1] the
bullionists were united in assigning responsibility for the excess,
as between the Bank of England and the country banks, wholly
or predominantly to the former. Boyd, in 1801, laid down the
formula which was to be the text of the bullionists: "The Bank
of England is the great source of all the circulation of the country; and, by the increase or diminution of its paper, the increase
or diminution of that of every country bank is infallibly regulated."[2] His argument rested on the postulate that the country
banks must keep a fixed percentage of reserves against their own
note circulation in Bank of England notes, whereas the Bank
of England was not subject to such a limitation.[3] In a note added
to the second edition, he conceded that the country banks, by
allowing their reserve ratio to fall, may have contributed independently to the then existing excess of currency, but he blamed
the Restriction, which left to holders of country bank notes the
possibility only of converting them into Bank of England notes
with which they were not familiar, for making this fall in reserve
ratio possible. He apparently believed that once this fall had taken
place, the Bank of England would again have control, through

---

sents an ingenious *a priori* argument in support of the greater tendency of
advances to government to raise prices than of the same amount of commercial
discounts, resting in effect on the greater velocity of circulation of the former
(*Letter to Lord Hamilton*, 1823, pp. 50-56). But there are grounds for believing
that during the Restriction period the advances to the government of the Bank
of England had an unusually low velocity of circulation, because of the practice
of the government of holding exceptionally large idle balances at the Bank of
England. See *infra*, p. 169.

[1] *Remarks on currency and commerce*, 1803, pp. 209 ff.; *Essay on the theory
of money and principles of commerce*, I (1807), 336 ff.

[2] *Letter to Pitt*, 1st ed., 1801, p. 20.

[3] *Ibid.*: "The circulation of country bank notes must necessarily be proportioned to the sums, in specie or Bank of England notes, requisite to discharge
such of them as may be presented for payment; but the paper of the Bank of
England has no such limitation."

regulation of its own issues, over the volume of country bank issues.[4]

Thornton reached the same conclusion, that the volume of Bank of England issues regulated the volume of country bank note issues, but by a more elaborate chain of reasoning. He applied to different regions within a country the Hume type of analysis of adjustment of international balances of payments.[5] If country banks took the initiative in increasing their issues, country prices would rise; the provinces would buy in London commodities which formerly they had bought locally; there would result an adverse balance of payments on London, which would be met through shipment of Bank of England notes to London or by drafts on the balances of country banks with London bankers. The impairment of their reserves would force the country bankers to contract their note issues.[6]

Thornton pointed out, however, that this did not mean that the proportion of country bank notes to Bank of England notes must always remain the same. This would hold true only if the areas of circulation of the two types of notes and also the relative volumes of payments to be made in the respective areas remained unaltered:

By saying that the country paper is limited in an equal degree, I always mean not that one uniform proportion is maintained between the quantity of the London paper and that of the country paper, but only that the quantity of the one, in comparison with the demand for that one, is the same, or nearly the same, as the quantity of the other in proportion to the call for the other.[7]

---

[4] *Letter to Pitt,* 2d ed., pp. 19-20, note. Boyd seems to have thought that an increase in holdings of cash by individuals in the country was the only way in which pressure on the country bank reserves could occur. In an appendix to the second edition (pp. 42-43), Boyd prints a letter from an unnamed correspondent taking him to task for attaching insufficient weight to the country-bank notes, which, according to this letter, had probably increased in greater proportion than Bank of England notes.

[5] Hume had noted incidentally the applicability of his analysis to the relations between the different provinces of a single country. See *supra,* p. 84.

[6] *Paper credit,* 1802, pp. 216 ff. Thornton also argues here that if bank credit became more easily available in the country while remaining restricted in London, mercantile houses with banking connections both in the country and in London would shift some of their borrowing from London banks to country banks, would demand Bank of England notes in exchange for the country bank notes thus obtained, and would thereby impair the reserves of the country banks and force them to contract their issues.

[7] *Ibid.,* p. 228.

Similar views were expressed by Horner,[8] King,[9] Ricardo,[10] the Bullion Committee,[11] Malthus,[12] and other bullionists.

Since the anti-bullionists denied any excess in the currency as a whole, they ordinarily showed little interest in the attempts of the bullionists to apportion responsibility for such excess. Some of the anti-bullionists agreed that convertibility of country bank notes into Bank of England notes was as effective a restriction on country bank note issue as convertibility into gold.[13] Others of them, however, apparently determined that if any blame was to be assigned it should not be to the Bank of England, denied that the amount of country bank notes was in any way dependent on the amount of Bank of England notes, and cited in confirmation the evidence of country bankers before the Bullion Committee that their reserves consisted only slightly of Bank of England notes and the apparent absence of correspondence between the fluctuations in the issues of the two types of paper money.[14]

Silberling and Angell reject the bullionist claim that the country bank note circulation was dependent on that of the Bank of England notes. Silberling ridicules the notion that if prices rise

---

[8] Review of Thornton, *Paper credit, Edinburgh review,* I (1802), p. 191.

[9] *Thoughts on the effects of the Bank restrictions,* 2d ed., 1804, pp. 101-11. King stated the argument, later to be stressed by the banking school, that country banks could not issue to excess because competition among the banks to issue their own notes would prevent any individual bank from expanding. See *infra,* pp. 238 ff.

[10] *High price of bullion,* 1810, *Works,* pp. 282 ff.

[11] *Report,* 1810, pp. 46, 67. The Bullion Committee nevertheless cited evidence tending to show that the reserve ratios of the country banks had fallen and that their note issues had therefore risen in greater proportion than the issues of the Bank of England, even after allowance for changes in the areas of hand-to-hand circulation of the two currencies. (*Ibid.,* pp. 68-71.) They also reached the erroneous conclusion that if country banks increased their note issues proportionately with the increase in Bank of England notes, "the excess of Bank of England paper will produce its effect upon prices not merely in the ratio of its own increase, but in a much higher proportion." (*Ibid.,* p. 68.)

[12] "Review of the controversy respecting the high price of bullion," *Edinburgh review,* XVIII (1811), 457-58.

[13] Cf. Coutts Trotter, *Principles of currency and exchanges,* 2d ed., 1810, pp. 22-23.

[14] Cf. Bosanquet, *Practical observations,* pp. 76 ff; Vansittart, *Substance of two speeches,* 1811, pp. 52-55. Bosanquet claimed that if prices rose in London as the result of increased issues by the Bank of England and its notes therefore flowed to the country, this might result in a contraction, but could never cause an augmentation, of the country bank note circulation, presumably on the ground that the Bank of England notes would necessarily displace country bank notes rather than supplement them.

in the provinces, it will result in a shift of purchases from the provinces to London: "London and the rest of England were not then, and are not now economic areas producing identical wares. If the price of iron or hops or wool rose in the provinces by reason of liberal credit accommodation to farmers and speculators, . . . it could not result in purchases from London of what London did not produce."[15] This is a valid criticism of the manner in which the bullionists expressed their argument, but leaves the essence of the argument untouched. A relative increase in country bank note issues will not lead the provinces to increase their purchases in London of *country* products, but it will, nevertheless, lead to a debit balance of payments of the country with London. The increase in spendable funds in the country will lead to increased purchases of *London* products by the provinces, and the rise in prices in the provinces will lead to decreased purchases of *country* products by London. When two regions have currencies convertible into each other at fixed rates and have commercial relations with each other, one of these regions cannot issue currency to any extent, irrespective of what the other does, without encountering serious exchange and balance of payments difficulties, even if the two regions do not have a single identical product.[16]

Silberling and Angell object further that the explanation given by Thornton and Ricardo is unilateral, instead of bilateral; it fails to take account of the upward effect on London prices of the release by the country to London of Bank of England notes and

---

[15] "Financial and monetary policy," *loc. cit.*, p. 419. Cf. Henry Burgess, *A letter to the Right Hon. George Canning*, 1826, p. 28: "The theory of the [Bullion] Committee . . . about an excess of country bank notes causing a local rise in prices and sending all people to London, to buy cheap commodities, seems to me equally luminous. . . . Who that had a correct notion of the working of the currency, would think of sending people from a distance in the country to London, to buy corn, cattle, cheese, wool, bacon, coal, lead, iron, etc. by an excess of country bank notes, as compared with Bank of England notes." Cf. also John Ashton Yates, *Essays on currency and circulation*, 1827, p. 37: "The local rise of prices in consequence of an increased issue of country bank notes must be enormous in order to bring corn or iron from London to Glamorganshire or Staffordshire. . . ."

[16] Cf. also the answer of George Woods: "For as commodities are cheaper where the excess has not taken place than where it has, so will they be taken to that part where a higher price can be obtained. If it be said that many goods, such as those from the East Indies, can be purchased only in London, I reply: the price of luxuries is dependent upon that of necessaries." (*Observations on the present price of bullion*, 1811, p. 21.)

balances with London bankers resulting from an expansion of country bank note issues. They contend, in rebuttal, that a rise in prices in the country resulting from an increased issue of country bank notes would spread to London.[17]

This is a valid criticism of Thornton.[18] It is not applicable, however, to Boyd[19] or Ricardo,[20] for both of these writers took it for granted that it was necessary for the country banks to maintain constant cash reserve ratios whether in Bank of England notes or not. If the Bank of England did not increase its issues, then the country banks could not at the same time increase their circulation and maintain a constant reserve ratio. It is this assumption of constancy in the country bank reserve ratios, to which neither Silberling nor Angell refers, which is the vulnerable point in the bullionist argument. If, as Boyd conceded, the country banks allowed their reserve ratios to fall, they could, as long as their reserves were not wholly exhausted, force their issues even while the Bank of England remained passive. If they tolerated a lowering of their reserve ratio, they could bring about a new price equilibrium and a new equilibrium in the balance of payments between London and the provinces, with the circulation greater, and prices higher than before, in each area. Even if the country banks expanded rapidly and extravagantly, and the Bank of England did not follow suit, it might be some time, as Joplin later pointed out,[21] before their reserves were exhausted, and in the interval before the collapse prices would be higher and the premium on bullion greater for England as a whole. The question still remains, however, as to what were the obligations of the Bank of England in such a situation.

Silberling further supports his argument that the issues of the country banks were not dependent upon those of the Bank of England by the claim that the country bank reserves consisted mainly of balances with London private bankers, while the reserves of the London bankers "were wholly uncontrolled by law and had never been more than very moderate sums; and their

---

[17] Silberling, "financial and monetary policy," p. 408; Angell, *Theory of international prices,* p. 46.

[18] Thornton was not unaware of the issue, but he failed to meet it satisfactorily. *Cf. Paper credit,* 1802, pp. 219 ff.

[19] See *supra,* p. 154.

[20] *Reply to Mr. Bosanquet's observations, Works,* p. 352.

[21] T. Joplin, *Outlines of a system of political economy,* 1823, p. 259.

ability to create credits was now but very little controlled by the Bank of England."[22] The London bankers, unless they were of a banking species hitherto unrecognized, must, in practice, have found it necessary to have on hand in case of need cash or its equivalent. But the only "cash" at the time was Bank of England notes, and its only equivalent at the time was a demand deposit with the Bank of England. The private bankers in London in fact began during the Restriction period the practice of opening accounts at the Bank of England and of rediscounting bills in their portfolios with the Bank, instead of, as before, selling exchequer bills or government stock on the open market, when they needed to replenish their cash reserves.[23] The then deputy governor of the Bank admitted to the Bullion Committee, in reply to a searching question on this point, that a considerable amount of the bills discounted with the Bank of England by the London private banks was country bank paper.[24] Willingness of the London bankers to allow their cash balances to run down would enable them to expand their credits to country banks in some degree, even if the Bank of England did not make available to them increased rediscount facilities. But since such expansion would involve a persistent drain of their cash to the Bank of England and to hand-to-hand circulation, it could not have been carried far without active Bank of England support. The Bank of England, moreover, could, by positive action, have prevented even such expansion of the volume of discounts of the London private banks as had been independent of increased discounts with the Bank of England.

Silberling and Angell fail completely to give any consideration to the proposition that while England had an inconvertible paper currency special responsibility attached to some agency, and presumably to the Bank of England as in effect a central bank, to keep the currency in good order, even if to do so it should prove necessary to countervail the activities of the country banks and the London private bankers. Silberling even goes to the length of characterizing as a "truly remarkable opinion," unfortunately, however, without indicating why, Ricardo's argument (as sum-

[22] "Financial and monetary policy," *loc. cit.,* p. 399.

[23] Cf. Joseph Lowe, *The present state of England in regard to agriculture, trade, and finance,* 2d ed., 1823, appendix, p. 20.

[24] *Bullion Report: Minutes of evidence,* pp. 171-72.

marized by Silberling) that "one of the causes of the 'excess' of Bank notes was the expansion of the country issues, which had thereby narrowed the field within which the Bank's issues could circulate; the latter overflowed, in other words, a contracted channel."[25] The Bank of England, it is true, was organized as a profit-making establishment. But it enjoyed valuable special privileges, and whatever some of its shareholders may have thought,[26] it was the general opinion of the time that it also had special obligations, what we should today term the obligations of a central bank. Silberling himself refers to the Bank of England of that period as a "central bank," and states that the Bank claimed to be a "regulator" of the currency. The Bank could not plead financial inability to carry out these obligations, for the "supposedly enormous profits," to which Silberling refers in a manner clearly intended to suggest that they existed only in the imagination of the bullionists, were genuine.[27] There is nothing obviously remarkable in the proposition that a central bank should contract when the rest of the banking system is dangerously expanding, in order to check and to offset that expansion. It should, on the contrary, be obvious that there is a fatal conflict between the regulatory functions of a central bank and determination on its part to maintain, willy-nilly, its accustomed proportion of the country's banking business.[28]

---

[25] "Financial and monetary policy," *loc. cit.*, p. 426.

[26] Cf. Daniel Beaumont Payne, *An address to the proprietors of bank stock* [1816], in *Pamphleteer*, VII (1816), 381: "Mr. Allardyce appears to have accurately understood, that 'it is the first and almost only duty of the court of directors, to promote the interest of the proprietors by all lawful ways and means.'"

[27] The Bank of England did not ordinarily report its profits even to its shareholders. But in 1797 the Bank was paying a dividend of 7 per cent on its capital stock. This was maintained until 1807, when it was increased to 10 per cent. In addition, six extra dividends or "bonuses" in government stocks or cash averaging over 5½ per cent were paid from 1799 to 1806, a stock dividend of 25 per cent was paid in 1816, and the Bank's premises were enlarged out of profits during the Restriction period. The average price of bank stock rose from 133½ in 1777 and 127½ in the crisis year, 1797, to 280 in 1809. (Mushet, *Effects produced on the national currency*, 3d ed., 1811, pp. 68-69; J. R. Mc-Culloch, *Historical sketch of the Bank of England*, 1831, p. 75.)

[28] To the extent that there was competition for issue between the country banks and the Bank of England, it was mainly regional competition. The two currencies circulated side by side only to a very limited extent, and when a note-issuing country bank was established in a new district, Bank of England notes would ordinarily not continue to circulate freely there. If as country banks extended the area of circulation of their notes the Bank of England

Silberling and Angell attempt also to demonstrate the lack of responsibility of the Bank of England for the increase in currency by an elaborate statistical comparison of the behavior of the Bank of England and the country banks. But if it is accepted that the Bank of England was a central bank, its responsibility for any excess of currency is *ipso facto* established, unless it can be shown that it used its powers of control to the utmost but that they did not suffice. What statistical analysis of this sort can at best show is the extent to which the actions of the other banks made it incumbent upon the Bank to exercise what powers of control it had, and in what degree and with what measure of success it did exercise them. Even such questions cannot be answered by a simple comparison of the short-term fluctuations of the two types of note issues. The Bank of England could have been wholly responsible for initiating and maintaining an inflationary trend during the period as a whole, while wholly irreproachable in its manner of dealing with short-term fluctuations about this trend. Allowance must be made, furthermore, for the changes in the areas of circulation of the two currencies and in the volume of trade and in the velocities of circulation in the two areas, and for the effects of the occasional collapses of the country bank circulation owing to discredit, before much can be learned from such comparison. These difficulties are disregarded by Silberling and Angell. But let us suppose them successfully surmounted. What then could be learned from a comparison of the fluctuations in the two types of issues?

The Bank of England could have followed any one of three alternative lines of policy with respect to the relationship between its own issues and those of the country banks, which can be distinguished as (1) regulatory, (2) passive or indifferent, and (3) sympathetic. If it followed a regulatory policy, this should show itself in a negative correlation between the fluctuations in the two types of issues, with the changes in the Bank's issues lagging behind those of the country banks. If the Bank took a passive or indifferent attitude toward the operations of the country banks, there should be no marked correlation, positive or negative, unless:

maintained its issue, there would tend to result an increase of Bank of England note circulation *within the area of circulation remaining to it.* Cf. Lord King, *Thoughts on the effects of the Bank restrictions,* 2d ed., 1804, pp. 102-5.

(a) the country banks, either from policy or from necessity, followed the Bank of England, when there should be a positive correlation between the fluctuations in the two types of issues, with the changes in the country issues lagging after the changes in the Bank issues; or (b), both the Bank and the country banks responded to the same factors in the general situation pulling for credit expansion or contraction, when there should be positive correlation between the fluctuations in the two types of issues, with the existence and the character of a lag depending on the time-order in which London and the provinces, respectively, felt the stimuli to expansion or contraction and the rapidity with which they responded to such stimuli. Finally, if the Bank followed a sympathetic policy, there should be positive correlation between the changes in the two types of issues, but with the changes in the Bank of England issues lagging after the changes in the country bank issues. This does not, of course, exhaust the range of possible relationships, since the types of relationship distinguished above need not in practice have been mutually exclusive, but could have been present in varied and varying combinations.

From his examination of the statistical data Silberling concludes that "the quarterly cyclical fluctuations in the country notes preceded . . . the discounts of the Bank of England (a much more accurate measure of accommodation than their notes)."[29] If this were the case, it would indicate that the Bank of England either had followed the "sympathetic" policy toward country bank issues, surely the least defensible of all if it was its function to keep the currency in order, or had had no policy at all but had reacted in the same way as the country banks, but more slowly, to the forces operating in the country at large to bring about a currency inflation. Silberling nevertheless presents this conclusion as an important element in his exoneration of the Bank from blame.

Angell, using Silberling's data, finds that the Bank of England note circulation "was a comparatively stable element" and that

---

[29] "Financial and monetary policy," *loc. cit.*, p. 420, note; "British prices and business cycles," *loc. cit.*, p. 243. If bank notes are rejected as a suitable measure of the "accommodation" granted by the Bank of England, they should be rejected also for the country banks.

"the great element of fluctuation in the volume of currency was, rather, the issues of the country banks. These issues usually expanded greatly before and during a rise in prices, while they contracted even more abruptly before and during a fall,"[30] i.e., the Bank of England followed a passive policy.

The statistical conclusions of both writers rest, unfortunately, on faulty data with respect to the country bank note circulation. There was no record of the actual amounts of notes issued, but the notes had to carry tax stamps, and all contemporary estimates were based on the official statistics of the tax stamps sold by the government, and on the estimated average life of the notes. Country bank notes were subject to tax only upon their original issue. Subject to some complex qualifications, prior to 1810 these notes could not be reissued after three years from the date of their original issue. This limitation was removed in 1810, on the assumption that on the average the notes would, because of wear and tear, have a life of about three years. If the notes could be presumed to last, prior to 1810, on the average for three years, if after 1810 all the notes could be presumed to last for the full three years, and if the country banks always succeeded in maintaining in circulation the full amount of notes for which they had purchased stamps, then the circulation at the beginning of any quarter would be equal to the amount of notes for which stamps had been sold during the preceding twelve quarters. There was no available mode of estimating the circulation which did not necessitate making doubtful assumptions of this kind.[31] Silberling's estimate of country bank note circulation, which Angell also uses, has, moreover, a special and catastrophic defect of its own. It consists merely of the amount, for each quarter, of £1 and £5 notes for which stamps had been sold in such quarter, *arbitrarily multiplied by ten,* i.e., with the decimal point moved one place to the

---

[30] *Theory of international prices,* p. 486.

[31] The country banks would always have to keep on hand some of their notes as till money or awaiting the possibility of their issue. The notes of banks which failed or suspended payments or for other reasons ceased to issue would be withdrawn before three years from the date of their original issue had elapsed. There were still other obstacles to making reliable estimates of the country bank note circulation from the statistics of stamp sales. Cf. the testimony of J. Sedgwick, Chairman of the Board of Stamps, *Report by the Lords Committee [on] resumption of cash payments,* 1819, appendix F, 7, pp. 408-15.

right, presumably as the result of an error in copying.[32] It bears no resemblance in its fluctuations to the other available estimates of country bank note circulation, as the following table shows:

TABLE II

Estimates of Country Bank Note Circulation for Specified Quarters

(In Millions of Pounds)

Third quarter of year	Based on aggregate sales of stamps during preceding twelve quarters[a]	Sedgwick's estimate[b]	Silberling's series[c]
1807.............	19.7		11.0
1808.............	17.5		14.9
1809.............	20.6	17.0	23.1
1810.............	22.9	21.8	13.1
1811.............	23.1	21.5	18.7
1812.............	19.2	19.9	15.3
1813.............	20.5	22.6	17.5
1814.............	22.1	22.7	14.5
1815.............	20.8	19.0	9.0

ᵃ *Report by Lords Committee* [on] *resumption of cash payments,* 1819, appendix F. 1, p. 396 (£1 and £5 notes only).

ᵇ *Ibid.,* appendix F. 8, pp. 408–15; based on assumption that in any given year there would be in circulation all the notes for which stamps had been sold during that year, two-thirds of the notes for which stamps had been sold in the preceding year, and one-third of the notes for which stamps had been sold in the next preceding year. (*All* notes.)

ᶜ Silberling, "British prices and business cycles," *loc. cit.,* p. 258 (£1 and £5 notes only).

Silberling claims for his series that "since this stamp duty involved expense to the issuing bankers, it is wholly probable that

---

[32] The following data for quarters chosen at random show adequately the nature of Silberling's series:

(1) First quarter	(2) Number of £1 notes stamped during quarter[a]	(3) Number of £5 notes stamped during quarter[a]	(4) Total value of £1 and £5 notes stamped during quarter[b]	(5) Silberling's series, millions of £[c]
1811.........	472,075	122,399	£1,084,070	10.8
1814.........	946,174	137,712	1,634,734	16.4
1818.........	954,268	217,383	2,041,183	20.4

ᵃ *Report of* [Commons] *Committee on resumption of cash payments,* 1819, appendix 32, p. 330.

ᵇ Column 2 + (5 × column 3).

ᶜ Silberling, "British prices and business cycles," *loc. cit.,* p. 258.

the volume of notes stamped each quarter affords a safe index, at any rate, of the variability of the actual issues."[33] But Silberling overlooks that the amount of stamps issued each quarter indicates at best only the amount of *new* notes which were issued during that quarter. Since it gives no indication of the amounts of *old* notes which went out of circulation during that quarter, it is a wholly unreliable index of the *net* change during the quarter in country bank note circulation. Silberling's series, as its method of compilation would lead one to expect, shows much greater quarter-to-quarter and year-to-year variability than do the other available estimates of country bank note circulation. These last do not indicate any appreciably greater instability in country bank note than in Bank of England note circulation. But even these other estimates are probably too defective to warrant any confidence on conclusions based on their use.[34]

x. Responsibility for Excess Issue: The Credit Policy of the Bank of England

Silberling finds other statistical evidence of the high quality of the Bank of England's management of its affairs during the Restriction: "the Bank's loans to the State tended to expand when discounts were moderate, and vice versa. In other words, the Bank granted accommodation to the government during the war rather sparingly and according to the state of their mercantile accounts. They put the business interests foremost and assumed a primary responsibility for the maintenance of British trade and industry, which, in an essentially commercial war, was of vast consequence."[1] But as can be seen from chart II and table III, all that the data show is that there was somewhat of an inverse correlation between the short-run changes in commercial discounts and advances to the government. As they stand, the data will equally well support the conclusion that commerce got only what was left after the government's demands had been satisfied. An even more plausible explanation of the inverse correlation between commercial discounts and advances to government, because it does not involve the attribution to the Bank of England

---

[33] "British prices and busines cycles," *loc. cit.,* pp. 242-43.

[34] Cf. Tooke, *A history of prices,* II (1838), 130-31.

[1] Silberling, "Financial and monetary policy," *loc. cit.,* p. 420, note.

of any consistent regulatory policy, is that advances to the government supplied commerce with funds as effectively as, though less directly than, commercial discounts. When the government borrowed freely from the Bank, the borrowed funds flowed into commerce and consequently lessened the demand of businessmen for discounts.[2] But while Silberling here praises the Bank for giv-

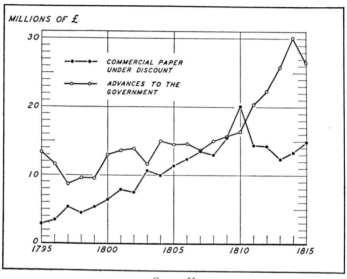

CHART II

ing commerce a preference over the government, and for treating the latter only as a residual claimant for credit, he later attacks the bullionists for their alleged failure to recognize the extent to which the Bank's expansion of its credit was due to the demands made upon it by the government.[3]

Angell, from the same data, derives a substantially different defense of the Bank's operations. Instead of finding that the Bank treated the government as a residual borrower, he claims,

---

[2] Officers of the Bank testified before the Commons Committee of 1819 that when the advances to the government were large, the demand for commercial discounts was generally small. (*Reports from the Secret Committee on the expediency of the Bank resuming cash payments,* 1819, pp. 27, 143.)

[3] "Financial and monetary policy," *loc. cit.,* pp. 425-27.

TABLE III (data of Chart II)

COMMERCIAL DISCOUNTS AND ADVANCES TO THE GOVERNMENT BY THE BANK OF
ENGLAND, 1795–1815

(In Millions of Pounds)

Year	Commercial paper under discount[a]	Advances to the government[b]
1795	2.9	13.3
1796	3.5	11.6
1797	5.4	8.7
1798	4.5	9.6
1799	5.4	9.5
1800	6.4	13.0
1801	7.9	13.6
1802	7.5	13.9
1803	10.7	11.6
1804	10.0	15.0
1805	11.4	14.5
1806	12.4	14.6
1807	13.5	13.7
1808	13.0	15.0
1809	15.5	15.7
1810	20.1	16.4
1811	14.4	20.4
1812	14.3	22.3
1813	12.3	25.8
1814	13.3	30.1
1815	14.9	26.5

[a] *Report from the [Commons] Committee . . . on the Bank of England charter,* 1832, appendix no.
59, p. 54.
[b] *Reports by the Lords Committee . . . [on] the expediency of the resumption of cash payments,*
1819, appendix A. 5, p. 309. (Yearly averages of returns for February and August of each year.)

probably justly,[4] that the Bank was not a free agent in deciding
the amount of credit it should grant to the government, and
concludes, from his analysis of the data, that the Bank in its
commercial discounts, "that part of the credit extensions over
which it had independent control," exercised "a moderating policy,
of restraint in boom times and of assistance in stringency. . . .
The Bank of England, in so far as its independent and uncontrolled loan-extensions were concerned, was largely blameless."[5]

[4] Cf. Chancellor of the Exchequer Vansittart, Hansard, *Parliamentary debates,* 1st series, XXIV (Dec. 8, 1812), 230: "the enormous profits of the
Bank had also been dwelt upon: to this he would bear testimony, that the
Bank was an unwilling party to those measures whence the profits accrued,
and which were forced upon it by the government of the country."
[5] *Theory of international prices,* p. 486.

What inverse correlation there was between the commercial discounts of the Bank and its advances to the government is consistent, in the absence of additional information, with a wide variety of interpretations of the credit policy of the Bank. All that can reasonably be inferred from the available data, statistical and non-statistical, with respect to the operations of the Bank is that during the Restriction period the Bank increased both its advances to the government and its commercial discounts substantially, that the increase in its commercial discounts was proportionately much greater than the increase in its advances to the government, that rising premiums on bullion, falling exchanges, and rising prices all failed to act as a check on the expansion by the Bank of its credit facilities of all types, and that the Bank directors told the truth when they insisted repeatedly that they followed no clearly-defined rule or principle in regulating their discounts except insistence that the commercial paper discounted should be "sound" and of short maturities. That the depreciation was, on modern, less exigent standards, only moderate, seems to have been due much more to the fact that the 5 per cent discount rate had become traditional and therefore was not lowered than to deliberate policy of the Bank. Even if it be granted that the Bank of England exercised a stabilizing influence, the evidence is lacking that it did so deliberately and as a matter of policy, and the record as to the premiums on bullion, the fall of the exchanges, and the rise of prices, demonstrates that it did not exercise it sufficiently, if these phenomena are regarded, as all the bullionists regarded them, as highly undesirable.

There is substantial ground for accepting Angell's plea in defense of the Bank's advances to the government that the Bank with respect to these was not a free agent. It nevertheless had much greater scope for regulating the currency through control of its commercial discounts than it made use of. Ample facilities for direct credit to private business had developed during this period outside the Bank of England both in London and in the provinces, and it is by no means clear that there was any longer any urgent need, as far as the nation's commerce and industry were concerned, for the Bank to grant any genuinely "commercial" discounts at all. Its "commercial discounts" increased, however, from 6.3 millions in 1800 to 15.3 millions in 1809 and

19.5 millions in 1810,[6] amounts which were never again reached until after 1914! The proportion of the Bank's commercial discounts to its total advances increased, from an average of approximately 25 per cent during the years 1794 to 1796 inclusive, to 33 per cent for 1797 to 1800, 42 per cent from 1801 to 1805, 50 per cent from 1806 to 1810, and 36 per cent from 1811 to 1815;[7] in 1820, after resumption, it fell to 19 per cent, a level which it appears barely to have maintained during the 1820's.[8]

Even these percentages apparently minimize the extent to which the Bank's expansion of its credit facilities provided funds for use by private industry rather than by government. The government during the Restriction kept a large proportion of the advances to it by the Bank, for the years 1807 to 1816 exceeding 50 per cent on the average,[9] on deposit with the Bank, presumably as an emergency reserve. The commercial discounts, on the other hand, were in the main drawn out immediately in cash, and the private deposits at the Bank of England during the same period averaged under 12 per cent of the commercial discounts.[10] It is likely, therefore, that the funds resulting from the commercial discounts had a greater velocity of circulation and consequently, *pro rata,* a greater influence on the level of prices, than the advances to the government.

Angell makes some attempt to determine the responsibility of price inflation in England for the fall in the exchanges and the premium on bullion by a comparison of their fluctuations with the fluctuations in the English price level, as shown by Silberling's index number of English prices for the period, but with admittedly inconclusive results.[11] Such a comparison is by its

---

[6] Some of the increase in "commercial discounts" may have been in rediscounts for London bankers, and some of it consisted undoubtedly of advances to subscribers to new issues of government stock, rather than of commercial discounts proper.

[7] Cf. Angell, *Theory of international prices,* p. 498, col. 15. Angell comments that "these percentages are on the whole surprisingly low" (*Ibid.,* p. 502) but does not indicate what his criterion of "lowness" is.

[8] Cf. the statistics of public and private securities held by the Bank, given in the *Report on the Bank of England charter,* 1832, appendix no. 5, pp. 13-25.

[9] Cf. *ibid.,* appendix no. 24, p. 35; appendix no. 5, pp. 13 ff.

[10] *Ibid.,* appendix no. 32, p. 41; appendix no. 5, pp. 13 ff.

[11] *Theory of international prices,* p. 484. Angell says, in this connection, that "contrary to the opinion of most contemporary writers, neither the specie premium nor the rise in the foreign exchanges were correct measures of the depreciation, if this last be measured by commodity prices. Both were much

nature without significance. Even a comparison of the fluctuations in the exchange rates with the *relative* fluctuations of English to foreign price levels would not yield conclusive results unless there was very marked agreement or disagreement in the fluctuations.[12]

That resort to price inflation is necessary if a great war is to be financed seems to Silberling so axiomatic that without argument he makes their failure to acknowledge this one of the most heavily stressed counts in his indictment of the bullionists.[13] There is no need to debate this issue here, but several considerations of which the bullionists were aware call for notice. Contemporary writers pointed out that England had financed successfully the Seven Years' War and the American War, both of which involved fairly comparable financial strain, without resort to price inflation involving serious depreciation of the currency in terms of bullion. Napoleon financed his side of the war on a strictly metallic currency basis. There was, moreover, a substantial rise in English prices even in terms of gold and silver, and England could, therefore, have had a substantial inflation even if she had remained on the gold standard.

---

too low." Since the bullionists did not in fact measure depreciation by the trend of English commodity prices, and the anti-bullionists either denied its existence or claimed that the premium on bullion and the fall in the exchanges *exaggerated* the extent of the depreciation, this passage is not easy to understand.

[12] Although Silberling's index number is a valuable contribution, it would not be satisfactory for this purpose even if a comparable Continental index number were available. Of the 35 commodities from whose prices the index is computed, only 11 are classed by Silberling as British commodities—including copper plates (or cakes or sheets) and tin blocks, essentially import commodities?—and none of these is a substantially fabricated commodity. ("British prices and business cycles," *loc. cit.*, p. 299.) For such comparisons, it is the relative trends of the prices of "domestic commodities" which are most significant. See *infra*, p. 385.

[13] Silberling's emphasis on the desirability of inflation under the then existing circumstances makes it hard to explain his anxiety to free the Bank of England from the charge that it was mainly responsible for bringing it about.

Chapter IV

THE BULLIONIST CONTROVERSIES:
II. THE DEFLATION PHASE

The guinea was made for man, and not man for the guinea.
—Thomas Attwood, A letter on the creation of money, 1817, p. 95.

I. THE RESUMPTION OF CASH PAYMENTS

The Bullion Report, which advocated resumption of cash payments at the old par within two years, was presented to Parliament on June 8, 1810, but was not taken up for discussion until July of the following year. In the latter part of 1810 there began a marked depression, the result largely of a collapse of the boom in the export trade which had followed the opening of Latin America to British trade. This depression continued into 1811, and was accompanied by the suspension of many country banks and by credit stringency. To relieve the situation the government, in March, 1811, issued £6,000,000 in exchequer bills to merchants on the security of commodities, in order to provide the merchants with acceptable paper for discount at the Bank of England or at other banks.[1] In the meantime the premium on bullion had been rising, and was not to reach its peak until 1813 for gold and 1814 for silver. These circumstances tended to strengthen the opposition to an early resumption of cash payments, and in the parliamentary session of 1811 the Horner resolutions embodying the conclusions of the Bullion Report were defeated by large majorities.

In 1813 and 1814 commerce and industry were in a prosperous state, and as the termination of hostilities impended the price of bullion began to fall. Napoleon's return from Elba and the resumption of hostilities in 1815 resulted in a rise of the premium

---

[1] The government had used this expedient to alleviate a credit stringency at least twice before, in 1782 and 1792.

on bullion, but a financial crisis, and a fall in prices and in the premiums on gold and silver, followed the definitive defeat of Napoleon at Waterloo.

These rapid changes within a few years in the fortunes of the paper pound appear to have converted many influential persons to the desirability of a return to a metallic standard. In 1816 the government enacted measures preparatory to a return to the gold standard at the old par. Silver coins were definitely relegated to a subsidiary status, thus completing the legal progress toward a monometallic gold standard begun in 1774. It was provided also that the authorization, by the Act of 1797 and later continuing legislation, of the issue of bank notes of smaller denominations than £5, should terminate within two years after the resumption of cash payments. But the government continued to refuse to obligate the Bank of England to resume cash payments, and both government and Bank were obviously waiting for the course of events to disclose the auspicious occasion for resumption. In 1816 gold fell to little above its mint price, and the Bank bought quantities of it at the market price and had it coined at a loss. In January, 1817, on its own initiative, it began partial resumption at the old par, giving gold upon demand for certain categories of its notes, under the authority of a provision in the Restriction Act of 1797 permitting the banks to pay notes under £5 in cash. But the exchanges soon after turned against England, with a resultant drain on the Bank's newly replenished gold reserves, and early in 1819 Parliament, at the suggestion of the newly-appointed committee referred to below, forbade the Bank to redeem any of its notes in gold.

Promises having been made on five different occasions of eventual resumption of cash payments, the House of Commons finally, in 1819, appointed a committee, under the chairmanship of Robert Peel the younger, to inquire into the expediency of the resumption of cash payments. A similar committee was appointed by the House of Lords. The House Committee, after hearing testimony of witnesses who, with one exception, were all favorable to resumption, recommended resumption with only one dissenting vote. In its report it took the desirability of resumption at the old par for granted, and confined itself to recommendations as to the time and manner of resumption. It recommended a gradual return to cash payments at the old standard, along lines which Ricardo had proposed. The government left the decision to the House, which, after but little debate, passed the Act of July 2, 1819, repealing the ancient restrictions on the export of coin and bullion and requiring the Bank to pay its notes in gold bars of a minimum weight of 60 oz. each, at rates per standard ounce which were to attain, by graduated stages, the old rate of £3. 17 s. 10½ d. per ounce by not later than May 1, 1821; after May 1, 1822, the Bank could pay its notes in gold coin or in ingots upon demand as it chose.

The price of gold fell to the mint price almost immediately, the exchanges turned in favor of England, and gold began to flow into the Bank. There was no demand whatsoever for the gold bars, and early in 1821 an act was passed, at the request of the Bank, which did not like the ingot plan, permitting it to cash its notes in gold *coin* after May 1, 1821.[2]

From 1816 on, there was a long period of economic distress, although with short intervals of prosperity. There had been voices raised before resumption, warning that it would bring evil consequences.[3] Once it was in effect, many persons attributed the distress to it, and there arose an extensive controversy over the expediency of the resumption and of the manner and occasion of bringing it about, which was actively to persist for many years, and was in fact not completely to end until after the middle of

[2] For more detailed accounts, see A. E. Feavearyear, *The pound sterling: a history of English money,* 1931, chap. ix; A. W. Acworth, *Financial reconstruction in England 1815-1822,* 1925, chap. vi.

[3] Thomas Attwood in particular protested vigorously against the casual manner in which what he regarded as the main question, i.e., whether there should be a metallic standard, and if so at what par, was answered by the Committees, and he predicted that the deflation necessary if return was made to the old par would not be as easily borne as the Committees supposed. "It is extraordinary," he exclaimed, ". . . to observe the coolness with which the Committees speak about the Bank of England, and country bankers, having sufficient time 'to call in their accommodations.' . . . 'To call in accommodations,' may be sport to them, and to the bankers, but it is death to the public. I wish that the Committees were to spend twelve months in a banking house, during the period of a general 'calling in of accommodations.' They would get more knowledge of human life, and of its ways and means, in that short period, than is to be learnt in all the books that ever were written from the beginning of the world." He pointed out that general liquidation was a much more serious proposition than liquidation by a single bank. (*A letter to the Earl of Liverpool, on the reports of the committees,* 1819, pp. 34 ff. Cf. also *ibid., A second letter . . . on the bank reports,* 1819.)

the century there occurred a reversal in the hitherto downward trend of the price level.

II. RESPONSIBILITY OF RESUMPTION FOR THE FALL IN PRICES

From a peak according to Silberling's index of 198 in 1814, the English price level fell to 136 in 1819, to 114 in 1822, to 106 in 1824, and to 93 in 1830. Ricardo had predicted that resumption would bring about a fall in prices not greater than the then prevailing premium on gold, or from 3 to 8 per cent.[1] After the event Ricardo conceded that resumption had probably caused a greater fall in prices than he had anticipated. He still contended, however, that if resumption had been managed in accordance with the plan which he had proposed, it would not have caused a greater fall in prices than 5 per cent. If resumption had actually caused a fall in prices greater than this it was because the Bank of England had so mismanaged the resumption as unnecessarily to bring about a rise in the world value of gold.[2] He held that there was no certain way of determining how much of the increase in the world value of gold was due to this mismanagement and how much to other causes, but he accepted as a plausible guess Tooke's estimate of 5 per cent as the additional fall in English prices resulting from the mismanagement of the Bank.[3] This would make the total reduction in English prices which according to Ricardo could be attributed to the resumption some 8 to 13 per cent, with the remainder of the fall attributable to other causes operating simultaneously to raise the world value of gold. At other times, however, Ricardo assigned to the Bank's mismanagement responsibility for a greater portion of the deflation of prices than Tooke's estimate would indicate.[4] In the absence of any index numbers, he could have had only a vague

---

[1] In testimony before the Commons Committee, March 4, 1819, 5 to 6 per cent (*Reports from the Secret Committee on the expediency of the Bank resuming cash payments,* 1819, p. 137; in testimony before the Lords Committee, March 26, 1819, 8 per cent (*Reports respecting the Bank of England resuming cash payments,* 1819, p. 202) ; in the House of Commons, May 24, 1819, 3 per cent (Hansard, *Parliamentary debates,* 1st series, XL, 743).

[2] Hansard, *Parliamentary debates,* 2d series, VII (June 12, 1822), 939 ff.

[3] *On protection to agriculture* [1822], *Works,* p. 470.

[4] Cf. Ricardo to Malthus, July 9, 1821: "Almost the whole of the pressure has arisen from the increased value which their [i.e., the Bank's] operations have given to the standard itself." *Letters of Ricardo to Malthus,* p. 185.

idea as to the extent of the fall in the price level which had occurred, and he seems to have seriously underestimated it.

In his ardent defense of resumption in principle, and also, though to a lesser extent, in his criticism of the management of resumption by the Bank, Ricardo occupied a somewhat isolated position. In the face of the depression which followed resumption, defenders of the resumption were few and these tended to rest their defense on the claim that a metallic standard of some sort was desirable, without undertaking to justify the restoration of the old par or to blame the Bank for the evils which they admitted had resulted from resumption as it had actually been brought into effect. Of the ardent bullionists who during the inflation period had insisted upon the desirability of a return to the metallic standard, some were now dead, or inactive as far as the currency controversy was concerned; and others, such as Wheatley and Lauderdale, when faced with falling prices, lost their earlier enthusiasm for a return to the metallic standard at the old par. Even so ardent a disciple of Ricardo as McCulloch thought that the return to cash payments at the old par had been a mistake. Much later in the century the Resumption Act of 1819 came to be generally regarded as a great achievement of economic statesmanship, but the economic distress which had followed it and the extensive literature of protest and criticism to which it gave rise had by then been largely forgotten.[5]

Ricardo, however, had given more hostages to fortune than the other bullionists. Not only had he been still active in 1819 in advocating resumption at the old par, when other bullionists had become silent or had advised devaluation, but he alone, or almost so, among the bullionists had insisted that the premium on bullion was a *measure* of the extent to which the suspension of cash payments had been responsible for the rise in English prices, and therefore he alone was now bound, if he were to be consistent, to maintain that it would also be a measure of the extent to which resumption of cash payments at the old par would lower prices. The other bullionists had not committed themselves to any quantitative estimate of the inflationary effect of suspension of cash

---

[5] Feaveryear's statement that "all the best-known writers of the nineteenth century praised the settlement of 1819 by which, after the currency inflation of the Napoleonic period, the old standard was restored" (*The pound sterling*, p. 137), if true at all, is true only for the second half of the century.

payments. They were now free to reject Ricardo's measure of the deflationary effect of resumption.[6]

It was later frequently alleged, mainly on the evidence of Heygate, a vigorous opponent in Parliament of the Resumption Act, that Ricardo, shortly before his death in 1823, had admitted to friends that he had been wrong in forecasting that resumption would cause a fall in prices of only 5 per cent.[7] This, however, seems doubtful. Ricardo, as we have seen, openly admitted that resumption, as actually carried out, had resulted in a greater fall of prices than 5 per cent, but he continued to deny, apparently to the end, that this greater fall had been an inevitable result of resumption.[8] When Ricardo stated that resumption would *cause* a fall of 5 per cent in English prices, he did not mean that resumption might not be *followed by* a much greater fall in prices. Other factors might well be operating simultaneously, but independently, to lower prices. Ricardo, moreover, when forecasting in 1819 the effect of resumption on prices, assumed proper management of the resumption,[9] and he always had reference to the level of prices and the premium on gold as they were in 1819, and not, as did some of his later critics, to the higher

---

[6] Cf. Mathias Attwood, *Letter to Lord Hamilton on alterations in the value of money,* 1823, p. 26: "The discussion of 1811 turned wholly on the question, whether any depreciation of money did or did not exist? The discussion of the present day is as to what was the extent of that depreciation."

[7] Cf. e.g., William Ward, *Remarks on the commercial legislation of 1846,* as cited in *The currency question,* 2d ed. (1847?), p. 20: "Now Mr. Ricardo lived to change this opinion, and shortly before he died expressed that he had done so; the late Sir W. Heygate was with him, and he said, 'Ay, Heygate, you and the few others who opposed us on the cash payments have proved right. I said that the difference at most would be only five per cent, and you said that at the least it would be twenty-five per cent.'" Cf. also Sir James Graham, *Corn and currency,* 4th ed., 1827, p. 39.

[8] It appears, therefore, that in the following passage, Porter goes too far in his denial of any change in Ricardo's opinion as to the effect of the resumption on prices: ". . . Mr. David Ricardo has been repeatedly held up as having recanted the opinion expressed by him, that the fall in prices to be brought about by returning to a metallic standard would be no more than the difference between the market and the mint prices of gold, which at the passing of Mr. Peel's Bill did not exceed 4 per cent. There is, in truth, no warrant whatever for this assertion, which, like many other figments, has been repeated until it has acquired the authority of truth." (George R. Porter, *Progress of the nation,* 1851 ed., p. 418.)

[9] Cf. Ricardo, in Hansard, *Parliamentary debates,* 2d series, VII (June 12, 1822), 944: ". . . his plan had not been adopted, and yet to it was referred the consequences which were distinct from it. . . ."

prices and higher premiums of the preceding years.[10] Ricardo had been charged during the inflation period with exaggerating the extent of the depreciation of paper and of the rise in prices. He was now to be charged, sometimes by the same persons, with minimizing the extent to which paper had been depreciated and therefore also the extent to which resumption had been responsible for the fall in prices which followed it.[11]

Ricardo had proposed that convertibility should be restored in terms of ingots of bullion instead of coin, and that the actual circulating currency should consist wholly of paper. In this way a metallic standard could be reestablished with a minimum drain on the world's supply of gold, and therefore with a minimum appreciation of the world value of gold.[12] The Bank, however, was unwilling to follow this plan and instead engaged in what Ricardo regarded as an unnecessary contraction of credit and accumulation of gold, thus raising its world value and forcing additional deflation of English commodity prices. Ricardo believed that if the Bank had acted in accordance with his plan it would not have found it necessary to add to the stock of gold which it already had in 1819: "There was nothing in the plan which could cause a rise in the value of gold, for no additional quantity of gold would have been required."[13] This alleged mis-

---

[10] Cf. *ibid.*, 945: ". . . to Mr. Peel's bill could only be imputed the alteration which had taken place in the currency between 1819 and the present period."

[11] Cf. Ricardo, *On protection to agriculture* [1822], *Works*, p. 467: "I believe it will be found, that many of those who contended, during the war, that our money was not depreciated at all, now endeavor to show that the depreciation was then enormous, and that all the distresses which we are now suffering have arisen from restoring our currency from a depreciated state to par." Cf. also Huskisson, in the House of Commons, Feb. 15, 1822 (Hansard, *Parliamentary debates*, 2d series, VI, 428): ". . . it is rather curious that the new converts, those who stoutly denied depreciation when it most glaringly existed, should now be the most strenuous to exaggerate the extent to which it was then carried."

[12] Ricardo's first suggestion of this plan was made in 1811. (*High price of bullion*, appendix to 4th ed., 1811, *Works*, pp. 300-01.) He developed it further in *Proposals for an economical and secure currency*, 1816, and advocated it before the Parliamentary Committees of 1819. On the history of the plan, see James Bonar, "Ricardo's Ingot Plan," *Economic journal*, XXXIII (1923), 281-304, and A. W. Acworth, *Financial reconstruction in England 1815-1822,* 1925, chap. vii.

[13] *On protection to agriculture* [1822], *Works*, p. 468. In February, 1819, the Bank held £4,200,000 of bullion; in August, 1819, £3,600,000. By February,

management of resumption by the Bank aroused strong feeling on the part of Ricardo.[14]

Table IV presents some statistical data on the operations of the Bank during the critical years of preparation for and actual establishment of cash payments. They appear in general to lend confirmation to Ricardo's criticism. But although the Bank's holdings of bullion increased greatly after 1819, they had been unusually low in that year. It is difficult to find a basis for an estimate of what would have been a conservatively safe gold reserve for the Bank at that time, in the absence of data as to the extent of the credit superstructure for which the Bank's bullion holdings were the base. If we use the ratio of its gold holdings to its own total demand liabilities as a measure of the status of the Bank's gold reserves, it would seem fairly clear that from 1821 to 1825 the Bank maintained larger reserves than were necessary. But with reserves at their peak in 1825, the Bank barely managed to survive the crisis of 1826 without suspension of cash payments. Even if the Bank's difficulties in 1826 were due to inexcusably reckless credit expansion on its part, the rapidity and the extent of the drain on its bullion reserves demonstrated that large reserves were necessary, given the quality of the Bank's management and the nervous state of public opinion with respect to the solidity of the paper circulation in times of financial strain. Information is lacking as to what the Bank's motives were in accumulating gold and in pushing it out into circulation, but one consideration seems to have been its desire

---

1821, the Bank had increased its bullion holdings to £11,900,000. (*Report . . . on the Bank of England charter, 1832*, appendix no. 5, pp. 13 ff.) In August, 1822, the bullion holdings of the Bank had fallen to £10,100,000. The Bank had meanwhile been using the permission granted to it in 1821 to pay out coin instead of bullion for notes, and had been actively withdrawing its small notes from circulation. Of the gold so paid out a large part, therefore, must have gone into English circulation in substitution for the canceled paper, and was thus withdrawn from the world supply. Ricardo in 1819 had advised the Bank not to buy bullion, but boldly to sell.—Hansard, *Parliamentary debates,* 2d series, VII (1822), 939.

[14] Cf. Ricardo to Malthus, July 9, 1821: "I very much regret that in the great change we have made from an unregulated currency to one regulated by a fixed standard we had not more able men to manage it than the present Bank directors. If their object had been to make the revulsion as oppressive as possible, they could not have pursued measures more calculated to make it so than those which they have actually pursued. . . . They are indeed a very ignorant set." *Letters of Ricardo to Malthus,* pp. 184-85.

TABLE IV

PRICE LEVEL AND BANK OF ENGLAND ACTIVITIES, 1810–1830

Year	Price level[a]	Total advances[b]	Note circulation[c]	Deposits[c]	Bullion[c]	Reserve ratio[d]
	(1790 = 100)	In Millions of Pounds				Per Cent
1810.........	176	35.7	22.9	13.1	3.4	9.4
1811.........	158	33.9	23.4	11.3	3.3	9.5
1812.........	163	36.4	23.2	11.8	3.1	8.9
1813.........	185	38.5	24.0	11.3	2.8	7.9
1814.........	198	42.9	26.6	13.7	2.2	5.5
1815.........	166	42.5	27.3	12.2	2.7	6.8
1816.........	135	34.6	26.9	12.2	6.1	15.6
1817.........	143	27.0	28.5	10.0	10.7	27.8
1818.........	150	29.0	27.0	8.0	8.3	23.7
1819.........	136	27.2	25.2	6.4	3.9	12.3
1820.........	124	22.2	23.9	4.3	6.6	23.4
1821.........	117	18.0	22.2	5.7	11.6	41.6
1822.........	114	17.1	18.1	5.6	10.6	44.7
1823.........	113	16.0	18.8	7.5	13.6	51.7
1824.........	106	14.8	19.9	10.0	12.8	42.8
1825.........	118	17.9	20.1	8.3	16.2	57.0
1826.........	103	17.6	23.6	7.1	4.7	15.3
1827.........	101	12.0	22.3	8.5	10.4	33.8
1828.........	97	10.8	21.7	9.7	10.4	33.1
1829.........	94	11.2	19.7	9.3	6.8	23.4
1830.........	93	10.6	20.8	11.2	10.2	31.9

[a] Silberling, "British Prices and Business Cycles, 1779–1850," *Review of economic statistics*, preliminary volume v (1923), supplement 2, pp. 232–33.

[b] *Ibid.*, p. 255. Simple averages of quarterly data.

[c] *Report from the [Commons] Committee . . . on the Bank of England charter*, 1832, appendix no. 5, pp. 13–25. Simple averages of data for two dates in each year.

[d] Percentage of bullion to sum of note circulation and deposits.

to rebut the charge that it was unduly concerned about its own profits.[15]

The Bank's abandonment of the bullion standard was more assuredly a mistake. The Bank, and other critics of Ricardo's plan, cited the absence of any immediate demand for ingots as a demonstration of its impracticability. But under the bullion standard, and in the absence of domestic gold hoarding, there could have been a demand for ingots only for industrial purposes and

[15] Cf. the testimony of William Ward, *Report . . . on the Bank of England charter*, 1832, *Minutes of evidence*, p. 143.

for export. The fact, therefore, that from 1819 to 1821, when the Bank was contracting its discounts, when paper was not at a discount, and when the exchanges were favorable, there was no demand for ingots, in no way reflected on the practicability or the desirability of the bullion standard. If the Bank had not withdrawn its small notes from circulation, there would have been no demand for *coin* or ingots.[16] The chief virtue of the ingot plan lay in the fact that at a time when the general return to metallic currencies was threatening to cause a price deflation, it would enable England to make her return to the gold standard with a minimum drain on the world supply of gold. It had the additional virtue that in times of depression, when there was still confidence in the paper currency but impaired confidence in the profitability of investment, the desire for cash liquidity could be met wholly in notes instead of in bullion, thus avoiding forced deflation by the Bank of England. It was open to the objection, however, that it would lessen the stabilizing influence of the pressure brought to bear on the Bank of England by an increase in active circulation during periods of credit expansion and of the leeway given to the Bank to expand credit in times of depression by the decline in active circulation and the consequent influx of gold to the Bank.

From February, 1819, to August, 1822, the Bank reduced its circulation of notes under £5 from £7,400,000 to £900,000, mostly by substituting gold coin for paper in circulation. This also was undoubtedly a mistake. In case of internal distrust, it was mostly the small notes which came back to the Bank for payment in gold, and these were therefore the part of the paper circulation which was most dangerous to the maintenance intact of the gold standard, and conservative opinion in England has always regarded notes of small denominations with misgivings. But the substitution of specie for paper could have been made more grad-

---

[16] Cf. the comment of "A country banker" in a letter printed in James Wilson, *Capital, currency, and banking,* 1845, p. 276:

When the ingot plan was put in practice, it became a dead letter, and for this plain and wholesome reason: the Bank of England had by contraction of her issues, raised the value of her paper to a par with gold, and the balance of trade being in our favor with foreign countries, not an ounce of gold was called for. Such, no doubt, would be the action of the ingot plan, were it now adopted; a dead letter when the exchanges were in our favor, and an effectual means of supplying gold when they came against us.

ual without serious risk. Some writers argued, further, that the gold standard could not be safely operated unless there was a secondary reserve of gold in the form of circulating coin from which external drains could be met,[17] but it is doubtful whether the Bank could ever draw in circulating gold quickly enough to serve as a means of meeting a severe external drain, and during an internal crisis in a country where gold circulates it is likely to be withdrawn from the banks into private hoards.

Samuel Turner, a director of the Bank of England at the time of the resumption, attempted to meet Ricardo's charge that the Bank after 1819 had added to the difficulties resulting from resumption by making excessive purchases of bullion by the argument that the Bank paid for the bullion in bank notes, and that in the absence of such purchase its owners would have taken the bullion to the mint to have it coined; the Bank's purchases therefore merely made the increase in circulation come more promptly than would have been the case if the holders of bullion had been obliged to wait until they could get coin in exchange for their bullion.[18] But the data in table III make it appear probable that the bullion would not have come to England at all if the Bank had not contracted its discounts and withdrawn its small notes, and that, instead of being exchanged at the Bank for notes, the bullion imports were used, directly or indirectly, to cancel indebtedness to the Bank and as a substitute circulating medium for notes. The Bank was not a purely passive agent, as its defenders claimed, but by maintaining its discount rate unchanged,[19] by sub-

---

[17] Cf. Erick Bollmann, *A letter to Thomas Brand, Esq., on the practicability and propriety of a resumption of specie payments*, 1819: "A specie bank, in a country destitute of a specie capital, seems to me a glaring misconception, falling little short of a downright absurdity" (p. 54). "To render the resumption of specie payments practicable and safe, the country must first be replaced in the situation in which it was previously to 1797; that is, it must be re-stocked with specie . . ." (p. 57). Cf. also, anon., *Observations on the reports of the committees*, 1819, pp. 49-50.

[18] Samuel Turner, *Considerations upon the agriculture, commerce, and manufactures of the British Empire*, 1822, p. 51. Cf. also, to the same effect, Thomas Tooke, *History of prices*, II (1838), 108. In an earlier publication, Turner had argued that there was no way in which the Bank could replenish its then depleted gold reserves except by purchase of gold at the market price with new issues of paper, thus further raising the premium on gold. (Samuel Turner, *A letter . . . with reference to the expediency of the resumption of cash payments*, 2d ed., 1819, p. 76.)

[19] Early in 1822 the Bank resisted pressure from the government to reduce its discount rate. Turner denied that the Bank in refusing to lower its discount

stituting specie for small notes, and by reducing its holdings of public securities, it was promoting deflation.

The government, however, must share responsibility with the Bank for any mistakes that were made in connection with the resumption of cash payments, at least prior to 1822. The Bank had been hostile to resumption in 1819, and embarked upon it only because compelled to do so. The Resumption Act had not been a government measure, but the government had not opposed it, and there is probably some basis for Mathias Attwood's charge[20] that the committee hearings of 1819 operated, whether intended to do so or not, to trap the opposition in Parliament to advocate measures which the government itself wished to have carried into effect, but for which it was reluctant to assume full responsibility. The committees and the government itself also yielded too readily, in spite of their misgivings,[21] to the Bank's insistence upon a drastic reduction of its floating debt to the Bank, a measure deflationary in its effect. The substitution of gold coin for small notes was made necessary by the provision in the Act of 1816 terminating the Bank's right to issue small notes two years after resumption of cash payments.[22] This provision received little or no mention when the Resumption Act was passed, and it has been suggested that its existence had been forgotten.[23] But the government was no doubt aware of its existence and in

---

rate below its traditional level of 5 per cent was promoting deflation. The fact that the market rate at the time was only 4 per cent proved, he thought, that there was no shortage of circulating medium. (*Considerations,* p. 52.) Ricardo also held that the Bank was not to be criticized for not lowering its discount rate. Ricardo apparently thought that open market operations in public securities were the proper means of regulating the amount of the Bank's note circulation. (See *infra,* p. 258.) The Bank rate of discount, he claimed, should always be kept equal with the market rate, and he apparently did not believe that a deviation of the Bank rate from the market rate, or of the Bank of England rate from that of the Banque de France, could affect the volume of circulation, the price level, or the international movement of gold. (*Protection to agriculture* [1822], *Works,* p. 474.) On June 20, 1822, however, the Bank finally gave way to parliamentary pressure and lowered its rate to 4 per cent, the first change in its rate since 1773.

[20] *Letter to Lord Hamilton,* 1823, p. 41.

[21] Cf. Hansard, *Parliamentary debates,* 1st series, XL (May 24, 1819), 687 ff.

[22] This was temporarily repealed in 1822, and finally reenacted in 1826, to take full effect in 1829.

[23] Cf. T. Joplin, *An analysis and history of the currency question,* 1832, p. 65: "Its existence had been forgotten, and was as unknown to the Ministers as to any other party. This is the only interpretation of the transaction . . . that can be given to it."

any case was alone responsible for it, and it was probably also due in part to pressure from the government that the Bank had built up its gold reserves by gold purchases even when gold was still at a premium.[24]

Whether Ricardo overestimated the influence on the world price of gold of the accumulation of bullion after 1819 by the Bank of England it seems impossible to determine. Mathias Attwood pointed out that Ricardo was not consistent in his treatment of inflation and of deflation. In accepting the premium on gold as an adequate measure of the rise in English prices caused by the suspension of cash payments, Ricardo in effect denied any importance to the inflationary influence on world gold prices of the release of a quantity of gold from English monetary use. "But if a purchase of bullion on the part of the Bank be capable of preventing bullion from falling, with an advance in the value of the currency, it must be equally clear, that a sale of bullion by the same body can prevent bullion from advancing along with a depreciation [i.e., in the value] of the currency."[25] It was Mathias Attwood's position, not that Ricardo was exaggerating the deflationary influence on prices of the Bank's accumulation of gold, but that, by virtue of his use of the premium on gold as a measure of the influence of the Bank's activities on prices, Ricardo had underestimated both the inflationary influence of suspension and the deflationary influence of resumption. Other writers maintained that, on the contrary, Ricardo was overestimating the deflationary influence on prices of the Bank's accumulation of gold, since even at their peak the bullion holdings of the Bank of England were only an insignificant fraction of the estimated world stock of gold and silver, and since much of the gold acquired by the Bank had probably come out of English hoards rather than from the stocks of other countries.[26] But the comparison should be between, on the one hand, the English absorption for monetary purposes of non-hoarded gold, *including the gold which went into English circulation through the agency of*

[24] Cf. the memorandum of Huskisson to Lord Liverpool, Feb. 4, 1819, in C. D. Yonge, *The life and administration of Robert Banks, second earl of Liverpool*, 1868, II, 382-83.

[25] *Letter to Lord Hamilton*, 1823, p. 36.

[26] Cf. Tooke, *History of prices*, II (1838), 131-43; McCulloch, *Historical sketch of the Bank of England*, 1831, pp. 26-27.

the Bank, and, on the other hand, not the world's *total* stocks of gold and silver, but the world's *monetary* stocks of gold and silver, but with greater emphasis on gold. The fact that the greater part of the world was then in fact, if not in law, on a silver standard basis makes it seem at least plausible that resumption as it was carried out involved a significant absorption of gold by England.

But whether or not Ricardo did exaggerate the deflationary effect of the English absorption of gold on world gold prices, he probably underestimated rather than overestimated the deflationary influence on *English* prices of the resumption of cash payments. In taking 1819 for his base year, Ricardo overlooked the probability that the mere anticipation of early resumption would depress prices, and that the fall in the premium on gold and the decline in prices from 1816 to 1819 were also therefore to be regarded as in part at least the consequence of the agitation for resumption. One writer, George Woods, had pointed out some time before that prices would not rise in full proportion to the increase in paper issue, the physical volume of trade remaining the same, if "speculators . . . invest their capital in bank paper . . . in anticipation of being ultimately paid in specie or bullion."[27] For the same reason prices could fall before actual resumption, the paper issues and the physical volume of trade remaining the same, if speculators were hoarding paper or dishoarding gold in anticipation of resumption. But Ricardo, like most of the writers of the period, paid little or no attention to the effects of speculative factors on the value of paper money in terms of bullion or of commodities. One writer claimed also that prior to the resumption of cash payments, mechanical inventions and the subsidy to labor from the poor rates had operated to keep the money costs and therefore the prices of export manufactures down and to increase the total volume of exports, and thus to give a temporarily high exchange value to the English currency,[28] but it is not clear that these factors ceased to operate, or operated in lesser degree, after 1819.

The defenders of the resumption were justified, however, in

---

[27] George Woods, *Observations on the present price of bullion,* 1811, p. 9. Cf. also, David Prentice, *Thoughts on the repeal of the Bank restriction law,* 1811, p. 50.

[28] Thomas Paget, *A letter . . . to David Ricardo . . . on the true principle of estimating the extent of the late depreciation in the currency,* 1822, p. 12.

denying that it had been responsible for all of the decline in prices which occurred after 1816, or even after 1819, especially as this decline continued until the 1850's.[29] Other countries which had been on a paper basis with inflated prices during the war returned to a metallic basis at old parities after its termination and therefore participated with England in the scramble for bullion, which was not available in sufficient quantities to support the existing price levels. The long-continued decline in the English price level after resumption is probably to be accounted for, moreover, by a failure, for the world as a whole, of the production of gold to keep pace with the growth of commerce and industry. The post-Napoleonic fall in prices appears not to have been confined to England, but to have been a world-wide phenomenon.

But whether or not the resumption of cash payments was causally responsible for part or all of the decline in the English price level, in resuming cash payments at the old par England was surrendering the means by which that downward trend could have been checked if not wholly avoided. This argument was at the basis of much of the criticism of the return to a metallic standard. Even Ricardo conceded that the Bank had some power to check a fall in prices, as long as its notes were inconvertible, which it did not have under a metallic standard, and that this was an advantage. But it was an advantage offset, according to him, by the disadvantages of an inconvertible currency.[30]

III. THE ECONOMIC EFFECT OF CHANGING PRICE LEVELS

There was general agreement at the time that changes in price levels resulted in arbitrary and inequitable redistribution of wealth

---

[29] Cf. Malthus, *The measure of value stated and illustrated,* 1823, pp. 67-68:
This rise . . . in the value of the currency has been by no means so considerable as those are inclined to make it, who would measure it by the fall of agricultural produce; nor is it so inconsiderable as those imagine who would measure it solely by the difference between paper and gold. But whether this difference is the whole of what can be fairly attributed to the Bank Restriction and the return to cash payments, or not, it may by no means be the whole change which has taken place in the value of the currency, when compared with an object which has not changed.

[30] "The Bank having the power to issue paper unchecked could certainly mitigate the inconvenience resulting from a sudden fall [of prices]. . . . When the Bank was unchecked, they had the power of arresting that reduction [of prices]; an advantage counterbalanced by other disadvantages." (Lords Committee, *Report,* 1819, p. 204.)

and income. There appeared, however, during this period some new arguments in support of the doctrine that falling prices had adverse effects on the *volume* of wealth and production which made them particularly undesirable, and that rising prices might bring advantages for production and wealth-accumulation to compensate for their inequitable influence on distribution. The general trend of these arguments was such as to constitute at least a partial defense of the wartime inflation and to strengthen the opposition to resumption at the old par. Whether by implication or expressly, these doctrines gave encouragement to the advocates of a national paper currency free from the limitations to which an international metallic currency was subject. To Ricardo these doctrines were for this as well as for other reasons unpalatable, and later "orthodox" economists, following in his path, tended to ignore or to ridicule them. They were, no doubt, carried to extreme and even absurd lengths. They represent, nevertheless, a substantial contribution to economic analysis which in later years had to be rediscovered.

According to Thomas Attwood, it was the lack of uniformity in a fall in prices which made it injurious:

> If prices were to fall suddenly, and generally, and equally, in all things, *and if it was well understood, that the amount of debts and obligations were to fall in the same proportion, at the same time,* it is possible that such a fall might take place without arresting consumption and production, and in that case it would neither be injurious or beneficial in any great degree, but when a fall of this kind takes place in an obscure and unknown way, first upon one article and then upon another, without any correspondent fall taking place upon debts and obligations, it has the effect of destroying all confidence in property, and all inducements to its production, or to the employment of laborers in any way.[1]

A contraction of the currency, on the other hand, was injurious because the rigidity of costs prevented it from being followed immediately by a reduction in prices. During the interval consumers, finding themselves possessed of reduced funds, would buy less physical quantities of goods. Workmen would thus lose employment, "until the action of intense misery upon their minds, and of general distress upon all, shall so far have reduced their

---

[1] *Prosperity Restored,* 1817, pp. 78-79. Italics in the original.

monied wages and expenses, as to reduce the price [of their product] . . . within the reduced monied means of the capitalist."[2]

Wheatley, abandoning his original views, now argued similarly that falling prices, unless they resulted from increasing per capita output, were a burden on farmers and manufacturers because rent, wages, and taxes would not fall in proportion:

All the distress arises from an inability to make good the contracts, which individuals entered into with each other and the state when prices were high, and nothing can remove the embarrassment, but altering the contracts, lowering rent, wages, and taxes, according to the reduction of prices, or raising prices to their former standard by increasing our currency to its former amount.[3]

These and other writers argued in like manner that an increase in the quantity of money operates to increase employment and prosperity. The argument took two forms. In one of them, the "forced-saving" doctrine now first introduced in England,[4] it is held that the increase in money results in an increase in commodity prices unaccompanied by a corresponding increase in the prices of the factors. There results a forced saving on the part of the recipients of the relatively fixed incomes, not in the monetary sense of an increase in the amount of unspent funds, but in

---

[2] Thomas Attwood, *Observations on currency, population, and pauperism,* 1818, p. 10.

[3] John Wheatley, *A Letter . . . on the distress of the country,* 1816, p. 16. Cf. also: C. C. Western, *A letter . . . on the cause of our present embarrassment* [sic] *and distress, and the remedy,* in *Pamphleteer,* XXVII (1826), 228-229; G. Poulett Scrope, *The currency question freed from mystery,* 1830, p. 2; ibid., *On credit-currency, and its superiority to coin,* 1830, pp. 20 ff. Malthus (*Principles of political economy,* 1820, pp. 446-47) appears also to attribute the decline of production resulting from a fall in prices to the lag of wages behind prices and the consequent destruction of the incentive to investment, but his analysis is much inferior to Thomas Attwood's.

[4] An elaborate exposition of the doctrine of forced saving is to be found in a book published in 1786 by one of the minor French physiocrats, Saint Peravy. Unlike most of the English writers, Saint Peravy expounds the doctrine in terms of an expansion of a metallic currency. When an increased amount of money first enters into the circulation, it raises the prices of products without immediately raising contract rents, wages, etc. Producers, therefore, have an extra profit, which they invest in an increase in production, but the general public suffers temporarily a corresponding diminution of *real* income. Saint Peravy regards the increased investment as a desirable phenomenon, but he asserts that unless other countries experience an equal increase in their stock of currency, their competition will prevent a rise in prices, which must be equal in all countries. Guérineau de Saint Peravy, *Principes du commerce opposé au trafic,* 1re partie, 1786, pp. 80-83.

the opposite sense of a decrease in the amount of real consumption while money expenditures are maintained. The increase in money is retained by entrepreneurs, who invest it in additional production. In the other form of the argument, commodity prices do not rise immediately or do not rise in as great proportion as the increase in money, and the money left over is available for additional expenditures and consequently for the employment of additional labor. This form of the doctrine, of course, was not novel, but goes back to Hume, and even earlier to William Potter and John Law,[5] and rests on the assumption that there are idle resources.

The first stages of the development in England of the doctrine of forced saving have been ably traced by Hayek.[6] He finds the first statement in print of the doctrine in the following passage from Henry Thornton:

It must be also admitted that, provided we assume an excessive issue of paper to lift up, as it may for a time, the cost [read *prices*?] of goods though not the price of labor, some augmentation of stock will be the consequence; for the laborer, according to this supposition, may be forced by his necessity to consume fewer articles, though he may exercise the same industry. But this saving, as well as any additional one which may arise from a similar defalcation of the revenue of the unproductive members of the society, will be attended with a proportionate hardship and injustice.[7]

Jeremy Bentham had shortly before completed an extended exposition of the same doctrine, but it remained in manuscript form until published in 1843 as his *Manual of political economy*.[8] According to Bentham, if an increase of money passes in the first instance into hands which employ it "productively," it results in reduced consumption, because of higher prices, on the part of all who use their income for "unproductive expenditure," until the new money reaches hands which will use it unproductively. During this interval the reduced consumption of wage earners and

---

[5] Cf. *supra*, pp. 37-38.

[6] F. A. von Hayek, "A note on the development of the doctrine of 'forced saving,'" *Quarterly journal of economics*, XLVII (1932), 123-33.

[7] *Paper credit*, 1802, p. 263.

[8] An abstract of his forced-saving doctrine is presented in Bentham, *The rationale of reward*, 1825, pp. 312-13.

recipients of fixed incomes results in corresponding additions to the national stock of capital.[9]

Hayek refers also to reasoning along similar lines by Malthus, Dugald Stewart, Lauderdale, Torrens, and Ricardo,[10] with the caution that he would "not be surprised if a closer study of the literature of the time revealed still more discussions of the problem." Some important additions can be made to Hayek's citations, including both further discussions of the problem by the writers whom he has cited[11] and discussions by other writers, and most notably by Joplin.[12]

In the other form of the doctrine that an increase in money meant an increase in production, it was argued that an increase in the quantity of money would increase the monetary volume of purchases more rapidly than it would increase prices, with the result that there would be a substantial interval during which the increase of spendable funds would be absorbed by increased employment in the production of consumers' goods rather than by increased prices.[13] In this form of the doctrine, the increase

---

[9] *Manual of political economy,* in *The works of Jeremy Bentham,* John Bowring ed., 1843, III, 44 ff. Bentham here surely exaggerates the importance of the identity of the hands into which the money first flows.

[10] Hayek's citations are: Malthus, "Depreciation of paper currency," *Edinburgh review,* XVII (1811), 363 ff.; Stewart, in a memorandum on the Bullion Report sent to Lord Lauderdale in 1811, but first published in *The collected works of Dugald Stewart,* 1856, VIII, 440 ff.; Lauderdale, in a letter to Dugald Stewart which is quoted in the preceding reference; Torrens, *An essay on the production of wealth,* 1821, pp. 326 ff.; Ricardo, *High price of bullion,* appendix to 4th ed. [1811], *Works,* p. 299, and *ibid., Principles of political economy,* 3d ed., *Works,* p. 160.

[11] Torrens, *Essay on money and paper currency,* 1812, pp. 34 ff.; Malthus, review of Tooke, *Quarterly review,* XXIX (1823), 239; Lauderdale, *Further considerations on the state of the currency,* 1813, pp. 96-97; Ricardo, see *infra,* pp. 195 ff.

[12] John Rooke, *A supplement to the remarks on the nature and operation of money,* 1819, pp. 68-69; Tooke, *Considerations on the state of the currency,* 2d ed., 1826, pp. 23-24; Joplin, see *infra,* pp. 190 ff.

[13] Cf. T. P. Thompson, "On the instrument of exchange," *Westminster review,* I (1824), 200; Henry Burgess, *A letter to the Right Honorable George Canning,* 1826, pp. 79-82; G. Poulett Scrope, *On credit-currency and its superiority to coin,* 1830, p. 31. Wheatley, in 1803, had denied that an increase in the quantity of money could bring about an increase in production, since this could occur only if it took more time to increase commodity prices than to increase production, which was not the case. (*Remarks on currency and commerce,* 1803, pp. 19 ff.) The answer, of course, is that it takes, or may take, more time for prices to increase sufficiently to absorb *all* of the increase in the quantity of money than for *some* increase of production to be initiated.

in money results in increased real consumption, whereas in the forced-saving form it results in increased investment, but in both forms it makes possible increased employment.

The contributions of Joplin to the discussion are interesting because of the way in which, in the midst of much confused analysis, there appear concise statements anticipating some of the "innovations" in both terminology and concepts of present-day monetary theory. Hayek credits Wicksell with "a contribution of signal importance" by his rediscovery of Thornton's doctrine of the effect of the rate of interest, through its influence on the volume of bank loans, on the volume of money, and his combination therewith of the doctrine of forced saving resulting from an increase in the quantity of money.[14] But Joplin has claims of priority in this respect. Hayek has himself pointed out[15] that Joplin in 1823 and later had ably analyzed the influence of the rate of interest on the quantity of money. Joplin not only stated clearly the doctrine of forced saving, but on the basis of these two doctrines reached conclusions as to the proper criteria of currency management which in their essentials seem to anticipate Hayek's "neutral-money" doctrine.

Joplin stated the forced-saving doctrine in several of his writings. There follows one such statement:

If a person borrows one thousand pounds of a banker who issues his own notes, the banker has seldom any means of knowing whether he has lent him money that has been previously saved or not. He lends him his notes, and if either he or some other banker should not have previously had a thousand pounds' worth of notes deposited with them, he has at once added a thousand pounds to the capital and a thousand pounds to the currency of the country. To the party who has borrowed the money, he has given the power of going into the market and purchasing a thousand pounds' worth of commodities, but in doing this he raises their price and diminishes the value of the money in previous circulation to the extent of one thousand pounds, so that he acquires the commodities by depriving those of them who held the money by which they were represented and to whom they properly belonged. On the other hand, if a person pays a thousand pounds into the hands of a banker, and the currency is contracted to that extent, both one thousand pounds of capital and

---

[14] *Prices and production,* 1931, p. 20.
[15] *Ibid.,* pp. 15-16.

one thousand pounds of currency are destroyed. The commodities represented by the money thus saved and cancelled, are thrown on the market, prices are reduced, and the power of consuming them is obtained by the holders of the money left in circulation.[16]

Joplin does not approve of forced saving. It involves a fraud on those who were holders of money prior to the increase in its issue. At first it results in a stimulus to trade such as "in all probability would more than compensate the holders of the money in previous circulation for the loss they incurred," but if the increase of issue continues, definite injury and injustice results.[17] "Legitimately a banker can never lend money which has not been saved out of income. Money saved represents commodities which might have been consumed by the party who saves it. Interest is paid for the use of the commodities and not for the money."[18] If banks have the power to issue money, the amount of such issue is determined by the rate of interest which the banks charge on loans. If forced saving is to be avoided, banks should charge "the natural rate of interest," which he defines as the rate which keeps savings and borrowings equal.[19] Under a purely metallic currency in its most perfect state, the quantity of money (and/or the scale of value) would be "fixed and unchangeable" and banks would be able to lend only what others had saved. But where banks acquired the right to issue paper currency not fully covered by gold, the quantity of money, "which ought, if possible, to be as fixed as the sun-dial, came to depend upon the credit of bankers with the public, and the credit of the public with the bankers, upon the supply of bills, the value of capital, and innumerable contingencies, which ought no more to affect the amount of currency in circulation than the motions of the sun."[20] To remedy this situation he would confine the circulation of paper money to

---

[16] *An illustration of Mr. Joplin's views on currency,* 1825, p. 28. Joplin reprints this passage from a letter to the *Courier* of Aug. 23, 1823. He restates the doctrine in his *Views on the subject of corn and currency,* 1826, pp. 35 ff., and again in his *Views on the currency,* 1828, p. 146, where he expressly distinguishes between "forced economy" and "voluntary economy."

[17] *Views on the subject of corn and currency,* 1826, pp. 36-37. Cf. also *An illustration of Mr. Joplin's views,* 1825, pp. 28-29, 37. Bentham had also treated forced saving as an undesirable result of changes in the quantity of money: "national wealth is increased at the expense of national comfort and national justice." (*Works,* III, 45.) Cf. also the citation from Thornton, *supra,* p. 188.

[18] *Views on the subject of corn and currency,* 1826, p. 35.

[19] *An illustration of Mr. Joplin's views,* 1825, pp. 28-29, 37.

[20] *Views on the subject of corn and currency,* 1826, p. 37.

certificates of deposit of bullion exchangeable for and issued only in exchange for bullion.[21]

Other doctrines were presented during this period which tended similarly to lead to the conclusion that the inflation of the war period had contributed to the augmentation of the national wealth or the national income. Bentham had argued that if taxation fell on funds which otherwise would have been spent on consumption, and if the proceeds of the taxes were not spent unproductively by the government, the "forced frugality" on the part of the tax-payers would operate to increase the national wealth.[22] Lauderdale, to the same effect, argued that the sinking-fund involved a "forced accumulation of capital . . . annually raised by taxation," thus "transferring from the hands of the consumers a portion of their revenues to commissioners, who are bound by law to employ it as capital, whilst, if it had remained in the hands to whom it naturally belonged, it would have been expended in the purchase of consumable commodities." Like Bentham, Lauderdale disapproved of this "forced accumulation," but not on the grounds of equity to which Bentham appealed. Lauderdale claimed that when the government's current expenditures fell below its revenues, there resulted a diminution of "effectual demand" and consequently of production. While the war continued,

---

[21] *Ibid.*, pp. 63 ff.

[22] The objection to forced saving which in his own discussions of the phenomenon Hayek emphasizes so strongly, namely, that it results in a distortion of the capital structure of the country and thus in an eventual loss of the added investment, was not raised in the early literature, although somewhat later James Wilson seems to have in part anticipated Hayek's doctrine to some extent. (*Capital, currency, and banking*, 1847, pp. 147 ff.) But the early writers were dealing with a deflation-depression, marked by unemployed resources and by underinvestment rather than overinvestment, and under such circumstances there is no *a priori* reason for expecting the added investment resulting from forced saving to prove wasteful in the long run. There seems to underlie the contrary doctrine the tacit assumption that while much which goes on during a boom is highly irrational even from the individualistic point of view, all that individuals do of their own accord during a depression is sensible and proper. But if one accepts instead what seems to be the sufficiently plausible assumption that the behavior of mankind is as likely to be irrational during depression as during prosperity, and that overinvestment is the outstanding manifestation of this irrationality during the boom and underinvestment during the depression, then forced saving (in so far as the manner of bringing it about does not induce voluntary savers to refrain from investment) is as much indicated as a corrective measure during a depression as would be currency contraction, or its equivalent, forced hoarding, during a boom.

[22] *Manual of political economy, Works*, III, 44.

he wanted the government to carry on its increased wartime expenditures by borrowing, and without forcing individuals, through taxation, to decrease their expenditures.[23] After the war had ended, he urged the government to offset the decline in military expenditures by increased civil expenditures on public works, in order to restore the demand for labor.[24]

William Blake similarly argued that increased government expenditures financed by borrowing operated to increase prices, profits, and production, by bringing into activity capital which if left in private hands would have remained "dormant," by which he meant apparently that it would have been kept either as idle cash or as idle stocks of goods. He explained the post-war difficulties as due to "the transition from an immense, unremitting, protracted, effectual demand, for almost every article of consumption, to a comparative cessation of that demand."[25]

John Rooke believed that spending on consumption contributed to prosperity whereas savings, apparently even if invested, did not. He therefore held that the cessation of military expenditures, unless offset by deliberate currency inflation, would operate to cause deflation and depression, especially if these military expenditures had been financed by borrowing:

As the funds which had supported them [i.e., soldiers] in a military capacity, particularly in England, were partly derived from borrowed money, the savers who had supplied this money did not become spenders in the place of government; nor would the war-taxes which were remitted immediately pass into circulation through the medium of consumption, the basis of all income.[26]

---

[23] Lord Lauderdale, *Sketch of a petition to the Commons House of Parliament,* 1822, pp. 5-7. Lauderdale was afraid of underconsumption. Writing in 1798, he had already attacked the sinking-fund on similar grounds. If the government financed its military expenses by borrowing from the Bank of England, this resulted in an increase of circulation. Taxes on income to liquidate these loans reduced the demand for bank notes by cutting down private expenditures. Since "all encouragement to reproduction depends on demand" and "demand can alone be created by expenditure," he concluded that "funding is the best and most prudent means of defraying the extended expenses of modern warfare." (*A letter on the present measures of finance,* 1798, pp. 18-24.)

[24] Cf. his "Protest," *Journals of the House of Lords,* LII (Dec. 17, 1819), pp. 961-62.

[25] *Observations on the effects produced by the expenditure of government,* 1823, pp. 60-67, 88.

[26] *Remarks on the nature and operation of money,* 1819, pp. 37-38. Cf. also pp. 58-59: "There is never any fear that the people will not have any inclination to save; the greatest difficulty is to get men to spend unnecessarily."

In one of his earliest essays, John Stuart Mill denied Blake's argument that it was the cessation of the government's war expenditures which brought about the depression:

. . . every argument is [fallacious] which proceeds upon the supposition that a fund becomes a source of demand by being spent, while it would not have become so by being saved. A loan is a mere transfer of a portion of capital from the lender to the government: had it remained with the lender it would have been a constant and perennial source of demand: when taken and spent by the government, it is a transitory and fugitive one.[27]

---

[27] Review of Blake's *Observations, Westminster review,* II (1824), 39.

This identification of saving with investment by the saver, involving a denial either of the possibility or of the possible importance of hoarding, was common among the classical economists. Cf. Ricardo, *Notes on Malthus* [1820], p. 231: "I know no other way of saving, but saving from unproductive expenditure to add to productive expenditure"; *ibid.,* p. 245; "Mr. Malthus never appears to remember that to save is to spend, as surely, as what he exclusively calls spending." Cf. also "Mr. Owen's plans for relieving the national distress," *Edinburgh review,* XXXII (1819), 473: "With the exception of a few insane misers who hoard their treasures, all persons are desirous of consuming whatever wealth they can command, either productively with a view to improving their condition, or else unproductively with a view to immediate enjoyment." (Ricardo believed that Torrens was the author of this article—cf. *Letters of Ricardo to . . . Trower,* p. 108—but it was more probably written by McCulloch). Cf. also John Craig's objection to Lauderdale's argument that the postwar depression was due to a decrease in demand resulting from the cessation of government spending in excess of its revenue: ". . . circulating capital is annually consumed as regularly as income, though by a different set of people; capital by hired workmen, the produce of whose labor restores it, with a profit, to its proprietor; income by the proprietor himself, without any kind of reproduction, for his own gratification. No new demand therefore arises from changing capital into income, but merely an alteration of the persons by whom it is consumed, together with this material difference, that there is no longer any new production in consequence of that consumption." (*Remarks on some fundamental doctrines in political economy,* 1821, p. 214.) ". . . our own profuse expenditure during the war, . . . never, in any possible circumstances, can be the parent of even a temporary semblance of national prosperity." (*Ibid.,* p. 219.)

Malthus attributed the depression, apparently, to an increase in saving unaccompanied by a corresponding increase in investment, and thought that, given the absence of sufficient incentive for investment under prevailing conditions, the remedy was to be found in increased private expenditures on consumption. (*Principles of political economy,* 1820, 463 ff.) It seems much more probable, however, that the amount of saving was less—rather than greater—during the depression than during the prosperous war years, but that the decline in ability to save in the post-war years was associated with an even greater decline in willingness to invest such savings as were made.

The only member of the Ricardian school I have found who gave any attention to the fact that saving might have other motives than securing interest on

Mill is here tacitly assuming that the government borrowed funds which the lenders would otherwise have themselves invested. But Blake had argued that if left in private hands these funds would have remained "dormant," i.e., would have been kept either as idle hoards of cash or as idle stocks of commodities. He could even more effectively have argued that the funds borrowed by the government were in large part created by the banks for the purpose of being lent to the government and therefore might not have existed at all in the absence of the government borrowings.[28] Mill also objected that Blake's contention that there could be oversaving rested on the reasoning that although the savers were the only persons who could purchase the (net?) products of their investment, men saved because they did not wish to consume. Mill replied, that on the contrary, men saved because they wished to consume more than they saved.[29] Mill is here once more clearly identifying saving with investment. He overlooks the possibility that men may save without investing because for the time being they wish neither to consume nor to invest, but merely to preserve their capital resources without risk of loss through unprofitable investment, and that this is especially likely to be the case when prices are falling rapidly and no investment seems profitable or secure.[30]

It is not surprising that Ricardo, with his loyalty to the metallic standard and his temperamental reluctance to explore the short-run and intermediate phases of economic process, also did not take kindly to these doctrines.[31] His references to them are few,

current investment, and who showed some recognition that the "transmutation of savings into capital" was not an automatic and certain process was William Ellis.—"Employment of machinery," *Westminster review,* V (1826), 106 ff.

[28] Cf. John Ashton Yates, *Essays on currency and circulation,* 1827, p. 28: ". . . the bankers who issue the paper not only lend the real capitals which are deposited with them, but they lend their own credit. . . ."

[29] Mill, *Westminster review,* II (1824), 43.

[30] Cf. Thomas Attwood, *A letter . . . on the creation of money,* 1817, p. 13: "The contractive action then [i.e., 1810] commenced, and ever since then, until the present period, in a greater or less degree, there has been a greater reward in indolence than in industry, there has been a greater profit in locking up money in a chest, than in any possible way in which human knowledge, care, and industry could have employed it." Cf. also C. C. Western, *A letter . . . on the cause of our present embarrassment* [sic] *and distress,* in *Pamphleteer,* XXVII (1826), 228-29.

[31] Ricardo appears to have seen, and taken issue with, Bentham's *Manual of political economy* before it reached the printed stage. Cf. the statement of the Duc de Broglie to Senior: "I remember a conversation at Coppet, which lasted

and tend to be obscurantist in nature. As in other cases, he alternated between outright denial of their validity, on the one hand, and qualified admission of their correctness for the short run but with minimization of their importance, on the other hand.

To Malthus's argument, that an increase in the quantity of money would operate to transfer purchasing power from those with fixed money incomes, an "idle and unproductive class," to farmers, manufacturers, and merchants, and would thus result in an increase of capital, Ricardo replied that an increase of prices resulting from such increase of money, by reducing real fixed incomes, might reduce the savings of those receiving such incomes to an equal degree instead of reducing their consumption.[32]

In answer to questions put to him by the Lords Committee in 1819, Ricardo dealt further with the question of forced saving. He denied that bank credit created capital:

Credit, I think, is the means which is alternately transferred from one to another, to make use of capital actually existing; it does not create capital; it determines only by whom that capital should be employed . . . Capital can only be acquired by saving.[33]

Asked what in his opinion was the difference between "a stimulus . . . by fictitious capital[34] arising from an overabundance of

---

for one or two days, between Ricardo and Dumoht, as to Bentham's political economy. Dumont produced many manuscripts of Bentham's on that subject. There were few of his doctrines to which Ricardo did not object, and, as it seemed to me, victoriously." (N. W. Senior, *Conversations with M. Thiers,* 1878, II, 176.)

[32] *High price of bullion,* appendix to 4th ed. [1811], *Works,* p. 299. Cf. also, *ibid., Notes on Malthus* [1820], pp. 212-16. To the extent that this occurred, there would be no net increase in investment as the result of currency expansion. This argument, however, could scarcely be applied to wage earners, who could be assumed to spend the bulk of their earnings whatever their level might be.

[33] Lords Committee, *Report,* 1819, pp. 192-93.

[34] The first Earl of Liverpool had applied this term merely to signify paper money in his *Treatise on the coins of the realm* [1805], 1880 reprint, p. 255, and Huskisson had quoted him in this sense, substituting "factitious," however, for "fictitious," in 1811. (Hansard, *Parliamentary debates,* 1st series, XIX, 731.) But Lauderdale had used the term in his letter to Dugald Stewart in 1811, and again in his *Further considerations on the state of the currency,* 1813, with reference to the phenomenon of forced saving: "It has been argued, and hitherto the reasoning has remained incontroverted, that an excess of paper produces its injurious effects on the exchange with foreign countries and in increasing the value of commodities, not by its operation of circulating medium, but by creating a mass of fictitious capital." (*Further considerations,* p. 96.)

paper in circulation, and that which results from the regular operation of real capital employed in production," he merely replied:

I believe that on this subject I differ from most other people. I do not think that any stimulus is given to production by the use of fictitious capital, as it is called.

He conceded that an increase in paper money circulation, by changing the proportions in which the national income is divided in favor of the saving classes, "may facilitate the accumulation of capital in the hands of the capitalist; he having increased profits, while the laborer has diminished wages." This is not an acceptance of the forced-saving doctrine, for the increase of investment is held to result indirectly and voluntarily from the redistribution of real income from a non-saving to a saving group, rather than directly and involuntarily from the rise in the consumer's cost of living. Ricardo, moreover, added that "This may sometimes happen, but I think seldom does."[35]

Although Ricardo conceded that a sharp fall in prices was a serious evil, the only undesirable consequence of such a fall which he emphasized was the arbitrary redistribution of wealth which resulted therefrom.[36] He admitted also that economic depression was likely to follow the end of war, but he attributed it to a relative shift in the demands for particular commodities, to which the capital equipment of the country had not yet had time to adjust itself.[37] Ricardo's position on these questions was closely related to his acceptance of the James Mill-J. B. Say doctrine that production, if properly directed, created the demand for its product, and that a general insufficiency of demand to absorb all of the possible output of industry was impossible. This doctrine leads naturally to a denial that a fall in prices would operate to

Since Lauderdale was a member of the Lords Committee of 1819, he may have been the person who put the question to Ricardo.

[35] Lords Committee, *Report*, 1819, pp. 198-99.

[36] Cf. John Rooke, *A supplement*, 1819, p. 15: "Neither Mr. Wheatley, nor Mr. Ricardo, appears to have had any conception of the effects produced upon public wealth by an expanding, or a contracting currency." Wheatley's later writings must have been unknown to Rooke.

[37] Ricardo, *Principles of political economy*, 3d ed., *Works*, p. 160. Malthus asked Ricardo to specify the industries offering unused opportunities for the profitable investment of capital. (Malthus, *Principles of political economy*, 1820, pp. 333-34.)

restrict production or a rise in prices to increase it. It rests on concepts of "supply" and "demand" too physical and an implicit assumption of price and money-cost flexibility too unrealistic to serve adequately the purposes of analysis of short-run disturbances in a monetary economy. If "supply" and "demand" are interpreted, as they should be, not as simply quantities of commodities but, in the modern manner, as *schedules of quantities which would be produced or purchased, respectively, at specified schedules of prices,* it becomes easy to see that if money costs are inflexible the schedules of demand prices may fall more rapidly than the schedules of supply prices, with a consequent reduction, not only in prices, but also in volume of sales, in output, in employment, in willingness of capitalists to invest, and in willingness of bankers to lend even if there were would-be borrowers.

Malthus was convinced that there was something wrong in the James Mill doctrine, including its Ricardian version. He failed, however, ever satisfactorily to expose the fallacy which underlay it, because he was himself insufficiently emancipated from the purely physical interpretation of "supply" and "demand." In the following passage, confused though it is, it appears to me that he comes nearest to exposing this fallacy successfully:

The fallacy of Mr. Mill's argument depends entirely upon the effect of quantity on price and value. Mr. Mill says that the supply and demand of every individual are of necessity equal. But as supply is always estimated by quantity, and demand only by price and value; and as increase of quantity often diminishes price and value, it follows, according to all just theory, that so far from being always equal, they must of necessity be often very unequal, as we find by experience. If it be said that reckoning both the demand and supply of commodities by value, they will then be equal; this may be allowed; but it is obvious that they may then both greatly fall in value compared with money and labor; and the will and power of capitalists to set industry in motion, which is the most general and important of all kinds of demand, may be decidedly diminished at the very time that the quantity of produce, however well proportioned each part may be to the other, is decidedly increased.[38]

It was not Malthus[39] but the two Attwoods, and especially

[38] Review of Tooke, *Quarterly review*, XXIX (1823), 232, note.

[39] J. M. Keynes, however, finds Malthus's doctrines on these matters entitled to less qualified praise. Cf. "Commemoration of Thomas Robert Malthus,"

Thomas Attwood, who first explained in reasonably satisfactory fashion the dependence of the "demand and supply" of price theory on the state of the currency:

. . . while it is certain that a reduction of the quantity of money in circulation necessarily occasions a reduction in the monied prices of all commodities; it is of equal necessity, that the price of no commodity whatever can decline, without some alteration in its relative proportion of supply and demand. The manner, therefore, in which a lessened quantity of money reduces monied prices, is by operating on those ulterior principles by which supply and demand are themselves governed. A scarcity of money makes an abundance of goods. Increase the quantity of money, and goods become scarce. The relative proportion between money and commodities can never alter without producing these appearances. Mr. Tooke, and Mr. Ricardo, will find in this obvious principle an exposition of many of the difficulties and inconsistencies in which they have involved the subject.[40]

Money is as necessary to constitute price, as commodities: increase the supply of money, and you increase the demand for commodities; diminish the supply of money, and you diminish the demand for commodities. The supply of commodities is the demand for money, and the supply of money is the demand for commodities. The prices of commodities, therefore, depend quite as much upon the "proportion" between the supply of, and demand for, money, as they do upon the "proportion" between the supply of, and demand for, commodities. This is a truth which Sir Henry Parnell has altogether overlooked, and his neglect in this respect has led him into a labyrinth of errors. He has considered the supply of, and demand for, commodities as acted upon by some obscure, uncontrollable, and capricious principles, having no reference to the state of the currency, and none to the legislative enactments, which, at one period, have introduced cheap money and high prices, and, when enormous monied obligations have been contracted in such cheap money, have then, at another period, introduced dear money and low prices, and have

---

Economic journal, XLV (1935), 233: "A hundred years were to pass before there would be anyone to read with even a shadow of sympathy and understanding his powerful and unanswerable attacks on the great Ricardo. So Malthus' name has been immortalized by his *Principle of Population,* and the brilliant intuitions of his more far-reaching *Principle of Effective Demand* have been forgotten."

[40] Mathias Attwood, *Letter to Lord Archibald Hamilton,* 1823, pp. 48-49. Attwood clearly means, by scarcity of goods, scarcity relative to demand at the hitherto prevailing price; not reduction of output. He has been arguing that an increase in the quantity of money will increase output, not decrease it.

thus strangled the industry of the country by compelling it to discharge monied obligations which its monied prices will not redeem.[41]

IV. RICARDO'S POSITION ON THE GOLD STANDARD

Although Ricardo believed that stability of its purchasing power was the criterion for an *ideal* standard of value, the effect of the suspension of cash payments on the purchasing power of the pound received no emphasis in his appraisal of the consequences of the suspension. In the first place, he thought the measurement of general purchasing power impossible.[1] Secondly, he attached great importance, on ethical grounds, to the maintenance of contractual obligations, and regarded it as vital that creditors should be enabled to collect, upon the maturity of their claims, the amount of gold specified by or contemplated by the contractors. He regarded it as unjust to withhold from a creditor the benefit of any rise in the purchasing power of his monetary claim as long as he was obliged to assume the risk of any fall in its purchasing power.[2]

---

[41] Thomas Attwood, *The Scotch banker,* 2d ed., 1832, pp. 70-71. (Except for a different title-page, the second edition is identical with the first edition of 1828.) Cf. also *ibid., A letter . . . on the creation of money,* 1817, pp. 18 ff., where he incidentally makes the modern distinction between transaction velocity and income velocity of money, estimating roughly the former at 50 and the latter at 4 per annum. For a sympathetic account of Thomas Attwood's doctrines, see R. G. Hawtrey, *Trade and credit,* 1928, pp. 65-71.

[1] Cf. *Proposals for an economical and secure currency* [1816], *Works,* p. 400.

[2] Cf. *Reply to Mr. Bosanquet's observations* [1811], *Works,* p. 326; *Proposals for an economical and secure currency* [1816], *Works,* p. 403.

To the argument that departure from the metallic standard involved injustice to bondholders, Thomas Attwood later replied that when bondholders lent their money, they knew that their debts were in terms of pounds sterling, whose metallic content had been altered in the past and was liable to alteration in the future. If they wanted to make certain that they would be repaid the same amount of bullion as they had lent, they should have stipulated "in a special contract, that their debts and dividends should be paid in so many ounces of silver or of gold, and not in the variable medium of the pound sterling. They never thought of such a contract as this, but were content to advance their money in the usual way, taking a large interest, and generally a large premium, as a consideration for the depreciation of money which they naturally saw was in progress." (*Observations on currency, population, and pauperism,* 1818, pp. 178-79.) This is, of course, specious reasoning. The absence of such stipulations in contracts was due, not to a conscious assumption of risk of alteration of the standard, but to the absence of recognition that there was any risk of such an alteration. In earlier centuries, when the risk had been apparent, such stipulations, akin to the modern "gold clauses," had been at least occasionally introduced into contracts.

It is a mistake to suppose, however, that Ricardo assumed or believed that gold always maintained a constant purchasing power, and that a premium on gold over paper always meant that paper had fallen in value and never meant that gold had risen in value, views frequently attributed to him by anti-bullionists and apparently ascribed to him by Silberling in the following passage: "Ricardo assumed that gold was still effective as a legal standard and could never itself rise in price in terms of paper. It was always paper that fell, not gold . . . that rose."[3] Ricardo never denied that it was possible for the value of gold to fluctuate, and claimed for it only that it was more stable in value than any other commodity:

A measure of value should itself be invariable; but this is not the case with either gold or silver, they being subject to fluctuations as well as other commodities. Experience has indeed taught us, that though the variations in the value of gold and silver may be considerable, on a comparison of distant periods, yet, for short spaces of time, their value is tolerably fixed. It is this property, among other excellencies, which fits them better than any other commodity for the uses of money.[4]

Ricardo complained, in fact, that while all his argument rested on the fluctuations in the *price* of gold, his opponents insisted on raising objections based on the fluctuations in its *value*. Although he was justifiably skeptical of it, he did not deny that an increase in the value of gold had occurred during the war; he claimed only that it was irrelevant to the question of whether depreciation of the paper currency had occurred.[5]

The violent currency and price fluctuations which followed the termination of hostilities led Ricardo later to admit that gold and silver were more variable in their value even in short periods of time than had generally been recognized. He still insisted, however, that the variations in the value of gold were irrelevant to

---

[3] "Financial and monetary policy," *Quarterly journal of economics*, XXXVIII, 424.

[4] *High price of bullion, Works*, p. 270, note.

[5] Cf. Ricardo to Horner, Feb. 5, 1810, *Minor papers on currency*, p. 40; Ricardo to McCulloch, March 25, 1823, *Letters of Ricardo to McCulloch*, p. 146. Ricardo thought that "whether in point of fact gold really rose or paper really fell, there is no criterion by which this can positively be ascertained." (*Ibid.*) Cf. also Hansard, *Parliamentary debates*, new series, VII (June 12, 1822), 947.

the bullionist case, and that in spite of these variations gold and silver still provided the most stable standard of value available.[6] It was apparently Ricardo's position that since gold and silver were in general more stable in value than an inconvertible paper currency would be, in case of departure from a metallic standard the paper currency should ordinarily be so regulated as to give to it the value which a metallic currency would have had under like circumstances, even if this should occasionally result in a greater instability of the value of the currency than would have prevailed if the paper currency had not been so regulated.

Malthus, in the same spirit, maintained that even if gold had risen in its world value during the Restriction, as some critics of the Bullion Report had claimed, it would nevertheless be desirable to restore the paper currency to parity with gold.[7] Although sufficiently loyal to the metallic standard, John Stuart Mill refused to go so far, though his refusal, given his denial that the circumstances which would justify this heresy had ever existed, was rather academic:

. . . Mr. Blake is of opinion, that instead of causing a variation,

---

[6] "This admission only proves that gold and silver are not so good a standard as they have been hitherto supposed,—that they are themselves subject to greater variations than it is desirable a standard should be subject to. They are, however, the best with which we are acquainted." (*Proposals for an economical and secure currency* [1816], *Works*, p. 402.)

"The bullionists, and I among the number, considered gold and silver as less variable commodities than they really are, and the effect of war on the prices of these metals were [sic] certainly very much underrated by them. The fall in the price of bullion on the peace in 1814, and its rise again on the renewal of the war on Bonaparte's entry into Paris are remarkable facts, and should never be neglected in any future discussion on this subject. But granting all this it does not affect the theory of the bullionists." Ricardo to Trower, Dec. 25, 1815, *Letters of David Ricardo to Hutches Trower and others*, 1899, p. 12. Cf. similarly, Francis Horner, in a speech in the House of Commons on May 1, 1816 (Hansard, *Parliamentary debates,* 1st series, XXXIV, 145): "The opinions which he had formerly given had received a strong and unexpected confirmation by late events; but he had already modified the opinion which he had formerly given as to the price of gold. When by the depreciation of the currency, gold was permanently separated from paper, it was subject to all the variations in price of any other article of merchandise."

[7] "Review of the controversy respecting the high price of bullion," *Edinburgh review,* XVIII (1811), 451. Cf. *Substance of two speeches of Henry Thornton, Esq.,* 1811, p. 72: "It was said that gold itself had risen; but even if it had, gold being the standard, we were bound to hold to it; we had held to it in the general fall, and we ought to abide by it in its general rise also."

it [the Bank Restriction] prevented that which would necessarily have taken place, if the currency had continued on a level with its nominal standard. We ourselves, if we could believe the Bank Restriction to have had this effect, should be among the warmest of its defenders and supporters.[8]

v. Reform without Departure from the Metallic Standard

The currency difficulties of the period, and especially the violent fluctuations after 1815 in the premium on gold, in commodity prices, and in business conditions, gave rise to a number of proposals for reform of the currency, with greater stability of its value as the objective. We will deal first with those proposals which involved a restoration and maintenance of a metallic standard of some sort, and then with those more radical proposals which involved the complete abandonment of a metallic standard and the substitution of a stabilized paper standard.

From at least 1809 on, proposals had been made that further depreciation of the currency should be checked, and at the same time a disastrous fall in prices avoided, by returning to the gold standard at the then prevailing price of gold in terms of paper, instead of at the old par. The Bullion Committee held that devaluation would be a "breach of public faith and dereliction of a primary duty of Government,"[1] while Huskisson characterized it as "a stale and wretched expedient."[2] Ricardo, writing in September, 1809, when, it should be noted, a marked depreciation had been prevailing for less than a year, not only termed devaluation "a shocking injustice," but for some reason which he does not make clear, claimed that it would not remove the premium

---

[8] Review of Blake's *Observations*, 1823, *Westminster review*, II (1824), 47. Blake, in 1823, had recanted some of his previously published views, and now claimed that it had been gold which had risen in value, and not paper which had fallen. (*Observations on the effects produced by the expenditure of government*, 1823, pp. 17, 79.) As Mathias Attwood pointed out (*Letter to Lord Hamilton*, 1823, pp. 68-69), Blake was hopelessly confused. Blake insisted that gold had risen in value and that paper had not fallen, although he conceded that there had been a rise in commodity prices in terms of paper, and that this rise was greater than the rise of gold in terms of paper.

[1] *Bullion Report*, p. 74.

[2] Huskisson, *The question concerning the depreciation of our currency stated*, 1810, p. 18.

on gold over paper and would result in a further rise in commodity prices.[3]

Devaluation was not without its advocates in 1819, but they failed to receive a sympathetic hearing in influential circles. There was considerable impatience at the failure of the government to redeem the pledge which it had repeatedly given from 1814 on that resumption would be carried out at the old par as soon as practicable; and the decrease of the premium on bullion in 1819 to a point where the paper currency was almost at a par with gold, and the widespread feeling that the resumption of cash payments at anything less than the mint par would serve still further to increase the reputedly excessive profits of the Bank of England, also operated strongly to prevent devaluation from becoming a practical issue at the critical moment when policy was to be decided. Ricardo was therefore in accord with parliamentary sentiment in giving little or no consideration to the desirability of resumption of cash payments at a higher mint price for gold than the old par. In his testimony before the Parliamentary Committees of 1819 Ricardo still advocated resumption at par, with no reference to devaluation that I have been able to find.[4] But in a speech in Parliament in 1820, Ricardo stated that if the premium on gold had not fallen to 5 per cent while the 1819 Committees were sitting, he would have favored an alteration of the standard in preference to a return to cash payments at the old standard,[5] and he later made similar statements.[6]

By Silberling and Angell, this is taken as evidence of a revo-

---

[3] "The hint thrown out of altering the mint price to the market price of gold, or, in other words, declaring that 3 l. 17 s. 10½ d. in coin, shall pass for 4 l. 13 s., besides its shocking injustice would only aggravate the evil of which I complain. This violent remedy would raise the market price of gold 20 per cent above the new mint price, and would further lower the value of bank notes in the same proportion." *Three letters on the price of gold* [1809], J. H. Hollander, ed., 1903, p. 18.

[4] Cf., however, Silberling, "Financial and monetary policy," *loc. cit.*, p. 437; Angell, *Theory of international prices*, p. 56, note.

[5] "At the time when that discussion took place, he certainly would rather have been inclined to have altered the standard than to have recurred to the old standard. But while the Committee was sitting, a reduction took place in the price of gold, which fell to 4 l. 2 s. and it then became a question whether we should sacrifice a great principle in establishing a new standard, or incur a small degree of embarrassment and difficulty in recurring to the old." Hansard, *Parliamentary debates*, 2d series, I (May 8, 1820), 191.

[6] Ricardo to Wheatley, Sept. 18, 1821, in *Letters of David Ricardo to Hutches Trower and others*, p. 160; *On protection to agriculture* [1822], *Works*, p. 468.

lution in Ricardo's views, corresponding to a change in his personal economic status from that of presumably a large holder of fixed-income securities to that of a landed proprietor. But Ricardo's will shows that he still had very large holdings of securities at his death, and the apparent change in his views can be explained in a much more creditable—and credible—way. When he attacked devaluation in 1809, the pronounced depreciation in the currency had prevailed only for a few months. By 1819 it had prevailed for some ten years, and many of the existing contracts had been entered into on the basis of such depreciation. What would be glaring injustice in the one situation might well be defended as the closest approach to justice available in the other situation.[7]

During the period of rising prices, the bullionists, Ricardo included, had always explained the mode of operation of a metallic standard as if, under given conditions in the world at large, it dictated to a country adhering to it a specific quantity of currency and a specific range of commodity prices. After 1815, however, Ricardo made it clear that he regarded the gold standard as not absolutely inflexible, but as permitting for short intervals of time some degree of latitude with respect to the quantity of currency and the level of prices which could be maintained under it. His charge that the Bank had so managed resumption as to bring about a greater contraction of the currency and a sharper fall in prices than was necessary would be unintelligible if he did not hold such views.[8] In 1816 he proposed a remedy for the periodic

---

[7] Cf. Ricardo, in the House of Commons, June 12, 1822 (Hansard, *Parliamentary debates,* 2d series, VII, 946, italics not in original) :

If, in the year 1819, the value of the currency had stood at 14 s. for the pound note, which was the case in the year 1813, he should have thought that upon a balance of all the advantages and disadvantages of the case, it would have been as well to fix the currency at the then value, *according to which most of the existing contracts had been made* . . .

[8] Cf. Hansard, *Parliamentary debates,* 2d series, VII (June 12, 1822), 939 (Ricardo speaking) :

His hon. friend had said, that whilst the Bank was obliged to pay its notes in gold, the public had no interest in interfering with the Bank respecting the amount of the paper circulation, for if it were too low, the deficiency would be supplied by the importation of gold, and if it were too high, it would be reduced by the exchange of paper for gold. In this opinion he did not entirely concur, because there might be an interval during which the country might sustain great inconvenience from an undue reduction of the Bank circulation.

scarcities in currency which occurred prior to the dates of payment by the government of the quarterly dividends on the public debt.[9] He thought that the rigid rules for granting loans followed by the directors of the Bank made commercial discounts unsuitable as an instrument for the regulation of the volume of currency, and therefore recommended that the managers of the currency should engage in open-market operations when expansion or contraction of the currency was desirable.[10]

Walter Hall argued that if there were a return to the gold standard—which he vigorously opposed—the Bank of England should maintain generous specie reserves, so that it would not be necessary for it to make its note issue fluctuate in exact correspondence with specie movements. Whenever an unfavorable balance of payments occurred which was due to temporary factors, the Bank should permit gold to flow out without contracting its issues.[11]

John Rooke, although an advocate of more thoroughgoing currency stabilization than was possible on a fixed metallic basis,[12] insisted that there were limited possibilities of price stabilization even on a fixed metallic basis:

A plain view of actual events would, therefore, seem to point out the justice and propriety of augmenting the circulating medium when prices have a tendency to fall, and of diminishing it when they have a tendency to rise. There is always a direct mode of acting at hand. A greater or less amount of bank paper may always be forced out of or into circulation, as occasion may require, and to a given extent, without causing the price of gold to vary. It evidently does not follow at all times, that an increase of bank paper will occasion a rise in the market rate of gold, since that depends upon the circumstance, whether the circulation of the paper money be carried to its greatest possible extent, which is seldom the case.[13]

Torrens also claimed that the gold standard permitted some scope for flexibility of the quantity of the currency, within the limits of the gold points. If a return were made to the gold standard, it would be desirable that the range between the gold

---

[9] *Proposals for an economical and secure currency* [1816], *Works*, pp. 410-11.
[10] Hansard, *Parliamentary debates*, 1st series, XL (May 24, 1819), 744; *Plan for the establishment of a national bank* [1824], *Works*, p. 512.
[11] Walter Hall, *A view of our late and of our future currency*, 1819, pp. 48 ff.
[12] See *infra*, pp. 208-09.
[13] *An inquiry into the principles of national wealth*, 1824, pp. 214-15.

points should not be too small. He therefore urged the retention
of the laws against the melting and export of coin, as operating
to raise the gold export point. For the same reason, he opposed
Ricardo's plan of substituting ingots of bullion for gold coin.
Coin was a "less eligible article of export" than bullion, and
therefore would not reflect as closely as bullion the fluctuations in
the foreign balance of payments.[14]

In 1812 Torrens had advocated raising the tariff as a means of
making resumption of cash payments possible without resulting
in a fall in the English price level. He conceded that this would
involve a loss of the advantages of the "territorial division of
employment," but he maintained that the evil of a fall in prices
was greater than the benefit from foreign trade.[15] Another writer
made a similar proposal in 1818:

> A more rapid method however of increasing the price of com-
> modities, may be found in the adoption of a paper currency; which,
> if aided by uniform duties on importation, will not entirely drive
> out of circulation the precious metals. By this means they may be
> kept at par with the paper, so long as the amount of paper issued
> does not exceed its due proportion to the rate of the import duties.[16]

In 1819 the Bank of England urged that if it were to be
required to make gold payments, it should not be at a fixed rate,
but at the market price of gold in paper, whatever that might be
when its notes were being presented for payment in gold.[17]
Ricardo pointed out the obvious flaw in this proposal: The Bank,
by regulating its issue of paper, could determine the price of
gold in paper, and therefore would not be subject to any real

---

[14] *A comparative estimate of the effects which a continuance and a removal
of the restriction upon cash payments are respectively calculated to produce,*
1819, pp. 36 ff.

[15] *An essay on money and paper currency,* 1812, pp. 56 ff., 295.

[16] Anthony Dunlop, "Sketches on political economy," *Pamphleteer,* XI (1818),
424.

[17] In response to a question sent to the Bank by the 1819 Lords Committee,
the directors replied: "The attainment of bullion by purchase in the market at
£3. 17s. 6d. is, in the estimation of the Court, so uncertain, that the Directors, in
duty to their Proprietors, do not feel themselves competent to engage to issue
bullion at the price of £3. 17s. 10½d.; but the Court beg leave to suggest, as an
alternative, the expediency of its furnishing bullion of a fixed weight to the
extent stated, at the market price, as taken on the preceding foreign post day, in
exchange for its notes; provided a reasonable time be allowed for the Bank
to prepare itself to try the effect of such a measure." Lords Committee, *Report,*
1819, appendix a.8, p. 314.

limitation on its note issue.[18] Only slightly less naïve was George Booth's proposal.[19] He advocated a paper standard currency. He vaguely suggested that a paper currency must *de natura* retain a constant general purchasing power, but gave no hint as to what he would do if the purchasing power of the paper currency should in fact fluctuate. But because of the liability to forgery of paper money of small denominations, he would retain gold and silver coinage. The standard would be the paper money, of which £1 would equal 20 silver shillings. The quantity of silver in a silver shilling would be made to vary with the market price of silver in paper money, so as to maintain parity of value between a paper pound and the quantity of silver in 20 silver shillings. The existing gold guineas were to be retained unaltered in their metallic content, but the number of shillings, paper or silver, which the guinea was to represent was to be varied according to the market price of gold in shillings. Booth failed to specify, however, any criterion for regulating the quantity of paper shillings in order to maintain stability of their purchasing power.

John Rooke, in 1824, made a somewhat similar proposal, which was not guilty, however, of the crucial omission in Booth's scheme of any plan for the regulation of the paper money issues.[20] Rooke advocated a convertible paper currency so regulated in its amount as to have stable purchasing power. He proposed that, as the purchasing power of the paper currency increased, the amount of paper money should be increased, and vice versa. The market price of gold in paper should be permitted to fluctuate freely, but convertibility of the paper currency should be maintained by changing the value in shillings or the denominations of the gold coins whenever necessary. The paper money would thus have a constant purchasing power, but the gold coins would have a variable value both in shillings and in general purchasing power. Rooke preferred, as the criterion for stabilization of the purchasing power of the currency, the "annual price of farm labor" to the price of any other commodity or set of commodities, because it has few or no short-term fluctuations. But he conceded that "the prices of

---

[18] *On protection to agriculture* [1822], *Works*, p. 470.

[19] George Booth, *Observations on paper currency*, 1815, pp. 22 ff., 36 ff.

[20] *An inquiry into the principles of national wealth*, 1824, pp. 216-17, 226-27, 460 ff. Irving Fisher has acknowledged Rooke as an anticipator of his own "compensated dollar" plan.

other things might be taken into account as well as labor, if doing so would give more exactness to the exchangeable value of the currency."[21]

Henry James, in 1818, advocated continuance of the Bank Restriction in order to avoid deflation.[22] In 1820 he recommended stabilization of the purchasing power of the currency in terms of wheat and agricultural labor, but did not make any concrete suggestions as to the method of stabilization.[23]

Joplin was in general a strong adherent of a metallic standard currency, but he nevertheless recommended that gold payments should be stopped temporarily during periods of crop shortages, if otherwise the external drains of gold would result in sharp declines in prices.[24]

VI. PAPER STANDARD CURRENCIES

All of the proposals described above provided for the continuance in some degree of a metallic basis for the currency. But advocates were not lacking of a complete break with the metallic standard and the adoption of an inconvertible paper currency. All of the defenders of the suspension of cash payments had thereby demonstrated their preference for an inconvertible paper over a metallic standard at least during the continuance of a great

---

[21] *Ibid.*, p. 462. In 1819, Rooke had advocated a continually depreciating currency: "A system which secures a constant depreciation in the real value of money, is alone calculated to accelerate national wealth." (*Remarks on the nature and operation of money,* 1819, p. 57.) But later in the same year he withdrew his support of a depreciating currency, because it "carries along with it in its train, evils and irregularities that, ultimately, may more than counterbalance the good to be derived from its adoption." (*A supplement to the remarks,* 1819, p. 4.) He advocated instead a stable monetary system "conforming to the prices of the last 16 years," and presented in outline the proposals which in his later work he developed in greater detail. As in his later work, he proposed that stabilization be accomplished in terms of the wages of farm labor, but because of the delay in the adjustment of farm wages to changes in prices of commodities and also because of the problem created by fluctuations in harvests, he suggested that wages in export industries be followed as a guide; presumably for short-term fluctuations. (*Ibid.,* pp. 88 ff.)

[22] *Considerations on the policy or impolicy of the further continuance of the Bank Restriction Act,* 1818.

[23] *Essays on money, exchanges, and political economy,* 1820, p. 203. In a later work, he advocated raising the price of silver in paper currency as prices fell, and in the same proportion, thus approaching closely to Rooke's proposal. (*State of the nation,* 1835, p. 173.)

[24] *Views on the subject of corn and currency,* 1826, p. 76.

war involving heavy foreign remittances. One anti-bullionist even appeared to find the superiority of the inconvertible paper currency over the metallic standard under wartime conditions to lie in the fact that the former was not set up or regulated in accordance with any deliberate plan.[1] Many of the anti-bullionists claimed that England profited during the war from having a currency independent of international entanglements, and therefore free from the necessity of adjusting itself to all the wartime fluctuations in England's balance of payments.[2] The suspension of cash payments, as one writer put it, gave England "the advantages of an insulated currency, under the circumstances of an expensive war."[3] But while the war continued, most of the supporters of the Restriction defended inconvertibility only as an emergency measure, and looked forward to an eventual return to a metallic standard. The writers who then ventured to declare for an inconvertible paper currency as a permanent institution were few in number and do not appear to have attracted any following. Among them were: advocates of an "abstract currency" divorced from the precious metals, which in some unexplained way would always maintain a proper value and be issued in the correct volume;[4] crude inflationists, for whom no amount of money could be excessive;[5] and others who laid chief stress on the importance of having a currency which was not liable to flow abroad irrespective of internal needs.[6] But when the war had

---

[1] "For these reasons, I am inclined to think, that the wants of men, and the ingenuity exercised in remedying them as they occur, have in this, as in most other instances, formed, upon the whole, a better system of currency for this country at present, and better adapted to the circumstances of the time, than any statesman, or political economist, however able and well informed, could have devised in his closet. . . . The thing is done first; the reason why it should be so done, is found out afterwards. . . . Where currencies of paper have failed in other countries, it is generally where speculative men have formed the plans for establishing them." (The Earl of Rosse, *Observations on the present state of the currency of England*, 1811, pp. 87-88.)

[2] Cf. the similar arguments of seventeenth-century writers, *supra*, p. 39.

[3] J. C. Herries, *A review of the controversy respecting the high price of bullion*, 1811, p. 96.

[4] E.g., Thomas Smith, *An essay on the theory of money and exchange* [1807], 2d ed., 1811; Glocester Wilson, *A defence of abstract currencies*, 1811; *ibid.*, *A further defence of abstract currencies*, 1812.

[5] E.g., Sir John Sinclair, *Observations on the Report of the Bullion Committee*, 3d ed., 1810; *ibid.*, *Remarks on a pamphlet by William Huskisson*, 2d ed., 1810.

[6] E.g., John Raithby, *The law and principle of money considered*, 1811, p. 111: "The currency of a country ought to be of a nature, the perpetual and

ended, and especially when resumption of cash payments was accompanied by sharply falling prices, the advocates of an inconvertible paper currency became fairly numerous, although apparently never influential with the government. Of greater interest were the writers who, prior to 1830, advocated some form of stabilized paper standard.

An anonymous writer as early as 1797 had proposed a system of control of the inconvertible paper currency through the use of the interest rate, although he failed to make clear whether or not his proposal contemplated a *variable* interest rate as the regulator of the quantity of the currency, and he failed to formulate an intelligible criterion of the proper quantity of currency. He proposed that all bank notes should be suppressed and that national paper money, issued in exchange for government securities, should be substituted for bank notes. The Bank of England should be obliged to accept for deposit *at interest* whatever quantity of national paper money individuals should offer it, and the government should be obliged to accept from the Bank all the paper money above what the Bank found necessary for carrying on its business. The government should pay interest to or receive interest from the Bank according as to whether the government was indebted to the Bank or the Bank to the government.[7]

Although John Wheatley had been one of the most outspoken critics of the suspension of cash payments, his belief in the metallic standard diminished under the impact of the fall in prices accompanying the approach and the realization of resumption of cash payments.[8] In his writings from 1816 on, he expressed preference at times for a currency so regulated as to maintain constancy in the price level, at other times for a currency constant in quantity. But stability of prices was apparently his ultimate objective, for he indicated that, where population was increasing

necessary tendency of which is to rest at home"; Lord Stanhope, in a Resolution presented to the House of Lords: Not only gold and silver, "but likewise every one of the other articles of merchandise by means of which British debts to foreign nations can be discharged, is . . . an improper and an unfit legal standard to serve as a fixed, invariable, and permanent measure of the relative value of different commodities and things within the country itself, which is the grand and essential end and object of an internal circulating medium. . . ." Hansard, *Parliamentary debates,* 1st series, XX (July 12, 1811), 911.

[7] *The iniquity of banking,* part II, 1797, pp. 42 ff., 59 ff., 62.

[8] For his advocacy, in 1807, of the voluntary use of a tabular standard for long-term contracts, see *infra,* pp. 282-83.

and there was a corresponding growth of production, the quantity of money should be increased in the same proportion, so as to prevent prices from falling. This would seem to lead to a regulated paper currency, but in 1816 he still advocated a return to the gold standard, on such a basis as to restore the 1813 level of prices: "a currency of coin is neither liable to sudden excess, to defraud the creditor, nor sudden contraction, to defraud the debtor. . . . With a circulation of paper it is impossible to prevent a constant variation in the amount of our currency. In times of confidence the banks issue too much, in times of distrust they issue too little."[9] In 1819 he still advocated resumption. The evil of deficiency of currency, which produces low prices, was greater than the evil of excess, which produces high prices, but under inconvertibility the currency system was liable to both deficiency and excess. All that was necessary to get a proper currency system was to abolish small notes, which were most liable to variation in their quantity, and to build up the stock of gold very gradually so as not to cause a sharp contraction of prices and so as not to involve other countries in difficulties.[10] But in 1822 he argued that sterling should have been allowed to remain depreciated until the world price level had risen to equilibrium with the English price level. If under inconvertibility the amount of the paper currency had been kept constant, it would have been better that resumption of cash payments should never take place. He now advocated that there be increased issue of paper until the 1812-13 level of the price of corn had been restored, and that thereafter there should be only such changes in the quantity of currency as would be necessary to maintain prices and incomes at this level, with the metallic standard, presumably, definitely abandoned.[11]

Thomas Attwood may not have had any great zeal for a stabilized paper currency, and his real objective seemed to be whatever increase in currency and prices should prove necessary to bring about full employment, without limitations prescribed in advance.[12] But he was deeply convinced that falling prices were

[9] John Wheatley, *A letter . . . on the distress of the country,* 1816, pp. 14-25, 43-44.

[10] *Ibid., Report on the reports of the Bank committees,* 1819, pp. 4, 45, 50-51.

[11] *An essay on the theory of money and principles of commerce,* vol. II, 1822, pp. 121 ff., 131 ff.

[12] He asks the question: why not issue money ad infinitum? and replies:

a serious evil which could not be avoided except through an inconvertible paper currency, and his stabilization suggestions seem to have been made in the hope that they would make his plea for an inconvertible paper currency more palatable to public opinion. They are nevertheless of considerable interest. Attwood recommended an inconvertible paper currency issued by the government and its quantity regulated through open-market purchases and sales of its own securities by the government.[13] As the criterion for the stabilization of the currency he wavered between the price of wheat,[14] the general rise or fall in the prices of commodities,[15] the rate of interest,[16] and the wages of agricultural labor.[17] He clearly was not prepared to commit himself definitely to any one criterion. Regulation of the amount of the currency should be entrusted to a legislative commission, and should be carried out not by "laws of maximum and minimum but by judicious legislative operations upon the issue of bank notes, or other national paper."[18] He recognized that if wages of labor were used as the standard for stabilization, there would be time-lags between changes in the quantity of currency and resultant changes in wages. He suggested, therefore, that, to supplement wages, the market rate of interest should be used as a more sensitive index of the effects of changes in the quantity of currency, the rate of interest to be used as a "temporary" and the wages of labor as a "permanent" guide in the regulation of issues.[19]

Attwood realized that it might not prove easy to reverse the trend of prices, and that more would be necessary than simple authorization to the banks to issue more paper:

It would be of no use to act upon the "rag makers," without at the

---

"Whenever . . . the money of a country is sufficient to call every laborer into action, upon the system and trade best suited to his habits and his powers, the benefits of an increased circulation can go no farther. . . ." Beyond that point, further stimulus is "nugatory or injurious." (*A letter . . . on the creation of money*, 1817, p. 68.)

[13] *Prosperity restored*, 1817, pp. 129-130; *Observations on currency, population, and pauperism*, 1818, pp. 164-67; *The late prosperity, and the present adversity of the country, explained*, 1826, pp. 34-35.

[14] *Prosperity restored*, pp. 129-30, 135.

[15] *Ibid.*, p. 136.

[16] *Ibid.*, p. 183.

[17] *Ibid.*, pp. 184, 193-94; *Observations on currency*, pp. 166-67.

[18] *Prosperity restored*, pp. 163 ff.

[19] *Observations on currency*, pp. 204-05.

same time acting also upon the public mind; for unless the public are willing to borrow the "rags," the "rag maker" cannot issue them. It is therefore necessary to act upon both parties; the one must be stimulated to *borrow,* and the other to *lend.* Both these dispositions are rather stagnant at present, and are becoming daily more so. Prudent and safe men are afraid to borrow money, because they cannot safely and beneficially employ it. Bankers are afraid to lend it, because they know that it cannot be safely employed, and because they remember the late panic, when they were compelled to pay everybody, whilst nobody could pay them.[20]

Although all of the prominent members of the classical school were adherents of a fixed metallic standard, I have not been able to find any serious attempt during this period to meet these claims that a better currency standard was available. There was then, as there has continued to be since, a marked tendency on the part of the exponents of the fixed gold standard to rely on dogmatic assertions of the injustice of any other system and of the impossibility of devising any system of currency which would have more stability of value than the precious metals.[21] Attempts to stabilize the value of money beyond what metallic money would do of itself, they asserted, were impracticable, and were straining after unattainable perfection: "It does not seem the design or intention of the Author of the world, that . . . stability [of the currency] should be perfect and invariable";[22] "to demand a standard abstractedly free from variation, is like seeking for better bread than is made of wheat."[23] As has already been pointed out, James Mill, Ricardo, and their disciples, also tended to minimize both the extent and the evil consequences of changing price levels, and thus to foster the attitude that the metallic standard, variable though it was, met adequately the requirements of a good currency standard.

During this period the adherents of a fixed metallic standard did not expressly claim as an advantage of such a standard that

---

[20] *The Scotch banker,* 2d ed., 1832, p. 101.

[21] Ricardo, in 1819, asserted that a currency less variable than a metallic standard one could not be attained by any system "that I have ever even imagined." (Commons Committee, *Report,* 1819, p. 138.)

[22] Samuel Read, *An inquiry concerning the nature and use of money,* 1816, p. 83.

[23] T. P. Thompson, "On the instrument of exchange," *Westminster review,* I (1824), 197.

it was an international rather than a purely national standard.[24] The bullionists had laid great emphasis on the fall in the exchanges as evidence of the undesirable mode of operation of the inconvertible paper currency, but primarily or solely because exchange depreciation indicated internal depreciation in terms of bullion. I have found only one instance of even bare mention by a bullionist of instability of the exchanges as an evil in itself,[25] and I have failed to discover what specific disadvantages, if any, the bullionists believed would result from a fluctuating exchange other than the fluctuations in the bullion value of the currency and in relative price levels as a whole at home and abroad which would be associated with it.

Few of the anti-bullionists conceded that fluctuating exchanges were an evil, and when they did they insisted that the advantages of a stable exchange could be acquired or retained only at an excessive cost, without as a rule indicating what they regarded as the disadvantages of a fluctuating exchange. As one paper-money advocate exclaimed, under a metallic standard: "The natural order of things will be reversed. Instead of a steady currency and fluctuating exchanges, we shall have steady exchanges, and a fluctuating currency!!"[26] One anti-bullionist, Walter Hall, did, however, carry the discussion a little further. He was not prepared to concede that the disadvantages of a fluctuating exchange were very serious: "What may be the value of a steady exchange, I shall consider hereafter; but it seems to me it will cost too dear, if the price to be paid for it is a fluctuating currency."[27] "After all, what is this mighty evil of an unfavorable exchange, that so much should be lost and hazarded for it."[28] Clearly identifying

---

[24] Malthus is the only exception I have found. He stated that it was desirable to have an internationally common standard, even if it meant falling prices, but did not give any reasons. "Review of the controversy respecting the high price of bullion," *Edinburgh review*, XVIII (1811), 450-51.

[25] George Woods, *Observations on the present price of bullion*, 1811, p. 53: "The only other disadvantageous consequence of the present system appears to be *the unsteady par of exchange*, and the unsettled relative value of currency, constantly at the mercy of a small body of men." (Italics not in original.)

[26] Erick Bollmann, *A second letter . . . on the practicability of the new system of bullion-payments*, 1819, p. 25, note.

[27] Walter Hall, *A view of our late and of our future currency*, 1819, p. 56.

[28] *Ibid.*, p. 59. For claims by other anti-bullionists that an "unfavorable" exchange was desirable as a bounty to exports and a check on imports, see Daniel Wakefield, *An investigation of Mr. Morgan's comparative view of the public finances*, 1801, pp. 51-52; anon., *Reply to the author of a letter . . . on*

a fluctuating with a falling exchange, he conceded that it results in a disadvantage to the consumer of imported goods in the form of higher prices, but he argued that this burden would be diffused equally over the whole community, and would be counterbalanced to the country as a whole by the advantage which resulted to the manufacturer and exporter, whereas the forced sales and the decline in prices which would result from the contraction of the currency for which falling exchanges were a substitute would fall heavily on the merchant and the manufacturer, and would cripple for a time the productive activities of the country.[29] He had earlier argued that changes in taxes result in serious changes in the relations between particular prices and thus change "the relations of society,"[30] and had thus shown that he recognized that changes in relative prices as well as changes in price levels as a whole could have serious consequences, but his attempt to show that this did not apply to the changes in relative prices which would result from a depreciating exchange cannot be regarded as satisfactory. But superficial and inadequate as was his analysis of this vital phase of the problem, it was the only explicit recognition of it which I have found, not only in the literature of the bullionist controversy, but in such of the English nineteenth-century literature on the currency problem as I have examined.

It cannot be claimed for the literature of the bullionist controversy that it afforded a satisfactory answer to the issue, prominent now as then, as to the comparative merits of a metallic (and international) monetary standard, on the one hand, and a non-metallic (and national or "insulated") standard, on the other. The defenders of the metallic standard contented themselves with an appeal to arbitrary dogmas and to moral issues, and with the claim that the limitations imposed by a metallic standard were a safeguard against the inflationary possibilities of an irresponsibly or incompetently managed paper standard currency. The exponents of a *national* paper standard made out a better case for what I am inclined to regard as theoretically a moderately inferior

---

the *pernicious effects of a variable standard of value,* 1819, pp. 34-35: "While the exchange is adverse it operates as a bounty on the export of all our manufactures; and stimulates, by additional profits, the industry and skill of the nation; and though this adverse exchange has its disadvantages, yet, as it has its benefits also, let us not throw the latter away. . . ."

[29] Walter Hall, *op. cit.,* pp. 53, 60.

[30] *Ibid.,* p. 16.

and under ordinary practical conditions a seriously inferior cause. They presented valid and novel arguments for the economic advantages of the freedom afforded by an independent monetary standard to escape a deflation (or inflation!) induced by external factors, to cope with a deflation resulting from internal factors and intensified by the prevalence of rigidity downwards in the prices of the factors of production, and, in general, to provide a country with the quantity of means of payment deemed best for it as against having that quantity dictated to it by external factors beyond its control. If the exponents of the paper standard, however, had intellectually somewhat the best of the argument, it was largely because of the failure of their opponents to set forth what seem to me to be the most important arguments for stability of the exchanges. The important issue lies between stable and unstable exchanges, and between a metallic standard and a paper standard only as and if the former in operation provides stable exchanges and the latter in operation fails to do so. First, fluctuating exchanges result in risks and uncertainties for foreign trade and foreign investment which are economically costly and for which the development of forward exchange markets and other facilities for hedging against exchange fluctuations provide only a strictly limited palliative. Second, although a paper standard currency managed without reference to the foreign exchanges could reduce the amplitude of short-term fluctuations in the *general* price level as compared to what they would ordinarily be under an international monetary standard, it would thereby tend to increase greatly the amplitude of short-term fluctuations *relative to each other* of sectional price levels—export commodities, import commodities, domestic commodities—as compared to what is conceivable under an international monetary standard. It was only under the stimulus of the recent great depression, however, that the analysis of these problems was carried much beyond the point at which it was left by the bullionists and their critics, and the present-day discussion seems to be tending to shift the issue from stable versus unstable exchanges to permanently stable versus shiftable exchanges. This is a much more significant issue, since almost no country for which foreign trade was of great importance has ever been willing for long to tolerate freely fluctuating exchanges, and stronger grounds can be presented for substituting a shiftable anchor for a permanently fixed one than for doing without an anchor at all.

Chapter V

ENGLISH CURRENCY CONTROVERSIES,
1825-1865

The student who turns from the literature of the Heroic Age of British monetary controversy in order to attempt a study of the original sources relating to the antecedents of our modern banking situation will find himself confronted with a jungle of blue books and Parliamentary discussions, pamphlets and tracts and leading articles: a jungle at first sight so impenetrable that he may well despair. For it is characteristic of the period of middle-class ascendancy after 1832 that it produced much heat and little light; many massive volumes of evidence and statistics, but no classic reports; much legislation but, for a long time at least, no final solution of the various problems to be faced.
—T. E. Gregory, Select statutes, I, ix.

I. INTRODUCTION

The downward trend of the English price level, which persisted without any sustained reversal from 1815 to the 1850's, was for English industry and labor only partially compensated by the progress in manufacturing technique and the fall in the prices of imported raw materials. The occasional prosperous intervals were ordinarily terminated by sharp financial crises, and were followed by intervals of depression and unemployment. There was general agreement that these business fluctuations were inherent in the new structure of industry, but there was also a widespread conviction that they had been accentuated by chronic mismanagement—or misbehavior—of the currency. It became apparent soon after resumption of cash payments that strict adherence to a fixed metallic standard was not sufficient to assure the smooth and beneficent working of the currency system. The Bank of England succeeded throughout the period in maintaining convertibility of its paper notes, but on several occasions only with great difficulty and after resort to emergency measures. In

1825, in 1836, and again in 1839, suspension of convertibility was avoided only by a narrow margin. In 1847, and 1857, and 1866, the Bank was again in serious difficulty. Each period of special strain gave rise to an extensive controversy, turning on the quality of the Bank's management of its affairs and on the principles which should be followed in the management of the currency.[1] That the currency was operating badly no one disputed, although there were not a few who would have agreed with Cobden that "managing the currency [was] . . . just as possible as the management of the tides, or the regulation of stars, or the winds,"[2] and that all that government could do, therefore, would be to place it on a wholly metallic basis, and then let "automatic" processes run their course.

During this period the English banking system underwent important structural changes. In the belief that it was mainly the small notes which were presented for redemption in gold during periods of financial stress, the renewal in 1822 of the right to issue notes under £5 was repealed by an act passed in 1826. To promote the establishment of financially stronger country banks, an act of the same year authorized the establishment in the provinces of note-issuing banks with an unlimited number of partners. An act passed in 1833 exempted the Bank of England, in so far as its discounts of short-term paper were concerned, from the legal maximum interest rate of 5 per cent under the usury laws, and thus gave it the power to use the discount rate as an instrument of credit control. This act also made the Bank's notes legal tender except by the Bank itself as long as the Bank maintained convertibility into gold, and definitely proclaimed— what had previously been questionable—the right to establish in the London area non-note-issuing banking establishments with more than six partners. The joint-stock banks grew rapidly in number and in importance, both in the provinces and in London. By the 1850's there were at least three joint-stock banks in London with deposits in excess of those of the Bank of England. The Bank of England had gradually given up most of its ordi-

---

[1] By far the most helpful surveys of the English currency controversies of the period that I have found are T. E. Gregory's introduction to the 1928 reprint of Tooke and Newmarch's *History of Prices* and his introduction to his *Select statutes, documents and reports relating to British banking, 1832-1928*, 1929.

[2] *Report from Select Committee on banks of issue*, 1840, p. 39.

nary commercial discount business, and its "private deposits" came to consist largely of bankers' balances held with the Bank as the equivalent of cash reserves.

Finally, there was passed the Bank Charter Act of 1844, commonly referred to as Peel's Act, which was to remain the charter of English banking until the Great War. This act required the Bank formally to segregate the issue department from the banking department,[3] and limited the issue department to a maximum issue of notes uncovered by bullion of £14,000,000, above which amount it could issue notes only in exchange for gold (or, within certain limits, silver). Country banks then issuing notes were permitted to continue such issue not to exceed the amount then in circulation, but the law made provision for the gradual absorption by the issue department of the Bank of England, as an addition to its uncovered issue, of the bulk of the note circulation of the country banks. Except as to note issue, the banking department of the Bank of England was left wholly free from statutory regulation, as were also the then existing private banks on all matters of consequence except the right to issue notes.

II. The "Currency School"-"Banking School" Controversy

The currency controversies of this period were carried on mainly by the members of two groups, with divergent views, who came to be known as the "currency school" and the "banking school," respectively.[1] The most prominent members of the currency school were Lord Overstone (Samuel Jones Loyd), G. W. Norman, R. Torrens, and William Ward. Thomas Tooke, John Fullarton, James Wilson, and J. W. Gilbart were the leaders of the banking school. There was not complete unanimity of doctrines within each group, and the currency school, under the impact of their opponents' criticisms, modified their doctrines

---

[3] The Bank had on its own initiative made such a separation in its accounts in 1840.

[1] William Ward, a member of the currency school group, referred to its main doctrine in 1832 as "the principle of the currency." Samuel Jones Loyd, in testimony before the Committee on Banks of Issue in 1840, referred to the doctrines of the two groups as the "currency principle" and the "banking principle," respectively. After 1840, the groups holding these views were commonly distinguished by the labels "currency school" and "banking school."

fairly substantially in the course of the controversy. An attempt is nevertheless made in the next few pages to summarize the general position of the two schools, as a preliminary to a more detailed examination of such of the particular doctrines expounded in the course of the controversy as are of importance for the theory of international trade. The discussion between the two schools turned wholly, however, on short-run issues. On the question of what determined the quantity and the value of a metallic currency in the long run, both schools followed the "classical" or "Ricardian" doctrines.

The currency school maintained that under a "purely metallic currency" any loss of gold to foreign countries or any influx of gold from abroad would result immediately and automatically in a corresponding decrease or increase, respectively, in the amount of currency in circulation. The actual currency was a "mixed currency," that is, convertible paper notes were a constituent element of the currency. A mixed currency would operate properly only if it operated precisely as would a metallic currency, i.e., only if any efflux or influx of gold resulted in a corresponding (absolute, not proportional) decrease or increase in the quantity of the currency—*the* "currency principle." But a mixed currency would not operate in this manner automatically and immediately unless the issue of paper money were deliberately regulated so as to make the changes in its quantity conform to the changes in the quantity of gold held by the issuing agencies. In the absence of such regulation, paper money would at times be issued to excess, at other times unduly contracted; the maintenance of convertibility would not be definitely assured; the improper fluctuations in the currency would accentuate the tendency inherent in the economic structure toward recurrent booms and crises.

Since the ultimate objective of the currency school was that the value of the monetary unit, or the level of prices, should be the same under a "mixed currency" as it would be under a purely metallic currency, this could be accomplished by their rule of making the fluctuations in the amount of bank notes correspond to the fluctuations which would occur in the amounts of specie under a purely metallic currency only if the velocity of circulation of bank notes and of specie would under like circumstances be identical. This was apparently overlooked by the members of the currency school,[2] although it may be that they took for granted that there would be such identity.[3]

The banking school denied almost all of these propositions. Generally waiving the question as to whether it was desirable that a mixed currency should operate precisely as would a purely metallic currency, they denied that a purely metallic currency would operate in the manner claimed by the currency school. They pointed out that under a purely metallic currency there existed in addition to specie, and under a mixed currency there existed in addition to specie and paper notes, a large quantity of bank deposits and bills of exchange which, they claimed, were also "currency" and in any case operated on prices in the same manner as did bank notes and specie. Under a purely metallic currency, moreover, some of the gold was not in circulation, but was in "hoards," in modern times held mainly in the bullion reserves of the Bank of England and other banks. Changes in the amounts of these hoards could not possibly have any effect on prices.[4] Even under a purely metallic currency, therefore, a gain or loss in the nation's stock of gold need not result in corresponding fluctuations of the currency, but might merely change the amount of gold in hoards, or might be offset by an inverse fluctuation in the amount of deposits. Without control of hoards and of deposits, limitation of the note issues could not suffice, therefore, to attain the objective of the currency school of enforcing correspondence between the fluctuations in the total circulation and the fluctuations in the total stock of gold. The banking school did not present an alternative program of statutory control of

---

[2] Cf., however, Sir Charles Wood: "The real question to be solved is, how to regulate the quantity of the paper circulation, so as to keep its value identical with what the value of the metallic currency would be. It is not necessary, perhaps, that a paper circulation should be of precisely the same quantity as the metallic currency which would be required if the paper did not exist, because the greater convenience of paper money may render it possible that the same functions shall be performed by a less quantity of paper as easily as by a greater quantity of gold or silver." (Hansard, *Parliamentary debates,* 3d series, LXXIV (May 20, 1844), 1356.

[3] For reasons why such identity need not exist, see *supra,* p. 131.

[4] Cf. Fullarton, *On the regulation of currencies,* 2d ed., 1845, p. 140: "[The currency school] never even allude to the existence of such a thing as a great hoard of the metals, though upon the action of the hoards depends the whole economy of international payments between specie-circulating communities, while any operation of the money collected in hoards upon prices must, even according to the currency hypothesis, be wholly impossible."

the currency. They held that statutory control of the deposits was not demanded by anyone, was impossible, and even if possible was undesirable. The amount of paper notes in circulation was adequately controlled by the ordinary processes of competitive banking, and if the requirement of convertibility was maintained, could not exceed the needs of business for any appreciable length of time—*the* "banking principle." If unsound banking practices did occasionally lead to excess grant of credit, this brought its own corrective penalties. In any case it could not be prevented by legislative measures, and especially by mere limitation of note issue.

The bullionists, it will be remembered, had insisted that under an inconvertible paper money currency the issues should be so regulated as to conform to the aggregate circulation of specie and paper which could be maintained under a convertible currency, but usually maintained—or took it for granted, without argument —that if the requirement of convertibility were enforced there was no need of further regulation to insure against excess—or deficient—issue of paper money.[5] The anti-bullionists, on the other hand, had ordinarily maintained that a paper currency could not be issued to excess whether convertible or not, if issued only by banks as loans on the security of good short-term commercial paper. The currency and the banking schools both rejected the anti-bullionist doctrine that an inconvertible paper money could not be issued to excess.[6] The currency school went further; they claimed that even a convertible paper currency could be issued to excess, not permanently, but for sufficiently long periods to endanger the maintenance of convertibility and to generate financial crises. The "currency principle," i.e., the doctrine that a mixed currency should be made to operate as would a "purely metallic" currency, did resemble, however, the bullionist doctrine that an inconvertible paper currency should be made to operate as would a convertible currency, and was obviously derived from it.

[5] Cf., however, Ricardo, *supra,* p. 205. The currency school were not aware that on this point they could derive support from Ricardo.

[6] A clear statement of the grounds on which they held that a paper currency could be issued to excess if inconvertible but not if convertible is not to be found in the writings of the banking school. Their reasoning seems to have been, however, that under convertibility the national price level, and therefore the quantity of money, was even in the short run internationally determined, whereas under inconvertibility this external limitation would not be operative.

The currency principle appears first to have been formulated during the 1820's. Joplin, in 1823, proposed a system of regulation of the issue of paper notes whose essence was the requirement of 100 per cent bullion reserves, so that "a paper circulation, by this system, would dilate and contract precisely in the same manner as a metallic currency."[7] Henry Drummond, in 1826, similarly urged that the amount of paper money should be kept constant, so that all variations in the quantity of the currency should consist of corresponding variations in the quantity of specie.[8]

III. THE "PALMER RULE"

In 1827 the Bank of England adopted a rule—later commonly known as the "Palmer rule" or the "rule of 1832" because it was first publicly explained, in 1832, by the then governor of the Bank, J. Horsley Palmer—which aimed at making the fluctuations in the English currency conform with those which would occur under a purely metallic currency by keeping its security holdings, including discounted paper, constant. At the same time, although apparently wholly independently, Pennington, a confidential adviser of the Treasury on currency matters, had recommended the same rule in a memorandum to Huskisson, then Chancellor of the Exchequer. The problem as Pennington saw it was to make the paper currency operate as would a "purely metallic currency": "The great objection to a paper currency arises from the extreme difficulty of subjecting its expansion and contraction to the same law as that which regulates the expansion and contraction of a currency purely metallic."[1] He offered as a solution that the Bank of England should be given an exclusive monopoly of note issue (or direct control over the issues of the other banks) and should hold a fixed amount of securities. There could then be no variations in its outstanding note circulation without corresponding variations in its holdings of bullion:

Nothing more would be necessary than that the bank should con-

---

[7] Thomas Joplin, *Outlines of a system of political economy*, 1823, p. 276.

[8] Henry Drummond, *Elementary propositions on the currency*, 4th ed., 1826, p. 47.

[1] James Pennington, *Memorandum* (privately printed), 1827, p. 8. The memorandum is reprinted in Pennington, *A letter . . . on the importation of foreign corn*, 1840, pp. 82 ff.

stantly hold a fixed amount of the same unvarying species of securities. If its outstanding liabilities amounted, at any particular time, to £26,000,000, and if, against these, it held £18,000,000 of government securities and £8,000,000 of bullion, then, by confining itself to the £18,000,000 of securities, the action of the foreign exchange would necessarily turn upon the gold: at one time the bank might have six, at another time ten, and at another eight millions of treasure; and in all cases, its paper would contract and expand according to the increase or diminution of its bullion.[2]

The Palmer rule was essentially the same. When the exchanges were at par and the currency "full," the Bank should try to have a bullion reserve of one-third of its combined note and deposit liabilities, so that its current assets should be one-third bullion and two-thirds securities. Thereafter all that would be required would be to maintain the securities at a constant amount. An influx of gold from abroad would thus act to increase the note circulation by a corresponding amount; an efflux of gold or a demand for coin for internal circulation would result in a corresponding decrease in note circulation. The internal circulation, specie plus paper, would thus remain constant unless acted upon by external gold movements.[3]

This rule had the fatal defect that it took no account of the necessity of also maintaining deposits constant if the maintenance of securities at a constant amount was to guarantee correspondence between the fluctuations in bullion and the fluctuations in note circulation. If the deposits were permitted to fluctuate, then as the bullion holdings fluctuated the note circulation might remain constant, or might fluctuate in the reverse direction. Under an inconvertible paper currency, a case could be made for the general policy of keeping the securities constant, *if* departure from this rule to offset variations in the velocity of circulation of notes and deposits were permitted, and *if* provision were made for adjustment of the amount of securities to the secular trend of production resulting from growth of population and capital. But under an international metallic standard, adherence to the rule of keeping the securities constant could lead to serious and lasting disequilibrium between the internal and the

---

[2] *Memorandum*, p. 14.
[3] Cf. the testimony of Mr. Palmer, *Report from the [Commons] Committee of Secrecy on the Bank of England charter,* 1832, p. 11.

world price levels, and therefore to exhaustion or to indefinite accumulation of gold reserves.[4]

It is not easy to understand Pennington's original position in this connection. The objective of control stated by him seems to involve an unqualified acceptance of the currency principle. But the method of control which he advocated, like the Palmer rule, would have made the fluctuations in notes *plus deposits* correspond with the fluctuations in specie reserves, whereas the currency principle called for correspondence between the fluctuations in notes alone and the fluctuations in specie reserves. It especially seems to call for explanation that Pennington, who was an important factor in drawing attention to the importance of deposits as a means of payment, should have advocated a rule which would permit of withdrawal through the deposits of all the specie reserves without calling for any positive corrective action on the part of the Bank. When Pennington later, in 1840, published his memorandum, his views had apparently undergone some modification. He now made it appear that by a "purely metallic currency" he had meant one which consisted only of specie, and that by "paper circulation" he had meant *notes and deposits*.[5] This would bring his rule of control into conformity with his objective. Against the currency principle proper he protested that it would make the fluctuations in the currency (= notes and deposits) exceed the fluctuations which would occur under a simple specie currency, with the result that "the public will be exposed to very great alternations of comparative ease and difficulty in the operations of the money market."[6] What he now supported, apparently, was a provisional adherence to the Palmer rule, which would limit the fluctuations in *notes and deposits* to the fluctuations in specie reserves, with departure from it in the form of open-market sales of securities only when otherwise dangerous depletion of the specie reserves would occur.[7]

---

[4] G. W. Norman later claimed that the Bank authorities were aware, when they adopted the Palmer rule, that it would allow an external drain of gold to be met by a diminution of deposits instead of by a contraction of note circulation, but thought it nevertheless the best principle available and practicable. (*Remarks upon some prevalent errors, with respect to currency and banking*, 1838, pp. 79 ff.)

[5] *Letter . . . on the importation of foreign corn*, 1840, pp. 89-90.

[6] *Ibid.*, p. 100.

[7] Cf. *ibid.*, pp. 98-99.

Pennington later claimed that there was no danger that the reserves of the

As was to be expected, the affairs of the Bank went badly while the Palmer rule was in operation. From 1836 to 1839 in particular, while the rule was presumably being followed, the Bank was in serious difficulties much of the time. The Bank found at times that gold was being withdrawn for export through the deposits without any compensating reduction in the note circulation. It also found itself unable—or unwilling—to keep its securities constant, and it even increased its securities while a drain of gold was under way. Its difficulties were due in part to misguided violations of its own rule,[8] but in part they were due also to the utter impracticability of the rule under a metallic reserve currency whenever greater contraction of the currency (notes and

---

Bank of England could be seriously depleted through withdrawal of deposits, while the amount of note circulation remained undiminished:

> This . . . could only happen to a very small extent, for a large portion of those deposits consists of the reserves of the private banks, which they are obliged to keep in hand, and which, in times of pressure and alarm, they find it expedient to increase rather than diminish. If, instead of leaving these reserves in the hands of the Bank, they withdrew them in the shape of bank notes, in order to keep them in their own tills, the operation would obviously be altogether a nugatory one. It would be holding their reserves in one shape, instead of in another. ("Letter from Mr. Pennington on the London banking system," in John Cazenove, *Supplement to thoughts on a few subjects of political economy,* 1861, p. 53, note.)

[8] Palmer later defended the violations of the rule by the claim that they were all due to deliberate adjustment to exceptional circumstances. (J. Horsley Palmer, *The causes and consequences of the pressure upon the money-market,* 1837; *ibid., Reply to the reflections, . . . of Mr. Samuel Jones Loyd,* 1837; also, his testimony before the Committee on banks of issue, 1840, *Report,* pp. 103 ff.) But circumstances which the Bank regarded as exceptional appeared to recur with surprising frequency. It is not clear what the motives of the Bank were in its departures from its own rule. Longfield pointed out that in case of an external drain: "The securities [under the Palmer rule] were to be kept even [i.e. not increased] for the convenience of the public, not the safety of the bank. The bank would be still more secure if it were active, and reduced its securities whenever an adverse state of the exchanges, or any other circumstance, leads to a demand for gold." ("Banking and currency, IV," *Dublin University magazine,* XVI (1840), 619.) On the same principle, expansion of its security holdings would under these circumstances serve the "convenience" of the public even better. But the income of the Bank would also profit from maintenance or expansion of its security holdings. As Samson Ricardo queried, "May not a slight consideration for the Bank Stock proprietors sometimes interfere with a strict adherence to the principle laid down?" (*Observations on the recent pamphlet of J. Horsley Palmer,* 1837, p. 27.) In justice to the Bank directors, however, it should be noted that it was a rule of the Bank that no director should hold more than £2000 of the Bank's stock, the minimum qualifying amount.

deposits) should be requisite than the rule of keeping the securities constant would permit.

Torrens and Overstone were critical of the Palmer rule, although they held that the departures from it had been such as to accentuate rather than moderate its shortcomings. They pointed out that if the currency principle were to be carried out, gold movements should not be permitted to operate on the deposits alone. When the Bank found that its gold reserves were being drawn out through its deposits, it should have reduced its note circulation by "forcible operation on its securities," i.e., by deliberate contraction of its discounts or by sale of government securities in the open market. They held that maintenance of securities at a constant amount, instead of enforcing correspondence between the fluctuations in the amounts of bullion holdings and of note circulation, prevented the Bank from establishing such correspondence.[9]

According to Torrens and to Overstone, the error in the Palmer rule was that it aimed at keeping the *whole* of the Bank securities constant, including those upon which "the Bank lent its deposits," and that it permitted gold flows to act on the *whole* of the liabilities, including the deposits. The Bank, on the contrary, should keep constant only those securities upon which it put out its notes, i.e., should keep constant the amount of its uncovered note circulation. Only then would variations in the Bank's note circulation necessarily correspond with the variations in its bullion holdings.[10] To enforce this procedure on the Bank, and to make certain that the securities held as backing for the notes should be segregated from those held as backing for the deposits, the banking and issue departments of the Bank should be formally separated, and the latter should be confined to the exchange of notes for bullion and of bullion for notes, pound for pound, except for a fixed maximum of notes to be covered by securities.[11] The cur-

---

[9] Cf. Torrens, *A letter to . . . Lord Melbourne, on the causes of the recent derangement in the money market,* 2d ed., 1837, p. 29; Overstone, *Reflections suggested by . . . Mr. J. Horsley Palmer's pamphlet* [1837], reprinted in Overstone, *Tracts and other publications on metallic and paper currency,* J. R. McCulloch ed., 1857, p. 29.

[10] Torrens, *Supplement to a letter . . . on the derangement in the money market,* 1837, p. 6, and appendix, pp. 4, 5; Overstone, *Reflections,* 1837, in *Tracts,* pp. 7-9.

[11] Torrens, *A letter to Thomas Tooke, Esq., in reply to his objections,* 1840, pp. 5 ff.; Overstone, *Reflections* [1837], in Overstone, *Tracts,* pp. 38-39.

rency school undoubtedly wanted the note issue powers of the country banks to be withdrawn, or at least drastically restricted, but they did not enlarge upon this phase of the question,[12] as a precaution, perhaps, against providing further stimulus to the already vigorous opposition of the country bankers to the currency school proposals.

IV. THE BANK ACT OF 1844

The Act of 1844 put into effect these proposals of the currency school. But any expectations which may have been held that the provisions of the act were sufficient to insure protection against currency disturbances were destined to meet with early disappointment. The Bank of England took too seriously the freedom from statutory regulation of its banking department under the act, and proceeded immediately to reduce its discount rate from 4 to 2½ per cent, the lowest rate in its history up to that time, and to expand its commercial discounts.[1]

Its reserves in the banking department soon began to fall. In 1847, the public, noting the decline in these reserves, and aware that under the Act of 1844 the Bank would be unable to meet the claims of its depositors with its own notes or with specie once the reserves of the banking department had been exhausted, took alarm, and proceeded to draw out their deposits. The Bank's attempts to check the drain by rationing, successive increases in the discount rate, sale of securities, and borrowing from the market, did not succeed. On October 22, 1847, the reserves in the banking department had fallen to £2,376,472, and a panic was in full sweep in the country. The Bank was still confident that it could continue to meet its payments, but the government, in order to allay the panic, stepped in, authorized the Bank to issue notes uncovered by gold in excess of the statutory maximum, and requested the Bank to discount freely, but at a high rate of interest.

---

[12] Cf. G. W. Norman, *Letter to Charles Wood, Esq., M. P. on money*, 1841, p. 95: "I advisedly pass over the question, should the treasure in the Bank of England increase and decrease in equal proportion with its own notes or in equal proportion with the whole paper-money of the country?"

[1] Palmer testified before the Lords Committee on the Commercial Distress in 1848 that the Bank had lowered its discount rate to 2½ per cent in September, 1844, "from the circumstance of its being supposed to be the proper course for the Bank to take to employ a given portion of the reserve in the banking department for the benefit of the proprietors." *Report*, p. 108.

The panic ceased at once, gold began to flow back to the Bank, and no issue in excess of the statutory maximum was actually made. But it had been demonstrated that under the Act of 1844 gold could be withdrawn from the Bank by means of the deposits as well as by presentation of its notes for payment in specie, and that in a period of alarm knowledge that the power of the Bank to issue notes was legally restricted could operate to promote such withdrawal. In 1857 and 1866, suspension of the Bank Act was again invoked to prevent exhaustion of the reserves in the banking department. The Act of 1844 *may* have established an absolute guarantee of convertibility of the note issue, subject only to the condition that the amount of notes voluntarily remaining in the hands of the public did not fall below £14,000,000.[2] It clearly failed to guarantee adequately good management of its credit operations on the part of the Bank of England.

The necessity of suspending the Bank Act three times within twenty-five years of its enactment was disappointing to its currency school advocates, but they denied that it justified the claims of the banking school that the currency school doctrines had been erroneous and that the act was injurious in its effects. Overstone even denied that the divergent fluctuations after 1844 in the note circulation of the Bank and in its bullion holdings disproved the contention of the currency school that the Act of 1844 would automatically enforce a correspondence between these fluctuations. He was able to show that when prior to the passage of the act he had supported the rule of forcing correspondence between the bullion holdings of the Bank and the note circulation *in the hands of the public*, instead of between the bullion holdings of the Bank and the notes *outside the issue department*, he had done so only because until 1844 information was not available as to the holdings of its own notes by the Bank as "till money." Had such information been available, he would have included notes held by the Bank in the banking department in the "circulation" whose fluctuations should be made to correspond with the fluctuations of the bullion holdings of the Bank.[3] The Act of 1844 did guar-

---

[2] Subject to this condition, it did provide an absolute guarantee of convertibility, if in case of default by the Bank in meeting the liabilities of the banking department the holders of Bank notes would legally have a prior claim on the gold remaining in the issue department, a disputed question.

[3] *The evidence, given by Lord Overstone, before the Select Committee of the House of Commerce of 1857, on bank acts,* 1858, pp. 119 ff.

antee absolute correspondence between the variations in the amount of notes outstanding at the issue department and the amount of bullion held by the issue department.

The great fault of the currency school was the exaggerated importance which they encouraged the public to attribute to the automatic regulation of the issue department as contributing to a proper functioning of the Bank of England as a whole. In his speech introducing the Bank Act in the House of Commons, Sir Robert Peel had stated: "With respect to the banking business of the Bank, I propose that it should be governed on precisely the same principles as would regulate any other body dealing with Bank of England notes."[4] In his opinion regulation of the operations of the issue department would suffice—or perhaps more accurately, would be likely to suffice—to assure sound management of the currency. In this respect Peel went further than his currency school supporters, and he later admitted that he had been overoptimistic.[5] Torrens and Overstone had never committed themselves to the doctrine that regulation of the note issues was a remedy for all banking ills, although this was often charged against them, both by contemporary and by later critics of the currency school. They had recognized that careful management by the Bank of its discounts would be necessary if its banking department reserves were not to be exhausted through drawing down of deposits. In their discussion of the Palmer rule, they had pointed out that suitable management of its discounts was an essential element in the proper functioning of the Bank. But they had believed that the Act of 1844, by requiring segregation of part of the bullion reserve as cover for the notes, beyond achieving its primary objective of assuring convertibility of the note issue, would force the Bank to give close attention to the fluctuations in the unsegregated or marginal reserve held in the banking department, and therefore to act more promptly to check a threat-

---

[4] Hansard, *Parliamentary debates, third series*, LXXIV (May 6, 1844), 742.

[5] "I say, then, that the bill of 1844 had a triple object. Its first object was that in which I admit it has failed, namely, to prevent by early and gradual, severe and sudden contraction, and the panic and confusion inseparable from it, but the bill had two other objects of at least equal importance; the one to maintain and guarantee the convertibility of the paper currency into gold—the other to prevent the difficulties which arise at all times from undue speculation being aggravated by the abuse of paper credit in the form of promissory notes. In these two objects my belief is, that the bill has completely succeeded." Hansard, *Parliamentary debates,* 3d series, XCV (Dec. 3, 1847), 657.

ening drain of gold.[6] They now held that the difficulties of 1847 were due to mismanagement of the Bank, not to the Act of 1844, and that had it not been for the Act of 1844 the Bank would have carried its imprudence even further:

> It was a case of banking mismanagement on the part of the Bank of England acting upon the community, at that moment peculiarly susceptible of alarm under vague and ignorant apprehensions of the effect of the new law. . . Danger from undue exhaustion of the bullion is the evil against which the Act undertakes to protect the community; against an improper exhaustion of the banking reserve, and the consequent inconveniences, it is the duty of the Bank of England to take timely and effectual measures of precaution.[7]

But if the currency school were prepared to admit that proper functioning of the banking system required proper management by the Bank of England of its credit operations as a whole as well as of its note issues, why did they content themselves with proposals for the regulation of the note issue only? The answer lay partly in the fact that their primary objective was guarantee of convertibility of the note issue, and this the Act of 1844 substantially accomplished. As Overstone claimed: the Act of 1844 "has preserved the convertibility of the bank note; the purpose for which it was passed, and that which alone its authors promised that it should do."[8] The currency school tended also to minimize or to deny the importance of bank credit in other forms than notes as a factor influencing prices, or, as in the case of Torrens, to claim that the fluctuations in the deposits were governed closely by the fluctuations in the note issues.[9] They had a hankering also for a simple, automatic rule, and could find none

---

[6] Cf. Torrens, *A letter to Thomas Tooke*, 1840, pp. 10-11: "The difference between us is this: you contend that the proposed separation of the business of the Bank into two distinct departments, would check over-trading in the department of issue but would not check over-trading in the department of deposit; while I maintain, on the contrary, that the proposed separation would check over-trading in both departments." Cf. also Overstone, *Thoughts on the separation of the departments of the Bank of England* [1844], *Tracts*, pp. 263 ff.; *ibid.*, *Evidence . . . before the . . . Committee of the House of Commons*, 1858, pp. 163-64; Sir William Clay, *Remarks on the expediency of restricting the issue of promissory notes*, 1844, p. 71.

[7] [Overstone], *Letters of Mercator on the Bank charter act of 1844*, 1855-1857, pp. 57-58.

[8] *Correspondence between the Right Hon. Lord Overstone, and Henry Brookes, Esq.*, 1862, p. 36.

[9] See *infra*, p. 250.

suitable for governing the general credit operations of the Bank.[10] They also had laissez-faire objections to extending legislative control of the banking system any further than seemed absolutely necessary.

The currency school held that their critics exaggerated the significance of suspension of the Bank Act. Overstone had prior to passage of the act conceded that, in case of an internal panic, suspension of the act would be desirable. In such a case, resort must be had to "that power, which all governments must necessarily possess, of exercising special interference in cases of unforeseen emergency and great state necessity." But an explicit provision in the act authorizing its suspension in an emergency would be objectionable, for it would tend to convert into a routine and anticipated procedure what should be regarded as only an emergency measure.[11] Later he argued that the suspensions which had occurred were of small consequence. During a panic an interval would elapse before a contraction of the note circulation would be offset by an inflow of gold from abroad: "To meet this temporary difficulty, which was purely technical and not depending upon any principle, an important provision of the Act was for a short time suspended."[12]

The banking school objected to the Bank Act of 1844, both that it was no remedy against overexpansion of bank *credit* and that overexpansion of convertible bank *notes* was impossible. But they never supported any proposals for legislative control of the volume of bank credit, partly because they thought it impracticable, partly because, like the currency school, they objected to such control on general laissez-faire grounds. In spite of the past record of the English banking system, which they interpreted as

---

[10] Cf. Sir William Clay, *Remarks*, 1844, p. 26.

[11] *Thoughts on the separation of the departments*, 1844 (written in 1840), *Tracts*, pp. 282-84.

[12] *Correspondence between . . . Lord Overstone, and Henry Brookes, Esq.*, 1862, p. 23. The public, in fact, soon became convinced that in case of need the statutory limitation of the uncovered note issue of the Bank would not be permitted to stand in the way of the Bank's extending credit when it was urgently needed to prevent a panic, but would be suspended. Cf. Governor Weguelin of the Bank of England, in *Report from the Select Committee on Bank acts,* 1857, part II, p. 3: "This power [of suspension] having been once exercised already, there is no cause to apprehend a panic, such as occurred in 1847. The public believe that it would be exercised again under similar circumstances."

unfavorably as did the currency school, they apparently saw no alternative but reliance on the hope that the English bankers would in time learn to do better:

If the country banks have erred at all, it has not been in their conduct as banks of issue, but in their conduct as banks for discounts and loans; a matter altogether different and distinct, with which the legislature has no more to do than with rash speculations in corn or cotton, or improvident shipments to China or Australia.[13]

Were it possible, by any legislative proceeding, to restrain effectually the errors and extravagances of credit, that would be the true course to a really beneficial reform of our banking system. But these errors and extravagances are unfortunately rather beyond the pale of legislation, and can only be touched by it incidentally, or by a sort of interference which would be more vexatious and intolerable than even the evil which it sought to correct.[14]

The banking school were not willing to concede any merit whatsoever to the Act of 1844. They either denied that it would force the Bank to contract its issues more promptly in case of an external drain,[15] or, if they granted this, they denied that this was an advantage.[16] John Stuart Mill took an intermediate position. While in general hostile to the Act of 1844, he conceded that when an external drain took place, the act forced upon the Bank a prompter contraction of credit than it might carry out in the absence of the act. But he held that where the drain was due to a temporary factor and would soon cease of its own accord, such contraction was undesirable. The act, moreover, hindered the Bank from taking the steps which would give relief when a crisis had already occurred.[17]

V. The Possibility of Overissue of Convertible Bank Notes

The Bank Act of 1844, in setting a maxium limit for the note issues of the country banks and in providing for the eventual

---

[13] Samuel Bailey, *A defence of joint-stock banks,* 1840, pp. 85-86, cited, with approval, by Tooke, *An inquiry into the currency principle,* 2d ed., 1844, p. 93.

[14] Fullarton, *On the regulation of currencies,* 2d ed., 1845, p. 195. Cf. also J. W. Gilbart, *A practical treatise on banking,* 1st American (=5th English) ed., 1851, p. 92.

[15] James Wilson, *Capital, currency, and banking,* 1847, pp. 22 ff.

[16] Cf. J. W. Gilbart, *A practical treatise on banking,* 1851, p. 94.

[17] J. S. Mill, *Principles of political economy,* bk. iii, chap. xxiv. Cf. also his testimony in *Report from the Select Committee on the Bank acts,* part I, 1857, pp. 180 ff.

absorption of their circulation by the Bank of England, was carrying out the recommendations of the currency school. The bullionists, it will be remembered, had denied the possibility of a relative overissue of country bank notes if they were convertible upon demand into Bank of England notes or specie. But the boom of 1824-25 and the resultant crisis of 1826 opened the eyes of many to the expansion possibilities even under convertibility, and the currency school on this point did not adhere to the bullionist doctrine. They insisted that the country banks could expand their issues relatively to the Bank of England note circulation for a long enough period to create difficulties, without being adequately checked by the resultant adverse balance of payments with London. *A fortiori,* they held that the Bank of England and the country banks, acting together, could issue to excess even under convertibility.

Torrens on this question held views closer to those of the banking school than to those of his currency school associates. He claimed that when a relative overissue of country bank notes occurred, country notes would be presented to be exchanged for bills on London, which would in turn be exchanged for gold for export; the balance of payments both with London and with foreign countries would turn against the provinces, and the country banks would quickly find themselves compelled to contract their issues. Similarly, when the Bank of England directors "decreed a contraction of the currency, the provincial banks of issue, instead of resisting, obeyed and suffered."[1]

Norman replied that Torrens did not make sufficient allowance for "friction" when he claimed that the Bank of England had complete control over the country bank issues.[2] Overstone argued that Torrens's conclusion rested on two assumptions, neither of which was valid: that the districts in which the two types of notes circulated were distinct and completely separated from each

---

[1] *A letter to . . . Lord Melbourne,* 2d ed., 1837, p. 48. He conceded a qualifying circumstance: if the adverse balance of payments of the provinces with London was met by shipments to London of Bank of England notes which had been in circulation in the country, the circulation and prices would rise in London as well as in the country, and the country banks would find themselves able to maintain for a time their increased circulation without losing all their reserves. To assure control of the circulation, therefore, it was necessary that the Bank of England should supply either all of the country circulation or none of it.

[2] *Remarks upon some prevalent errors,* 1838, p. 53.

other,[3] and that there was no delay before a contraction of Bank of England issues exercised its full effect on the reserves of the country banks. To Torrens's statement that when the Bank of England decrees contraction, the country banks of issue, instead of resisting, obey and suffer, he replied that "the country banks first resist, then suffer, and in the end submit.[4]

Torrens similarly claimed that nothing the Bank of England could do could increase the circulation by one pound beyond the amount decreed by the "necessary and natural law which governs the amount at which a convertible currency can be maintained." If the Bank issued more notes it would displace an equal amount of bullion thereby driven abroad.[5] Torrens and the remainder of the currency school thus meant different things by "excess" of note issue. Torrens by "excess" of note issue must have meant an amount of issue which was greater than was consistent with the retention of bullion in reserves or in circulation as coin at its existing and presumably appropriate volume and would therefore result in an *immediate* export of bullion. The currency school as a whole meant by excess of note issue an amount of issue such as to make the total circulation of notes and coin combined greater than could be *permanently* maintained consistently with maintenance of convertibility and of the gold standard. The latter explained the phenomena resulting from an excess note issue in terms of lags between the original excess issue and the consequent rise in prices, external drain of gold, and impairment of the Bank's bullion reserves. Torrens would here have no commerce with lags, and he gave no consideration to the possibility of a significant intervening period of excess aggregate circulation. It is not apparent, however, that Torrens ever realized the extent of the divergence of his views from those of the other prominent currency principle advocates, or the essential harmony between this phase of his analysis and that of the banking school writers whom he was vigorously attacking.

Against the possibility of overissue the banking school appealed to the alleged "law of reflux," which amounted to nothing more than that the notes issued by a banking system on loan at interest

---

[3] As we have seen, Torrens conceded that this assumption might not accord with the facts.

[4] *Remarks on the management of the circulation* [1840], *Tracts*, pp. 96 ff.

[5] *The principles and practical operation of Sir Robert Peel's bill*, 1848, p. 49.

to their customers would return to the banks in liquidation of these loans when they matured, and therefore any excess "would come back to the banks."

New gold coin and new conventional notes are introduced into the market by being made the medium of *payments*. Bank-notes, on the contrary, are never issued but on *loan*, and an equal amount of notes must be returned into the bank whenever the loan becomes due. Bank-notes never, therefore, can clog the market by their redundance, nor afford a motive to anyone to pay them away at a reduced value in order to get rid of them. The banker has only to take care that they are lent at sufficient security, and the reflux and the issue will, in the long run, always balance each other.[6]

To Fullarton's "vaunted principle of reflux," Torrens made an inadequate reply. If the Bank issued notes by discount of 60-day paper, there would be an interval of sixty days before an increase of notes would return to the Bank.[7] But Fullarton had pointed out that there was no necessity "that the particular securities on which those notes were advanced should also furnish the channel for their return."[8] As earlier loans matured during the 60-day interval, the Bank *could* contract its circulation by failing to replace them with new loans. What Fullarton certainly failed and Torrens apparently failed to see was that the "reflux" gave the Bank the power, but did not compel it, to contract its issues, and that by granting new loans as rapidly as old ones matured, the Bank could keep any quantity of notes out for any length of time, provided only that its bullion reserves were not exhausted, and that the Bank lent on terms attractive enough to find willing borrowers.[9]

The essential fallacy of the banking school doctrine had already

---

[6] John Fullarton, *On the regulation of currencies*, 2d ed., 1845, p. 64 (italics in original). See also Tooke, *History of prices*, IV (1848), 185. Tooke denied only that banks could issue *notes* to excess and agreed that they could lend to excess in the form of deposits and bills of exchange. (*An inquiry into the currency principle*, 2d ed., 1844, p. 158, note.)

[7] *The principles and practical operation of Sir Robert Peel's bill of 1844*, 1848, pp. 106 ff.

[8] *On the regulation of currencies*, 2d ed., 1845, p. 96.

[9] Cf. T. P. Thompson, "On the instrument of exchange," *Westminster review*, I (1824), 197: ". . . the confining either a private or public bank to discounting bills at dates however short, will be no limitation. For it amounts to a permission to issue in perpetuity as much paper as men can be persuaded to borrow, under the formality of from time to time renewing the contract."

been exposed during the bullionist controversy by Ricardo and others. It lay in its assumption that the "needs of business" for currency were a definite quantity independent of the state of business psychology and the activities of the banks. The banking school were right in insisting that the volume of bank credit was dependent on the willingness of businessmen to borrow, as well as on the willingness of banks to lend. But the willingness of businessmen to borrow depended on their anticipations of the trend of business, on the interest rate, and on their anticipations as to the willingness of the banks, in case of need, to renew loans upon their maturity. The banks, by lowering their interest rates, or consciously or unconsciously lowering their credit standards, could place more loans, and the increase of loans, by increasing prices and physical volume of sales, would in turn increase the willingness of businessmen to borrow. As Joplin had pointed out in 1826, bankers ordinarily do not see this, because they do not see that they themselves as a group had created the conditions which make an expansion of credit possible and appear to make it "necessary":

> Bankers, indeed, have the idea that their issues are always called forth by the natural wants of the country, and that it is high prices that cause a demand for their notes, and not their issues which create high prices and vice versa. The principle is absurd, but it is the natural inference to be deduced from their local experience. They find themselves contracted in their issues, by laws which they do not understand, and are consequently led to attribute the artificial movements of the currency to the hidden operations of nature, which they term the wants of the country.[10]

The banking school also argued, as against the possibility of overissue, that if any bank issued in excess of its usual amount it would find the balances running against it at the clearinghouse and would be forced to contract its issue. That the power to overissue of a single bank, operating in competition with other banks, was closely limited, had long been known. It had been pointed out as far back as 1773 that if a single bank increases its note

---

[10] *Views on the subject of corn and currency,* 1826, pp. 45-46. Joplin is arguing that there are limitations on the power of issue of *individual* banks, and that the bankers perceive this, but that they do not perceive that these limitations do not apply to the banking system as a whole.

issue it at first causes a drain on the reserves of the other banks in its district, but that in time its balances to other banks become unfavorable and it is forced to contract its discounts in order to replenish its reserves.[11] Lord King made the same point in 1804: "An excessive issue of notes by any particular banker is soon detected, if not by the public, at least by the interested vigilance of his rivals; an alarm is excited; and he is immediately called upon to exchange a very large portion of his notes in circulation for that currency in which they are payable."[12]

In the 1820's, in reply to the use of this argument to demonstrate the impossibility of overissue, a number of writers drew a distinction between what a single bank acting alone could do and what a large group of banks, or an entire banking system, could do, acting simultaneously.[13] The Committee of 1826 on Joint-Stock Banks heard much evidence to the effect that the practice of the Scotch banks of making a periodic demand on each other for payment of their respective notes in cash, bills on London, or exchequer bills, was a complete safeguard against excess issue. The questions put to some of the witnesses indicate that the doctrine that banks acting together *could* issue to excess, though not accepted either by the questioners or the witnesses, was already current.[14]

In the same year, a number of writers denied the claims that were being made on behalf of the Scotch banks, that their regular procedure of presenting each other's notes for payment provided a guarantee against overissue, on the ground that if the

[11] Adam Dickson, *An essay on the causes of the present high price of provisions*, 1773, pp. 46-47.

[12] *Thoughts on the effects of the Bank restrictions*, 2d ed., 1804, p. 100.

[13] According to C. A. Phillips, writing as late as 1920 (*Bank Credit*, 1920, p. 32): "the accepted statements of banking theory, with scarcely an exception, have made no such distinction [i.e., between the power of issue of a single bank and of a banking system acting in harmony], with the result that confusion, obscurity, and error prevail with reference to the most fundamental principles of the subject."

[14] Cf. *Report on Joint-Stock Banks*, 1826, p. 269: "Q. Do you think that this is a sufficient check against the possibility of an overissue by any particular bank? A. I think no particular bank can overissue. Q. Do you think that, if all the banks were to combine, they could, by any means, force more notes permanently into circulation than the transactions of the country required? A. I think it quite impossible; the notes which are not required for the use of the country would instantly be returned to the banks." Cf. also, *ibid.*, pp. 59, 213.

banks all increased their issues simultaneously and in the same degree, they would not have adverse clearing balances against each other and therefore could overissue indefinitely.[15] These writers overlooked or, in the case of Doubleday, denied, that, while simultaneous and equal expansion by the Scotch banks would not result in adverse clearing balances among themselves, it would result, at least after a time, in adverse balances with London. It is to their credit, however, that they perceived and expounded the important principle that there is less check to overexpansion by banks when they act in unison than when they act singly, and that it is an error to infer, from the limitations upon expansion to which a single bank acting alone is subject, that overexpansion for a time is impossible for an important group of banks, or *a fortiori* for a banking system as a whole, when acting in unison. After 1826, this principle was frequently stated,[16] and it was adopted by the currency school as one of the elements in their reply to the banking school doctrine that overissue was impossible under convertibility. It became an important element in the then-prevailing theory of business fluctuations that alternating waves of optimism and pessimism resulted in overtrading and speculation followed by collapse and contraction, and that the bankers, who as a group shared the optimistic or pessi-

---

[15] Cf. J. R. McCulloch, "Fluctuations in the supply and value of money," *Edinburgh review*, XLIII (1826), 283:

> . . . the mutual exchanges that are made, twice a week, by the Scotch bankers, of each other's notes in their possession . . . though in many respects an useful and convenient regulation, is quite ineffectual, either to prevent the excessive issue of the notes of any one banking company, in which the public has confidence, or to prevent a general over-issue. If the different banks were to increase their issues in the same, or nearly the same proportion, the whole currency of the country might be doubled, were that otherwise practicable, in the course of twelve months, without the notes of any one company becoming excessive in relation to the others; for, as the increased amount of notes that might be payable by a particular company would, under such circumstances, be met by the equally increased amount that would be receivable by it, the balance to be paid in cash or bills on London, would not really be greater than it had been before the augmentation.

Cf. also Henry Burgess, *A letter to . . . George Canning*, 1826, pp. 45-46; Thomas Joplin, *Views on the subject of corn and currency*, 1826, pp. 44-45; Thomas Doubleday, *Remarks on some points of the currency question*, 1826, pp. 30-31.

[16] Cf., e.g., Sir Henry Parnell, *Observations on paper money, banking, and overtrading*, 2d ed., 1829, pp. 88-89; A merchant, *Observations on the crisis, 1836-37*, 1837, p. 19.

mistic views of their customers, fed the cycle by simultaneous expansion or contraction of their credits.[17]

Several writers, however, went further, and insisted that even a single bank could overissue for a time, and that credit expansion initiated by a single bank might spread to other banks. Mc-Culloch, in 1831, started from the hypothetical case of ten banks in London, each with a note issue of £1,000,000. If one of them should increase its issue to £2,000,000, there would result a fall in the exchanges and a demand for gold. But the demand on the overissuing bank would be only in the same proportion to its issue as on the other banks. If to check the drain of gold general contraction takes place, then, when the reserves had been replenished the bank which had expanded its issue would find itself with a circulation of £1,818,000, and the other banks would have a circulation of only £909,000 each. The other banks "would certainly be tempted to endeavor to repair the injury done them by acting in the same way." Even a single bank can expand, therefore, and, more important, may arouse the other banks to a defensive expansion.[18] McCulloch failed to point out that a single bank which expanded its note issue while other banks remained passive or contracted would suffer a drastic impairment of its reserves. He now also insisted, for reasons which are not clear but which arose probably more from considerations of Scotch patriotism than of Scotch logic, that, while expansion by a single London bank was possible, this did not hold for Scotch banks.

Scrope denied that McCulloch's reasoning was sound either for London or for Scotch banks. He did not explicitly raise the issue of the effect on the reserves of the expanding bank, but he

---

[17] Cf. Sir Henry Parnell, *Observations on paper money*, 2d ed., 1829, p. 90; Overstone, *Reflections, suggested by . . . Mr. . . . Palmer's pamphlet* [1837], in *Tracts*, p. 32; Sir William Clay, *Remarks on the expediency of restricting the issue of promissory notes*, 1844, pp. 34 ff. Cf. also, "The Bank of England and the country banks," *Edinburgh review*, XLV (1837), 76:

• The radical defect, in fact, in the constitution of the Bank, consists in its participation too much in the feelings and views of the mercantile class. It is managed by merchants, and we need not wonder that it should sympathize with them. It may, however, be inferred, with almost unerring certainty, that the Bank is acting on erroneous principles, when its conduct is warmly approved by the merchants, and conversely. Whenever the city articles of the metropolitan papers teem with eulogies on the conduct of the Bank, we may be quite certain that mischief is abroad.

[18] J. R. McCulloch, *Historical sketch of the Bank of England*, 1831, pp. 48-50. Cf. also Henry Burgess, *A letter to . . . George Canning*, 1826, pp. 45-46.

claimed that a bank could expand its issue relatively to other banks only by discounting at a lower rate, or on inferior security, than its competitors, and that to maintain its increased circulation it must continue to discount on more favorable terms. "But if, as is presumable, the other banks are going as far in both these ways as a sound practice will permit, . . . the bank in question cannot go beyond them without risks, such as no stable or solvent establishment would hazard."[19]

Sir William Clay, in the hearings before the 1838 Committee on Joint-Stock Banks, received an affirmative reply to the following question put by him to a witness:

Is there not this circumstance with regard to a competition in the issue of money, that although it may be true that one bank, of many (issuing in competition in Dublin, we will say), if it issued more in a larger proportion than its rival banks, would have its notes returned upon it; and is it not true that that would not operate as a check, if all, in the spirit of competition in a period of excitement, were also disposed to issue largely?

Longfield, citing this question and answer, objected that they took insufficient account of the part which even a single bank could play in bringing about an expansion of the circulation. If a single bank in a particular region expanded its discounts and permitted its cash reserve ratio to fall, there would result a gold drain from the banks of the region as a whole either to hand-to-hand circulation or for export, which all the banks in that region would feel in proportion to their circulation. If the other banks kept their discounts constant, they would find their reserves falling in greater proportion than their circulation (because since their circulation was several times larger than their reserves, the loss of a given amount of cash through presentation of notes for payment would represent a greater relative reduction in their reserves than in their circulation). To maintain their former reserve ratio, they must drastically contract their discounts. The expanding bank, if it had sufficient capital to withstand the drain on its own reserves, could by this procedure drive the other banks out of business. If the other banks in self-defense expanded their discounts, and allowed their reserve ratios to fall, there would

---

[19] G. Poulett Scrope, *A plain statement of the causes of, and remedies for, the prevailing distress,* 1832, pp. 13 ff. These risks, presumably, were of losses through bad debts, not of impairment of cash reserves.

result a general expansion of credit and circulation in the district. "Thus a bank may be driven in self-defense to take up the system of overtrading adopted by its competitors, and where there are several joint-stock banks of issue, the country will suffer under alternations of high and low prices, of confidence and panic, of great excitement and general depression of trade." Competitive issue of bank notes might therefore operate as a stimulus to, instead of as a protection against, the periodic recurrence of general overexpansion and overcontraction of the circulation.[20]

VI. THE ROLE OF DEPOSITS, BILLS OF EXCHANGE, AND "CREDIT" IN THE CURRENCY SYSTEM

It was, as we have seen, the position of the banking school that bank notes and bank deposits were both means of payment and parts of the circulating media, and that, since the proposals of the currency school dealt only with bank notes and left bank deposits free of control, they were bound to operate unsatisfactorily if put into practice. In a memorandum to Tooke in 1829, Pennington insisted that the deposits of London bankers performed exactly the same function as did the notes of country bankers: "the book credits of a London banker, and the notes of a country banker, are but two different forms of the same species of credit."[1] This statement by Pennington is often credited with being the first statement of the identity between the economic functions of notes and deposits. It undoubtedly exerted a considerable influence not only on the members of the banking school, but also on the currency school, and especially on Torrens.[2] But

---

[20] M. Longfield, "Banking and currency, II," *Dublin University magazine,* XV (1840), 218-19. Cf. Overstone, *Remarks on the management of the circulation* [1840], *Tracts,* pp. 98-99: "The desire to extend his own issue is the motive of each issuer; this motive will lead each party to meet an expansion of issue on the part of others by a corresponding expansion on his own part; but it will also lead him to look upon contraction in any quarter as a favorable opportunity, not for contracting, but for expanding his own issues, with the view and in the hope of possessing himself of the ground from which his rival has receded."

[1] "Paper communicated by Mr. Pennington," printed as appendix no. I in Thomas Tooke, *A letter to Lord Grenville,* 1829, pp. 117-27.

[2] Pennington repeated his argument in a paper sent to Torrens, which the latter published as appendix no. ii to his *A letter to . . . Melbourne on the causes of the recent derangement in the money market,* 2d ed., 1837, pp. 76-80.

Pennington was merely repeating an old doctrine. At the very beginning of paper money in England, it was recognized that the transfer of bank notes and the transfer of book credits at the bank were alternative means of making payments.[3] During the restriction on cash payments at the beginning of the nineteenth century the part played by the expansion of bank deposits in bringing about rising prices and the premium on bullion never became a subject of controversy, but a number of writers, both bullionist and anti-bullionist, in their analysis of the monetary process, assigned to bank deposits a role identical with that of bank notes. Boyd, in 1801, held that the "open accounts" of London bankers were, equally with country bank notes, an "addition to the powers of the circulating medium of the country." Bank notes were the "active circulation" of the banks; book credits were the "passive circulation" because they circulated only as their owners issued orders upon the bank.[4] Thornton in 1802 treated bank deposits as a substitute for paper money.[5] James Mill, in 1807, accepted "the common cheque upon a banker" as in the same class with the bank note, both being "currency," but neither being "real money."[6] Lord Stanhope in 1811 presented a resolution in the House of Lords to authorize the Bank of England to establish branches throughout England, and to substitute for bank notes book credits with the Bank, to be legal tender and transferable without cost. Stanhope claimed for this proposal that it would avoid the disadvantage of paper money of its liability to forgery, and the disadvantage of metallic currency, of the influence on its quantity of the international balance of payments.[7] He clearly regarded bank deposits as identical with bank notes in their monetary significance. Torrens, who was later

---

Torrens, under Pennington's influence, finally accepted most of the banking school doctrine with respect to the role of bank deposits.

[3] Cf. *A discourse concerning banks*, 1697, p. 6; *A vindication of the faults on both sides* [1710], in Somers' *Tracts*, 2d ed., 1815, XIII, 5.

[4] *Letter to Pitt*, 2d ed., 1801, p. 22, and appendix, p. 9. In testimony before the Lords Committee of 1797 Boyd had denied that discounts by private bankers were an addition to the circulating medium; they were only one of the many ways in which "the circulating medium really existing may be employed." (*Report of the Lords Committee of Secrecy*, 1797, p. 54.)

[5] *Paper credit*, 1802, p. 55.

[6] Review of Smith, "Essay on the theory of money and exchange," *Edinburgh review*, XIII (1808), 52.

[7] Hansard, *Parliamentary debates*, 1st series, XX (July 12, 1912), 908 ff.

radically to change his monetary views, in 1812 claimed that checks and bills of exchange were more important elements in the circulation than bank notes.[8] Samuel Turner pointed out that "A country bank was a kind of clearing-house, where, without any actual interchange of notes or money, the greater part of all payments between man and man was effectuated by mere transfers in the books of their bankers."[9] Senior stated that deposits subject to check were more important banking instruments for making payments than were bank notes.[10] Other writers, while denying to bank deposits the dignity of constituting an independent element in the circulating medium, conceded that they were "economizing devices," which rendered a smaller amount of bank notes sufficient to mediate a given volume of monetary transactions.[11]

There might be debate among economists today as to whether bank deposits are "money" or are "currency." There would be general agreement, however, that they are, like bank notes, means of payment and therefore a part of the circulating medium. Many early writers, however, insisted that bills of exchange were also part of the circulating medium. Henry Thornton, in 1797, included as "means of payment," not only coin and bank notes, but also bills of exchange "when used as such," i.e., when they served as a means of final settlement of a transaction.[12] An anonymous author wrote in 1802 that "Cash, or ready money, when considered as the medium of payment in a commercial country, comprehends every species of negotiable paper. . . ."[13] Ravenstone stressed the importance of bills of exchange as a means of payment, and declared that "I do not know how this species of paper has entirely escaped the attention of those who have treated this subject."[14] Burgess,[15] Parnell,[16] and subsequently many other

---

[8] *An Essay on money and paper currency,* 1812, p. 289, note.

[9] *Considerations upon the agriculture, commerce and manufactures of the British Empire,* 1822, p. 54.

[10] N. W. Senior, *Three lectures on the transmission of the precious metals,* 2d ed., 1830, pp. 21-22.

[11] Cf. the *Bullion Report,* 1810, p. 63.

[12] *Report of the Lords Committee of Secrecy,* 1797, p. 71.

[13] *Of the utility of country banks,* 1802, p. 3.

[14] Piercy Ravenstone, *A few doubts as to the correctness of some opinions generally entertained on the subjects of population and political economy,* 1821, p. 376.

[15] Henry Burgess, *A letter to . . . George Canning,* 1826, p. 21.

[16] Sir Henry Parnell, *Observations on paper money,* 2d ed., 1829, p. 73.

writers, included bills of exchange as parts of the circulating medium.

Some writers included "credit" as a part of the circulating medium, but meant by "credit" bank credit, and regarded it not as an item additional to bank notes and bank deposits, but as the source from which the two latter items arose.[17] But other writers, most notably J. S. Mill, included credit in a broader sense as an element of "purchasing power":

> The purchasing power of an individual at any moment is not measured by the money actually in his pocket, whether we mean by money the metals, or include bank notes. It consists, first, of the money in his possession; secondly, of the money at his banker's, and all other money due to him and payable on demand; thirdly, of whatever credit he happens to possess. To the full measure of this three-fold amount he has the power of purchase. How much he will employ of this power, depends upon his necessities, or, in the present case, upon his expectations of profit. Whatever portion of it he does employ, constitutes his demand for commodities, and determines the extent to which he will act upon price. . . . Bank notes are to credit precisely what coin is to bullion; the same thing, merely rendered portable and minutely divisible. We cannot perceive that they add anything, either to the aggregate of purchasing power, or to the portion of that power in actual exercise.[18]

Modern writers on money as a rule include specie, government or bank notes, and bank deposits payable on demand by check, as constituting "money," or the "circulating medium," or the stock of "means of payment." They exclude bills of exchange and promissory notes, and treat checks as merely the instruments whereby bank deposits are transferred or "circulate." But during the early part of the nineteenth century bills of exchange for small amounts were still commonly used in some parts of England, and especially in Lancashire, as a means of payment between individuals, and sometimes passed through many hands in settlement of transactions before they matured and were canceled. To the extent that the receivers of these bills passed them on to others

---

[17] Fullarton, *per contra,* maintained that only coin with an intrinsic value equal to its face value was "money," and that all other instruments of exchange, including bank notes, bank deposits, and bills of exchange, were "credit." (*On the regulation of currencies,* 2d ed., 1845, pp. 35 ff.)

[18] J. S. Mill, review of Tooke and Torrens, *Westminster review,* XLI (1844), 590-91.

before their maturity in payment of debts or as payment for purchases, they functioned just as did bank notes and were properly to be included in the circulating medium. As one contemporary writer, Edwin Hill, pointed out, anticipating Francis Walker's dictum that "Money is that money does," the correct test of whether something is "currency" or not is not what it is, but what it does; bills of exchange, to the extent that they settled transactions without involving the use of any other medium, acted as currency.[19] But even when bills of exchange do not pass from hand to hand, they are still entitled to be ranked with checks as instrumentalities whereby bank deposits are transferred, provided, as was generally the case in England, these bills were made payable at the acceptor's bank and when they matured were passed through clearings and credited to and debited against bank accounts in the same manner as checks.

In including personal command over credit and individual claims on other individuals as part of the stock of "purchasing power," J. S. Mill went too far. If valid individual claims to immediate payment are included as means of payment, then individual liabilities to immediate payment should be subtracted therefrom. Since these items are necessarily equal, they cancel each other, although they may in practice affect in different degree the willingness of the creditors and the unwillingness of the debtors to use their cash balances in other transactions. The case of command of credit in making purchases presents more difficulty. If all who can purchase on credit were simultaneously to do so, prices would rise even if demand deposits and notes in circulation remained unchanged in volume, for it is purchases which raise price levels, rather than payments for purchases. But the maintenance of the higher level of purchases requires, after some interval, an augmentation of the volume of payments, and this in turn re-

---

[19] Edwin Hill, *Principles of currency,* 1856, pp. 105-06. R. H. Walsh later improved on this analysis by pointing out: (1) that credit instruments reduce the *number* of transactions for which "money" is needed only when they are exchanged for goods or services and increase the number when they are exchanged for money: (2) but that even when the use of credit instruments increases the number of transactions in which money must be used, as when to make a payment in another locality a person buys with money a bill of exchange which the recipient cashes for money, the *amount of time* during which money is employed to effect the transfer may be less than if no bills of exchange were used.—"Observations on the gold crisis," *Journal of the Dublin Statistical Society,* I (1856), 186.

quires either more means of payment or their greater "velocity" or rapidity of use. But the whole discussion as to what is and what is not "money" retains the appearance of significance only while velocity considerations are kept in the background. What mattered for the currency school-banking school controversy was the extent and the causes of the fluctuations in the volume of payments, i.e., of amount of money times its payment velocity, and therefore the wrongful inclusion as money of something which did not serve as a means of payment was of little consequence if its velocity coefficient was recognized to be zero. Moreover instruments which were not money at some particular moment could be so at some other moment. In this connection bills of exchange, time deposits, and overdraft privileges could be regarded as a sort of "potential money." The quality which one writer attributed solely to bills of exchange, as the result of which "they can be either kept in the circulation, *as media of payment,* or withdrawn from the circulation, and held for a time *as interest-bearing investments,*"[20] was possessed also by time deposits, which could without much delay be transformed into demand deposits.

That differences in their velocity of circulation were the significant basis on which bank notes, deposits, and bills of exchange could be distinguished from each other with respect to their possession of the qualities of "currency" was by no means overlooked during this period. The existence of such differences was, indeed, the main ground on which the currency school refused to include deposits and bills of exchange, with their comparatively low velocity of circulation, on a parity with bank notes as parts of the circulating medium. This could be conceded to the currency school, however, without accepting their conclusion that deposits and bills of exchange should be treated as not constituting *any* part of the circulating medium, and should have led only to the assignment of greater weight to a given quantity of bank notes than to the same quantity of deposits. This was in effect done by several writers. Gilbart, for instance, although insisting that deposits were means of payment just like bank notes, argued that the extent to which they perform the functions of money must be measured, "not by the amount of the deposits, but by the amount of the transfers." Because only deposits payable on

[20] E. Hill, *Principles of currency,* 1856, p. 107 (italics in original).

demand could be transferred, he considered only such deposits as a part of the currency.[21] Longfield, similarly, held that the greater velocity of circulation of bank notes was a significant, but the only significant, difference between deposits and notes, in so far as their influence on prices was concerned.[22] J. W. Lubbock expounded the same doctrine for cash, checks, and bills, with the aid of an algebraic formula which has close resemblance to Irving Fisher's celebrated "equation of exchange."[23]

Although the members of the currency school all supported a system of currency regulation which would place the issue of bank notes under rigorous control but would leave deposits wholly

---

[21] "The currency: banking," *Westminster review*, XXXV (1841), 99-100.

[22] "Banking and currency, IV," *Dublin University magazine*, XVI (1840), 613.

[23] [J. W. Lubbock] *On currency*, 1840, pp. 29 ff.

Lubbock's formula is $\Sigma a\chi + E = A + mB + nC$,

where $\Sigma a\chi =$ the sum of transactions (a) at prices (χ) during a given interval of time;

$E =$ the sum of transactions not involving prices (gifts, tax payments, payment of acceptances, etc.);

$B =$ the total amount of bills of exchange in existence during the given interval of time;

$mB =$ the total amount of use of these bills during the given time interval in the settlement of transactions;

$A =$ the total amount of check transactions;

$C =$ the total amount of cash;

$nC =$ the total use of cash during the given time interval.

The terms m and n are thus velocity coefficients. There had been earlier algebraic (or arithmetic) formulations of the equation of exchange in which the velocity of circulation of the means of payment had been expressly provided for. (Cf. Henry Lloyd, *An essay on the theory of money*, 1771, p. 84; *The theory of money; or, a practical inquiry into the present state of the circulating medium*, 1811, pp. 42 ff.; Samuel Turner, *A letter . . . with reference to the expediency of the resumption of cash payments*, 2d ed., 1819, pp. 12-13.) But Lubbock was, it seems, the first to provide separate terms for, and expressly to provide for, different rates of velocity of the different items in the circulating medium. Lubbock also makes some penetrating comments on the relations between the variables in his equation and on the need for and difficulty of finding the quantitative values for all of these terms.

The alternative "cash-balance" approach to the problem of money goes back, as Marshall pointed out, to Petty and Adam Smith. It was expounded elaborately by Postlethwayt (*The universal dictionary of trade and commerce*, 4th ed., 1774, article "Cash"). It makes an occasional appearance in the literature of the period under examination. Senior makes incidental use of it. It is developed at some length by Richard Page in testimony before the Committee on Banks of Issue, 1840 (*Report*, pp. 64-65), and Longfield comments on Page's discussion in his "Banking and currency," *Dublin University magazine*, 1840 (XVI), 613.

free from interference, they did not agree on the grounds which justified this discriminatory treatment of deposits and notes.[24]

Torrens freely conceded that bank deposits and bank notes were coordinate means of payment and acted similarly on prices. He claimed, however, that payments in specie and notes bore a constant proportion to payments by check and that an expansion of deposits could therefore not take place without an increase of gold or notes;[25] regulation of the volume of note issues thus automatically involved regulation of the volume of bank deposits.[26] Sir William Clay conceded the similarity between bank deposits payable upon demand and bank notes,[27] and even admitted that the latter were a subsidiary circulating medium, and one whose importance was bound to decrease.[28] He nevertheless insisted that the issue of bank notes needed to be and could be closely controlled. As for deposits, however, he knew of no practicable means of controlling their volume, and in any case there was no desire for such control in any quarter.[29]

---

[24] Cf. *Report from [Commons] Select Committee on banks of issue*, 1840: evidence of Lord Overstone (Loyd), pp. 212, 281 ff.; Norman, p. 143; Sir Charles Wood, pp. 50 ff. On one point they were in agreement. The holder of a bank note was more entitled to protection against loss than the holder of a check. Bank notes were a common medium of hand-to-hand circulation, used by all classes, including persons who were in no position to inform themselves as to their quality or to bear a loss. Checks, on the other hand, were used mainly by businessmen and the well-to-do, who could better protect themselves against loss.

[25] Even if the proportion of payments in specie and notes to payments by check remained constant, this would be valid only if the relative velocities of circulation of deposits and notes also remained constant.

[26] *Reply to the objections of the Westminster review*, 1844, pp. 16-17. To this argument the banking school replied by citing statistical data purporting to show marked short-run divergencies between the fluctuations in deposits, in note circulation, and in volume of bills of exchange outstanding. Cf. Wm. Newmarch, "An attempt to ascertain the magnitude and fluctuations of the amount of bills of exchange . . . in . . . circulation," *Journal of Statistical Society of London*, XIV (1851), 154 ff., and, for an attempt by an adherent of the currency school to meet this argument, cf. G. Arbuthnot, *Sir Robert Peel's Act of 1844 . . . vindicated*, 1857, p. 30.

[27] *Remarks on the expediency of restricting the issue of promissory notes*, 1844, pp. 14 ff.

[28] "Notes, indeed, may be considered as ancillary to deposits, their functions commencing where those of deposits end; they are required only because banking is not universal, and will always diminish in quantity as the practice of banking is more widely diffused. The same considerations of economy and convenience, which have led to the substitution of notes for metallic money, tend evidently, although no doubt with inferior force, towards the further substitution of deposits transferable by cheques for a note circulation." (*Ibid.*, p. 19.)

[29] *Ibid.*, pp. 26-27.

Norman's main argument against the inclusion of deposits as a part of the currency was that the velocity of circulation of deposits was much less than that of bank notes or coin.[30] He also claimed that the volume of deposits and bills of exchange was dependent on the volume of underlying credit, which in turn was regulated by the amount of bank notes and coin, and that in any case the influence on prices of these "economizing expedients" was only "trifling and transient."[31] It was no more reasonable, moreover, to object to proposals for regulating note issues because the "economizing expedients" were left unregulated than it would be, in the absence of paper money, on similar grounds to object to the regulation of coin.[32] Norman argued also that all that the currency school proposed was that the currency should be made to operate as if it were a purely metallic currency; but even under such a currency, i.e., even if bank notes did not exist, "the trade in money, like other trades, would be occasionally out of joint, although not probably so often or to so great an extent as now."[33]

Overstone's case for limiting regulation to note issues also consisted mainly of this argument that if a currency system which included bank notes could be made to operate as would a currency system in which bank notes did not exist, that was all that could be expected of it:

The utmost that can be expected from a paper-currency is that it shall be the medium of adjusting the various transactions of a country without greater inconvenience to the community than would arise under a metallic circulation.[34]

---

[30] Cf. his evidence, *Report from Select Committee on banks of issue*, 1840, p. 205:

The banking deposits of the United Kingdom may be estimated at the very least to exceed 100 millions sterling; and I confess, the notion that that amount of banking deposits would perform the same quantity of monetary functions as would be performed by an equal amount of bank notes and coin (which is the true test of these being really money), seems to me to be a supposition completely inadmissible; and if I was not convinced upon general grounds, would induce me to be persuaded that it is an incorrect hypothesis to consider banking deposits as so much money, and as performing an equal quantity of monetary functions, as the same amount of coin or bank notes.

[31] *Letter to Charles Wood, Esq., on money, and the means of economizing the use of it*, 1841, pp. 42 ff., 82 ff.

[32] *Ibid.*, p. 74.

[33] *Ibid.*

[34] Overstone, *Reflections suggested by a perusal of Mr. . . . Palmer's pamphlet* [1837], *Tracts*, p. 36.

Deposits, debts owing, indeed credit in any form, may be made the means of purchasing and paying, of adjusting transactions; and they may therefore, in one sense, be considered as forming a part of what has been called "auxiliary currency." But the whole superstructure of "auxiliary currency" forms a subject, distinct from that of the management of the circulation. It may be raised equally upon a metallic or a paper circulation, and the fluctuations which it may undergo are subject to laws distinct from those which ought to regulate the substitution of paper for metallic money.[35]

The final outcome of the discussion was that the currency school agreed with the banking school that deposits and other forms of "auxiliary currency" or "economizing expedients," as well as bank notes, could be a source of difficulty, but that the two groups appraised differently the relative importance of variations in the two types of means of payment as causes of currency and credit disturbances. The currency school were not prepared to support government regulation of the credit operations of the banking system, but believed that statutory limitation of the note issues would bring a substantial measure of improvement. The banking school refused to support statutory restrictions on either bank deposits or bank notes, and maintained that the strict limitation of the amount of uncovered note issue would either have no effect or would operate to accentuate rather than to moderate the fluctuations in business conditions.[36]

It is not sufficient, to refute the currency school argument, to show that note circulation and bank deposits have divergent fluc-

---

[35] *Ibid., Second letter to J. B. Smith, Esq.* [1840], *Tracts,* p. 201.

[36] J. S. Mill claimed that the restriction of note issues would be nugatory, because to the ordinary man whether credit assumed the form of bank notes or not was a mere matter of convenience. "Is it supposed that having credit, and intending to buy goods by means of it, he will be disabled from doing so because a banker is prohibited from one particular mode of giving him credit?" This would make it appear that the restriction of note issues would have no important consequences. But he nevertheless predicted that it would cause the interest rate to fluctuate more, and during crises would accentuate the shortage of credit.—Review of Tooke and Torrens, *Westminster review,* XLI (1844), 591 ff.—It is not evident how these views can be reconciled. But the possibility that strict limitations on the volume of particular types of means of payment may fail to accomplish their purpose because of resort in greater degree to the use of the unrestricted types, the invention of new types, or more rapid rate of use of the restricted types, appears sufficiently real to warrant more consideration than is ordinarily given to it. Conversely, artificial stimuli to the use of one type of means of payment may result in offsetting declines in the use of other types.

tuations, or even that there are divergent fluctuations in the volumes of payments by means of bank notes and checks, respectively, if, as the currency school assumed to be the case, the relative use of notes and checks is at any one moment, given the circumstances and habits then prevailing, fairly definitely fixed, and if the regulation of the quantity of notes does not of itself operate to induce a change in these relations. But given their price- and business-stabilizing objectives, the currency school should have proposed such a method of regulation of note issue as would have resulted at all times, if velocity is left out of account, in the desired aggregate volume of *means of payment,* or taking velocity into account, in the desired aggregate volume of *payments.* Since the different stages of a business cycle are marked by variations in the proportions between bank notes and deposits, mere limitation of the amount of uncovered note issue would not suffice, and no method of regulation of note issue would suffice which did not make provision for cyclical changes in the ratio between bank notes and deposits and in their relative velocities, as well as for any changes in these ratios which the regulation of one type of means of payment might itself tend to bring about. Since these provisions could not be reduced to a simple formula, regulation of note issue alone, though it might still operate on the whole to make a "mixed currency" conform more closely to a "purely metallic currency" than if left wholly unregulated, would fail to bring about the desired results with respect to prices and the volume of business activity. An additional difficulty, with respect to the timing of regulatory measures, would arise, if, as appears to have been the case, the fluctuations in deposits preceded, instead of being simultaneous with or following, the fluctuations in note issues, so that if attention was confined to note issue alone the danger signals would come too late.[37]

---

[37] Cf. J. M. Keynes, *A treatise on money,* 1930, II, 264:

To regulate the volume of bank-notes is a very clumsy, slow, indirect and inefficient method of regulating the volume of bank-money. For while it may be true that the volume of the bank-notes bears, at any time, a more or less determined relationship to the volume of bank-money, the relationship has been steadily changing, quantitatively speaking, over long periods as a result of changes of monetary habits and customs; whilst over short periods there is a serious time-lag, the volume of bank-money generally changing first, so that a control over the volume of notes operates too late —after the evil has been done by a change in the volume of bank-money which may have taken place some months earlier.

During this period, however, the relative importance of bank notes in the English circulating medium, while steadily decreasing, was much greater than it is today. It is possible, moreover, to defend the currency school against these criticisms, even if deposits are acknowledged to be coordinate with notes as means of payment, if their objective of limiting the fluctuations in the volume of means of payment to such as would exist under a "purely metallic currency" is accepted as adequate, and if it is conceded that the variations in the proportions of deposits to *specie and notes* under a "mixed currency" would correspond, *caeteris paribus,* to the variations in the proportions of deposits to *specie* under a "purely metallic currency."

VII. The Technique of Credit Control

The Record of the Bank of England.—In appraising the record of the Bank of England during this period, allowance must be made for the lack of an adequate statistical account of the operations of the Bank and also for the absence of any serious attempt on the part of the Bank publicly to defend its record. It nevertheless appears to me that the evidence available warrants the verdict that during the period from about 1800 to about 1860 the Bank of England almost continuously displayed an inexcusable degree of incompetence or unwillingness to fulfill the requirements which could reasonably be demanded of a central bank. During the restriction of cash payments, it not only permitted the paper pound to depreciate, prices to rise, and the exchanges to fluctuate, but it repeatedly denied that there was any relationship between these phenomena and its own activities. William Ward relates that when he became a director of the Bank in 1817, he "could trace nothing directly that could fairly be said to constitute a plan or system" of credit management. It was not until 1827 that the Bank, upon Ward's motion, rescinded a resolution which it had solemnly adopted in 1819, which appeared to deny any connection between the volume of its note issues and the level of the foreign exchanges.[1] The Bank even after 1827 apparently continued to be without any reasoned policy as to its discount rate, for Ward, in 1840, could still write:

---

[1] Cf. William Ward, *On monetary derangements,* 1840, pp. 11 ff., and his evidence in *Report . . . on the Bank of England charter,* 1832, p. 143.

I have often pressed on the Court the necessity of regarding the market rate of interest, but I generally found it an unwelcome subject. Low interest was said to encourage speculation; and on my enquiring the principle by which the rate should be governed, I was told in answer, to look to the practice of our forefathers.[2]

The growing authority of Horsley Palmer and G. W. Norman in the counsels of the Bank in the 1830's brought more enlightened pronouncements to the public, but does not appear to have improved the practice of the Bank. The adoption of the Palmer rule was a flagrant error, and the rule was repeatedly violated in such manner as to make things worse instead of better. The passage of the Act of 1844 by huge majorities was evidence of a general lack of confidence in the ability of the Bank properly to carry out its responsibilities to the public. When the Act of 1844 came into effect, the Bank at once proceeded to act as if the freedom from external control which the act left to the banking department had also rendered unnecessary any internal control. During this entire period, the management of the Bank showed an almost incomplete inability to profit not only from its own recent experience, and from the advice so freely offered to it by outsiders, much of it excellent, but even from "the practice of their forefathers" in the eighteenth century.[3] The Bank then knew

---

[2] *On monetary derangements,* p. 13.

[3] Two doctrines expounded in 1867 by Thomson Hankey, a former governor of the Bank of England, are of interest as revealing what views could still be held in Bank circles at that late date. First, he denied that the Bank of England had any responsibility to come to the assistance of the market in times of monetary pressure: "The more the conduct of the affairs of the Bank is made to assimilate to the conduct of every other well-managed bank in the United Kingdom, the better for the Bank and the better for the community at large." (*The principles of banking,* 1867, pp. 18 ff.) This was, in effect, a denial that the Bank of England was a "central bank." Second, he held "that the amount of ready money, or even to use the larger expression, of floating capital, in the country at any one moment is a fixed quantity; whatever part is taken or appropriated to the use of any one class, is so much abstracted from all others, or at least from some one of the others. . . ." (*Ibid.,* p. 30.) This was in effect a denial of the power of the banking system to create or destroy means of payment. Not much could rightly be expected in the way of effective credit control from a central bank in which such views prevailed.

It is possible also that the poor record of the Bank during this period was in part the result of a failure of its governors adequately to distinguish between their responsibilities as central bank officials and their interests as private business men. The roll of governors during this period was not a distinguished one. A contemporary writer noted that of the nine governors of the Bank of

that there was a connection between their discount policy and their note issue, on the one hand, and the level of the foreign exchanges, on the other, and that a contraction of their discounts would operate to improve the exchanges and to check an external drain of gold. It recognized the difference between an internal drain due to impairment of confidence and an external drain due to a relative excess of note issue, and it was aware that different remedies were appropriate for the two cases: courageous extension of credit in the former and contraction of credit in the latter. Until the Bank was exempted in 1833 from some of the provisions of the Usury Acts, variations in the discount rate above 5 per cent were not available to it as an instrument of credit control, but it made use of informal rationing,[4] of systematic borrowing from the market, and probably also of open-market operations, during the eighteenth century.

Variations in Discount Rate vs. Rationing.—From the beginning of the nineteenth century, writers had expressed regret that the Usury Laws prevented the Bank from substituting variations in the discount rate for rationing as an instrument of credit control.[5] When in 1833 the Bank was exempted from the Usury Laws, in so far as its loans of three months' maturity or under were concerned, it was done with the approval of the Bank[6] but apparently not at its request, and the Bank did not make systematic use of this new instrument until after 1844, and even then with a view too much to its own profit and not

England during the period 1830-1847, six became insolvent in 1847 or earlier. (Jonathan Duncan, *The mystery of money explained,* 2d ed., 1863, p. 147. Cf. also T. H. Williams, "Observations on money, credit, and panics," *Transactions Manchester Statistical Society,* 1857, p. 60.)

[4] In at least one instance of credit pressure, it resorted to formal and systematic rationing. Cf. the Resolution of the Court of Directors, Dec. 31, 1795:

"That in future, whenever the bills sent in for discount, shall on any day amount to a larger sum than I shall be resolved to discount on that day, a *pro rata* proportion of such bills in each parcel as are not otherwise objectionable, will be returned to the person sending in the same, without regard to the respectability of the party sending in the bills, or the solidity of the bills themselves. The same regulation will be observed as to [promissory?] notes." Cited from *The life of Abraham Newland, Esq.,* 1808, p. 39.

[5] Cf. Henry Thornton, *Paper credit,* 1802, p. 287; Francis Horner, review of Thornton, *Edinburgh review,* I (1802), 195.

[6] Cf. *Report from the Committee of Secrecy on the Bank of England charter,* 1832, evidence of Mr. Palmer, pp. 16 ff.; Mr. Norman, p. 170.

enough to its responsibilities as a central bank.[7] The discovery by the Bank that the discount rate was an effective instrument of control seems to have surprised it,[8] although dozens of writers had been scolding it for years for its failure to use it more extensively.

The arguments then used for the substitution of variations in the discount rate for rationing were that rationing was arbitrary and capricious in its mode of behavior, and that the fear to which it gave rise, that credit facilities in sufficient quantities would be unavailable on any terms in case of credit stringency, tended to promote panic. Formal rationing seems to have been practiced only at times of unusual credit strain. But even after the Bank had adopted variations in the discount rate as its chief instrument of control, it still upon occasion made use of rationing, in the form of shortening of the maturities of the paper which it would accept for discount, as a supplementary instrument of control.[9]

Open-Market Operations.—The present-day literature on banking commonly treats open-market operations, or the purchase and sale of securities by the Bank on its own initiative as a means of currency and credit control, as a recent development whether as idea or as practice.[10] Given its legally and traditionally fixed rate of discount, there was for the Bank of England even during the eighteenth century no alternative to rationing of discounts except open-market selling operations and borrowing from the market when it wished for any reason to increase its bullion reserves. Since rationing meant refusal to its regular commercial customers of discount of what had hitherto been fully acceptable commercial paper, it was a drastic step which it could never readily have taken in the absence of emergency conditions. We

---

[7] Cf. the criticism of the Bank in this respect by the Lords Committee on commercial distress, 1848, *Report*, pp. xxxv-xxxviii.

[8] Cf. the evidence of G. W. Norman, *Report from the Select Committee on Bank acts*, 1857, part I, p. 319: "We have found, contrary to what would have been anticipated, that the power we possess, and which we exercise, of raising the rate of discount keeps the demand upon us within manageable dimensions. There are other restrictions which are less important. The rate we charge for our discounts, we find, in general, is a sufficient check."

[9] Cf. the letter of T. M. Weguelin, Governor of the Bank of England, in *Report from the Select Committee on Bank acts*, 1857, part II, p. 3.

[10] Cf. e.g., J. M. Keynes, *A Treatise on Money*, 1930, II, 170: "Those days [i.e., 1893-94] when 'open-market' policy had not been heard of."

know that during the Restriction period the Bank bought exchequer bills in the open market whenever it thought the circulation inadequate for the needs of the country but found no demand for additional discounts at the traditional rate.[11] Ricardo regarded the volume of commercial discount business of the Bank as too small to serve as an adequate regulator of the volume of the currency, and he held that the conservative discount policy of the Bank made it necessary that it be in a position to use other means than increase in its commercial discounts to increase the amount of the currency, if this was to be maintained under a metallic standard at a sufficiently high level.[12] He took it for granted that under a metallic standard open-market operations would be relied upon by the central bank whenever it desired to reinforce or to offset the effects of automatic gold movements.[13] After the resumption of cash payments, open-market operations were without question the main instrument of credit control used by the Bank.[14] It was reluctant to resort to the drastic step of formal

---

[11] Cf. the testimony of Samuel Thornton, *Report from the Secret [Commons] Committee on the expediency of the Bank resuming cash payments,* 1819, p. 152.

[12] Hansard, *Parliamentary debates,* 1st series, XL (May 24, 1819), 744.

[13] "If the funds of the Commissioners become so ample as to leave them a surplus which might be advantageously disposed of, let them go into the market and purchase publicly Government securities with it. If, on the contrary, it should become necessary for them to contract their issues, without diminishing their stock of gold, let them sell their securities, in the same way, in the open market." (*Plan for the establishment of a national bank* [1824], *Works,* p. 507.) "If the circulation of London should be redundant, . . . the remedy is also the same as that now in operation, viz. a reduction of circulation, which is brought about by a reduction of the paper circulation. That reduction may take place two ways; *either by the sale of exchequer bills in the market,* and the cancelling of the paper money which is obtained for them,—or by giving gold in exchange for the paper, cancelling the paper as before, and exporting the gold. The exporting of the gold will not be done by the Commissioners; that will be effected by the commercial operation of the merchants, who never fail to find gold the most profitable remittance when the paper money is redundant and excessive. If, on the contrary, the circulation of London were too low, there would be two ways of increasing it,—*by the purchase of government securities in the market,* and the creation of new paper money for the purpose; or by the importation and purchase, by the Commissioners, of gold bullion, for the purchase of which new paper money would be created. The importation would take place through commercial operations, as gold never fails to be a profitable article of import when the amount of currency is deficient." (*Ibid.,* p. 512. Italics not in original.)

[14] The banking school tended to deny that purchase or sale of securities would have any effect on the volume of note circulation, on the ground that it would affect solely or mainly the volume of deposits. Cf. Fullarton, *On the regulation*

rationing of discounts when it wished to contract its credit operations, and it had no means other than open-market operations of
increasing the volume of outstanding bank credit when the demand for discounts at the traditional and legally the maximum
permissible 5 per cent rate was insufficient either for credit control objectives or for its own income objectives. Under the
Palmer rule, which called for the maintenance of the securities
held by the Bank at a constant amount once the desired balance
had been attained, the only scope for open-market operations
would be to offset variations in the amount of commercial paper
held by the Bank by counter-variations in the holdings of governments. The critics of the Palmer rule, when they insisted that
"forcible operations upon the securities" would sometimes be
necessary to check a drain of gold, or to make the note circulation expand to the same amount as did the gold reserves in case
of an influx of gold, meant by such operations sales and purchases
of government securities in the open market as well as contraction or expansion of commercial discounts. Norman, in fact,
testified in 1832 that, given the restrictions of the Usury Laws,
open-market operations were the only practicable means of regulating the note issue,[15] and Palmer, before the same committee,
stated that if contraction was necessary the Bank would sell
exchequer bills first, and would contract its discounts only as a
last resort and only if the market rate of discount exceeded the
legal maximum.[16] It was common knowledge at the time that
open-market operations were the main reliance of the Bank when
it wished to act on the volume of its credits outstanding.[17] Prob-

---

of currencies, 2d ed., 1845; pp. 96 ff.; James Ward, *The true action of a purely
metallic currency*, 1848, p. 43.

[15] "I certainly think that if the issues were to be regulated in one way or the
other, I should much prefer exchequer bills. Under present circumstances, I
consider it quite impossible, without at times doing immense mercantile mischief, to attempt to regulate them by discounts. The usury laws alone are quite
decisive upon that point." (*Report . . . on the Bank of England charter*, 1832,
p. 170.)

[16] *Ibid.*, pp. 16-17.

[17] Cf. the evidence of Overstone, *ibid.*, p. 249; Richard Page, *Banks and
bankers*, 1842, p. 231. Cf. also E. S. Cayley, *Agricultural distress—silver standard*, 1835, p. 42 (a reprint of a speech in the House of Commons): "Whenever
the Bank (it is well known) wishes to enlarge its circulation, it buys up
exchequer bills, sending out its notes in their place. On the other hand, when
it wishes suddenly to diminish its circulation, it sells exchequer bills." Cf., however, Henry Parnell, *A plain statement of the power of the Bank of England*,

ably more important was the fact that prior to the passage of the Act of 1844 the Bank of England never lowered its commercial discount rate below 4 per cent, and after resumption of cash payments the market rate, except at crisis periods, was as a rule substantially lower than the Bank rate.[18] The Bank, in consequence, lost most of its commercial discount business, and except at times of financial pressure what remained consisted largely of special accounts paying less than the nominal rate.[19]

There was little discussion, however, of the technique of open-market operations. One writer claimed that when the Bank wished to contract its note issue, the order of its operations was, first, to raise the discount rate, second, to sell government securities, and finally, if these did not suffice, resort to "putting on the

2d ed., 1833, pp. 57-58: "When circumstances arise to make it necessary to lessen the amount of paper in circulation, the process by which it must be effected, is by issuing a less amount in accommodating trade; for when the price of the funds is greatly depressed, as is always the case when a large contraction of paper is indispensable, the Directors cannot sell exchequer bills, or other securities, without incurring an increase of loss. . . ."

[18] Cf. A. H. Gibson, *Bank rate; the banker's vade mecum*, 1910, pp. 56-57. Palmer, however, had testified in 1832 that the Bank charged only 3 per cent to country banks for the discount of their bills (*Report . . . on the Bank of England charter*, 1832, p. 33), and it seems clear that a substantial fraction of the Bank's discounting was done at less than the regular rate whenever this exceeded the market rate. The Bank, on the other hand, had a number of ways of evading the legal maximum of 5 per cent. (Cf. *The evidence, given by Lord Overstone before the . . . committee . . . of 1857, on Bank acts*, 1858, pp. 104-05.)

[19] Testifying in 1848, Governor James Morris of the Bank of England gave the following explanation of the reasons for the more extensive resort by the Bank after 1844 to variations in the discount rate: .

Previous to September, 1844, the minimum rate of discount charged by the Bank of England was for a long period not less than 4 per cent; the consequence was, that when money was abundant, and the current rate of interest below 4 per cent, the only means the Bank had of getting out its notes was by the purchase of securities; when the current rate of interest was high, a demand naturally arose for discount at the Bank, and the Bank was then obliged to resort to the sale of securities for the purpose of obtaining notes from the public to meet the demand. This practice of buying securities when money was abundant and the price high, and of selling securities when money was scarce and the price low, caused a loss to the Bank and incon[venience] in the money-market which it was desirable to avoid; it was also considered advantageous that a portion of the Bank's deposits should be constantly employed in the discount of bills, and constantly, therefore, under control. (*Report from the [Commons] Secret Committee on commercial distress*, 1848, *Minutes of evidence*, pp. 199-200.)

screw" or rationing.[20] It was pointed out that from the point of view of the Bank open-market operations suffered from the disadvantage that ordinarily it would be when securities were low in price that sales would be in order and when they were high that purchases would be made.[21] During the crisis of 1847, the Bank, to escape the capital loss which would be involved in selling government stock, and to avoid arousing as much attention in the money market as would be involved in openly borrowing from the market, sold government securities for cash and at the same time bought an equal amount forward, thus in effect borrowing from the market.[22] In 1875, and later, it appears to have resorted to analogous practices.

Internal and External Gold Drains.—The banking school regarded it as one of the defects of the Bank Act of 1844 that it failed to provide different treatment for an internal and an external drain on the Bank's gold, but in both cases aimed at forcing a corresponding contraction in the note circulation. They maintained that an internal drain due to mistrust called for an expansion instead of a contraction of credit.[23] Palmer, in 1840, made a further distinction between external drains due to temporary causes which could be allowed to correct themselves and external drains due to a fundamental disequilibrium of price levels which could be corrected only by forcing down prices through contraction of credit:

---

[20] R. Cockburn, *Remarks on prevailing errors respecting currency and banking,* 1842, p. 16.

[21] James Ward, *The true action of a purely metallic currency,* 1848, p. 39. David Salomons thought that the Bank made a mistake in ordinarily using exchequer bills instead of government stock in its open-market operations, as the latter would depreciate less under forced sale. He suggested, therefore, that the Bank arrange to borrow stock from the Savings Bank Commissioners when needed for open-market sales. (*A defence of the joint-stock banks,* 2d ed., 1837, pp. 34-35.) He fails to make clear why he thought that short-term securities would depreciate more during a crisis than long-term bonds, but apparently he believed that exchequer bills had a thinner market and that short-term rates rose more during a crisis than did long-term rates.

[22] See R. G. Hawtrey, *The art of central banking,* 1932, p. 151, and the testimony of James Morris, Governor of the Bank, in *Report from the Secret Committee [of the House of Commons] on the commercial distress,* 1848, pp. 199-200.

[23] In 1857, the Governor of the Bank, Weguelin, criticized the Act of 1844 on the same grounds. See his letter in *Report from the Select Committee on bank acts,* 1857, part II, pp. 1, 2.

I think the Bank are always called upon to look for the cause of the drain as far as they can form an opinion upon it when it commences, and to act upon the best opinion they can form of the occurrences then passing. There are two causes that will act upon the bullion of the country; one I take to be the deranged state of prices between this and other countries; the other, distinct payments which are to be made to foreign countries without any derangement of the general prices; if of the latter character, . . . that payment being made, and the commerce of the country not being deranged, I believe the bullion and currency would gradually resume their former state. If, as in the year 1825, a great derangement of prices existed, then it would only be by an adjustment of those prices, with reference to foreign countries, that the drain of bullion would be stopped.[24]

J. S. Mill drew similar distinctions between internal drains, external drains which were self-corrective in character, and external drains which could be checked only by a change in relative price levels, and criticized the Act of 1844 on the ground that it forced the Bank to apply identical treatment to all three types of drains.[25] He claimed that a mechanical rule for the regulation of note issue was objectionable because it would prevent different treatment of the different types of drains,[26] and he held that there would ordinarily be no difficulty for the Bank in determining the character of a drain, as the cause of a drain was generally notorious.[27]

---

[24] *Report from Select Committee on banks of issue,* 1840, p. 138.

[25] *Principles of political economy* [1848], Ashley ed., p. 665; *ibid.,* in *Report from the Select Committee on bank acts,* part I, 1857, p. 182. James Ward (*The Bank of England justified in their present course,* 1847, pp. 24 ff.) also claimed that the rule of contracting the circulation when a drain of gold occurred was properly applicable only when the drain was external and was due to international price disequilibrium. Fullarton in an elaborate discussion of drains containing much which is valuable argued that all drains were ultimately self-correcting, and that in the main the Bank of England had power to check a drain only after most of the damage had been done and the drain would in any case soon have ceased. (*On the regulation of currencies,* 2d ed., 1845, pp. 136-73.)

[26] Cf. also Lord Ashburton (Alexander Baring), *The financial and commercial crisis considered,* 4th ed., 1847, p. 15: External drains arise from different causes and therefore call for different treatment; "nothing can be more absurdly presumptuous than to substitute machinery in such a case for human intelligence." Also John G. Hubbard (Baron Addington), *The currency and the country,* 1843, p. 19.

[27] *Report from the Select Committee on bank acts,* part I, 1857, p. 189. Cf. Mill's memorandum to the French *Enquête,* 1867, V, 591:

Une banque dirigée par des hommes capables, dès que sa réserve com-

The distinction between external drains according to their causes is valid and important, but Mill exaggerated the ease with which they could be so distinguished in practice, especially in a period of scanty statistical data.[28] A drain, moreover, which is distinctly of one type in its origin, may imperceptibly become a drain of another type, or may, by causing alarm, give rise to another type of drain as well.[29]

Mill was in error also when, following Tooke, he held that while prior to 1844, and also under a purely metallic currency, a drain would generally be met from the "hoards" of bankers and merchants, under the Act of 1844 it must necessarily come out of the circulation.[30] A contemporary writer pointed out the ambiguous way in which Mill here used the term "circulation." Mill's account of the manner in which the Act of 1844 must operate was correct only if by "circulation" he meant the "gross circulation" outside the issue department. But this gross circulation included the notes and bullion held by the banking department as well as whatever reserves of notes or bullion were held outside the Bank of England. These reserves outside the issue department, however, constituted "the identical hoards from which, as he so truly argues, when speaking of a [purely] metallic currency, nearly all drains must be taken." Mill's criticism of the Act of 1844 would be valid therefore only if under it drains must come from the "active" or net circulation, which was not the case.[31] The Bank, in other words, was still able, under the Act

mence à s'en aller, trouvera dans sa connaissance des antécédents commerciaux le moyen de reconnaître les causes particuliers qui ont produit l'écoulement; elle saura si le numéraire tend à sortir en quantité indéfinie ou seulement en quantité définie.

[28] Cf. William Fowler, *The crisis of 1866: A financial essay,* 1867, p. 44: The directors of the Bank, and other men of practical experience, do not agree with Mr. Mill as to the facility of distinguishing the causes of a drain of bullion.

[29] Cf. I. C. Wright, *Thoughts on the currency, 1841,* p. 11: "under our present system, a foreign drain is always likely to produce a domestic one." Cf. Overstone, *Letters of Mercator on the Bank charter act,* 1855-57, pp. 54-55: "A drain of bullion may arise from the joint operation of several causes; indeed it is seldom otherwise. Who is to say how much of the drain arises from one cause, and how much from another cause? Such a distinction is utterly impracticable. . . . A drain of bullion, whatever the cause of it, would produce a contraction of metallic money; it ought, therefore, to be met by a corresponding contraction of the paper money" [apparently because such was the purpose of the Act of 1844].

[30] *Principles,* Ashley ed., p. 665.

[31] William Hooley, "On the bullion reserve of the Bank of England," *Transactions Manchester Statistical Society,* 1859-60, p. 85.

of 1844, to discriminate in its treatment between different kinds of drains, and to meet drains out of its reserves without contracting its "active" circulation when it thought it desirable, if it kept adequate reserves in its banking department. Mill, however, later admitted in effect that at least as far as external drains was concerned the Bank of England could still deal with them as it had had the power to do before 1844, if it retained *in its banking department* as large reserves as before 1844 had sufficed for the Bank as a whole.[32]

Adequate Reserves.—Gold reserves yield no income, and banks operating for profit tend to reduce them to the lowest level that seems consistent with safety. In countries with central banks, all other banks tend to rely upon the central bank to provide the bulk of the gold reserves for the system as a whole. The Bank of England was never legally charged with this responsibility, and its obligations to its shareholders, who during this period still held its stock primarily because they wanted dividends and not as a social duty or because prestige attached to being a "Bank proprietor," necessarily loomed large in the minds of its directors. The other banks, on the other hand, behaved as if the Bank of England were a true central bank, with full responsibilities for looking after the gold reserves of the nation. When the Bank's charter was renewed in 1833, the government made a stiff financial bargain with the Bank, which reduced its earning power and made still more onerous for it the maintenance of any surplus reserves. The rapid growth of joint-stock banks in London further deprived the Bank of England of a large part of its commercial discount business, which had hitherto been the most remunerative form of employment of its funds. As a result of these circumstances, the English credit structure was marked, during the nineteenth century, by an extraordinarily low ratio of gold reserves to aggregate gross demand liabilities of the banking system. English banking statistics for this period are too meager to make possible an accurate determination of this ratio, but it seems that, disregarding the probably negligible amounts of coin and bullion held as reserves by the joint-stock and private banks, it fell at times to as low as 2 per cent and never between 1850 and 1890 exceeded 4 per cent.

---

[32] *Principles*, Ashley ed., p. 674. The relevant passage was not in the first edition, and Ashley omits to indicate the date of its first appearance.

From the late 1820's[33] on to the end of the century a con-
tinuous succession of writers called attention to the inadequacy of
the gold reserves, but without any visible results. One writer
pointed out that the interest of the public in an adequate gold
reserve was so great as to render the cost of its maintenance a
matter of very minor importance from the national point of
view. He took it for granted that the terms of the 1833 Bank
Charter made the maintenance of an adequate reserve a greater
burden for the Bank than it could bear. He therefore recommended that the Bank should be required to establish, at the
expense of the government, an additional reserve, not to be
encroached upon without a warrant from the Treasury.[34] Richard
Page saw that the ambiguous status of the Bank was a source of
danger: "The double interests and duties of the Bank—as the
proper institution for regulating the currency, and conducting a
profitable banking business—are incompatible. The two things
may often consist, but times will occur when they cannot be
preserved together."[35] He warned that the economy of the use
of the precious metals had already been pushed too far, and
that means should be found to restore the reserves to a satisfactory level:

A banker is now encouraged to keep but a small amount of specie
by him; all his transactions resolve themselves into and are based
upon ready money, and yet he is relieved of all labor and anxiety in
procuring specie. The charge and responsibility of that obligation are
taken from his shoulders, and put upon the Bank of England. The
customers for gold in the market are therefore reduced to a single
body; who, if the gold comes, take it in, but confess that they do
not conceive it a part of their duty to go out of their way to obtain
it. This is an evil. If every banker was obliged to market for himself,
we should soon find our condition amended.[36]

Every recent improvement in banking has gone upon the principle
that we should retain gold as a standard, but bring it forward as
seldom as possible, and scarcely ever touch it. The perfection of the

---

[33] Cf. Burgess, *A letter to . . . George Canning,* 1826, pp. 110, 123; Tooke, *History of prices,* II (1838), 330-31, and his evidence in *Report from Select Committee on banks of issue,* 1840, pp. 355 ff.

[34] R. Cockburn, *Remarks on prevailing errors respecting currency and bank-ing,* 1842, pp. 57 ff.

[35] *Banks and bankers,* 1842, p. 221.

[36] *Ibid.,* p. 308.

theory would be a refinement of the thing into nothing, a spiritualizing away of the reality, until gold and no gold became one and the same. Such improvers would make it "small by degrees, and beautifully less," until it had vanished altogether, and ceased to exist otherwise than argumentatively.[37]

The Bank Act of 1844 made the gold in the issue department of the Bank unavailable for external payments, except as the banking department had a disposable reserve of notes which it could exchange for issue department gold.[38] The crises of 1847 and 1857, and the necessity of suspending the act in these years, could in large part be attributed to the inadequate reserves against emergencies held by the Bank. There was no lack of advice to the Bank that its reserves needed strengthening, but such advice was frequently accompanied by the recommendation that the additional expense should be borne by the government, or by the large joint-stock banks.[39] One especially forceful statement was as follows:

---

[37] *Ibid.,* p. 400. Cf. also, Lord Ashburton (Alexander Baring), *The financial and commercial crisis considered,* 4th ed., 1847, p. 39, for a warning to the supporters of the gold standard to "consider whether the desire to refine too much on the absolute perfection of the standard may not endanger their having no standard at all, and leave them to lapse into the Birmingham mire of inconvertible rags."

[38] Cf. Richard Webster, *Principles of monetary legislation,* 1874, p. 123:
> An ample reserve of bullion is as necessary to the nation as is an ample storage of water to a city, but both should be provided, not simply to be looked at, but for use whenever the necessity arises. . . . The very essence of the utility of a reserve lies in its being available; to lock it up is to completely ignore the very reason for its maintenance. Vary the conditions on which it may be used by putting up the rate of interest, if necessary, but do not practically prohibit its use, or you at once attack the confidence which it alone can preserve.

[39] Cf. "Tristram Trye," *The incubus on commerce,* 1847, pp. 8-9 (if necessary, the country should bear a portion of the cost of procuring and maintaining the needed increase in the stock of bullion) ; Adam Hodgson, *Letter . . . on the currency,* 1848, pp. 14 ff. (there should be an extra reserve for emergencies, maintained at the public expense, to render unnecessary violent credit contractions) ; J. E. Cairnes, *An examination into the principles of currency,* 1854, pp. 73 ff.; J. S. Mill, in *Report from the Committee on bank acts,* 1857, part 1, p. 178.

T. H. Milner, after canvassing the possibilities as to the maximum external drain to which England was liable, concluded that £10,000,000 was an ample gold reserve for external purposes, in addition to a bullion reserve for internal purposes of one-third of the note issue. (*On the regulation of floating capital,* 1848, p. 90.) This would have required total reserves in 1848 of about £16,000,000 compared to actual reserves of under £14,000,000.

Hamer Stansfeld proposed, as a substitute for Tooke's scheme of an emer-

. . . we say with all the emphasis we can command, that the entire question of administering the monetary system of this country resolves itself into the magnitude of the bullion reserve of the Bank of England. The present system works badly, painfully, and dangerously, because it has at the bottom of it nothing more substantial than the five, six, or seven millions of reserve in the banking department. But let the reserve be raised to such a point that on the average of the year, or some more convenient period, it shall not be less than say fourteen millions, and the whole complexion of the case would be changed. A transmission of three or four millions of bullion goes a long way in these rapid days in adjusting even a large foreign balance; and even four millions taken out of fourteen is a very different measure, and leaves behind it a very different residue compared with four millions taken out of eight or nine. Moreover, it might be a by-law of the Bank Court that for any fall of half a million in the treasure below say twelve millions, the official rate should be raised a half per cent, or in some other proportion to be determined after due inquiry. It is pitiful and mean that a country like this, containing millions of people dependent on trade, cannot afford or manage to keep a bullion reserve so reasonably sufficient for the amount and uncertainties of the business carried on, that the arrival or departure of a few parcels of gold or silver produces commercial sunshine or storm.[40]

It has been said that Peel was aware that the metallic base of the currency was extraordinarily narrow, but did not think that either the Bank or the people would willingly bear the expense of broadening it.[41] The contemporary literature throws little light on what the attitude of the Bank was toward this vital question. Testifying before the Parliamentary Committee of 1840, Palmer had in effect admitted that the Bank had not found the Rule of 1832 practicable. Asked to suggest a better procedure for the

gency reserve maintained at the expense of the country, that a national bank be set up with authority to issue on loan at 4 per cent £1 notes to serve as substitutes for sovereigns whenever the rate of discount exceeded 5 per cent. When gold returned to the country and caused the rate of discount to fall, these notes would be presented and canceled, as it would no longer pay to hold them. (*A plan for a national bank of issue,* 1860, pp. 5-6.)

[40] N. W.; "The recent financial panic," reprint from *British quarterly review,* July, 1866, pp. 15-16. For earlier suggestions that the discount rate should be made to vary with the amount of bullion reserves in accordance with a more-or-less definite plan, see *Suggestions for the regulation of discount by the Bank of England,* 1847, and Tooke's proposals of 1848, summarized in T. E. Gregory, *An introduction to Tooke and Newmarch's A history of prices,* 1928, pp. 102-03.

[41] Adam Hodgson, *Letter . . . on the currency,* 1848, p. 13.

Bank, he replied: "I know of no other course which could be taken beyond holding a larger amount of bullion, but which I am not prepared to say the Bank could do, without means being devised to remunerate that establishment for the expenses and charges that would attend such a measure."[42] G. W. Norman, on the other hand, denied that surplus gold reserves were desirable. If the Bank had surplus gold reserves, it would not need to contract its issues at the commencement of a drain. But "a foreign drain, however arising, would always diminish, *pro tanto,* a [purely] metallic currency," and should therefore be made to operate likewise on a mixed currency. The lost gold could be recovered only by a proportional contraction of the issues, and this contraction would be less injurious if it came promptly than if it was delayed. Surplus reserves would make the regulation of the currency depend (in its timing?) "on the fancy or caprice of those who have to administer the currency; while I think that the contraction should be connected with a self-acting machinery, that it should be regulated simply by the state of the English currency, compared with that of the currencies of other countries as tested by the exchanges; in other words, that it should exactly conform to what would occur had we only metallic money."[43]

During this period discussion of the proper criterion of the adequacy of bullion reserves was generally in terms of the minimum *absolute* amounts of bullion which, in the light of past experience of external and internal drains, would afford full safety to the Bank. Treatment of the question in terms of the minimum safe *ratio* of bullion holdings to note circulation or to total demand liabilities of the Bank—or of the banking system— became common only toward the end of the century, and I have found only two contemporary discussions of the adequacy of reserves which were couched in terms of reserve ratios. One writer, while conceding that the Palmer rule did not call for

---

[42] *Report from Select Committee on banks of issue,* 1840, p. 136.

[43] *Letter to Charles Wood, Esq., M. P. on money,* 1841, pp. 92 ff. Norman later stated that during the 1850's the excess of bankers' balances with the Bank of England above what they thought necessary plus the excess above these bankers' balances of the bullion reserves of the Bank of England over what it thought necessary together rarely exceeded £4,000,000, so that a comparatively small external drain of gold was sufficient to force a rise in the interest rate. (*Papers on various subjects,* 1869, pp. 105-07.) He now welcomed, however, the suggestion that the joint-stock banks should share with the Bank of England the burden of maintaining adequate gold reserves. (*Ibid.,* p. 138.)

maintenance of the bullion reserve ratio at one-third of the demand liabilities, claimed that the public had nevertheless so understood the rule, and insisted that it was a better rule than that of maintaining the security holdings constant.[44] He proposed "that for the future the Bank of England govern her issues of notes (without reference at all to deposits) on the principle of holding one-third of gold against notes in circulation."[45] Another writer, in the same year, recommended that instead of following the Palmer rule the Bank aim at maintaining a 50 per cent reserve against its note circulation. He apparently set the required reserve at so high a ratio because of his recognition that bullion could be drawn out of the Bank through its deposits as well as by presentation of notes and his belief that consideration should also be given to the existence of private bank note circulation dependent upon the Bank of England for its ultimate bullion reserve. He conceded that a 25 per cent reserve ratio would be adequate if the Bank followed the rule of withdrawing £4 in notes for each £1 loss in bullion. He called his proposal the "principle of proportion," to distinguish it from "the principle hitherto assumed as the correct one, and which may be called the principle of diminution in equal amounts."[46]

The practice of extreme economy in the maintenance of bank reserves did have as an accidental by-product the beneficial effect that it guaranteed to the metallic standard world that as far as England was concerned there would be no hoarding of gold and that all gold reaching that country would quickly exercise an influence in the appropriate direction for international equilibrium on interest rates and the volume of bank credit. But it tended to intensify the growing tendency for instability of business conditions within England itself. Without willingness at times to maintain greater metallic reserves than were absolutely necessary to secure convertibility of the paper currency and without excess reserves which could be released during times of pressure as an alternative to credit contraction, there could be no "management" of a metallic standard currency in the interest of internal stabilization, and it is arguable that even the outside

---

[44] "A Merchant," *Observations on the crisis, 1836-37,* 1837, pp. 5 ff.

[45] *Ibid.,* p. 13.

[46] John Hall, *A letter . . . containing a new principle of currency,* 1837, pp. 10 ff. I am indebted to Mrs. Marion J. Wadleigh for this reference.

world had more to gain from greater internal stability in England than it would have had to lose by the occasional "sterilization" by the Bank of England of several million pounds of gold. While the English currency was undoubtedly even then a "managed" rather than a purely "automatic" one, the main objective of management appears to have been to achieve the maximum economy of reserves, i.e., the maximum banking profits, consistent with maintenance of convertibility. But the Bank of England was not set up as an eleemosynary institution, and during this period it probably could not have afforded to assume greater control responsibilities without financial guarantees from the government which could not be asked for without injury to its prestige and which would, moreover, probably not have been obtainable merely for the asking.

Foreign Securities as a Secondary Reserve.—In the hearings before the Committee of 1840, it was brought out that the Bank had given some consideration to the desirability of adopting the practice of holding foreign securities as a secondary reserve which would yield income while providing an emergency means of international payment. In reply to questions, Palmer and Norman agreed that foreign securities would serve equally with gold for this purpose, with the advantage over gold that they would earn interest while serving as a reserve. Palmer agreed also that the sale of foreign securities would be preferable to forced recourse to borrowing from foreign central banks as a means of checking an abnormal pressure on the gold reserves. Norman, however, thought that it would prove difficult in practice to find suitable foreign securities whose salability in the places with which the balances of payments were adverse could be relied upon, and Overstone was inclined to disapprove of the practice, on the ground that it would serve as an expedient to avoid resort to contraction of the note issue, which he regarded as the only sound method of dealing with an external drain of gold, and that it would tend to injure the credit of the Bank abroad.[47]

The discussion before the Committee of 1840 attracted some attention. James Ward claimed that the practice would prove highly profitable for the Bank of England—not only would for-

---

[47] *Report from Select Committee on banks of issue,* 1840, pp. 136, 159, 241.

eign interest-bearing securities be substituted for bullion, but purchases of the securities would be made when the exchanges were favorable to England and sales when the exchanges were unfavorable, with an additional profit, therefore, on the turn of the exchanges. If the Banque de France should also adopt this practice, then "the joint operation would in fact be the same as if each country kept a banking account with the other to draw upon for the payment of any balances between them without the necessity of actually sending gold backwards and forwards for the purpose; and it must be evident that such an arrangement would very much diminish fluctuations in the rates of exchange."[48]

Robert Somers, writing in 1857, comments as follows on a suggestion made in a letter to the *Times*, recommending that mint certificates of deposit of bullion be used as a means of making international payments and thus of saving the cost of transport of the actual bullion:

The bullionists [i.e., the currency school] are so formal in adherence to their principle, that they would consider gold in the British mint a proper basis of money, though the right to it belonged to, and was doing service in, another country; but surely gold in another country, the right to which resides in this, must be a fully better security for British currency to rest upon. This is a distinction constantly overlooked under the Bank charter act. It is not the right of property in bullion, not the control over its movements and its possession, but the mere place where it may happen to be lodged, that forms the sole guide of the Bank in regulating the rate of discount. Though the whole stock of bullion in the Bank of England were in the power of a foreign capitalist, and could be removed any hour he chose, the Act would recognize it as a valid basis of paper money; but if British capitalists sent their gold temporarily to France or America, and held securities equivalent to such gold, these securities would pass for nothing.[49]

It is true that under the Act of 1844 the Bank could not have counted gold earmarked to its account abroad, or holdings by itself of foreign securities, to say nothing of private holdings of foreign securities, as part of its bullion reserve in the *issue* department. But there was nothing in the Act of 1844 to prevent the

---

[48] James Ward, *The true action of a purely metallic currency*, 1848, p. 74, note. Cf. also J. W. Gilbart, "The Currency: Banking," *Westminster review*, XXXV (1841), 126.

[49] *The errors of the banking acts of 1844-5*, 1857, pp. 18-19.

Bank from treating gold earmarked abroad or holdings by itself of foreign securities as part of its *banking* department reserves, or, in appraising its reserve position, from taking into account holdings by the British public of foreign securities and holdings by foreigners of British securities.

Silver as a Reserve Metal.—The Bank of England before 1844 bought and sold silver and always included its silver holdings at the market value in its returns of bullion held. In 1819 the Bank had opposed Baring's recommendation of a bimetallic standard on the ground that "silver bullion answered equally their purpose of checking an adverse state of exchange and a demand of their gold from abroad, as if it were converted into a current coin."[50] The Bank in 1844 asked that it continue to be permitted to issue notes against silver and that it be permitted to count its silver holdings as part of its bullion reserves in the issue department. It claimed that foreign remittances could often be made more cheaply in silver than in gold, but that the variations in the market price of silver were too slight to compensate private concerns for holding it in stock, and were too slight also to compensate the Bank for holding it unless it could count it as part of its issue department reserve. The Act of 1844 gave the Bank the right to issue notes against silver not to exceed one-fourth of the gold held in the issue department, although the Bank had asked that this limit be set at not lower than one-third, and the Bank continued for a while to complain that the limit set by the act was too low.[51]

There is some evidence, however, that the attempt to operate a two-metal reserve under a monometallic standard had not been very successful. During the crisis of 1825, it apparently required the cooperation of the Banque de France to enable the Bank of England to exchange silver for gold.[52] According to Baring, during the crisis of 1847 the Bank at one time had upward of £1,500,000 in silver, for which it was unable to get gold in exchange.[53] In any case the Bank in 1850 ceased to issue against

---

[50] Lord Ashburton (Alexander Baring), *The financial and commercial crisis considered*, 1847, p. 38.

[51] Cf. *Report from the [Lords] Committee [on] the causes of the distress . . . among the commercial classes*, 1848, pp. xli ff.

[52] See J. H. Clapham, *An economic history of modern Britain*, 1926, I, 282, and the sources there cited.

[53] *The financial and commercial crisis considered*, p. 38.

silver, except for a minor resumption of the practice in 1860-61, when, to help the Banque de France, it exchanged £2,000,000 of gold for silver on the basis of a repurchase agreement.[54]

Cooperation between Central Banks.—The Bank of England found itself forced, no doubt very reluctantly, to appeal to the aid of foreign money markets on a number of occasions. In 1836 the Bank of England, by arrangement with the Banque de France, drew bills of credit on Paris for over £400,000. This transaction was not publicly acknowledged until 1840. In 1838, while the Bank of England was under pressure, it arranged with the Governor of the Banque de France, who was in London at the time, for credit in Paris to be drawn upon if needed. In 1839, as the gold reserves of the Bank of England were approaching exhaustion, the Bank of England took advantage of this arrangement. As the Bank of England was not accustomed to draw on foreign countries, and the Banque de France made loans only on bills of exchange bearing French names or on French public securities, the transaction was carried out with the aid of intermediaries. Baring Brothers, on behalf of the Bank of England, drew bills on twelve Paris bankers to the extent of £2,000,000, which the Banque de France, in accordance with the arrangement, discounted for these bankers. At the same time similar credits established in Hamburg brought the Bank £900,000 additional gold.[55] The necessity of resort to Paris for assistance, at a time, moreover, when relations with France were not too friendly, was regarded in England as rather humiliating, especially as it was reported that the followers of M. Thiers were boasting of the generosity of Frenchmen in coming to the assistance of the Bank of England when in difficulty while recommending that under no circumstances should such liberality be repeated in future.[56]

---

[54] Cf. *The bullion business of the Bank of England,* 1869, p. 20; Sir Felix Schuster, *The Bank of England and the State* (a lecture delivered in 1905), 1923, p. 34; *Economist,* XVIII (1860), 1301, 1357.

[55] For these transactions see: A. Andréadès, *History of the Bank of England,* 2d ed., 1924, p. 268; *Report from . . . Committee on banks of issue,* 1840, testimony of Mr. Horsley Palmer, pp. 120, 128; David Buchanan, *Inquiry into the taxation and commercial policy of Great Britain,* 1844, p. 295. During October, 1839, after £2,900,000 had thus been acquired abroad, the bullion holdings of the Bank amounted at one time to only £2,525,000.

[56] *The banker's circular* for Nov. 19, 1841, as cited by William Leatham, *Letters . . . on the currency,* 2d series, 1841, p. 12.

In 1847 the financial crisis and the shortage of gold were common to both London and Paris. By arrangement with the Banque de France, the Emperor of Russia and the Imperial Russian Bank bought from the Banque de France and other sources, with gold taken from the Russian reserves, Russian and foreign securities to the amount of £6,600,000, thus relieving the strain in the Paris and London money markets.[57] It does not appear, however, that the Bank of England was a direct party to this transaction, and it, in fact, indirectly gave assistance to the Banque de France in that year. The Banque de France, after giving consideration to proposals that it should engage in open-market sales of *rentes* in order to check the drain of gold which it was undergoing, decided not to, on the ground that such operations would reduce the circulation, but would not increase the metallic reserve. Instead, it raised its discount rate and engaged a banker to borrow 25,000,000 francs in London, on *rente* collateral, and used the proceeds to withdraw gold from the Bank of England.[58]

Cooperation between central banks in the management of metallic currencies was during this period exceptional rather than an established policy. On the contrary, it appears that ordinarily the central banks either paid little attention during this period to what was going on in other money markets, or else engaged in com-

---

[57] See *The currency question*, 2d ed., 1847(?), pp. 35-38, where the Russian decrees are reprinted in translation.

[58] Cf. Horace Say, "La crise financière et la Banque de France," *Journal des économistes*, XVI (1847), 200. It would be interesting to know whether the Banque de France consulted the Bank of England before engaging in this transaction, as it came at a most embarrassing time for the latter.

In addition to the 1826, 1836, 1839, and 1847 instances referred to in the text, the Bank of England appears to have received aid from the Banque de France or from other Paris banks in 1832, 1890, 1896, and 1897. The 1890 transaction resulted in a hostile interpellation in the French Chambre des Députés, but was defended by the French Minister of Finance on the ground that it was necessary to prevent harmful repercussions on France from the financial crisis in London. (*Journal officiel, débats parlementaires*, 5ᵉ leg., sess. ord., 1891, I, 16 ff.) The Bank of England in 1696, or shortly after its foundation, borrowed in Holland. (Andréadès, *History of the Bank of England*, 2d ed., 1924, p. 109.) In 1898 the Bank of England appears to have cooperated with the Banque de France in coming to the assistance of German banks. (Cf. *Revue d'économie politique*, XIII (1899), 165.) The first earmarking of gold by the Bank of England on behalf of a foreign central bank appears to have been in 1906, for the National Bank of Egypt, but it had earmarked gold for India on earlier occasions.

petitive increases of their discount rates and in raids on each other's reserves at a time of actual or anticipated credit stringency.[59]

There were only scattered references in the literature of this period to the need for international cooperation in credit management. Poulett Scrope, in 1830, found fault with the suppression of small notes by the Act of 1826, on the ground that it operated to cause a rise in the value of gold throughout the world and produced distress in the other great commercial nations as well as in England. He remarked that this international aspect had apparently failed to attract any attention, although "There have been times when a far less injury would have been resented by a declaration of war. But this fact is one only of many, showing how, in the close relations by which commerce knits nations together, each is interested in the welfare and good government of the other, almost, if not quite as much, as in her own."[60] Several writers pointed out that the growth of commerce and the increasing international mobility of capital was bringing about a greater interdependence of the world's money markets, with the result that single-handed regulation of its metallic currency by any country was becoming increasingly difficult. Because of this trend William Blacker predicted that "monetary panics will year after year become more frequent and more severe as long as a metallic basis is preserved, which, with the aid of steam, conveys the monetary convulsion from country to country with a rapidity which, for all practical effect, may be compared to a metallic wire passing through the lands of all nations conveying the electric shock almost simultaneously to the most remote quarters of the

[59] Cf. R. H. Patterson, "On the rate of interest . . . during commercial and monetary crises," *Journal of the Royal Statistical Society,* XXXIV (1871), 343. Cf. also Robert Somers, *The errors of the banking acts of 1844-5,* 1857, p. 95: "The manner in which the various commercial nations deal with the great mediums of exchange seems dictated by caprice rather than by any intelligent principle, and so far from adopting some general system in the interests of all, their monetary policy is conceived in hostility one to another." Somers, however, had in mind the monetary standards, rather than the day-to-day monetary practices, of the different countries. Cf. also the later comment of Luzzati: "Aujourd'hui, . . . les banques d'émission restent presque inaccessibles dans leur majesté solitaire, et ne communiquent qu'exceptionellement entre elles." "Une conférence internationale pour la paix monétaire," (*Séances et travaux de l'académie des sciences morales et politiques,* new series LXIX (1908), 363-64.)

[60] *The currency question,* 1830, pp. 32-33.

globe."[61] Another writer stressed the importance of the comparative rate of expansion of credit in different countries as affecting the severity and the area of monetary pressure which would follow. If the expansion was widespread, there would be a general scramble for gold when the pressure came.[62]

VIII. THE RELATION BETWEEN BANK OF ENGLAND OPERATIONS AND SPECIE MOVEMENTS

The Bank of England did not itself engage directly in import or export transactions in bullion or specie. It was obligated, however, to give specie upon demand in exchange for its own notes, and as a part of its regular routine it also upon demand gave notes in exchange for specie, cashed its depositors' checks in specie, and bought gold bullion of standard fineness at the fixed price of £3.17.9 per ounce. In addition, the Bank operated its bullion department on ordinary commercial principles, buying and selling silver bullion and gold bullion of other than the standard fineness at the prevailing market prices. Periods of business expansion were also as a rule periods of expansion of Bank note circulation, of increased indebtedness to the Bank of private bankers and other clients, and of decline in the Bank's specie reserves. As long as the Bank of England would freely discount, a credit expansion could go on indefinitely, without a rise in the rate of interest or depletion of the cash reserves of private[1] banks. A credit expansion, if peculiar to England, or relatively more marked there than abroad, would operate to stimulate imports and, through increased domestic absorption of supplies, to check exports, and would thus tend to create an unfavorable balance of payments. Even a credit expansion in which England was lagging behind the rest of the world might deplete specie reserves in England if it resulted in a substantial internal drain of gold to satisfy the demand for increased hand-to-hand specie circulation.

[61] *The evils inseparable from a mixed currency* [1st ed., 1839], 3d ed., 1847, pp. 128-29.

[62] T. H. Williams, "Observations on money, credit, and panics," *Transactions of the Manchester Statistical Society*, 1857-58, pp. 58-59.

[1] In the absence for England of a term corresponding to the American "member bank," I use "private bank" to designate banks and bankers of all kinds other than the Bank of England. The joint-stock banks, of course, normally did not borrow directly from the Bank of England, but they did borrow indirectly through bill brokers, and there were exceptional instances of their borrowing directly from the Bank of England.

The role of the Bank of England under such circumstances, whether she acted to protect her own specie reserves or to control the credit situation, was to check such credit expansion before it had reached a dangerous level. We are here concerned with the contemporary views as to the mechanism whereby the Bank of England could influence the flow of specie into and out of the country and thus into and out of her own coffers.

It was common doctrine that the market rate of interest influenced the flow of specie, a high rate operating to attract specie and a low rate to force it out, and that the Bank of England could regulate the flow of specie through its power over the market rate of interest. It was taken for granted that normally there were no idle funds outside the Bank of England, and that any reduction by the Bank of England of the volume of credit it had outstanding, whether accomplished through raising its discount rate, rationing, sales of securities in the open market, or borrowing from the market, would, other things being equal, force a rise in the market rate of interest.[2] It was pointed out, however, that at times the market was sufficiently independent of the Bank to make the Bank's discount rate ineffective as a controlling factor unless supported by open-market sales and, in extreme cases, by borrowing from the market.[3] On the other hand, there was recognition of the possibility that increases in the Bank rate might act as a deflationary factor not only directly through their influence on the volume of advances to the Bank's own customers, but also indirectly through their psychological influence on the market judgment as to business prospects and therefore on the willingness of private bankers to lend and of businessmen to borrow and on the velocity of circulation.[4]

---

[2] Cf. T. H. Milner, *Some remarks on the Bank of England,* 1849, p. 21: "there is never any spare capital out of the Bank." Cf. also "N" (Newmarch) in London *Times,* April 27, 1863, as cited in W. J. Duncan, *Notes on the rate of discount in London,* 1867, pp. 69-70.

[3] See *supra,* pp. 259-60.

[4] Cf. Overstone, *Thoughts on the separation of the departments of the Bank of England* [1844], in *Tracts,* p. 264:

> . . . a rise in the rate of interest . . . tends to produce a contractive effect upon the country circulation, and still more on the state of confidence and of the auxiliary currency [i.e., bank deposits and bills of exchange] which rests upon that confidence.

Cf. also Norman's evidence, *Report from Select Committee on banks of issue,* 1840, p. 158:

> . . . I do not look at a rise in the rate of discount merely as it affects the securities and the circulation of the Bank; it produces a much greater

Most of the discussions of the role of the interest rate referred only to short-run disturbances, including periodic business fluctuations, or "cycles,"[5] and the changes in interest rates were related to specie movements mainly in terms of their influence on the international movement of short-term funds, and their influence on relative prices was commonly held to be too slow-working to be an important factor in restoring international equilibrium.[6] Most emphasis was put on the international mobility of funds devoted to investment in securities, in response to relative changes in the market rates of interest in London and abroad,[7] but many other ways in which a relative rise of the English interest rate could attract short-term funds from abroad or check their flow to abroad were noted.[8]

---

and more important effect than that in its general influence upon credit; it limits all banking expedients; I have no doubt that it increases the reserves of bankers; it diminishes the efficiency, therefore, of a given amount of currency; it renders persons less willing to discount bills; and it makes merchants less disposed to buy, and more disposed to sell.

[5] See especially Hamer Stansfeld, *The currency act of 1844*, 1854, pp. 17-19, for an account of the business cycle emphasizing the status of the interest rate, the balance of trade, and the balance of payments at each stage of the cycle. Cf. also William Miller, *A plan for a national currency*, 1866, pp. 16 ff.

[6] Overstone gives the following account of the sequence of events resulting from an increase in the interest rate:

Contraction of circulation acts—first upon the rate of interest—then upon the price of securities—then upon the market for shares, &c.—then upon the negotiation of foreign securities—at a later period, upon the tendency to enter into speculation in commodities—and lastly, upon prices generally. These effects may be retarded or accelerated by other circumstances; possibly they may not occur precisely in the manner here stated; but this is something like the order of succession in which the effects of contraction of the circulation are gradually developed. (*Thoughts on the separation of the departments* [1844], *in Tracts*, 1857, p. 253.)

See also the substantially similar accounts in R. K. Douglas, *Brief considerations on the income tax and tariff reform, in connection with the present state of the currency*, 1842, p. 28, and Robert Somers, *The errors of the banking acts of 1844-5*, 1857, p. 10. Cf. also J. S. Mill, *Principles of political economy* [1848], Ashley ed., p. 497: ". . . it is a fact now beginning to be recognized, that the passage of the precious metals from country to country is determined much more than was formerly supposed, by the state of the loan market in different countries, and much less by the state of prices."

[7] Cf. T. H. Milner, *Some remarks on the Bank of England*, 1849, p. 16: "One per cent may make all the difference, whether capital be invested at home ·or in another country." See also, *infra*, pp. 403 ff.

[8] Cf. e.g., Tooke's evidence, *Report from Select Committee on banks of issue*, 1840, p. 359:

. . . the effect upon the exchanges of a rise in the rate of interest would be that of inducing foreign capitalists to abstain from calling for their

Most of the writers of the period conceded the efficacy of the Bank discount rate, if employed skillfully and forcibly enough, as a regulator of specie movements through its influence on the international movement of short-term funds and, to a less extent, on the commodity trade balance. A skeptical note, however, was struck occasionally in the literature. It was pointed out that in so far as the movement of short-term funds was concerned what mattered was only the *relative* height of market rates of interest in London and abroad, and that rates were likely to rise and fall simultaneously in the important money markets. It was later claimed, moreover, that the foreign central banks, and especially the Banque de France, for a time during this period systematically followed the practice of meeting increases in the English discount rate by increases in their own rates in order to protect their reserves.[9] A rise in the discount rate, moreover, might be interpreted as a signal of impending financial stress and thus instead of attracting funds to England might frighten them away.[10] One writer, otherwise favorable to its use, regarded it as a defect of the discount rate as a regulator of specie flows that it operated to check exports, presumably by making it more costly or more difficult to finance them.[11] Finally, the opponents of a metallic standard or of central bank control thereof tended either to deny in general terms the efficacy of the discount rate as

funds from this country, to the same extent as they otherwise might do, and it would operate at the same time in diminishing the inducements to capitalists in this country to invest in foreign securities, or to hold foreign securities, and it might induce them to part with foreign securities, in order to make investments in British stocks or shares. It would likewise operate in restraining credits from the merchants in this country by advances on shipments outwards, and it would have the effect of causing a larger proportion of the importations into this country to be carried on upon foreign capital.

[9] Cf. R. H. Patterson, "On the rate of interest . . . during commercial and monetary crises," *Journal of the Statistical Society of London*, XXXIV (1871), 343; Robert Somers, *The Scotch banks and system of issue*, 1873, pp. 177 ff.; Richard Webster, *Principles of monetary legislation*, 1874, p. 113.

[10] "History and exposition of the currency question," *Westminster and foreign quarterly review*, XLVIII (1848), 468, note; R. H. Patterson, *loc. cit.*

[11] William Hooley, "On the bullion reserve of the Bank of England," *Transactions of the Manchester Statistical Society*, 1859-60, p. 89:

One of the least satisfactory features of the present mode of effecting this object [the correction of the exchanges], by increasing the rate of interest and lessening the amount of accommodation, is, that its effect on imports cannot be felt until after the lapse of months, whilst its effect on exports is immediate, and unfortunately in the wrong direction, viz., restriction.

a regulator of specie movements, or to deny any need of such
control given the existence of a self-regulating mechanism, or
to claim that the regulation, whether effective or not in protecting specie reserves, was costly to internal prosperity when it involved increase in the discount rate and contraction of credit, or
to find still other objections to it.[12]

IX. CURRENCY REFORM PROPOSALS

All that the currency school aimed at, as we have seen, was
that the existing "mixed currency" should be made to operate
precisely as they supposed a "purely metallic currency" would
operate. By a "purely metallic currency," it should be remembered,
they meant one which would not include either government paper
money or bank notes, but under which bank deposits transferable by check or bill of exchange would still exist. The chief
characteristic of such a currency, they thought, was that every
influx of gold from abroad or efflux of gold to foreign countries
would immediately and automatically result in a corresponding
increase or decrease, respectively, in the amount of money in

[12] Cf. Robert Somers, *The errors of the banking acts of 1844-5*, 1857, p. 78:
    The time has come when the theory of regulating foreign trade by the
    Bank screw must be discarded. It is no longer suited to the state and cir-
    cumstances of commerce. Free trade has introduced a new and more
    natural regulator into the transactions of nations. We do not now specu-
    late in foreign trade so much as simply barter the produce and manu-
    factures of the United Kingdom for the goods of our neighbours. Our
    import and export trade have thus received a simplicity, an adaptation,
    and equality, which could not possibly be realized under a system of pro-
    hibition and protection. The connection of the most distant countries by
    railways and telegraphs, securing the utmost rapidity of motion and in-
    telligence, and the cosmopolitan attributes of capital, creating one money
    market and keeping trade equally active throughout the world, all co-
    operate with the principle of free commerce in harmonizing the exchanges
    and preventing those oscillations and inequalities in imports and exports
    which were formerly the frequent cause of monetary and commercial
    derangement.
Somers further objects to the discount rate-mechanism, that specie does not
necessarily flow to the high-rate market and may flow in the opposite direction
(p. 18) ; that when imports are discouraged by a rise in the discount rate,
exports are correspondingly checked by the resultant fall in purchasing power
of the countries which are the source of the imports (p. 77) ; that the increase
in the interest rate, by increasing capital costs, instead of increasing, impairs
the ability of English exporters to meet foreign competition (p. 78) ; and that
in general, more attention should be paid, in credit policy, to the needs of the
internal market than to specie flows.

circulation. The banking school pointed out that even under a "purely metallic currency" of this kind there would be "hoards" of gold of variable amounts, mainly in the form of bank reserves; that an influx of gold might go to augment the hoards instead of the specie and note circulation, while an efflux of gold might similarly come out of hoards instead of out of circulation; and that the influence of a variation in the metallic circulation on the level of prices might be offset or more than offset by an opposite variation in the amount of bank deposits. Many critics of the currency school, moreover, held that it was not desirable that a mixed currency should act precisely as would a purely metallic currency if that meant that it should undergo all the fluctuations in quantity and in value which would be experienced by a purely metallic currency. As one writer put it: "a mixed currency should not fluctuate as a metallic currency does. A metallic currency is undoubtedly the safest, possessing intrinsic value; but its liability to fluctuation in quantity arising from the state of the exchanges, and consequent drains, diminishes its claim to be considered the best type of a currency. Its liability to fluctuation is an evil to be counteracted and not adopted."[1] The banking school, however, had no legislative solution to offer. Imperfectly as the currency operated, legislative interference would only make things worse. Reliance must be had on the good sense and the competence of those who had charge of the credit operations of the banking system.

There were numerous writers, however, who shared the dissatisfaction of the banking school with the existing currency system even if made to operate in accordance with the specifications of the currency school, but who rejected the banking school doctrine that nothing could be done by regulation to make the currency more stable in its value. The Attwoods had acquired a considerable following, who became known as the "Birmingham school," at one time had an organization called the "National

---

[1] Letter of Hamer Stansfeld, in *Money market review*, Dec. 21, 1861, cited by Brookes in *Correspondence between . . . Lord Overstone, and Henry Brookes, Esq.*, 1862, p. 65. Cf. also the similar views in: J. W. Gilbart, "The currency: banking," *Westminster review*, XXXV (1841), 98; "The Bank charter act. Currency principles," *ibid.*, XLVII (1847), 432; J. S. Mill, *Principles of political economy*, Ashley ed., p. 670; *ibid.*, *Report from the Select Committee on the bank acts*, part I, 1857, p. 204; John Haslam, *The paper currency of England*, 1856, p. 34.

Anti-Gold Law League," modelled after the Anti-Corn Law League, and engaged in vigorous and sustained propaganda for the total abandonment of a metallic basis for the currency. But the Attwood doctrines deteriorated in the hands of their disciples, who in the main were crude inflationists and advocates of a national inconvertible paper money, free not only from what they regarded as an arbitrary and dangerous bond with gold,[2] but also from any other legislative restriction on its quantity. They had a naïve reliance on the sufficiency of competition to keep prices from rising excessively, irrespective of the quantity of the currency in circulation.[3] This group, and the many other crude inflationists who issued tracts during this period, we can reasonably ignore. A number of writers during this period, however, presented proposals providing either for the regulation of the quantity of the currency with a view to stabilization of its value, or for the adoption of practices which would lessen the evil consequences arising from fluctuating, and especially falling, price levels. There follows a brief account, with no pretensions to completeness, of the proposals for reforms of these types which were made during this period. It should be noted, however, that the government, and the more prominent economists of the time, such as J. S. Mill, McCulloch, Senior, Cairnes, and Torrens, either wholly ignored these writers or treated their proposals with derision or contempt.

Wheatley, in 1807, had made the following proposal for the voluntary use in long-term contracts of a tabular standard based on an index number of prices, as a protection against changes in the purchasing power of the monetary unit:

. . . in compositions of a permanent nature, some criterion should be assumed for the purpose of providing a graduated scale of the value of money, and . . . an increase or diminution of income should be allowed in conformity to the result. The present impoverishment of the crown is a sufficient warning against permanent compacts for a definite sum; and no public composition will, I trust, be hereafter

---

[2] Cf. Jonathan Duncan, *The national anti-gold law league. The principles of the league explained*, 1847, p. 9: "We have in circulation about 220 millions of provisionary notes and bills of exchange; these repose on the narrow basis of an inverted pyramid of gold; shake the basis, the whole superstructure tumbles to the ground."

[3] Cf. *ibid.*, p. 11: "In this national money wages and prices would rise to their taxation level, and competition would prevent them exceeding that level."

concluded, that does not contain within itself the power of revision as to the pecuniary compensation. In a late projected composition government very properly departed from the principle of a fixed income, and as a commutation for tithes, it was proposed to grant a stipendiary salary, according to the price of corn. The basis upon which the compensation was to be negotiated was perfectly just; but I have already shown the inefficiency of corn as an exclusive standard; and whenever it may be necessary for any object of extended policy to ascertain the relative value of money for a period of long duration, the principles, upon which Sir George Shuckburgh constructed his table of proportions, will be found the least objectionable.[4]

Joseph Lowe[5] in 1822, and Scrope[6] in 1833, made similar recommendations for the voluntary use of a tabular standard,[7] although without reference to Wheatley. Some years later an anonymous writer recommended what was in effect a compulsory tabular standard of payments. According to his scheme, the currency would consist of £100 exchequer notes, made legal tender, and issued by the government in return for the obligation to pay to the government annually the value in pounds of a quarter of wheat at the average of the preceding ten years' prices. If wheat should be judged not to be a sufficient base, then the average prices of 50 or 100 commodities could be used instead. If prices rose because of overissue of this currency, it would be in the interest of holders of these notes to turn them in.[8] The essence of the plan was the issue of inconvertible notes on loan

[4] *Essay on the theory of money,* I (1807), 328-29.

[5] *The present state of England,* 2d ed., 1823, pp. 331-46, appendix, pp. 85-101. On Lowe's proposals, see Correa M. Walsh, *The fundamental problem in monetary science,* 1903, p. 171.

[6] *Principles of political economy,* 1833, pp. 406-07; *An examination of the Bank charter question,* 1833, pp. 25 ff. Scrope acknowledged Lowe's priority. (*An examination,* p. 29, note.) Cf. also the reference to a similar proposal made by Charles Jones in 1840 in R. K. Douglas, *Brief considerations on the income tax and tariff reform,* 1842, pp. 22-23.

[7] Samuel Bailey expressed doubt as to the practicability of the proposals made by Lowe and Scrope. As was still common at the time, he was skeptical of the possibility of measuring changes in the purchasing power of the monetary unit by means of index numbers, and he pointed out other more genuine obstacles to a widespread adoption of the tabular standard even on a voluntary basis. (*Money and its vicissitudes in value,* 1837, pp. 165 ff.)

[8] "History and exposition of the currency question," *Westminster review,* XLVIII (1848), 480-81.

at rates of interest varying in the same direction as the variations in commodity prices.[9]

John Gray, in 1842, advocated a currency system which would stabilize wages, and which would enable creditors to obtain at the maturity of their claims at least the same amount of command over goods as the amount of money which they had lent had had at the time the loan was contracted.[10] To accomplish the latter purpose he would have a currency consisting of : bank notes freely issued by private banks but convertible upon demand into standard money; and of standard coins made to vary in weight inversely with variations in the market value of the metal of which they were composed. His proposal is a variant of the "compensated dollar" idea; the denominations of the coins are to be maintained unaltered, but their size is to be varied in such a manner as to keep their purchasing power over commodities constant.[11] He apparently did not see that this might conflict with his other objective of keeping wages constant.

William Cross, in 1856, advocated a paper currency convertible into gold, but into amounts of gold varied periodically in conformity with a weighted "index list" or index number of commodities, so as to maintain constant purchasing power for the paper currency. He would retain the sovereign as a gold coin of

---

[9] For other proposals for regulation of the quantity of an inconvertible currency by variations in the interest rate, cf. the 1797 pamphlet referred to, *supra,* p. 211, and the proposals of Thomas Attwood, *supra,* p. 213, and Norton, Pell, Bosanquet, and Blacker, *infra,* pp. 285 ff. John Taylor, in 1833, had proposed an inconvertible paper currency so regulated in its quantity as to maintain constant value in terms of coin, but did not specify the mode of regulation. (*Currency fallacies refuted,* 1833, p. 29.) One writer proposed a paper currency so regulated in its quantity as to stabilize the interest rate, thus putting the cart before the horse: "when a rising rate of interest proves that money is becoming dear, and that the legitimate profits of producers are sacrificed to the gains of the monied classes, paper substitutes for metallic money should be issued in sufficient abundance to bring down the value of money to its former standard" i.e., in terms of the interest rate. "The Bank charter act— currency principles," *Westminster review,* XLVII (1847), 452.

[10] *An efficient remedy for the distress of nations,* 1842, p. 18:

"A debt, then, is justly paid, and only justly paid, when it is compensated in money, of whatever kind, which gives back to the creditor as great a command over the necessaries, comforts, and luxuries of life, as the money, or other value, which created the obligation, gave to the borrower; provided always that the creditor get the benefit of all the public improvements and useful inventions that may have come into existence during the interval subsisting between the period of contracting the debt and that of extinguishing it."

[11] *Ibid.,* pp. 33-35, 84.

fixed size but of variable value in paper currency.[12] He believed that knowledge of liability to adjustment of the paper value of the gold coins (or of the gold value of the paper currency) would, through anticipations of businessmen, operate to reduce the need for such adjustments and to render potential changes "a preventative influence rather than a rectifying interference":

> On the other hand, during a general decline of prices, the observation of this circumstance would lead to anticipation of a reaction favorable to sellers at the next ensuing time for the adjustment of the standard, and thus tend to check the fall of prices and render any rectification unnecessary. For producers and holders of goods would refrain from pressing sales when they knew or believed that the value of their stocks would be increased . . . as soon as the over-enhancement of money should be reduced . . . by the legal rectification. In the same circumstances, capitalists would become more free in their accommodations, and merchants more liberal in their purchases, knowing money to be verging on the maximum, and commodities on the minimum value possible under the system of periodical adjustment.[13]

One writer advocated a paper currency convertible into gold at the variable market price of gold instead of at a fixed price. In order to stabilize the value of the paper currency in terms of commodities, he proposed that its issue should be controlled by an official body, with authority to increase it when the rate of interest rose above 5 per cent and to contract it when the rate of interest fell below 3½ per cent, but failed to reveal why he believed this would suffice to stabilize prices.[14]

Richard Page advocated a fixed issue of inconvertible paper money, with the limit fixed by Parliament and periodically adjusted to changes in the population and trade of the country.[15]

---

[12] *A standard pound versus the pound sterling*, 1856, pp. 13 ff.

[13] *Ibid.*, p. 30.

[14] Edward Norton, *The Bank charter act of 1844*, 3d ed., 1857, especially p. 52. Norton repeats these proposals in his *National finance & currency*, 3d ed., 1873, pp. 91-92. W. T. Thomson, in 1866, advocated a paper currency convertible into gold at the market price of gold, and issued only by the government, with a fixed maximum amount of issue. (*The Bank of England, the Bank acts & the currency*, by Cosmopolite, 1866.) Proposals for the convertibility of paper money into gold at the market price of gold instead of at a fixed rate, but without concrete suggestions as to the manner of regulation of the quantity of such currency or express recognition of the need for such regulation, had been common since the bullion controversy.

[15] *Report from Select Committee on banks of issue*, 1840, p. 90. This proposal

George Pell proposed a government legal tender paper currency, issued for a minimum period of one year on collateral securities, and with interest charged at the rate yielded by these securities at their fair appraised value at the time of issue of the currency. What the plan aimed at was "the prevention of fluctuations in the value, that is, in the purchasing power, of money at home," and the author believed that the deviations between the rate of interest paid for the money and the rate of interest which could be earned by its investment would automatically so regulate the quantity of currency issued as to attain this objective. He assumed that the currency would maintain constant purchasing power if the rate charged for its issue were always kept equal with the average yield of capital. As the current rate of yield of capital rose it would be to the advantage of bankers to obtain larger quantities of currency from the government; as the current rate of yield of capital fell, it would be to their advantage to lessen the quantity already obtained by repayments to the government.[16] He does not explain how these deviations between the yield of capital in the market and the rate charged by the government could occur if the government based its rate on the former, nor why stabilization of the purchasing power of the currency would be assured if the rate of interest at which currency was issued was always made equal to the current yield of capital.

Several writers proposed schemes designed to render the purchasing power of the currency stable in the short run, but not necessarily in the long run. Poulett Scrope insisted that there were important possibilities of short-run stabilization of the price level even under a fixed metallic standard through appropriate regulation of its note issues by the Bank of England. He anticipated so strikingly later views on this question that his exposition deserves quotation at some length:

When gold is, for commercial, financial, or political purposes, drawn away from this country in any quantity, it is chiefly from the treasure of the Bank that it is taken, and it is for the Bank

---

is supported by I. C. Wright, *Thoughts on the currency,* 1841, pp. 35 ff. Wright suggests a supplementary currency for foreign trade, consisting of "bullion notes" issued in exchange for gold, and reconvertible into gold at the market price of bullion.

[16] George H. Pell, *Outline of a plan of a national currency, not liable to fluctuations in value,* 1840, pp. 5 ff.

exclusively to determine, whether the drain shall or shall not have any influence on our home prices. If the Bank choose to keep up its circulation of paper to the same point as before, no effect is felt in our markets. It may even reverse the natural effect of the drain, which is to lower prices, by increasing its issues as the gold flows out, and thereby raising our prices to an unnatural height. When the gold returns on this country by the spontaneous reaction of the exchanges, it is for the Bank to determine whether it shall have any effect upon our circulation or not. If they buy the gold as it comes in, and yet make no corresponding increase of their paper, the money of this country is in no degree enlarged; and should the Bank contract its issues while purchasing gold, our prices are actually depressed at a time when the influx would naturally have raised them. . . . It is only when the Bank contracts its paper exactly as it parts with gold for a foreign drain, and expands it as the gold flows back again, that the effect of these local variations in the demand and supply of bullion are [*sic*] reduced to that which our metallic standard necessarily occasions, and which would happen all the same even though our circulation were purely metallic.

It is evident, then, that the power of the Bank over prices in the British markets is confined within no narrow limits through the obligation of paying its notes in gold; that by its conduct in extending and contracting its paper, and purchasing or selling bullion, the value of gold itself, first in this country and ultimately in others, is arbitrarily influenced to a very great extent; that the Bank has the power of determining the exchanges, and, consequently, whether gold shall flow into or out of this country; that, by accumulating gold at one time in its vaults, to the extent of fifteen or more millions, at another allowing them to be nearly emptied, before any attempt is made to restore the equilibrium, the Bank can influence the market for gold as well as that of every other commodity.[17]

Scrope no doubt saw that as long as convertibility was required the Bank could at best be able to prevent the price level from fluctuating in response to even short-term fluctuations in the balance of payments only within the limits of its available reserves of bullion or, when prevention of a *rise* in prices was its objective, within the limits of its financial ability to accumulate non-income-earning stocks of bullion, and that the Bank could not prevent the English price level from responding to a sustained trend in the world value of gold if convertibility of its paper into bullion at fixed rates were insisted upon. In any case, Scrope pro-

---

[17] *An examination of the Bank charter question*, 1833, pp. 41-42.

posed as an ideal currency—"as perfect a system of currency as can be devised"—an inconvertible paper money to be preserved at par with bullion ordinarily, but to be left free to deviate from par for short periods during which temporary fluctuations of the price level would otherwise occur.[18]

William Blacker advocated an inconvertible paper money to be issued by a government commission in discount of commercial bills at such a rate of discount as would be found by experience to keep the exchange at par under ordinary circumstances, but to be left free to vary from par at times of temporary disturbances in the balance of payments. He argued that by varying the rate of discount the currency commissioners could make the currency operate as they pleased, but thought it was a debatable question whether or not the currency should be made to follow long-run changes in the value of gold and silver.[19] J. W. Bosanquet similarly advocated a paper currency which would follow the long-run trends in the value of gold, but not its short-run fluctuations. To realize this objective, he would meet temporary external drains out of the reserves or by temporary issues of notes under £5 in exchange for specie in the hands of the public. If this did not suffice, he would have the managers of the currency temporarily suspend convertibility. If the exchange then continued unfavorable by as much as ½ of 1 per cent for two uninterrupted years with both Paris and Hamburg, he would have the rate of discount on advances raised, but not to more than 6 per cent. In case the exchanges remained favorable for a substantial period of time, he would have the rate of discount reduced. He believed that under such a system the English price level could be kept from responding to temporary fluctuations in the world value of gold and in the balance of payments without involving ordinarily an appreciable departure of the paper currency from parity with gold. He did not himself attach importance to the maintenance of convertibility of the paper currency, but he thought that public opinion was not prepared to consider a complete departure from the gold standard.[20]

---

[18] *Ibid.*, p. 63. For a more detailed account of Scrope's monetary doctrines, see Redvers Opie, "A neglected English economist, George Poulett Scrope," *Quarterly journal of economics*, XLIV (1929), 101-37.

[19] *The evils inseparable from a mixed currency* [1st ed., 1839], 3d ed., 1847, pp. 51, 65, 93-94.

[20] *Metallic, paper, and credit currency*, 1842, pp. 14 ff., 144 ff.

Supporters of an orthodox metallic standard frequently level against advocates of inconvertible paper currencies the criticism that their zeal for "management" or "stabilization" of currencies tends to be confined to periods when prices are falling, and that in general they show more concern lest prices fall than lest they rise. This criticism appears to have substantial justification for the period here studied.[21] But when the gold discoveries of the middle of the century resulted in rising prices and augmented gold reserves, some at least of the disciples of the Attwoods taunted the advocates of the currency principle with the charge that their policy was fostering an inflation which only a regulated inconvertible paper currency could prevent.[22]

---

[21] Cf. Thomas Attwood, testifying before the Committee on the Bank of England charter, 1832:

"Do you think the amount of circulation in the country ought to be always exactly the same?—No, I think it ought to possess an expansive character, but rarely a contractive one." (*Report,* p. 468.) Attwood, however, may have had in mind the secular trend upward of the physical volume of trade.

[22] Cf. *The money bag,* 1858, pp. 113-14. (*The money bag* was an ephemeral magazine, established to promote the cause of an inconvertible paper currency. It printed some interesting cartoons relating to the currency question.)

Chapter VI

THE INTERNATIONAL MECHANISM UNDER
A SIMPLE SPECIE CURRENCY

Besides that the speculation is curious, it may frequently be of use in the conduct of public affairs. At least, it must be owned that nothing can be of more use than to improve by practice the method of reasoning on these subjects, which of all others are the most important, though they are commonly treated in the loosest and most careless manner.—David Hume, "Of interest," *Political discourses*, 1752.

I. INTRODUCTORY

In this chapter an account will be presented of the history and the present status of the theory of the mechanism of adjustment of international balances, in terms throughout of the simplifying assumption of an international simple specie currency, i.e., with the circulating medium consisting solely of standard metallic money. It was in terms of this assumption that the theory was first presented, and it has served ever since as a convenient device whereby to segregate for separate treatment different problems connected with the mechanism. It should be noted that in this chapter, as throughout the book, the term "balance of payments" is used in its original sense of an excess of immediate claims on abroad over obligations to abroad, or vice versa, which must be liquidated by specie. It should be noted also that by a "disturbance" to international equilibrium will be meant a change in *one* of the elements in a preexisting equilibrium such as to require a new equilibrium, and that this change, whether it takes the form of a series of crop failures, of international tributes or loans, of new import duties, or of a relative change in the demands of the two countries for each other's products, is presumed to continue indefinitely, and its cessation is treated as a new change in the reverse direction. A wide variety of disturbances can be used to illustrate the theory of the mechanism of international trade, and each has its own sequence of stages and to some extent its own set of special problems. A selection must be made, therefore, and the reader is asked not to attribute to me or to the writers cited generalization of the conclusions reached from the analysis of cases specifically dealt with beyond what the context clearly shows to be intended.

The "classical" theory of the mechanism of international trade, as developed from Hume to J. S. Mill, is still, in its general lines, the predominant theory. No strikingly different mechanism, moreover, has yet been convincingly suggested, although there has been gain in precision of analysis, and some correction of undoubted error. In recent years, it is true, a number of writers have pointed out what they regard as major errors in the classical theory, and have claimed that to eliminate these errors would require major reconstruction of the classical doctrines. But the current notions as to what the classical doctrines actually were are, with respect to this as to other matters, largely traditional rather than the product of examination of the original sources, and even when, as sometimes happens, the critics do use classical texts as the basis for the interpretation of the classical doctrines, they confine their references almost wholly to Ricardo and to J. S. Mill, and to the compressed, elliptical, and simplified expositions of their doctrines which are to be found in short chapters, labeled as on international trade, in their *Principles*. But if an adequate notion of the classical doctrines as to the mechanism of international trade is to be had, it is necessary to examine the writings of other classical economists, and for Ricardo and J. S. Mill to read in their *Principles* beyond the chapters distinctly labeled as dealing with international trade and also to explore what they had to say on this subject elsewhere. It is also necessary to bear in mind that there were important differences of doctrine within the ranks of the classical economists themselves, so that on some important points it is impossible to find any one doctrine which can properly be labeled as *the* classical doctrine. The following account will, I trust, demonstrate that some at least of the much-emphasized discoveries and "corrections" of recent years either are to be rejected as erroneous or were current doctrine in the classical period.

II. THE MECHANISM ACCORDING TO HUME

In so far as the classical theory of the mechanism of international trade had one definite originator, it was David Hume.[1] His main objective in presenting his theory of the mechanism was to show that the national supply of money would take care of itself, without need of, or possibility of benefit from, governmental intervention of the mercantilist type. He started out with the hypothesis that four-fifths of all the money in Great Britain was annihilated overnight, and proceeded to trace the consequences. Prices of British commodities and British wages would sink in proportion; British commodities would consequently overwhelm foreign competition in foreign markets, and the increase in exports would be paid for in money until the "level of money" in Great Britain was again equal to that in neighboring countries. Assuming next that the money in Great Britain were multiplied fivefold overnight, he held that prices and wages would rise so high in England that no foreign countries could buy British commodities, while foreign commodities, on the other hand, would become comparatively so cheap that they would be imported in great quantities. Money would consequently flow out of England until it was again at a level with that of other countries. The same causes which would bring about this approach to a common international level when disturbed "miraculously" would prevent any great inequality in level from occurring "in the common course of nature." The same forces also would preserve an approximately equal level as between different provinces of the same country. An additional, though minor, factor, operating to correct "a wrong balance of trade," was the fluctuations in the foreign exchanges within the limits of the specie points. If the trade balance was unfavorable, the exchanges would move against England, and this would become a new encouragement to export. The entire mechanism was kept in operation by the profit motive of individuals, "a moral attraction, arising from the interests and passions of men," acting under the stimulus of differences in prices.

The mechanism, therefore, was according to Hume automati-

---

[1] In *Political discourses* [1752], in *Essays, moral, political, and literary*, 1875 ed., I, 330-345, and especially 333-335.

cally self-equilibrating, was intranational as well as international, was bilateral, involving adjustments both at home and abroad, and consisted of such changes in the volume of exports and imports, resulting chiefly from changes in relative prices but also in minor degree from fluctuations in exchange rates, as would bring about or maintain an even balance of trade, so that no further specie need move to liquidate a balance.

III. AN OMITTED FACTOR? RELATIVE CHANGES IN DEMAND AS AN EQUILIBRATING FORCE

In Hume's account, changes in price levels thus play the predominant role in bringing about the necessary adjustment of trade balances, and are assisted only by fluctuations in exchange rates, held to be a factor of minor importance. In recent years a number of writers, most notably Ohlin, have contended that such an account leaves out of the picture an important equilibrating factor. These writers insist that much, or even all, of the equilibrating activity commonly attributed to relative price changes is really exercised by the direct effects on trade balances of the relative shift, as between the two regions, in the amounts of means of payments or in money incomes; that when disturbances in international balances occur, the restoration of equilibrium will or can take place unaccompanied by relative price changes or accompanied by only minor changes in relative prices; and that such changes if they do occur will not be, or are not likely to be, or need not necessarily be—which of these is supposed to be the fact is not always made clear—of the type postulated in the later classical doctrine as expounded by J. S. Mill or Taussig. While none of these writers seems to have applied his doctrine to a currency disturbance such as postulated by Hume, where the need for at least temporary price changes of some kind would seem most obvious, it may be assumed, nevertheless, that they would hold Hume's analysis of the mechanism to be inadequate even when confined to such cases.

It will be conceded at once that, in the case, for instance, of the initiation of continuing unilateral remittances, the aggregate demand for commodities, in the sense of the amounts buyers are willing to purchase at the prevailing prices, will, in the absence of price changes, fall in the paying country and rise in the lending country,[1] and that unless there is an extreme and unusual distortion of the relative demands for different classes of commodities from their previous proportions this shift in demands will of itself contribute to an adjustment of the balance of payments to the remittances. The problem is rather to explain why this fairly obvious proposition should not sooner have received general recognition and to determine to what extent its recognition constitutes, as some contend, a major revolution in the theory of the mechanism requiring wholesale rejection of what the older writers had to say. To the first question, even though I have sinned in this connection myself, I have no answer, except that it is difficult to judge, after something has been clearly pointed out to us, how obvious it would or should be to others not so circumstanced. While, however, the account of the mechanism given by Hume and by many later writers gives no indication of recognition that the direct influence on the trade balance of relative changes in demands in the two countries would be an equilibrating factor, such recognition was by no means wholly lacking on the part of the major writers of the nineteenth century.

That imports pay for exports, and that an increase in imports, by providing foreigners with increased means of payment, would operate to increase exports, was pointed out even during the mercantilist period. But the following account will disregard incidental recognition of the relationship between amount of income and extent of demand, which has always been common, even with laymen, and will deal only with cases where such recognition is to be found incorporated as an integral part of a more or less formal exposition by nineteenth-century writers of the mechanism of adjustment of international balances.[2]

---

[1] This much must be regarded as implicit even in the Hume-Thornton-Taussig type of formulation, since otherwise the changes in prices which they postulate would have no immediate explanation. What is in issue is not, therefore, whether a relative shift in demands occurs, but whether this shift in demands, *of itself and aside from its effect on relative prices,* exercises an equilibrating influence.

[2] These writers, however, had been anticipated by an eighteenth-century Frenchman, Isaac de Bacalan, in a memoir written in 1764, although not published until 1903, after its discovery by Sauvaire-Jourdan:

Supposerons-nous qu'un seul État fournisse aux autres plus de marchandises qu'il n'en retire et que toutes les nations soldent avec cet État en argent? . . . Croit-on de bonne foi que cette situation serait durable, et que cet État absorberait peu à peu tout l'argent qui existe dans le

Wheatley, Ricardo.—Henry Thornton, in 1802, had applied the Hume type of explanation generally to any type of disturbance of the balance of payments, and specifically to the disturbance resulting from a crop failure which made necessary greatly increased imports of grain,[3] and to a change in the English demand for foreign commodities as compared to the foreign demand for English commodities.[4] Wheatley and Ricardo, on the other hand, denied that this explanation was applicable to such disturbances of a non-currency nature and offered different explanations of the mechanism of adjustment to such disturbances. While Wheatley's discussion was in part earlier, Ricardo's was less significant for the point at issue, and it will be convenient to dispose of it first. Ricardo denied that crop failures or the payment of subsidies would disturb the balance of payments at all and denied, therefore, that any mechanism of adjustment would be necessary.[5] The only justification for this position which he offered was that if a crop failure should be permitted to disturb the balance of payments, since the disturbance would prove to be temporary and after it was over things would be as they had been before, any movement of specie—and presumably also any corresponding change in relative price levels—would have to be offset later by a return movement of equal size, a waste of effort which would not be indulged in:

The ultimate result then of all this exportation and importation of money, is that one country will have imported one commodity in exchange for another, and the coin and bullion will in both countries have regained their natural level. Is it to be contended that these results would not be foreseen, and the expense and trouble attending

---

monde? Non, sans doute. L'augmentation de la quantité d'argent en diminue-rait le prix; le luxe croitrait et avec lui la consommation des denrées soit nationales, soit étrangères. Il en résulterait donc que cet État transporterait aux autres une moindre quantité de denrées et en retirerait une plus grande quantité. Ainsi il serait obligé à son tour de payer en argent et la circulation se rétablirait. ("Paradoxes philosophiques sur la liberté du commerce entre les nations" [ms. 1764], first printed in F. Sauvaire-Jourdan, *Isaac de Bacalan et les idées libre-échangistes en France*, 1903, p. 43.)
Cf. also Isaac Gervaise in 1720, *supra*, pp. 80-81.

[3] *Paper credit of Great Britain*, 1802, pp. 131 ff.

[4] *Ibid.*, pp. 242-43.

[5] *High price of bullion, Works*, pp. 268-69, and appendix to 4th ed., *ibid.*, pp. 291 ff. For a detailed analysis of Ricardo's argument and of Malthus's reply thereto, and for some later qualifications to his argument made by Ricardo in his reply to Malthus, see Jacob Viner, *Canada's balance*, pp. 193-201.

these needless operations effectually prevented, in a country where capital is abundant, where every possible economy in trade is practiced, and where competition is pushed to its utmost limits? Is it conceivable that money should be sent abroad for the purpose merely of rendering it dear in this country and cheap in another, and by such means to insure its return to us?[6]

This exaggerates the extent to which individual traders can foresee whether a drain of gold would be temporary or not, or would find it in their interest to check it even if they were convinced that it was temporary.[7] Seasonal movements of specie are still permitted to occur, even though their seasonal character is generally known.

Wheatley defended his denial that crop failures or foreign subsidy payments would disturb the balance of payments by more adequate reasoning. He maintained that crop failures, or the payment of subsidies, would immediately alter the relative demands of the two regions for each other's products in such manner and degree that the commodity balance of trade would at once undergo the manner and degree of change necessary to maintain equilibrium in the balance of payments. This shift in relative demand would result from the alteration brought about by the crop failure or the subsidy in the relative ability of the two countries to buy each other's commodities:

If, then, it be correct in theory, that the exports and imports to and from independent states have a reciprocal action on each other, and that the extent of the one is necessarily limited by the extent of the other, it is obvious, that if no demand had subsisted in this country from 1793 to 1797 for corn and naval stores, the countries that furnished the supply would have possessed so much less means

---

[6] Ricardo, *High price of bullion*, appendix, *Works*, p. 292. Cf. also Wheatley, *Report on the reports*, 1819, pp. 20-21, for a similar argument.

[7] Ricardo apparently thought that the fact that specie movements created more serious problems of adjustment for the country as a whole than would equivalent movement of other commodities would in some manner result in the liquidation of new foreign obligations in goods instead of in specie, but he did not indicate the mechanism whereby this would be brought about. Cf. Ricardo, *op. cit.*, p. 293: "Any of these commodities [i.e., other than gold] might be exported without producing much inconvenience from their enhanced price; whereas money, which circulates all other commodities, and the increase or diminution of which, even in a moderate proportion, raises or falls prices in an extravagant degree, could not be exported without the most serious consequences." But these consequences, if serious, would be serious not for the individual exporters of the specie, but for the community as a whole.

of expending our exports, as an inability to sell would of course have created an equal inability to buy. It is totally irregular, therefore, to infer, that our exports would have amounted to the same sum, had the import of the corn and naval stores been withheld, as those who provided the supply would have been utterly incapable of purchasing them.[8]

On similar grounds, Wheatley held that under an inconvertible paper currency the exchanges would not be affected by a crop failure or the payment of a subsidy, and could move against a country only if there had developed a relative redundancy of currency in that country.[9] Wheatley carried his doctrine so much further than he clearly showed to be justified that even the bullionists rejected it, and in doing so overlooked the important element of validity underlying it.

Longfield, Torrens, Joplin.—In 1840, Longfield, discussing the effect of increased imports of grain owing to a harvest failure in England, pointed out that this would result in a relative shift in the amounts of money available for expenditure in England and in the grain-exporting countries, and that this shift would contribute, even in the absence of price changes, to a rectification of the trade balance. Longfield denied, however, that this contribution would be sufficient to make price changes unnecessary:

A certain equilibrium exists between our average exports and imports. This is disturbed by the importation of corn. England suddenly demands a large quantity, perhaps six millions worth of corn. She may be ready to pay for them by her manufactures, but will those who sell it be willing to take those manufactures in exchange? Will the Prussian or Russian landowner, whose wealth has been suddenly increased, be content to expend his increased wealth in the purchase of an increased amount of English manufactures? We say that the contrary will take place, and that his habits will remain unchanged, and his increase of wealth will be spent in nearly the same manner as his former income, that is to say, not one fiftieth part in the purchase of English goods. His countrymen will, in the first instance, have the advantage of his increased expenditure. It will not be felt in England until after a long time, and passing through many channels. . . . Thus the English have six millions less than usual to expend in the purchase of the commodities which they

---

[8] *An essay on the theory of money,* vol. 1, 1807, p. 238.
[9] *Ibid.,* pp. 180-81 ; *Report on the reports,* 1819, pp. 21-29.

are accustomed to consume, while the inhabitants of the corn exporting countries have six millions more. . . . The commodities, therefore, which the Russians and Prussians consume, will rise in price,
while those which the English use will undergo a reduction. But a
very great proportion, much more than nineteen-twentieths of the
commodities consumed in any country, are the productions of that
country. English manufactures will therefore fall, while Russian and
Prussian goods will rise in price. The evil, after some time, works its
own cure.[10]

Torrens, in 1841-42, in the course of an attempt to demonstrate
that retaliation against foreign tariffs would be beneficial to England even if such retaliation did not lead foreign countries to
reduce their tariffs, placed main emphasis on the role of relative
price changes in adjusting the international balances to tariff
changes, but in his well-known Cuban illustration the restoration
of equilibrium was made to result directly from the relative shift
in the amounts of means of payment, as well as indirectly from
the relative shift in prices resulting from this shift in means of
payment. He assumed, first, that all the demands for commodities
in terms of money in each country had unit elasticity, and that
Cuba was exporting to England 1,500,000 units of sugar, at a
price of 30 shillings per unit, in return for 1,500,000 units of
English cloth, at a price also of 30 s. per unit. Cuba then imposes a duty of 100 per cent on cloth, with the result that the
price of cloth rises to 60 s. in Cuba, and the Cuban consumption
falls by 50 per cent, to 750,000 units. Sugar continues for a time
to flow to England at the original price and in the original quantity. There results an unfavorable balance of payments for England, and specie moves from England to Cuba. The price of sugar
rises, and the price of cloth falls. The Cuban consumption of
cloth increases to more than 750,000 units, apparently because of
both the fall in the price of cloth and the increase in the amount
of money available for the purchase of cloth in Cuba. Conversely,
the rise in the price of sugar and the decrease in the quantity of
money in England result in a decline in the English consumption
of sugar to less than 1,500,000 units. Specie continues to flow
from England to Cuba, the amount of money to fall in England
and rise in Cuba, the price of cloth to fall and the price of sugar

[10] "Banking and currency, Part I," *Dublin University magazine*, XV
(1840), 10.

to rise, until the exports of cloth to Cuba had expanded and the exports of sugar to England contracted sufficiently to restore equilibrium in the balance of payments between the two countries. Under this final equilibrium, Cuba would be importing annually 1,500,000 units of cloth, at a price before duty of 20 s., and after duty of 40 s. per unit, and would be exporting 750,000 units of sugar at a price of 40 s. per unit.[11] These results, it is to be noted, could not have resulted from the changes in prices alone, given the postulated elasticities of demand. They imply changes in money incomes in each country, and consequent changes in each country, the same in direction as the changes in money incomes, in the quantities which would be demanded of both commodities if the prices had remained unaltered.

Joplin, in his many tracts, repeatedly expounded the mechanism of adjustment of international balances in terms only of relative price changes, but in one passage, by exception, he stressed the direct influence on the course of trade of the relative change in demand for each other's commodities resulting from the transfer of money from one of the countries to the other, with the change in relative prices mentioned only as a by-product of, rather than as an essential factor in, the equilibrating process:

Now, when the balance of payments is against one and in favor of another nation, it arises from the inhabitants of the former having a greater demand for the productions of the latter, than the inhabitants of the latter have for the productions of the former. But after a transmission of the balance in money, an alteration must necessarily be experienced in the state of this demand. The inhabitants of the country from whence the money was sent would be unable, from their reduced monetary incomes, to purchase so large a quantity of the products of the money-importing country as before; while they, the inhabitants of the importing country, would be enabled, by the increase in their monetary incomes, to purchase more of the commodities of the nation from which the money had been received. Thus the trade would again be brought to a balance in money, and be thereby rendered an exchange of commodity for commodity: the nation receiving the money gaining by the improved terms on which the barter would be thereafter conducted.[12]

---

[11] R. Torrens, *The budget, a series of letters on financial, commercial, and colonial policy,* 1841-44, Letter II.

[12] Thomas Joplin, *Currency reform: improvement not depreciation,* 1844, pp. 14-15.

J. S. Mill, Cairnes.—John Stuart Mill, in the exposition of the mechanism which he gives in his *Principles*, appears to attribute to relative changes in prices sole responsibility for bringing about a trade balance such as would restore equilibrium in a disturbed balance of payments.[13] At one point, in fact, he appears explicitly to say so. Discussing a case where "there is at the ordinary prices a permanent demand in England for more French goods than the English goods required in France at the ordinary prices will pay for," he states that "the imports require to be permanently diminished, or the exports to be increased; *which can only be accomplished through prices.*"[14] At another point, however, he expressly includes, as a factor operating to restore equilibrium, the relative shift in the amount of monetary income in the two countries resulting from the transfer of specie. He is tracing the consequences of a cheapening of the cost of production of a staple article of English production:

The first effect is that the article falls in price, and a demand arises for it abroad. This new exportation disturbs the balance, turns the exchanges, money flows into the country . . . and continues to flow until prices rise. This higher range of prices will somewhat check the demand in foreign countries for the new article of export; and will diminish the demand which existed abroad for the other things which England was in the habit of exporting. The exports will thus be diminished; *while at the same time the English public, having more money, will have a greater power of purchasing foreign commodities.* If they make use of this increased power of purchase, there will be an increase of imports: and by this, and the check to exportation, the equilibrium of imports and exports will be restored.[15]

The ordinary interpretation of Mill's theory as explaining the adjustment of international balances solely in terms of relative

---

[13] *Principles of political economy* [1848], Ashley ed., bk. iii, chap. 21.

[14] *Ibid.*, p. 620. (Italics not in original.) There is an unfortunate ambiguity here, since it is impossible to say with certainty whether Mill meant that prices will necessarily operate alone to restore equilibrium, or merely that price changes were necessary.

[15] *Ibid.*, pp. 623-24. (Italics not in original text.) Mill notes also that foreign consumers "have had their money incomes probably diminished by the same cause" (*ibid.*, p. 624) but does not expressly point out that this will be an additional factor operating to reduce English exports and thus to restore equilibrium. Bresciani-Turroni (*Inductive verification of the theory of international payments* (1932, p. 91, note) points out the significance of the passage cited in the text.

price changes probably should be accepted, and this passage therefore regarded as indicating only an accidental perception by Mill at one moment of the presence in the mechanism of an additional factor rather than as a statement of an integral element in his theory. But it may be an error to do so. The exposition in the *Principles* is a restatement, in some respects less detailed, of an earlier exposition by Mill,[16] in which the relative change in monetary income in the two countries resulting from a movement of specie is expressly incorporated in the exposition of the mechanism as, together with the elasticities of demand in terms of money prices, determining the extent of the response to price changes of the volume of purchases of each other's commodities by the two countries. Even here the emphasis is mainly on relative price changes, but this can in part be explained by the fact that Mill treats a rise in the prices of a country's own products as necessarily involving also a rise in its money incomes,[17] as well as by the fact that he is here primarily concerned with the effects of disturbances on the "gains" from trade, rather than with the mechanism *qua* mechanism.[18]

Cairnes, in his better known expositions of the mechanism of international trade,[19] makes no reference to the relative shift in means of payment, or in demands for commodities in terms of money, as a factor contributing to the adjustment of international balances. But in an earlier essay he emphasized the role it plays, and showed that he was aware that he was adding something not in the usual version:

---

[16] *Essays on some unsettled questions,* 1844, Essay I.

[17] Cf. *ibid.,* p. 16: "As the money prices of all her other commodities [= her own products] have risen, the money incomes of all her producers have increased."

[18] Cf. *ibid.,* pp. 26-27 (Mill is discussing the effect on the gains from trade of an import duty imposed by England on German linen):

The equilibrium of trade would be disturbed if the imposition of the tax diminished in the slightest degree the quantity of linen consumed . . . the balance therefore must be paid in money. Prices will fall in Germany, and rise in England; linen will fall in the German market; cloth will rise in the English. The Germans will pay a higher price for cloth, and will have smaller money incomes to buy it with; while the English will obtain linen cheaper, that is, its price will exceed what it previously was by less than the amount of the duty, while their means of purchasing it will be increased by the increase of their money incomes.

[19] *Some leading principles of political economy newly expounded,* 1874, pp. 360 ff.; *Essays in political economy,* 1873, pp. 24 ff.

. . . it is not true that the motives to importation and exportation depend upon prices alone; and, should the fall in prices be very sudden and violent, I conceive its effect on the whole would be rather unfavorable than otherwise on the exportation of commodities. . . . if any circumstance should occur to render industry less profitable, or to diminish the general wealth of the country, the means at the disposal of the community for the purchase of foreign commodities would be curtailed. Without supposing any alteration in prices, therefore, the demand for such commodities would decline and consequently the amount of our imports would fall off. And conversely, if the opposite conditions should occur, if the wealth of the country were to increase, we should each on an average have more to spend; a portion of this increased wealth, without necessarily supposing any fall in prices abroad, would go in extra demand for foreign commodities; and our imports would consequently increase . . . and what takes place here will of course take place equally in foreign countries. It follows, therefore, that the relation between our exports and imports, and, by consequence, the influx and efflux of gold, depends not only on the state of prices here and abroad, but also on the means of purchase which are at the command, respectively, of home and foreign consumers.

.   .   .   .

[In the cases of crop failures, military remittances abroad, etc.] The transference of so much gold from this country to foreign countries—though it need not interfere to any great extent with the proceedings of commerce at home—yet alters the disposable wealth comparatively of this and other countries; their means of expenditure is proportionally altered, and consequently their demand for each other's goods. There is thus, in the circumstances attending a transmission of gold from this country, a provision made for its return, quite independently of the state of prices, *or of the circulation.* . . .[20]

Bastable, Nicholson.—Bastable in 1889 defended, against Mill, Ricardo's doctrine that an international loan would not result in a transmission of specie or in relative changes in prices, by invoking the direct effect of the relative change in "purchasing power" or money incomes in the two countries on their trade balances:

[20] *An examination into the principles of currency,* 1854, pp. 34-36. The words italicized by me involve a fallacy, since a relative decrease in monetary circulation in the paying country is necessary, even when relative price changes are not. See *infra,* p. 366.

Suppose that A owes B £1,000,000 annually. This debt is a claim in the hands of B, which increases her purchasing power, being added to the amount of that power otherwise derived. . . . [It is also doubtful whether in case of interest payments or repayments of previous loans] Mill is correct in asserting that the quantity of money will be increased in the creditor and reduced in the debtor country. The sum of money incomes will no doubt be higher in the former; but that increased amount may be expended in purchasing imported articles obtained by means of the obligations held against the debtor nation. . . . Nor does it follow that the scale of prices will be higher in the creditor than in the debtor country. The inhabitants of the former, having larger money incomes, will purchase more *at the same* price, and thus bring about the necessary excess of imports over exports.[21]

A few years later Nicholson presented a similar criticism of Mill's reasoning, worked out in some detail, and accompanied by a denial, based on crudely fallacious reasoning, that price changes and specie movements played *any* part in the mechanism.[22]

A number of the most important nineteenth-century writers on the theory of international trade thus recognized that relative shifts in the amounts of means of payment, or of incomes, exercised, independently of relative price changes, an equilibrating role in the mechanism of adjustment of international balances to disturbances.[23] But there were important divergences of doctrine between these writers. It was common doctrine for all of them that a change in relative money incomes resulting, say, from loans would contribute to the adjustment of the balance of payments to the loans through its influence on the relative demands of the two countries for each other's commodities. But one group (i.e.,

[21] C. F. Bastable, "On some applications of the theory of international trade," *Quarterly journal of economics*, IV (1889), p. 16. (Italics in original.) Ricardo, in his later correspondence with Malthus, while continuing to deny that a crop failure or a unilateral remittance would result in relative price changes, conceded that it would result in a movement of specie from the debtor to the creditor country sufficient to restore the normal relationships in each country between quantity of goods and quantity of money. (See my *Canada's balance*, pp. 195-96.)

[22] J. S. Nicholson, *Principles of political economy*, II (1897), 287-93. In the preface, Nicholson made an acknowledgment to Bastable "for his careful revision and criticism of the chapters on the theory of foreign trade."

[23] It may be significant, as indicating possible indebtedness, that of these writers Longfield, Cairnes, and Bastable had all been associated with Trinity College, Dublin, as students, or professors, or both, and Nicholson had received help from Bastable.

Ricardo, Longfield, J. S. Mill, Cairnes) either explained this shift in relative incomes as resulting from a prior transfer of money or conceded that a transfer of money would result from it, whereas another group (Wheatley, Bastable, and Nicholson, and, at one point, Cairnes) denied that any transfer of money need take place. One group (Longfield, Joplin, Cairnes, J. S. Mill) left an important place in the mechanism for relative price changes, whereas another group (Wheatley, Ricardo, Bastable, Nicholson) denied, or questioned, the necessity of relative price changes for the restoration of equilibrium.

In the later literature there continue to be presented explanations of the mechanism of adjustment which do and others which do not assign an equilibrating role to the relative shift in demands, and some writers who at one time take pains to point out its significance at other times permit it to drop out of their exposition and revert to an explanation in terms solely of relative price changes. Mainly owing to Ohlin, however, there has been a growing awareness of the issue, and an increasing readiness to give weight to this factor.

Taussig, Wicksell.—In an article published in 1917, and dealing primarily with the mechanism of adjustment under a paper standard currency, Taussig argued that in the case of an international loan under a metallic standard that part of the proceeds not used immediately by the borrowers in purchase of foreign goods would enter the borrowing country in the form of goods only after a remittance of specie from lender to borrower had raised prices in the borrowing country and lowered them in the lending country.[24] In a reply to this article, Wicksell claimed that the increased demand for commodities in the borrowing country, and the decreased demand for commodities in the lending country, would "in the main" be sufficient to call forth the changes in the trade balance necessary to restore equilibrium in the balance of payments. He held that it would not make any difference if the increased power of purchase in the borrowing country were directed toward its own products rather than imported products:

. . . this of course would diminish the imports, but if the value of imports surpasses the value of exports by precisely the amount bor-

---

[24] F. W. Taussig, "International trade under depreciated paper," *Quarterly journal of economics,* XXXI (1917).

rowed during the same time, there would be no occasion for sending or receiving gold.

Gold *would* move to the borrowing country, but only because, and *after*, it had acquired additional commodities, and not before the transfer of the loan in the form of goods.[25]

Taussig, in his brief rejoinder, confined his discussion in the main to other points and did not adequately meet the fundamental issue raised by Wicksell as to the role played by changes in demand in the equilibrating process. To Wicksell's denial of the necessity of specie movements at an early stage of the process of adjustment, he made an effective reply: "I find it difficult to conceive how 'increased demand for commodities' will cause a rise in the price of commodities, unless more money is offered for them; and no more money can be offered for them unless the supply of money is larger."[26] This may seem to imply an acceptance by Taussig of Wicksell's doctrine at least to the extent of recognition that changes in demand do play an equilibrating part aside from price changes, for if there is an increase in demand it operates to increase the amount taken at the *same* prices as well as to increase the prices, but I cannot find a clear statement to this effect either here or in his later writings. Taussig also pointed out that Wicksell's denial of the possibility that relative price changes could be an important equilibrating factor, since, transportation costs aside, commodities tend to have uniform prices everywhere, overlooked the existence of "domestic" commodities not entering into international trade, whose price movements could diverge from the movements of the prices of international commodities and thus contribute to the establishment of a new international equilibrium.[27]

"Canada's Balance."—In 1924, reviewing this discussion between Wicksell and Taussig, I conceded, as had Taussig in his original article, that to the extent that the new spendable funds

---

[25] Knut Wicksell, "International freights and prices," *ibid.*, XXXII (1918), 404-10. Wicksell is here following Ricardo. Cf. *supra*, p. 303, note 21.

[26] *Quarterly journal of economics*, XXXII (1918), 410-12.

[27] *Ibid.* Even if there were no "domestic" commodities, and if the prices of *all* commodities were necessarily uniform throughout the world, relative price changes could still be an equilibrating factor, since it is the relative changes in prices of *different* commodities in the same market, not the relative changes in prices of the *same* commodity in different markets, which is the important price factor in the mechanism. See *infra*, p. 319.

in the borrowing country resulting from the loan were used in the purchase of foreign commodities which otherwise would not have been imported there would be a contribution to adjustment independent of relative price changes. I also accepted the argument, which I attributed to Wicksell,[28] that the use of the proceeds of the loans to purchase home-produced commodities which otherwise would have been exported would similarly contribute to adjustment. I concluded, however, that there was no *a priori* reason to expect that these two factors would suffice to bring about adjustment, on the grounds that: (1) the theoretical expectation would be that in the absence of price changes the same percentage of the additional, as of the original, spendable funds would be used in the purchase of "domestic" or non-international commodities; and (2) unless in the absence of price changes *none* of the borrowed funds would be used in the purchase of "domestic" commodities, there could not be adjustment of the balance of payments without relative price changes.[29] As will appear later, this last proposition was an error, resulting from my failure, at this point,[30] to bear in mind that a diversion of productive factors from production of exportable commodities for export to production of domestic commodities for domestic consumption would, by restricting the volume of exports, contribute as much to the adjustment of the balance of payments as would an

---

[28] I cannot now find an explicit statement of this argument by Wicksell. Nicholson, however, had presented it in 1897.—See his *Principles*, II (1897), 289.

[29] *Canada's balance of international indebtedness*, 1924, pp. 204-06.

[30] In the analysis, later in the same book, of the influence on its export trade of Canada's import of capital, I did point out the equilibrating influence of this additional factor:

It is difficult to explain the decline in the percentage of exports to total [Canadian] commodity production, without reference to the capital borrowings from abroad. . . . The expansion of manufacturing not only absorbed an increased proportion of the Canadian production of raw materials, but it withdrew labor, from the production of raw materials which otherwise would have been exported, to the construction of plant and equipment and the fabrication, from imported raw materials, of manufactured commodities for domestic consumption. The development of roads, towns, and railroads, made possible by the borrowings abroad, absorbed a large part of the immigration of labor, and these consumed considerable quantities of Canadian commodities which would otherwise have been available for export. Changes in relative price levels resulting from the capital borrowings were also an important factor in restricting exports, operating coordinately with the factors explained above (*ibid.*, pp. 262-63).

equivalent increase of imports or of domestic consumption of products hitherto exported.

Keynes, Ohlin.—The discussion of the transfer aspect of the German reparations problem gave rise to intensified discussion of this issue, but the contributions of Ohlin and Keynes can alone be dealt with here. Ohlin, in an article published in 1928, laid strong emphasis on the role which a relative shift in demand for commodities, in terms of money, upward in the receiving countries, downward in Germany, would play in adjusting the German balance of payments to the reparations payments, thus making relative price changes adverse to Germany a subsidiary and probably unnecessary part of the mechanism, and easing the task of transfer of the reparations in the form of goods.[31] In this article, it appears to me, he took a position with respect to the lack of significance of relative price changes in the international mechanism more extreme than the treatment in his later book (which still seems extreme to me). He argued that when international unilateral remittances occurred a change in price favorable to the paying country was as likely to take place as one unfavorable to that country, and that in the absence of knowledge of the particular circumstances it must be presumed that no relative change in prices will occur.[32] He further claimed that even if a relative price change unfavorable to the paying country did occur, it would only be at the beginning of the payments, and would not persist long enough to be significant.[33]

In 1929, Keynes, in a pessimistic article on the possibility of transfer of the German reparations, which stressed the difficulties which Germany would encounter even if she succeeded in providing for the payments in her government budget, did not take into account, as a factor facilitating economic transfer of the payments, the shift in the demands for commodities which would result from an initial transfer of means of payment from Germany to the receiving countries. Ohlin replied, invoking this shift as a

---

[31] "The reparations problem," *Index,* April, 1928.

[32] *Ibid.,* p. 9: "There is no direct reason why A's export articles should go up in price or B's go down. In both it is a question of A's increased demand balancing B's reduced demand. In any case an increase in the total demand may just as well apply to B's as to A's international goods. Without a knowledge of the circumstances in each particular case we must presume that no such shifting of prices takes place."

[33] *Ibid.,* p. 10.

factor which would lessen the seriousness of the transfer problem, and there resulted a further exchange of views between the two writers, in which neither succeeded in converting the other.[34] Ohlin did not state his views as clearly as he has since presented them, and on one essential point he made an unnecessary concession to Keynes.

Keynes reasoned throughout, on the conventional lines, as if the only factor tending to adjust the German trade balance to its reparations obligations could be an increase in German exports relative to imports resulting from a fall in German prices relative to outside prices. Taking an extreme case to emphasize his point, namely, where the foreign (simple "Marshallian") elasticity of demand for products of Germany was assumed to be less than unity, and abstracting from the possibility of a reduction in the value of German imports, he concluded that "in this case, the more she exports, the smaller will be the aggregate proceeds. Again the transfer problem will be a hopeless business"—i.e., the reparations in this case could not be transferred even if relative price changes did occur. Keynes therefore concluded that the elasticities of demand of the two countries might be such as to make transfer in kind wholly impossible, and that for such transfer to take place in any case, "the expenditure of the German people must be reduced, not only by the amount of the reparation-taxes which they must pay out of their earnings, but also by a reduction in their gold-rate of earnings below what they would otherwise be," that is, German money wages, etc., must fall even aside from taxation thereof.[35] This Ohlin denied.

At a later stage of the controversy, Keynes explained that he had attributed little (no?) importance to changes in demand conditions, because he had assumed that Germany was not in a position to export large quantities of gold, and because if Germany did ship gold her products would have to share the benefits of the resultant increase in demands outside Germany with the products of the rest of the world, so that the gain to her export trade

[34] *Economic journal,* XXXIX (1929): J. M. Keynes, "The German transfer problem," 1-7; B. Ohlin, "The reparation problem: a discussion," 172-78; Keynes, "The reparation problem, a rejoinder," 179-82; Ohlin, "Mr. Keynes' views on the transfer problem: II, a rejoinder," 400-04; Keynes, "Views on the transfer problem: III, a reply," 404-08.

[35] *Ibid.,* p. 4.

would be negligible.[36] To this it could be replied that the ratio of gold shipments to aggregate reparations payments over the entire period would not have to be large, since a given transfer of gold will continue to keep up the level of foreign demand in terms of money for German goods by some fraction (or multiple) of itself per unit period as long as the gold stays abroad; it will operate not only to raise the foreign demand for German goods but to decrease the German demand for foreign goods; and if in the first instance all, or most, of the receiving country's increase in demand is directed to the products of third countries, these countries will acquire the specie surrendered by Germany, and their demands for foreign commodities, including those of Germany, will rise. But Keynes, apparently to the last, failed to understand Ohlin's argument that the initial transfer of specie, or its equivalent, would result in a relative shift in an equilibrating direction of the demands in terms of money prices of the two countries for each other's products, regardless of their elasticities. He still argued that if the world's demand for German goods had an elasticity of less than unity, "there is *no* quantity of German-produced goods, however great in volume, which has a sufficient selling-value on the world market, so that the only expedient open to Germany would be to cut down her imports."[37] But elasticity of demand of less than unity for German exports would set a definite limit on the value of such exports only if no increase in the foreign demand for German commodities in terms of money

---

[36] *Ibid.,* pp. 407 ff.

[37] *Ibid.,* p. 405. Pigou has expounded the same doctrine. Cf. "The effect of reparations on the ratio of international interchange," *Economic Journal,* XLII (1932), 533:

> Thus suppose that Germany is normally sending so much of her exports abroad and buying with them so much imports; and that, on the top of this situation, she is subjected to an indemnity whose amount is expressed in English goods. If the indemnity exceeds the previous sum of English exports sent to her by us, so that it cannot be paid by Germany's dispensing with these exports, and if also the English demand for German goods in respect of enlarged quantities has an elasticity less than unity, Germany cannot, however much she increases her exports to us, provide the means of paying the indemnity.

Whether Pigou uses "demand" here in the simple monetary sense or in the reciprocal demand sense, this would not necessarily be true since in either case the English demand for German goods might shift in a direction favorable to Germany as the result of the receipt by England of reparations payments.

resulted directly from the transfer abroad by Germany of specie.[38]

The failure of the two writers to make themselves clear to each other, and especially the failure of Ohlin to convert Keynes, was probably due in part to an ambiguous and otherwise unsatisfactory use by both writers of the treacherous term "purchasing power." Ohlin's argument that a relative shift in demand for each other's products would occur rested on the doctrine that the payment of reparations would commence with a transfer of "purchasing power" from Germany to the receiving countries and that the resultant relative change in the amounts of "purchasing power" in the respective areas would bring about this relative shift in demands for commodities. In reply, Keynes presents a hypothetical case, where Germany, having succeeded by some means in developing a net export surplus of £25,000,000, meets her reparations obligations to the extent of £25,000,000 out of the proceeds of this export surplus. Exploiting to the full the ambiguities of the term "buying power," he then claims that "the increased 'buying power,' due to the fact of Germany paying something . . . will have been *already* used up in buying the exports, the sale of which has made the reparation payments possible," whereas "Professor Ohlin has to maintain that the 'increased buying power' is *more* than £25,000,000, and—if his repercussion is to be important—appreciably more."[39] Ohlin, instead of pointing out that the increase of "buying power" in France which could be counted on to bring about real transfer of

---

[38] Ohlin later pointed this out (*Interregional and international trade*, 1933, p. 62).

In his later *Treatise on money* (1930, I, 340-42), Keynes returns to the problem briefly, but without much addition to his earlier argument. He here stresses the difficulty of surrender of gold by Germany; appears to interpret Ohlin's argument, perhaps rightly, as resting on the assumption that neither relative price changes nor specie movements are necessary for transfer of reparations if the proper credit policies are adopted in paying and receiving countries; and takes it for granted that a loss of gold by Germany, in the absence of a change in credit policy, means a lowering of money wages in Germany. But it is theoretically possible for reparations to be transferred without relative price changes, without changes in the usual gold reserve ratios in either country, without a fall in money wages in the paying country or a rise in the receiving country, through the mediation of an initial transfer of specie and its effects on relative demands for commodities in terms of money. See *infra*, pp. 338 ff., 366 ff.

[39] *Economic journal*, XXXIX, 181. (Italics in original.)

reparations would precede rather than follow the real transfer, and would not be "used up" by the French import surplus of a particular year, merely replied: "Surely it is easier to sell many goods to a man who has got increased buying power, even though after buying them he has no longer greater buying power than he used to have!"[40] a reply which conceded too much to Keynes, and left his argument intact instead of refuting it.

For Keynes, the real transfer of £25,000,000 of reparations was due to a fortuitous development of an export surplus by Germany, payment for which Germany was willing to accept in credits against her reparations liabilities. Suppose, however, that Germany's first step in her attempt to meet her reparations obligations was the payment of £25,000,000 *in gold* to France, and that in France this increase in gold had its normal effects on the total volume of means of payments. Suppose also that thereafter at each reparations payment date, Germany credited France anew with £25,000,000 in German funds at German banks. Frenchmen would now have both increased willingness to buy German goods at the same prices and increased power to pay for them in French currency, and there would therefore tend to be recurrent French import surpluses with respect to Germany. These import surpluses could be liquidated internationally by drafts against the reparations credits in favor of France periodically set up by the German government in German banks. As long as Germany continued, in the narrow financial sense, to meet her reparations obligations, the increase in the French willingness to buy and power to pay, as compared to the pre-reparations situation, would never be "used up," but would be everlasting. But the question of the place of willingness to buy and power to pay for foreign commodities in the mechanism of transfer of unilateral payments will be dealt with in a more fundamental manner later, after a needed digression on the role of price changes in the mechanism.

IV. PRICES IN THE MECHANISM: THE CONCEPT OF "PRICE LEVELS"

An adequate exposition of the role of price changes in the mechanism of international trade as it affects a particular coun-

---

[40] *Ibid.*, p. 402.

try would explain both what would be the necessary relationship under equilibrium between prices in that country and prices abroad, and in what manner if any fluctuations of prices would contribute to, or would be associated with, the restoration of equilibrium when it had been disturbed. In tracing the development of doctrine on these questions, it is once more convenient to begin with Hume. For our present purposes it is convenient to accept as the predominant criterion of equilibrium in international trade under an international metallic standard a situation in which there is an even balance of payments, i.e., no flow, and no tendency to flow, of bullion or specie from country to country.[1]

Hume held that when the balance of payments of England with the outside world was even, the "level of money" in England and in neighboring countries would also be equal, subject to minor qualifications. The mechanism of international trade operated to bring money to a common level in all countries, just as "all water, wherever it communicates, remains always at a level." Hume meant by "level of money" the proportion between money and commodities:

> It must carefully be remarked, that throughout this discourse, whenever I speak of the level of money, I mean always its proportional level to the commodities, labor, industry, and skill, which is in the several states. And I assert that where these advantages are double, triple, quadruple, to what they are in the neighboring states, the money infallibly will also be double, triple, quadruple.[2]

Modern usage makes it tempting to translate "level of money" by average value or purchasing power of money as against commodities in general, with some statistical average of prices as its reciprocal. But this would be an anachronism as far as Hume, or even as the classical school as a whole, was concerned. Hume wrote before the first attempt in England, that of Evelyn in 1798, to measure changes in price levels by means of statistical averages.[3] Even after 1798, the leading economists until the time of

---

[1] This definition, of course, would fit only either a static world in which the world stock of monetary gold was subject neither to accretion from mines nor to depletion by wear and tear or industrial use, or else a world in which each country produces the gold it needs for industrial consumption or to replace monetary wear and tear.

[2] *Essays*, 1875 ed., I, 335-36, note.

[3] Sir George Shuckburgh Evelyn, "An account of some endeavours to ascertain a standard of weight and measure," *Philosophical transactions of the Royal Society of London*, 1798, part 1, pp. 175-76.

Jevons either revealed no acquaintance with the notion of representing, by means of statistical averages, either a level of prices, or changes in such level, or found it inacceptable for various reasons, good and bad.[4] While a number of crude index numbers were constructed during the first half of the nineteenth century, none of the classical economists, with the single exception of Wheatley, would have anything to do with them.[5]

Hume's use of the term "level" troubled some of the classical economists. Wheatley claimed that Hume was inconsistent in arguing both that money everywhere maintained its level and that one country might retain a greater relative quantity than another, "which is incompatible with the nature of a level."[6] Ricardo, in his published writings, seems to have avoided the use of the term "level" for the general state of prices, although he used it in this sense freely in his private correspondence.[7] He refused to acknowledge that there was any satisfactory way of comparing the value of money, or of bullion, in different countries:

---

[4] Cf., e.g.: Ricardo, *Proposals for an economical and secure currency* [1816], *Works*, p. 400:

> It has indeed been said that we might judge of its value [i.e., the value of money] by its relation, not to one, but to the mass of commodities. If it should be conceded, which it cannot be, that the issuers of paper money would be willing to regulate the amount of their circulation by such a test, they would have no means of so doing; for when we consider that commodities are continually varying in value, as compared with each other; and that when such variation takes place, it is impossible to ascertain which commodity has increased, which diminished in value, it must be allowed that such a test would be of no use whatever.

Cf. also, Malthus, review of Tooke, *Quarterly review*, XXIX (1823), pp. 234-35: *ibid., Principles of political economy*, 1st ed., 1820, p. 126; William Jacob, *An historical inquiry into the production and consumption of the precious metals*, 1831, II, 375-76; Arthur Young, *An inquiry into the progressive value of money in England*, 1812, p. 134; Tooke, in *Report from Select Committee on banks of issue*, 1840, p. 337.

[5] Wheatley was sharply rebuked by Francis Horner for his reliance on Evelyn's index number, with which Horner found fault on the basis both of genuine shortcomings in its mode of construction and of objections, weighty and otherwise, to the index number logic.—"Wheatley on currency and commerce," *Edinburgh review*, III (1803), 246 ff.

[6] *Essay on the theory of money*, I (1807), 2-3. The inconsistency is not apparent. The equality of level which Hume posited was not between absolute quantities of money but between the proportions of quantities of money to quantities of commodities, i.e., prices, and he conceded the possibility of differences in these proportions only if money was hoarded, or, for metallic money, if paper money was also used, or where equality of proportions was disturbed by differences in transportation costs as between export and import.

[7] E.g., *Letters to Malthus*, pp. 16, 34, 57, 196.

When we speak of the high or low value of gold, silver, or any other commodity in different countries, we should always mention some medium in which we are estimating them, or no idea can be attached to the proposition. Thus, when gold is said to be dearer in England than in Spain, if no commodity is mentioned, what notion does the assertion convey? If corn, olives, oil, wine, and wool, be at a cheaper price in Spain than in England, estimated in those commodities, gold is dearer in Spain. If, again, hardware, sugar, cloth, &c., be at a lower price in England than in Spain, then, estimated in those commodities, gold is dearer in England. Thus gold appears dearer or cheaper in Spain, as the fancy of the observer may fix on the medium by which he estimates its value.[8]

Malthus denied that money necessarily maintained a uniform level in different countries, if by uniformity of level was to be understood necessary equality of the prices of some specified commodity or of the "mass of commodities."[9]

What then were the views of the classical writers with respect to the relationship of prices and of the value of gold in different countries? The following seems to be a correct interpretation of their general position: (1) When they speak of the value of money or of the level of prices without explicit qualification, they mean the array of prices, of both commodities and services, in all its particularity and without conscious implication of any kind of statistical average; (2) when they postulate a tendency for the uniformity of the value of money, or of prices, in different countries, they have reference only to particular identical commodities taken one at a time, and only to transportable commodities, and they claim such a tendency for uniformity only subject to allowance for transportation costs both for the commodities and for the specie; (3) where the monetary units are not the same, or where different standards are in use, they postulate uniformity in the prices of identical commodities only after conversion into a common currency unit at the prevailing rate of exchange, and they postulate uniform ratios between the prices of different transportable commodities in the currencies of the respective countries.[10]

---

[8] *Principles, Works,* p. 228.

[9] *Inquiry into the nature and progress of rent,* 1815, p. 46, note.

[10] The uniformity posited, it must be noted, is between sale or market prices in the two areas, not between cost prices.

Most of these propositions are implied in the following passage from Hume:

The only circumstance that can obstruct the exactness of these proportions, is the expense of transporting the commodities from one place to another; and this expense is sometimes unequal. Thus the corn, cattle, cheese, butter, of Derbyshire, cannot draw the money of London, so much as the manufactures of London draw the money of Derbyshire. But this objection is only a seeming one; for so far as the transport of commodities is expensive, so far is the communication between the places obstructed and imperfect.[11]

In spite of the obscurity of his exposition, it seems clear that Ricardo would have subscribed to these propositions, and that where occasional statements in his writings appear to conflict with them the inconsistency is only apparent. Thus Ricardo says at one point that "the value of money is never the same in any two countries" and that "the prices of the commodities which are common to most countries are also subject to considerable difference";[12] but the context shows that he had in mind the differences in different countries in the purchasing power of gold over particular commodities which were due to the cost of transporting gold, to bounties and tariffs, to the cost of transporting goods, and to the existence of non-transportable "home commodities" which, according to him, would be higher in price in countries where the effectiveness of labor in export industries and therefore also the wages of labor were comparatively high, and he included as an element in the value of money its purchasing power in terms of labor, which he assumed to be a non-transportable commodity.[13] In a letter to Malthus, Ricardo conceded that the situation suggested by Blake, where gold moved from France to England although the value of gold in terms of commodities was constant in France and rising in England, was possible though improbable, and explained the possibility of such divergent trends of the value of gold by reference to the transportation costs of commodities and the existence of non-transportable commodities.[14]

---

[11] *Essays*, 1875 ed., I, 336, note.
[12] *Principles, Works*, p. 81.
[13] Cf. *ibid.*, pp. 81 ff. Cf. also *High price of bullion*, appendix to 4th ed. [1811], *Works*, p. 293.
[14] *Letters of Ricardo to Malthus* [May 3, 1823], p. 151

Wheatley held that in the absence of tariff barriers "corn and manufactures . . . would always be brought, or have a constant tendency to be brought to the same proportion and price in all countries, with the exception of the charge of transit between them. A difference to the extent of this charge might always exist; but if trade were open, the difference in the price of corn and manufactures, in any two countries, could never exceed the expense of bringing in the one and taking out the other."[15]

The classical school and its important followers all held the same views on this point: after allowance for transportation costs, the market prices of identical transportable commodities must everywhere be equal or tend to be equal when expressed in or converted to a common currency.[16] When, therefore, critics of the classical theory have taken it to task on the ground that it explained the adjustment of international balances by the influence on the course of trade of divergent market prices in different markets of identical transportable commodities,[17] or

---

[15] *Essay on the theory of money*, II (1822), 103.

[16] Torrens (*The budget*, 1844 ed., Introduction, pp. liii ff.) shows that an attempt by Lawson to refute his argument based on the Cuban illustration rests on the "absurd assumption" that there could prevail great differences in price for identical commodities in Cuba and England, whereas his conclusions "had been deduced from the assumption, that (carriage and merchant's profit being excluded from the calculation, for the sake of simplicity and brevity) when the price of cloth fell to 20 s. per bale in England, it would be sold for 20 s. per bale in the markets of Cuba; and that, when the price of sugar in Cuba rose to 40 s. per cwt., it would be sold in the markets of England for 40 s. per cwt."

Whewell, in 1856, in what was presented as mainly an uncritical mathematical exposition of J. S. Mill's doctrines on international trade, formulated what he called the "principle of uniformity of international prices," to the effect that, transportation costs being abstracted from, "when the international trade has been established, the relative value of all commodities which are exported and imported is the same in the two countries."—"Mathematical exposition of some doctrines of political economy. Second memoir," *Transactions of the Cambridge Philosophical Society*, IX, part I (1856), 137-39.

See also, for similar reasoning: Longfield, *Three lectures on commerce*, 1835, p. 25; Cairnes, *Essays in political economy*, 1873, pp. 70 ff.; *ibid.*, *Some leading principles*, 1874, p. 409; Marshall, *Money credit & commerce*, 1923, p. 228; Taussig, "International freights and prices," *Quarterly journal of economics*, XXXII (1918), 411-12.

[17] E.g., Laughlin, *Principles of money*, 1903, p. 379: "Evidently, the classical theory counted on a change of all prices in England in such a manner that the whole English level would be, for a time, higher or lower than the general level in the United States, and would, in this manner, occasion new exports or new imports." Cf. also: Nicholson, *Principles of political economy*, II

when followers of the classical theory have attempted to defend it although themselves giving it such an interpretation,[18] they have misinterpreted the classical doctrine.

When costs connected with transportation, including tariff duties as such, are taken into account, prices in two markets for identical commodities can vary independently of each other within the limits of the transportation costs in either direction between these markets, except as a connection of both markets with a third market may impose narrower limits. Assuming only two markets, A and B, a cost of transportation from A to B of m, and from B to A of n, and a technological possibility of the production of the commodity in either A or B, and it is possible, (1) when P_a is the price in A, for the price in B to be anywhere from $P_a + m$ to $P_a - n$, and (2) when P_b is the price in B, for the price in A to be anywhere from $P_b + n$ to $P_b - m$. If the commodity is regularly moving from one market to the other, the price in the buying market must obviously be higher than the price in the selling market by exactly the cost of transportation, but the possibility of reversal of direction of movement, or of cessation or initiation of movement because of substitution in one country of domestic production for import or of import for domestic production, makes the double-transportation-cost range of possible relative variation in price potentially of practical significance.[19]

(1897), 288; Wicksell, "International freights and prices," *Quarterly journal of economics,* XXXII (1918), 405.

[18] Cf. A. C. Whitaker, "The Ricardian theory of gold movements," *Quarterly journal of economics,* XVIII (1904), 236 ff., and my comments thereon in *Canada's balance,* pp. 206 ff.

[19] Convinced apparently that a reversal in the direction of movement of a commodity is practically inconceivable, one writer has found something absurd in my statement of these elementary propositions in my *Canada's balance.*—See L. B. Zapoleon, "International and domestic commodities and the theory of prices," *Quarterly journal of economics,* XLV (1931), 425, note.—But such instances have occurred in the past, and it was the case of butter in Canada before 1913, which shifted from the export to the import class, which brought their possibility to my attention.

To my argument that a substantial range of fluctuation of the relative prices of the same commodity in two different markets is possible if the commodities are bulky or are subject to import duty, Bresciani-Turroni has replied: "Experience however shows that in many cases even for commodities for which transportation costs or import duties are very high there exists an equilibrium between prices in different countries and that goods move from one country to another as soon as the equilibrium is disturbed." (*Inductive verification of the theory of international payments,* 1932, p. 97, note.) He claims that for international commodities there is a "normal difference" in their prices in two

It may be objected that some difference, slight though it may be, must exist between the market prices of identical commodities in different regions, even in the absence of transportation costs, if there is to be any inducement to move the commodities from one region to the other. This is not true, however, with respect either to intranational or to international trade. When there is no intermediary between buyer and seller, the selling price and the buying price, f.o.b., are the same price whether the buyer is here or abroad. The only difference in price necessary to induce export from A to B of a particular commodity, transportation costs being assumed to be zero, is an excess in the actual or potential *supply* price at which B can procure the commodity from any source other than A in the quantities required by B over the price at which it can be procured from A.

Such changes in relative *sales* prices of *identical* commodities in different markets as may occur within the limits of the transportation costs and may result in the complete cessation or initiation of movement, or in a reversal of the direction of movement, of the particular commodities affected, can ordinarily be a minor, but only a minor, factor in bringing about adjustments of the course of trade to disturbances of moderate duration such as international loans. It is relative changes in the *supply* prices of identical commodities as between different potential sources of supply, and, above all, relative changes in the actual sales prices of *different* commodities which, through their influence on the direction and extent of trade, exercise a significant role in the mechanism of adjustment of international balances.

---

markets, corresponding to the costs of transportation and of duties, and that "When the actual spread in prices is not equal to this 'normal difference,' the disturbed 'parity' will soon be reestablished through movements of goods" (*ibid.*). What he says is indisputable, and has not been disputed, for commodities which do *continuously* move in international trade and always move only in *one* particular direction. But it does not cover adequately the full range of possibilities, and takes no account, in particular, of two possibilities, for, let us say, a commodity, wheat, which has been moving from country A to country B. First, the departure from "parity" in the price of wheat in country B may be such as to stop rather than to stimulate the movement of wheat, i.e., the price of wheat in B may fall below its import parity, with the result that import ceases, perhaps permanently. Secondly, the fall in the price of wheat in country B relative to its price in country A may be so great as to carry the price in B from import parity with respect to country A to export parity with respect to country A, i.e., may reverse the direction of movement of the wheat.

v. The "Terms-of-Trade" Concept

In the classical theory, the discussion of the role of variations in prices in the mechanism of adjustment of international balances relates not to relative variations in prices of identical commodities in different markets, but to relative variations in prices of different commodities in the same markets, and primarily to relative variations in prices as between export and import commodities. It concerns itself, therefore, with the effect of disturbances on what are now called the "terms of trade." Changes in the terms of trade were discussed, however, with reference to two essentially distinct though related problems; first, their role in the mechanism of adjustment and, second, their significance as measures of gain or loss from foreign trade. It is only the former of these problems that concerns us in this chapter.[1]

The most familiar concept of the terms of trade measures these terms by the ratio of export prices to import prices, what Taussig has called the "net barter terms of trade," and I prefer to designate as the "commodity terms of trade." The classical economists, however, had also another concept of terms of trade, for which they tacitly accepted the commodity terms of trade as an accurate measure, so that they used the two concepts as quantitatively identical although logically distinct. This second concept, which I would designate as the "double factoral terms of trade," is the ratio between the quantities of the productive factors in the two countries necessary to produce quantities of product of equal value in foreign trade.

From Hume on, there was general agreement that some or all types of disturbances in international balances would result in changes in the terms of trade, and that these changes would contribute to the restoration of equilibrium. As has been shown, Hume held that a relative change in the quantity of money in one country as compared to other countries would result in a rise in the prices of its products relative to the prices of foreign products, until, as the result of the influence of this relative change in prices on the course of trade and on the flow of specie, the "level of money" had again been equalized internationally.

---

[1] See *infra*, pp. 555 ff., for a detailed discussion of the terms of trade as an index of gain or loss from trade.

This was almost universally accepted doctrine during the next century. Thornton and Malthus claimed, with Wheatley and Ricardo dissenting, that a similar change in relative prices would occur and would operate to restore equilibrium in the balance of payments when it had been disturbed by a crop failure or the remittance of a subsidy, and this also came to receive wide acceptance, under the erroneous designation of the "Ricardian theory." Ricardo conceded, however, that there were some types of disturbance in an existing international equilibrium other than those originating in the currency which would affect the terms of trade, and he specified an original change in the relative demand of two countries for each other's products and a tariff change as disturbances of this sort.[2] There is ground for distinguishing in this connection between different types of disturbances, and Ricardo's distinctions have some measure of validity. In the account which follows of later treatments of the question, only the historically most important controversies are referred to.

Irish Absenteeism.—The economic consequences for Ireland of the absenteeism of Irish landlords was a burning issue in the eighteenth and nineteenth centuries and gave rise to extensive discussion. The Irish complaints against absenteeism often rested on mercantilist arguments to the effect that the remittance of the rents abroad represented an equivalent loss of specie to Ireland. The English classical economists, notably McCulloch, tended to be satisfied that when they had demonstrated that the remittances were ultimately transferred in the form of goods rather than in specie they had also demonstrated that absenteeism was not economically injurious to Ireland. An early instance of this argument follows:

When it is considered that, if in the natural order of things, undisturbed by such a measure as the restriction on specie, the remittances to absentees, by causing a balance of pecuniary intercourse

---

[2] Cf. his evidence before (*Lords*) *Committee on resumption of cash payments,* 1819, p. 192:

"Q. Do you mean that you doubt whether an increase of foreign demand has not always a tendency to increase the production and wealth of a nation?

"A. In no other way than by procuring for us a greater quantity of the commodities we desire in exchange for a given quantity of our own commodities, or rather for a given quantity of the produce of our land and labor."

against Ireland, would force an export from thence wherewith to pay it, and restore the level, it may be fairly concluded that the absentees, by bringing over their money to England, force the manufacture or produce to follow them, which, but for their coming, they would necessarily have caused to be used at home, the only difference is, that the produce or manufactures which their incomes naturally promote, would come to be consumed or used in England, in the stead of being consumed or used in Ireland; and thus the encouragement to the productive industry of Ireland may be said to operate in both cases . . .[3]

Longfield[4] introduced into the controversy the question of the effect of absenteeism on the Irish terms of trade, apparently for the first time in print.[5] He insisted that it was important to examine whether the increase in Irish exports resulting from absenteeism took place "in consequence of a diminished demand [for Irish products] at home, or an increased demand abroad," and claimed that the former was the case, because Irish landlords living abroad would not have the same demand for Irish commodities and services as would the same landlords if living in Ireland. In order to induce acceptance of the rents in goods instead of money, therefore, the Irish tenants would have to offer more

---

[3] *Report from the Committee on the circulating paper of Ireland,* 1804, p. 20. Cf. also, to the same effect: Lord King, *Thoughts on the effects of the Bank restrictions,* 2d ed., 1804, pp. 85-86; J. R. McCulloch, "Essay showing the erroneousness of the prevailing opinions in regard to absenteeism," reprinted from *Edinburgh review,* November, 1825, in his *Treatises and essays,* 2d ed., 1859, pp. 223-49 (in a new introduction, McCulloch says of this essay that "It helped to stem the torrent of abuse, and has yet to be answered," p. 224); N. W. Senior, *Political economy,* 4th ed., 1858, pp. 155 ff.; J. Tozer, "On the effect of the non-residence of landlords, &c. on the wealth of a community," *Transactions of the Cambridge Philosophical Society,* VII (1842), 189-96 (a mathematical study which begs the crucial question: "When the proprietor becomes non-resident the capital $C_2 + C_2'$ will be disengaged, because his absence destroys the demand on which its employment depended; but a new demand for such commodities as can be exported with advantage will be created by the absence, because the rent of the proprietor must now be exported"); J. L. Shadwell, *A system of political economy,* 1877, pp. 395-96.

[4] M. Longfield, *Three lectures on commerce and one on absenteeism,* 1835, pp. 82, 88 ff., 107 ff. He discusses along similar lines the effect of an import duty on the terms of trade. *Ibid.,* pp. 70, 105.

[5] This claim is made for Longfield by Isaac Butt, *Protection to home industry,* 1846, p. 93. Cf., however, J. S. Mill, *Some unsettled questions in political economy* [written 1829-30], 1844, p. 43: "Ireland pays dearer for her imports in consequence of her absentees; a circumstance which the assailants of Mr. M'Culloch, whether political economists or not, have not, we believe, hitherto thought of producing against him."

goods to liquidate their indebtedness to absentee landlords than would be necessary if the landlords lived in Ireland, i.e., there would have to be a fall in the prices of Irish export products relative to the prices of imports.[6]

Tariff Changes.—Torrens's discussion of the effect of a tariff on the terms of trade has already been referred to.[7] In his basic illustration, Torrens assumed unit elasticities of demand for sugar and cloth in both countries, production of sugar only in Cuba and of cloth only in England, and production under conditions of constant costs for both countries, and he concluded that both the commodity and the factoral terms of trade would move in favor of Cuba, the tariff-levying country. His argument was on the whole received unsympathetically by most of the economists of his time, because it seemed to them to undermine the case for free trade.[8] But their criticisms, in so far as they were deserving of consideration at all, bore only on the conformity of the assumptions to real conditions. Of these criticisms, the most important was the argument by Merivale that if sugar could be produced in England as well as in Cuba, or if a third country which could produce sugar were brought into the hypothesis, the English elasticity of demand for *Cuban* sugar would be greatly increased, and the shift in the terms of trade in favor of Cuba would in consequence be much lessened in degree.[9] The only favorable comments on Torrens's argument were by an anonymous writer in the *Dublin University magazine*,[10] who may perhaps have been Longfield, and by J. S. Mill, who made the publication of Torrens's *The budget* the occasion for the publication of his own *Essays on some unsettled questions*, which had been written some fifteen years before, and of which the first essay presented a similar argument as to the effect of import duties on the terms of trade.

---

[6] *Three lectures on commerce*, p. 82.

[7] *The budget,* 1841-1844, *passim.* See *supra*, pp. 298-99.

[8] A request by Torrens in 1835 to discuss some question—probably the one here under discussion—was rejected unanimously by the Political Economy Club on the ground, according to Mallet, that it turned "upon an impossible case" and "did not go to establish but to disturb a principle, that of free trade, upon grounds altogether hypothetical."—Political Economy Club, *Minutes of proceedings*, VI (1921), 270. Cf. also *ibid.*, pp. 54, 284.

[9] Herman Merivale, *Lectures on colonization and colonies,* 1842, II, 308 ff.

[10] XXIV (1844), 721-24.

VI. THE PRICES OF "DOMESTIC" COMMODITIES

While the distinction between "domestic" commodities and those entering into international trade dates at least from Ricardo,[1] and subsequent writers made clear that international uniformity in the prices of identical commodities after allowance for transportation costs was a necessary condition under equilibrium only for "international" commodities,[2] Taussig was the first to lay emphasis on the significance for the mechanism of adjustment of international balances to disturbances of changes in the level of domestic commodity prices as compared to the prices of international commodities. In 1917, Taussig argued that some of the proceeds of an international loan would ordinarily be directed in the first instance to the purchase of domestic commodities, instead of import commodities. But in order that the loan should be transferred wholly in the form of goods, it was necessary that there should develop an excess of imports over exports equal to the amount of the borrowings, and this could not occur if part of the proceeds of the borrowings continued to be directed to purchases of domestic goods. The increased purchases of domestic goods would raise their prices, however, relative to other commodities, and the rise in prices of domestic commodities as compared to international commodities, as well as the rise in export prices as compared to import prices, would operate to decrease exports, increase imports, sufficiently to effect a transfer of the loan in the form of goods.[3]

In my *Canada's balance*, I conceded that the increase in means

---

[1] Cf. *supra*, p. 315.

[2] Cf. R. H. Mills, *Principles of currency and banking*, 2d ed., 1857, p. 38: "there is, besides, a large proportion of every man's income expended on subjects which do not admit of exportation, as house-rent, many articles of diet, attendance, and various other matters. Of all these the prices vary considerably in different countries, and the general level of price is much higher in some than it is in others."

Cf. also J. E. Cairnes, *Leading principles*, 1874, p. 409.

[3] F. W. Taussig, "International trade under depreciated paper," *Quarterly journal of economics*, XXXI (1917); cf. also *ibid.*, "Germany's reparation payments," *American economic review, supplement*, X (1920), 39.

Graham used a similar classification of commodities in the analysis of the mechanism under depreciated paper.— "International trade under depreciated paper. The United States, 1862-1879," *Quarterly journal of economics*, XXXVI (1922), 220-73.

of payment in the borrowing country would, even in the absence of price changes, result in both a decrease in exports and an increase in imports. I claimed, however, that in the absence of price changes and of special circumstances it was to be expected that the borrowings abroad would not disturb the proportions in which the total purchasing power in the borrowing country, including that derived from the loan, would be used in buying domestic and foreign commodities; and I claimed further that without a change in these proportions the direct effect of the transfer of means of payment would not suffice fully to adjust the balance. I held, therefore, that there would have to occur relative price changes of the type postulated by Taussig, namely, for the borrowing country, a rise of export prices relative to import prices and of domestic commodity prices relative to both export and import prices.[4]

To my statement that, in the absence of price changes, it was theoretically to be expected that increase in the amounts available for expenditure by the borrowing country would not result in a change in the proportions in which these expenditures were distributed among the different classes of commodities, it has been objected that "there are ample grounds to dispute this view,"[5] and that "there is every reason to believe, on the contrary, that borrowings abroad would disturb the proportions."[6] But this statement was not intended to be a denial of the obvious fact that there were an infinite number of proportions in which the increased funds could conceivably be divided among the three classes of commodities, nor even as an assertion that in the absence of price changes the probability that the proportions in which the expenditures were divided among the three classes of commodities would not be disturbed was greater than the probability that these proportions would be disturbed, i.e., was greater than all the other probabilities combined. The probability that the

---

[4] *Canada's balance,* pp. 205-06.

[5] Roland Wilson, *Capital imports and the terms of trade,* 1931, p. 80. Wilson continues: "Professor Viner himself has since abandoned it, preferring to regard such a distribution of the added purchasing power derived from the loan as *merely* one of an infinite number of possible distributions." (Italics mine.) This does not correctly state my position at present, or at any other time.

[6] Harry D. White, *The French international accounts, 1880-1913,* 1933, p. 20. Cf. also Carl Iversen, *International capital movements,* 1935, pp. 230 ff.

proportions would be disturbed is obviously infinitely greater than the probability that they would not be. If an indifferent marksman aims at a distant target, the probability that he will hit the bull's-eye is, on the basis of experience, small. But it is nevertheless much greater than the probability that he will hit any other single spot in the universe, and if a forecast of his shot must be made, the probable error will be minimized if, in the absence of a known bias in his marksmanship or in the conditions governing his shooting, it is forecast that he will hit the bull's-eye.[7] The assumption that, in the absence of price changes and of known evidence to the contrary, the amounts available for expenditure in each country would after their increase or decrease be distributed among the different classes of commodities in the same proportions as before still seems to me more reasonable than any other specific assumption. It represents what Edgeworth in another connection described as "a neutral condition between two conditions of which neither is known to prevail."[8] But this assumption was not sufficient to justify such definite conclusions as I drew from it, and in occupying themselves with the assumption instead of with the partly erroneous inferences I based upon it my critics have directed their ammunition at the wrong target.

The existence of domestic commodities affects the mechanism of adjustment only as it affects the manner in which the amounts available for expenditure are apportioned as between native[9] and foreign products. The assumption of the existence of domestic commodities is not essential to any valid theory of the general mechanism of adjustment of international balances to disturbances; and certainly no quantitative proposition as to their importance relative to international commodities need be incorporated in an abstract explanation of the mechanism. But if "domestic" commodities do exist, certain important consequences ensue, and it becomes necessary to take specific account of them in the analysis. For a commodity to be a "domestic" commodity, be it noted, it is not necessary that its prices be wholly inde-

[7] Cf. J. S. Mill's treatment of the division of the gain in international trade, where the same problem of the *a priori* probabilities arises: "The advantage will probably be divided equally, oftener than in any one unequal ratio that can be named; though the division will be much oftener, on the whole, unequal than equal." (*On some unsettled questions*, 1844, p. 14.)

[8] Edgeworth, *Papers relating to political economy*, II, 363.

[9] I use "native" to include both "domestic" and "exportable" commodities.

pendent of the prices of similar commodities abroad, or of the prices of competitive or of complementary international commodities at home. If this were the case, there could obviously be no "domestic" commodities in a world in which all prices are parts of an interrelated system. It suffices to make a commodity a "domestic" commodity if it ordinarily does not cross national frontiers and if its price is not tied directly to the prices of similar commodities abroad in such manner that there is always a differential between them approximating closely to the cost of transportation between the two markets.[10]

That in the United States, for instance, there is an extensive and important range of commodities (including services) available for purchase whose prices are capable of varying within substantial limits while the prices of identical or similar products or services in other countries remain unaltered, seems to me so obvious that it would not require restatement had it not been disputed. One writer[11] has claimed, however, not only that the existence of a substantial range of domestic commodities is a vital assumption of the ordinary theory of the mechanism but that such an assumption is contrary to the facts. But the evidence he offers in support of his argument consists only of an irrelevant demonstration that the prices in different markets of identical commodities actually moving in international trade in constant directions are bound together in a close relationship.

VII. THE MECHANISM OF TRANSFER OF UNILATERAL PAYMENTS IN SOME RECENT LITERATURE

Recent discussion of the problem of the effect of international unilateral payments on the terms of trade has made it clear that the older writers (including myself) had not sufficiently explored

---

[10] For large countries, a commodity may be an international commodity near the frontier, but a domestic commodity in the interior, and some commodities may for practical purposes be hard to classify. The distinction, nevertheless, is both theoretically and practically valid. Commodities which are transportable can for our purposes be identified as domestic commodities of a particular country if their prices within that country remain as a general rule within their import and export points. Cf. the penetrating discussion by Theodore J. Kreps, "Export, import, and domestic prices in the United States, 1926-1930," *Quarterly journal of economics*, XLVI (1932), 195-207.

[11] L. B. Zapoleon, "International and domestic commodities and the theory of prices," *Quarterly journal of economics*, XLV (1931).

the problem and had failed to realize its full complexity. There follows an account of some recent attempts at a more definitive solution of the problem.[1]

Wilson.—Wilson examines the effects on relative prices, and especially on the commodity terms of trade, of a continued import of capital, with the aid of an elaborate series of arithmetical illustrations of an ingenious type.[2] He concludes that relative price changes will ordinarily be necessary for restoration of equilibrium, but that the type of change will depend on the particular circumstances of each case, and may be unfavorable to the paying country. He believes that he demonstrates that the changes in export and import prices, *relative to each other,* make no direct contribution to bringing about a transfer of the loan in the form of goods instead of in money, but that the role of these changes is solely to determine for each country to what extent the transfer shall take place through a change in exports or a change in imports, and to bring the two countries to a uniform decision, and that it is the relative changes in prices between domestic and international commodities which, together with the shift in demands resulting from the transfer of means of payment from lender to borrower, brings about the transfer of the loan in the form of goods.[3] Wilson's account marks a distinct advance over previous attempts, because it takes more of the variables simultaneously into account and deals with some of them with a greater measure of precision of analysis than had previously been achieved. While he carries the problem forward toward a solution, there are, however, some defects in his mode of analysis which seriously detract from the significance of the concrete results which he obtains.

---

[1] A useful account of the more recent literature, with special emphasis on the terms-of-trade issue, is given by Carl Iversen, in his *Aspects of the theory of international capital movements,* 1935, pp. 243-99. His own position is in all essentials identical with Ohlin's, and his survey of the literature is presented in terms of two sharply contrasting bodies of doctrine, the wrong or "classical" doctrine, on the one hand, and the correct or "modern" doctrine, on the other. The inclusion in the "classical" doctrine of special treatment of the prices of domestic commodities he seems to regard as a peculiar aberration, accidentally in the right direction, of the "classical" writers.

[2] Roland Wilson, *Capital imports and the terms of trade,* 1931, chap. iv.

[3] *Ibid.,* pp. 75-76. That this proposition is incorrect can be sufficiently shown by the reductio ad absurdum to which it would lead if there were no domestic commodities.

Wilson's mode of analysis and the nature of the results which he obtains can for present purposes be made sufficiently clear by reference to two of his arithmetical examples, I and IV,[4] which are here presented in somewhat modified form to simplify the exposition. It is assumed in both examples that production is under conditions of constant cost; that in the absence of price changes the transfer of the payments will not change the proportions in which either country would desire to distribute its expenditures as between the classes of commodities available to it; and that the amount to be paid is 9 monetary units. In Wilson's example I there are no domestic commodities in either country, while in his example IV there are domestic commodities in each country. Purchases are measured in monetary units uniform for both countries. The paying country's export commodity is represented by P, and its domestic commodity by D_p; the receiving country's export commodity is represented by R, and its domestic commodity by D_r.

WILSON'S EXAMPLE I: NO PRICE CHANGES NECESSARY

Commodity	Paying country		Receiving country	
	Purchases before payment	Purchases after payment if no price changes occurred	Purchases before payment	Purchases after payment if no price changes occurred
P................	60	54	30	36
D_p................	..	..	..	..
D_r................	..	..	..	..
R................	30	27	15	18
Total............	90	81	45	54

Granted Wilson's assumptions, his example I is an adequate demonstration of the possibility that payments can be transferred without resulting in any movement of the terms of trade. Under the conditions given, the receiving country is willing in the absence of price changes to increase its purchases of each of the commodities to an extent just sufficient to offset the decreases in

[4] *Ibid.*, pp. 70, 72.

purchases by the paying country, and therefore no price changes are necessary for the restoration of equilibrium. This example suggests a general principle already formulated by a previous writer in this connection that "If the borrower wants what the lender does without, no change in prices is necessary."[5] It is to be noted, however, that in example I one of the countries spends a substantially larger amount on foreign than on native commodities. It will be found upon experimentation that, given the assumption that in the absence of price changes the international loan or tribute will not cause either country to desire a change in the proportions in which it had hitherto distributed its expenditures between native and imported commodities, the transfer of the loan or tribute will necessarily result in a movement of the terms of trade unfavorable to the paying country unless before reparations the unweighted average ratio of expenditures on native to expenditures on foreign commodities for the two countries combined is unity or less, an improbable situation when there are domestic commodities.

In example I there were assumed to be no domestic commodities. To show that his conclusion—that the transfer of payments will not necessarily involve a movement of the terms of trade against the paying country and may even involve a movement of the terms of trade in its favor—is not dependent on the assumption that there are no domestic commodities, Wilson presents his example IV, in which domestic commodities are introduced for both countries but otherwise the same assumptions are followed as for example I.

Comparing separately for each commodity the amounts which in the absence of price changes the two countries combined would be willing to purchase after the payments with the amounts they purchased before the payments, Wilson concludes that while the price of the receiving country's domestic commodity would rise, and the price of the paying country's domestic commodity would fall, the aggregate demand for the receiving country's export commodity will at unaltered prices have fallen more (from 60 to 58) relatively than the aggregate demand for the paying country's export commodity (from 50 to 49) and therefore the price of the former will probably have to fall relatively to the price of the

---

[5] [H. K. Salvesen] "The theory of international trade in the U.S.A.," *Oxford magazine,* May 19, 1927, p. 498.

latter to restore equilibrium. For the relations of the price levels of the internationally-traded commodities, he reaches the general conclusion that: "No matter what be the original proportions of total demand, *that class of goods will be higher relatively in price to the other, for which the borrowing country has the greater relative demand as compared with the lending country.*"[6]

No significance can be attached, for constant cost conditions, to the results derived by Wilson from his example IV, since it fails to take into consideration the necessary relationship between the prices in each country of domestic and export commodities resulting from their competition for the use of the same factors of production. If in either country the prices of domestic commodities rose or fell relative to export commodities, factors of production would be diverted from the low-price to the high-price industry until the earning power of the factors in the two industries was equalized, and under constant costs this would mean that in neither country could there be relative changes

WILSON'S EXAMPLE IV: TERMS OF TRADE MOVE AGAINST RECEIVING COUNTRY

Commodity	Paying country		Receiving country	
	Purchases before payment	Purchases after payment if no price changes occur	Purchases before payment	Purchases after payment if no price changes occur
P.................	20	18	30	31
D$_p$...............	40	36	..	..
D$_r$...............	..	..	210	217
R................	30	27	30	31
Total...........	90	81	270	279

between the prices of domestic and export commodities. What the direction of relative change of the prices of the products of the respective countries will be as the result of international payments will depend on what effect the payments have on the relative aggregate demands of the two countries for *all* the products, and therefore for the factors of production, of the respec-

---

[6] *Ibid.*, pp. 73-74. (Italics in original.)

tive countries. In Wilson's example IV, the payment results, in the absence of price changes, in an increase in the aggregate demand for the products of the receiving country (275 after the payment as compared to 270 before the payment) and in a decrease in the aggregate demand for the products of the paying country (85 after the payment as compared to 90 before the payment). The prices of the factors, and consequently the commodity terms of trade, must therefore move against the paying country if equilibrium is to be restored.

To an objection to his analysis made by some unspecified person[7] to the effect that the flow of gold from lending to borrowing country, by raising money prices and incomes generally in the borrowing country, and lowering them generally in the lending country, will make the prices of the productive services and therefore also of their products, in domestic and export industries alike, rise in the borrowing country and fall in the lending country, Wilson replies that: "mere changes in money costs of production are not sufficient in themselves to cause a change in prices. If prices are to be affected by changes in costs of production, it can only come about through a change in the relative demand and supply of those goods whose money costs of production are affected," and that the relative changes in price which such changes in cost would tend to produce would tend to be checked by diversion of expenditures to or from other classes of goods not so affected.[8] This reply bears only on the *degree* of relative price changes needed, whereas the issue is whether *any* price changes are needed, and if so, in what directions. It, moreover, misses the character of the valid objection to which his analysis is open, which is not the common but fallacious argument that relative changes in the amounts available for expenditure in the two countries must necessarily result in changes in the same direction in the prices of the productive services and therefore also in the money costs of production of the two countries,[9] but that changes in the relative aggregate demands for the commodities of the respective countries will do so. If, as is possible, but, as will later

---

[7] I suspect that I am supposed to be the guilty person.

[8] *Ibid.*, pp. 76-77.

[9] If I correctly interpret him, R. F. Harrod, in his review of Wilson's book, attempts to meet Wilson's example IV by just this argument. *Economic Journal,* XLII (1932), 428 ff.

be shown, improbable, a transfer of funds on loan from country A to country B results in an increase in the aggregate demand of the two countries for A's products and a decrease in their aggregate demand for B's products, it will be the prices of A's, and not of B's, factors of production which will rise.

Yntema.—Yntema applies to the problem a powerful mathematical technique, and analyzes it on the basis of a wide range of assumptions.[10] For cases such as those contemplated by the older writers, he reaches conclusions substantially in accord with theirs, especially with reference to the relative movement of the prices of the domestic commodities of the two countries and of their double factoral terms of trade.[11] But Yntema's analysis rests throughout on certain assumptions which seriously limit the significance of his results. He assumes that when a relative change in the amount of money in two countries occurs as a result of loans or tributes or other disturbances in the international balances, there will occur in the country whose stock of money has increased a rise not only in all of that country's demand schedules (in the simple Marshallian sense), but also in the prices of the factors of production and in the supply schedules of that country's products, and that there will similarly occur in the country whose stock of money has decreased a fall not only in all of that country's demand schedules, but also in the prices of its factors of production and in the supply schedules of that country's products, though these rises or falls need not be uniform in degree within each country. But a rise in all the demand schedules of a country does not necessarily lead to or require a rise in its supply schedules or in the prices of its factors of production. What will be the effect of an international transfer of income on the *direction* of the relative movement of the prices of the factors in the two countries is itself the question relating to the equilibrating process awaiting solution, but in Yntema's analysis it is unfortunately decided by arbitrary assumption. Yntema's conclusion that under constant cost the terms of trade must necessarily shift in favor of the receiving country results from his assumption that the prices of the factors and the money costs of production will neces-

---

[10] T. O. Yntema, *A mathematical reformulation of the general theory of international trade,* 1932, especially chap. v.

[11] Which Yntema calls the "resources terms of trade." See *ibid.*, pp. 19-21.

sarily rise in the receiving country. As has been argued above, this is not a valid assumption.

Ohlin.—In his important treatise,[12] Ohlin gives an elaborate account of the mechanism, whose most important contribution is the convincing demonstration that not price changes only, but also relative shifts in demands resulting from the transfer of means of payment, are operative in restoring a disturbed equilibrium in the balance of payments. On the question immediately at issue, i.e., the specific mode of operation of relative changes in sectional price levels in the mechanism of adjustment, he is extremely critical in tone in his treatment of the older writers, although as long as he adheres to the traditional assumptions he follows the traditional reasoning and conclusions only too closely. Ohlin claims that the older writers exaggerated the importance of relative price changes in the equilibrating process both because they overlooked the direct influence on purchases of the shift in means of payment and because the ordinarily high elasticity of foreign demand for a particular country's exportable products makes a small change in price exert a large influence on the volume of trade. Subject to the qualification that I believe I have shown that recognition of its validity was not nearly as rare among the classical expositors of the theory of international trade as he appears to take for granted, I concede his first point. But on the second point, at least a partial defense can be made of the position of the older writers. When two factors are necessarily associated in a complex economic process, there is rarely a satisfactory criterion for measuring their relative importance, even if all the quantitative data that could be desired were available. Ohlin appears to regard the relative degree of price change as between different classes of commodities as an appropriate measure of the importance of such price changes in the equilibrating process. A more appropriate criterion, if it could be applied, would be the proportion of (1) the equilibrating change in the trade balance which results from relative price changes to (2) the total change in the trade balance necessary to restore equilibrium. Since foreign demands for a particular country's products ordinarily have a high degree of elasticity, small price changes in the right direction can exert great equilibrating influence. But the emphasis

---

[12] Bertil Ohlin, *Interregional and international trade,* 1933, especially pp. 417-33.

which Ohlin gives to the question of the degree of change seems to me a novel one, as far as discussion of mechanism is concerned, and I cannot recall a single instance in the older literature where a definite position was taken as to the extent of the price changes necessary to restore a disturbed equilibrium.

Taking the case of international loans,[13] Ohlin assumes, as a first approximation, that "all goods produced in a country require for their manufacturing 'identical units of productive power' consisting of a fixed combination of productive factors." The lending country B must make initial remittances to the borrowing country **A**. The assumptions as to the effects on demands are not clearly stated, but seem to be as follows: the aggregate demands in terms of money prices of the two countries combined (1) for the export goods of A and (2) for the export goods of B, are each assumed to remain unaltered;[14] (3) the demand in A for A "domestic" goods increases; (4) the demand in B for B "domestic" goods decreases. This "implies" a shift in demand from B factors to A factors, which "raises the [relative] scarcity of the A unit, which means that every commodity produced in A becomes dearer than before compared with every commodity produced in B. The terms of exchange between A's export goods and B's change in favor of A."[15] So far, therefore, there is no correction of the older doctrines with respect to the *kind* of price changes necessary to restore equilibrium. But Ohlin attributes these results to the assumption that all industries use identical "units of productive power," and remarks that it is because they have expressed costs in such units that "men like Bastable, Keynes, Pigou, and Taussig have stopped at the preliminary conclusion in §5 and have found a variation in the terms of trade certain in all cases, at least where the direction of demand is not of a very special sort."[16]

---

[13] *Ibid.*, pp. 417-20 (chap. xx, §5).

[14] Cf. *ibid.*, p. 418: "the assumption, which has been tacitly made above, that the combined demand of A and B for the export goods from either is in the first place unchanged by the borrowings."

[15] *Ibid.*

[16] *Ibid.*, p. 425, note. Cf. also Carl Iversen, *International capital movements,* 1935, p. 289:

Expressing costs in terms of "units of productive power" and similar concepts, one cannot, of course, push the analysis beyond a demonstration that this unit, i.e., productive factors as a whole, becomes more scarce in the capital-importing country, less scarce in the capital-exporting country.

These results, however, arise not from the assumption of the use in each country of identical "units of productive power," but from Ohlin's assumption that the transfer of funds does not of itself lead to any alteration in the aggregate monetary demand for the export commodities of the respective countries. Even with both these assumptions, they are not *necessary* results, if it be granted that, without price changes, the increase in funds in A may lead to a *decrease* in the demand for A "domestic" goods, or that the decrease in the funds in B may lead to an *increase* in the demand for B "domestic" goods, or both, consequences by no means inconceivable, as, for instance, if A's and B's domestic goods are both predominantly low-grade necessaries of the sort heavily consumed only when there is economic pressure.[17] But Ohlin would probably regard—and not without justification—such movements of demand as "of a very special sort" and therefore not calling for consideration.

Abandoning the assumption of identical "units of productive power" and substituting the assumption that different industries use different factors, and use the same factors in different proportions, Ohlin shows that by introducing additional assumptions of non-competing factoral groups, the existence of idle resources, the tendency of the prices of the products to rise more rapidly than the prices of the factors in an expanding industry, and so forth, instances are possible where the commodity terms of trade turn against rather than in favor of the borrowing country.[18]

It is to be noted that some of these assumptions are of a non-equilibrium nature, i.e., can be valid only temporarily. But granted that Ohlin has shown the *possibility* that the terms of trade, when such assumptions are made, will turn *against* the borrowing country, what about the probabilities? Every one of these added factors is as likely, *a priori,* to accentuate the movement of the terms of trade in favor of the borrowing country as to operate to move them against the borrowing country. Take only one example, sufficiently representative of the others: Ohlin argues that the factors used relatively largely in expanding industries are

---

And on this premise it is inevitable that the terms of trade will move against the latter country.

[17] I.e., if in each country "domestic" goods are, with respect to export and import goods, "inferior commodities."

[18] *Ibid.,* pp. 420 ff.

likely to rise in price, while those used relatively largely in declining industries are likely to fall in price; in the borrowing country, the domestic commodity industries will be expanding, because of the increased demand for their products, while the export commodity industries will be declining, presumably because of decreased demand in the lending country for their products; the prices of the factors used largely in the domestic commodity industries therefore will rise, while those used largely in the export commodity industries will fall. In the lending country, reverse trends will be operating. The export commodities of the borrowing country therefore will decline in price relative to the prices of the export commodities of the lending country; i.e., the terms of trade will move against the borrowing country. But the export commodity industries of the borrowing country are not, *a priori,* more likely to decline than to expand. The foreign demand for their products, it is true, will tend to fall, but Ohlin overlooks that the home demand for their products will tend to rise, and that there is no obvious reason why the latter tendency should be expected to be less marked than the former and to be insufficient to offset the former.

The "orthodox" conclusions as to the *kind* of price change which would tend to result from international borrowing thus emerge from Ohlin's critical scrutiny almost unscathed. When he adheres to the usual assumptions, Ohlin reaches the same conclusions. When he departs from them, he succeeds in showing that different results are *possible.* But he does not succeed in showing that they are *probable*, or even that they are not improbable.

Pigou.—In a recent article Pigou has attacked the problem in terms of marginal utility functions, and has reached the conclusion that, under constant costs, there is a strong presumption, but not a necessity, that the commodity terms of trade (which he calls the "real ratio of international interchange") will turn against the paying country as the result of reparations.[19] Pigou's results, it will later be shown, can in part at least be reached by an alternative procedure which is simpler and has the additional virtue that it does not involve resort to utility analysis. But Pigou's analysis can be made to serve the useful function of bringing into clear view the utility implications of this alternative procedure, and thus warrants detailed examination and elaboration.

---

[19] "The effect of reparations on the ratio of international interchange," *Economic journal,* XLII (1932), 532-43.

Pigou assumes a paying country, Germany, and the rest of the world, which he calls "England," but since the existence of neutral countries, neither paying nor receiving reparations, gives rise to complications which this procedure disregards, I will proceed, for the time being, as if there are only two countries, Germany, the paying country, and England, the receiving country. Pigou makes the following additional assumptions: only one commodity produced in each area; "constant returns" (i.e., constant technological costs); dependence of the utility of any commodity on the quantity of that commodity alone; and linear utility functions throughout.

Pigou writes $\frac{X}{Y}$ for the commodity terms of trade before reparations, and $\frac{X+P+R}{Y+Q}$ for the terms of trade after reparations, where: X, Y, represent the annual pre-reparations physical quantities of English exports and imports, respectively; $X+P$ —P being negative—represents the annual quantity of English exports (or German imports) after reparations payments have been initiated; R represents the annual reparations payments measured by their value in English goods; and $Y+Q$ represents the annual quantity of English imports (or German exports) after reparations payments have commenced. He further writes nX, nY, for the "representative" Englishman's pre-reparations exports and imports, respectively, and mX, mY, for the "representative" German's pre-reparations imports and exports, respectively. He then writes:

$\phi(nY)$ for the marginal utility of (nY) German goods to the representative Englishman;

$f(nX)$ for the marginal disutility to him of surrendering (nX) English goods;

$F(mX)$ for the marginal utility of (mX) English goods to the representative German;

$\psi(mY)$ for the marginal disutility to him of surrendering (mY) German goods.

Then, in accordance with Jevon's analysis,

$$\frac{\phi(nY)}{f(nX)} = \frac{X}{Y} = \frac{\psi(mY)}{F(mX)} \tag{i}$$

$$\frac{\phi\{n(Y+Q)\}}{f\{n(X+P)\}} = \frac{X+P+R}{Y+Q} = \frac{\psi\{m(Y+Q)\}}{F\{m(X+P)\}} \tag{ii}$$

In order that the new terms of trade should be equal to the old, it would therefore be necessary that

$$\frac{\phi(nY)}{f(nX)} = \frac{\psi(mY)}{F(mX)} = \frac{\phi\{n(Y+Q)\}}{f\{n(X+P)\}} = \frac{\psi\{m(Y+Q)\}}{F\{m(X+P)\}} \qquad \text{(iii)}$$

which, for linear functions, implies[20] that

$$\frac{\phi'}{f'} = \frac{\psi'}{F'} \qquad \text{(iv)}$$

It can similarly be shown that reparations will cause the terms of trade to turn in favor of Germany if $\frac{\phi'}{f'} > \frac{\psi'}{F'}$, and to turn against Germany if $\frac{\phi'}{f'} < \frac{\psi'}{F'}$.

VIII. A Graphical Examination of Pigou's Analysis[1]

The examination of Pigou's algebraic analysis, and especially of its economic implications, can be facilitated by the use of

---

[20] Pigou says that these implications are very simple (*ibid.*, p. 534) and does not trouble to demonstrate them. A demonstration may not be superfluous for some readers:

$$\frac{\phi'}{f'} = \frac{\dfrac{\phi(nY) - \phi\{n(Y+Q)\}}{nQ}}{\dfrac{f(nX) - f\{n(X+P)\}}{nP}} \qquad \text{(v)}$$

$$\frac{\psi'}{F'} = \frac{\dfrac{\psi(mY) - \psi\{m(Y+Q)\}}{mQ}}{\dfrac{F(mX) - F\{m(X+P)\}}{mP}} \qquad \text{(vi)}$$

From (iii)

$$\frac{\phi(nY) - \phi\{n(Y+Q)\}}{f(nX) - f\{n(X+P)\}} = \frac{\psi(mY) - \psi\{m(Y+Q)\}}{F(mX) - F\{m(X+P)\}} \qquad \text{(vii)}$$

and

$$\frac{nQ}{nP} = \frac{mQ}{mP} \qquad \text{(viii)}$$

$$\therefore \qquad \frac{\phi'}{f'} = \frac{\psi'}{F'}$$

[1] I have benefited from the criticism of Professor G. A. Elliott, of the University of Alberta, of the diagrams here presented, and chart V, in par-

graphical illustrations. In chart III the left-hand diagram relates to the representative Englishman and the right-hand diagram to the representative German. Commodity units of the respective commodities are so chosen, for each country separately, as to be equal in price prior to reparations. For the English and the German "representative" consumer, respectively, the quantity purchased before reparations of his own country's commodity is

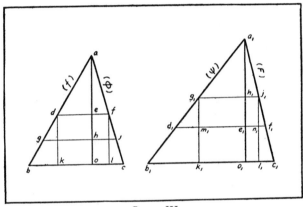

CHART III

measured on the *df* or d_1f_1 axis, to the left from the *oa* or o_1a_1 axis, and the quantity purchased before reparations of the imported commodity is measured on the same axis but to the right from the *oa* or o_1a_1 axis. For the representative consumer in each country the marginal utilities of the different commodities are measured vertically from the *bc*, or b_1c_1, axis. The curve of marginal utility to the representative English consumer is, therefore, *ab* for the native commodity and *ac* for the imported commodity, and a_1b_1 and a_1c_1 are similarly the curves of marginal utility to a representative German of the German and the English

ticular, incorporates a modification made as the result of his criticism. He has since published a treatment of the problem along lines similar to those adopted here, but it unfortunately became available to me too late to permit its use as a check on my results. Cf. G. A. Elliott, "Transfer of means-of-payment and the terms of international trade," *Canadian journal of economics and political science,* II (Nov. 1936), 481-92.

commodities, respectively. Since the utility functions are assumed to be linear, ab, ac, a_1b_1, and a_1c_1, are all drawn as straight lines.

In chart III there is substituted, for the two "marginal *disutility* of surrendering" functions which Pigou uses (i.e., $f(nX)$ and $\psi(mY)$), the corresponding marginal *utility* curves, ab and a_1b_1. The substitution does not call for a change in the numerical value of the slope, and by placing the ab and a_1b_1 curves on the left side of the oa, o_1a_1 axes, i.e., by making their inclinations positive, change of signs is also avoided. Since $\phi' =$ the slope of ac, $f' =$ the slope of ab, $\psi' =$ the slope of a_1b_1, and $F' =$ the slope of a_1c_1, Pigou has demonstrated that the terms of trade of Germany will not change, will move against Germany, or will move in favor of Germany according as

$$\frac{\text{the slope of } ac}{\text{the slope of } ab} = , <, \text{ or } > , \frac{\text{the slope of } a_1b_1}{\text{the slope of } a_1c_1}.$$

Unless, however, some presumptions can be established as to the relative slopes of the various utility curves, no progress has been made toward determining the probable effects of reparations payments on the terms of trade. To establish such presumptions Pigou resorts to two additional sets of presumptions, first, that before reparations each country spends more on native than on imported goods, and second, that the utility functions within each country are "similar."

The presumption that each country before reparations spends more on its own products than on foreign products is equivalent to making $de > ef$ and $d_1e_1 > e_1f_1$ in chart III. Pigou adopts it, presumably, on the ground that such is almost invariably the actual situation. The general prevalence of this situation results, however, chiefly from restrictions on foreign trade, from the existence—by no means universal—of greater international than internal costs of transportation from producer to consumer, and, above all, from the fact that included in the native commodities of each country are "domestic" commodities, or commodities which because of regional differences of taste or non-transportability cannot find a market outside their country of production. But Pigou presumably abstracts from trade restrictions and transportation costs, and he explicitly excludes "domestic" commodities by his assumption that "there is only one sort of good made in the reparation paying country and only one sort made in the rest of the world." In the absence of these factors, there would be no *a priori* presumption that there was any difference in either area in the amounts spent for native and for imported commodities if the two areas were equal in size, size being measured in terms of the pre-reparations value of output or of consumption. If the two areas were unequal in size, the most reasonable assumption would appear to be that, at the pre-reparations equilibrium, prices of the commodities would be such as to induce each country to spend more on the larger country's than on the smaller country's product. To justify acceptance of a general presumption that each country spends more on its own than on imported products it is necessary to recognize the existence of trade restrictions, transportation costs, and above all, "domestic" commodities. It will be shown, moreover, that while an excess in each country before reparations of expenditures on native over expenditures on imported commodities, of itself, whatever its cause, tends to make $\frac{\phi'}{f'} < \frac{\psi'}{F'}$, i.e., to contribute toward a situation in which reparations will make the terms of trade turn against the paying country, to the extent that such excess is due to higher international than internal transportation costs or to import duties this tendency *unfavorable* to the paying country will, given linear utility functions, be more than offset by the counter-tendency of the transportation costs and import duties to cause deviations from "similarity" of the utility functions within each country in directions *favorable* to the paying country.

By "similarity" of the utility functions within each country, Pigou must mean that, numerically, $\phi' = E(f')$ and $F' = G(\psi')$, where E is the pre-reparations ratio of the expenditures of a representative Englishman on English goods to his expenditures on German goods, and G is the pre-reparations ratio of the expenditures of a representative German on German goods to his expenditures on English goods. When the commodity units within each country are so chosen as to be equal in price before reparations, this is equivalent to the assumption that within each country first units of the different commodities have equal utilities, i.e., that in chart III the lines ab, ac start from the oa axis at some common point a, and the lines a_1b_1, a_1c_1 start from the o_1a_1 axis at some common point a_1.

For the two-country case, the assumptions of linearity and of "similarity" within each country of the utility functions turn out to involve as a corollary the familiar assumption in other discussions of this problem that, in the absence of relative price changes, changes in the amounts available for expenditure in the respective countries resulting from reparations payments will not affect in either country the proportions in which these expenditures are apportioned between native and foreign commodities. Before reparations the representative Englishman bought ed units of English commodities and ef units of German commodities. Since the commodity units in chart III have been so chosen as to make the pre-reparations prices of the two commodities equal, their marginal utilities must have been equal to a representative English purchaser of both, i.e., $kd = lf$. Therefore, d, e, f, must be points on a horizontal straight line. Suppose that in the absence of relative price changes the representative Englishman, after reparations, buys hg units of English commodities and hj units of German commodities. If no changes have occurred in their relative prices, the two commodities must still have equal marginal utilities to him, i.e., g, h, j, must be points on a horizontal straight line. From the geometry of triangles it follows that $\frac{ed}{ef} = \frac{hg}{hj}$, i.e., that, in the absence of relative price changes, changes in the amount of his aggregate expenditures will not affect the proportions in which the representative Englishman distributes them as between English and German commodities. Similarly, $\frac{e_1 d_1}{e_1 f_1} = \frac{h_1 g_1}{h_1 j_1}$, i.e., in the absence of relative price changes, changes in the amount of his aggregate expenditures will not affect the proportions in which the representative German distributes them as between German and English commodities.

That for the two-country case the assumptions of linearity and of similarity within each country of the utility functions plus the assumption of an excess before reparations for the representative consumer of each country of his purchases of native over his purchases of foreign commodities suffice to establish Pigou's conclusion that reparations will necessarily cause the terms of trade to turn against the paying country, i.e., that $\frac{\phi'}{f'} < \frac{\psi'}{F'}$, can also readily be demonstrated from chart III. Suppose that in chart III, $ed > ef$ and $e_1 d_1 > e_1 f_1$. Then, since: numerically, $\phi' : f' : : ed : ef$;

numerically, $\psi':F'::e_1f_1:e_1d_1$; and $\phi'<O$; $F'<O$; $f'>O$;
$\psi'>O$; $\therefore \dfrac{\phi'}{f'}<\dfrac{\psi'}{F'}$.

The assumption of "similarity" of the utility functions is a reasonable one, not because "similarity" is in fact probable, but because in the absence of specific information the "dissimilarity" which is likely to exist is, *a priori,* as likely to be in the one direction as in the other. Given the proportions in which expenditures in each country before reparations are divided between native and imported commodities, dissimilarities existing within either or both countries will tend to make reparations turn the terms of trade against or in favor of the paying country according as they take the form of lower or of higher ratios of the utility of initial units of native to the utility of initial units of imported commodities, the units of the commodities being so chosen, for each country separately, as to be equal in their pre-reparations prices.

Chart IV illustrates the bearing of "similarity" of utility functions on the problem. The proportions in which expenditures in each country are divided before reparations between native and imported commodities are made the same as in chart III, i.e., $ed > ef$ and $e_1d_1 > e_1f_1$. Reparations payments, nevertheless, would leave the terms of trade unaltered, i.e., $\dfrac{\phi'}{f'} = \dfrac{\psi'}{F'}$. This results from the assumptions in the chart that, when for each country such commodity units are chosen as will make their pre-reparations prices equal, to the representative Englishman the utility of a first unit of the English commodity is sufficiently greater than the utility of the first unit of the German commodity (i.e., $oa > oA$) and to the representative German the utility of a first unit of the German commodity is sufficiently greater than the utility of the first unit of the English commodity (i.e., $o_1a_1 > o_1A_1$) to make $\dfrac{\phi'}{f'} = \dfrac{\psi'}{F'}$.

It can be seen from chart IV that, other things equal, the greater before reparations the average ratios of excess of the consumption of native over the consumption of imported commodities in the two countries, the greater must be the average ratio of excess in the two countries of the initial utility of the imported commodity over the initial utility of the native commodity if the terms of trade are not to be turned against the paying country by reparations payments. Although the pre-reparations ratios of consumption of native to consumption of imported commodities assumed in chart IV are much lower than would ordinarily be found in practice, the ratio of excess of the initial utility of native over the initial utility of imported commodities had to be substantial for each country (or on the average for the two countries combined) if reparations payments were not to turn the terms of trade against the paying country. If with uniform commodity units in both countries the ratio between the

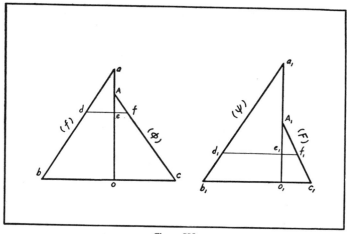

Chart IV

prices of the two commodities was identical in both countries—as would be the rule for internationally traded commodities in the absence of trade barriers or transportation costs—it would be difficult, if not impossible, to find plausible grounds for holding that such substantial "dissimilarities" of utility functions were likely to prevail in practice.

IX. SOME ELABORATIONS ON THE BASIS OF PIGOU'S ANALYSIS

Duties on imports, however, whether levied by the paying or the receiving country, and *a fortiori* when levied by both, do tend to result in higher initial utilities in each country for native than for imported commodities, and although they also tend to result in an excess of expenditures on native over expenditures on foreign commodities, they operate to make reparations turn the terms of trade in favor of, instead of against, the paying country. Import duties, regardless of which country levies them, operate to make the imported commodity relatively dearer than the native commodity in each country, as compared to what the situation would be in the absence of the duties. If in each country the units of the two commodities are so chosen as to be equal in price before the imposition of the duty, then, with the units used for the English commodity in England and the German commodity in Germany left unaltered, after the imposition of the duty the size of the unit used for the German commodity in England and the size of the unit used for the English commodity in Germany will both have to be decreased if the units used for the two commodities within each country are to be kept equal to each other in price. In terms of the graphical illustrations here used, it will follow that the initial utility of the imported commodity will be lower in each country after the duty than before, the initial utility of the native commodity remaining unaltered. A situation with respect to "dissimilarities" of the utility functions within each country corresponding in kind to that illustrated in chart IV will thus tend to result.

This reasoning is illustrated, for the case of an English import duty, in chart V. It is there assumed that initially there are no trade restrictions in either England or Germany, that there are no "domestic" commodities, and that in each country the representative consumer spends as much on imported as on native commodities. It is also assumed that in each country the utility functions are linear and originally "similar," so that when commodity units are so chosen as to be equal in their original prices, the utilities of initial units are also equal. Then $\frac{\phi'}{f'} = \frac{\psi'}{F'}$, so that Germany could make reparations payments to England without affecting the terms of trade.

Suppose, however, that before the obligation to pay reparations comes into effect, England imposes a revenue import duty of 50 per cent ad valorem on the German commodity. Let us assume that as a result the price of the German commodity to the English consumer rises by one-third relative to the price of the English commodity, i.e., one unit of the English commodity now has the same price in England as three-fourths of a unit of the German commodity, duty-paid. If, while the unit used for the English commodity in England is left unchanged, a new unit three-fourths as large as the old one is now used for the imported commodity so as to make units of the two commodities equal in value at the new relative prices, there will be a new utility function, *a'c'*, for the imported commodity, with *oa'* 75 per cent of *oa*, and *oc'* 33 1/3 per cent greater than *oc*.

If the levy of a 50 per cent duty on the German commodity

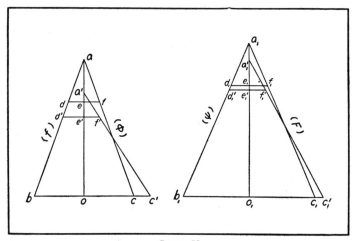

CHART V

causes its price in England duty-paid to rise by one-third relative to the price of the English commodity in England, then in Germany, with units unchanged, the price of the English commodity must rise one-eighth relative to the price of the German commodity, i.e., one unit of the German commodity now has the same price in Germany as eight-ninths of a unit of the English commodity.[1] If the unit used for the German commodity in Germany is

---

[1] In this illustration, the reasonable assumption has been made that in the duty-levying country the imposition of the duty will result in the price of the imported commodity rising relative to the price of the native commodity by less than the amount of the duty. This assumption, that the terms of trade move in favor of the duty-levying country as the result of the duty, affects the degree, but not the direction, of change in the terms of trade to be expected from reparations payments. If the duty caused no change in the terms

left unchanged, but a new unit eight-ninths as large as the original one is now used for the English commodity in Germany so as to make the units of the two commodities equal in value at their new relative prices, there will be a new utility function, a'_1c_1', for the English commodity in Germany, with o_1a_1' eight-ninths of o_1a_1, and o_1c_1' nine-eighths of o_1c_1. Since ϕ' and F' are now both smaller numerically and therefore greater algebraically than they were before the imposition of the duty, while f' and ψ' are unaltered, therefore $\dfrac{\phi'}{f'} > \dfrac{\psi'}{F'}$ in the new situation, and, even in the case illustrated by chart V, where the imposition of the duty causes the representative consumer in each country to spend more on native than on imported commodities,[2] the levy of the duty creates a situation in which reparations payments would make the terms of trade turn in favor of Germany.

It can be similarly shown that export taxes levied by either or both countries and an excess of international over internal transportation costs for the commodities of either or both countries, even when they result in an excess in each country of expenditures on native over expenditures on foreign commodities, by tending to make native commodities relatively cheap in each country and thus tending to make the initial utility of native commodities greater in each country than the initial utility of imported commodities of equal price, tend likewise, given linear functions, to create a situation in which reparations payments will turn the terms of trade in favor of the paying country. Export

---

of trade, there would be no change in a_1c_1 as the result of the duty, but ac would move further toward the horizontal than indicated in chart V, i.e., there would be no change in F', but the numerical reduction of ϕ' would be greater than there indicated.

[2] The duty has these results only if $d'f'$, $d_1'f_1'$, are above the intersections of ac and $a'c'$ and a_1c_1 and $a_1'c_1'$, respectively. It should be explained that $d'f'$, which represents the new income of the Englishman measured in units of English goods or their (new) value equivalent in German goods, must be drawn so as to be equal to $df + 1/3 \, e'f'$. On $d'f'$, $d'e'$ represents the number of English goods and $e'f'$ the number of German goods (in their new units) which would be purchased by the representative Englishman with his new income. Measured in units of English goods alone, the new income would be the same as the old, or df. But since on all purchases of German goods the government collects one-third of the duty-paid price ($=$ one-half of the price before duty), which is presumably not lost to the representative Englishman but returns to him as remission of other taxes or in some other form, $d'f'$ must equal $df + 1/3 \, e'f'$. In the German section of the diagram $d_1'f_1'$ must be drawn so as to be equal to d_1f_1.

or import subsidies, granted by either or by both countries, and an excess of internal over international transportation costs for the commodities of either or both countries, tend, on the other hand, by making native commodities dear in each country relative to imported commodities, to create a situation in which reparations will turn the terms of trade in favor of the receiving country in spite of an excess in each country of expenditures on foreign over expenditures on native commodities.

The existence of "domestic" commodities also operates to create a presumption that reparations payments will turn the terms of trade against the paying country, but in this case by increasing the proportion of expenditures in each country on native commodities without affecting the relative utilities of initial units of native and imported commodities. To adapt Pigou's analysis to the existence of domestic commodities, the utility functions for a representative consumer of the products of his own country must be interpreted as representing the marginal utility curve of a composite commodity made up of one or more units of each of the different native commodities, with the units so chosen as to be equal in pre-reparations price, and with the number of units of each commodity entering into the composite commodity made proportional to their respective importance in domestic consumption. If the assumptions of constant costs and of similarity and linearity of utility functions for "representative" consumers are adhered to, and if the possibility that reparations payments may change the identity of the "representative" consumer is disregarded, the weighting of the different native commodities in making up the composite native commodity presents no difficulty, since under these assumptions relative variations in the prices or the volume of consumption of the constitutent items of the composite native commodity cannot result merely from a change in the total expenditures of the representative consumer. The introduction in either country of domestic commodities will operate with respect to that country to reduce the slope of the curve of marginal utility to a representative individual of the composite native commodity, i.e., the existence of domestic commodities will operate to reduce the relevant f' and/or ψ'. Since $\dfrac{\phi'}{f'} <0$, and $\dfrac{\psi'}{F'} <0$, it follows, therefore, that where there are only two countries, the existence of "domestic" commodities in either country will tend to make $\frac{\phi'}{f'} < \frac{\psi'}{F'}$, and therefore will tend to make reparations payments turn the terms of trade against the paying country.

If either of the countries is incompletely specialized, i.e., if it imports a portion of its consumption of some commodity, say cloth, which it also produces at home, a special case arises where the ratio of $\frac{\phi'}{f'}$ to $\frac{\psi'}{F'}$ does not suffice to determine the effect of reparations on the terms of trade even on the assumptions of linearity and "similarity" within each country of the various utility functions. Regardless of the ratio of $\frac{\phi'}{f'}$ to $\frac{\psi'}{F'}$, the incompletely specialized country, whether it be the paying or the receiving country, can check any tendency for the terms of trade to move against it by cutting down on its exports and shifting the productive resources thus freed to the production of cloth. Under constant costs the prices of other foreign commodities could not rise relative to cloth as long as cloth was still being produced abroad, and the prices of other native commodities could not fall relative to cloth as long as more cloth could be produced at home. Before the terms of trade could turn against the country which before reparations had been incompletely specialized, it would be necessary therefore that she should be producing nothing except ("domestic" commodities and) cloth and that the other country should have completely abandoned the production of cloth. [3]

If the assumption of linearity of the utility functions is abandoned the solution of the problem becomes much more difficult. But in the two-country case, the departures from linearity are as likely *a priori* to be in directions strengthening the presumption that reparations payments will cause the terms of trade to turn against the paying country as to weaken it, and Pigou has shown in effect that if $\frac{\phi'(nY)}{f'(nX)}$ is much greater numerically than $\frac{\psi'(mY)}{F'(mX)}$

it will take substantial deviations from linearity in directions working favorably for the terms of trade of the paying country to keep reparations payments from turning the terms of trade against her.[4]

---

[3] Cf. *infra*, pp. 448 ff.
[4] Pigou, *Economic journal*, XLII (1932), 535.

The use of the concept of a "representative" German or Englishman in utility analysis raises familiar difficulties. Its use in this particular problem involves a tacit evasion of the difficulty arising if the payment of reparations results in a redistribution of the available spending power within either or within both communities of such a nature that the individual who could reasonably be taken as "representative" before the payments began was no longer "representative" after they had begun. Any redistribution in spending power in Germany resulting from the making of reparations payments would operate to make the terms of trade move unfavorably or favorably to Germany according as the reduction in spending power fell relatively more heavily or less heavily on individuals for whom, as compared to other Germans, the $\frac{\psi'}{F'}$ ratio, or the ratio of the slope of their utility curve for German goods to the slope of their utility curve for English goods, was large or small numerically. Similarly, any redistribution in spending power in England resulting from the receipt of reparations payments would operate to make the terms of trade move favorably or unfavorably to Germany according as the increase in spending power accrued more heavily or less heavily to individuals for whom, as compared to other Englishmen, the $\frac{\phi'}{f'}$ ratio, or the ratio of the slope of their utility curve for German goods to the slope of their utility curve for English goods, was small or large numerically. In the absence of special information, it is hard to see any basis for any presumption that the changes in distribution of spending power in either country would be in one direction rather than the other.

I have so far assumed that there are only two countries. If in addition to the countries directly participating in the reparations payments there are other countries connected with them through trade relations, additional complications arise which Pigou, who does not differentiate "England" from "non-Germany," but takes his "representative Englishman," with his significant ratio $\frac{\phi'}{f'}$, as representative of all non-Germany, fails to mention. If there are three or more countries, there is no longer only one significant set of commodity terms of trade, but there are at least four distinct sets, namely, the terms of trade: (1) between Germany and the rest of the world, including England; (2) between England and the rest of the world, including Germany; (3) between Germany and England, and (4) between the neutral area and the rest of the world.

Since the reparations payments go only to Englishmen proper, the change in the relative distribution of spending power as between Englishmen and other non-Germans as the result of reparations will, even with the assumptions of linearity and of "similarity" of the utility functions within the entire non-German area, prevent Pigou's $\frac{\phi'}{f'}$ ratio, although adequately representative of the utility functions of all non-Germany before reparations, from being representative after reparations, and will render inadequate Pigou's criterion for the effect of reparations payments on the terms of trade of Germany, unless before reparations the ratios corresponding to Pigou's $\frac{\phi'}{f'}$ ratio were identical for both the representative Englishman and the representative neutral. If before reparations the ratio for the representative Englishman corresponding to Pigou's $\frac{\phi'}{f'}$ for all non-Germany was smaller algebraically than the similar ratio for the representative neutral, then the terms of trade would turn against Germany as the result of reparations not only when before reparations Pigou's condition of $\frac{\phi'}{f'} < \frac{\psi'}{F'}$ was met, but also if $\frac{\phi'}{f'} = \frac{\psi'}{F'}$ and even, within limits, if $\frac{\phi'}{f'} > \frac{\psi'}{F'}$. On the other hand, if before reparations the ratio for the representative Englishman corresponding to Pigou's $\frac{\phi'}{f'}$ was greater algebraically than the similar ratio for the representative neutral, the terms of trade would turn in favor of Germany as the result of reparations not only when before reparations $\frac{\phi'}{f'} > \frac{\psi'}{F'}$, but also if $\frac{\phi'}{f'} = \frac{\psi'}{F'}$, and even, within limits, if $\frac{\phi'}{f'} < \frac{\psi'}{F'}$. But since, *a priori,* the probability that the ratio corresponding to Pigou's $\frac{\phi'}{f'}$ will be greater algebraically for the representative Englishman than for the representative neutral is no greater than the probability that it will be smaller, and, because of the existence of "domestic" commodities, Pigou's $\frac{\phi'}{f'}$ is likely to be *much* smaller algebraically than $\frac{\psi'}{F'}$, the presumption that the terms of trade will turn against the paying country survives the introduction of third countries into the problem. If England and the third country produce the same commodity (or commodities), there is no basis for trade between these two countries, and the terms of trade between Germany and the outside world as a whole must be identical with those between Germany and England. The third country, therefore, will share with England any improvement or impairment in the terms of trade with Germany which may result for England as the result of her receipt of reparations from Germany.

If the third country produces the same commodity (or commodities) as Germany, similar conclusions would be reached as in the preceding case, except that the fortunes of the neutral country would now be pooled with those of the paying country instead of with those of the receiving country. If either England or Germany produces "domestic" commodities as well, this would operate, in the manner already explained, to make reparations payments result in the terms of trade turning against Germany, but whether or not the neutral country produced "domestic" commodities would not affect the direction of change in the terms of trade of Germany with the outside world as the result of reparations.

If the third country, however, produces distinctive exportable commodities of its own, the method of approach needs to be modified somewhat. To take first the terms of trade of Germany with the outside world, "non-German" data are to be used wherever in the case of only two countries English data would be used, and the problem will then correspond to the case where England and the neutral country produce identical commodities, except that given the pre-reparations ratio of $\frac{\phi'}{f'}$ representative of all non-Germany, the greater numerically the slope of the representative Englishman's utility curve for the neutral country's commodity as compared to the slope of his curve for the German commodity, the more favorable will be the situation for Germany with respect to the terms of trade. Similarly, for the terms of trade of England with the rest of the world, "non-English" data are to be used wherever in the case of only two countries German data would be used, and the problem will then correspond to the case where Germany and the neutral country produce identical commodities, except that, given the pre-reparations ratio $\dfrac{\psi'}{F'}$ representative of all non-England, the greater numerically the slope of the representative German's utility curve for the neutral country's commodity as compared to the slope of his curve for the English commodity, the less favorable will be the situation for England with respect to the terms of trade. To take next the terms of trade of England with Germany, they will remain unchanged, move in favor of England, or move in favor of Germany, given Pigou's assumptions, according as $\dfrac{\phi'}{f'} = , < ,$ or $> \dfrac{\psi'}{F'}$, where ϕ' and f' relate to the slopes of the utility curves of the representative Englishman for English and German commodities, respectively, and ψ' and F' relate to the slopes of the utility curves of the representative German for English and German commodities, respectively, i.e., regardless of the slopes of their respective utility curves for neutral country commodities or of the slopes of the utility curves of the representative neutral for the commodities of England and Germany.

To take, finally, the terms of trade of the neutral country with the rest of the world, the payment of reparations by Germany to England will leave them unchanged, will move them in favor of the neutral country, or will move them against the neutral country, *caeteris paribus,* according as the slope of the utility curve for the neutral country's commodity is numerically equal, smaller, or greater for the representative Englishman than for the representative German, and, *caeteris paribus,* according as the pre-reparations volume of imports of neutral commodities is equal, greater, or smaller for England as a whole than for Germany as a whole, in proportion to their total expenditures.

X. An Alternative Solution

That it is possible to attack the problem without resort to utility analysis is demonstrated in chart VI in terms of a two-country case, based on the assumptions that in each country before reparations more is spent on native than on imported commodities, that the proportions in which expenditures are distributed between native and imported commodities remain unaltered in both countries, in the absence of relative price changes, as the amount available for expenditures changes, that production is carried on under constant cost conditions, and that there are no trade barriers or transportation costs. The "amount available for expenditure," it is to be noted, is measured not in money but in units of the native commodity, or their equivalent in value, which can be bought with the money available at the prevailing prices.

Through any point, *e*, on a vertical line *mn* draw a horizontal line *df*, such that the distance *df* represents the aggregate number of units of commodities which England can purchase with her national income before reparations at the prevailing prices, when the physical units of the commodities are so chosen that the Eng-

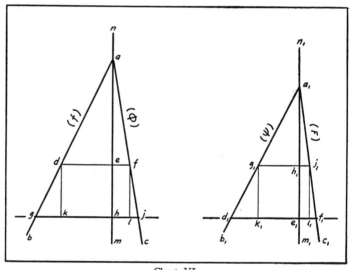

Chart VI

lish and the German commodity are equal in price, and such that *de* and *ef* represent the amounts of English and of German commodities, respectively, which the English would consume before reparations at the prevailing prices. Through any point on *mn* below *e* draw another line *gj* such that, in the absence of price changes, *gj*—*df* would represent the amount of reparations received by England, and gh and hj would represent the amounts of English and of German commodities, respectively, which the English would consume after reparations. Draw lines connecting g with d and j with f, and project them until they intercept mn. If a change in the amount England has available for expenditure does not, in the absence of price changes, and within the range of observation, change the proportions in which England would divide her expenditures between English and German commodities, i.e., if $gh : hj :: de : ef$, then the projections of gd and jf will intercept mn at some common point a, above e.

Through any point e_1 on another vertical line m_1n_1 draw a horizontal line d_1f_1 such that the distance d_1f_1 represents the aggregate number of units of commodities which Germany can purchase before reparations at the prevailing prices when the physical units of the commodities are the same as in the other part of the diagram, and such that d_1e_1 and e_1f_1 represent the amounts of German and English commodities, respectively, which the Germans would buy before reparations at the prevailing prices. Through any point on m_1n_1 above e_1 draw another line g_1j_1 such that, in the absence of price changes, $d_1f_1 - g_1j_1$ would represent the amount of reparations paid by Germany, and g_1h_1, h_1j_1, would represent the amount of German and of English commodities, respectively, which the Germans would buy after reparations. Draw lines connecting d_1 with g_1 and f_1 with j_1 and project them until they intercept m_1n_1. If a change in the amount Germany has available for expenditure does not in the absence of price changes change the proportions in which Germany divides her expenditures between German and English commodities, i.e., if $g_1h_1 : h_1j_1 :: d_1e_1 : e_1f_1$, then d_1g_1 and f_1j_1 when extended upward will intercept m_1n_1 at some common point a_1 above h_1.

Suppose now that $de > ef$, and that $d_1e_1 > e_1f_1$, i.e., that before reparations each country spent more money on its own than on the other country's commodities. To show that on these assumptions reparations must turn the terms of trade against Germany, it is necessary to show that, in the absence of relative price changes, the two countries combined would, after reparations, want to buy more of England's commodities and less of Germany's commodities than before reparations, i.e., that, in the absence of relative price changes: (1) the amount by which England would want to increase her consumption of English commodities was greater than the amount by which Germany would want to decrease her consumption of English commodities, or that $gk > l_1f_1$; (2) that the amount by which Germany would want to decrease her consumption of German commodities was greater than the amount by which England would want to increase her consumption of German commodities, or that $d_1k_1 > lj$.

By assumption,

$$gh : hj :: de : ef;$$ (1)
$$de = kh; ef = hl;$$ (2)
$$\therefore gk : lj :: de : ef.$$ (3)

By assumption,

$$de > ef;$$ (4)
$$\therefore gk > lj, \text{ and, similarly, } d_1k_1 > l_1f_1.$$ (5)

Since reparations results in an increase in England's spendable funds equal to the decrease in Germany's spendable funds,

$$gk + lj = d_1k_1 + l_1f_1$$ (6)
$$\therefore gk > l_1f_1, \text{ and } d_1k_1 > lj$$ (7)

Reparations payments will, therefore, in the absence of relative price changes, result in this case in a shortage, relative to demand, of English commodities, and a surplus, relative to demand, of German commodities, and the establishment of a new equilibrium, adjusted to the reparations payments, will require a relative rise in the prices of English commodities, i.e., a movement of the commodity terms of trade against Germany.

If in either or in both countries the proportion in which expenditures between native and imported commodities, in the absence of relative price changes, varies with variations in the aggregate amount of spendable funds, such variations will operate favorably or unfavorably for Germany's terms of trade according as, in the case of Germany, the proportion spent on German goods increases or decreases with a *decrease* in the amount of spendable funds and as, in the case of England, the proportion spent on German goods increases or decreases with an *increase* in the amount of spendable funds. Deviation in the proportions of the expenditures in a direction favorable to Germany in either or in both countries will not suffice, however, to turn the terms of trade in favor of Germany, given an excess before reparations in the expenditures of each country (or in both combined) on native commodities over their expenditures on imported commodities, unless such deviations are sufficiently marked to make reparations payments result in the aggregate for both countries, in the absence of relative changes in prices, in a relative increase in the demand for German commodities over the demand for English commodities.[1]

A concrete case may be cited to illustrate the type of situation in which the terms of trade might turn in favor of the paying country as the result of reparations. First, suppose that the paying country, Germany, produces two kinds of commodities, one a "domestic" commodity, primarily a necessary, and the other a luxury, which is exported but is not consumed heavily at home, and imports from England what is essentially a luxury commodity. As the spendable funds of Germany are cut down by reparations payments, there would probably occur, in the absence of relative price changes, a proportionately greater reduction in the German purchases of the luxury import than of the necessary "domestic" commodity. Suppose, in turn, that England also produces two kinds of commodities, one a "domestic" commodity, primarily a necessary, and the other a luxury, which is exported but is not consumed heavily at home, and imports from Germany what is a luxury commodity. As the spendable funds of England are increased by the reparations receipts, there would probably occur, in the absence of relative price changes, a proportionately greater increase in the English purchases of the imported luxury than of the necessary "domestic" commodity. These deviations from proportionality, both working in favor of Germany, could conceivably be sufficiently marked to make the terms of trade turn in favor of Germany as the result of reparations, even if before reparations each country spent much more on native than on foreign commodities. This would be certain to be the situation if the English demand for native commodities was such that, with prices unchanged, the English purchases of native commodities would fall absolutely when the English incomes increased, and if the German demand for native commodities was such that, with

---

[1] I.e., unless in chart VI, the deviations in the two countries from the proportions in which they originally distributed their expenditures between German and English goods would, in the absence of price changes, be sufficiently favorable to Germany to make $lj > d_1k_1$ and $gk < l_1f_1$.

prices unchanged, the German purchases of native commodities would rise absolutely when the German incomes decreased, demand phenomena which are no doubt highly improbable, but are not inconceivable.[2]

Demand and supply curves in terms of money prices of the ordinary Marshallian type cannot legitimately be used in the solution of the reparations transfer problem, since they abstract from the interrelationships between demands, supplies, and incomes.[3] Nor can the problem be solved through the use of Marshallian reciprocal-demand curves without additional information, since the problem turns on what happens as the result of reparations payments to the position and shape of the reciprocal-demand curves, and this depends on the utility functions in both countries, and cannot be determined without reference, direct or indirect, to these functions.[4]

It has so far been assumed that in every industry production is carried on under conditions of constant costs. By virtue of this assumption, it has been possible to carry out the analysis without explicit reference to costs without impairing the validity of the conclusions reached. Under constant technological costs money costs can change only as the prices of the factors of production change, and, assuming no change in the supplies of the factors, their prices can change only as the aggregate demands for them from all the industries using them change. It was therefore necessary to take account only of the apportionment by the two countries of their expenditures as between their own products and foreign

---

[2] In this case, in terms of chart VI, although $gj > df$, and $g_1j_1 < d_1f_1$, in each instance by the amount of reparations payments, nevertheless $gh < de$, and $g_1h_1 > d_1e_1$.

[3] Cf. *infra*, pp. 582 ff.

[4] Cf. D. H. Robertson, "The Transfer Problem," in Pigou and Robertson, *Economic essays and addresses*, 1931, p. 171: "they [i.e., Keynes, Pigou, Taussig] have nowhere, so far as I know, explained clearly the reactions of a reparation payment on the shape and position of the Marshall [reciprocal-demand] curves."

Marshall, nevertheless, offers a solution by means of his reciprocal-demand curves of what is, for present purposes, a problem identical with that of the effect of reparations payments, namely, the effect of the transfer of interest payments. His solution, must, however, be rejected, as wholly arbitrary. He leaves the receiving country's curve unaltered, and shifts the paying country's curve to the right by an amount, equal at all points of the curve, to the amount of interest payments. Cf. Marshall, *Money, credit & commerce*, 1923, p. 349, fig. 19.

products, and their mode of apportionment of their expenditures as between their "domestic" and their export commodities had no bearing on the problem. Under constant costs, moreover, the double factoral terms of trade would be affected by reparations payments in precisely the same way, both as to direction and as to degree, as the commodity terms of trade. But if some, or all, industries operate under varying costs as their output is varied, it is possible in each country for the prices of domestic and of export commodities, respectively, to move in different degrees and even in different directions as the result of a change in the volume of expenditures, so that the movement of the prices of the "domestic" commodities of the two countries may differ in direction or in degree from the movement of their export commodity prices, and the factoral terms of trade may move differently, in degree, and when the commodity terms of trade move *against* the receiving country, even in direction, from the commodity terms of trade. This will hold even if there is effective mobility of the factors within each country, i.e., if the marginal value productivity and the rate of remuneration of each factor are equal in all industries in which it is employed, provided different industries use the factors in different and variable combinations. But if prices at which any factor is available are for any reason not uniform in all industries, or if there are factors which are specialized for certain industries, then the range of possible relative variation of the prices of "domestic" and of export commodities in each country will be still greater.

The task of tracing the effect of international payments on the terms of trade when production is carried on under conditions of varying cost as output is varied appears to be one of discouraging complexity. Even after resort to the utmost simplification of which the problem admits there remain more variables to be dealt with than either arithmetical illustrations or ordinary graphic methods can effectively handle. Though general solutions may be obtainable by algebraic methods, it seems evident that they are not easily obtainable, and in any case they are not within my power. There seems no good *a priori* reason to suppose, however, that any of these additional factors has an inherent tendency to operate more in favor of the paying than of the receiving country, as far as the terms of trade are concerned.

I venture the prediction, therefore, that when the problem is solved for more complex cases involving varying costs as output is increased, the following conclusions derived from analysis of the simpler cases dealt with above will be found not to require substantial modification: (1) that a unilateral transfer of means of payment may shift the commodity terms of trade in either direction, but is much more likely to shift them against than in favor of the paying country; (2) that the double factoral terms of trade will ordinarily shift in the same direction as the commodity terms of trade, but under increasing costs in all industries, when the commodity terms of trade shift in favor of the paying country, the double factoral terms of trade will nevertheless shift in favor of the receiving country, or will shift in less degree than the commodity terms of trade in favor of the paying country; and (3) that the tendency of the terms of trade to move against the paying country will be more marked, *caeteris paribus,* the greater the excess in each country, prior to the transfer, of consumption of native products to consumption of imported products, to the extent that such excess is not due to trade barriers or to higher international than internal transportation costs.

XI. Types of Disturbance in International Equilibrium

In the examination of the probable effects on the terms of trade of a lasting disturbance of a preexistent international equilibrium, there is one basis of distinction between types of disturbances which calls for special emphasis. Disturbances are to be distinguished according as they originate in a relative change in the amounts, measured in units of constant purchasing power over native goods, available for expenditure in the two areas, or as they originate in a relative change in the demands of the two countries for each other's products in terms of their own products resulting from changes in taste or in conditions of production, or from changes in tariffs, subsidies, internal taxes, or transportation costs.[1] The analysis presented above of the effects on the terms of trade of reparations payments is applicable without serious modification to all lasting disturbances of the first class, i.e., involving an initial relative shift in the amounts available for expenditure, whether this shift is due to loans, tribute, or sub-

---

[1] Cf. T. O. Yntema, *A mathematical reformulation of the general theory of international trade,* 1932, chap. v, especially pp. 61-62, 71-72.

sidy, but is not applicable to disturbances of the second class, where, however, analysis in terms of reciprocal demand curves is appropriate in most cases.

Whereas in the first class of disturbance a relative change in the amounts available for expenditure in the two countries is the *source* of the disturbance and a relative change in the demands of the two countries for each other's products is the *result* of the disturbance, in the second class of disturbance a relative change in the demands is the original cause of the disturbance and a relative change in the amounts available for expenditure is part of the process of adjustment to the disturbance. The case of a new revenue import duty, levied by one of the countries, may be taken as sufficiently illustrative of the effects of disturbances of the second class on the terms of trade. Let us suppose only two countries, only two commodities, no tariffs, no transportation costs, and an even balance of payments between them. One of the countries, England, now imposes a duty on imports of the German commodity. Before the duty the two commodities exchanged for each other at the same rate in both countries. After the duty the German commodity will rise in price to the English consumer relative to the English commodity. Let us assume that this relative rise is at first equal to the amount of the duty. The English will therefore buy smaller physical quantities than before of the German commodity and larger physical quantities than before of the English commodity. Suppose that the reduction in the volume of their sales to England will tend to cause Germans to reduce their total expenditures to the same amount, and that part of this reduction will be applied to German commodities. The willingness to buy German goods at the prevailing price (in England plus duty) will therefore decline in both countries; the willingness to buy English goods will increase in England, and decrease in Germany; with the increase in the former (corresponding to the total decrease in English purchases of German goods and therefore, by assumption, to the total decrease in German purchases of German and English goods combined) exceeding the decrease in the latter country.

Two consequences will follow: (1) Germany will have an adverse balance of payments with England, and specie will move from Germany to England; (2) the price of the German commodity will fall in both countries relative to the English, so that in England it will, without duty, be lower than it was before the duty was imposed, and, including duty, will exceed the pre-duty price by less than the amount of the duty. In other words, the commodity terms of trade will have moved against Germany, with an international transfer of specie as part of the process whereby this comes about. The effect of the duty on the terms of

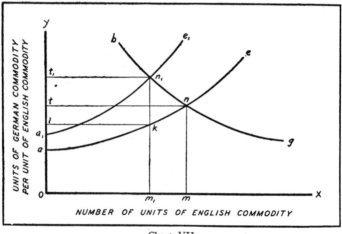

Chart VII

trade is illustrated in chart VII, an application in a slightly modified[2] form of Marshall's foreign trade curves.

The quantity of the English commodity is measured from o on the ox axis, and the relative price of the English commodity, in terms of number of units of the German commodity for one unit of the English commodity, is measured from o on the oy axis. The curve ae represents the quantities of the English commodity which before the duty England would be willing to export at the indicated rates of exchange of the English for the German commodity, and the curve bg represents the quantities of the English commodity which Germany would be willing to import at the indicated rates of exchange of the English for the German commodity. Equilibrium will be established at the terms of trade

---

[2] Cf. *infra*, pp. 541-42.

of mn or ot units of the German commodity for one unit of the English commodity.

If now England should levy a duty of 40 per cent ad valorem on imports of the German commodity, payable by the importer and used by the government to remit other taxes, the English export supply curve adjusted to the duty will be a_1e_1, with a_1e_1 uniformly 40 per cent higher than ae with reference to the ox axis. The new equilibrium rate of exchange of English commodities for German will in the English market (i.e., after payment of duty) be m_1k, or ol, units of German goods for one unit of English goods. The new terms of trade, or the rate at which Germany will be able to exchange its commodity for the English commodity, will be m_1n_1, or o_1t_1, units of the German commodity for one unit of the English commodity, which will also correspond to the relative prices of the two commodities within Germany. The terms of trade will thus be turned against Germany by the English import duty.

It can similarly be shown that an English protective duty, a German export bounty, higher German or English internal taxes on German than on English goods, a shift in taste in either country in favor of English goods, or a relative reduction in the cost of producing the German commodity, will in like manner turn the terms of trade against Germany, whereas a German revenue or protective duty, an English export bounty, lower German or English internal taxes on German than on English goods, a shift in taste in either country in favor of German goods, or a relative reduction in the cost of producing the English commodity, will turn the terms of trade in favor of Germany.

An endless variety of further distinctions between types of disturbances can of course be drawn. Tributes and loans, for instance, are to be distinguished from each other by the fact that, since the former are as a rule involuntary and the latter voluntary, the problem of adjustment in the "paying" country is likely to be more serious in the former than in the latter case. Loans, moreover, call almost immediately for interest payments and eventually for amortization payments in the opposite direction from the loans, whereas this is not true of tributes. Loans are to be distinguished according to whether they are made out of income or out of capital, and according to whether the proceeds are used in the borrowing country for immediate consumption or for investment, since the nature of the source and of the mode of use of the loan will affect the manner in which adjustment is made to the change in the amount of funds available for expenditure, and will affect also the relative availability of the different classes of commodities toward which the expenditures are directed. In actual experience the initial disturbances may come in various combinations, or may originate at home or abroad, or simultaneously in both, and, depending on the nature of the original disturbance and perhaps on other circumstances, what at one time operates as the source of the disturbance and gives rise to the need for adjustment may at other times be the equilibrating factor, with corresponding changes in the time-sequence of phenomena. Thus price changes, capital movements, changes in demand, for example, may at one time be disturbing factors, at other times equilibrating ones, and except when there are drastic disturbances whose origin is fairly obviously to be associated with contemporary events external to the mechanism of international trade itself, it will ordinarily be fruitless to try to distinguish equilibrating from adjusting factors. Some writers have attempted to generalize, however, as to the "disturbing" or "equalizing" character of specific elements in international balances. Thus Keynes, for instance, has maintained that historically the international movement of long-term capital has adjusted itself to the trade balance rather than the trade balance to capital movements,[3] whereas Taussig[4] has supported the opposite, and traditional, view. There is no apparent *a priori* reason why the dependence should not be as much in one direction as the other, and the question of historical fact can be settled only, if at all, by comprehensive historical investigation. It is possible, however, to set forth theoretically the types of circumstances which would tend to make the one or the other the more probable direction, and to find striking historical illustrations in support of such analysis. It seems clear to me, for instance, that in the case of Canada before the war the fluctuations in the trade balance were much more the effect than the cause of the fluctuations in the long-term borrowings abroad, whereas in the case of New Zealand the fluctuations in her balance of indebtedness

---

[3] "The German transfer problem," *Economic Journal*, XXXIX (1929), 6.

[4] Cf. *International trade*, 1927, pp. 312-13. Cf. also Carl Iversen, *Aspects of the theory of international capital movements*, 1935, pp. 181 ff.

since the war seem to be clearly the result rather than the cause of the fluctuations in her trade balance. In New Zealand a marked degree of dependence of the national income on the state of the crops and the world-market prices of a few export commodities, with sharp year-to-year fluctuations in the crops and in prices, makes it necessary to choose between highly unstable expenditures on consumption or domestic investment, on the one hand, and substantial fluctuations in the net external indebtedness of the country, on the other, and the choice seems to be predominantly in favor of the latter. Examination of such data as are readily available strongly confirms, however, the orthodox doctrine that, at times when "fear" movements of capital are not important, short-term capital movements are much more likely than long-term capital movements to be "equilibrating," and that major long-term capital movements have, as Taussig maintains, mainly been "disturbing" rather than "equilibrating" in nature.

The foregoing discussion, it should be repeated, has dealt solely with the long-run effects of a lasting variation in one of the elements of an original equilibrium on the terms of trade. It should be noted also that changes in the terms of trade have been treated as purely objective phenomena, without reference to the differences in hedonic significance which may be attached to them according to the types of disturbance from which they result.

XII. Specie Movements and Velocity of Money

The classical economists were agreed that (abstracting from the process of distribution of newly-mined bullion) there were no specie movements under equilibrium conditions, and that specie moved only to restore and not to disturb equilibrium, or, as Ricardo put it, gold was "exported to find its level, not to destroy it."[1] But on the range of circumstances which could disturb equilibrium in the balance of payments so as to require corrective specie movements they were, as we have seen, not in agreement. Wheatley, as much later Bastable and Nicholson, held that the balance of payments would adjust itself immediately, and without need of specie movements, to disturbances of a non-currency nature, through an immediate and presumably exactly equilibrating relative shift in the demand of the two regions for each

---

[1] *High price of bullion*, appendix, *Works*, p. 293.

other's commodities. Granted that a relative shift in demand as between the two countries may, without the aid of relative price changes, restore an equilibrium disturbed, say, by an international tribute, it is an error to suppose that the shift in demand can ordinarily occur, under the assumption, be it remembered, of a simple specie currency, without involving a prior or a supporting transfer of specie from the paying to the receiving country. The new equilibrium requires that more purchases measured in money be made per unit of time in the receiving country and less in the paying country; as has been shown above, it is by its effect on the relative monetary volume of purchases in the two countries that the relative shift in demands exercises its equilibrating influence. Unless as and because one country becomes obligated to make payments to the other velocity falls in the paying country and rises in the receiving country, these necessary relative changes in purchases and in demands will not occur except after and because of a relative change in the amount of specie in the two countries, and such changes in velocity are at least not certain to occur, nor to be in the right directions if they do occur. Acceptance of the doctrine that a relative shift in demand schedules may suffice, without changes in relative prices, to restore equilibrium in a disturbed international balance does not involve as a corollary that specie movements are unnecessary for restoration of equilibrium, as Wheatley, Bastable, Nicholson, and others seem to have supposed. The error arises from acceptance of a too simple version of the quantity theory of money, in which price levels and quantities of money must move together and in the same direction regardless of what variations may occur in other terms of the monetary equation. In its most extreme application this erroneous doctrine has led to the conclusion that if unilateral payments should perchance result in a relative shift in price levels in favor of the *paying* country, the movement of specie will be from the receiving to the paying country![2]

---

[2] Such doctrine has actually been applied by Pigou, by Haberler, and by others following them, to the reparations transfer problem. In Pigou's analysis there is failure to notice that even if prices rise in Germany and fall in England as the result of reparations payments by Germany to England, there must nevertheless be a reduction in Germany and an increase in England in the relative amount of money income available for final expenditure and therefore in the amount of money work to be done. (Pigou, "The effect of reparations on the ratio of international exchange," *Economic journal,* XLII (1932),

It has been generally overlooked, however, that the velocity of money, or the ratio of the amount of purchases per unit of time to amount of money, has an important bearing on the extent of the specie movement which will be necessary to restore a disturbed equilibrium. It is not purchases, or transactions, in general which are significant for the mechanism of adjustment, but only purchases of certain kinds. If, for instance, a particular house has changed ownership as between *dealers* through purchase and sale three times in one year, and not at all in the next year, neither the transactions in one year nor their absence in the next year have any direct significance for the international mechanism. What matters is only the volume of expenditures which for the unit period operate to remove the purchased commodities from the market. Such purchases we will call final purchases, to distinguish them from transactions which do not consist of purchase and sale of commodities and services or which, if they do involve such purchase and sale, result merely in transfer of ownership from one person to another who will in turn before the unit period of time is over sell or be ready to sell the commodity or service, whether in the same form or not does not matter, to a third person. It is the relative change as between the two countries in the volume of final purchases, so defined, which plays a direct and equilibrating role in the mechanism of adjustment of international balances to disturbances.

Under the assumption of a simple specie currency, the significant velocity concept for the analysis of the mechanism of international trade is accordingly the ratio of final purchases per unit of time to the amount of specie in the country, which we will call the "final purchases velocity of money." This concept

---

542-43.) Haberler seems to reach his conclusion that if reparations result in a relative rise in prices in the paying country the movement of specie will be *to* instead of *from* the paying country on the basis of a tacit assumption that price level and quantity of money must vary in the same direction regardless of other circumstances. In his treatment of the reparations transfer problem, Haberler writes:

It is theoretically possible for the terms of trade to change in favor of Germany so that the prices of German exports rise and the prices of German imports fall. This leads to the rather paradoxical result that gold flows into Germany, and the transfer mechanism thus eases the situation of the country paying reparations. This is not a very probable case, but it would arise if the increase of foreign demand were for German exports, and the fall in Germany's demand related to imports. (*Theory of international trade,* 1936, pp. 75-76.)

is to be distinguished not only from the familiar velocity concept, or the "transactions velocity of money," but also from the "income" or "circuit" velocity of money concept. This latter is for our purposes a more serviceable concept than the "transactions velocity," since it disregards many kinds of transactions which are of no direct significance for the international mechanism. It is nevertheless not a wholly satisfactory concept for the present purpose. For any limited period of time "income" is not only difficult of measurement but almost incapable of definition. It does not matter, moreover, for the mechanism of international adjustment whether what is spent comes from current net income or from disposable capital funds, borrowings, internal or external, or "negative income" or business losses eventually to be defrayed by the creditors. Nor does it matter whether the expenditures are for consumption or for maintenance or expansion of investment, except indirectly as this may affect the productive resources of the country or the apportionment of expenditures as between different classes of commodities. What matters for present purposes is primarily the ratio to the volume of money of the expenditures per unit of time which, for that unit of time, make an equivalent reduction in the willingness to spend of the purchasers.[3] The final purchases velocity of money will of course necessarily be much smaller than the transactions velocity. It may be smaller or larger than the income velocity. It will tend to be smaller than the income velocity in so far as the latter covers income not spent or invested at home but hoarded or lent abroad. It will tend to be larger than the income velocity in so far as the latter fails to take account of maintenance and replacement expenditures, disinvestment expenditures, or expenditures of the proceeds of external or internal borrowings.

Since the relative change in the amount of final purchases in the two areas is an important equilibrating factor in the process of adjustment to a disturbance in their international balances, then, assuming no change to occur in either country in the final purchases velocity of money, the greater is the weighted average final purchases velocity of money in the two countries combined, the smaller will be the amount of money necessary to be transferred to restore a disturbed equilibrium, other things remaining

---

[3] An essentially similar concept is used for the same purposes by Ohlin (*Interregional and international trade,* 1933, pp. 378, 407, note).

the same. If, as the result of a transfer of specie to meet the first instalments of new and periodic obligations of one country to the other, a sudden change occurs in the amount of money in each country, and the volume of final purchases in each country does not immediately respond proportionately to the change in the amount of money, the amount of transfer of money to the receiving country will for a time have to be greater than the amount of such transfer ultimately necessary, and after the velocities in the two countries have recovered their normal levels, but before the periodic payments have terminated, a partial return of money to the paying country will occur. If, on the other hand, change in the amount of money tends to be accompanied with change in its velocity in a corresponding direction, a smaller initial transfer of money will suffice for the time being, but as the velocities recede to their normal levels more money will have to be transferred from the paying to the receiving country to maintain their relative volumes of final purchases at the new equilibrium level. In all cases, the amount of specie transfer necessary for adjustment to a disturbance will depend on the velocities of money in the two areas as well as on the manner in which the demands for different classes of commodities behave as the amounts of money are varied. Except under very unusual conditions, however, adjustment of the balance of payments to new and continuing unilateral remittances will require some initial transfer of specie from the paying to the receiving country.

The final purchases velocities in the two countries not only help to determine the amount of specie transfer necessary for adjustment, but they also help to determine what effects the remittances shall have on the *absolute* price levels in the two countries combined. If in the receiving country money has a higher velocity than in the paying country, the transfer of means of payment will result in a higher level of prices for the two countries combined, and vice versa. It is even conceivable, though not of course probable, that reparations payments may result in higher (or in lower) prices in *both* of the countries. Failure to take into account the possibility of different velocities in the two countries has led some writers to deny this even as a theoretical possibility.[4]

---

[4] Cf. Rueff's "principle of the conservation of purchasing power," according to which the transfer of a given amount of "purchasing power" (i.e., specie?)

TABLE V

EFFECTS OF INTERNATIONAL TRANSFERS IN ABSENCE OF PRICE CHANGES:
VARIATIONS IN VELOCITY[a]

Commodity	Receiving country		Paying country	
	Willing to purchase	Available for export	Willing to purchase	Available for export
Before Transfer				
Domestic and export...	2000	1000	500	1000
Import...............	1000		1000	
	3000	1000	1500	1000
After Transfer: Case A				
	Velocity before and after transfer = 1		Velocity before and after transfer = 1	
Domestic and export...	2400	600	300	1200
Import...............	1200		600	
	3600	600	900	1200
After Transfer: Case B				
	Velocity before and after transfer = 2		Velocity before and after transfer = 1	
Domestic and export...	2600	700	350	1300
Import...............	1300		700	
	3900	700	1050	1300
After Transfer: Case C				
	Velocity before and after transfer = ½		Velocity before and after transfer = 1	
Domestic and export...	2240	520	260	1120
Import...............	1120		520	
	3360	520	780	1120

[a] All quantities measured in monetary units per month; loan at rate of 600 units per month.

The role of specie movements and of the velocity of money in the mechanism of adjustment to disturbances is illustrated in table V, in which it is assumed that before reparations the unweighted average ratio of expenditures on native to expenditures on foreign commodities for the two countries combined is unity, and that, in the absence of price changes, reparations payments will not disturb the proportions in which expenditures are distributed between native and foreign commodities in either country. Under these conditions reparations payments, as we have seen, would not disturb the terms of trade. The pre-reparations equilibrium is disturbed by the imposition on one of the countries of the obligation to pay reparations to the other for an indefinite period of time at the rate of 600 monetary units per month.

In case A, the final purchase velocity of money per month, both before and after[5] the beginning of the reparations payments is unity in both countries, and prior to the transfer the final purchases per month are 3000 in the receiving country and 1500 in the paying country. There must therefore have been, in the initial equilibrium situation, 3000 monetary units in the former, and 1500 in the latter, country. A transfer of 600 monetary units from the paying to the receiving country takes place when the payments begin, and the resultant shifts in demands bring about an adjustment of the balance of payments of the two countries to the tribute without necessitating any change in prices. In case B the velocity of money per month both before and after the beginning of the tribute payments is 2 in the receiving country and 1 in the paying country, and prior to the transfer there are 1500 units of money in each of the countries. To restore equilibrium, a transfer of only 450 units of money is necessary. But since the

---

between two countries cannot result in a change in the aggregate power to purchase, measured in money, of the two countries.—Jacques Rueff, "Mr. Keynes' views on the transfer problem," *Economic journal*, XXXIX (1929), 388-99.

[5] Theoretically, other things being equal, and especially the "transactions velocity" of money remaining constant in each country, the final purchase velocity of money should be expected to fall slightly in the paying country and to rise slightly in the receiving country as the result of reparations, since in the paying country there will be production involving the use of money but not resulting in "final purchases," and in the receiving country there will be final purchases not involving, directly or indirectly, domestic production, and therefore absorbing less than the normal amount of means of payment for their mediation.

transfer of money is from a low-velocity to a high-velocity country, it results in an increase in the world level of prices and of
money incomes. As in case A, however, equilibrium is restored
without any change in the terms of trade. In case C the velocity
of money is $\frac{1}{2}$ in the receiving country and 1 in the paying
country, and prior to the transfer there are 6000 units of money
in the receiving country and 1500 in the paying country. To
restore equilibrium a transfer of 720 units of money is necessary.
But since the transfer of money is from a high-velocity to a low-
velocity country, it results in a decrease in the world level of
prices and of money incomes. As in the previous cases, however,
equilibrium is restored without any change in the terms of trade.
Whatever other cases were chosen, the same conclusion would
be indicated that the effect of a transfer of payments on *relative*
prices is independent of the velocities, provided that such changes
in money incomes as are offset by corresponding changes in prices
are assumed not to affect the apportionment of expenditures
among different classes of commodities.[6]

In the older literature, analysis of this sort of the role of
velocity of money in the mechanism of adjustment of interna-

---

[6] The results presented in these cases are not arbitrary, nor merely possible,
but follow necessarily from the assumptions explicitly made in connection
therewith. In case C, for example, the results as to the apportionment of
expenditures and the distribution of money between the two countries after
adjustment has been made to the payments are obtained as follows. Write:
i_r for the amount available for expenditure in the receiving country before
transfer ($= 3000$).
i_p for the amount available for expenditure in the paying country before transfer ($= 1500$).
I_r for the amount available for expenditure in the receiving country after
transfer.
I_p for the amount available for expenditure in the paying country after transfer.
x for the ratio of the weighted average velocity after transfer to the weighted
average velocity before transfer, for the two countries combined.
Then

$$2I_r + I_p = 2i_r + i_p = 7500 \tag{i}$$
$$I_r = xi_r + 600 \tag{ii}$$
$$I_p = xi_p - 600 \tag{iii}$$

Solving for x, I_r, and I_p, $\tag{iv}$

$$x = \frac{69}{75}; \ I_r = 3360; \ I_p = 780$$

Allocation of I_r and I_p to the different classes of commodities in the proportions in which it is assumed each country would distribute its expenditures in
the absence of relative price changes yields the remainder of the data necessary to
determine whether relative changes in prices are necessary for the new equilibrium, and, if so, in what direction.

tional balances is to be found, if at all, only by implication. In the more recent literature, also, discussion of this phase of the mechanism is scanty. Ohlin's treatment of velocity is imbedded in his exposition of the mechanism as a whole, but there seems to me to be agreement between our accounts in so far as they cover the same ground. D. H. Robertson, in a short essay,[7] which nevertheless contains in germ much of what has here been more elaborately expounded with reference to the transfer mechanism, also treats the velocity factor, in so far as he carries his analysis, in the same manner in which it is here treated. But concerned presumably more with establishing certain possibilities than with surveying the range of probabilities, he applies his analysis only to assumptions so extreme as to lead him to highly improbable conclusions. In an analysis of the effects of reparations payments by Germany to America on specie movements, terms of trade, and aggregate income in the two countries, he introduces an annual velocity of money factor, assumed to be unity and invariable in each country, and which represents the ratio of annual income, or annual expenditure, to the stock of money. From an arithmetical illustration he concludes that the payment by Germany of reparations need involve no transfer of money, no alteration in the terms of trade, and no change in "gross monetary income" in either country. Substituting "final purchases" for "gross monetary income," and taking only the data which he presents for America, his illustration is as follows:

America

> *Before Reparations Payments*
> Final purchases of £1,600 buy 900 American goods + 100 German goods and pay £600 taxes.
> Gold stock £1,600. $V = 1$.
> Price of American goods = £1.

> *During Reparations Payments at the rate of £600 per year*
> Final purchases of £1,600 buy 900 American goods + 700 German goods.
> Gold stock £1,600. $V = 1$.
> Price of American goods = £1.

How extreme the assumptions are on which all of these results

---

[7] "The transfer problem," in Pigou and Robertson, *Economic essays and addresses*, 1931, pp. 170-81.

depend is not made apparent only because they are not brought clearly into the open in either the illustration or the accompanying text. The illustration assumes that the government of America uses the proceeds of the reparations payments to remit taxation, but it presumably continues to render the same services to the community, for otherwise £600 of spending power would be unaccounted for. As far as final purchases or "gross money incomes" are concerned, the apparent absence of an increase when reparations are received is due solely to the fact that real income in the form of government services for which previously £600 was paid by individuals in taxes is now met by the reparations income of the government and therefore does not appear in the accounts of *private* monetary income. As far as money stocks are concerned, the absence of any increase in the receiving country can be explained only if the periodic receipt of the reparations payments and their use by the government in hiring personnel and buying materials with which to carry out its functions requires no use of the country's stock of money, whereas collection of taxes equal in amount to the reparations plus use of the tax receipts in the identical fashion in which the proceeds of the reparations are used would involve the use of £600 throughout the year. As far as the commodity terms of trade are concerned, the absence of any change is to be explained by the assumption that although in the receiving country no prices have changed and spending power has increased by £600, no increase will occur in that country in the amount of its own goods or governmental services demanded by its people.

XIII. COMMODITY FLOWS AND RELATIVE PRICE LEVELS

Graham and Feis hold that the explanation of the mechanism of adjustment of international balances to capital borrowings offered by the classical economists and their modern followers omits reference to a factor operating to bring about relative shifts in price levels in the direction opposite to that posited in this explanation. Graham claims that since the effect of a loan is to shift goods from the lending to the borrowing country, the volume of goods relative to the volume of gold will be increased in the borrowing country and decreased in the lending country, and therefore the prices will tend to fall in the former and rise in the latter. On the assumption that the first phase of the mechanism is a transfer of gold from the lending country to the borrowing country unaccompanied by a transfer of goods, and that the transfer of goods is a later phase, Graham, calling the former the "short-range" effect of capital movements and the latter the "long-range" effect, concludes that "the short and long range effects of borrowings will run in opposite directions."[1] He had earlier applied the same reasoning to the problem of the adjustment of international balances to capital imports under an inconvertible paper currency, on the assumption that the quantity of money in each country is held constant.[2] Feis accepts Graham's argument:

The effects of the goods movements upon price levels would, therefore, tend to be in the opposite direction to those produced by changes in the volume of purchasing power in each of the countries concerned, as Professor Graham has pointed out. Apparently, two conflicting tendencies are present in each country during the process of adjustment. These tendencies may or may not be simultaneous and equal in strength.[3]

This reasoning seems erroneous to me. The conclusion of these writers results from a mechanical application of the $\frac{M}{T} = P$ formula of price determination to the international trade mechanism, on the implicit assumptions that the price level is result and not cause, and that the changes in M and the changes in T are unrelated and independent factors in the mechanism,[4] and

---

[1] In a review of my *Canada's balance, American economic review*, XV (1925), 108. I had suggested, as an explanation of a tendency which seemed to be apparent in the Canadian experience for the relative rise in prices in the borrowing country to diminish in extent as borrowings continued at an even rate, that the longer the interval between a relative price change and the actual trade transactions the fuller would be the response to such price change, and, therefore, that the degree of relative price change required to bring about adjustment of the trade balance in the first year of a period of borrowings at an even rate would tend to be more than was required in later years. Graham offered his argument as a better explanation of the shrinkage in the relative change in prices.

[2] "International trade under depreciated paper. The United States, 1862-79," *Quarterly journal of economics*, XXXVI (1922), 223.

[3] Feis, "The mechanism of adjustment of international trade balances," *American economic review*, XVI (1926), 602 ff. (at p. 603).

[4] In Graham's exposition, this is suggested by his failure to discuss the determinants of the size of the specie flow and by his reference to his analysis of the depreciated paper case, where he had arbitrarily assumed that the

Feis, at least, explicitly attributes the same assumptions to the classical school.[5] But in the classical theory, as in the preceding exposition, the establishment of international equilibrium is regarded as primarily a problem of international adjustment of prices, and the direction and extent of flow of specie, and therefore also the relative amounts of money in the two countries, instead of being treated as independent factors, are held to be determined by the relative requirements for money of the two countries given their equilibrium price levels and their respective physical volumes of transactions requiring mediation through money. The bearing of the commodity flows in the mechanism, therefore, is not their influence on the relative price levels, but is, instead, their influence on the quantity of specie flow necessary to support the price relations required for equilibrium.

Let us suppose that when the lending first begins the lending country ships sufficient commodities on consignment to the borrowing country to bring its export surplus to equality with its volume of lending per unit period, but that, in consequence of the influx of goods, prices as a whole fall in the borrowing country to a level lower than is consistent with the maintenance of its import surplus at the required amount. A new or intensified flow of specie must thereupon occur from lending to borrowing country, so as to bring prices (and demands) in the borrowing country to a level adequately high to result in a continuing import surplus equal to the borrowings.[6]

---

quantities of money in each country would be held constant, an assumption which makes any analogy from the mechanism under depreciated paper a fallacious one in this connection for the mechanism under the gold standard.

[5] Cf. *ibid.*, p. 605: "The classical account of the process of adjustment both in its original sources and as presented in the preceding pages, rests upon the implicit assumption that income and price levels are the passive result of other influences. They are commonly said to be determined by the relationship between the volume of goods (trade) and the volume of purchasing power (and its velocity) within a country. . . ."

[6] Cf. G. W. Norman, *Letter to Charles Wood, Esq., M.P. on money,* 1841, p. 20:

There is one circumstance worth attention on account of its tendency to increase the transmission of specie under an adverse exchange. The articles of export which might replace gold and silver are usually few in number, speaking practically, and the increased quantity of such goods received by the creditor country lowers their price in it to an extent which, partially at least, lessens the effect produced by the enlargement of its currency.

If Norman means by this passage that a sufficient large flow of specie must

"Capital" movements, it is true, if they consist of funds which in the absence of such movement would have been invested at home, and if they result in an increase in the amount of investment in the borrowing country as compared to what would have been the situation in the absence of the borrowings, will eventually result in a relative increase in the output of the marketable commodities of the borrowing country as compared to those of the lending country and, therefore, will to this extent tend to result in a relative fall in the price level of the borrowing country. But Graham's and Feis's argument rests on the supposed effect on relative price levels of the commodities actually transferred, rather than on the effect on relative price levels of the relative changes in the *output* of commodities in the two countries.

XIV. EXCHANGE RATES

Hume conceded that the fall in the exchange value of a country's currency when for any reason there was adverse pressure on its balance of payments tended to exercise an equilibrating influence by providing an extra incentive to commodity export and a deterrent to commodity import. He held, however, that this could be but a minor factor in the process of adjustment, and although he gave no reasons it may be presumed that he saw that under a metallic standard the maximum possible range of variation of the exchanges, i.e., between the specie export and import points, was so limited as to make it extremely unlikely that such variation could exert an appreciable direct influence on the course of trade.[1] Since his time the maximum range of variation has become still narrower under normal conditions because of reduction in the cost of transporting specie, and scarcely anyone today would dispute that under an international metallic standard exchange variations are a negligible factor as far as their direct

occur to offset any otherwise disequilibrating influence on prices of the flow of commodities, then the position taken here corresponds with his.

[1] Hume, *Political discourses* (1752), in *Essays moral, political, and literary,* 1875 ed., I, 333, note. Cf. W. Whewell, "Mathematical Exposition of certain doctrines of political economy. Third memoir," *Transactions of the Cambridge Philosophical Society,* IX, part II (1856), 7: "The rate of exchange may be looked upon as an instrument which measures the force of that current [i.e., gold movements], and does not add anything to that force, or produce any effect of its own, except, it may be, to regulate and reduce to steadiness the casual and transient impulses."

influence on commodity trade is concerned.[2] It has sometimes been suggested, however, that this narrowing of the range between the gold points has not been an unalloyed benefit, since by its facilitation of specie shipments it has contributed to the instability of national credit structures. Proposals have been made, starting with Torrens in 1819,[3] artificially to widen the margin between the specie points, by seigniorage charges, premiums on gold for export, different buying and selling prices for gold at the Central Bank, generous tolerance for underweight in the internal specie circulation, differential buying or selling prices for the gold of the particular degrees of fineness most in supply or demand abroad, and other similar devices, and such practices have, for this or other reasons, been followed. To the extent that such practices exist, the range of possible exchange fluctuations under a metallic standard, and therefore the possible influence of exchange variations on the course of trade, can of course be somewhat increased. In effect this is an attempt to retain the advantages of an international metallic standard while escaping in part one of its incidents, namely, the direct dependence of the national stock of money, or of the specie reserves upon which it rests, on the state of the foreign exchanges. But the same advantages of partial freedom of the quantity of the circulating medium from dependence on the vagaries of the exchanges can be more safely, and especially for an important financial center whose effectiveness depends largely on its ability to attract foreign short-term funds, more cheaply obtained, by the maintenance of excess specie reserves, than by artificial widening of the range between the gold points. Even with such widening, moreover, unless it were carried to much greater lengths than has ever been customary, the direct influence of exchange rate fluctuations on the course

---

[2] I at one time interpreted J. H. Hollander, as did also Taussig, as holding that exchange rate fluctuations within the limits of the specie points were the effective factor in bringing about a transfer of international borrowings in the form of commodities instead of specie. (See Hollander, "International trade under depreciated paper," *Quarterly journal of economics,* XXXII [1918], 678, and my *Canada's balance,* 1924, p. 150.) But upon a rereading I am now inclined to interpret him as holding that the adjustment takes place automatically, without any moving factor, as in Ricardo's version, or perhaps with an automatic and precisely adequate relative shift in demand implied as the moving factor, with the variations in the exchange rates just happening, and serving no function in the mechanism.

[3] See *supra,* pp. 206-07.

of commodity trade would still be negligible. But even small variations in the exchanges can exert an appreciable influence on the movement of short-term capital funds, and through them on the mechanism of adjustment. This phase of the mechanism is discussed in the next chapter, in connection with the discussion of the relation of banking processes to the mechanism.

In their discussion of the foreign exchanges, the writers on the theory of international trade with apparently almost complete unanimity expound a particular error of minor practical importance but revealing lack of due precision in exposition or thought. They hold that when the balance of payments is even, the exchanges will be at their mint par.[4] The correct statement is that when the balance of payments is even the exchanges will be somewhere within the export and import points. The mint par has significance for the exchanges only as a base point from which to determine the specie export and import points. Equilibrium between the amount of foreign bills demanded and offered is as likely to be reached at any one as at any other rate within the limits of the specie points. Except for the approximately fixed limits to the range of possible fluctuation of the exchanges under an international metallic standard, there is no basis for differentiating the theory of the foreign exchanges between two currencies having a common metallic standard, on the one hand, and between two currencies on different standards, on the other hand.

xv. A Criticism of the Purchasing-power Parity Theory[1]

Owing more, probably, to good fortune than to superior insight, the classical economists escaped almost completely the fatal

[4] The only instance I have noticed in the literature of explicit correction of this error is in Harry D. White, *The French international accounts, 1880-1913,* 1933, 156, note, where the perpetration of this error in my *Canada's balance* is properly rebuked. I was in excellent company, however. Ricardo, J. S. Mill, Bastable, Marshall, Taussig, have all, at one time or another, made the same error.

[1] The criticism presented here corresponds in most respects to that to be found in the following, among other, sources: G. W. Terborgh, "The purchasing-power parity theory," *Journal of political economy,* XXXIV (1926), 197-208; T. O. Yntema, *A mathematical reformulation of the general theory of international trade,* 1932, pp. 18-19; C. Bresciani-Turroni, "The 'purchasing power parity' doctrine," *L'Égypte contemporaine,* XXV (1934), 433-64;

error of formulating their theory of the international relationships of prices in terms of simple quantitative relationships between average price levels. But since 1916, Professor Gustav Cassel has expounded, and obtained wide acceptance of, a simple formula purporting to express the relationship to each other of national statistical price levels, which he called the purchasing-power parity theory. Some writers have found in this formula nothing but a restatement of the English classical theory, but it differs substantially from any version of the classical theory known to me.

The following citation embodies an early formulation of his theory by Cassel, and the one which first gained for it wide attention:

> Given a normal freedom of trade between two countries, A and B, a rate of exchange will establish itself between them and this rate will, smaller fluctuations apart, remain unaltered as long as no alterations in the purchasing power of either currency is made and no special hindrances are imposed upon the trade. But as soon as an inflation takes place in the money of A, and the purchasing power of this money is, therefore, diminished; the value of the A-money in B must necessarily be reduced in the same proportion. . . . Hence the following rule: when two currencies have been inflated, the new normal rate of exchange will be equal to the old rate multiplied by the quotient between the degrees of inflation of both countries. There will, of course, always be fluctuations from this new normal rate, and in a period of transition these fluctuations are apt to be rather wide. But the rate calculated in the way indicated must be regarded as the new parity between the currencies. This parity may be called the *purchasing power parity*, as it is determined by the quotients of the purchasing powers of the different currencies.[2]

Howard Ellis, *German monetary theory, 1905-1933,* 1934, part III. Cf. also Jacob Viner, "Die Theorie des auswärtigen Handels," in *Die Wirtschaftstheorie der Gegenwart* (Wieser Festschrift), IV (1928), 117-18.

[2] Gustav Cassel, "Memorandum on the world's monetary problems," International Financial Conference, Brussels, 1920, *Documents of the Conference,* V, 44-45. (Italics in the original.)

If a and b represent two countries, E represents the number of units of b's money which exchanges for one unit of a's money, P represents the index number of prices, and o and I the base and the given years, respectively, then according to Cassel:

$$\frac{E_1}{E_o} = \frac{\frac{bP_1}{bP_o}}{\frac{aP_1}{aP_o}}$$

Cassel has expounded the theory primarily in terms of paper currencies and with special bearing on the effects of currency inflation on exchange rates. But if true for paper currencies, there is no apparent reason why it should not apply equally to gold standard currencies. Since under an international gold standard the possible range of variation of the exchanges is narrowly limited by the gold points, it should follow that under such a standard the possibility of substantial divergence of movement of price levels, in direction or in degree, in different countries is correspondingly limited. It would seem further that if substantial relative changes in the purchasing power of two currencies must generally result in corresponding inverse changes in the rates at which these currencies exchange for each other, then under equilibrium conditions metallic standard currencies must have equal purchasing power in terms of units of identical gold content,[3] unless adequate reason can be found for holding that all the factors other than relative price levels capable of exerting an enduring influence on the exchanges were already present in the year arbitrarily chosen as the base year, had already exercised all of their possible influence on the exchange rates, and would never disappear or weaken. It is easy to conceive, however, of changes in cost or demand conditions or both, in one or the other countries, or both, which so change the relative demands of the two countries for each other's products in terms of their own as to bring about an enduring and substantial relative change in their levels of prices, including the prices of domestic commodities and services, even under the gold standard. The existence of non-transportable goods and services in one country which have no exact prototype in the other, moreover, makes it difficult to see not only how there could be any necessity under the gold standard that the price levels be identical in the two countries, but how the two price levels could be compared at all with any approach to precision.

Cassel nevertheless accepts readily the corollaries of his doctrine:

Even when both countries under consideration possess a gold stand-

---

[3] I.e., using the same symbols as in note 2, *supra*:

$$E_1 = \frac{{}^b P_1}{{}^a P_1}; \qquad E_o = \frac{{}^b P_o}{{}^a P_o}$$

ard, the rate of exchange between them must correspond to the purchasing power parity of their currencies. The purchasing power of each currency has to be regulated so as to correspond to that of gold; and when this is the case, the purchasing power parity will stand in the neighborhood of the gold parity of the two currencies. Only when the purchasing power of a currency is regulated in this way will it be possible to keep the exchanges of this currency in their parities with other gold currencies. If this fundamental condition is not fulfilled, no gold reserve whatever will suffice to guarantee the par exchange of the currency. Under stable currency conditions and when no radical alterations in the conditions of international trade take place, no great or lasting deviation from purchasing power parity is possible.[4]

Some writers have held that the purchasing-power parity theory is invalid if applied to *general* price levels, but that it could be made acceptable, and in fact reduced to the status of a truism, if it were confined to the price levels of commodities directly entering into international trade, and if abstraction were made, as does Cassel, from relative changes in transportation costs or tariff rates. The following quotation from Heckscher is representative of this point of view:

The conception that the exchanges represent relative price levels, or, what is the same thing, that the monetary unit of a country has the same purchasing power both within the country and outside it, is correct only upon the never existing assumption that all goods and services can be transferred from one country to another without cost. In this case, the agreement between the prices of different countries is even greater than that which is covered by the conception of an identical purchasing power of the monetary unit; for not only average price levels but also the price of each particular commodity or service will then be the same in both countries, if computed on the basis of the exchanges.[5]

Cassel, however, rejects this view, and insists that the doctrine will not hold if applied to international commodities alone, since if the prices of all B's export commodities were doubled, all other prices in B and all prices in A remaining unchanged, the exchange value of B's currency would fall by much less than

---

[4] Cassel, *Post-war monetary stabilization*, 1928, pp. 31-32.

[5] E. F. Heckscher (and others), *Sweden, Norway, Denmark and Iceland in the world war*, 1930, p. 151.

half. Before the exchange could fall to this level, other commodities hitherto produced only for home consumption could be profitably exported by B, and its imports of A's commodities would have fallen, and thus a further drop in its exchanges would be prevented.[6]

Cassel is right in maintaining that the doctrine need not hold if applied to the price levels of a *variable* range of international commodities. But it need not hold even if applied to a fixed assortment of international commodities. Suppose that there are only two countries, that no new commodities enter into international trade, that no commodities already in international trade change the direction of their flow or disappear from trade, and that there are no tariffs or freight costs, so that all international commodities command identical prices in all markets, in terms of the standard currency when this is uniform and exchange is at par, or in terms of the currency of either of the countries converted from the other, when necessary, at the prevailing rate of exchange. Even in this case, the doctrine that the exchange rates will vary in exact inverse proportion with the relative variations in the index number of prices of international commodities in the two countries would not only not be a truism, but would not necessarily or ordinarily be true if, as would be most appropriate, *weighted* index numbers were used and the basis for the weighting were, not the relative importance of the commodities in international trade (which, with only two countries, would mean identical weights for both countries) but their relative importance in the consumption or the total trade, external and internal, of the respective countries. In fact, it would be possible for the exchange rate under these conditions to change even if no change

---

[6] Cassel, *Theory of social economy,* 1932, pp. 662-63. Cassel proceeds to make a concession which seems to me to involve a surrender of the one element in his theory which differentiates it from other theories, namely, his insistence that the long-run exchange value of a currency depends solely on the average level of prices in the two countries. He says: "However, the general internal purchasing power of the B currency has, of course, fallen, and to that extent one must expect a corresponding fall in the rate of exchange. Over and above that, *there will perhaps take place a further fall in the rate as a consequence of a distribution of the general rise of prices which may be particularly unfavorable for the external value of the B currency.*" (*Ibid.,* p. 663. Italics not in original.) Unless Cassel has in mind only a temporary effect, he is here conceding that the exchanges need not move in the same direction or degree as the relative change in general price levels.

occurred in any price, provided there were changes in the weights in the two countries, or even if no change occurred in any weight, provided there were any changes in prices, notwithstanding the necessity under the conditions assumed that any price changes should be identical in both countries.

The only necessary relationships between prices in different countries which the classical theory postulated, or which can be formulated in general terms, are the international uniformity of particular prices of commodities actually moving in international trade when converted into other currencies at the prevailing rates of exchange, after allowance for transportation costs and tariff duties, and the necessity of such a relationship between the arrays of prices in different countries as is consistent with the maintenance of international and internal equilibrium.

The one type of case which would meet the requirement of exact inversely proportional changes in price levels and in exchange rates would be a monetary change in one country, such as a revaluation of the currency, which would operate to change all prices and money incomes in that country in equal degree, while every other element in the situation, in both countries, remained absolutely constant.[7] Cassel, however, argues for at least the practical validity of his theory, as applied to actual history, on the ground that it is substantially confirmed by the facts, since under the gold standard there do not occur even over long periods wide divergences in the trends of the indices of different countries, and under fluctuating paper currencies the divergences between the actual trends of the indices and the purchasing-power parities calculated in accordance with his formula are not great and tend to disappear. He claims that the disturbances such as capital flows or tariff changes which operate to prevent purchasing-power parity from establishing itself are rarely powerful enough, as compared to the influence of the comparative purchasing power of the respective currencies, to result in a wide divergence from purchasing-power parity and are moreover likely to be temporary in character. His defense of the theory is essentially empirical rather than analytical.

It is no doubt true that the comparative purchasing power of two paper currencies in terms of all the things which are purchasable in their respective countries is at least ordinarily the most

---

[7] Cf. T. O. Yntema, *A mathematical reformulation of the general theory of international trade*, 1932, pp. 18-19.

important single factor in determining the exchange rate between the two currencies and must ordinarily be powerful enough to keep divergences of the exchange rate and purchasing power parity from reaching such lengths as, say, a rate only 50 per cent or as much as 200 per cent of the rate called for by the purchasing-power parity formula. It is also true that the exchange rate, which means approximately the comparative mint prices of gold, is ordinarily the most important single factor in determining the price levels of countries on an international gold standard. But the divergences between actual exchange rates and those required by the purchasing-power parity formula are in fact frequently substantial, and the "disturbances" from which such divergences result need not by any means be temporary in character, so that a longer period would lessen the divergence, but may in fact be progressive in character through time. Nor can these divergences be satisfactorily explained by defects in the available index numbers. On the contrary, the indices ordinarily used are unweighted wholesale price indices, and these are notoriously heavily loaded with the staple commodities of international commerce, whose prices are most likely to have uniform trends in different countries. Examination of such few indices as are constructed on a broad enough basis to give some representation to domestic commodities and services indicates, what is to be expected, that the more comprehensive the index the wider tends to be the divergence of the actual exchange rate from the purchasing-power parity rate. Use of weighted indices also ordinarily results in a widening of the indicated deviation of the exchanges from the purchasing-power parity rate.

Cassel's theory purports to be not merely a statement of relations between quantities, but also an explanation of the order of causation, with exchange rates being determined by relative price levels, rather than vice versa. Under an international metallic standard in the long run, for any one country, and especially if it is a small country, its price level will be determined for it largely by factors external to it and impinging upon it through specie movements.[8] Under paper standards not substantially pegged to gold, whether *de jure* or *de facto*, it is impossible to formulate the issue intelligently without reference to the princi-

---

[8] Cf. Robert Adamson, "Some considerations on the theory of money," *Transactions of the Manchester Statistical Society*, 1885, p. 58:
. . . I cannot read the literature of this subject without seeming to feel

ples on which the quantity of money in each country is regulated, and if, as is, however, rarely the case, there is no clear governing principle, and the play of circumstances, such as the state of the national budget, pressure from business, or more or less arbitrary or traditional discount policies, are allowed to be the determining factors, there will be mutual influence of prices on exchange rates and of exchange rates on prices, with no satisfactory way of apportioning to each set of influences its share of responsibility for the actually resultant situation.

Cassel has defended his failure to give attention to the factors which even in the long run can operate to create divergence between the actual exchange rate and the purchasing-power parity rate on the ground that his theory threw the emphasis on what was during the war and post-war period of extreme inflation overwhelmingly the most important factor in determining exchange rates, namely, currency inflation. Under such circumstances, the proper procedure for the economist apparently is to forget about the minor factors:

The art of economic theory to a great extent consists in the ability to judge which of a number of different factors cooperating in a certain movement ought to be regarded as the most important and essential one. Obviously in such cases we must choose a factor of permanent character, a factor which must always be at work. Other factors which are only of a temporary character and may be expected to disappear, or at any rate can be theoretically assumed to be absent, must for that reason alone be put in a subordinate position.[9]

that in the ordinary explanations of prices by reference to fluctuations in the quantity of money, and of circulation, etc., are not only curious reversals of the true theory, but practical dangers. They concentrate attention on the secondary factor, assign all importance to it, and tend toward the practical doctrine that remedies are to be sought in some artificial manipulation of the money system. I would not deny [sic] for a moment that the money system of a country is without influence on the course of its prices; no two facts can coexist in mutual dependence without some reciprocal influence being exercised, but the influence seems to me to be secondary in its action and relatively insignificant. It only acts because, through deeper lying causes, there is already a determined range of prices. The comparative efficiency of a country as one member of the great trading community is what in the long run determines the scale of prices in it, and it is to the variations in the conditions affecting its efficiency that we must turn for final explanation of the movements which on the surface appear as changes in an independent entity, money.

[9] Cassel, *Post-war monetary stabilization,* 1928, p. 29. Machlup has recently expressed similar views in the course of a review of Ellis's book:

No objection can be made to this, if it is to be understood to mean merely that minor factors should be treated as minor factors. But if it is presented as justification for the omission of mention of minor factors, and even for express denial that they are operative, on the ground that their recognition weakens the persuasive power of one's argument, then this amounts merely to saying that bad theory may make good propaganda, and is a debatable proposition at that.[10]

The purchasing-power parity theorists, of course, overstated their case of unilateral causation (inflation-prices-exchange rates). But it was necessary to do so at a time when the monetary authorities tried to deny any responsibility for the depreciation by maintaining that the intense "need" for imported goods and the misbehavior of wicked speculators were to be blamed. The concession that, under dislocated currencies, certain shifts in the relative intensity of the demand for the other countries' goods may bring about a (slight) change in foreign exchange rates was *entirely out of place* at a time when foreign exchanges were continuously rising to some fantastic multiple of their original level. (*Journal of political economy,* XLIII [1935], 395. Italics mine.)

[10] Cf. R. G. Hawtrey, *Currency and credit,* 3d ed., 1928, p. 442:

But to recommend a dogma on account not of its inherent validity but of its good practical consequences is dangerous. When people discover its theoretical weaknesses they may not only reject the dogma, but neglect the practical consequences.

Chapter VII

THE INTERNATIONAL MECHANISM IN RELA-
TION TO MODERN BANKING PROCESSES

> . . . *many writers have perplexed themselves and their readers by founding theories on exceptional circumstances. Others have been led astray by statistics—the characteristic form of modern research.* . . .
> —G. Arbuthnot, "Sir Robert Peel's Act of 1844 . . . vindicated," 1857, p. vii.

1. AUTOMATIC VS. MANAGED CURRENCIES

The assumption of a simple specie currency followed in the preceding chapter made it possible to deal with the international mechanism as an "automatic" mechanism, if by "automatic" is meant freedom from discretionary regulation or management. But if there are non-specie elements in the currency, and if the ratio of the non-specie to the specie elements is variable and subject to the discretionary control of a central authority, there result differences of some importance in the short-run mode of operation of the mechanism from the manner in which it would operate under a simple specie currency. Although most present-day writers seem to believe either that the non-automatic character of the modern gold standard is a discovery of the post-war period or that it was only in the post-war period that the gold standard lost its automatic character, currency controversy during the entire nineteenth century concerned itself largely with the problems resulting from the discretionary or management elements in the prevailing currency systems. The bullion controversy at the beginning of the nineteenth century turned largely on the difference in the mode of operation in the international mechanism of a managed paper standard currency, on the one hand, and of a convertible paper currency, on the other, with the latter treated generally, but not universally, as if it were automatic. Later, the adherents of both the currency and the banking schools distinguished carefully between the way in which a supposedly automatic "purely metallic" currency (which, in addition to specie, included bank deposits but not bank notes) would operate and the way in which the Bank of England was actually operating a "mixed" currency (which, in addition to specie and bank deposits, included bank notes). Both schools were hostile to discretionary management. The currency school thought that the currency could be made nearly automatic again merely by limiting the issue of bank notes uncovered by specie. The banking school held that there was no acceptable way of escape from the discretionary power of the Bank of England over the volume of deposits, although the "banking principle," according to which the issue of means of payment could not be carried appreciably beyond the needs of business under convertibility, set narrow limits to this discretionary power. Later discussion centered largely about the rules which the Bank of England should follow in using the discount rate and its other instruments of control to regulate the currency.

Even the terms "automatic," "self-acting," "managed," "discretionary," or their equivalents, as applied to currency systems are of long standing, as the following sample quotations from the literature of the currency school-banking school controversy show:

In the case of a [convertible] paper currency an attempt is made from considerations of convenience and economy to substitute paper notes in the place of metallic coins. In making this exchange we adopt a circulating medium which has no intrinsic value, and we therefore lose that self-acting security which we had with a metallic circulation, for the due regulation of its amount and the maintenance of its value. It therefore becomes necessary that we should resort to some artificial system or rule, which shall secure with respect to a paper currency that regulation of its amount which in a metallic currency necessarily results from its intrinsic value.[1]

. . . from the moment that we employ figurative language at all, and speak of gold "flowing" and "fluctuating" as if it were water, or "circulating" as if it were blood, no metaphor seems so significant, or to apply so aptly to the character of the notion of the precious metals as the expression "automatic." This word indicates an action which is not determined by any particular exercise of an extrinsic volition,

---

[1] Overstone, *Further reflections on the state of the currency,* 1837, pp. 33-34.

but one proceeding from, and attaching to, the functional, intrinsic and uncontrollable energies of the organ, or thing, which acts. The thing which acts in this case is the universal appetite of the human mind, and the effects produced on gold make it seem to be animated by that appetite, and to seek its end in active obedience to it. . . . I conclude therefore thus far that the idea of a safe paper currency is incompatible with the idea of any thing savoring of control, guidance, discretion, or government, and that it is a principle essential to a safe paper currency that the issue and resorption of it should be purely automatic.[2]

There are some who object *in limine* to all "regulation of the currency," as it is termed, but such objection is founded in error; because currency being legal tender it . . . is the creature of law or "regulation"; wherefore to withdraw "regulation" altogether would be to cease to have legal tender; an impracticable alternative. . . .

But regulation is of two kinds, viz., discretionary, and self-acting. Thus, on the one hand, the Bank of England both possesses and exercises the power of regulating the currency at its discretion, by altering its rate of discount. . . . Whilst, on the other hand, self-acting regulation is afforded by the exportation of gold at one time in relief of excess, and its importation at another, in relief of insufficiency, such operations being undertaken upon ordinary mercantile principles; the trader simply seeking his own profit, and not concerning himself in the least about the regulation of anything whatever.[3]

If a currency system could be imagined under which the specie reserves of the banking system as a whole were always maintained without central bank regulation at a constant ratio to its demand liabilities to the public, there would be only one significant difference between such a currency and a simple specie currency as far as the international mechanism was concerned. Whereas under a simple specie currency fluctuations in the quantity of specie would result in equal fluctuations, both absolutely and relatively, in the amount of means of payment, under a fixed fractional reserve currency fluctuations in the quantity of specie would result in equi-proportional but absolutely greater fluctuations in the amount of means of payment. The absolute amount of specie movement necessary for adjustment of the balance of

[2] John Welsford Cowell, *Letters . . . on the institution of a safe and profitable paper currency*, 1843, pp. 45-46.
[3] Edwin Hill, *Principles of currency*, 1856, pp. 2-3.

payments to a disturbance of a given monetary size would be less under a fractional reserve currency than under a simple specie currency.

Under both types of currency the international mechanism would be "automatic" in the sense that its mode of operation would not be influenced by the discretionary management of a central authority, but would be the result of the voluntary responses of a host of individuals to changes in prices, interest rates, money incomes, money costs, and so forth. Under both types of currency, therefore, it would be possible to formulate a fairly precise description of the mechanism of international adjustment on the basis either of assumptions as to the nature of rational individualistic behavior under the circumstances specified or of the assumption of persistence in the future of such patterns of behavior, whether rational or not, as had been found upon investigation to have prevailed in the past.

Where the ratio of the amount of the currency to the amount of specie is subject to the discretion of a central authority, however, the international mechanism becomes subject to the influence of the decisions or activities of this authority and thus loses some at least of its automatic character. If the controlling agency were operating on the basis of a clearly formulated and simple policy or rule of action, which was made known to the public, it would be possible to describe the international mechanism as it would operate under such policy. But central banks do not ordinarily disclose their policy to the public, and the evidence seems to point strongly to a disinclination on the part of central bankers as a class to accept as their guide the simple formulae which are urged upon them by economists and others, or to follow simple rules of their own invention. All central banks find themselves at times facing situations which appear to demand a choice between conflicting objectives, long-run versus short-run, internal stability versus exchange stability, the indicated needs of the market versus their own financial or reserve position, and so forth, and they seem universally to prefer meeting such situations *ad hoc* rather than in accordance with the dictates of some simple formula. Whatever may be the merits of this attitude, it results in practice in behavior by central banks which fails to reveal to the outsider any well-defined pattern upon which can be based predictions as to their future behavior.. Theorizing about the nature of the international mechanism in so far as it is subject to influence by the operations of central banks cannot therefore be forthright and categorical, but must resort to analysis of the consequences for the mechanism in different types of situations of the particular choices which central bankers may conceivably make among the various species of action—or inaction—available to them in such situations. But whatever central banks do or refrain from doing, and for whatever reasons or absence of reason, their mere existence with discretionary power to act suffices to give some phases of the international mechanism, and especially the specie-movement phase, a "managed" and variable and largely unpredictable relationship to the other phases of the mechanism.

If there is no central bank or its equivalent, and if there are a large number of genuinely independent banks with power to issue bank money, whether in the form of demand deposits or of notes, and with their specie reserves left completely or substantially free from statutory regulation, the specie-movement phase of the international mechanism can still be regarded as automatic if the average specie reserve ratio of the banking system as a whole is at any moment determined by the aggregate effect of the autonomous decisions of a large number of individuals or firms. The ratio under such circumstances of the total amount of means of payment to the amount of specie will be a variable one, but there will be some elements of regularity in this variability, discoverable by historical investigation if not by *a priori* cogitation alone. But this does not seem to be a common situation. In the absence of a central bank, as in the United States before the establishment of the Federal Reserve system or in Canada before 1935, either the great bulk of the banking business was in the hands of a small number of large banks necessarily following, because of their size and fewness, an essentially uniform course with respect to reserve ratios, or a few of the largest banks operated as rediscount agencies for the many small banks and the latter adhered closely to a customary or legal minimum cash reserve ratio, leaving to a few large banks the chief responsibility for the maintenance of adequate national specie reserves. From the point of view of the international mechanism, it is by no means clear that such a system differed significantly *in practice* from a system operating under formal central discretionary control, or that what differences did exist were uniformly such as to point to the desirability of formal central control as it has been exercised in the past. In any case, there is ordinarily under both systems some measure of more or less centralized and discretionary control over the amount of means of payment and its ratio to the amount of specie, and the mode of operation of this control is under both systems unlikely to follow any simple pattern.

Under an international metallic standard, there are various possible objectives of the central bank. (1) It may be the policy of the bank to enforce adherence of the banking system to a fixed minimum (and possibly also maximum) specie reserve ratio. (2) Or its objective may be to minimize the amount of its own non-income-earning specie reserves while maintaining at all times unquestioned convertibility of its demand liabilities. This objective calls for frequent and prompt central bank intervention to check inward or outward specie movements, with a general tendency to force close correspondence in timing and direction between the fluctuations in the national stock of means of payment and the fluctuations in the foreign exchanges. It seems to have been a dominant element in the policy of the Bank of England during the nineteenth century. (3) Another possible objective may be to minimize the frequency of central bank intervention, and to confine intervention to those occasions when price or other rigidities or the prevalence of distrust result in a dangerous depletion of reserves or in an accumulation of excess reserves to an extent burdensome to the central bank or dangerous to the position of foreign central banks. The Banque de France appears to have followed this objective with substantial constancy during the latter half of the nineteenth century. It operates to reduce the significance of the central bank, whose powers are used to support the automatic processes only to protect itself from danger and to counteract the automatic processes only to protect its profits or to protect other central banks from danger. (4) Finally, another possible objective is to exploit the possibilities of internal stabilization, whether of prices, or of amount of means of payment, or of physical volume of business activity, through control of the quantity of means of payment within the limits set by adherence to an international monetary standard. Under such a policy the automatic forces would be left alone or reinforced when they were operating in a stabilizing direction, but would be counteracted when they were acting in an unstabilizing direction, within the limits of safety with respect to maintenance of convertibility. Pursuit of this objective would involve willingness of the central bank to accumulate idle specie reserves or to permit without interference the substantial depletion of reserves. While this objective has undoubtedly been upon occasion a factor in determining the operations of central banks, it does not seem ever, at least during the nineteenth century, to have been a formally adopted and consistently applied aim of central bank policy, with the brief, and partial, exception of the period of adherence by the Bank of England to the "Palmer rule."

In terms of the distinction, examined in detail in later sections, between primary fluctuations in the amount of means of payment or those resulting directly from specie flows, on the one hand, and secondary fluctuations in the amount of means of payment, or those resulting from fluctuations in the volume of loans and investments of the banking system, gold outflows would always tend to involve primary contraction and gold inflows to involve primary expansion, but whether these primary fluctuations would be accompanied by operations of the central banks tending to produce secondary fluctuations and whether these secondary fluctuations would be in a direction supporting or offsetting the primary fluctuations, would depend on what objectives the central bank was pursuing. In terms of the classification of possible objectives of central bank policy made above, the appropriate operations of the central banks would be as indicated in tabular form on page 395.

II. Primary and Secondary Expansion of Means of Payments

Under a metallic standard currency system which contains both specie and non-specie elements, changes in the total stock of means of payment in the country may result either from changes in the amount of specie or from changes in the amount of non-specie currency, or from both. The amount of specie can increase as the result of an inflow of specie or bullion from abroad, of the coining of domestically-produced bullion, or of the diversion of

---

⁴ The types of secondary operations of an offsetting character should perhaps be further subclassified, so as to distinguish partially offsetting, exactly offsetting ("neutralizing"), and over-compensating secondary fluctuations.

Central bank objective	Central bank operations	
	Gold outflow (Primary contraction)	Gold inflow (Primary expansion)
(1) Fixed reserve ratio	Secondary contraction	Secondary expansion
(2) Minimum reserves	Secondary expansion while excess reserves persist; secondary contraction when reserves are below minimum	Secondary expansion to check accumulation of excess reserves
(3) Minimum intervention	Secondary contraction when reserves approach safety minimum	Secondary expansion when needed to protect foreign central banks
(4) Stabilization	Secondary expansion if undesired deflation under way or "reflation" desired; secondary contraction if undesired inflation under way or deflation desired	Secondary contraction if undesired inflation under way or deflation desired; secondary expansion if undesired deflation under way or "reflation" desired

bullion from industrial to monetary use. The amount of non-specie currency (assuming foreign issues are not generally accepted) can increase through increased issue of paper money by the government to meet current expenditures or to redeem debt obligations, or through an increase by the banking system as a whole of its note and/or deposit liabilities to the outside public by the grant of loans, purchase of securities, or payment of its own operating losses or unearned dividends in "bank money." Changes in the amount of means of payment will be here distinguished as "primary" or "secondary" according as they result from changes in the amount of specie or from changes in the amount of uncovered non-specie currency, and an attempt will be made to demonstrate that examination of the international mechanism with the aid of this distinction serves both to expose some current misinterpretations of the doctrines of the older writers and to bring out more clearly the nature of the banking aspects of the mechanism under modern conditions. To simplify the exposition, the following assumptions, involving only minor quantitative departures from the actually prevailing conditions under the gold standard, will be made: (1) that changes in the amount of specie result only from international movements of specie or bullion; (2) that bullion or specie is never borrowed or lent internationally by banks *on their own account*; and (3) that non-specie currency, including both notes and deposits, is issued only by banks and only as loans, in the purchase of securities, or in the exchange of one form for another form of currency. Further to simplify the exposition, it will be assumed that all actual specie is in bank reserves and that there is no non-monetary use of gold.

Given these assumptions, primary expansion or contraction of the means of payment can result only from, and must be equal to, the inflow or outflow of specie from or to the outside world. Let us suppose that as the result of increased commodity exports an inflow of specie occurs, and that the owners of such specie exchange it at the banks for either bank notes or bank deposits. This constitutes a primary expansion of the currency. If the banks increase their loans and investments—whether or not because of the increase in their specie reserves is immaterial—a further increase in bank money occurs which constitutes a secondary expansion. If for any reason the banks should reduce the amount of their loans and investments while their specie holdings were increasing, the primary expansion would be at least in part offset, and could conceivably be more than offset, by a simultaneous secondary contraction, so that the net expansion, if any, of the currency would be smaller than the primary expansion.

In tracing the development of doctrine with relation to the respective roles in the international mechanism of what are here designated as primary and secondary fluctuations of the currency, it is important to take note of the assumptions of the writers as to the kinds of means of payment comprised in the currency system. In the earliest expositions of the international mechanism, such as those of Hume and his predecessors, the analysis was as a rule carried on in terms of a simple specie currency, where there could be only primary expansion or contraction, and analysis in these terms continued to be common, both among the writers of the classical period and to the present day, when the objective was a simple and concise formulation with emphasis on other than the banking aspects of the mechanism. The further back in time we go, therefore, the greater the stress on primary fluctuations, with secondary fluctuations often left completely unmentioned. Systematic analysis of the international mechanism in terms of the role of fluctuations in the non-specie as well as in the specie elements of the currency began only[1] with the bullionists, including Ricardo. The bullionists commonly, though not universally, failed to give attention to deposits as a part of the national stock of means of payment, but their discussion of the mechanism under a metallic standard was expounded in terms of a predominantly paper circulation, with fractional specie reserves generally assumed to be maintained at a constant ratio of the total circulation. The bullionists therefore held that under a metallic standard specie movements would be accompanied by absolutely greater fluctuations in the amount of the total (specie and note) circulation, i.e., that, in the terminology here used, both primary and secondary fluctuations in the currency, in the same direction, were a part of the international mechanism. Later, the currency school held that: (1) in the absence of statutory regulation the relation between the short-run fluctuations in the total (specie and note) circulation and the fluctuations in specie was a variable one as to both direction and degree and subject to the caprice of the Bank of England; (2) the proper relationship was one in which the fluctuations in total (specie and note) circulation would be in the same direction as and absolutely equal to the fluctuations in the national stock of specie, i.e., there should be no secondary expansion or contraction through the medium of note issue; and (3) this rule would be violated if the Bank allowed an external drain of gold to operate, in part or in whole, on the amount of its deposit liabilities instead of on the amount of its note circulation. The currency school thus called for the same relationship between fluctuations in total note circulation, on the one hand, and fluctuations in specie reserves, on the other, which the Palmer rule required for fluctuations in total note *and deposit* circulation, on the one hand, and fluctuations in specie reserves, on the other hand. Since ordinarily, in case of an outflow of specie, if the Bank remained passive the primary contraction would be divided between the note circulation and the deposits, the currency school, and the Bank Act of 1844, in effect insisted upon a procedure which would require the Bank to support primary contraction by additional secondary contraction, whereas the Palmer rule called only for primary contraction. The

---

[1] Cf., however, Isaac Gervaise's treatment of "credit," in 1720, *supra*, p. 81.

banking school, on the other hand, held that it was possible for the Bank, without violating the currency principle or the Bank Act of 1844, to offset a primary contraction through the note issue by a secondary expansion through the deposits, so that the total stock of means of payment could still fluctuate differently in degree, and even in direction, from the total stock of specie, a position theoretically valid if the contention of the banking school be granted that the proportions of payments by notes and payments by checks could be freely varied by the banking system or by the public to counteract the restrictions on the amount of note issue.

Some recent writers have interpreted the classical doctrine as wholly overlooking what is here designated as primary fluctuations and as assigning to secondary fluctuations alone a direct role in the international mechanism. This interpretation appears to rest on the notion that the older writers regarded specie flows into or out of the reserves of the banks as having no effect on the total circulating medium except as, by affecting the reserve status of the banks, they induced the banks to expand or contract their loans, or, in other words, to engage in secondary expansion or contraction. In fact, however, the writers of the first half of the nineteenth century tended, as has been argued above, to overemphasize the role of primary fluctuations in the mechanism and to ignore or minimize the role of supporting secondary expansion or contraction, and, except in the case of the banking school, this was especially true for secondary fluctuations which took the form of fluctuations in the amount of deposits. That writers of the period explicitly recognized that flows of specie into or out of the banks constituted direct changes in the amount of the national stock of means of payment when the banks acquired specie through the surrender of notes or deposits or surrendered specie in exchange for notes or checks on deposits, the following citations should suffice to demonstrate:

If, during the prevalence of an unfavorable foreign exchange, the balances [of London bankers with the Bank of England] are reduced by cheques drawn upon the Bank, and finally by payments in gold, for exportation, then—unless the bankers themselves export the gold on their own account, which seldom or never happens—the balances due to their various depositors, and consequently the quantity of money in the metropolis, is as effectually reduced as if the outstanding notes of the Bank were reduced by the redemption of securities in its possession, and the bankers' deposits at the Bank to remain unaltered.

On the other hand, during the prevalence of a favorable foreign exchange, and the consequent influx of gold from abroad, whether the imported gold is held by the bankers, or placed by them in deposit at the Bank, the quantity of money in the metropolis is as effectually increased as it would be if the Bank of England were to give notes in exchange for the gold.[2]

. . . let us assume . . . that the bank, while holding £1,000,000 in coin, discounts bills and opens cash credits to the amount of £2,000,000. Now it is evident that in this case the 1,000,000 sovereigns deposited with the bank perform a double function. They constitute a money-in-hand power of purchasing, as regards the original depositors, who may draw them out on demand [i.e., primary expansion], and they form the basis of the credit-power of purchasing, which the holding of them enables the banker to extend to the customers to whom he grants discounts and cash credits [i.e., secondary expansion].[3]

[In case of a crop failure] the first import of provisions would very probably be paid for in bullion. I will assume that it is paid for at once, to the extent of £4,000,000; the effect of that is, that £4,000,000 of notes are canceled; the money of this country is diminished £4,000,000 in amount.[4]

In the earlier literature on the international mechanism there is one element of doctrine which does appear to give some semblance of validity to the interpretation of the classical school doctrines as ignoring the primary phase of the fluctuations in the currency resulting from specie movements, namely, the "hoards" doctrine of Fullarton, Tooke, and their followers, including, with qualifications, John Stuart Mill. These writers held that gold drains ordinarily come out of the hoards, consisting mainly of banking reserves, rather than out of the active coin or note circulation, and that the specie may be more largely withdrawn through checks on deposits than by presentation of notes for conversion into gold. It is by no means clear, however, that by

[2] James Pennington, in a letter published in Tooke, *A History of Prices*, II (1838), 377-78.

[3] Torrens, *Reply to the objections of the Westminster review*, 1844, p. 12.

[4] *The evidence, given by Lord Overstone, before the Select Committee . . . of 1857*, 1858, p. 181.

their hoards doctrine these writers intended to deny that specie movements ordinarily involved corresponding primary fluctuations in notes and deposits combined. J. S. Mill did, at one point, state that if the Bank of England kept adequate specie reserves a temporary gold drain could be met from these reserves without involving a "contraction either of credit or of the circulation."[5] But as I understand the context, what Mill had in mind was that if the Bank had adequate reserves it would be in a position to permit gold to go out by way of its deposits without either a reduction in its *note* circulation or a reduction in its "credit" or the amount of its loans and investments, i.e., that while a gold outflow would under these circumstances involve a primary contraction of the deposits it would not be necessary to make it result also in a secondary contraction of the notes or deposits. Fullarton also does not seem to have intended to deny that an inflow of gold into the Bank's reserves would constitute, or involve, a corresponding primary expansion of the circulation;[6] what he claimed was that this primary expansion would, or might, soon thereafter be offset by a counter secondary contraction.[7]

It was the later rather than the earlier, or classical, writers who tended to neglect the primary fluctuation phase. The growth of deposit banking in England resulted in a rapid growth of the ratio of bank money to specie, and in the latter half of the nineteenth century the total specie reserves appear always to have constituted less than five per cent of the total note and deposit liabilities to the public of the English banking system. Under these circumstances the primary effects of specie movements on the amount of the national stock of means of payment, unless they were of highly abnormal magnitude, could not be an important factor in maintaining international equilibrium, and it would be the supporting secondary expansion or contraction of

---

[5] *Principles,* Ashley ed., p. 670.

[6] Cf. *On the regulation of currencies,* 2d ed., 1845, p. 78: "for every ounce of gold received into the Bank of England, a corresponding weight in coin, or an equivalent in bank-notes [or in deposits?], is issued to the public."

[7] Cf. *ibid.,* p. 79: "The Bank meanwhile will have its notes flowing in fast, in payment of the bills of exchange previously in its hands, as they successively become due, while there will be no vent for its notes in fresh discounts; and the result of the whole will be, that, at the end perhaps of a week, the Bank will find itself with a million more of coin in its coffers, and a million less of securities." (I.e., the primary expansion of £1,000,000 would, after a week, be offset by a secondary contraction of £1,000,000.)

means of payment which would bear the main responsibility for keeping or restoring an even balance of payments. There resulted from these conditions a natural tendency for writers to pass over lightly or even wholly to ignore the primary effects of specie movements on the size of the national stock of means of payment, and to lay sole or main emphasis upon the secondary expansion or contraction induced by changes in the specie reserve position of the banking system.

The following passage from Sidgwick presents an early and unusually clear instance of total omission of—and therefore at least an implied denial of the operation of—the primary effects of specie movements :[8]

An increased supply of gold . . . tends ultimately to lower the purchasing power of money relatively to commodities generally ; but, in the first stage of the process that leads to this result, the increment of coin—or in England of notes representing the new gold in the issue department of the Bank—must pass through the hands of bankers,[9] and so increase the amount of the medium of exchange that they have to lend. Hence the price paid for the use of money will tend to fall, and this fall to cause increased borrowing, and consequent extended use of the medium of exchange ; and then through the resulting rise in prices generally, the greater part of the new coin or bank-notes will gradually pass into ordinary circulation. Thus the fall in the purchasing power of money, consequent on an influx of gold, will normally establish itself through an antecedent and connected fall in the value of the use of money.

In most modern expositions of the international mechanism, both English and American, the primary effects of specie movements are similarly left unmentioned, or by implication denied.

[8] Henry Sidgwick, *The principles of political economy,* 1st ed., 1883, p. 265. The same passage appears unchanged in the later editions.

[9] Angell comments on this passage: "No particular proof is offered to show why this is necessarily so. What we should now call the 'direct' effects of influxes of gold are rather passed by ; that is, the effects proceeding from outlays by the gold importers themselves, other than through the mediation of the banks." (*Theory of international prices,* p. 118, note.) This seems to be recognition of the omission by Sidgwick of what I call the "primary expansion" phase of the mechanism. But Angell comments on the passage as a whole, apparently with reference to Sidgwick's recognition of the role of interest rate fluctuations in the mechanism, that "it is at once apparent . . . that we have here something quite new in English theory." (*Ibid.,* p. 118.) As has been shown above, however, recognition of the part played by interest rate fluctuations was common during the currency controversies earlier in the century.

Explicit denial of the role of primary fluctuations, however, appears to be about as rare as explicit recognition of their role. Laughlin expressly denied that specie flowing into bank reserves, would operate to raise prices if it did not result in increased bank loans,[10] and Whitaker agreed with him on this point, but claimed that the inflow of specie *would* result in an increase in bank loans.[11] Marshall, on the other hand, apparently alone among modern writers until very recently, mentioned specifically both the primary fluctuation and the secondary fluctuation of the mechanism. He pointed out that while for England with its low ratio of specie to bank money the primary phase was unimportant, this might not be true for other countries where the actually circulating medium still consisted in large part of specie:

England is, in my opinion, but I speak with great diffidence, a specially bad example for India to follow in matters of currency. For, first, currency is but a small part of the means of payment used in England; and under most, though not all, conditions, bank money is the main means of payment; and that is elastic. Secondly, an imperative demand for increased currency is rare in England; and, when it does occur, it is on a very small scale relatively to England's total business and resources. The importation of the amount of ten millions of sovereigns makes an enormous difference in Lombard Street, but it is a mere nothing relatively to England's total business. Whereas, if the same difficulty arises in a country in which the main payments have to be made with currency itself, you want an importation of currency, or an increase of currency, standing in some moderately high relation to the total business of the country. . . .[12]

The following passage from Henry Seager seems to indicate recognition by him of both primary and secondary phases of the gold-flow mechanism:

Suppose . . . that the importation of gold has been induced by the low prices at which commodities are being sold in the importing country. Such importation will before long itself cause prices to rise, there being more money to serve as a medium of exchange than

---

[10] J. L. Laughlin, *Principles of money*, 1903, p. 387.

[11] A. C. Whitaker, "The Ricardian theory of gold movements," *Quarterly journal of economics*, XVIII (1904), 241 ff.

[12] Alfred Marshall, "Evidence before the Indian Currency Committee" [1899], reprinted in *Official papers by Alfred Marshall*, 1926, p. 282. ("Currency" is to be interpreted here as specie.) Cf. also *ibid.*, *Money credit & commerce*, 1923, p. 229.

before, while the withdrawal of gold from other countries will in time cause their prices to fall. These results will follow the more promptly because ordinarily the new gold will find its way into bank reserves and will add to the use of credit as a medium of exchange much more largely than it adds to the country's supply of standard money. In the same way its exportation will serve ordinarily to deplete bank reserves and to cause a contraction of credit that will lessen the supply of media of exchange by much more than the amount of gold lost.[13]

III. SHORT-TERM LOANS IN THE INTERNATIONAL MECHANISM

International short-term lending takes many forms; interbank credits, transfers of deposits, purchase of foreign bills of exchange, purchase of foreign treasury bills, commercial credits, purchase of long-term securities in a foreign market with the expectation of their early resale abroad, etc. Whatever form it takes, the international movement of short-term funds derives its importance for the mechanism of adjustment of international balances from the fact that these funds are highly mobile and in the absence of financial or political disturbance respond quickly, especially as between well-developed money markets, to even moderate relative fluctuations in interest rates. Since outward drains of gold ordinarily tend to result in rising rates of interest or at least to occur under circumstances which cause a rising rate of interest to be associated with them, and since inflows of gold are ordinarily similarly associated with falling rates of interest, the short-term funds and the specie are likely to move in opposite directions. Such movements of short-term funds in a reverse direction from the actual or incipient movement of specie are helpful to the international mechanism of adjustment in two main ways.

To take first the less important type of case, the balance of immediate obligations of any country is likely to be undergoing constant fluctuation and to be repeatedly shifting from a debit to a credit status. The most marked instances of such fluctuations in the balance of immediate obligations are to be found in countries whose export and import trade have marked and divergent seasonal patterns. If such countries did not resort to international

---

[13] *Principles of economics,* 1913, p. 370.

short-term credit operations, specie would repeatedly have to be exported in substantial quantities to liquidate a debit balance, only to return soon thereafter upon the development of a credit balance. If such countries have well-developed money markets, such credit operations will take place through the ·initiative of individual banks or traders, in response to the seasonal relative shifts in interest rates at home and abroad. These operations will be further stimulated, moreover, by seasonal fluctuations in exchange rates resulting from the seasonal fluctuations in the trade balance. This goes counter to the doctrine sometimes expounded that the cost of shipping gold, or the deviation of the exchanges from the mint par, acts as a deterrent to the movement of short-term funds in response to small differentials in interest rates.[1] This doctrine overlooks the fact that the movements of short-term funds and of gold are frequently, and perhaps in the majority of cases, in opposite directions rather than in the same direction, and that when the former is the case the turn of the exchanges which is to be anticipated is a stimulus rather than a deterrent to short-term movements of funds. An individual in a country whose currency is above par in the exchange market who lends in terms of the foreign currency to a country whose currency is below par stands to profit not only from whatever interest differential he can obtain but also from the gain on the turn of the exchanges which may be expected to occur, and for which he can wait before recalling his funds.[2] When the movement of short-term funds is in the opposite direction from the actual or incipient movement of gold, it operates to reduce the extent of the gold movement to a corresponding degree.

Secondly, a major disturbance of international equilibrium requiring for its complete adjustment a more or less enduring contraction of means of payment and deflation of prices in some country may come so suddenly, or may have been so long neglected by the banking authorities of that country, that if short-

---

[1] Cf., e.g., G. J. Goschen, *The theory of the foreign exchanges*, 1861, pp. 129-30, and R. G. Hawtrey, *The art of central banking*, 1932, p. 142.

[2] If the gain which can be anticipated on the turn of the exchanges exceeds the loss on the interest differential, it will pay even to transfer funds from the high to the low interest rate market. The amount of differential in interest rates necessary to move short-term funds in the same direction as the gold movements will be greater than the amount of differential in interest rates necessary to move them in the opposite direction from the gold movements.

term loans could not be made abroad a large amount of gold would have to be exported at once and bank credit contracted suddenly and sharply, with the danger that a major crisis would result. By resort to borrowing on short-term abroad, the necessary drain of gold can be spread over a longer period and even reduced in its total amount, and bank credit can be more gently and gradually contracted, thus avoiding or moderating the internal crisis.

This cushioning effect of short-term loans is especially important for long-term capital-exporting countries, where the flotation of foreign issues is likely to be irregularly spaced. Suppose, for instance, that country A floats the first of a series of great long-term loans in country B, whose balance of payments had previously been in approximate equilibrium. Even if the flotation of the loan were followed immediately by a substantial transfer of specie from B to A, and by supporting secondary expansion of means of payment in A and secondary contraction of means of payment in B, it would still ordinarily take some time before the demands for and the prices of commodities in the two countries would shift sufficiently to effect a transfer of the remainder of the loan in the form of commodities. In the meantime there would have been a heavy and unnecessarily large specie movement, an excessive credit expansion in the borrowing country, and an even more disturbing credit deflation in the lending country. But if the short-term money markets of the two countries are flexible and responsive to differentials in money rates, there will be a rise in short-term interest rates in B and a fall in A which will induce A to lend B on short term some of the funds it has borrowed from B on long term. The adverse balance of immediate obligations of B to A will thus be lessened; the flow of specie from B to A will be reduced; and the long-term loan will obtain transfer in the form of commodities more smoothly and with less disturbance to the economies of the two countries, even if more slowly.

The role of short-term capital movements as an equilibrating factor is limited, however, by the imperfect international mobility of such funds. While, in the absence of "fear movements," the international movement of short-term funds *tends* to bring about equality of short-term interest rates in different money markets, the amount of short-term funds which will move across national frontiers in response to moderate differentials in interest rates is for many frontiers always, and for all frontiers frequently, insufficient in quantity to bring about actual equality of interest rates or to reduce to-and-fro movements of gold to a minimum.[3]

When a central bank, in order to check an expansion of bank credit, raises its discount rate or engages in selling operations in the open market, the resultant rise in the market rate of interest tends to attract foreign funds. It has become the custom to say that an inflow of short-term funds under these circumstances may offset or even more than offset the efforts of the central bank to bring about contraction in the amount of means of payment,[4] but this overlooks the fact that the foreign funds will flow in only as the market rate becomes higher than it was previously. The inflow of short-term funds under these circumstances will provide the member banks with increased reserve assets and thus lessen their dependence on the central bank, and will operate to reduce the degree of response of the market rate to the central bank rate. But the market rate must rise *somewhat* if foreign funds are to be attracted, and at this higher rate the amounts borrowers are willing to borrow will presumably fall, while the higher cost of their borrowed reserves will check the willingness of the banks to lend.

It is true, however, that variations in the market rate of interest in response to variations in the specie reserve position of the banking system, whether these variations in the market rate of interest occur automatically or as the result of central bank manipulations of its discount rate, do tend to convert the fluctuations in the exchange rates from such as would exercise a direct equilibrating influence on the trade balance to such as would exercise a direct disequilibrating influence on the trade balance. Suppose that a relative shift in demand for commodities results in an adverse trade balance and an adverse balance of payments

---

[3] Axel Nielsen warns against exaggerating the international mobility of short-term capital: it is only a fraction of the short-term funds that is truly "cosmopolitan,"—*Bankpolitik*, II (1930), 279 ff., as cited by Carl Iverson, *Aspects of the theory of international capital movements*, 1935, p. 239.

[4] Cf., e.g.: A. F. W. Plumptre, "Central banking machinery and monetary policy," *The Canadian economy and its problems*, 1934, p. 197; A. D. Gayer, *Monetary policy and economic stabilization*, 1935, pp. 10-11; W. Edwards Beach, *British international gold movements and banking policy, 1881-1913*, 1935, pp. 17-18.

for England. Let us first assume that no change occurs in the English market rate of interest. Sterling will fall in the foreign exchange markets, with a consequent stimulus to English exports and check to English imports. Let us next assume that the external drain of specie results in a relative rise in the English market rate of interest, and that this attracts a flow of short-term funds to England, which stops the external drain of specie and causes sterling to rise in the exchange markets, possibly to higher than the mint parities. The direct equilibrating influence of the exchange rate fluctuations on the English trade balance is lost, and may even give place to a direct disequilibrating influence. So limited, however, is the possible range of exchange rate fluctuations under an international metallic standard that their direct influence on trade balances must be of negligible proportions, and it cannot be regarded as an important drawback to the use of variations in the discount rate to maintain or restore equilibrium in international balances that it prevents exchange rate fluctuations from exercising a direct equilibrating influence.

While short-term lending has a useful role to play in the international mechanism, it is capable, nevertheless, and more so than any other element in the mechanism, of operating perversely. International short-term lending still awaits its historian, but there have been notorious cases, and especially in recent years, where the erratic and unpredictable movement of short-term funds has influenced the international mechanism during a period of stress very much in the manner in which loose cargo operates on a ship during a storm. The high degree of international mobility of short-term funds becomes a liability instead of an asset when there is alarm in the air, for short-term funds are quick to fly to foreign countries in search of safety when there is alarm at home, and are even quicker to be called back home when there are signs of trouble abroad.

Disturbances to international equilibrium resulting from the excessive mobility—or timidity—of short-term funds appear to be an ancient phenomenon. During the Napoleonic Wars, for instance, there were substantial fluctuations in the foreign holdings of British securities which were at the time believed by some to have been due more largely to the rise and fall of confidence in the military fortunes of England or in the future of the paper pound than to relative fluctuations in the interest rate,[5] and which may therefore have operated rather to accentuate than to moderate the fluctuations in the gold value of the inconvertible paper pound.[6] Later in the century, the growth in the international movement of funds attracted considerable attention, but most observers regarded this development as a wholly desirable one.[7] Some writers held that the development of international movement of short-term funds had rendered specie movements, changes in price levels, and even adjustments of trade balances unnecessary except in major disturbances.[8] An occasional note of warning was struck,

---

[5] Cf., however, Henry Thornton, with reference to what would happen under a metallic standard and with no legal restrictions in interest rates if England's exports were curtailed by embargoes or other wartime disturbances:

Doubtless much of our gold coin would be taken from us; and, perhaps, a larger quantity of this than of other articles. The whole, however, would not leave us; a high rate of interest would arise, and this extra profit on the use of gold, which would increase as its quantity diminished, would contribute to detain it here—some foreigners, probably, transferring property which would take the shape of the precious metals, or continuing to afford to us the use of it for the sake of this high interest. (*Substance of two speeches . . . on the bullion report*, 1811, p. 10.)

[6] Cf. (Commons) *Report . . . on the expediency of the Bank resuming cash payments*, 1819, appendix no. 43, p. 354; Sir John Sinclair, *The history of the public revenue of the British Empire*, 3d ed., III [1804], appendix no. 5, pp. 160-63; John Hill, *An inquiry into the causes of the present high price of gold bullion in England*, 1810, p. 36; G. R. Porter, *The progress of the nation*, new ed., 1851, pp. 628-29.

[7] Cf. David Salomons, *A defence of the joint-stock banks*, 2d ed., 1837, p. 12:

. . . I . . . assert that their transmission [i.e., of British funds for investment abroad] has on the whole been favorable to commerce, that they have tended to regulate the exchanges, instead of having had an injurious effect on them; and many most important payments could not have been made, without the powerful assistance derived from the export of foreign stock, as the most ready means of payment. It will be, indeed, difficult to show how such descriptions of foreign funds, for which a ready market exists on the Continent as well as in London, could at all injuriously affect the exchanges. Such funds are, in truth, a universal currency, and payments either at home or abroad can be made by their transmission, and the balance of trade as readily adjusted, as by an import or export of the previous metals.

[8] Cf. Fullarton, *On the regulation of currencies*, 2d ed., 1845, p. 149:

Since the practice, however, of investing capital in foreign securities has become general in this country, a new element has been introduced into the economy of our exchanges. The capital required for the liquidation of a foreign debt may be transmitted as well in the form of a marketable security for money, as in gold or merchandise. And, as the price of such securities rises and falls with the fall and rise of the market rate of interest, and the securities themselves accordingly are in a continual course of transition from places where the rate of interest is high to places where it

however. Milner, for instance, although he regarded the development as on the whole a desirable one, saw that international capital movements could act as a disturbing as well as an equilibrating factor, and therefore recommended state control of the export of capital either directly or through regulation of the English discount rate with reference to prevailing rates abroad, both with a view to conserving ample capital resources for English industry and to guard against undue pressure on the English balance of payments.[9] It was pointed out also that if there was distrust of the financial situation funds might flow from the high-rate to the low-rate money market, and that attempts by the former to check the drain by raising the discount rate still further might serve only to increase the distrust and to accentuate the drain.[10] But scarcely a voice was raised during the nineteenth century in England to warn the banking authorities that short-term indebtedness to foreigners should be treated as special claims against specie reserves, and that extra precautions should be taken to provide the means to meet such claims.[11] The fact that in English pre-war banking practice neither the Bank of England nor the clearinghouse banks sold their own bills to banks abroad and that the English holdings of short-term claims on the rest of the world were certainly in ordinary times and probably at all times substantially in excess of the foreign holdings of short-term claims on England was at least a partial justification of this complacency. But there were always, nevertheless, substantial holdings of sterling bills abroad, and substantial deposits of foreign funds with London "foreign" banks, and when for any reason foreigners asked for their funds the clearinghouse

---

is low, the fluctuations of interest have become an engine of some importance in the regulation of the exchanges, and, to the extent of their action, are found certainly a more manageable and safe instrument for facilitating foreign payments and correcting irregularities in the distribution of the precious metals, than the fluctuations of price.

Cf. also, *supra,* pp. 278 ff.

[9] T. H. Milner, *Some remarks on the Bank of England,* 1849, pp. 17 ff., 42. He claims that "the regulation of foreign investment is . . . the effectual key to the regulation of the monetary affairs of the country." (*Ibid.,* p. 18.)

[10] Cf. "History and exposition of the currency question," *Westminster and foreign quarterly review,* XLVIII (1848), 468, note: "the depression of English securities may as often induce the foreign capitalist to withdraw his gold from England, by alarming him for its safety, as to send it here for profitable investment."

[11] Cf. *supra,* p. 271, for one such warning in 1857.

banks and the Bank of England were indirectly called upon to meet these demands. The development in the post-war period of the practice by central and other banks of deliberately holding part of their reserves on deposit or otherwise invested in foreign money markets added to the danger, first, because it increased the amount of short-term foreign funds held in the money markets most used for this purpose, namely, London and New York, and, second, because bank funds, and especially funds regarded by the creditor banks as constituting part of their reserves, were more likely than the funds of private investors to be withdrawn simultaneously and suddenly upon the appearance of some signs of lack of safety in the investment or of impending need of extra financial resources at home. There was little outward sign of recognition by banking authorities in the countries having particularly large external short-term indebtedness that such liabilities required special treatment.[12] Bank authorities of these countries do not appear even to have made much effort to keep informed as to the amount and trend of such indebtedness, until, as the depression beginning in 1929 continued and became more intense, there occurred extraordinarily great flights of short-term funds from country to country, in which the central banks[13] participated at least as actively as did other banks and private individuals.[14]

---

[12] Cf., however, *Thirteenth annual report of the Federal Reserve Board*, 1927, p. 16:

> Dollar balances in New York have been built up not only by foreign industrial corporations and commercial banks but also by European and South American central banks, which in many instances are authorized by law to keep a portion of their reserves in the form of foreign exchange in countries with stable currencies. These dollar balances of foreign central banks, whether they are invested or kept on deposit, are in liquid form and subject to immediate withdrawal at any time. If they were to be withdrawn in gold in whole or in part the demand for the gold, though it would first be felt by the commercial banks, both member and nonmember, would promptly reach the federal reserve banks as the only holders of gold in any considerable amount. These balances are, therefore, potential sources of demand upon the federal reserve banks for gold out of their reserves, the central banking reserves of the United States, which have thus become indirectly a part of the reserves against bank credit and currencies in other countries. The existence in America of these foreign balances consequently presents a condition in the banking situation to be taken into account in determining the federal reserve system's credit policy with a view to maintaining the country's banking system in a position to meet demands for gold from abroad without disturbing business and credit conditions in this country.

[13] In their hasty abandonment of the gold-exchange standard, the European

Where the agencies concerned are private individuals or business firms, there is no easy solution for the problem of excess mobility of short-term funds, since direct regulation of such movement would be troublesome, costly, and, unless reinforced by censorship of communications, easily evaded. But the chief offenders have been banks, including central banks operating under the so-called gold-exchange standard, and here certain fairly practicable remedies seem to be indicated. The only legitimate functions of the gold-exchange standard are to facilitate international payments and to eliminate the expense of to-and-fro gold movements occurring within short intervals of time. But the claim often made for it, that it enables poor countries to adhere to the gold standard without bearing the burden of maintaining non-income-earning gold reserves, makes a virtue out of the gold-exchange standard's defect. Either the expense of carrying such reserves is transferred to the country in which the reserve funds are invested, or else that country assumes dangerous liabilities against its own reserves without adopting protective measures. Properly administered, the gold-exchange standard would approximate in its mode of operation to reciprocal earmarking of gold. Central banks would still count their holdings of claims on foreign banks as part of their reserves. But they would treat their own liabilities and the liabilities of member banks to foreign banks as demand claims against their own reserves, and would enforce very high specie reserve ratios against such liabilities. No central bank would invest funds at interest in another

---

banks of issue, according to a computation of the Banque de France, reduced their holdings of foreign short-term funds from 48,464,405,000 francs French on January 1, 1931, to 3,921,500,000 francs French on November 30, 1933, or by more than 95 per cent. The ratio of such funds to the total reserves of these banks fell during the same period from about 35 per cent to about 2½ per cent. (Cf. *Federal Reserve bulletin,* March, 1934, p. 164.)

[14] From March 31, 1931, to the middle of July, 1931, withdrawals of foreign short-term funds from Germany amounted to over 1,000,000,000 marks, or over 20 per cent of the total short-term foreign indebtedness of Germany at the earlier date—"The Wiggin report," Annex V, *Economist,* CXIII (Aug. 22, 1931), supplement, p. 6. From June 30, 1931, to November 30, 1931, the American dollar acceptances in Europe—mostly in Germany—were reduced from about $500,000,000 to about $300,000,000 (*New York Times,* Jan. 4, 1932, p. 32). These withdrawals would of course have been even greater and more rapid if the debtors had met all the demands made upon them by their creditors. During this period, money rates were substantially higher in Germany than in the creditor countries, i.e., funds were moving from a high-rate money market to low-rate money markets.

country except in or through the mediation of the central bank of that country, at the request of such central bank, and to aid it during a crisis rather than to earn interest on reserve assets. Such a reform would not be costless, and would not completely remedy the situation, but it would reduce to much smaller proportions one of the major defects of the international gold standard as it has operated in modern times.

The Gold Delegation of the League of Nations has defended the use of the gold-exchange standard as a means of economizing for poor countries the cost of maintaining gold reserves, and has proposed, as a remedy for the problem of the excess mobility of short-term funds, that "it is necessary for lending countries to assure that foreign lending does not exceed or fall short of their net active balance on income account."[15] Taken literally, this would mean that any country having a favorable balance of immediate obligations on commodity and service account should feel obligated to lend sufficiently abroad to prevent any inflow of gold, and presumably also that any country having an unfavorable balance on commodity and service account should feel warranted in borrowing sufficiently abroad to prevent any outflow of gold. Gold flows, under such a regime, would either not occur at all, or would occur only in connection with the liquidation of old debts. This is surprising doctrine to be found in a document intended to be a plea for the maintenance and rehabilitation of the international gold standard. Under such a regime, balances, favorable or unfavorable, on income account would never be liquidated.[16]

[15] League of Nations, *Report of the Gold Delegation of the Financial Committee*, 1932, p. 52.

[16] The validity of this interpretation depends on how the Gold Delegation would deal with a situation such as the following: country A has a favorable balance of trade with country B, and in accordance with the rule laid down lends to B the funds with which to meet that balance. Next week, B repays this debt. Is the payment on capital account, and therefore such as to justify gold shipments, or is it on income account, and therefore to be countered by country A by a new loan to country B or to some third country? If the former answer is correct, then the proposal of the Gold Delegation amounts merely to the recommendation that specie movements should never occur immediately whenever there is not an even balance of payments on income account, but should always be delayed until they can take the form of liquidation of capital liabilities. If the latter answer is correct, as seems to me to be the case, then no gold movements would ever occur except in connection with the amortization of borrowings not made to liquidate preexisting indebtedness on income

IV. PRIMARY AND SECONDARY EXPANSION IN CANADA, 1900-13

"Canada's Balance."—The Canadian experience before the war during a period of great import of capital provides an opportunity for the examination of the role of primary and secondary expansion in the international mechanism in a gold standard country where the banking system keeps part of its reserves in the form of holdings of outside short-term funds. In a study I made of the Canadian mechanism from 1900 to 1913,[1] I reached the following conclusions with respect to the monetary aspects of the mechanism. The Canadian borrowings obtained transfer into Canada smoothly and without noticeable friction in the form of a net commodity and service import surplus, as the result of relative price changes (and shifts in demands) which were of the character indicated as to be expected by the older writers. The price and demand changes resulted from a relative increase in the amounts of Canadian bank money, deposits and notes, and these increases resulted in turn mainly from the exchange by Canadian borrowers abroad of the proceeds in foreign funds of their borrowings abroad for Canadian bank deposits or notes. The Canadian banks brought into Canada in the form of specie only such part of their newly-acquired foreign funds as was required to maintain their specie reserve ratios in Canada at their customary level. The remainder of the foreign funds thus acquired by the banks, to the extent that they were not absorbed in paying for the growing Canadian import surplus, was left abroad by the Canadian banks, largely in the form of call loans in New York, as additions to their "outside" or "secondary" reserves. Except toward the end of the period, when a marked credit expansion occurred in Canada, the increase in the outside reserves was not used by the Canadian banks as a basis for expansion of their loans in Canada. With the exception that fluctuations in the outside reserves operated in the Canadian mechanism in the manner attributed to specie movements in the classical doctrine, I concluded that the Canadian mechanism corresponded in all its

---

account, while borrowings could be made only for the purpose of such liquidation.

[1] *Canada's balance of international indebtedness 1900-1913,* 1924, chap. VIII.

important aspects to the mechanism as formulated in the classical doctrine.

In my study I did not use the "primary," "secondary" terminology developed in the preceding sections of this chapter. Applied to the Canadian data, the meaning of primary expansion would have to be broadened, so as to include increases in Canadian bank deposits and notes resulting from the exchange by Canadian borrowers abroad of foreign funds for Canadian bank money, whether the Canadian banks exchanged these foreign funds for specie and brought the specie into Canada or held the foreign funds as secondary or outside reserves, as the economic significance of the two types of reserves was, dollar for dollar, the same. Restated in terms of the primary and secondary terminology, my explanation of the monetary phases of the Canadian mechanism was, therefore, that foreign borrowings by Canadians, to the extent that their proceeds in foreign funds were not used up immediately in paying for import surpluses, resulted in a primary expansion of Canadian means of payment through the exchange of foreign funds for Canadian bank money, and that the Canadian banks converted only a fraction of these foreign funds into specie. To secondary expansion, resulting from the expansion of bank loans in Canada, I attributed importance, as a supporting factor reinforcing the primary expansion, only for the last few years of the period.

Angell's Criticism of the Account in "Canada's Balance." —Angell[2] and a number of writers who follow him, have raised some important objections against my account of the Canadian mechanism. Angell finds fault with my conclusion that fluctuations in the outside reserves played the same role in the Canadian mechanism as that assigned to gold movements in the classical doctrine. His failure to state in what respects he believed the actual Canadian mechanism was different from that postulated in the classical doctrine makes it difficult to deal with this criticism. But I believe that he here interprets the classical doctrine as assigning a role only to secondary fluctuations, and as ignoring totally the primary fluctuations. In any case, he attributes to me

---

[2] J. W. Angell: review of *Canada's balance* in *Political science quarterly*, XL (1925), 320-22; "The effects of international payments in the past," National Industrial Conference Board, *The inter-ally debts and the United States*, 1925, pp. 140-53; *The theory of international prices*, 1926, pp. 170-74, 505-10.

the proposition that it was secondary expansion which did the work in the Canadian mechanism, although I am now convinced that I overemphasized the primary phase, both with reference to the facts in Canada and with reference to the classical doctrine.

Angell's own interpretation of the Canadian mechanism is that the expansion of Canadian deposits which operated to adjust the Canadian trade balances to the borrowings was a primary expansion, but a primary expansion of a very special sort, resulting from the exchange of *sterling* funds, but of no other sort of outside funds, for Canadian deposits. Although I carefully explained in my study that the outside reserves consisted "of funds loaned on call in New York *and London*, and net balances kept with New York *and London* banks,"[3] he always interprets my propositions with respect to "outside reserves" as if I meant them to apply only to New York funds, and uses the term in this way himself. To understand his account of the Canadian mechanism and his criticism of my account, it is necessary, therefore, to remember that Angell excludes sterling funds from "outside reserves," wrongly attributes the same exclusion to me, and treats fluctuations in the Canadian bank holdings of sterling and of New York funds, respectively, as if they had radically different significance for the mechanism.

Angell's objections to my account of the Canadian mechanism are for the most part covered by the following paragraph :[4]

. . . Viner's verification of the general theory . . . I think . . . breaks down on this question of the intermediary financial mechanisms. Neither the statistical data submitted nor the reasoning based upon them show any clear sequence *from* the outside reserves *to* credit and price conditions within Canada itself. Outside reserves moved closely with bank deposits in Canada, and showed no independent relationship to prices. Rather, the sequence must have been that which Viner himself rather hesitantly suggests at another point.[5]

---

[3] *Canada's balance*, p. 177. (The italics were not in the original text.) Cf. also *ibid.*, p. 164, and the explanation given of the constituent items in my "secondary reserves" series in chart II, pp. 166-67, as "Call loans elsewhere than in Canada, and net balances due from banks outside Canada."

[4] *Theory of international prices*, pp. 172-73. (Italics in the original text.)

[5] Angell's impression that there were two versions derives from the distinction which he makes between the significance for the mechanism of fluctuations in the holdings of sterling and of New York funds, respectively, a distinction I did not make.

The Canadian borrowers, having sterling funds at their disposal, deposited them with the Canadian banks (except in so far as the loans were spent in England). These funds, thus converted into Canadian currency and credit, were spent in Canada and induced a rise in prices; a rise which roughly adjusted the commodity balance of trade to the volume of new borrowings. The Canadian banks recouped themselves by selling the sterling funds in New York, the proceeds being left there or taken back to Canada as needed. It does not appear from the data, however, that these changes in the *New York* balances had any direct and independent effect upon conditions within Canada. By providing potential additional metallic reserves, their increase made a Canadian credit expansion *possible*, but there is no convincing evidence, inductive or deductive, to show that it provided the initial stimulus to expansion.[6] The stimulus came, rather, from the original increase in bank deposits within Canada itself.

Angell thus interprets the Canadian expansion of deposits as being solely[7] a primary expansion, resulting (solely?) from the

---

[6] Angell means presumably by "credit expansion" what I here call secondary expansion, and by "direct" effect on the volume of Canadian deposits what I here call primary expansion. Angell's failure to notice the meaning and importance I attached to the fluctuations in "foreign loan deposits" is responsible not only for his own error in attributing to me the doctrine that secondary expansion was the important factor, but for a similar error on the part of a number of other writers who have obviously accepted Angell's account of my position as accurate. Cf. especially, Iversen, who takes me to task for neglecting what I did my utmost to emphasize, and, I now believe, in fact overemphasized: "Here again Viner seems to underestimate the implications of his restatement, which clearly suggests a *direct* connection between foreign loans and volume of purchasing power." (*Aspects of the theory of international capital movements,* 1935, p. 236. Italics in original.)

[7] That this is a correct interpretation of Angell's position is indicated by the following and other similar passages: "The crux of the explanation is the proposition that the importation of capital increases the supply of bills offered in the local exchange market for discount relative to the demand, thus increasing the bank's average holdings of such bills. A *corresponding* increase in the volume of bank deposits results, and if it is on a large scale produces the indicated effects on prices and the commodity balance of trade." (*Theory of international prices,* p. 173, note. Italics not in original text.) If the fluctuations in deposits "corresponded" with the fluctuations in holdings of foreign "bills," the fluctuations in deposits would be solely primary. Angell sometimes speaks of the bills being "discounted," and sometimes of their being "exchanged" for deposits, and treats these as identical phenomena. The latter was the usual procedure, as the bills were predominantly sight bills, frequently drawn on an outside agency of a Canadian bank. Under the former procedure, an original secondary expansion would be transformed, after a few weeks, into a primary expansion when the bills became due and their proceeds were used by their owners to liquidate their indebtedness to the Canadian banks. The volume of

exchange of *sterling* funds for Canadian deposits, while he attributes to me the doctrine that the Canadian expansion of deposits was (solely?) a secondary expansion, i.e., resulted from an expansion of bank loans in Canada, into which the banks were led by the increase in their holdings of outside reserves in the form of New York funds. He presents no evidence to support his account of the role I assigned to secondary expansion, and it has no other basis, I am convinced, than Angell's assumption that when I found similarity between the role of fluctuations in the outside reserves in Canada and the role of gold movements in the classical mechanism, I must have had in mind the use of gold reserves as a basis for expansion of deposits through loans. I had in mind, on the contrary, what I now call the primary phase of gold movements in the mechanism. Instead of stressing secondary expansion in the Canadian mechanism, I ignored it except for the last few years of the period studied. And instead of comparing the fluctuations in total deposits, or in loans, or in total deposits minus outside reserves, with the fluctuations in outside reserves, as would have been appropriate if the secondary fluctuations were regarded as important, I paid no attention to the fluctuations in the *aggregate* volume of bank loans in Canada, and I compared the fluctuations in outside reserves with the fluctuations in "foreign loan deposits," i.e., total deposits *minus* loans, i.e., the deposits *not* resulting from Canadian bank loans.[8]

The distinction which Angell draws between the role of sterling funds and the role of New York funds in the Canadian mechanism seems to me without basis, either in theory or statistically. Sterling funds and New York funds were equally "outside reserves." The fluctuations in the net holdings of sterling funds were throughout the period small in amount, as the Canadian banks *immediately* converted sterling funds, if in excess of the small

---

Canadian deposits would not change, but the offsetting bank assets would change from loans to holdings of foreign funds.

[8] The relationship I trace for Canada between the "outside reserves" and the "foreign loan deposits" corresponds closely to the relationship emphasized in recent years by students of Australian and New Zealand banking between the holdings of London funds by Australasian banks and the variations in the excess of domestic deposits over domestic advances. Cf. e.g., A. H. Tocker, "The measurement of business conditions in New Zealand," *Economic record,* I (1925), 51 ff.; K. S. Isles, "Australian monetary policy," *ibid.,* VII (1931), 1-17; Roland Wilson, "Australian monetary policy reviewed," *ibid.,* 195-215.

amounts needed as working balances for remittance purposes, into New York funds or into specie. It was, moreover, the *maintenance*, and not merely the *acquisition*, of outside funds, upon which the volume of primary Canadian deposits depended, since the reduction of outside reserves to meet the need for foreign payments would, for the banks, be balanced by a corresponding amount of debits charged against the deposits of Canadian customers for whom the foreign payments were being made. Even when first acquired, furthermore, not all the outside funds were sterling funds, since somewhat over 30 per cent of the total Canadian borrowings during the period were made elsewhere than in England (chiefly in the United States). The conversion of sterling funds into New York funds simply happened to serve the convenience of the Canadian banks, and had no other significance. Held in New York, their outside funds could earn higher rates of interest than in London and in case of need could be converted into gold and brought into Canada overnight with a minimum risk of exchange loss.[9]

Angell further interprets me as holding that the expansion of Canadian deposits (always?) came later in time than the expansion of outside reserves. He again presents no evidence to support this interpretation but it is probably only a logical inference from his erroneous attribution to me of the proposition that the expansion of Canadian deposits was a secondary expansion, induced by the improved secondary reserve position of the Canadian banks. He maintains that, on the contrary, the expansion of deposits preceded the expansion of outside reserves.[10]

Angell's claim that in fact the increase in Canadian deposits was prior to the increase in outside reserves seems to be the product of the following chain of reasoning: (1) Canadian borrowings were (solely?) from England and therefore yielded sterling funds; (2) the Canadian borrowers exchanged these sterling

---

[9] Cf. *Canada's balance*, p. 155.

[10] Cf. especially, *Theory of international prices*, p. 174:

But I think that Professor Viner's data warrant the inference—despite the opposite conclusion which he himself draws—that the classical theory is erroneous with respect to the role of gold flows, under modern conditions. The correction of the maladjustment in trade produced by the loans did not come from the effects of the gold flows, or of changes in the outside bank balances. It came from the effects of the original (and prior) increase in Canadian bank deposits.

funds for Canadian deposits; (3) some time after[11] such exchange had occurred, the Canadian banks converted the sterling funds into New York funds; (4) New York funds were, but sterling funds were not, "outside reserves" nor apparently, even "outside bank balances"; (5) the (primary) increase in Canadian deposits was therefore prior to the increase in "outside reserves." Since, however, sterling funds were, dollar for dollar, just as much "outside reserves" as were New York funds; since Canadian borrowings occurred in the United States as well as in England, so that some of the outside reserves were originally acquired in the form of American dollars; and since the Canadian banks converted newly-acquired sterling funds into New York funds almost instantaneously rather than after a substantial delay, this argument collapses. The primary expansion in Canadian deposits was neither prior to the expansion in outside reserves, as Angell claims, nor after it, the view which he attributes to me, but was, as I contended, simultaneous with it.

Feis, after citing with approval Angell's conclusion that the increase in Canadian bank deposits is the "original" and "prior" factor operating to correct the Canadian balance of payments, attempts to explain more explicitly than did Angell what is to be understood by "original" and "prior" .[12]

By "original" Dr. Angell meant to distinguish, I venture to interpret, the immediate credit expansion from any increase that might result later from the strengthening of gold reserves; by "prior" is meant prior in time to any such increase of gold reserves.

That the primary expansion in Canadian bank deposits resulting from the exchange of the proceeds of foreign borrowings for Canadian deposits—which it is misleading to refer to as "credit expansion" since its significant characteristic was that it was *not* Canadian credit expansion—would be prior to any secondary expansion of Canadian bank deposits resulting from the improvement in the reserves is obvious. But how could this primary ex-

---

[11] Angell seems to ,think that the Canadian banks converted their sterling funds into New York funds only after the increase in Canadian deposits had resulted in a rise in prices and an increase in the Canadian import surplus. (Cf. quotations from Angell, pp. 416 and 418, note 10, *supra.*)

[12] Herbert Feis, "The mechanism of adjustment of international trade balances," *American economic review*, XVI (1926), 597. Feis explains that he uses the term "gold reserves" to include both the specie reserves held in Canada and the "outside reserves."

pansion also be prior to the increase in outside reserves? Feis states that the (primary) expansion of Canadian bank deposits and the increase in outside reserves are "both results of the same borrowing operations. In that vital sense they are interdependent; in other ways they may be said to be independent. They, therefore, must be recognized as playing separate parts in the mechanism of adjustment."[13] But this, while not very helpful, suggests simultaneity rather than priority.[14] The increase in outside reserves and the primary increase in deposits *must* have occurred simultaneously unless, indeed, if it should be found that in banking practice the bank clerks regularly debit the bank before they credit the customer, or vice versa, someone could be found who would attach significance to a priority of this sort and would expect it to reveal itself in "lags" in monthly (or annual!) banking data.

Carr presents the following as a summary of my findings:

The surplus of bills on London created by English loans to Canada never attained great enough proportions to force sterling rates to the gold import point for Canada. Instead of permitting London bills to accumulate on the Canadian market and depress exchange quotations, the Canadian banks sold them to New York, and thereby built up their New York balances or "outside reserves." But on the basis of these outside reserves the Canadian banks were able to extend credit at home. Price inflation resulted as if gold had been imported. In other words, a substitute was found for the gold flow in the Canadian case in the form of increased outside reserves. The sequence of events, then, according to Professor Viner, was this: (1) foreign borrowing, (2) increase in outside reserves, (3) extension of credit at home.[15]

The notion that the motive of the Canadian banks in exchanging London funds for New York funds was to prevent a depres-

---

[13] *Ibid.* pp. 598-99.

[14] Feis, however, seems to have followed Angell in excluding sterling funds from the "outside reserves," and in taking it for granted that there was a substantial lag between the accumulation by the Canadian banks of sterling funds and their conversion into New York funds, and thus may merely be repeating Angell's argument. Cf. Feis, *op. cit.,* p. 598: "Canadian banks sell their London funds to New York banks, thereby accumulating outside reserves." Such sales would leave the outside reserves unchanged in amount and would change only their form.

[15] Robert M. Carr, "The role of price in the international trade mechanism," *Quarterly journal of economics,* XLV (1931), 711.

sion of sterling exchange on the (non-existent!) Canadian sterling exchange market is assuredly not mine.[16] The notion that outside funds constituted outside reserves only if they were New York funds should have been credited to Angell, but not to me. Finally, secondary expansion of Canadian deposits through an expansion of domestic bank loans[17] induced by an improved bank reserve position was not an important element in my explanation of the expansion of Canadian means of payments. The only element in my account which Carr here correctly reports, therefore, is that increases in the outside reserves operated as a substitute for inflows of specie.

White interprets my findings as differing "from the orthodox explanation in that credit expansion instead of following the increases in bank reserves appears to have preceded them." He nevertheless does not regard the objection made by Angell and Carr to my account "on the score of chronological sequence" as serious, on the ground that since the Canadian banks treated outside reserves as if they were specie, the difference of the Canadian mechanism from the classical doctrine was due simply to "a modification arising from modern banking practice."[18] If, as seems to be intended by White, "credit expansion" is understood to mean expansion of bank money, whether primary or secondary, and "bank reserves" is understood to mean only *specie* reserves in *Canada*, that was exactly my position.[19] But it is not relevant to Angell's or Carr's criticism "on the score of chronological sequence." It was my supposed account of the chronological order of variations in the *non-specie* or "outside" reserves and in *primary* deposits, and not in the *specie* reserves and *total* deposits, with which Angell and Carr took issue.[20]

Angell's Statistical Analysis.—Angell supports his findings as to the sequence of events in the Canadian mechanism by an

---

[16] Cf. *supra*, p. 418.

[17] This, I assume, is what Carr means by "extension of credit at home."

[18] Harry D. White, *The French international accounts 1880-1913*, 1933, pp. 11-12.

[19] Cf. *Canada's balance*, pp. 164-77.

[20] White apparently at times interprets the "orthodox" doctrine, which he accepts for himself and attributes also to me, as involving only secondary fluctuations in the amount of means of payment. Cf. White, *op. cit.*, pp. 7-8: "A year or even more may elapse before the increased reserves in the gold receiving country result in increased demand liabilities."

analysis of the statistical data.[21] Since he presents no data on the outside reserves, whether sterling funds, or New York funds, or total holdings, no light is thrown by this analysis on the manner in which he reached his conclusions as to the place of the outside reserves in the mechanism. On the basis of his statistical analysis, he presents two (inconsistent) sets of conclusions as to the chronological sequence of events: first, that the net import surpluses follow the net borrowings "with a lag of a year";[22] and second, that (a) "the changes in bank deposits *followed*, with a lag up to a year, the changes in the excess of net capital imports [= net borrowings] over final means of payment [= import surpluses]; and that the magnitudes involved were roughly similar when the lag is allowed for. . . . The latter set of fluctuations evidently dominate the first set"; and (b) the increases in the import surpluses followed, also with "a lag of about a year," the increases in bank deposits,[23] with an aggregate lag, therefore, of up to two years between an increase in borrowings and an increase in the import surplus. Since Angell holds that the increase in deposits was prior to the increase in New York funds, there would therefore be also, according to his account, a lag of up to a year to over a year between the fluctuations in borrowings and the fluctuations in New York funds.

Angell attributes the lag which he finds between the increases in borrowings and increases in import surpluses to two factors which received due recognition in my study: "first, to the interval between the announcement of each new loan (at which time it was usually credited to Canada) and its actual flotation; and second, to the lag between the accumulation of the capital abroad and the appearance of the resulting changes in the commodity balance."[24] Both factors are valid. For security flotations, however, the interval between announcement of the loan and payment by subscribers of the final instalment rarely, if ever, exceeded three months, and, presumably because the winter season in Canada is unsuitable for heavy construction, few important flotations occurred in the late autumn. This lag, therefore, would

---

[21] *Theory of international prices,* appendix B, pp. 505-10, and "The effects of international payments in the past," *loc. cit.,* pp. 140-53.

[22] *Theory of international prices,* p. 506.

[23] *Ibid.,* p. 508. (Italics are in original.)

[24] *Ibid.,* p. 506.

scarcely reveal itself in calendar year statistical series. But direct investments in Canadian branch plants, etc., would commonly attract attention at and be assigned to the time when plans were announced, while the actual execution of the plans, and transfer of the necessary funds, might well take a year or longer. The second factor should ordinarily have been more important. The Canadian import surpluses should be expected to lag after the Canadian borrowings, since it would ordinarily take some time before the proceeds of the foreign borrowings would be completely absorbed in payment of adverse trade balances. But if Canadians borrow abroad in a given year more than the excess of what they spend abroad over what they sell abroad, and if they do not take any of the unspent borrowings in the form of specie, the unspent borrowings must be held either by Canadian individuals or by Canadian banks in the form of increased holdings of foreign funds. Assuming in turn that Canadian *individuals* hold only negligible and comparatively constant amounts of foreign funds and that upon the acquisition of such funds they promptly exchange them with Canadian banks for Canadian funds in the form of bank deposits, then the excess in any year of Canadian net borrowings abroad over Canadian import surpluses must result in simultaneous and corresponding increases in Canadian primary deposits and in the outside reserves of the Canadian banks, my original position. What then of Angell's statistical finding that there was a lag of up to a year of the changes in deposits after the changes in unspent borrowings? The fact that Angell, when he is not dealing with deposits, finds a lag of only a year between borrowings and the import surpluses on which they are finally spent, but finds a lag of up to two years between the borrowings and the import surpluses when he is dealing with deposits, and that none of the lags he finds stands out clearly in his charts, itself suggests that the one year lag of deposits after the initial accrual of unspent borrowings may be spurious. But whatever Angell's charts may appear to show, the defects both in my estimates upon which these charts are based and in Angell's use of them are such as to make the charts have little bearing on the questions of chronological sequence which he attempts to answer by means of them.

To obtain the amount of unspent borrowings of each year, or what he calls the "excess of net capital imports over final means

424 *Studies in the Theory of International Trade*

of payment," Angell subtracts my estimates of the Canadian commodity and service import surpluses of each year from my direct estimates of the net amounts of Canadian borrowings abroad for the corresponding years.[25] This is logically correct procedure. But if the estimates of (a) net borrowings and (b) import surpluses were absolutely accurate, the excess of net borrowings over import surpluses should for each year be identical with the increase in the Canadian bank (plus private) holdings of outside funds. Estimates (a) and (b), however, are each *net* series, or series of differences between pairs of other series. Thus series (a) is a series of the differences between series (a₁), borrowings by Canada, and series (a₂), loans by Canada; and series (b) is a series of the differences between series (b₁), imports into Canada, and series (b₂), exports by Canada. Now each of the series, a₁, a₂, b₁, b₂, is inevitably subject to an appreciable margin of probable error, and the series (a) and (b) are therefore subject to much greater margins of probable error. When we come to the final series consisting of the differences between series (a) and (b), the margin of probable error must be regarded as too great to warrant reliance upon it for important conclusions. If estimates of international balances are to be used at all there must not be too much squeamishness about their accuracy, but I presented my direct estimates of Canadian borrowings only with the most serious reservations, especially with reference to their allocation to particular years, which is vital here. In my original study I advisedly made little use of them as a basis for interpreting the mechanism.

Let us suppose, however, that there are no *unknown* errors or omissions in the series used by Angéll. Angell's "net capital imports" series is constructed by subtracting from my direct estimates of Canadian borrowings abroad my estimates of Canadian investments of capital abroad. But unfortunately for the purposes of his analysis, the latter series included as Canadian investments abroad the net increases in Canadian bank holdings of outside funds.[26] Since the changes in the Canadian bank holdings of out-

---

[25] To get his "net capital imports" series Angell also subtracts the net interest payments by Canada from the borrowings. Since he also excludes the net interest payments from his "final means of payment" series, these operations cancel out and do not affect his "excess of net capital imports over final means of payment" series.

[26] Cf. Angell, *Theory of international prices*, p. 510, table 1, col. 2; *ibid.*, "The

side funds constitute the changes in the amounts of untransferred borrowings, Angell's successive operations reduce to subtraction of one estimate of the total borrowings, transferred and untransferred, from another estimate of the total borrowings, transferred and untransferred, and treatment of the remainders as the untransferred borrowings. If all the estimates were accurate, there would be no remainders. Angell's series of "excess of net capital imports over final means of payment" is in fact a series of substantial sums. But subject to the qualifications that there are assumed to have been no important fluctuations in the holdings of outside funds by *individual* Canadians and that Angell does not include non-commercial items such as capital brought in by immigrants as "capital imports" or funds requiring economic transfer, these remainders represent merely the net errors and omissions in the several series of estimates from which they are derived, and have no other significance.

A hypothetical illustration will perhaps bring out more clearly why Angell's series of "excess of net capital imports over final means of payment" represents, subject to the two qualifications indicated above, only the net errors in my various series. Suppose that, in a particular year, the Canadian gross borrowings abroad amount to $100,000,000; the new investments abroad by Canadians other than banks amount to $10,000,000; the net increase in holdings of outside funds by the Canadian banks amount to $20,000,000; and the Canadian commodity and service import surplus amounts to $70,000,000. The excess of net borrowings over the import surplus, or the amount of untransferred borrowings, would in that year then be $20,000,000, which is necessarily the same as the amount of increase in the holdings of outside funds by the Canadian banks. But by Angell's procedure, namely, subtracting (a) the import surpluses from (b) the net borrowings *minus the increase in the holdings of outside funds by the Canadian banks*, the excess of net borrowings over the import surplus, or the amount of untransferred borrowings,

---

effects of international payments in the past," *loc. cit.*, p. 141, table 22, col. 13 ("net capital imports") = col. 4 (my direct estimates of Canadian borrowings abroad) *plus* col. 3 (interest received by Canada) *minus* col. 8 (my estimates of Canadian investments abroad) *minus* col. 9 (interest paid by Canada). For the inclusion in my estimates of Canadian investments abroad (col. 8 in Angell's table 22) of the net increases in Canadian bank holdings of outside funds, see *Canada's balance*, pp. 92-93, table XXIV, and p. 94, table XXV.

would appear to be zero. Suppose, however, that the actual amounts remain as above, but that the Canadian import surplus is wrongly estimated at $60,000,000 instead of at its true amount of $70,000,000; computed by Angell's method the excess of net borrowings over the import surplus, or the amount of untransferred borrowings, would appear to be $10,000,000, or the amount of the error in the estimate of the Canadian import surplus.

Accepting Angell's computations, Carr comments:

An excess of net capital imports [over the commodity and service import surpluses] amounting to only 1.6 per cent of the total appears much too small to have provided Canada for the entire period with the increase in purchasing power necessary for carrying on a growing domestic trade at the sustained higher price levels. This fact is also embarrassing to the classical analysis, for it is only through the medium of the excess of net capital imports that the rise in Canadian prices can be accounted for.[27]

For the reason already given, the excess of borrowings over import surplus as computed by Angell must be regarded as meaningless except as a measure of the net error in the various estimates. The smallness of its ratio to the total amount of borrowings should therefore prove embarrassing only to those who attach significance to it. For individual years it is, in fact, embarrassingly large for me as the person responsible for the estimates on which it is based. If by "increase in purchasing power necessary for carrying on a growing domestic trade at the sustained higher price levels," Carr means increase in monetary reserves, he overlooks the fact that included in the import surpluses as computed in *Canada's balance* and used by him was a total net import for the period of $113,000,000 of gold coin, as compared to a total stock of gold coin in Canada at the beginning of the period of only $19,000,000,[28] and that the outside reserves of the Canadian banks increased during the period from $39,000,000 to $130,000,000, or an increase of $91,000,000.[29]

A Statistical Reexamination of the Canadian Experience.

[27] "The role of price in the international trade mechanism," *Quarterly journal of economics,* XLV (1931), 718.

[28] Cf. *Canada's balance,* p. 30, table II, col. IX, *minus* col. VIII. White has pointed this out with reference to Carr's argument. (*The French international accounts,* p. 15, note 1.)

[29] *Canada's balance,* p. 187, chart III.

—The major obstacle to the use of direct estimates of borrowings in the analysis of the transfer mechanism is the absence, ordinarily, of sufficient information on which to base acceptable estimates of short-term credit transactions, such as international purchases and sales of securities through stock exchanges, short-term loans by others than banks, and trade debts incurred in one calendar year and not liquidated until the next calendar year. Incomplete segregation in the reported figures of loan flotations of the portions of the proceeds used to amortize older loans presents another source of possible error. While the changes in outside reserves of the Canadian banks cannot be regarded as an accurate measure of the relation of Canadian borrowings to economic or real transfers, they are as reliable a measure of the changes in the amounts of untransferred borrowings as can be derived from the data made available in my Canadian study. In tables VI and VII are presented some of the results of a reexamination of the Canadian experience. To the data presented in my original study are here added the amounts of bank loans in Canada, as representative of secondary fluctuations in the volume of means of payment in Canada. There is also some rearrangement of the data along lines similar to those followed by Angell. What I believe to be a further improvement is based on the distinction which White makes between *net* and *total* gold flows.[30] In my original study I used for my banking series the amounts of deposits, reserves, etc., as reported for the last business day of each year, and the differences in the figures for successive years thus represented the *net* year-to-year changes. White claims that for purposes of tracing the influence of gold flows on trade balances the influence on demands for commodities of gold which entered, say, in February and departed in November would not be accounted for by data as to net annual changes in the amount of gold. To account for the influence of an inflow of gold which remained only for part of the statistical unit period, he concludes that total annual gold flows instead of net annual changes in the amount of gold should be used in analysis. But the substitution of total gold flows for net gold flows is not the proper method of giving to gold which was within the country for only part of a year its due weight, since this method would give to gold which

---

[30] *The French international accounts*, pp. 30-31.

TABLE VI

(Averages of Amounts Reported Monthly in Millions of Dollars)[a]

Year	1	2	3	4	5	6
	Deposit and note liabilities in Canada[b] (Increases = Primary + Secondary Expansion)	Bank loans in Canada[c] (Increases = Secondary Expansion)	"Foreign Loan Deposits" (Increases = Primary Expansion) $(1 - 2)$	Reserves		
				Gold and Dominion notes held by banks[d]	Outside reserves[e]	Total reserves $(4 + 5)$
1900[f]...	344	310	34	30	39	69
1901....	374	324	50	32	52	84
1902....	411	354	57	35	60	95
1903....	449	408	41	43	51	94
1904....	496	449	46	50	58	108
1905....	551	483	68	53	74	127
1906....	631	561	69	61	76	137
1907....	671	630	42	71	59	130
1908....	664	584	80	78	94	172
1909....	786	608	178	96	156	252
1910....	914	717	196	105	152	257
1911....	998	800	198	120	134	254
1912....	1122	919	203	133	143	276
1913....	1135	985	149	137	119	256

[a] Computed from data in monthly banking supplements of *Canada gazette.*

[b] Notes in circulation, balances due to Dominion and provincial governments, demand and time deposits in Canada. (Notes of other Canadian banks held by the banks should be subtracted, but were not separately listed in the returns.)

[c] Call and short loans in Canada, current loans in Canada, loans to Dominion, provincial, and local governments, and overdue debts.

[d] Includes amounts held outside Canada, not separately reported before July, 1913.

[e] Due from banks in United Kingdom and in foreign countries and call and short loans elsewhere than in Canada *minus* due to banks in United Kingdom and in foreign countries.

[f] Averages of amounts reported for last six months only.

stayed in the country for a day equal weight with gold which stayed in the country for 360 days if entrance and departure were in the same calendar year, and would give a negative weight to gold which had entered in the previous year and stayed 360 days of the given year and a positive weight to gold which entered on the last day of the year. The procedure required to answer White's objection to the use of net year-to-year changes as of a given day is to substitute for them the year-to-year changes in the average amounts of gold within the country during the year as a whole. For Canada, an adequate approximation to such averages is made possible by the use for each year of the averages of the monthly returns made by the banks. The reasoning which makes use of such averages preferable to use of end-of-the-year data for gold applies equally to other banking series bearing on the amount of means of payment.

The close relationship, as different aspects of the same banking operations, between the primary fluctuations in bank money in Canada (the fluctuations in "foreign loan deposits") and the fluctuations in outside reserves, is made clearly evident in table VI. With one negligible exception, the fluctuations were always in the same direction and there was also substantial correspondence in size of fluctuation. The discrepancies between the two series are to be explained mainly by: the fluctuations in Canadian bank holdings of gold and Dominion notes, which represented substantially substitutions as between "cash" reserves and outside reserves; accruals to or drafts on the outside reserves by the regular banking operations conducted by the Canadian banks outside Canada, chiefly in Newfoundland and the West Indies, which are not segregated in the official returns; and (minor) fluctuations in the Canadian bank purchases of and sales of securities within and outside of Canada.

Table VI indicates that primary and secondary expansion of means of payment in Canada both contributed to the creation of a situation in which the necessary import surpluses could develop, although the secular growth of the bank loans in Canada, associated with the general economic development of the country and with the rise of prices in Canada as part of a world rise, operates to magnify the apparent importance of the secondary expansion as a factor in the mechanism of adjustment to the borrowings. From the data in tables VI and VII it is possible to argue that at times at least the import surpluses resulted from original secondary expansion, and that the borrowings were engaged in to obtain the foreign funds necessary to liquidate trade balances already incurred and to restore reserves encroached upon in paying for past debit trade balances.[31] But this is quite con-

---

[31] That this sometimes occurred appears more clearly in the monthly data.

TABLE VII

Net Acquisition of Outside Funds by Canada, and the Disposition Made of Them, 1901–1913

(In Millions of Dollars)

	1	2	3	4	5
Year	Net acquisition of outside funds[a]	Amount of net economic transfer[b]	Increase or decrease (−) in Canadian bank holdings of outside funds[c]	Total accounted for (2 + 3)	Amounts unaccounted for (−) or overaccounted for (1 − 4)
1901.........	−4	−9	19	10	14
1902.........	14	2	1	3	−11
1903.........	38	43	−7	36	−2
1904.........	29	58	23	81	52
1905.........	65	49	3	52	−13
1906.........	70	73	−6	67	−3
1907.........	47	132	−22	110	63
1908.........	139	53	91	144	5
1909.........	166	84	23	107	−59
1910.........	216	168	−41	127	−89
1911.........	248	254	6	260	12
1912.........	183	303	−5	298	115
1913.........	367	251	7	258	−109
Totals......	1578	1461	92	1553	−25

[a] Canadian borrowings abroad, direct estimate (*Canada's balance*, p. 139, table XLIV) *minus* Canadian investments abroad exclusive of changes in outside reserves of Canadian banks (*ibid.*, p. 94, table XXV and chart II, pp. 166–67) *plus* credit balances and *minus* debit balances of noncommercial transactions (*ibid.*, p. 61, table X) *minus* net interest payments by Canada (*ibid.*, p. 101, table XXVIII, col. 4 and p. 94, table XXV, final column).

[b] Commodity import surpluses inclusive of coin and bullion (*Canada's balance*, p. 33, table III) *plus* service debit balances exclusive of interest payments (*ibid.*, pp. 102–03, table XXIX).

[c] *Canada's balance*, p. 187, chart III, col. 3, annual changes, as of December 31 of each year, in due from banks in United Kingdom and in foreign countries *plus* call and short loans elsewhere than in Canada *minus* due to banks in United Kingdom and in foreign countries.

sistent with the orthodox explanation,[32] which recognizes the possibility that import surpluses may result from an internal (i.e., secondary) expansion of deposits made in anticipation of, or at least later supported by, borrowings abroad whose proceeds go to liquidate debit trade balances already incurred and to build up de-

[32] Cf. especially, Taussig, *International trade*, 1927, pp. 207–08.

pleted reserves. It should also be remembered that fortuitous shifts in the Canadian demands as between different classes of commodities or changes in the foreign demand for Canadian exports may bring about substantial year-to-year changes in the Canadian trade balance without prior changes in the amount of Canadian means of payment, and that changes in the "final purchase velocity" of the means of payment would also influence the trade balance, even in the absence of changes in the amount of deposits or prior changes in borrowings. As far as the general trends are concerned, the Canadian experience does show that the growth of the import surplus was preceded by a growth in the amount of means of payment in Canada,[33] that this growth in means of payment was both primary and secondary, that the primary fluctuations in the amount of means of payment were relatively more marked than the secondary fluctuations, and that there was a variable time-lag between borrowings abroad and economic transfer, with the recorded, or long-term, borrowings usually but not always preceding the economic transfer chronologically.

In table VII the amounts of funds requiring transfer, including not only net borrowings proper, after deduction of interest obligations, but also unilateral remittances and monetary capital brought in by immigrants, are compared with the actual amounts of net economic transfer, or the import surpluses, including the excess of imports over exports of services other than interest as well as of commodities. If all of these items were accurately estimated, and if individual Canadians held no balances abroad, an excess or deficiency in any year of the amounts of funds requiring economic transfer to Canada over the amounts of net economic transfer would be reflected by a corresponding change, in size and direction, in the holdings of outside funds by the Canadian banks. Column V reveals how serious is the lack of correspondence between these series as far as the figures for individual years are concerned, although for the period as a whole the total discrepancy, $25,000,000, is less than 2 per cent of the estimated total net acquisition of outside funds requiring transfer to Canada during the period. The discrepancies for individual years are to be explained, I believe, mainly by defects in the allo-

---

[33] Although the data are not here presented, this was not only an absolute growth but a growth relative to the trend of bank deposits in the United States and England.

cation to particular years of net long-term borrowings, by the impossibility of accounting from the available data for short-term financial transactions of various kinds which overlapped two or more calendar years, by incomplete success in deducting from the reported amounts of new loans floated the portions thereof used to amortize old loans, and by the impossibility of making allowance, in the estimates of outside reserves, for the call loans in New York by Canadian banks without agencies there, made directly from and reported as of their Canadian head offices.

v. The International Mechanism and Business Cycles

In the older literature there are to be found only scattered and incidental references to the repercussions on the international mechanism of cyclical fluctuations in business activity. Within the last few years the question has been more seriously tackled, but in the instances which have come to my attention the treatment has frequently been based on a somewhat mechanical application of a particular—if not peculiar—cycle theory to a superficial analysis of the mechanism of international trade. Given the disturbed—though in my opinion exceedingly promising—state of business cycle theory at the moment and the absence of the necessary inductive spadework on the international aspects of business fluctuations, it seems to me that we must await further developments in both directions before we can expect very fruitful results from any attempt systematically to incorporate cycle theory into the theory of international trade, or, a more important task, to apply international trade theory to cycle theory. A cursory survey of the recent literature bearing on this question suggests, however, some comments of a primarily methodological order.

In the formulation of an *a priori* description of the relation of cyclical fluctuations to the international mechanism, it is necessary to make clear which of the following possibilities is assumed to be the fact: that the cyclical fluctuations in the country in question are (a) peculiar to it, conditions in the outside world being assumed to be stable, or (b) are synchronized with, or (c) lag behind, or (d) precede fluctuations in the same direction in the outside world. Each of these situations would, *a priori*, be expected to have associated with it a different cyclical pattern in the international aspects of the economic phenomena of the country in question. Since any particular country may at one time be in one of these situations and at another time in another, or, as is most probable, may generally be in one of these situations with respect to some phases of business activity and in some other of the situations with respect to other phases of business activity, attempts such as are to be encountered in the literature to formulate a single and precise pattern of relationship between cyclical fluctuations and specific elements of the international mechanism without discrimination between the situations here differentiated seem to me to be based on an excessive simplification of the problem.

Recognition of the existence of close relationship between the cyclical fluctuations of business activity and the behavior of the various items in the international balances was common during the currency school-banking school controversy. As a rule, however, it was tacitly assumed either that the cyclical fluctuations in volume of means of payment, prices, etc., were confined to England (which corresponds to my assumption [a] above) or that the cycle came earlier and was more pronounced in England than abroad (which corresponds substantially to my assumption [d] above). An expansion of means of payment in England was therefore treated as resulting in a relative rise in prices in England, a decline in exports and increase in imports, a relative rise in interest rates in England, and specie exports and short-term borrowing from abroad to liquidate the adverse balance of payments. Given the assumptions this was correct analysis, but it was certainly not made sufficiently clear by those presenting such analysis that they recognized the dependence of their conclusions on the particular type of relationship, with respect to timing, direction, and degree, assumed to exist between the fluctuations within England and those in the outside world.

This can be illustrated by contrasting the probable pattern of behavior of the international phenomena when the cycle comes earlier and is more pronounced in England than abroad, as is usually assumed by these writers, with what the pattern would be if the cycle came later in England and was less pronounced than abroad. Taking first the expansion phase, in both situations the amount of means of payment in England, prices, interest rates, output, and imports, would be rising. But imports would be rising relative to exports in the first case, falling in the second, and the balance of payments on trade account would be moving against England in the first case, in her favor in the second, with reverse movements of specie in the two cases. A corresponding contrast between the two cases holds for the contraction phase.

For similar reasons, it seems a mistake to assume that there is one definite pattern of relationship between business fluctuations and international capital movements. During the expansion phase of a cycle in a particular country the volume of investment will increase. If that country is normally a capital-exporting country and is having an earlier or more marked expansion of business activity than the outside world, the ratio of investment at home to export of capital should be expected to rise. On *a priori* grounds alone, there would seem to be somewhat of a presumption that the volume of export of capital would fall absolutely as well as relatively to total investment, since domestic interest rates would be rising relative to interest rates abroad. It is even conceivable that the international movement of capital may under these circumstances reverse its usual direction, capital being borrowed from abroad or withdrawn from abroad instead of being exported.[1]

It is easy, however, to conceive of a different pattern. Paradoxical though it may seem at first glance, the increased export of capital may be the cause, and may in fact constitute the bulk, of the internal expansion of business activity, where the export of capital and the export of capital goods are so closely associated that a marked expansion of capital directly involves a substantial increase in the production of capital goods. To the extent that international capital movements result directly and immediately in movements of capital goods in a corresponding direction they tend to operate as an inflationary rather than a deflationary factor in the capital-exporting country, and perhaps also as a deflationary instead of an inflationary factor in the capital-importing country. It is the fraction of the capital movement which takes the form of a specie movement which exercises the deflationary influence in the capital-exporting country and the inflationary in-

[1] Cf., however, Wesley Mitchell, *Business cycles,* 1927, p. 447:
. . . prosperity, with its sanguine temper and its liberal profits, encourages investments abroad as well as at home, and the export of capital to other countries gives an impetus to their trade.

fluence in the capital-importing country. The specie phase of a capital movement represents for the exporting country domestic saving with which *domestic* investment is at least not directly associated, and for the importing country it represents domestic investment unaccompanied by *domestic* saving. The capital-goods phase of a capital movement, on the other hand, may represent for the exporting country an increase in *domestic* investment whose products are, in part only, to be transferred abroad, and for the importing country may result in decreased domestic investment.[2]

Given this wide range of possibilities, I see no *a priori* grounds for expecting to find a significant correlation, whether positive or negative, between the fluctuations in the export of capital by particular countries and the fluctuations in their general level of business activity, unless there is ground for assuming that capital-exporting countries are typically countries whose business cycles always precede or always lag after world cycles, or are countries in which fluctuations in the volume of foreign investment are major factors in initiating fluctuations in the internal level of business activity rather than by-products of the latter.[3]

Similar reasoning leads also to skepticism as to the validity of the grounds on which it is often argued nowadays that free trade exercises in general a stabilizing influence. It is held that foreign trade exercises a moderating influence on the amplitude of the cycle, since internal expansion tends to result in an adverse trade balance, with its deflationary pressure, while contraction tends to result in a favorable trade balance, with its inflationary stimulus.[4] This moderating influence, however, operates exclusively in the country where the infection starts or is making most rapid progress. For other countries the trade balance is, with capital movements, sympathetic price trends, and psychological contagion, a

---

[2] Cf. K. Wicksell, *Lectures on political economy*, 1935, II, 100-02; Marco Fanno, "Credit expansion, savings and gold export," *Economic journal*, XXXVIII (1928), 126-31; and, for gold movements, Saint-Peravy, in 1786! (*Supra*, p. 187.) ("Investment" is used here to mean expenditures for productive purposes.)

[3] Cf., for substantially similar conclusions, J. W. Angell, *Theory of international prices*, 1926, pp. 174, note; 396-97; 527-28; and the additional references listed in his index, p. 561, under "Cyclical movements of business."

[4] Cf., e.g., Folke Hilgerdt, "Foreign trade and the short business cycle," in *Economic essays in honour of Gustav Cassel*, 1933, pp. 273-91.

major vehicle for the international spread of the infection. I would agree that high tariffs bear an important share of the responsibility for the recurrence of major booms and depressions, but on different considerations. Without rigid price structures, major business cycles are inconceivable, and high tariffs are an important factor in making price rigidity possible.

Chapter VIII

GAINS FROM TRADE: THE DOCTRINE OF
COMPARATIVE COSTS

It is always to be remembered that the failure of an argument in favor of a proposition does not, generally speaking, add much, if any probability, to the contradictory proposition.—Jevons, Principles of Science.

I. THE NATURE AND ORIGIN OF THE DOCTRINE

The classical theory of international trade was formulated primarily with a view to its providing guidance on questions of national policy, and although it included considerable descriptive analysis of economic process, the selection of phenomena to be scrutinized and problems to be examined was almost always made with reference to current issues of public interest. This was true even of the classical discussions of the mechanism of international trade, but it was more conspicuously true in the field which is sometimes called "the theory of international value," where the problems were expressly treated with reference to their bearing on "gain" or "loss" to England, or on the distribution of gain as between England and the rest of the world. Recognition of its "welfare analysis" orientation is essential to the understanding and the appraisal of the classical doctrine. Although the classical economists did not clearly separate them, and shifted freely from one to the other, they followed three different methods of dealing with the question of "gain" from trade: (1) the doctrine of comparative costs, under which economy in cost of obtaining a given income was the criterion of gain; (2) increase in income as a criterion of gain; and (3) terms of trade as an index of the international division and the trend of gain. This chapter will deal with the doctrine of comparative costs.

The doctrine of comparative costs originated as an improvement and development of the eighteenth-century criticism of mercantilist policy, and it has continued to command attention mainly because of its use as the basic "scientific" argument of free-trade economists in their attack on protective tariffs. Protectionists have an obvious motive for attacking the doctrine, but it has also been rejected by economists whose animus seems to arise from the fact that it was one of the outstanding products of the English classical school, by economists who deal with it as an exercise in pure price theory and as such find it unsatisfactory, and by economists who believe that they have at their command a superior technique than it affords for the appraisal of commercial policy. Never widely accepted on the Continent, the doctrine now is clearly on the defensive everywhere.

The doctrine of comparative costs maintains that if trade is left free each country *in the long run* tends to specialize in the production of and to export those commodities in whose production it enjoys a comparative advantage in terms of real costs, and to obtain by importation those commodities which could be produced at home only at a comparative disadvantage in terms of real costs, and that such specialization is to the mutual advantage of the countries participating in it. In the exposition of the doctrine the "real" costs are expressed as a rule in terms of quantities of labor-time, but with the implication, as throughout the classical theory of value, that these quantities of labor-time correspond in their relative amounts within each country to quantities of subjective cost. The legitimacy of this assumption that labor-time costs are proportional to real costs is examined at length later in this chapter, and for the present will not be questioned.

There has been some measure of confusion as to the nature of the comparisons between costs which the doctrine contemplates. According to Cairnes:

. . when it is said that international trade depends on a difference in the comparative, not in the absolute, cost of producing commodities, the costs compared, it must be carefully noted, are the costs in each country of the commodities which are the subjects of exchange, not the different costs of the same commodity in the exchanging countries.[1]

But it is not costs at all which are directly to be compared, but *ratios between costs*, and it is unessential whether the cost ratios which are compared are the ratios between the costs of

---

[1] J. E. Cairnes, *Some leading principles of political economy*, 1874, p. 312.

producing different commodities within the same countries or the ratios between the costs of producing the same commodities in different countries.

Commodity	Real costs per unit	
	Country A	Country B
A.................	m	r
B.................	n	s
C.................	p	t

In the illustration given above, it does not matter whether the ratios compared are $\frac{m}{n} \! : \! \frac{r}{s}, \frac{m}{p} \! : \! \frac{r}{t}, \frac{n}{p} \! : \! \frac{s}{t}, \frac{n}{m} \! : \! \frac{s}{r}, \frac{p}{m} \! : \! \frac{t}{r},$ and $\frac{p}{n} \! : \! \frac{t}{s},$ on the one hand, or $m \! : \! r$, $n \! : \! s$, and $p \! : \! t$, on the other hand. In the first set of comparisons, country A has its greatest comparative advantage in the production of that commodity whose cost in A appears as the numerator in the first term of the lowest of these ratios, and its greatest comparative disadvantage in the production of that commodity whose cost in A appears as the denominator in the first term of the lowest of these ratios. In the second set, country A has its greatest comparative advantage in the production of that commodity whose cost in A appears as the first term in the smallest of these ratios, and its greatest comparative disadvantage in the production of that commodity whose cost in A appears as the first term in the highest of these ratios. Whatever numerical values are assigned to the unit real costs, both these methods of comparison will necessarily produce identical results, though the first method will ordinarily be found much more convenient to use. If the first method is used, the units used in the measurement of cost need not be identical or even comparable in the two countries. It is then not necessary, for instance, to know whether m is greater or less than r, or whether n is greater or less than s.

In the beginnings of free-trade doctrine in the eighteenth century the usual economic arguments for free trade were based on the advantage to a country of importing, in exchange for native products, those commodities which either could not be produced at home at all or could be produced at home only at costs absolutely greater than those at which they could be produced abroad. Under free trade, it was argued or implied, all products, abstracting from transportation costs, would be produced in those countries where their real costs were lowest. The case for free trade as presented by Adam Smith did not advance beyond this point.

In an earlier chapter, however, it has been shown that several writers prior to Adam Smith, and especially the author of *Considerations on the East-India Trade*, 1701, stated the case for free trade in terms of a rule which would provide the same limits for profitable trade as does the doctrine of comparative costs, the rule, namely, that it pays to import commodities from abroad whenever they can be obtained in exchange for exports at a smaller real cost than their production at home would entail. Such gain from trade is always possible when, and is only possible if, there are comparative differences in costs between the countries concerned. The doctrine of comparative costs is, indeed, but a statement of some of the implications of this rule, and adds nothing to it as a guide for policy.[2]

Many of the classical economists, both before and after the formulation of the doctrine of comparative costs, resorted to this eighteenth-century rule as a test of the existence of gain from trade. Ricardo incorporated it in his formulation of the doctrine of comparative costs:

Though she [i.e., Portugal] could make the cloth with the labor of 90 men, she would import it from a country where it required the labor of 100 men to produce it, because it would be advantageous to her rather to employ her capital in the production of wine, for which she would obtain more cloth from England, than she could produce by diverting a portion of her capital from the cultivation of vines to the manufacture of cloth.[3]

---

[2] Cf. F. Y. Edgeworth, *Papers relating to political economy*, 1925, II, 6: "Foreign trade would not go on unless it seemed less costly to each of the parties to it to obtain imports in exchange for exports than to produce them at home. This is the generalized statement of the principle of comparative cost, with respect to its positive part at least."

[3] *Principles of political economy*, in *Works*, pp. 76-77. For other instances of resort to this rule by classical economists for the purpose of establishing the existence of gain from trade, or, in some cases, measuring its extent, see R. Torrens, *The economists refuted* [1808], reprinted in his *The principles and practical operation of Sir Robert Peel's Act of 1844*, 3d ed., 1858, pp. 53-54; James Mill, *Commerce defended*, 1808, pp. 36-38; N. W. Senior, *Political economy*

Malthus had credited as a factor contributing to the prosperity of the United States her ability to sell "raw produce, obtained with little labor, for European commodities which have cost much labor."[4] To this, Ricardo replied:

> It can be of no consequence to America, whether the commodities she obtains in return for her own, cost Europeans much, or little labor; all she is interested in, is that they shall cost her less labor by purchasing them than by manufacturing them herself.[5]

This explicit statement that imports could be profitable even though the commodity imported could be produced at less cost at home than abroad was, it seems to me, the sole addition of consequence which the doctrine of comparative costs made to the eighteenth-century rule. Its chief service was to correct the previously prevalent error that under free trade all commodities would necessarily tend to be produced in the locations where their real costs of production were lowest.

In his *Principles*, first published in 1817, Ricardo presented the doctrine of comparative costs by means of what was to become a famous illustration, in which the quantity of wine which required for its production in England the labor of 120 men could be produced in Portugal by 80 men, while the cloth which in England required the labor of 100 men could be produced in Portugal by 90 men. Portugal would then import cloth from England in exchange for wine, even though the imported cloth could be produced in Portugal with less labor than in England.[6]

Credit for the first publication of the principle of comparative costs is generally given to Ricardo. Leser,[7] however, in 1881, assigned to Torrens the credit of discovery of the doctrine on the

---

[1st ed., 1836], 4th ed., 1858, p. 76; J. R. McCulloch, *Principles of political economy*, 4th ed., 1849, p. 147; J. S. Mill, *Principles of political economy* [1848], Ashley ed., p. 585.

[4] Malthus, *Principles of political economy*, 1st ed., 1820, p. 428.

[5] Ricardo, *Notes on Malthus' "Principles of political economy"* [1820], Hollander and Gregory editors, 1928, p. 209.

[6] *Principles, Works*, pp. 76-77.

[7] "Torrens hat . . . eine andere grossartige Entdeckung gemacht, die aber auch nicht an seinen Namen, sondern an den des Ricardo geknüpft zu werden pflegt . . . Wir haben hier genau die vielbewunderte Auseinandersetzung vor uns, die Ricardo . . . gegeben hat. . . ." (E. Leser, *Untersuchungen zur Geschichte der Nationalökonomie*, I, 1881, pp. 82-83, note.)

strength of the following passage in Torrens's *Essay on the External Corn Trade*, 1815:

> If England should have acquired such a degree of skill in manufactures, that, with any given portion of her capital, she could prepare a quantity of cloth, for which the Polish cultivator would give a greater quantity of corn than she could, with the same portion of capital, raise from her own soil, then tracts of her territory, though they should be equal, nay, even though they should be superior, to the lands in Poland, will be neglected; and a part of her supply of corn will be imported from that country. For, though the capital employed in cultivating at home might bring an excess of profit over the capital employed in cultivating abroad, yet, under the supposition, the capital which should be employed in manufacturing would obtain a still greater excess of profit; and this greater excess of profit would determine the direction of our industry.[8]

Leser's comment attracted no notice, but some years later credit for priority in formulating the doctrine of comparative cost was again claimed for Torrens, this time by Professor Seligman.[9] Professor Hollander has replied, in defense of Ricardo's claims, that much of the evidence in support of Torrens presented by Seligman was not relevant or was of questionable weight; that even after the appearance of Ricardo's *Principles* Torrens never realized the full significance of the comparative cost doctrine and never made explicit use of it; and that Ricardo's claims to priority could not be overcome merely by the fact that Torrens, in a single paragraph, had correctly stated the doctrine "in outline" before Ricardo had published his *Principles*.[10]

Torrens clearly preceded Ricardo in publishing a fairly satisfactory formulation of the doctrine. It is unquestionable, however, that Ricardo is entitled to the credit for first giving due emphasis to the doctrine, for first placing it in an appropriate setting, and for obtaining general acceptance of it by economists. Hollander, moreover, appears to be justified in his contention that

---

[8] Torrens, *An essay on the external corn trade*, 1815, pp. 264-65; cf. also p. 266.

[9] E. R. A. Seligman, "On some neglected British economists," *Economic journal*, XIII (1903), 341-47; reprinted in Seligman, *Essays in economics*, 1925, pp. 70-77.

[10] J. H. Hollander, *David Ricardo: a centenary estimate*, 1910, pp. 92-96. Cf. also the further discussion by Seligman and Hollander, "Ricardo and Torrens," *Economic journal*, XXI (1911), 448 ff.

the doctrine was never an integral part of Torrens's thinking. While Torrens again stated the doctrine, and stated it very well, in at least two of his publications,[11] and incidentally first used the term "comparative cost" in connection with the doctrine,[12] these later statements are frankly presented as improvements on Torrens's earlier views resulting from the discussion of the problem by other economists. Torrens's grasp of the doctrine, moreover, was not so firm that he could not occasionally display confusion about its meaning and implications.[13]

Much of the evidence from Torrens's writings which Seligman cites to demonstrate that he was an exponent of the doctrine of comparative costs shows only, as Hollander says, that Torrens accepted the argument that international division of labor was beneficial, or that he accepted the principle that it paid to import commodities if they could thus be obtained at lower cost than the cost of producing them at home, a principle which I have shown above to have had its origin early in the eighteenth century.

The only claim to priority over Ricardo with reference to the doctrine of comparative costs which Torrens made[14] was based on the passage in the 1815 edition of the *Essay* already cited above. Hollander surmises that even this earlier passage itself may owe something to discussion of the question with Ricardo, but until it is at least made clear that Torrens and Ricardo were already acquainted in 1815, not much weight is to be attached to

---

[11] *Essay on the external corn trade*, 4th ed., 1827, in a section, "Effects of free trade on the value of money," pp. 394-428, first added in this edition; *Colonization of South Australia*, 1835, pp. 148 ff.

[12] Seligman stated that: "Neither Torrens nor Ricardo uses the term 'comparative cost.' This term was introduced by Mill in his *Unsettled Questions* in 1844." (*Economic journal*, XXI (1911), 448.) Hollander points out that Torrens did use the term "comparative cost," but in a different connection, in his *Essay on the external corn trade*, 3d ed., 1826, p. 41, and claims that James Mill first used the word "comparative" in connection with the theory of international trade. (*Economic journal*, XXI (1911), 461.) But Torrens did use the term "comparative cost" correctly in the 4th edition of his *Essay on the external corn trade*, 1827 (p. 401), and Ricardo, in all the editions of his *Principles*, had used the phrases "comparative disadvantage as far as regarded competition in foreign markets" (*Works*, p. 101) and "comparative facility of . . . production" (*ibid.*, p. 226). Terminological usage by the classical economists must have been so influenced by their oral discussions as to make the record of priority in print have little bearing on the question of priority in use.

[13] Cf. *infra*, pp. 487-88.

[14] *Essay on the external corn trade*, 4th ed., 1827, p. vii.

this possibility. On the other hand, Torrens's own claim to priority should not be given too great emphasis, since Torrens was erratic both in his claims and in his acknowledgments, and could be abundantly quoted against himself.[15]

Ricardo's illustration implies a number of important assumptions which, in conformity with his usual practice, he never expressly states. His conclusions have been criticized both on the ground that they do not follow from his assumptions, and on the ground that the assumptions necessary for the validity of his conclusions are unrealistic and that with their abandonment or correction the conclusions would cease to hold. It is more or less obvious that Ricardo based his analysis on the following assumptions: ample time for long-run adjustments; free competition; only two countries and only two commodities; constant labor costs as output is varied; and proportionality of both aggregate real costs and supply prices within each country to labor-time costs within that country. Those criticisms or corrections of Ricardo's analysis which do not involve a rejection of his assumptions will be examined first, and the more fundamental criticisms which question the validity of his assumptions will be dealt with later.

II. The Division of the Gain from Trade

An Alleged Error in Ricardo.—Ricardo has been charged with claiming, on the one hand, that all the gain from trade goes to one of the countries[1] and, on the other hand, that all the gain goes to *each* country,[2] instead of finding it to be divided between the two countries.

---

[15] Cf., e.g., Torrens, *Tracts on finance and trade*, no. 2 (1852), 17: "In his chapter upon foreign trade, that profound and original writer [i.e., Ricardo] propounded for the first time, the true theory of international exchange." Torrens, it is true, apparently has reference here rather to the terms of trade question than to comparative costs, but he had also claimed priority with respect to terms of trade doctrine.

[1] "In the view of the question presented by Mr. Ricardo, the advantages derived from foreign trade were confined to only one of these countries." (Torrens, *The principles and practical operation of Sir Robert Peel's Act,* 3d ed., 1858, preface to 2d ed., pp. xiii-xiv.) This same charge is repeated by J. W. Angell, *The theory of international prices,* 1926, pp. 54, note; 67.

[2] "Mr. Ricardo . . . unguardedly expressed himself as if each of the two countries making the exchange separately gained the whole of the difference between the comparative costs of the two commodities in one country and in

The data given in Ricardo's arithmetical illustration are as follows:

Country	Amount of labor required for producing a unit of	
	Cloth	Wine
Portugal............	90	80
England............	100	120

In order that all the benefit from trade should go to England, English cloth must exchange for Portuguese wine in the ratio of 1 unit cloth for 9/8 unit wine. In order that all the benefit should go to Portugal, English cloth must exchange for Portuguese wine in the ratio of 1 unit cloth for 5/6 unit wine. But Ricardo states that English cloth will exchange for Portuguese wine in the ratio of 1 cloth for 1 wine: "Thus England would give the produce of the labor of 100 men [= 1 cloth] for the produce of the labor of 80 [= 1 wine]."[3] At this ratio, the gain would be divided approximately evenly between the two countries. Ricardo, therefore, was guilty of neither error attributed to him.

James Mill, in the first edition of his *Elements of political economy*, did commit the error of attributing all the gain to each of the countries, but he corrected it in the third edition, 1826.[4] Einaudi at one time attributed the error to Ricardo as well as to James Mill, and on the strength of a suggestion of Torrens's raised the question whether it was not James Pennington who first perceived and corrected the error.[5] Sraffa,[6] in reply, pointed out that Ricardo had not been guilty of the error, and

the other" (J. S. Mill, *Essays on some unsettled questions of political economy*, 1844, pp. 5-6.)

[3] Ricardo, *Principles, Works*, pp. 76-77.

[4] James Mill, *Elements of political economy*, 1st ed., 1821, pp. 86-87; 3d ed., 1826, p. 122.

[5] L. Einaudi, "James Pennington or James Mill: an early correction of Ricardo," *Quarterly journal of economics*, XLIV (1929-30), 164-71.

[6] Cf. P. Sraffa, "An alleged correction of Ricardo," *ibid.*, 539-44, and Einaudi's acceptance of Sraffa's account, *ibid.*, 544-45. Cf. also my review of Angell's *Theory of international prices* in the *Journal of political economy*, XXXIV (1926), 609, where I had previously shown that Ricardo was not guilty of this error.

that J. S. Mill, in his *Autobiography*,[7] had stated that his father made the corrections in the 1826 edition of his *Elements* as the result of criticisms made by himself and by George Graham in 1825.

Another co-worker of J. S. Mill's, William Ellis,[8] early in the same year, 1825, had presented an arithmetical illlustration similar to those used by James Mill, and had concluded therefrom that the gain would be equally divided between the two countries. It seems, therefore, that the error was detected about the same time by several members of the group associated with James Mill.

Relation of Comparative Costs to the Terms of Trade.— In Ricardo's illustration, the two commodities exchange for each other under trade in a ratio almost exactly halfway between their comparative cost ratios in the two countries.[9] Ricardo does not indicate whether he regards this precise ratio as required by the conditions of the problem as he had stated them, or how the actual ratio would in practice be determined. Ellis in 1825 and James Mill in 1826 also stated that the gains from trade would be equally divided between the two countries. McCulloch presented the doctrine of comparative costs in terms of an arithmetical illustration under which the ratio of gain was equal for both countries.[10] It is doubtful whether these writers attached any special significance to these arbitrary[11] terms of trade, since in the early writings of the classical school, and especially in the works of Longfield and Torrens, recognition can be found of the fact that the location of the equilibrium terms of trade was variable and depended on the relative strength of the demand of

---

[7] J. S. Mill, *Autobiography*, 1873, pp. 121-22.

[8] "Exportation of machinery," *Westminster review*, III (1825), 388-89.

[9] Ricardo states that cloth and wine will exchange for each other in the ratio of 1 cloth for 1 wine. The ratio exactly halfway between the ratios of comparative costs of the two commodities in the two countries would be 1 cloth for $\frac{47}{48}$ wine.

[10] *Principles of political economy*, 4th ed., 1849, p. 147 (also in earlier editions).

[11] Cf., however, Angell, *Theory of international prices*, p. 305:

He [i.e., Achille Loria] seems to hold that international values will be fixed midway between the two points of maximum and minimum gain, for the one country and the other. This can perhaps be regarded, however, as a legitimate deduction from the principle of comparative costs.

J. S. Mill held that the gains would be divided equally more often than in any other specific ratio. Cf. *supra*, p. 325, note 7.

the two countries for each other's products. Pennington, however, seems to have been the first explicitly to point out in print that the comparative costs set maximum and minimum rates for the terms of trade, and that within these limits the operation of reciprocal demand could fix the terms of trade at any point.[12]

Torrens had long been insisting vigorously that the terms of trade were determined by reciprocal demand, and his emphasis on this in connection with the tariff controversy in the 1840's[13] had aroused considerable opposition on the part of economists who found Torrens's application of it as an argument against unilateral reduction of tariffs distasteful. The interest aroused by Torrens's discussion led J. S. Mill to publish in 1844 some essays written in 1829 and 1830, of which one dealt with the same problem. It was from his exposition in the *Essays*,[14] repeated and developed later in the *Principles*,[15] and not from Longfield, Torrens, or Pennington, that later economists took over the doctrine. No country would give in exchange for a unit of a foreign commodity A more units of a commodity B than it could produce at a real cost equal to that at which a unit of A could be produced at home. The comparative costs set the limits, therefore, within which the two commodities could exchange for each other, but the actual ratio is set by the reciprocal demand of the two countries for each other's products. The greater the demand for B in terms of A in the country with a comparative advantage in the production of A, the closer, other things being equal, would the rate of exchange of A for B approach to their relative costs of production in that country. The greater the demand for A in terms of B in the country with a comparative advantage in the production of B, the closer, other things being equal, would the rate of exchange of A for B approach to their relative costs of production in this other country. Under equilibrium conditions,

---

[12] James Pennington, *A letter . . . on the importation of foreign corn*, 1840, pp. 32-41. Cf. also J. S. Mill, *Essays on some unsettled questions* (written 1829-30), 1844, p. 12.

[13] Especially in *The budget*, 1841-44, *passim*.

[14] *Essays on some unsettled questions*, 1844, Essay I. Mill claims for himself not "the original conception, but only the elaboration" of the part played by reciprocal demand. (*Ibid.*, preface, p. v.) He says that this question was not dealt with by Ricardo, "who, having a science to create, had not time, or room, to occupy himself with much more than the leading principles." (*Ibid.*, p. 5.)

[15] *Principles of political economy*, 1848, bk. iii, chap. xviii. Repeated in all editions.

however, the value of the exports must equal the value of the imports. Of the possible ratios of exchange between A and B, that one would be the actual ratio which made it possible to meet this condition, i.e., that ratio at which the quantity of A offered by one country would equal the quantity of A which the other country would be willing to take.

Trade at One of the Limiting Ratios.—Nicholson later pointed out, with the aid of a series of arithmetical illustrations, that if there were only two countries and two commodities, and if the relative magnitudes of the two countries were not the same, the terms of trade would probably settle at or near the comparative costs of the larger country, i.e., the smaller country would get all or nearly all the gain from trade. He suggested that the omission of consideration of the relative size of the two countries had resulted in some measure of confusion in J. S. Mill's analysis.[16] Graham has more recently repeated this argument, although without reference to Nicholson. Graham has carried the argument further by pointing out explicitly that approximate equality in importance of the commodities as well as of the countries was necessary if under the conditions stated each country was to get a substantial share of the benefits from trade.[17] Graham asserts, on the basis of this argument, that the situation which to J. S. Mill was only an "extreme and barely conceivable case," namely, that all the benefit should go to one of the countries, was, under the conditions of constant costs, only two countries, and only two commodities, rather the normal case. He agrees with J. S. Mill that division of the benefit is the normal case, but only because ordinarily more than two commodities enter into trade, so that when the terms of trade are moving against a country because of excessive export of one commodity, it begins to export other commodities in which its comparative advantage is less, and thus checks the adverse movement of its terms of trade. He concedes, however, that Bastable has recognized these probabilities in trade between a small and a large country, but criticizes his manner of dealing with the problem.[18]

Graham's reasoning is sound, but his criticism of J. S. Mill is

[16] J. S. Nicholson, *Principles of political economy*, II (1897), 302.
[17] F. D. Graham, "The theory of international values re-examined," *Quarterly journal of economics*, XXXVIII (1923), 55-59, 79.
[18] *Ibid.*, pp. 63-65.

only partially justified. The passages in Mill's *Principles* which he attacks are quotations, presented as such, from Mill's *Essays* written long before. In the same chapter of the *Principles* in which these quotations appear, in a section first added in the third edition (1852), Mill explicitly raises the same problem, and gives the same answer as does Graham. He asks why, in a particular illustration given by him, he should assume that trade would result in the benefit being divided instead of all of it going to one of the countries. He answers that in such a case the country which gets all the benefit from trade would probably find it to its advantage to import from the other country additional commodities in which that other country had a comparative advantage, although a lesser one than in its original export commodity, in exchange for additional quantities of its own export commodity, until a state was reached where the other country no longer produced any of the commodity which it imported and the terms of trade had become such as to divide the benefit between the two countries. "And so with every other case which can be supposed."[19] Pennington had already, in 1840, pointed out that the entrance of more commodities and more countries into trade would tend to prevent the terms of trade from establishing themselves at a point at which all of the gain goes to one of the countries.[20]

The Possibility of Partial Specialization.—Graham[21] cites as another error in Mill's analysis, the following passage:

Cost of carriage has one effect more. But for it, every commodity would (if trade be supposed free) be either regularly imported or regularly exported. A country would make nothing for itself which it did not also make for other countries.[22]

Graham shows that if trade is at one of the limiting ratios this is erroneous even on the assumption of constant costs, since a country which trades on terms corresponding to its own relative costs of production may be, and is likely to be, producing at home some portion of its consumption of the commodity which it imports. It seems clear, however, that while Mill at first held that

---

[19] *Principles,* Ashley ed., p. 601, note.
[20] *A letter . . . on the importation of foreign corn,* 1840, p. 41.
[21] Graham, "The theory of international values re-examined," *loc. cit.,* pp. 67 ff.
[22] Mill, *Principles,* Ashley ed., p. 589.

complete specialization would necessarily follow from free trade in the absence of transportation costs, he later adhered to it only on the assumption that trade did not take place at one of the limiting ratios, when the proposition would be correct. In correcting, in the third edition of his *Principles*, his earlier doctrine that with trade in only two commodities the terms of trade would ordinarily be such as to divide the benefit between the two countries, he also corrected this error. In the case which he assumes of trade at one of the limiting ratios, he makes one of the countries specialize only partially in the commodity which it exports. If Germany had a comparative advantage in linen and England in cloth, and if at the ratio of exchange equal to their relative costs of production in Germany the latter was willing to take more cloth than England could supply, then if no third commodity entered into the trade "England would supply Germany with cloth up to the extent of a million" and "Germany would continue to supply herself with the remaining 200,000 by home production."[23] Whewell had previously shown, on the basis of Mill's own illustrations, that on the assumptions of constant costs, only two commodities, and only two countries, one of the countries was likely to find itself in a position where it derived no gain from trade, and that such country might specialize only partially in the production of the commodity in which it had a comparative advantage.[24]

Graham points out that Bastable also asserted the impossibility of only partial specialization under conditions of constant costs, only two countries, and only two commodities.[25] Here again, however, he has not read his author carefully enough. In dealing with what he calls the "special case" of trade between a small and a large country Bastable had clearly, although inconsistently with his general denial, asserted the possibility—as far as the context indicates, perhaps even the probability—that the larger country will only partially specialize in the production of the

---

[23] Mill, *Principles,* Ashley ed., p. 601, note.

[24] William Whewell, "Mathematical exposition of some doctrines of political economy. Second memoir," *Transactions of the Cambridge Philosophical Society,* IX, part I (1856), 141. This memoir was read in 1850, and printed in the same year for private circulation. Since it was primarily a criticism of Mill's doctrines, Mill may have been acquainted with it.

[25] Graham, "The theory of international values re-examined," *loc. cit.,* p. 60; Bastable, *The theory of international trade,* 4th ed., 1903, pp. 29, 35, 177, 178.

commodity in which it has a comparative advantage.[26] In 1897, moreover, Edgeworth criticized Bastable's position, and showed that Mangoldt had long before demonstrated the possibility of partial specialization by one of the countries,[27] and in an appendix added in the third edition Bastable conceded his error.[28]

Ricardo had supported his argument for the benefit of international specialization in accordance with comparative costs by the following analogy with trade between two persons:[29]

Two men can both make shoes and hats, and one is superior to the other in both employments; but in making hats, he can only exceed his competitor by one-fifth or 20 per cent—and in making shoes he can excel him by one-third or 33 per cent;—will it not be for the interest of both, that the superior man should employ himself exclusively in making shoes, and the inferior man in making hats?

Pareto, citing this passage from Ricardo, argued that it was erroneous in its implication that *complete* specialization would necessarily be advantageous, as compared to no specialization at all. He showed by means of arithmetical illustrations that complete specialization would under some circumstances result in more of one commodity but less of the other, as compared to no specialization, and that, depending on the relative demands for these commodities, the increase in one commodity might not be sufficient to offset in value the deficit in the other commodity.[30] This has occasionally been interpreted as a partial rejection of the principle of comparative costs as an argument for free trade.[31]

---

[26] Bastable, *ibid.*, p. 43: "It therefore follows that the production of both *x* and *y* will continue to be carried on in B, while A will give its entire efforts to the production of *y*, and will therefore obtain almost the entire gain of the trade." (The same passage appears in the 2d ed., 1897, p. 43.) Bastable says "almost the entire" instead of the entire gain, because he is assuming that *y* is produced in B at different costs of production, and that it is therefore "probable that B will receive some advantage, since the production of the most costly part of *y* will be abandoned by it."

[27] Edgeworth, review of 2d ed. of Bastable, *Economic journal*, VII (1897), 398-400. Nicholson had also pointed out the possibility of partial specialization in the same year. (*Principles*, II (1897), 302.)

[28] Cf. Bastable, *Theory of international trade*, 4th ed., 1903, p. 179, note.

[29] *Principles, Works*, p. 77, note.

[30] V. Pareto, *Manuel d'économie politique*, 2d ed., 1927, pp. 507-14.

[31] Cf., e.g., Angell, *Theory of international prices*, p. 256, who says that Pareto shows that specialization does not lead to a total output which is necessarily greater in value than that secured under non-specialization, and that the principle of comparative costs is therefore "not universal in its application, and may involve a *non sequitur*."

If it were so intended, it could, of course, easily be refuted by showing that specialization in accordance with comparative costs, to the extent that such specialization would tend to be carried under free trade, would not, under the conditions stated, result in a loss. But it seems an injustice to Pareto to interpret him in this way. His criticism appears to be directed only against the proposition that *complete* specialization is necessarily profitable as compared to no specialization. Pareto himself shows that where complete specialization would not be profitable it would not take place even under free trade.[32]

Ricardo's statement that it would be to the interest of two *individuals* to specialize completely if each had a comparative advantage in the production of one of the commodities seems an inadequate basis, moreover, upon which to convict him of the belief that complete specialization would necessarily be profitable to each of two *countries* if they had comparative differences in costs of production. It so happens that the sentence cited by Pareto to show that Ricardo held this belief follows immediately in Ricardo's text an express stipulation that partial specialization by one of the countries is a possibility:

It will appear, then, that a country possessing very considerable advantages in machinery and skill, and which may therefore be enabled to manufacture commodities with much less labor than her neighbors, may, in return for such commodities, import *a portion of* the corn required for its consumption, even if its land were more fertile, and corn could be grown with less labor than in the country from which it was imported.[33]

Another writer, A. F. Burns, later repeated Pareto's demon-

---

[32] *Manuel*, p. 513.

[33] *Principles, Works*, p. 77, note. (Italics not in original text.) It may reasonably be objected that Ricardo was not adhering to the constant cost assumption in his reference to the possibility of partial specialization in the production of corn, but the passage, given its location in Ricardo's text, serves at least to show that he was not placing any emphasis on complete specialization as a necessary result of specialization in accordance with comparative advantage.

Wicksell, in a review of Pareto, agreed that if the commodities were not of equal importance there would be only partial specialization, but he characterized Pareto's criticism of Ricardo as captious, and commented that Ricardo was not writing fairy tales for children.—Knut Wicksell, "Vilfredo Paretos Manuel d'économie politique," *Zeitschrift für Volkswirthschaft*, XXII (1913), 148-49. (I am indebted to G. J. Stigler for this reference.)

stration that complete specialization may be unprofitable.[34] This writer goes further, however, than did Pareto, for he definitely argues as if specialization along the lines of comparative advantage necessarily involves complete specialization, and then claims that whenever such specialization results in more of one commodity but less of another it is impossible to show that free trade has been profitable. He overlooks the fact that if the specialization is voluntary it will not be carried to the point where the marginal unit exported is worth less on the market than what is obtained in exchange for it, and, therefore, that while there may be no profit from trade for one of the countries under the conditions stated, there must be profit for at least one of the countries, and there can be loss to neither, if in each country the prices of its own products are proportional to their real costs.

III. TRADE IN MORE THAN TWO COMMODITIES

The problems connected with the doctrine of comparative costs have usually been examined under the simplifying assumptions that there are only two commodities and only two countries, in the belief that while the introduction of more commodities or countries into the problem would complicate the analysis it would require no serious qualitative change in the conclusions reached on the basis of the simpler assumptions as to the nature and profitability of international specialization.[1] This position seems to me substantially correct, although certain problems relating to foreign trade tend to be neglected when these assumptions are followed.

Graham has, however, put forth the claim that because of its adherence to the assumptions of only two countries and only two commodities, "the classical theory of international values seems . . . to be open to grave objections, objections which, while they do not subvert its foundations, nevertheless call for a substantial

---

[34] A. F. Burns, "A note on comparative costs," *Quarterly journal of economics,* XLII (1928), 495-500. Cf. the criticisms of his argument by G. Haberler, "The theory of comparative cost once more," *ibid.,* XLIII (1929), 380-81, and by the present writer, "Comparative costs: a rejoinder," *ibid.,* XLII (1928), 699.

[1] Cf. J. S. Mill, *Principles,* Ashley ed., p. 588: "Trade among any number of countries, and in any number of commodities, must take place on the same essential principles as trade between two countries and in two commodities."

modification of its conclusions,"[2] and in a later article[3] he has expressed his criticism in still stronger terms. Some of his criticisms are well taken, and expose genuine weaknesses in the classical expositions of the theory. As Graham explains, however, his objections are mainly directed against the reciprocal-demand theorizing of J. S. Mill and Marshall, and not against the doctrine of comparative costs, which is alone the concern of this chapter. The classical economists, moreover, departed from the rigid assumption of only two commodities more often than Graham would lead one to suppose. Several instances, in which analysis in terms of more than two countries bore on the relationship between comparative costs and terms of trade, are examined below.

Longfield appears to have been the first to attempt to extend the Ricardian analysis so as to deal explicitly with more than two commodities. Where there are only two commodities, then, given the comparative costs, there is no question as to which commodity each country will respectively import and export. But when there are more than two commodities the question as to what commodities will be exported and what imported by each of the countries cannot be so readily answered. Longfield's solution, although not entirely satisfactory, approached closely to what later became the accepted one. He abstracts from transportation costs, and from all elements in real costs but labor costs, and assumes tacitly that when trade is under way all prices will be identical in the two countries. He then assumes tentatively that wages in each country are uniform in all occupations. He offers, apparently without realizing it, several different and inconsistent solutions. He first asserts that wages in the two countries will be proportional to the *average* productivities of labor in the two countries. If English labor, presumably before trade, is on the average three times as productive as French labor, and therefore English money wages three times as high as French wages, then in all those industries in which English labor is, say, four times as productive as French labor money costs will be comparatively low, and these commodities will be exported; while in those industries in which English labor is not more than twice as productive as French

---

[2] F. D. Graham, "The theory of international values re-examined," *Quarterly journal of economics,* XXXVIII (1923), 54-55.
[3] "The theory of international values," *ibid.,* XLVI (1932), 581-616.

labor, money costs will be comparatively high, and these commodities will be imported. "Commerce will flow according as the proportion [of labor productivity] in particular trades is below or above the average proportion."[4]

Later he argues that if, while England was exporting the product of industries in which her labor was twice as productive as that of foreign countries, she acquired a threefold superiority in some other new industries, then her greater superiority in the new industries would make the old ones unprofitable. Labor in the old industries would have to be paid at the same rate as in the new, or at three times the rate prevailing abroad, and as its productivity in the old industries was only twice that of foreign labor, foreigners could produce the old products more cheaply in terms of money costs.[5]

Still later he provides a slightly different solution:

. . . if a nation enjoyed an immense superiority in the production of two or three articles of very general demand, the wages of her laborers might be, in consequence, so high that she could not compete with the rest of the world in any other manufacture, under a system of free trade. Let us suppose the productiveness of English labor to be ten times as great as that of any other nation, in the production of tin, calico, coals, cutlery, and pottery. The wages of her laborers will, in consequence, be much greater than those in any other nation; suppose them eight times as great, and suppose that English labor is only twice as productive as foreign labor, in the manufacture of other commodities. These latter, therefore, will be fabricated in the rest of the world, at the fourth part of the price which it will cost to make them in England.[6]

Longfield here presented correctly two important elements of the correct solution, namely, that for each country the commodities exported would be in the upper and the commodities imported would be in the lower range of its potential products with respect to comparative advantage in real costs, and that comparative money wage rates in the two countries would determine the precise line of division between export and import commodities. Where he failed, however, was in not providing a satisfactory explanation of the mode of determination of the ratio between

[4] M. Longfield, *Three lectures on commerce*, 1835, pp. 50-56.

[5] *Ibid.*, pp. 63-64.

[6] *Ibid.*, pp. 69-70.

wages in the two countries. His first two solutions are both obviously arbitrary and incorrect. Wages in the two countries would be proportional neither to the average productivities in all pre-trade employments, nor to the productivities in the two countries in the relatively most productive employment of *one* of the countries. His final formula, where he makes the wage rate in England exceed the wage rate abroad by a somewhat smaller ratio than the ratio of superiority of English labor over foreign in those employments in which England is comparatively most efficient, is correct as far as it goes, but is insufficient basis for a definite solution of the problem. This was an important step forward, but Longfield's contribution unfortunately attracted no attention, and other leading writers did not deal at all with the problem of what determines the relative level of money incomes in different countries or accepted an unsatisfactory solution offered by Senior.

Senior argued that within any country the level of money wages in all occupations—proper allowance being made for differences in the attractiveness of different occupations—was determined by the wages which labor could earn in the export industries, and that the comparative levels of wages in the export industries of different countries were determined by the comparative prices which the export products of the different countries could command in the world markets.[7] This became standard doctrine, although it left unanswered the question, given more than two commodities, as to how it was determined what would be the export industries. The prevailing level of wages would obviously be a factor in determining which industries could find export markets for their products. But to explain the determination of which industries should be export industries by reference to the general wage level, and to explain the general level of wages by reference to the level of wages prevailing in the export industries, would obviously be reasoning in a circle. Senior's argument sufficed to show that under equilibrium conditions wages in the non-export industries must be equal to wages in the export industries and that wages in different countries must be proportional to the value productivities of labor in the export industries of the respective countries. Senior failed to show, however, that

---

[7] N. W. Senior, *Three lectures on the cost of obtaining money*, 1830, pp. 11-30.

wages in the non-export industries were determined by wages in the export industries instead of both sets of wages being the common product of a number of factors.

In the writings of Ricardo and the two Mills no approach to a solution of this problem is to be found. Torrens, in an elaborate discussion bearing evidence of indebtedness to Senior and Longfield, made some progress. He pointed out that the extent to which a country could confine its exports to the commodities in whose production it was at or near the upper limit of its scale of comparative advantage depended on the extent of the foreign demand for these commodities. The wider the range of commodities which it had to export in order to employ its labor to the best advantage, the lower, other things equal, would be its relative level of money wages as compared to other countries.[8] Cairnes also attacked the problem, and reached the correct conclusion that while the general level of wages and foreign trade were intimately connected, the connection was one not of simple cause and effect operating in a single direction, but of joint dependence on the "productiveness of industry" as a whole and on the demands for different commodities.[9] He left vague, however, the precise nature of the interrelationships between productivities, wage levels, and international specialization.

A minor writer, P. J. Stirling, attempted to deal with the problem,[10] but did not carry it as far as had Longfield. He claimed that the two countries would find it to their interest to exchange at each other's "par," or on terms proportional to the cost of production of the exchanged commodities. "The terms of the exchange are regulated by the relative efficiency of the labor of the two countries in the production, not of all commodities, but of those commodities in the production of which their efficiency is most nearly equal." He thus assimilated the theory of international value to the theory of domestic value, completely where there is some product whose cost is identical in the two countries,

---

[8] R. Torrens, *Colonization of South Australia,* 1835, pp. 148-74, and especially pp. 169-74. What is here given is to be regarded as an interpretation of the general drift of Torrens's argument rather than a close paraphrase of his actual language.

[9] *Some leading principles of political economy,* 1874, pp. 334-41. Ohlin also points this out. (*Interregional and international trade,* 1933, p. 281.)

[10] P. J. Stirling, *The Australian and Californian gold discoveries,* 1853, pp. 211 ff.

and approximately where there is no such product. He presented the following case:

1,000 days labor will produce in

England	Mexico
50 iron	50 iron
25 tin	400 silver
50 wheat	100 wheat
150 cloth	75 cloth

Tin and silver are commodities peculiar to England and Mexico, respectively, and iron has identical costs in both countries. England will export cloth and import wheat, in the ratio of 150 units cloth to 100 units wheat, or the reciprocal of the ratio of their costs of production in the countries where they can be respectively produced at a comparative advantage. Although he does not expressly say so, silver and tin will also presumably exchange in the reciprocal of the ratio of their costs of production, or 400 units silver for 25 units tin, and iron will not move in trade. He says that if the English output of iron should increase to 55 units per 1000 days labor, other things remaining the same, then the rate at which English cloth would exchange for Mexican wheat would be 150 units cloth for 110 units wheat, which, it will be noted, makes the double factoral terms of trade with respect to these two commodities conform to the reciprocal of the ratio between the costs in the two countries of the commodity, iron, in which these costs approach most closely to equality. This is of course a purely arbitrary solution. But it has at least the one point of merit that it posits that the commodities which each country will export and import, respectively, will lie in the upper and the lower range of its series in terms of comparative advantage.

The necessary further step toward a satisfactory solution was taken by Mangoldt.[11] He shows that, cost of production being regarded as constant, each country will specialize in the production of a group of one or more commodities, that the commodities within each of these groups will exchange for each other in proportion to their real costs of production, and that the terms on which the commodities belonging to the two different groups will exchange for each other will be determined by the effect of

[11] H. von Mangoldt, *Grundriss der Volkswirthschaftslehre,* 2d ed., 1871, pp. 209-30. I follow here Edgeworth's excellent summary and commentary. *Papers relating to political economy,* II, 52-58.

the reciprocal demand of the two countries for each other's export commodities on the relative money rates of remuneration of the productive factors in the two countries. To find a basis for determining which country will export any particular commodity, Mangoldt posits the existence of a commodity such that, when its real costs in each of the respective countries are multiplied by the rates of remuneration prevailing there, there will result a

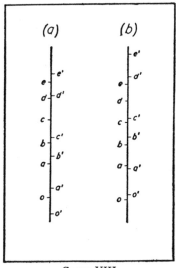

CHART VIII

money cost which is equal in both countries. Mangoldt presents his argument by means of laborious arithmetical illustrations, but it seems preferable to expound it with the aid of Edgeworth's ingenious logarithmic illustration, which, among other advantages, dispenses with the necessity of positing a commodity which is just on the margin of export or import.

Let the two columns of letters on either side of the vertical line in chart VIII (a) represent the logarithms of the real costs of the commodities a, b, c, d, e, in the two countries, with the left-hand column representing costs in country I and the right hand column representing costs in country II. Locate the points *a, b, c, d, e* by marking off from a fixed point *o* the logarithms of the real costs of the respective commodities in country I. Assume that the right-hand column can be made to slide freely up and down while the left-hand column is held rigid. From any fixed point o' on this sliding column mark off in the same way and on the same scale as for country I the points a', b', c', d', e', representing the logarithms of the real costs of the respective commodities in country II. Slide the right-hand column up or down to make oo' equal the logarithm of the ratio of wages in country II, (w_i), to wages in country I, (w_{ii}), so that

$$oo' = \log \frac{w_{ii}}{w_i},$$

putting o' below o when wages in country II are lower than wages in country I, as in Chart VIII(a), and putting o' above o when wages in country II are higher than wages in country I, as in chart VIII(b).[12] The relative rates of wages in the two countries, and therefore the distance of o' below or above o, will be determined by the reciprocal demand of the two countries for each other's products, which in turn will be partially determined by the comparative costs. Real costs in the two countries remaining the same, any shift in their reciprocal demand for each other's products would result in a change in relative wages in the two countries and therefore in a corresponding shift, upward or downward, in the movable right-hand column in chart VIII(a). If the demand of country I for country II's products in terms of its own products increased, other things remaining the same, the right-hand column in VIII(a) would slide upward, and vice versa. The vertical distances from o, when the right-hand column is adjusted properly, of the points a, a', b, b', etc., will then show the logarithms of the money costs of production of the different commodities in the two countries in terms of a common currency unit.

Since the reciprocal demands are not shown in this chart, it does not show how the comparative wage rates are determined. It shows, however, given the real costs in each country and the comparative wages as determined by reciprocal demand, what commodities each country will export and import, respectively,

<hr />

[12] Edgeworth presents only chart VIII (a) as drawn above. If wages were equal in both countries, then $\log \frac{w_{ii}}{w_i}$ would be zero, and o and o' would be on a level with each other.

and on what terms. If the wage rates are as indicated in chart VIII (a), the money costs of production will be higher in country I for commodities a, b, and c, and lower in country I for commodities d and e, than in country II. Country I will therefore export d and e, and import a, b, and c. The commodity terms of trade as between each pair of export and import commodities will be indicated by their comparative prices: e.g., the number of units of commodity a obtained by country I in return for 1 unit of d will be $\frac{\text{antilog } od}{\text{antilog } oa'}$; the number of units of b obtained by country I in return for one unit of e will be $\frac{\text{antilog } oe}{\text{antilog } ob'}$, and so forth. If there were a commodity with equal money costs of production in both countries, that commodity might be exported or imported by either country, might not move at all in foreign trade, or might be exported from one country to the other while being produced in both countries, quite consistently in each case with the conditions stated.

Whatever commodities country I will export and whatever ones she will import, the ratio of the logarithms of the real costs, and therefore also the ratio of the real costs in country I to the real costs in country II, will be lower for each of the commodities exported by country I than for any of the commodities imported by country I. Thus in (a) of the above chart, where country I exports commodities d and e and imports commodities a, b, and c, $\frac{od}{o'd'}$ and $\frac{oe}{o'e'}$ are both smaller than $\frac{oa}{o'a'}$, $\frac{ob}{o'b'}$, or $\frac{oc}{o'c'}$.[13] But as Edgeworth points out:[14]

This theory brings into view an incident which is apt to be masked as long as we confine ourselves to the case of two commodities, . . . namely, that it is not in general possible to determine *a priori*, from a mere observation of the [real] costs of production in the respective countries before the opening of the trade, which commodities will be imported and which produced at home. . . . Thus if *o'* in the figure be pushed up a little, the distances *o'a'*, *o'b'*, etc., being preserved con-

---

[13] Cf., for another and in some respects more general method of dealing with this problem, Haberler, "The theory of comparative cost once more," *Quarterly journal of economics,* XLIII (1929), 378-80, and *The theory of international trade,* 1936, pp. 136-39, 150-52.

[14] *Papers relating to political economy,* II, 55.

stant, e will become an export (from country no. I) instead of an import. But the position of o' depends not only the cost of production in each country, but also on the law of demand in each country for the different commodities.

This can perhaps be more clearly brought out by a comparison of (a) and (b). The scales of comparative costs are the same in both (a) and (b), but because of different reciprocal demands in the two cases the ratio between wages in country I and wages in country II is higher for (a) than for (b). As a result, country I exports only commodities d and e in case (a), as compared to commodities, b, c, d, and e in case (b).

IV. TRADE BETWEEN MORE THAN TWO COUNTRIES

The older writers rarely departed from the simplifying assumption that only two countries participated in foreign trade, and there are therefore only a few instances to be examined of discussion of the problems of international trade in terms of more than two countries.

William Ellis, in an attempt to meet the argument current in his time that England would suffer injury if competition with her staple export industries should develop abroad, introduced for the first time a third country into arithmetical illustrations of the type used by Ricardo and James Mill in their exposition of the doctrine of comparative costs.[1] He began with England and France engaged in trade, with England having a comparative advantage in cottons and France in silk. He then showed that the entrance into the trade of a third country, Brazil, with a comparative advantage in sugar, did not result in a loss to England. This, of course, did not meet the issue, and to have made his point he would have had to show that England could not lose from the entrance of Brazil into trade even if Brazil's comparative advantage was in the same commodity, cotton, as England's.[2]

---

[1] "Exportation of machinery," *Westminister review*, III (1825), 390.
[2] Cf. N. W. Senior, *Three lectures on the cost of obtaining money*, 1830, pp. 25-26:

> Many economists have maintained that no country can be injured by the improvement of her neighbors. If the continent, they say, should be able to manufacture cottons with half the labor which they now cost in England, the consequence would be, that we should be able to import our supply of cottons from Germany or France at a less expense than it costs us to

In his only reference to a third country, J. S. Mill first considered the effect on the terms of trade of England with Germany of the entrance into trade of a third country exporting the same commodity as Germany, namely, linen, and concluded that in consequence England would get her linen more cheaply in terms of English cloth. He then assumed that the third country produces neither linen nor any other commodity in demand in England, but has a demand for English cloth, and produces commodities which are in demand in Germany, and concluded that here also England's terms of trade with Germany would improve as the result of the entrance of the third country into trade, as Germany would have to induce England to take more of her linen in order to obtain the means of paying for her imports from the third country.[3] This seems to me to be correct reasoning as far as it goes. But there are other possibilities, unfavorable for England, which Mill left unmentioned, as, for instance, if this third country had no demand for English cloth but was herself a potential exporter of cloth and importer of German linen.

Torrens, in *The Budget*, had argued that if Cuba imposed a duty on English cloth, the restoration of equilibrium in the trade balance of the two countries would require a relative fall in the price of English cloth as compared to Cuban sugar. Merivale replied that if an alternative source for sugar was available to England, although at a somewhat higher price than that at which Cuban sugar was available before the imposition of the Cuban duty on cloth, the rise in the price of Cuban sugar and the fall in the price of English cloth "would soon bring into play the competition of the next cheapest country producing the same commodities as Cuba." While the Cuban duty, therefore, would affect adversely the terms of trade of England, the injury to her would

---

manufacture them, and might employ a portion of our industry now devoted to the manufacture of cottons, in procuring an additional supply of some other commodities. . . . But it must be remembered that England and the continent are competitors in the general market of the world. Such an alteration would diminish the cost of obtaining the precious metals on the continent, and increase it in England. The value of continental labor would rise, and the value of English labor would sink. They would ask more money for all those commodities, in the production of which no improvement had taken place, and we should have less to offer for them. We might find it easier to obtain cottons, but we should find it more difficult to import everything else.

[3] J. S. Mill, *Principles*, Ashley ed., pp. 591-92.

be much less than if Cuba were the only source of sugar.[4] Torrens, in reply, criticized some of the details of Merivale's argument, but conceded that on Merivale's assumption that sugar could be obtained from other sources at a price not much higher than the Cuban price prior to the imposition of the Cuban duty on English cloth, the terms of trade would not shift seriously against England.[5]

Cairnes claimed that, while if there were only two countries with wide differences in their comparative costs of producing the staple articles of trade there would be a very considerable range within which the terms of trade could be determined under the influence of comparative costs, if there were more countries competition from one or more of these countries would prevent the terms of trade from settling at either of the limiting rates.[6] This is valid as a probability, but Cairnes proceeded to too rigorous a conclusion:

. . . it is not the difference in the comparative costs of production in each pair of trading countries that fixes the limits to the possible variations of international values under the influence of reciprocal demand, but, among all countries mutually accessible for commercial intercourse, the difference of comparative costs, as it exists in the particular countries in which that difference is least. The limits of variation are thus set by the minimum, not by the maximum, difference in comparative cost among the various exchanging and competing countries.[7]

There is no such necessity. Assume the following situation:

Commodity	Units of real cost per unit of product		
	Country I	Country II	Country III
M................	1	2	3
N................	2	1	1

[4] Herman Merivale, *Lectures on colonization and colonies,* II (1842), 308-11.
[5] *The budget,* 1841-44, pp. 357-63.
[6] *Some principles of political economy newly expounded,* 1874, p. 352. This proposition is closely related to Graham's doctrine that where a number of countries are participating in trade, the terms of trade will be determined, within narrow limits, by the cost conditions alone. See *infra,* pp. 548-552.
[7] *Some leading principles,* p. 352.

If at the ratio of three of N for one of M country III is willing to supply all of commodity N which all three countries want, then this will be the effective rate of exchange of the two commodities, and trade between country I and country III will take place on terms corresponding to the "maximum difference

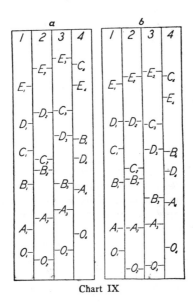

Chart IX

in comparative cost among the various exchanging and competing countries."

Triangular (or multiangular) trade has been examined by Graham,[8] Taussig,[9] von Mering,[10] and earlier writers,[11] by means of arithmetical examples of one type or another. Edgeworth's logarithmic illustration, modified so as to apply to more than

---

[8] Graham, "Theory of international values re-examined," *Quarterly journal of economics,* XXXVIII (1923), 68-86.

[9] F. W. Taussig, *International trade,* 1927, pp. 97-107.

[10] O. F. von Mering, "Ist die Theorie der internationalen Werte widerlegt?" *Archiv für Sozialwissenschaft,* LXV (1931), 257-65; *ibid., Theorie des Aussenhandels,* 1933, pp. 35-37.

[11] Cf. A. E. Cherbuliez, *Précis de la science économique,* 1862, I, 382 ff.; Bastable, "Economic notes," *Hermathena,* VII (1889), 120-21, and *Theory of international trade,* 4th ed., 1903, pp. 40-41.

two countries, seems to me, however, to be better suited to the purpose than arithmetical illustrations.

Chart IX is constructed on the same principles as chart VIII, except that four countries are included, instead of only two. What commodities each country will export and import and on what terms will be determined by the comparative costs in conjunction with the comparative wage rates, and the latter in turn will be determined, in part, by the reciprocal demands. For chart IX (a), the following situation will prevail under equilibrium conditions:

Country	I	II	III	IV
Exports.........	A	C	B	D
Imports.........	C, D	A, B, D, E	A, C, D, E	A, B, C

In addition, country I may either export or import or not trade in commodities B and E, and country IV may either import or export or not trade in commodity E, these commodities being on the margin of trade for those countries. The ratios in which the commodities will exchange for each other will, of course, be the reciprocals of their price ratios in a common currency. Their prices will be the antilogs of the logarithms of lowest money costs represented by the vertical distances from O_1 on a right line, as indicated below:

Commodity	A	B	C	D	E
Price = antilog of............	O_1A_1	O_1B_3	O_1C_2	O_1D_4	O_1E_1

In IX, (b) all the real costs are the same as in (a), but because the reciprocal demands are different in (b) from what they are in (a), money costs, prices, and the conditions of trade are also different, as compared to (a). Under equilibrium conditions, the following situation will prevail in (b):

Country	I	II	III	IV
Exports.......	A	C	B	D, E
Imports.......	B, C, D, E	B, D, E	A, C, D, E	A, B, C

In addition, country II may either import, export, or not trade in commodity A, this commodity being on the margin of trade for that country. The prices of the commodities will be as follows, measured as before by the antilogs of the indicated vertical distances:

Commodity	A	B	C	D	E
Price = antilog of............	O_1A_1	O_1B_3	O_1C_2	O_1D_4	O_1E_4

For country I, the change in the demand situation from (a) to (b) improves its terms of trade with the outside world, i.e., enables it to get B, C, D, and E in greater quantities per unit of its export A, or per unit of real cost, than before.

V. TRANSPORTATION COSTS

The theory of international trade is usually expounded on the assumption that there are no transportation costs, and this has occasionally been made a basis of criticism. But abstraction from transportation costs is also a common feature of the exposition of the theory of trade in a single market—"closed economy"—and such abstraction does not appear to be logically less permissible in the one case than in the other. Notwithstanding, moreover, the common assumption that transportation costs are relatively much more important in foreign than in domestic trade, it is by no means clear that such is the general situation. Cases are common where internal freight costs from producer to consumer are higher than international freight costs from producer to consumer, as can be seen from a study of the transportation item in the reports on costs of production in different countries made by the United States Tariff Commission.[1] The role of transportation costs, both of products and of factors of production, in con-

---

[1] Cf. also C. F. Bickerdike, "International comparisons of labor conditions," *Transactions of the Manchester Statistical Society*, 1911-12, p. 77: "I suggest that if we consider the broad facts regarding the bulk of important mineral and agricultural products, it is open to question whether the average bushel of wheat, pound of meat, ton of coals or of steel has to incur much if any greater expenses of transport before it reaches the final consumer in the United Kingdom than in reaching the final consumer in the United States."

tributing to regional differences of prices is an important field for study. It has not, however, been historically the particular responsibility of the theory of international trade, and judging what has so far been done in this field, under the name of *Standortslehre*, it is not yet apparent, in spite of the claims of its expo-

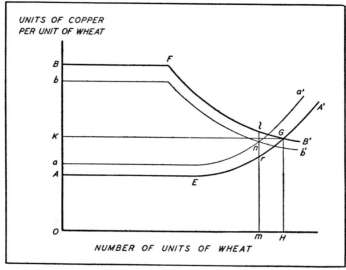

Chart X

nents,[2] that the indebtedness will be by the theory of international trade to *Standortslehre* rather than the other way round.

The relation of transportation costs to production costs and the terms of trade can be illustrated by chart X, a slight modi-

---

[2] Cf., e.g., Hermann Schumacher, "Location of industry," *Encyclopaedia of the social sciences*, IX (1933), 592: "[The theory of location] adds fulness to the general theory of division of labor, imparting a scientific character to discussions of international division of labor, so that it has even been termed the core of the theory of world economy." Cf. also Alfred Weber, "Die Standortslehre und die Handelspolitik," *Archiv für Sozialwissenschaft*, XXXII (1911), 667-88, where the treatment of location by the theory of international trade is discussed in terms which reveal utter miscomprehension of the most elementary propositions of that theory. As to Ohlin's dictum that "The theory of international trade is nothing but *internationale Standortslehre*" (*Interregional and international trade*, 1933, p. 589), he must have in mind either a *Standortslehre* or a theory of international trade (or both) which has but slight resemblance to what is to be found in the existing literature bearing these labels.

fication of Marshall's graphic method of dealing with foreign-trade problems. In country A a given amount of labor can produce either one unit of copper or one unit of wheat, and in country B a given amount of labor can produce either 3/2 units copper or ½ unit wheat. Country A will export wheat, and country B will export copper. In the absence of transportation costs, wheat will exchange for copper on terms within the limits of 1 wheat = 1 copper (= OA in chart) and 1 wheat = 3 copper (= $OB = 3 \times OA$, in chart). AA' represents the export supply curve of wheat in terms of copper of country A. BB' represents the import demand curve of wheat in terms of copper of country B. The chart as drawn implies that in the absence of trade (or with trade on terms of 1 wheat = 1 copper) country A would consume ($OA \times AE$) units of copper, and that in the absence of trade (or with trade on terms of 1 wheat = 3 copper) country B would consume BF wheat.

The actual transportation is assumed to be provided by the exporter. The charges for transportation are assumed to be 1 unit wheat payable in the export country for each 9 units of wheat transported and 1 unit copper payable in the export country for each 5 units of copper transported. With the transportation costs in the specified amounts, the possible limits of the terms of trade will be 1 wheat = 1.2 or Oa copper and 1 wheat = 2.7 or Ob copper. Country A's export supply curve for wheat in terms of copper will be aa', and country B's import demand curve for wheat in terms of copper will be bb'. The equilibrium terms of trade, which would have been 1 wheat = OK copper in the absence of transportation costs, will be 1 wheat = mr copper, net after payment of transportation costs, for country A, and 1 wheat = ml copper, net after payment of transportation costs, for country B. It is to be noted that with the existence of transportation costs the terms of trade net after payment of transportation costs will be different for the two countries, the difference being absorbed in meeting the costs of transportation. Given elasticities greater than unity for both the foreign-trade curves, volume of trade will be smaller and the net terms of trade will be less favorable for both countries when there are transportation costs than when these are zero. In the present case the existence of transportation costs will reduce the amount of wheat imported by country B from OH to Om units, and will reduce the amount of copper imported by country A from $(OH \times OK)$ units to $(Om \times Or)$ units.[3] The division of the costs of transportation as between the two countries will, as J. S. Mill contended, be determined by "the play of international demand."[4]

VI. INCREASING AND DECREASING COSTS

Ricardo, in his statement of the doctrine of comparative costs, assumed that costs of production were constant as output was varied, and this assumption has been followed, explicitly or implicitly, in much of the later literature, and in this chapter so far. Where costs are constant no issue arises as between average and marginal costs, since these are identical. If costs to the individual producer increase as output is increased, the doctrine of comparative costs still holds, but must be stated in terms of comparative marginal costs.

---

[3] The transportation costs relevant here are not the total transportation costs, but only the excess, if any, of international over internal transportation costs, in each case from the point of production to the point of consumption. For example, Aa represents the excess of the amount of the copper which country A has to pay for the cost of transporting one unit of foreign copper as compared to the amount of copper which would be absorbed in meeting transportation costs of one unit of domestically produced copper. Where internal freight costs are higher than international freight costs, the range between the limiting terms of trade will be wider, and the volume of foreign trade will be greater, than if no freight costs, internal or international, existed. In fact, differences in freight costs may create a comparative advantage which in the absence of freight costs would not exist at all. For a fuller treatment of the influence of transportation costs on the terms of trade, it would be necessary, of course, to deal with transportation as representing two or more additional commodities produced under conditions of joint cost, namely, inward and outward freights and freights according to commodity.

[4] *Principles,* Ashley ed., p. 589.

In an obscure and patently confused argument, Sidgwick attempted to show that the existence of transportation costs of commodities provided the sole basis for a theory of international values different from the theory of domestic values. (Henry Sidgwick, *The principles of political economy,* 1st ed., 1883, pp. 214-30; 2d ed., 1887, pp. 202-16, in somewhat different form.) Sidgwick refuses to go behind money costs of production, and his argument, I believe, reduces itself to the proposition that the prices in any country of the products of any two (or more) countries, after allowances for transportation costs, are proportional to their money costs of production in their countries of origin, a proposition which no one would deny, and which is embodied, implicitly when not explicitly, in the classical doctrine of comparative costs instead of, as Sidgwick supposed, constituting a correction thereof. For a more extended comment, see the original version of this chapter, "The doctrine of comparative costs," *Weltwirtschaftliches Archiv,* XXXVI (1932, II), 373-77.

If there are no external economies or diseconomies of large production, pecuniary or technological, i.e., if a producer who keeps his own output constant experiences no change in costs as the result of a change in the output of his industry as a whole, then either in an isolated country or under free trade labor will tend to be distributed among the respective industries until, at equilibrium, its marginal value return *to the industry as a whole* per unit of labor is equal in all industries. Assuming only two commodities and two countries and labor as the only factor of production, abstracting as usual from transportation costs, and assuming that before trade country A has a comparative advantage in marginal cost in the production of commodity M, it will be to the advantage of country A under trade to transfer its labor from the production of N to the production of M until the point is reached where its comparative marginal cost advantage ceases.[1] Under constant cost, there is an apparent[2] gain from trade, measured in saving in cost on the imported commodity, even on the marginal unit of trade, unless the terms of trade correspond to the relative costs of production of the country in question, when there is no gain for that country from any part of the trade. But under increasing costs, the saving in costs is confined to the inframarginal units of trade.[3]

Under constant costs, a country will not both import and pro-

---

[1] Unless before that point is reached country A has already transferred all of its labor to the production of M or country B has already transferred all of its labor to the production of N and cannot supply country A with all of the units of N which A is prepared to take. The former may be the case if country A is much smaller, and the latter may be the case if country A is much larger, than country B. It will be assumed that neither is the case.

[2] Even under constant costs, there will be no gain from the marginal unit of trade, since trade will be carried to the point at which the possibility of gain is exhausted. There will still be a gain at the margin measured in terms of cost alone, however, but the value of the export commodity will have risen relative to the value of the import commodity, so that although additional units of the foreign commodity could be obtained by import for an expenditure of labor less than that at which they could be produced at home, the market value of additional imports would be less than the value of the amount of the export commodities which would have to be given in exchange for them. Even before the marginal unit is reached, while the saving in cost as compared to domestic production will be evidence that there is gain from trade, there will be no close relationship between the amount of saving in cost and the amount of gain, and the latter will never be greater and will usually be smaller than the former.

[3] Cf. the discussion on this point between Edgeworth, *Economic journal,* VII (1897), 402, note 2, and Bastable, *Theory of international trade,* 4th ed., 1903, pp. 196-97. Cf. also, *infra,* p. 547, note 24.

duce for itself any commodity unless the price relations between that and other commodities produced in that country correspond to their relative costs of production in that country, i.e., unless that country is deriving no benefit from the import of that particular commodity. This does not hold true, however, for commodities produced under conditions of increasing costs, when simultaneous importation and domestic production of a commodity indicate that all (except the marginal unit) of the imports are obtained at lower real costs than those at which they could be produced at home. Under increasing costs, both (all) commodities can conceivably be produced simultaneously under equilibrium conditions in both (all) countries. When trade is carried to the equilibrium point under increasing costs, i.e., to the point where each country is fully exploiting the possible gains from trade, the ratios of marginal real costs as between the two (all) countries will be the same for all commodities being simultaneously produced in both (all) of these countries, and it will be the comparative differences in the marginal costs which would result if the existing trade were altered in volume or direction, rather than any prevailing difference in actual marginal costs, which would explain the existing trade.

It should be apparent that charts such as charts VIII and IX above, which were constructed on the assumption of constant costs, would not be applicable to illustrate the problem of international specialization where increasing costs are operative. Since the marginal costs in each industry and country would vary with the output, there would not be a single and fixed scale of costs for the different commodities in each country. If, as was likely, the rate of increase of marginal costs as output increased differed from commodity to commodity, and differed for the same commodity from country to country, there would be no fixed order of rank of the commodities in terms of comparative marginal costs for each country, as their ranks would tend to change with substantial changes in the outputs of the respective commodities. As has already been pointed out, under equilibrium conditions specialization would be carried to the stage where the relative scales of marginal costs would be uniform for all the countries producing the respective commodities.

Schüller has made an elaborate critique of free trade which rests in large part on considerations which must be regarded as essentially short run in character or as inconsistent with free competition, and therefore as outside the scope of the present discussion.[4] Such, for instance, is his argument that factors of production which are displaced from their original employment by foreign competition ordinarily fail in substantial degree to find alternative employment. His argument also that commercial policy may either attract productive resources from abroad or induce them to emigrate, and that the former is desirable and the latter undesirable, whatever its validity—and his argument is exceedingly one-sided, since if the injury to one industry from free trade in its product tends to drive its factors out of the country, the benefit to other industries and to consumers should in like manner tend to induce immigration and check emigration of the factors not engaged in this industry—is also outside the scope of this article. But an essential portion of his case is made to rest on the existence of a wide range between the money costs at which different producers within an industry can produce their output. In the long run, and even in the short run under free competition, there must necessarily be a tendency for equality of marginal money costs for all producers in a given industry, and it is these marginal costs, and not the average costs which Schüller alone considers, which are the regulator of value. None of his inferences unfavorable to free trade as a long-run policy which depend for their validity on the simultaneous existence of different costs for different producers therefore has any force.[5]

It has frequently been claimed by economists that if a country has a comparative advantage in costs in an industry or industries subject to increasing costs as output is increased and has a comparative disadvantage in an industry or industries subject to decreasing costs, it may not be to the interest of this country to specialize in accordance with comparative costs. All of the attempts which have been made to demonstrate this proposition follow the same general line of argument. It will be conceded beforehand that there is a trace of validity in this proposition,

---

[4] R. Schüller, *Schutzzoll und Freihandel,* 1905. Cf. the criticism of Schüller's analysis by G. Haberler, *The theory of international trade,* 1936, pp. 253 ff.

[5] The analysis by Kemper Simpson, "A re-examination of the doctrine of comparative costs," *Journal of political economy,* XXXV (1927), 465-79, in this case favorable to free trade, seems to me to be similarly defective through its employment of particular expenses curves, or "bulkline" cost curves, as if they were analogous to the cost and supply curves of orthodox price theory.

but a very faint one, long-run considerations alone being understood to be relevant.

In the long run, specialization in accordance with *marginal cost to the industry or country* must be to the advantage of a country, in so far as costs are made the criterion of advantage. If a country is at a comparative advantage in marginal costs in an industry subject to increasing costs, the transfer of a marginal unit of the productive factors from the decreasing-cost to the increasing-cost industry must necessarily yield to that country a greater increment of whichever commodity it prefers to have than this marginal unit of the productive factors would yield if left in the decreasing-cost industry. Let the country with the comparative advantage in the increasing-cost industry be designated by M, the increasing-cost product by a, and the decreasing cost product by b. At the given stage of specialization in this country, let $\frac{1}{X_a}$ be the marginal cost per unit of a in terms of units of the productive factors, and let $\frac{1}{X_b}$ be the marginal cost of b. Then X_a, X_b will be, respectively, the number of units of a and of b produced at the margin by one unit of the productive factors. Suppose further that at the given stage of specialization in M, X_a units of a can be exchanged in foreign trade for Y units of b. Since by hypothesis M still has a comparative marginal advantage in the production of a, then $Y > X_b$, and by using the marginal unit of the factors of production to produce a rather than b, M gains either $Y - X_b$ units of b, if what it wants is more units of b, or $X_a - \frac{X_b}{Y}(X_a)$ units of a, if what it wants is more units of a. In either case, M gains by further specialization in the production of a. The only basis on which specialization under these conditions of marginal cost might be unprofitable to M would be if specialization and trade were not governed by industry marginal costs.

All of the many attempts to demonstrate the possibility that specialization in accordance with comparative costs by a country with a comparative cost advantage in increasing-cost industries and a comparative cost disadvantage in decreasing-cost industries may be unprofitable for it have much in common, and only three of the more elaborate ones will be examined here, and only one in detail.[6] Nicholson makes such an attempt,[7] which is open to other criticism, but which can be disposed of on the ground that his analysis is not completely in marginal-cost and marginal-return terms. He posits the case of a country with a comparative advantage in the production of wheat subject to increasing costs and a comparative disadvantage in manufacturing subject to decreasing costs. As the result of the opening of trade, manufacturing becomes unprofitable, and the factors are shifted to wheat-growing, manufactures being imported in exchange for wheat. There results for the country, in an extreme case, no increase in the amount of wheat available for consumption and a decrease in manufactures. Nicholson bases his conclusions on marginal-cost analysis as far as wheat is concerned, but on average-cost analysis for manufacturing. Had he applied marginal-cost analysis to both, he could not have obtained results of this kind.

Francis Walker obtains similar results by means of arithmetical computations in terms of money income from charts showing monetary-demand and average-cost curves before and after trade.[8] His procedure is defective in almost every conceivable particular. He at no point carries his analysis to a stage consistent with long-run equilibrium. He fails to provide for full employment of all the factors both before and after trade. He keeps all of his analysis on a superficial monetary level, and makes no attempt to allow for changes in the significance of the monetary unit as the result of trade, even though he includes "consumers' surpluses" measured in money in his computations. His results are totally devoid of significance.

Graham[9] also obtains similar results by a method of analysis not differing in any essential from that used by Nicholson, although he makes no reference to him. Graham, however, sets forth his argument in much greater detail, with less ambiguity in use of terms, and with at least passing reference to the objec-

---

[6] In addition to the three examined here, there may be cited Alfred Marshall, "Some aspects of competition" [1890], reprinted in *Memorials of Alfred Marshall*, A. C. Pigou ed., 1925, pp. 261-62; T. N. Carver, "Some theoretical possibilities of a protective tariff," *Publications of the American Economic Association*, 3d series, III, no. 1 (1902), 169-70.

[7] J. S. Nicholson, *Principles of political economy*, II (1897), 307-09, 317-18.

[8] F. Walker, "Increasing and diminishing costs in international trade," *Yale review*, XII (1903), 32-57.

[9] F. D. Graham, "Some aspects of protection further considered," *Quarterly journal of economics*, XXXVII (1923), 199-216.

tions which might be raised against his reasoning on value-theory grounds. He supports his argument with arithmetical illustrations, which will be reproduced here with modifications which do no violence to the original but facilitate their appraisal.

Case I. Incipient Specialization :[10] 4 wheat = 3½ watches

Country A	Country B
(200)	(200)
1 day's labor = 4 wheat	1 day's labor = 4 wheat
(200)	(200)
1 day's labor = 4 watches	1 day's labor = 3 watches

The comparative advantage of country A is in watches and of country B in wheat, and in so far as comparative costs alone are concerned trade may take place between the two countries on any terms within the limits of 4 wheat = 3 watches and 4 wheat = 4 watches. The actual ratio is assumed to be 4 wheat = 3½ watches and when trade is initiated a small amount of trade takes place at that ratio, country A exporting watches and importing wheat. Both countries appear to gain from the trade, country A getting 4 wheat at a cost in labor with which she could produce only 3½ wheat at home, and country B getting 3½ watches at a cost in labor with which she could produce only 3 watches at home.

Case II. Intermediate Specialization: 4 wheat = 3½ watches

Country A	Country B
(100)	(300)
1 day's labor = 4.5 wheat	1 day's labor = 3.5 wheat
(300)	(100)
1 day's labor = 4.5 watches	1 day's labor = 2 watches

Trade is carried further, on the same terms of exchange of wheat for watches, country B increasing her specialization in the production of wheat and country A in the production of watches. But in both countries the production of wheat is subject to increasing costs and the production of watches to decreasing costs. Each unit of trade still seems to yield gain to both the participants, since country A gets each 4 units of wheat at a

---

[10] The figures in upper brackets represent the amounts of labor employed in each industry. They are not to be found in the original illustrations, but are added by the present writer to show more clearly the degree of specialization reached at each stage.

labor cost at which she could only produce 3½ wheat at home, and country B gets 3½ watches at a labor cost at which she could produce only 2 2/7 watches at home. But country B is really losing from the trade, since as she increases her total output of wheat and decreases her total output of watches, the productivity of labor falls in both industries. If in case I the total trade consisted of an exchange of 4 wheat for 3.5 watches and in case II the total trade consisted of an exchange of 320 wheat for 280 watches, then in case I country B would have as its total income 796 wheat + 603.5 watches, and in case II only 730 wheat + 480 watches.

This is as far as Graham goes with his illustrations, but if the argument is sound, and if it is assumed—and there is no reason why it should not be—that the indicated trends of cost as output is varied continue to operate, they can be, and must be, carried still further, with rather spectacular results.

Case III. Full Specialization: 4 wheat = 3.5 watches

Country A	Country B
(1)	(399)
1 day's labor = 5 wheat	1 day's labor = ½ wheat
(399)	(1)
1 day's labor = 5 watches	1 day's labor = ¼ watch

Except for 1 unit of labor, each country is now completely specialized in the employment in which it is at a comparative advantage. But it is profitable to the participants in trade to carry specialization to the fullest extent possible, for if the day's labor still engaged in producing watches in country B were to be diverted to growing wheat, it could with the ½ unit wheat so obtained secure in exchange 7/16 of a watch, instead of only the ¼ watch which it can produce directly. Country B has nevertheless lost severely as the result of specialization in accordance with comparative advantage. If in case III it exchanges a total of 120 wheat for 105 watches, its income will consist of 79.5 wheat + 105¼ watches, as compared to 730 wheat + 480 watches under partial specialization (case II), 796 wheat + 603.5 watches under only incipient specialization (case I), and 800 wheat + 600 watches in the total absence of trade! Trade, which economists have regarded as a beneficent activity, appears under these conditions to be for one of the countries rather a form of economic suicide, and the protectionist a wise benefactor.

These extraordinary results are the consequence, and wholly the consequence, of value-theory reasoning, implicit or explicit in Graham's argument, which is either unambiguously erroneous or is of very limited practical significance. As his argument has so far been reproduced it rests on analysis in terms of average money costs for both the increasing-cost and the decreasing-cost industries. Graham concedes that in the increasing-cost industry marginal and not average costs will guide the producer, and that if the figures for output which he gives for wheat are marginal, then the increase of rent to landlords will be an offsetting item not accounted for in his analysis, which may more than compensate for the loss to B shown by his illustrations. He claims, however, that his conclusion that country B under the conditions assumed must lose by free trade is "inevitable" if his figures for wheat costs are interpreted as figures of average cost,[11] provided the marginal costs are not such as to make trade unprofitable to the individuals participating therein at the terms of trade assumed by him. Graham here both concedes too much and claims too much. His interpretation of marginal cost as the cost of the most expensive unit to produce is faulty, and the excess of the marginal cost of wheat over its average cost would necessarily be much higher than he indicates, and therefore the range of trade profitable to individual traders in B, granting his other assumptions, much less than he indicates. On the other hand, he concedes too much when he says that the increase in rent to landlords when the output of wheat is increased will be an offsetting item which may more than compensate for the loss to B shown by his illustrations. The loss to B shown there exceeds the increase in the cost of producing wheat and includes this plus the increase in the cost of producing watches. But rent in terms of wheat cannot increase with an increase in the production of wheat unless the average cost exclusive of rent rises, and the increase in average

---

[11] It is easy to show that the illustrations are in several respects inconsistent with equilibrium unless they are so interpreted. Graham, for example, keeps the relative values of wheat and watches constant while varying their relative costs in country B. Assuming, as he does, that average costs are significant in the determination of watch values, but marginal costs in the determination of wheat values, this assumed constancy in the relative values of watches and wheat would be impossible as the ratios of average watch costs to marginal wheat costs in B varied. His illustrations are consistent, however, with maintenance of constancy in the ratios between average watch costs and marginal wheat costs in both A and B, if generously interpreted.

cost of wheat, inclusive of rent, must therefore be greater than the increase in average rent per unit of wheat.

Regardless of whatever defects there may be in Graham's handling of the costs of wheatgrowing, his general conclusions would still be acceptable if his treatment of the costs of watchmaking could be accepted as satisfactory. It is in his treatment of decreasing costs that the fatal flaw in his argument is to be found. A decrease in unit costs as output is increased may be due either to "internal" economies, i.e., economies accruing to an individual producer because *he* expands his output, or to "external" economies, i.e., economies accruing to an individual producer because the industry as a whole is expanding its output. Graham says that "the reasoning in the text simply assumes that a decreasing unit cost is obtained by an expansion of the production of watches; whether the cause of it be external or internal economies is immaterial to the theory. . . ."[12] It is, on the contrary, very material to the theory, as Knight has shown in a reply to Graham's argument to which the present analysis is greatly indebted.[13]

Suppose, first, that the economies in the watch industry are internal. Then, since the larger the scale of plant the lower the unit costs, competition will be inconsistent with long-run equilibrium, and there will be a tendency toward the monopolization of the industry by a single concern. The principle governing the relation of cost to price is, of course, different for a monopoly than for a competitive industry, but marginal rather than average cost remains the determining factor of price and no resources will be transferred from watchmaking to wheatgrowing if a loss in value of product results therefrom. But even if, by exception, we depart from long-run assumptions and take the situation prevailing while competition still continues to be effective in the watchmaking industry, it still remains true that no resources will be transferred from watchmaking to wheatgrowing if the transfer would involve a loss in value of product. Any producer of watches in country B who reduces his output of watches to produce wheat instead loses thereby the marginal output in watches and gains only the marginal increment of wheat. If, as indicated in cases I

[12] *Ibid.*, p. 204, note.
[13] F. H. Knight, "Some fallacies in the interpretation of social cost," *Quarterly journal of economics*, XXXVIII (1924), 592-604.

and II above, 100 units of labor are diverted in country B from producing watches to producing wheat, the transfer of the units of labor would involve a loss of 400 watches to get 250 wheat at a time when 400 watches are worth 457 wheat. Assuming internal economies in the watch industry, there simply would be no such transfer of labor. Had Graham dealt with his problem in terms of marginal costs and marginal returns for both industries, he could not have obtained results unfavorable to free trade.

If, however, the economies are external, then the individual producer will not take them into account in regulating his contribution to the output of the watch industry as a whole. The decrease in unit costs to the other producers if he should enter the industry, and the increase in unit costs to the other producers if he should withdraw from the industry, will not affect his decisions. In such a case those changes in marginal cost to the industry as output of the industry changes which are due to the accrual or loss of external economies will play no part in the regulation of the industry's output, and a conceivable case can be made out for Graham's conclusion, but with a very limited field for its practical application.

In the first place, if the external economies are a function of the size of the world industry, and not of the national portion of it, as may well be the case, they will still be retained by a national industry which shrinks in size if this shrinkage is offset by a corresponding expansion of the foreign industry. Suppose that as the watch industry as a whole expands and increases its purchases of watchmaking machinery, such machinery can consequently be obtained at lower unit prices. If there is free trade in machinery, this economy in machinery costs will not be lost to the watch industry in a particular country merely because it is shrinking in size, if there is no shrinkage in the size of the watch industry as a whole.

Second, if the external economies resulting from size of the industry are purely pecuniary, and if what they reflect is merely bargaining advantage for a large industry in hiring *domestic* factors or buying *domestic* materials, then they are not real national economies and nothing is lost to the country when they disappear.

A conceivable case for protection on the basis of the existence of external economies in an industry which from the individual producer's point of view is at a comparative disadvantage in costs can be made out, therefore, only where these external economies are (a) dependent on the size of the national and not the world industry and (b) are technological rather than pecuniary, or, if pecuniary, are not at the expense of domestic sellers of services or materials to the industry. The scope for the application of the argument is extremely limited, especially as it seems difficult even to suggest plausible hypothetical cases of the existence of genuine technological external economies. Instead of providing a substantial "scientific" basis for the popularity of protection among the vulgar, as Graham seems to think, his thesis reduces to little more than a theoretical curiosity.

A similar theoretical case can be made for an export tax on the product of an industry subject to external technological diseconomies, on the ground that the marginal cost to the individual producer which regulates prices and the course of trade will be less than the marginal cost to the industry as a whole and to the country in the case of such an industry, and that its scale of operations should therefore be contracted. Conceivably important instances of external technological diseconomies are to be found in the grazing, hunting, and fishing industries, where no rent is charged for the use of valuable natural opportunities and they tend therefore to be overexploited with resultant waste, in competitive digging of wells over a common pool of oil, and in general when competition tends to raise costs rather than to lower them. But for both external economies and external diseconomies, what case there is for interference with competition applies to trade as a whole, and to export trade only as a part of such trade. Since external technological diseconomies tend to result in prices disproportionately low as compared to real costs, the only ground on which it can be argued that there is a basis for discrimination between domestic and foreign trade is that non-interference with the domestic trade results in unduly low prices to *domestic* consumers, whereas non-interference with the foreign trade results in unduly low prices to *foreign* consumers.

Knight goes still further in his rejection of Graham's argument. He claims that there cannot be external economies for a concern ("business unit") A which are not internal economies for another concern B within the same industry; that under these circumstances the industry will tend to be a monopoly and that the principles which will then regulate value will not be those appropriate to competitive conditions.[14] I see no logical necessity that external economies to one concern must be internal economies to any other concern, whether in the same or in another industry. But suppose it be granted that external economies to industry C are internal economies to industry D, and suppose it be granted further that industry D is under monopoly control. It will still be possible that as C's demand for D's produce increases, D's prices will decrease, if production by D is subject to decreasing costs. External economies can therefore still accrue to industry C even though these economies, external to C, are internal for another, monopolized, industry D.

Knight claims further that even if decreasing costs existed in the watch industry, country B specializing in wheat would get the same benefit from these economies by importing the watches from A as by producing them at home.[15] This would be true only if as B proceeded with its specialization in wheat the terms of exchange between watches and wheat moved against watches sufficiently to offset the opposite movement of their relative marginal costs *to the industries as a whole* in B. Now the whole point of the argument from external economies is that where they exist, relative prices need conform only to relative marginal costs to individual producers and need not conform to relative marginal costs to the industries as a whole. The price of watches, if watch-making is subject to external economies, will be higher than their marginal money cost to the industry as a whole.

Haberler has characterized Graham's argument as but a variant of the infant-industry argument for protection.[16] But the validity of Graham's thesis, if it is valid at all, is not dependent upon short-run considerations. Decreasing marginal costs are not necessarily nor typically a short-run phenomenon,[17] and it is Graham's contention that if an industry is operating under decreasing costs it may pay to protect it even if it has a permanent and irremovable comparative disadvantage in costs.

---

[14] "Some fallacies in the interpretation of social cost," *loc. cit.*, pp. 597-98.

[15] "On decreasing cost and comparative cost. A rejoinder," *ibid.*, XXXIX (1925), 333.

[16] Haberler, "Die Theorie der komparativen Kosten," *Weltwirtschaftliches Archiv*, XXXII (1930, II), 356.

[17] Though I would now concede that they are a possible phenomenon even in the short run, and that the argument by which this possibility is ordinarily denied is defective.

VII. PRICES, MONEY COSTS, AND REAL COSTS

The doctrine of comparative costs was stated by Ricardo and his followers in terms of "real" costs as distinguished from money costs. It has been interpreted by some modern writers as if it denied that prices, or money costs, or "expenses of production," had anything to do with the course of foreign trade, and as if a reformulation of the theory of international trade in terms of prices or of money costs would of itself involve a correction of Ricardo or would introduce into the theory an element not already included in the classical expositions thereof. This view, however, involves a total miscomprehension of the classical theory.

For all the classical writers it was common doctrine, as has already been argued,[1] that under free trade, and in the absence of transportation costs, prices of identical internationally-traded commodities would be uniform in all countries when expressed in the same currency. It was also common doctrine that the prices of commodities produced within a country would be, or would tend to be, proportional to their money costs of production, that differences in supply prices were the immediate determinant of the course of trade, and, therefore, that differences in money costs of production determined the course of trade. They extended their analysis to real costs not as a substitute for analysis in terms of money costs, but in order to show that, although trade was immediately governed by price and money-cost differences, these differences in prices and money costs reflected differences in real costs and were therefore significant for welfare appraisals.[2] The real-cost analysis was intended, therefore, to give significance to the analysis in pecuniary terms, and not to replace it.

For the classical school, the immediate determinant of whether a particular commodity will be obtained abroad or at home, or

---

[1] Cf. *supra*, pp. 314 ff.

[2] In considering the profitability of trade for a particular country, it is to be noted, its own money costs matter only as they are proportional to the real costs, whereas the real costs of the outside world matter only as they are reflected in foreign supply prices. It does not matter to an importing country why its imports are cheap, provided they can be relied upon to remain cheap. The proper basis for determining the profitability of trade to a particular country, therefore, is the comparison of its own relative real costs for different commodities with foreign relative supply prices of the same commodities.

exported, is the *absolute* difference in the prices at which domestic and foreign producers are willing to furnish it.[3] Actual market prices being assumed to be everywhere equal in the absence of transportation costs, commodities will be exported or imported according as their domestic *supply prices* or money costs of production are *absolutely* lower or higher than their foreign supply prices or money costs of production expressed in the same currency. Some writers, however, transferring Ricardo's comparative-cost doctrine too abruptly into the realm of money costs and prices, have argued that trade is, or should be, governed by comparative differences in money costs even in the absence of absolute differences in money costs.

A glaring case is an anonymous pamphlet published in 1818, which has been reprinted and recommended to the favorable attention of modern scholars by Arnold Plant.[4] The main thesis of the pamphlet is that it is profitable to merchants to export a commodity, A, selling at a higher price at home than abroad and to import a commodity, B, if the ratio of the home price of A to the home price of B is lower than the ratio of the foreign price of A to the foreign price of B:

The advantage of any trade, where one article is to be exported, and either mediately or immediately to be exchanged for another to be imported, depends on the proportion between the quantities of the two articles that may be bought for the same price in the one market being effectually different from the proportion between the quantities of the same two articles that may be bought in the other market for one and the same price: that article, the home price of any proposed quantity of which will buy less of the other article (at home) than the foreign price of the *same* quantity of that article will

---

[3] Cf. Ricardo, *Principles, Works*, p. 100: "The motive which determines us to import a commodity, is the discovery of its relative cheapness abroad: it is the comparison of its price abroad with its price at home." *Ibid.*, p. 78: "Every transaction in commerce is an independent transaction. Whilst a merchant can buy cloth in England for £45, and sell it with the usual profit in Portugal, he will continue to export it from England."

[4] *A letter on the true principles of advantageous exportation* [1818], reprinted in *Economica*, XIII (1933), 40-50. Plant, in his introduction, says of it that "here is a formal, generalized statement of the main principle [of comparative cost] by an obvious master of precise theoretical exposition," and that "The anonymous author of this tract should take his place with Ricardo, J. S. Mill, Longfield, Mangoldt and Edgeworth as one of the outstanding exponents of the theory of international trade in the nineteenth century."

abroad, being the one to export, and the other the one to import: in other words, that article (of the two) which is, relatively to the other, cheaper at home than abroad, being the one to export, and the other the one to import.

Observe: it matters nothing whether the article, thus comparatively cheaper, be *really* cheaper or dearer than in the other market; but only that it should be cheaper, if paid for in that other article. As for example, silk stockings, bought with brandy in England, may be cheaper than in France. A gallon of brandy may buy more than in France; though perhaps, absolutely, silk stockings may be as cheap in France as in England, or cheaper.[5]

But if the supply price of silk stockings is higher in England than in France, no sensible merchant will voluntarily export stockings to France in exchange for brandy when money can be exported instead.[6] As Plant points out, the author's exposition, much of it algebraic, is of excellent quality. Unfortunately, however, the algebra is wasted on the exposition of a fallacy. This and other similar instances,[7] of failure to see that it is *absolute* differences and not merely comparative ones which matter when it is prices and money costs and not real costs which are under consideration, were sometimes the result of a laudable desire to

---

[5] *Ibid.*, p. 45. (Italics in original text.)

[6] The author meets this objection by conceding that while the profit would be greater if money were exported instead of stockings, there would still be some profit in exporting the stockings in exchange for brandy. (*Ibid.*, p. 48.) But why not export the money, which would appear less troublesome as well as more profitable? Better doctrine on this point was expounded by a contemporary writer, in the following passage:

> Whoever exports an article, sells it for as high a price as he can obtain; but he must find the commodity he brings back, after paying his own expenses, at least equal in value to what he exported: if this were not the case, he would lose by the trade, and would give it up. If money is the article brought back, the money must be capable of purchasing at least an equal quantity of the commodity exported, or the trade would be abandoned. (Thomas Hopkins, *Economical enquiries relative to the laws which regulate rent, profit, wages, and the value of money,* 1822, p. 84.)

[7] Cf., e.g., W. Cockburn, *Commercial œconomy: or the evils of a metallic currency,* 2d ed., 1819, p. 5:

> If a merchant were to purchase a quantity of cotton goods for £100, and send them to Petersburgh and sell them for £50, it would appear at first sight almost certain, that he had made a bad commercial experiment. But the fact might be otherwise. If with his £50 he were to purchase hemp, which hemp, on its arrival in London, sold for £200, the speculation on the whole would turn out beneficial.

meet the argument, that in the absence of protection a country might find it impossible to withstand foreign competition abroad or in its domestic market because its price level was too high, by demonstrating that export could be profitably carried on regardless of the general price level. The classical economists would of course have met this argument in another manner, by contending that England could not long maintain a price level so high as to shut off all exports and that forces would operate automatically, through gold movements, to restore a relationship between the English and the outside price levels under which a normal volume of exports could be maintained with profit to the individual exporters.

Walras, in his only treatment of the theory of international trade, made almost exactly the converse error, and applied to costs in terms of quantities of the factors reasoning valid only for costs in money terms:

Notre pays serait arrivé, en dernière analyse, à faire du blé en faisant du drap. Il aurait ainsi substitué les coéfficients de fabrication de l'étranger aux siens propres pour le blé, en même temps que l'étranger opérait la substitution inverse pour le drap. Là est l'essence du libre échange, et les deux substitutions sont corrélatives.[8]

What Walras's proposition amounts to is that under trade the prices of the products of the two countries must be proportional to their real costs. Instead of being universally valid, this proposition will be valid only in the special case where—assuming labor to be the only cost—wage rates are uniform in both countries under trade. The only generally valid proposition which can be made as to the real costs at which imports are obtained is that they will be lower than—or in the limiting case equal to—the real costs at which they could have been produced at home. If each country has an absolute advantage in the production of its export commodity, and if wage rates are not uniform in both countries, one of the countries will obtain its import commodity at a real cost to itself *lower* than its real cost in its country of origin while the other country will obtain its import commodity at a real cost to itself *higher* than its real cost in its country of origin. If one of the countries is at an absolute disadvantage in the pro-

---

[8] Léon Walras, *Études d'économie politique appliquée*, 1898, p. 296.

duction of both commodities, that country cannot possibly obtain its import commodity at a real cost to itself as low as that at which it is produced in its country of origin.

Ricardo, assuming perfect occupational mobility of the factors at home and imperfect international mobility of the factors, held that while the relative values of home-produced commodities were governed by their relative real costs of production, this rule did not hold for commodities produced in different countries:

> The same rule which regulates the relative value of commodities in one country does not regulate the relative value of the commodities exchanged between two or more countries. . . . In one and the same country, profits are, generally speaking, always on the same level; or differ only as the employment of capital may be more or less secure and agreeable. It is not so between different countries.[9]

Other classical economists as a rule took this proposition over from Ricardo without question.[10] It seems, however, to have worried Torrens. While he stated the doctrine himself at times, he seemed at one time to believe that in doing so he was disagreeing with Ricardo,[11] perhaps because he had heard McCulloch ex-

---

[9] *Principles, Works,* pp. 75-76. Assuming as he presumably does here that the proportion of labor to capital is within a country uniform in all industries, and that wages are uniform in all occupations, uniformity of the interest rate in all occupations involves proportionality of prices of domestically produced commodities to labor-time or "real" costs.

[10] Edgeworth, later, called it the "negative clause" of the principle of comparative costs, and held it to be superfluous: "that the value of articles in the international market is not proportioned to the cost—the 'efforts and sacrifice'—incurred by the respective producers, is superfluous, if the definition here proposed is adopted. Why should there be any correspondence between cost and value in the absence of the conditions, proper to domestic trade, on which that equality depends?" *Papers relating to political economy,* 1925, II, 6.

[11] Cf. the report of his speech in the House of Commons, July 3, 1832, Hansard, *Parliamentary debates,* 3d series, XIV, 19:

> Now the error in this case [referring to an argument that it did not matter to England whether a foreign country took goods or money in exchange for its own goods] sprang out of another of still more universal acceptation; namely, that great maxim of the Ricardo school of economists, that as the value of a commodity in the home market depended on the cost—the labor—of production, so must it be in a foreign market. He would maintain, that though this principle was true of domestic policy, yet that it was not it that regulated the exchangeable value in a foreign market. What we received in return for our goods in foreign markets did not depend on the cost of producing those foreign articles, but on the demand that existed in the foreign market for our commodities.

pound it incorrectly,[12] and still later he raised the question as to whether the doctrine was valid at all.[13]

Sidgwick, it will be remembered,[14] took issue with the doctrine that the relative values of the products of different countries were not proportional to their relative costs, but in his argument he seemed to mean money cost rather than real cost by "cost," whereas in the Ricardian doctrine "cost" meant real cost. At one point, however, Sidgwick presents some conclusions which would be true if he used cost to mean real cost, but would not be true if he used cost to mean money cost.[15] He repeats an illustration of J. S. Mill's, where England exports cloth in exchange for Spanish wine, and adds a third commodity, corn, which is produced in both countries. He argues that since in England, where both cloth and corn are produced, their values must be determined by their relative costs of production, and similarly in Spain the values of corn and wine must also be determined by their relative costs of production, therefore the relative values of cloth and wine must also be determined by their relative costs of production, if there are no transportation costs. If values here mean prices and if "costs" mean "money costs," this is correct, and Mill would have agreed. Since the price of corn must be the same in both countries, and since in England the price of cloth:

---

[12] Cf. Mallet's account of the discussion at the Political Economy Club, April 5, 1832, Political Economy Club, *Minutes of proceedings,* VI (1921), 234:

> The discussion at last ran into a question of value, what constituted value in exchange—and on this rock it split, and left us all at sea. McCulloch, boldly standing by Ricardo's doctrine, that equal quantities of labor are equal in value all over the world—and Torrens and Malthus treating it as a ridiculous notion.

[13] In 1844 there was discussed at the Political Economy Club the question put by Torrens: "Was Ricardo correct in stating that 'the same rule which regulates the relative value of commodities in the country, does not regulate the relative value of the commodities exchanged between two or more countries'?" Torrens was not present, but McCulloch is reported as having held that Ricardo's chapter on foreign trade was faulty, and that in practice only such commodities are imported as foreign countries produce more cheaply, whether in terms of money costs or of real costs not being indicated.—Political Economy Club, *Minutes of proceedings,* VI (1921), 291.—It seems that McCulloch never accepted Ricardo's doctrine that comparative disadvantage in real cost could make importation profitable even though accompanied by absolute advantage in real cost, and his exposition of the doctrine appears always to have been in terms of absolute, as well as comparative, advantage. (Cf. McCulloch, *Principles of political economy,* 4th ed., 1849, chap. v.)

[14] *Supra,* p. 470, note 4.

[15] Sidgwick, *Principles,* 2nd ed., 1887, pp. 205-07.

price of corn: : money cost of cloth: money cost of corn, and in Spain the price of wine: price of corn: : money cost of wine: money cost of corn, therefore the price of cloth: price of wine: : money cost of cloth: money cost of wine. So far there is no difficulty, except in seeing why Sidgwick thought that he was differing from Mill. But at this point Sidgwick appends a note which is not intelligible if he is not using cost to mean real cost, and is simply a concession of his whole case against Mill if he is so using it: "It does not of course follow that the wine and cloth will exchange for each other in proportion to their respective costs; since, if (as Mill supposes) labor and capital are imperfectly mobile, the cost of producing corn may be different in the two countries."[16] If Sidgwick is conceding that the prices of wine and cloth will not be proportional to their real costs of production, he is accepting Mill's entire case. If he is denying that the prices of wine and cloth will be proportional to their money costs of production, he is denying his own theory of value, and apparently contradicting the accompanying text.[17]

VIII. DEPENDENCE OF COMPARATIVE COST DOCTRINE ON A REAL-COST THEORY OF VALUE

The Ricardian exposition of the doctrine of comparative costs stated costs in terms of units of labor-time and assumed that the values of commodities produced within a country would be proportional to their labor-time costs. The same procedure was followed by many of the leading exponents of the doctrine of comparative costs, and this chapter has so far not questioned its validity. But the labor-cost theory of value could find few, if any, serious defenders today, and many writers have claimed either that the doctrine of comparative costs must be rejected because of its dependence on a labor-cost theory of value, or else that it

---

[16] *Ibid., Principles,* 2d ed., p. 207, note.

[17] If it be assumed that at this stage of his argument Sidgwick has unconsciously lapsed into using the term "cost" in Mill's sense of real costs, then a suggestion by Edgeworth (*Papers,* II, p. 30) offers a means of reconciling his main text with this note. If "determined by cost of production" be read to mean merely "affected or influenced by cost of production," then, of course, the relative values of the products of different countries can be "determined" by their real costs of production without being proportional to them. This would reconcile the note with the text, but would make Sidgwick agree wholly with Mill when he was giving the same meaning to the terms he uses.

must be restated in terms of "modern" value theory without reference to labor costs. The remainder of this chapter deals with various phases of this question.

There are serious difficulties here for the doctrine of comparative costs, but they arise from the necessary dependence of its normative aspects on some form of "real-cost" theory of value and not from its relationship with the "labor-cost" theory of value, which can easily be severed. The association of the comparative-cost doctrine with the labor-cost theory of value is a historical accident, a result merely of the fact that Ricardo, in his pioneer exposition of it, expressed real costs in terms of quantities of labor. Except for Ricardo, none of the classical expounders of the doctrine of comparative costs, with the relatively unimportant and partial exception of James Mill, was an exponent of a labor-cost theory of value. Ricardo, himself, made important qualifications from the start for the influence of capital costs on relative values, and attached increasing importance to them as time went on. Malthus and Torrens expressly rejected the labor-cost theory. Senior and Cairnes dealt with real costs in terms of "labor and abstinence"[1] or "labor and capital." J. S. Mill in his earliest writings dissociated himself from the strict labor-cost theory, and in his *Principles* expressly rejected it in his discussion of general value theory, although he expounded the doctrine of comparative costs, as did Cairnes, as a rule, in the terminology of the labor-cost theory. Later writers, such as Bastable and Edgeworth, substituted "units of productive power," or similar expressions, for quantities of labor in expounding the doctrine,[2] or else, like Marshall,[3] made "quantities of labor" stand for combinations of the factors. Taussig, almost alone among modern writers, has adhered, with qualifications, to a labor-cost theory of value, but with full recognition of the objections which have been made against it, and on the ground not that these

---

[1] Cf. Senior, *Three lectures on the cost of obtaining money,* 1830, p. 4: ". . . an equal expenditure of wages and profits, or, in my nomenclature; . . . an equal sum of labor and abstinence. . . ."

[2] Cf. Edgeworth, review of Bastable's *Theory of international trade* in *Economic journal,* VII (1897), 399, note.

[3] Cf. Marshall, *Money credit & commerce,* 1923, p. 323: "Differences in the skill required for different occupations, and in the amount of capital by which each man's labor needs to be assisted, are neglected (or else the values of the several classes of labor and stocks of capital are expressed in terms of the value of labor of a standard efficiency)."

objections are theoretically invalid but that their practical importance can reasonably be questioned. The Economists who in general would deny that prices were necessarily proportional to labor costs may have fallen back on the labor-cost formula when expounding the theory of international trade because of the aid this formula provides in avoiding—or evading—serious logical difficulties in appraising from a welfare point of view the consequences of trade. While, therefore, evidence seems completely lacking which will support Knight's dictum that "historically the whole doctrine of comparative cost was a prop for a labor-cost theory of value,"[4] the converse proposition is arguable that historically the labor-cost theory of value has been used, even by writers who did not believe in it, as a prop for the doctrine of comparative costs. But now that there is almost universal and vigorous rejection of the labor-cost theory, its historical association with that theory is proving for the comparative-cost doctrine a hindrance rather than an aid to its general acceptance. Although for some of its critics this would make little difference, it is therefore important to emphasize that the doctrine of comparative costs has for most of its exponents derived its cogency from their acceptance of a real-cost theory of value which was not simply a labor-cost theory of value, even when expressed in its terms.

Before proceeding to an examination of the possibility of upholding the validity of the doctrine of comparative costs on the basis of real-cost theorizing, I should make it clear what meaning I attach to the phrase "real-cost theory of value." I understand by a "real-cost theory of value" a theory which holds that there is at least a strong presumption of rough proportionality between market prices and real costs, and that therefore propositions which depend for their validity on the existence of such rough proportionality are not for that reason to be regarded as invalid unless and until evidence is produced tending to show that in the particular situation under examination no such approach to proportionality between prices and real costs exists. Real-cost theorizing, therefore, even if valid, yields presumptions, but only presumptions, as distinguished from certainties. But presumptions are all that economic theory can be expected to yield in this field. But even if no presumptions as to proportionality of prices to

---

[4] "Some fallacies in the interpretation of social cost," *Quarterly journal of economics,* XXXVIII (1924), 599, note.

"real costs" can be established, general value theory must, of course, take account of "real costs" in so far as they exist and influence relative prices in any manner. Demolition of the "real-cost theory of value," therefore, does not have as an appropriate sequel abandonment of "real-cost" analysis.

The question next arises as to what is to be understood by "real costs." As applied to Ricardo's labor-cost theory, it would appear to mean cost in terms of day's labor, or the labor technical coefficients of production, where "real" would serve merely to distinguish quantities of the services of the factors necessary for production from money expenses of production, in the same manner in which "real" is applied to income to distinguish the commodities which money income can buy from the money income itself. It is clear, however, that the classical writers, when dealing with questions of public policy, were concerned with subjective costs, or "disutilities," and that although they generally assumed that disutilities were proportional to quantities of the services of the factors, they meant by real costs all subjective costs directly associated with production. The irksomeness of labor, whether in comparison with leisure or with some other kind of labor, and the "abstinence" associated with voluntary postponement of consumption, were for them the important real costs. They recognized, of course, that the economic process involved choice between products as well as choice between activities, but they treated choice between products as an income phenomenon and not as a cost phenomenon. When dealing with costs, they assumed income to remain constant, and examined the means by which it could be procured at the minimum cost. When dealing with income, they assumed cost to remain constant, and examined the means by which income could be maximized. That this was the only possible, or even the best, procedure, whether with respect to terminology or to mode of analysis, there would be no point in insisting upon, since there is always a choice of terms and of methods of analysis, and which is chosen is often determined mainly by some intellectual fashion of the moment. While there were imperfections in their doctrine, the only one I see which can conceivably be attributable to their technique was the one pointed out by Barone and Pareto,[5] their unsatisfactory method of han-

[5] See *infra*, p. 509.

dling land services (or, in general, services supposed not to involve real costs) as a factor in production.[6]

The course of international trade is governed immediately by prices. Unless the prices of commodities within a country are at least roughly proportional to their real costs, the doctrine of comparative costs is insufficient to establish a presumption in favor of free trade and, in fact, may provide a presumption in favor of interference with trade in order to bring it into conformity with comparative real costs.[7] The following sections examine the bearing on the doctrine of comparative costs of certain factors which are commonly held to operate against the existence of any significant correspondence between money costs and real costs, namely, differences in wage rates in different employments, and the use of the factors of production in different proportions in different industries.

IX. Differences in Wage Rates in Different Occupations

If different wages are paid to different kinds of labor and these different kinds of labor are used in different proportions by different industries, or if the same kind of labor is paid different

---

[6] Assume that as the result of an export bounty to an industry using much land but little labor, the same imports are obtained in return for commodities containing less labor services but more land services than those previously exported. I suppose that Ricardo would say in this case that the export bounty resulted in the country getting the imports at less real cost, and was therefore beneficial, and would overlook any reduction in domestically produced income resulting from the withdrawal of land from production for domestic consumption to production for export. It is conceivable, however, that Ricardo, if the point had been raised, would have made the necessary correction in his income analysis.

[7] Ricardo expressly recognized, with special reference to taxation, that in so far as relative prices were influenced by factors not representing real cost, the case for free trade no longer held. Cf. *On protection to agriculture* [1822], *Works,* p. 463:

It is only when commodities are altered in relative value, by the interference of government, that any tax, which shall act as a protection against the importation of a foreign commodity, can be justifiable. . . . It may be laid down as a principle, that any cause which operates in a country to affect equally all commodities, does not alter their relative value, and can give no advantage to foreign competitors, but that any cause which operates partially on one does alter its value to others, if not countervailed by an adequate duty; it will give advantage to the foreign competitor, and tend to deprive us of a beneficial branch of trade.

wages in different industries, then, assuming labor to be the only factor of production, prices of commodities produced within a country, though proportional to wages costs, will not be proportional to labor-time costs. It will follow that the course of trade under free trade will be governed by wages costs (i.e., labor-quantity costs times wage rates) and not, as posited by Ricardo, by comparative labor-quantity costs. This was seen and clearly stated by Longfield:

> The next circumstance which gives a direction to the stream of commerce, is, that the relative wages of labor in one country may vary by a different law from that which is observed in another. In one country, honesty and skill may be rare and high-priced qualities, and add much to the relative wages of the laborer who is required to possess them. In another country, the general comfortable condition of the people may render the laborer most unwilling to encounter severe toil, and a great increase of price may be necessary to induce him to engage in a disagreeable or unhealthy occupation. In this latter country, honesty, and that attentive disposition which quickly produces skill, may be the general qualifications of the people. On this supposition, if no disturbing causes exist, manufactures which require honesty and skill, will exist in the latter country; as the laborers possessing those qualities will sell their labor cheaper in proportion to its productiveness. In these two circumstances all commerce may be said to originate—namely, a difference in the proportion of the productiveness of labor of different kinds, in different countries; and the different scales by which the relative wages of labor vary in different countries.[1]

But when Longfield proceeded to deal with the advantages to be gained from free trade, he tacitly assumed that a country with an absolute advantage in money costs in the production of a particular commodity would also have a comparative advantage in real costs with respect to that commodity, and made no further mention of the complication which he had previously introduced.[2]

---

[1] *Three lectures on commerce*, 1835, pp. 56-57. Ohlin (*Interregional and international trade*, 1933, p. 32) cites a similar passage from Longfield's earlier *Lectures on political economy*, 1834, pp. 240-41, and asks the reader to note "that Longfield does *not* think of cheapness relative to effectiveness, as did the classical economists." The passage I have cited shows that Longfield, *to his credit*, did think of cheapness relative to effectiveness ("cheaper in proportion to its productiveness").

[2] *Three lectures on commerce*, pp. 60 ff. Cf. for a similar procedure, J. S. Eisdell (*Treatise on the industry of nations*, 1839, I, 343) who acknowledges his indebtedness to Longfield.

Cairnes pointed out that international trade is proximately regulated by prices and not by comparative real costs, and that the prices of commodities produced within a country by different non-competing groups will not be proportional to real costs in terms either of quantities of labor expended thereon or of "labor sacrifice."[3] But Cairnes apparently did not see the problem which this created for the free-trade doctrine, or else deliberately abstracted from it, for later he states that "it has been seen that nations only trade with one another when by doing so they can satisfy their desires at smaller sacrifice or cost than by direct production of the commodities which minister to them,"[4] whereas all that he had shown was that they trade with one another when the imported commodities can thereby be obtained at a saving in money costs. In his discussion of the tariff issue he tacitly makes the assumption, against which he had objected as illegitimate when dealing with general value theory and with the theory of international trade, that wages costs throughout the range of a nation's industries are an adequately accurate measure of relative real costs.[5] Thus even the economist most responsible for directing attention to the significance of differences in wages in different occupations ignored these differences when dealing with the tariff problem.

The problem does not appear to have received any further attention until we come to Professor Taussig's treatment. Taussig presents a clear and unambiguous demonstration, with the aid of arithmetical illustrations, of how differences in wages in different occupations may cause relative prices to diverge from relative labor-quantity costs, and how in consequence international specialization under free trade may not conform with comparative advantage in terms of labor-time costs.[6]

Taussig, however, claims that there is at least a rough correspondence between the hierarchy of occupations in advanced

---

[3] *Some leading principles of political economy,* 1874, pp. 322-24.

[4] *Ibid.,* p. 375.

[5] *Ibid.,* pp. 375-406.

[6] *International trade,* 1927, pp. 43-60. Cf. also for a similar, though less complete, treatment, his earlier "Wages and prices in relation to international trade," *Quarterly journal of economics,* XX (1906), 497 ff. (reprinted in his *Free trade, the tariff and reciprocity,* 1920, pp. 89-94), and his *Principles of economics,* 1911, I, 485-86; II, 154-57.

countries,[7] and that the exceptions, though important, are essentially temporary in character. He concedes that differences between countries in this hierarchy will operate to make the course of trade diverge from what it would be if prices were regulated by labor-time costs, and gives some concrete examples of such divergence. He maintains, however, that if the hierarchies are identical in different countries, "trade will develop as it would if prices within each country were governed by labor costs alone." I believe that Taussig has shown that the greater the approach to similarity in different countries in the hierarchy of wages the smaller will be the deviation of trade from the course it would follow if wages within each country were uniform, but that he has failed to show that with complete similarity in the hierarchies there would be *no* deviation from the course trade would follow if wages within each country were uniform in all occupations.

Taussig presents his reasoning with the aid of a series of arithmetical illustrations based on two somewhat different types of assumptions with respect to the nature of the non-competing groups. He illustrates the first type by the following example :[8]

Country	Labor-time costs (in days)	Wages per day (in $)	Total wages (in $)	Produce	Domestic supply price (in $)
United States......	10	1.00	10.00	20 wheat	0.50
	10	1.50	15.00	20 linen	0.75
Germany.........	10	0.66⅔	6.66	10 wheat	0.66⅔
	10	1.00	10.00	15 linen	0.66⅔

In this illustration there are differences in wages as between the different industries, but the order and percentage degree of difference are identical in the two countries. Taussig concludes

[7] Unless the hierarchy was in each country relatively stable through time (as both Adam Smith and Ricardo believed it to be) or changed substantially only in response to world-wide forces, this would not be true. That it is substantially true in fact seems to have been the conclusion of C. F. Bickerdike from a detailed study of the wage statistics of several countries ("International comparisons of labor conditions," *Transactions of the Manchester Statistical Society*, 1911-12, pp. 62-63).

[8] *International trade*, 1927, p. 47.

that the course of trade will be precisely the same as if supply prices within each country were regulated by labor-time costs. Ohlin has pointed out, however, that while the commodities exported and imported by each country remain the same the terms of trade may be different in the two cases. With labor-time costs regulating, i.e., with wages the same in both occupations, trade can take place anywhere within the limits of 1 wheat for 1 linen and 1 wheat for 1.5 linen. With the differences in wages in the two industries trade can take place only within the limits of 1 wheat for 2/3 linen and 1 wheat for 1 linen, a change to the disadvantage of the country with a comparative advantage in the product of the low-wage industry.[9] But Taussig has shown that the deviation from trade in accordance with comparative labor-time costs will tend to be less when the direction and degree of difference in wages in the two industries are the same in the two countries than when they are not the same.

In his second type of illustration, Taussig deals with differences in wages of different classes of labor, each of which finds employment throughout the range of industry. He then shows, successfully as far as I can see, that if the hierarchy is the same in different countries both as to rank and as to percentage differences in wages, and if all industries in both of the countries use labor coming in the same proportions from the different social classes of labor, the course of trade, although then as always immediately regulated by prices and money costs, will be precisely the same as if it were governed by labor-quantity costs.[10] The assumptions on which this conclusion rests seems to me, however, seriously to restrict its significance, especially as departure from any one of them would force a modification of the conclusion. But Taussig's analysis turns rather on the existence of fixed scales of relative wages than on the question of occupational mobility of labor,[11] and it seems to me that more fruitful results can be ob-

---

[9] B. Ohlin, "Protection and non-competing groups," *Weltwirtschaftliches Archiv*, XXXIII (1931, I), 42-43.

If there were more than two commodities as potential articles of trade, even the commodities imported and exported by each country would not necessarily be wholly the same in the two cases.

[10] See especially the arithmetical illustration in Taussig, *International trade*, p. 51.

[11] If immobility of labor were tacitly assumed in his illustrations, then the specialization posited therein would be impossible.

tained by the application to the problem of Taussig's general mode of analysis of the origin and significance of differences in wages.[12]

First, differences of wages in different occupations may be what Taussig has called "equalizing" differences, i.e., may be wholly due to and proportional to differences in the attractiveness, or irksomeness, of the occupations, and not to the absence of complete mobility between the occupations. Specialization in accordance with money costs will then also be in accordance with comparative real costs measured in terms of "disutilities" or of irksomeness of the occupations or of the living conditions associated with such occupations, even though it is not in accordance with comparative labor-time costs. In such cases the doctrine of comparative real costs holds unequivocally, in spite of the differences in wage rates in different occupations.[13]

Next, let us suppose that the differences in wages are due to absolute labor monopolies in the high-wage groups, and that the hierarchy of labor is according to industry or product, rather than, or more than, across industry in general.[14] Given the ab-

---

[12] Cf. Taussig, *Principles of economics*, 1911, II, chap. 47. The analysis which follows is indebted to the article by Ohlin just cited, though there is some difference in conclusions. It is in part a restatement of the argument in my review of Manoïlesco, *The theory of protection and international trade*, 1931, in the *Journal of political economy*, XL (1932), 121-25. Manoïlesco had shown that if under free trade money incomes of workers were higher in manufacturing than in agriculture, and if manufactured products were imported and agricultural products exported, protection to manufactures would enable the country to get its manufactured products at lower labor-time costs by domestic production than by import.

[13] In my review of Manoïlesco's book, in which he argued that the higher money earnings of labor in manufacturing than in agriculture justified protection for manufacturing industries which under free trade could not survive, I had contended, along the same lines as above, that if a greater labor-time cost of obtaining manufactured products by import in exchange for exports of agricultural products instead of by domestic manufacture was more than offset by the greater disutility of labor in manufacturing than in agriculture, there would be no case for an import duty on the manufactured product. In a reply to this objection, Manoïlesco merely repeats his demonstration that protection may result in a saving in *labor-time* costs, and overlooks, or perhaps denies, the necessity of weighting the labor-time costs by what Pareto called their "ophelimity coefficients" in order to get the real costs. (Mihail Manoïlesco, "Arbeitsproduktivität und Aussenhandel," *Weltwirtschaftliches Archiv*, XLII (1935, I), 41-43.)

[14] Haberler has commented that it is noteworthy that I do not mention the important case of "differences in the quality of the labor supplied by the different groups." He comments that: "It falls outside the scope of the real-cost theory, to which Viner adheres—apparently from reverence for tradition; or at

sence of the possibility of movement of labor from the low-wage to the high-wage industry, then the amount of labor available for the latter industry has only the limited degree of variability resulting from the dependence of the amount of labor offered for employment by the members of the high-wage group on the wage obtainable. Abstracting from such variability of the amount of labor as is internal to the group and not due to migration of labor from other groups, if the high-wage industry is at a comparative advantage in terms of real costs but, because of the limitations on the number of laborers who have access to employment in that industry, competing products continue to be imported, the imposition of a tariff on its product will not appreciably affect the volume of its domestic production, and its significant results will be confined to changes in the volume of foreign trade, the relative prices of commodities, and the relative wages paid in different industries. The inequality in wages would be further accentuated, and the power of the monopoly labor group to exploit the rest of the community would be increased, but there would be no improvement in the apportionment of labor among the different occupations.

Finally, suppose that there is complete mobility between occupations, but that by law, custom, or trade-union regulation wages in some of the industries which are in a position of comparative advantage in terms of real costs are maintained at so high a level that the domestic market for their products is shared with imports of competing products. Under these conditions a protective duty on imports of the commodities produced by the high-wage industries would increase the amount of employment provided by those industries and would result in a shift of labor from occupations of lower to occupations of higher productivity. The conditions of this hypothesis would not be consistent with long-run assumptions, but recent experience has shown that wages in some occupations can persist for long periods at levels high enough seriously to restrict the volume of employment, even when the only alternatives for those not securing employment therein are either

least it can be included only under quite definite assumptions." (*Theory of international trade,* 1936, p. 196, note 2.) There is no such omission, since "labor monopolies" would cover both those contrived and those due to scarcity of persons having the requisite qualities, and for the purpose in hand all that is relevant is the existence of monopoly, whatever be its cause.

unemployment or the acceptance of much lower wages in other occupations.

These examples do not exhaust all the possibilities, but they bring out sufficiently the range of possibilities that the existence of different rates of wages in different occupations will make import duties profitable. The results of this analysis may be recapitulated in the following propositions:

(1) Equalizing differences in wages do not cause trade to diverge from the lines of comparative advantage in terms of real or subjective costs, even if they do cause trade to diverge from the lines of comparative advantage in terms of labor-time costs.

(2) Where differences in wages are due to a labor monopoly in the high-wage occupation, import duties on the product of the high-wage industry will not result in a transfer to that industry of labor from low-wage industry, will not therefore improve the situation from the point of view of production, and will impair it further from the point of view of distribution if inequality is regarded as an evil.

(3) Where there is occupational mobility but wages are fixed by regulation or custom at too high a level in some industry with a comparative advantage in terms of real costs, an import duty on the product of that industry will enable it to employ more labor. But free trade plus flexibility of wages will result in an even closer approach to the presumptively optimum distribution of labor among the different occupations.

The doctrine of comparative costs emerges, therefore, very nearly intact even from a test about whose results some of its most ardent adherents have had misgivings. Although reached by a somewhat different method, the foregoing results amply confirm the conclusion of Professor Taussig that the existence of differences in wages does not suffice to overturn the doctrine of comparative costs.[15]

X. Variable Proportions of the Factors and International Specialization

Ohlin, the most outstanding and vigorous of the critics of the doctrine of comparative costs, bases his criticism on an interpre-

---

[15] *International trade*, p. 61.

tation of the doctrine as representing the attempt of the classical school to explain the forces which determine the specific nature of the course of trade and of international specialization. Except for one paragraph, he has given no sign of recognition that this was not the sole nor even the main purpose of the doctrine, and this paragraph, appearing as the final paragraph of a book of 590 pages in which the doctrine is treated throughout as erroneous and irrelevant, is clearly a last-minute afterthought.[1] Ohlin's own explanation of the forces which determine the nature of international specialization is in its general lines admirable, and, I am convinced, will help to set the pattern of future discussion of this question. Ohlin goes into considerable detail but the general framework of his theory can be summarized in several sentences. A country exports those commodities which it can produce at lower money costs than any other country and imports those commodities which other countries can produce at lower money costs. What the relative money costs of production of different commodities will be in any country depends on the relative prices of the different factors of production, on the productivity functions of these factors, and on the extent to which production is carried in the different industries, and some of these in turn depend on the demands, domestic and foreign, for the various commodities. On empirical grounds, however, the conclusion may be reached that the most important single factor explaining the nature of international specialization is the differences as between different countries in the relative abundance, and therefore in the relative prices, of different factors. These international differences in the relative prices of different factors tend to result in the money costs of production of particular commodities being low in those countries where the factors entering heavily into the production of these commodities are relatively abundant and therefore low in price.[2]

---

[1] *Interregional and international trade,* 1933, p. 590.

[2] Ohlin recognizes that different rates of remuneration in different industries will also be a factor in determining the nature of a country's specialization. He would grant also, I suppose, that relative differences between countries in the prices of the factors and in their effectiveness result in differences in the methods by which the same commodities are produced, as well as in differences in the commodities produced, and that the abundance and quality of "free goods" is an important element in determining the productivities of the "scarce" factors.

In his general mathematical exposition of international equilibrium, Ohlin treats as the same factor in the two regions "only factors of identical quality in

Although Ohlin presents this analysis in a controversial manner and as a radical correction of the errors of the classical school, the appearance of conflict between his own position in this respect and that of the classical writers and their followers is in large part the result of Ohlin's treatment of the doctrine of comparative costs in terms of labor costs as the only classical attempt to explain the forces determining the nature of international specialization and of his failure to allow for the fact that this doctrine was directed primarily to answering another question, the question of gain or loss from foreign trade. Ohlin is correct in his claim that the doctrine of comparative costs when expounded in terms of a single factor, or of fixed and uniform combinations of the factors, cannot serve effectively to explain the influence on the course of international trade of the differences in the proportions in which the different factors enter into the production of different commodities and the differences as between different countries in the relative abundance of the different factors. But he goes further, and claims that by their adherence to the doctrine of comparative costs the classical school were prevented from even dealing with these considerations:

There is no doubt that varying productive factor equipment is the main cause of those inequalities in [money] costs of production and commodity prices which lead to trade. . . . The fact that the productive factors enter into the production of different commodities in very different proportions and that therefore (relative prices of the factors being different in different countries) an international spe-

the two regions" (*ibid.,* p. 560, note), thus abstracting from the necessity of dealing expressly with the role in international trade of comparative differences in "effectiveness" of the factors as between the different industries and regions. (For the purposes of international trade theory, the "effectiveness" of a factor should be understood to mean its marginal physical productivity function with respect to variations both in the amount of that factor and the amounts of the other factors associated with it in production.) Ohlin, in his criticism of Taussig's analysis, seems to forget, for the time being, that Taussig had not made the same abstraction, but that, on the contrary, he had always placed marked emphasis on the importance of comparative differences in "effectiveness." Unless it is assumed that each factor, in each industry, has identical "quality" or effectiveness in the two regions, Ohlin's contention that international trade would be impossible if Taussig's assumption of identical relative scales of wages and interest in the two regions were applicable to *all* factors, or if Taussig's assumption of identical proportions of labor and capital in all industries were applicable to *all* factors and *both* regions (*ibid.,* pp. 561-62), is incorrect in both cases. In each case, the existence of comparative differences in effectiveness would suffice to provide a basis for trade.

cialization of production is profitable, is so obvious that it can hardly have escaped notice. Yet this fact has been given no attention in international trade theory. There can hardly be any other explanation than the dominance of the Ricardian labor cost theory—in the form of the doctrine of comparative cost—which is built on the explicit assumption of proportionality between the quantities of all factors except land in all industries. This precludes the study of varying proportions.[3]

Ohlin, accordingly, finds it not surprising that the influence on the course of trade of differences between countries in the relative abundance of the different factors was "first touched upon, not by the English classical school, but in French works."[4] Unfortunately for his thesis, however, the only French work which he cites is Sismondi's *De la richesse commerciale*, published in 1803, while with the exception of the *Wealth of Nations* the earliest work of the classical school in the field of international trade came later than 1803. Sismondi, moreover, was at this time still a rather slavish disciple of Adam Smith and may conceivably have found his inspiration even on this question in the *Wealth of Nations*.[5] Of early writers in English, Ohlin cites only Longfield[6] as offering an explanation of international specialization in which differences as between countries in the relative abundance

---

[3] *Interregional and international trade,* pp. 30-31. It obviously does *not* preclude the study of varying proportions between labor and land. Ohlin lays special emphasis on the variable proportions between labor and *capital,* as a reaction, no doubt, against the Ricardian assumption—at times—of fixed proportions between labor and capital. But the Ricardian analysis is more vulnerable in its treatment of land as an element in cost than in its treatment of capital. I venture the guess, moreover, that the relative abundance of natural resources as compared to all other factors taken together has been in the past, and continues to be today, a much more important element in determining the nature of international specialization than the relative abundance of capital as compared to labor. Cf., to the same effect, N. G. Pierson, *Principles of economics* (translated from the Dutch), II (1912), 195.

[4] *Ibid.,* pp. 30-31.

[5] Cf. *Wealth of nations,* Cannan ed. II, 100:

Our merchants frequently complain of the high wages of British labor as the cause of their manufactures being undersold in foreign markets; but they are silent about the high profits of stock. They complain of the extravagant gain of other people; but they say nothing of their own. The high profits of British stock, however, may contribute towards raising the price of British manufactures in many cases as much, and in some perhaps more, than the high wages of British labor.

[6] See *supra,* p. 494.

of different factors are treated as important, but he apparently does not regard Longfield as a "classical" economist.

The classical economists, it is true, revealed no great interest in the detailed explanation of the forces which determined the nature of the international specialization existing in their time. But they did not wholly ignore the question, and when they did touch on it their adherence to the doctrine of comparative costs did not prevent them from dealing with it on lines similar in essentials to those followed by Ohlin.

In the course of critical comment on Adam Smith's doctrine that capital employed in agriculture gave more employment to labor than capital employed in other industries, Ricardo explained as follows the forces determining the nature of international specialization:

> In the distribution of employments amongst all countries, the capital of poorer nations will be naturally employed in those pursuits, wherein a great quantity of labor is supported at home, because in such countries the food and necessaries for an increasing population can be most easily procured. In rich countries, on the contrary, where food is dear, capital will naturally flow, when trade is free, into those occupations wherein the least quantity of labor is required to be maintained at home: such as the carrying trade, the distant foreign trade, and trades where expensive machinery is required; to trades where profits are in proportion to the capital, and not in proportion to the quantity of labor employed.[7]

In dealing with the effect of a tax on agricultural raw materials which raised their price relative to other elements entering into production, Ricardo states:

> . . . as the value of commodities is very differently made up of raw material and labor; as some commodities, for instance, all those made from the metals, would be unaffected by the rise of raw produce from the surface of the earth, it is evident that there would be the greatest variety in the effects produced on the value of commodities, by a tax on raw produce. As far as this effect was produced, it would stimulate

---

[7] *Principles, Works*, p. 211. In a footnote Ricardo adds: "If countries with limited capitals, but with abundance of fertile land, do not early engage in foreign trade [i.e., the carrying and entrepôt trade?], the reason is, because it is less profitable to individuals, and therefore also less profitable to the State." I was a familiar doctrine in the eighteenth century that only countries like Holland, rich in capital and poor in natural resources, could specialize in the entrepôt trade.

or retard the exportation of particular commodities, . . . it would destroy the natural relation between the value of each . . . and therefore rather a different direction might be given to foreign trade.[8]

Malthus, dealing with the question of why in England, as compared to the Continent, wages were relatively high, or, as he put it, the value of money was relatively low, offered the following answer:

The lower value of money in England compared with the value of money in most of the states of Europe, has appeared to arise principally from the cheapness of our exportable manufactures, derived from our superior machinery, skill, and capital. The still lower value of money in the United States is occasioned by the cheapness and abundance of her raw products derived from the advantages of her soil, climate, and situation . . . neither the difference in profits, nor the difference in the price of labor, is such as to counterbalance this facility of production, and prevent the abundance of exports.[9]

McCulloch, to illustrate the effect on foreign trade of changes in the rate of wages, presents a hypothetical case in which wages and facilities of production are equal in France and England for all of a range of commodities, so that both countries are on equal terms in the export trade of these commodities to the United States. He assumes also that capital, in the form of durable machinery, enters into the cost of production of these commodities in different proportions for different commodities. He next supposes that wages rise in England while they remain stationary in France, and concludes that "England will henceforth have a decided advantage over France in the production and sale of those commodities that are produced chiefly by machinery; while France will, on her part, have an equally decided advantage over England in the production and sale of those commodities that are chiefly the direct produce of the hand." He finds, moreover, that this hypothetical case fits the facts:

---

[8] *Principles, Works,* pp. 100-01.

[9] *Principles of political economy,* 2d ed., 1836, pp. 106-07. The above quotation reproduces only part of the relevant material. See also the first edition of the *Principles,* 1820, pp. 104-5. Cf. also Malthus, *The measure of value,* 1823, p. 47: "It is evident, therefore, that the values which determine what commodities shall be exported, and what imported, depend . . . partly upon the quantity of labor employed in their production, partly upon the ordinary rates of profits in each country, and partly upon the value of money." Malthus explains that by "value of money" he means the "money price of labor." (*Ibid.,* p. 46.)

The bulk of our exports consists of cotton goods and other products of machinery; whereas the bulk of the exports of France consists of the productions of her soil, and of jewellery and fancy articles, principally the product of manual labor. It is, therefore, difficult to suppose that a rise of wages should be fatal to the foreign commerce of a country, except by reducing profits, and creating a temptation to employ capital abroad. It can hardly fail, however, to turn it, to some extent at least, into new channels: for if, on the one hand, it raises the value of certain descriptions of commodities and checks their exportation, on the other, it proportionally lowers the value of other descriptions, and fits them the better for the foreign market.[10]

Cairnes, in a discussion of the type of specialization in which a new country would tend to engage, gave consideration to the relative abundance of capital and natural resources:

The class of commodities in the production of which the facilities possessed by new communities, as compared with old, attain their greatest height, are those of which timber and meat may be taken as the type, and comprises such articles as wool, game, furs, hides, horns, pitch, resin, etc. The characteristic of all such products is, that they admit of being raised with little previous outlay, and, therefore, with comparatively little capital, and in general require for their production a large extent of ground. Now capital is the industrial agent which new countries are least able to command, while they commonly possess land in unlimited abundance. There can, therefore, be no difficulty in perceiving that, for the production of the class of commodities mentioned above, newly-settled communities are especially adapted, and that, consequently, the value of all such commodities will be in them exceptionally low.[11]

---

[10] J. R. McCulloch, *Principles of political economy,* 2d ed., 1830, pp. 355-56 (also in later editions). McCulloch is taking for granted, along Ricardian lines, that the quantity of money remains constant, and that a rise in money wages must consequently be accompanied by a fall in interest rates.

[11] *Some leading principles of political economy,* 1874, pp. 119-20.

In connection with his discussion of the relation between wage levels and the course of foreign trade, Cairnes (*ibid.,* p. 327, note) pointed out that a general change in the rate of wages in a country, by resulting in relative changes in the money cost of production as between industries in which fixed capital was important and industries in which outlays on wages were important, would affect the course of trade. On the ground that "these are details . . . into which it is scarcely necessary to enter in arguing the general question of the effect of wages on foreign trade," he did not attempt to explain in detail the nature of the changes which would occur. He claimed, however, that a fall in wages "might easily have the effect of checking instead of promoting the exportation of an article if it happened to be one in the production of which fixed capital was largely employed."

These references to recognition of the influence of the relative abundance of the factors are confined to writers generally recognized as belonging to the classical school, and can be extended by citations from minor writers of the classical period,[12] as well as by citations from later writers, American and Continental, who were more or less under the classical school influence.[13] Such recognition has been an especially prominent feature of Taussig's analysis,[14] although in his earlier treatments there seems to be no reference to the relative abundance of capital. An allied problem, which Taussig dealt with at length,[15] the influence of differences in the relative supplies of the different factors on the techniques whereby different countries produce the *same* commodities, does, however, seem to have been left almost completely untouched by the early classical economists. It was, nevertheless, a question of widespread interest at the beginning of the nineteenth century, especially in connection with the contrast between the prevalent "high" farming in England and extensive cultivation in the United States. Not only did almost every traveler attempt to explain these differences in technology in terms of the relative abundance of the respective factors, but acute discussion of the question is to be found in the correspondence or other writings of such early American statesmen as Benjamin Franklin, George Washington, and Thomas Jefferson.

---

[12] Cf., e.g., Thomas Hopkins, *Economical enquiries,* 1822, pp. 84-86; Lord Stourton, *Three letters . . . on the distresses of agriculture,* new ed., 1822, pp. 62-64; John Rooke, *Free trade in corn,* 2d ed., 1835, pp. 22-23; J. S. Eisdell, *Treatise on the industry of nations,* 1839, I, 343.

E. G. Wakefield cited, in 1833, the following passage from the London *Times* as representing a prevalent English opinion (*England and America,* 1833, II, 47-48):

> All political writers in this country have visited with censure the present policy of the American general government in attempting by high protecting duties to force the establishment, or to encourage the extension, of manufactures in the United States. With the high price for labor that exists in the United States, with their scanty supply of monied capital, with their unlimited range of uncultivated or half improved soil, it was almost a crime against society to divert human industry from the fields and the forests to iron forges and cotton factories.

[13] E.g., Francis Bowen, *American political economy,* 1870, p. 484; N. G. Pierson, *Principles of economics,* II (1912), 192-95; Angell, *Theory of international prices,* 1926, p. 472. Ohlin (*op. cit.,* p. 33) makes acknowledgements to an important contribution (in Swedish) by Heckscher, in 1919.

[14] *Protection to young industries,* 2d ed., 1884, pp. 7-12; *Some aspects of the tariff question,* 1915, chap. iii and *passim*; *International trade,* 1927, chap. vii.

[15] Especially in his *Some aspects of the tariff question,* 1915.

XI. Variable Proportions of the Factors and Comparative Real Costs

Proportionality of real costs to money costs is an essential premise of the doctrine of comparative costs, but the existence of more than one factor of production, the use of the different factors in different proportions by different industries or by the same industry under different circumstances, and the absence of any objective and generally-accepted method of equating the "real" or subjective costs involved in the use of units of different productive factors, present formidable obstacles to the demonstration of the existence of any simple pattern of relationship between real and money costs. Must the doctrine of comparative costs therefore be abandoned, as some modern writers contend?

It is remarkable how completely the early exponents of the doctrine of comparative costs were able to avoid discussing this fundamental issue without encountering hostile comment from opponents of the free-trade principle in whose support the doctrine was expounded. When the doctrine was formulated in terms of labor-time costs, this involved the implicit assumptions that prices were proportional to subjective labor costs, and that no other real costs were involved in the productive process, assumptions which clearly never commanded wide acceptance as conforming to reality. Those writers, who, like Senior and Cairnes, wrote in terms of the proportionality of prices to "labor and abstinence" costs, or who, like Bastable, Edgeworth, and Marshall, accepted money costs of production as proportional to the number of "units of productive power" used in the production of the respective commodities, and accepted the quantity of such units of productive power as a measure of the "real" costs involved in production, never explained how subjective costs associated with the use of different factors of production could be equated with one another.[1] Although it is hard to believe that

---

[1] Unless Edgeworth's vague reference to "proper index-numbers" is accepted as an explanation: "The conception [of "units of productive power"] might be facilitated by imagining each country to employ a monetary standard corrected by proper index-numbers, so that the efforts and sacrifices incurred in procuring a unit of the standard money should be constant." Review of Bastable, *Theory of international trade, Economic journal*, VII (1897), 399, note.

it was the first in fact, the earliest criticism of the doctrine of comparative costs along these lines that I have been able to find was by Lexis, in 1891.[2] Lexis pointed out that the doctrine as expounded by Ricardo rested on labor-cost theory of value assumptions, and that these assumptions required for their validity the unlikely circumstances that labor and capital should in each country enter into the production of all commodities in uniform proportions.

A few years later, Pareto, commenting on Cairnes's exposition of the doctrine, objected to the ambiguity of his treatment of the significant aspect of costs as "sacrifice," and to his lumping together of "labor" and "abstinence" as if they were homogeneous quantities capable of summation. He claimed that the significant cost factors which determined prices and the allocation of resources among different employments were the individual *"coûts en ophélimité,"* both direct and indirect, the "direct" costs being the "real" costs of the classical school and the "indirect" costs the utility from the consumption of the (best) alternative product B which must be forgone when product A is produced instead.[3] The "indirect" costs of Pareto are therefore the subjective equivalent of the alternative product costs of recent neo-Austrian theorizing. Unlike the neo-Austrians, however, Pareto introduced the "indirect" costs into his analysis as a supplement to, instead of as a substitute for, the "real" or "direct" costs, although he attributed to the former a much greater importance in influencing economic behavior than to the latter. Also unlike the later writers who have introduced alternative product-cost theory into the theory of international trade as a correction of the comparative-cost theory in terms of real costs, Pareto succeeded in exposing a genuine error in the comparative-cost doctrine when expounded in terms of "direct" costs alone, namely, the error of giving no consideration to the indirect costs of exports to the extent that such exports are produced by land, or other factors, with which no "direct" costs are associated but which could otherwise have been used to produce other (or the same?)

---

[2] W. Lexis, article "Handel," in Schönberg, *Handbuch der Politischen Oekonomie,* 3d ed., II (1891), 902.

[3] V. Pareto, *Cours d'économie politique,* II (1897), 210 ff. Pareto makes acknowledgments to Barone for the extension of his cost analysis to include the *"ophélimité indirect."*

commodities for domestic consumption.[4] The doctrine of comparative costs, to meet this criticism, would have to be restated in terms of "real" costs plus those indirect costs not already covered in the real-cost accounting.

In the last few years the value theory assumptions of the doctrine of comparative costs have been subjected to extended criticism, most notably by Ohlin,[5] Haberler,[6] and Mason.[7] Taussig, on the other hand, has defended the value assumptions of the doctrine as sufficiently in accordance with the facts to provide a substantial foundation for the conclusions made to rest thereon.[8]

Taussig concedes that the real costs or the "sacrifices" associated with labor and capital are "in their nature incommensurable,"[9] as they are not, or are not in the same degree, as between different types of labor. He makes no attempt to reduce them to commensurability or to find a basis for restating the doctrine of comparative costs in terms of labor-plus-capital real costs. He attempts to show, however, that over a wide range of cases where labor and capital both enter into production, the presence of capital charges will not make the comparative money-cost ratios different from what they would be in the absence of capital charges.[10] Where this is the case, then the course of trade—i.e., the commodities which each country imports or exports and the limiting ratios within which they can exchange for each other—will be the same as if there were no capital costs.

Taussig succeeds in showing that there are many cases in which the introduction of capital costs, although it changes absolute money costs or even relative money costs within a country, leaves comparative money costs the same as they would be if there were no capital costs. All of these cases fall under one

---

[4] Pareto, *ibid.*, p. 211. The error did not carry over, I believe, into the foreign-trade analysis of the classical school from the income side, but I can find no explicit recognition of the issue before Pareto.

[5] Ohlin, "Ist eine Modernisierung der Aussenhandelstheorie erforderlich?" *Weltwirtschaftliches Archiv*, XXVI (1927, II), 97-115; *ibid., Interregional and international trade*, 1933, appendix iii, pp. 571-90, and *passim*.

[6] Haberler, "Die Theorie der komparativen Kosten," *Weltwirtschaftliches Archiv*, XXXII (1930, II), 356-60; *ibid., The theory of international trade*, 1936, especially, pp. 175-98.

[7] E. S. Mason, "The doctrine of comparative cost," *Quarterly journal of economics*, XLI (1926).

[8] Taussig, *International trade*, 1927, chap. vii.

[9] *Ibid.*, p. 67.

[10] *Ibid.*, pp. 61-66.

general category, however, where, assuming that there are no other expenses at the margin except wages and interest, the ratio between the percentages of wage (or interest) expense to total marginal expense for the two commodities is the same in both countries.

Let the two commodities be designated by a and b, respectively, the two countries by 1 and 2 respectively, wage cost at the margin by w, capital cost at the margin by c, and total marginal cost per unit by t. Then:

$$w_{a,1} + c_{a,1} = t_{a,1} \qquad w_{a,2} + c_{a,2} = t_{a,2}$$
$$w_{b,1} + c_{b,1} = t_{b,1} \qquad w_{b,2} + c_{b,2} = t_{b,2} \tag{1}$$

In order that the course of trade shall not be altered by the introduction of capital costs, as compared to what it would be if there were only wages costs, then the following equation must hold:

$$\frac{\dfrac{w_{a,1}}{w_{a,2}}}{\dfrac{w_{b,1}}{w_{b,2}}} = \frac{\dfrac{t_{a,1}}{t_{a,2}}}{\dfrac{t_{b,1}}{t_{b,2}}} \tag{2}$$

But equation (2) will hold only when the following equation, which can be derived from equation (2), will hold:

$$\frac{\dfrac{w_{a,1}}{t_{a,1}}}{\dfrac{w_{b,1}}{t_{b,1}}} = \frac{\dfrac{w_{a,2}}{t_{a,2}}}{\dfrac{w_{b,2}}{t_{b,2}}} \tag{3}$$

i.e., equation (2) will hold only when the ratio between the percentages of wage expense to total expense in the production of the two commodities in country 1 is equal to the corresponding ratio in country 2. It is obvious that, even if the interest rate is not different in the two countries, there will be many cases in which equation (3) will not hold.

Since there are fairly substantial differences in interest rates between countries, and since even if interest rates were internationally uniform there would still be possibilities of divergence between comparative total money costs, on the one hand, and comparative wage (and real labor) costs, on the other, it would appear that the doctrine of comparative costs in terms of labor costs is subject to serious modification when account is taken of the participation of capital in the productive process. Taussig does not deny the existence of this logical difficulty for the doctrine of comparative costs in terms of labor costs, but claims, on empirical grounds, that its significance is limited:[11]

The quantitative importance of the capital charge factor in international trade is probably not great. As the whole tenor of the preceding exposition indicates, the range of its influence is restricted to a special set of circumstances. Within that range, its influence is further limited by the absence of wide inequalities in the rate of return on capital. Interest, while it does vary somewhat from country to country, does not vary widely between the leading countries of western civilization; and it is in the trade between these, and in the competition between them for trade with other countries, that the interest factor is most likely to enter with its independent and special effects . . . we are justified in concluding that this element in the economic situation, like the element of persistent differences in wages to different workers, does not lead to a radical modification of our first conclusions.

It would not be seriously contended by anyone today—if ever —that the doctrine of comparative costs in terms of labor costs lays down an exact and universally applicable rule of policy, any deviation from which necessarily involves national loss. It could still be held that the doctrine provides a generally valid rule of policy, to be departed from only upon clear demonstration in particular instances that there exist special circumstances which make the rule inapplicable in those circumstances, if for most products entering into foreign trade wages costs were so predominant a part of the total costs that the differences as between different products in the percentages of wages costs to total costs were narrowly limited in range. Ohlin counters this mode of defense of Taussig's position by citing the range of capital per worker in manufacturing industries in the United States from $10,000 in the chemical industry to $1700 in the tobacco industry.[12] This is not, however, as crushing a rebuttal as it seems to be. The significant ratios for the labor-cost version of the doctrine of comparative costs are between the proportion of

---

[11] *Ibid.*, pp. 67-68.
[12] *Interregional and international trade*, p. 572.

wages costs to total costs, and not between the amounts of capital used per laborer. Assuming that interest and wages *shown as such on the books of the particular industries* are the only costs, assuming further that the interest rate is 5 per cent per annum and the average annual wages per laborer $1200, the data cited by Ohlin show a range of percentages of wages cost to total cost of from 70 per cent to 93 per cent. If wages cost never fell below 70 per cent of total cost, a trade policy which accepted labor costs as the only real costs, money costs as a rough but ordinarily adequate index of comparative wages cost, and wages cost as a rough but ordinarily adequate index of comparative real cost, would not go far wrong.

Ohlin also cites estimates of the value of output per 1000 hours of labor in American industry ranging from $548 in the yarn and thread industry to $10,870 in the die and punch industry, with the implication that the disparity is due to the much greater role of capital in some industries than in others.[13] Such estimates, it may safely be taken for granted, are based on the accounts of the concerns which carry out the final stages of production of the enumerated commodities, and therefore do not include in the labor costs of these commodities the labor ingredients in the expenditures of these concerns for materials, equipment, transportation, building rent, capital equipment, and even taxes, insurance, and banking services charged as "interest." The apparent ratio of wages costs to total costs of automobiles will be much higher if calculated from the accounts of an integrated concern producing the automobiles from the materials stage to the finished car stage than if computed from the accounts of an assembly plant. In the same manner, interest charges are concealed in the costs of materials, etc. If calculations of ratios of wages cost to total cost are to be used to test the validity of the doctrine of comparative costs in terms of labor costs, they must either include the element of wages for past labor contained in materials and other expenses, or, a more practicable and more relevant procedure, they must be made only for specified stages or segments of the productive processes of the various commodities, and must be based on comparisons of wages costs to "value added by manufacture" rather than to gross value

---

[13] *Ibid.*

of the product. Ohlin maintains that the "orthodox" theory considers only current, not past labor.[14] If this were so, it would be an obvious error which should not be incorporated in one's own analysis. But whether we take Ricardo[15] or Taussig[16] as the authoritative exponent of the "orthodox" theory, past labor costs are included in the labor costs of that theory. Whatever properly computed data would show, the data offered by Ohlin inflict no serious damage on the doctrine of comparative costs in terms of labor costs.

The plight of the comparative-cost doctrine appears still less serious, moreover, if it is granted, as I believe it must, that a real-cost theory of value should provide for real capital costs as well as for labor costs. If interest charges are different fractions of total expenses in different industries, then if money costs were to be proportional to real costs they could not be proportional to labor costs alone. Specialization in accordance with money costs may still be in conformity with real costs if these include both labor and capital costs, even when it is clearly not in conformity with labor costs alone. The logical difficulty for the doctrine of comparative costs created by interest charges is not that they can be shown to result in a deviation of money costs from real costs, but rather that there is no satisfactory way of showing whether money costs which include both wages and interest costs do or do not conform to real costs.

It must be conceded, therefore, that the existence of variable proportions between labor costs and capital costs and the absence of any procedure by which a bridge can be built between real labor costs and the subjective costs connected with capital or "waiting" makes it impossible to postulate a close relationship

---

[14] *Ibid.*, p. 582, note.

[15] Cf. Ricardo, *Notes on Malthus* [1820], p. 37:

Besides omitting the consideration which I have just mentioned [i.e., intensity of labor] he [i.e., Malthus] surely does not reckon on the labor bestowed on machines, such as steam engines, etc., on coal, etc., etc. Does not the labor on these constitute a part of the labor bestowed on the muslins?

[16] Cf. Taussig, *International trade*, 1927, pp. 68-69. Cf. also, *ibid., Some aspects of the tariff question*, 1915, p. 38 (italics in the original):

When the effectiveness of labor is spoken of, the effectiveness of *all* the labor needed to bring an article to market is meant; not merely that of the labor immediately and obviously applied (like that of the farmer), but that of the inventor and maker of threshing-machines and gangplows, and that of the manager and worker on the railways and ships.

between prices and real costs,[17] and restricts the case for trade on the basis of cost analysis to the proposition that in so far as such relationship can be traced the analysis as a general rule points conclusively to the profitability of trade. The area of doubt can be still further narrowed by cost analysis where it can be shown that *all* of the technical coefficients of domestic production of a particular commodity are higher than the corresponding technical coefficients of the export commodities in exchange for which the commodity in question would be obtained under free trade, or where, if most, but not all, of the technical coefficients of domestic production are higher, those which are lower can be regarded as of minor importance and those which are higher are much higher and those which are lower are little lower. The case for free trade can be still further strengthened by resort to analysis from the side of *income* instead of *cost*, as will be shown in the next section of this chapter and in the next chapter. Before I proceed to the income side of the picture, it will be convenient, however, to examine still another method of cost analysis which, on the surface, seems to dispose of the complications for a real-cost theory of value resulting from the use of different factors of production in variable proportions.

Given effective occupational mobility of the factors and equal attractiveness of the occupations, each factor will tend to be apportioned among the various employments until its marginal value productivity in each is equal, i.e., until the prices of the different commodities are proportional to their marginal real costs in terms of any single factor, which corresponds with their marginal single technical coefficients. Let x_1, x_2, be the outputs of commodities 1 and 2; let y_1, y_2, be the total amounts of labor-time used in the production of x_1, x_2, respectively, and z_1, z_2, be the total amounts of "capital-waiting" used in the production of x_1 and x_2, respectively; and let p_1, p_2, be the prices of commodities 1 and 2, respectively. Then $\dfrac{\delta y_1}{\delta x_1}$, $\dfrac{\delta y_2}{\delta x_2}$ will be the marginal costs of commodities 1 and 2, respectively, in terms of real labor costs, and $\dfrac{\delta z_1}{\delta x_1}$, $\dfrac{\delta z_2}{\delta x_2}$ will be the marginal costs of commodities 1 and 2, respectively,

[17] Land costs are not "real" costs as the term is here used. They must be dealt with, therefore, by means of income analysis, or by adding them to the real costs. See *supra*, pp. 493, note 6; 509-10.

in terms of real capital costs, and, under equilibrium, commodity units of equal price will have equal marginal real labor costs and equal marginal real capital costs, or:

$$\frac{p_1}{p_2} = \frac{\dfrac{\delta y_1}{\delta x_1}}{\dfrac{\delta y_2}{\delta x_2}} = \frac{\dfrac{\delta z_1}{\delta x_1}}{\dfrac{\delta z_2}{\delta x_2}}.$$

These marginal costs in terms of single factors have meaning, however, only with reference to changes in output so small that they can reasonably be assumed to be brought about by changes in the amount used of a single one of the factors. Substantial changes in output would normally be brought about by substantial changes in the amounts used of all, or of most, of the factors, when the significant marginal costs would be aggregates of a number of different factoral costs, instead of costs associated with one factor only. This approach, therefore, is inapplicable to substantial changes in the allocation of resources as between different industries, whereas significance can be attributed to the doctrine of comparative costs only as, and if, it is applicable to substantial changes in such allocation.

XII. "Opportunity Cost" Analysis as a Substitute for Real Cost Analysis

The Austrian school presented a theory of value in which "real costs" as understood by the English classical economists had no place, and, except for technological coefficients of production, no cost analysis was included. The original Austrian theory of value did not so much contest as ignore the existence of "real costs" and the considerations which led the English classical school to assign to them an important influence over relative prices.[1] Yielding to the pressure of controversial discussion, the Austrians eventually made some minor concessions to such influence, but failed to incorporate these concessions satisfactorily into their general theory,[2] and continued to present their

---

[1] For an admission of this by Böhm-Bawerk, see his "One word more on the ultimate standard of value," *Economic journal*, IV (1894), 720-21.

[2] Böhm-Bawerk, as far as I know, never abandoned his original position that money costs of production are determined solely by (technological costs and)

theory on the basis of a set of special assumptions whose responsibility for most of its distinctive features they never emphasized and, I believe, never recognized.[3]

The Austrian theory of value has recently taken on a new lease of life under distinguished and enthusiastic sponsorship under the designation of the "opportunity cost" or "alternative [product] cost" or "displaced [product] alternative" theory of value. This originally was except for the label an identical reproduction of the Austrian theory of value. In response to criticism, it is now incorporating real-cost considerations into its analysis more fully than did the original Austrian school, although its exponents have denied the legitimacy of such considerations more unrestrainedly than did the original "Austrians." This opportunity-cost theory has recently been applied to the theory of international trade as a substitute for the doctrine of comparative costs in terms of real costs, and has occasionally been presented as accomplishing all that the latter professed to do while escaping all of its difficulties. I will first examine the criticisms by the opportunity-cost theorists of the legitimacy and relevance of real-cost analysis, and then consider the positive substitute they offer for it.

The opportunity-cost theorists interpret "real costs" or "disutilities" as signifying "pain costs" (often as signifying *labor*-pain costs only), and they apparently deny that pain costs have any bearing on prices, or perhaps any existence. Whether or not there is such a thing as "pain," and if there is, whether or not its presence at the margin or earlier is a factor in determining the quantity of work or saving which will be done, are questions

the demands for the factors of production. But if disutilities can influence values, as he conceded, they can do so only through their influence on money costs. Wieser, making concessions to the irksomeness of labor as a value-determining factor, concluded that "Services of equal utility, but of different degrees of hardship, are so regulated in regard to value that the more troublesome labor is more highly appraised" (*Natural value*, 1893, p. 198) but failed to explain how this extraordinary result was brought about.

[3] They assumed, for instance, uniform rates of pay in all occupations for each kind of productive service, and fixed amounts of labor irrespective of the rates at which its services were remunerated. The quantity of capital, in the sense of the amount of postponement of consumption, or, given the amounts of the other factors, in the sense of the "average length of the productive period," they took to be a function of the rate of interest, but by confining their emphasis to the *increase in product* which resulted from a lengthening of the productive period they avoided the necessity of treating postponement or abstinence from immediate consumption as a cost even though it were irksome.

which the economist is, as such, incompetent to answer, whether in the affirmative or in the negative. Fortunately, however, no answer to these questions is required by a theory of value of any species which has ever had wide currency. "Real cost" or "disutility" has not, as far as I know, ever been used as a synonym for "pain" in some precise psychological sense, and in real-cost analysis pleasure relinquished and pain endured are alike treated as real costs, without attempt to distinguish them, and without any purpose which such distinction could serve. I am not even certain that Ricardo, or J. S. Mill, or Cairnes, or Taussig ever used the term "pain" in their analyses. In so far as the pleasure-pain terminology was used, the usage of the ordinary classical economist, though never rigorously defined as far as I know, seems to have been essentially that of Bishop Berkeley many years before:

> Sensual pleasure, quâ pleasure, is good and desirable by a wise man. But if it be contemptible, 'tis not quâ pleasure but quâ pain, or cause of pain, or (which is the same thing) of loss of greater pleasure.[4]

Every problem in economic welfare is a problem in the maximization of the surplus of income, in some sense significant for welfare, over outgo, also in some sense significant for welfare. The classical school, in the doctrine of comparative costs, attacked welfare problems from the point of view of how the outgo necessary to obtain a given unit of income could be minimized, and as outgo, or real cost, they included pleasures surrendered of certain though not all kinds, the one kind omitted being the pleasure derivable from an alternative product. They also, as we shall see in the next chapter, dealt with problems of welfare, including the problem of trade policy, from the income angle, from the point of view of maximizing the total income from a given outgo in terms of real cost, where the forgone pleasure derivable from an alternative product was treated as an alternative income, not as a cost. The two approaches are complemetary, rather than contradictory. Provided every element affecting relative prices is given proper consideration, it does not matter, except on purely terminological considerations, whether they are treated as costs or as forgone incomes. But the opportunity-cost theory,

---

[4] "Commonplace book," Berkeley, *Works,* Fraser ed., 1871, IV, 457.

as originally expounded, not only left out of consideration some important factors affecting price, but denied, by implication at least, that they were entitled to consideration.

Second, the opportunity-cost theorists stress the fact that prices are the outcome of the choices of individuals as between alternatives, with the implication that this differentiates their theory from real-cost theory. I know of no individualistic theory of exchange value, ancient or modern, which is not a theory of the consequences for relative prices of the choices made by individuals between alternatives, and the differences between the various theories are essentially differences in the range of alternatives choice between which they treat as significant for price formation. The notion occasionally encountered that the classical economists believed that in some way real costs fashioned prices to conform to themselves without the intervention of choices between alternatives exercised by individuals in the market seems to me a myth which cannot be substantiated by chapter and verse or any other sort of evidence.

The opportunity-cost doctrine, in its original form and in the only form in which its pretensions to being a revolutionary departure from real-cost value theorizing have any basis, treated choice between alternative *products* (or choice between the utilities derivable from the consumption of alternative products) as the only choice significant for price determination. In this theory the only true cost is foregone product, and relative prices are held to be determined solely by preferences between products and by the technical coefficients of production. In real-cost value theorizing, preferences as between products play a role in the determination of values, but so also do preferences between occupations for their own sakes, as activities, pleasurable or painful, and because of the modes and locations of life necessarily associated with them, and also preferences between employment and (voluntary) non-employment of the factors, and even between existence and non-existence of the factors. In the comparative-cost doctrine, where the problem of trade policy is dealt with from the point of view of under what foreign-trade policy a unit of a given commodity will be procured at the minimum real cost, the problem of choice between alternative *products* is abstracted from, but free scope is left for consideration of all the other relevant alternatives between which choice must be made. In situations, however, where, for whatever reason, any choice between occupations, or between employment and non-employment, is a matter of indifference to the individuals concerned, comparison of the products of alternative allocations of the productive services will alone be relevant both for the explanation of the determination of relative prices and for the appraisal in welfare terms of the relative desirability of alternative allocations. In such situations, only analysis on the income side is necessary, and real-cost analysis is irrelevant. The classical school, as will be shown in the next chapter, did have recourse to analysis on the income side, but their main emphasis was on costs, and where, as in the case of land use, real costs were absent or unimportant, their analysis was defective. But even in such situations, the opportunity-cost form of the income approach has no obvious advantages as compared to an outright income approach, and has the disadvantage that by its forced restriction to two commodities and its stress on physical quantities it distracts attention from the complications presented by a variety of alternative products and from the utility or welfare aspects of variations in the components and in the distribution of the real income.

The opportunity-cost theory was first applied to the problem of gain or loss from foreign trade as a substitute for the doctrine of comparative real cost by Haberler,[5] who claimed for it that it was adequate for the purpose and had the advantage over the doctrine of comparative costs that the use of the factors in variable proportions presented no difficulties for it. In his presentation, Haberler made use of a production-indifference curve, and the indifference-curve approach has been further elaborated, on similar lines, by Lerner[6] and Leontief.[7] I will endeavor to show, by an examination of the indifference-curve approach, that the opportunity-cost analysis faces difficulties on the "real income" side of the problem analogous to those involved in real-cost analysis, and

---

[5] "Die Theorie der komparativen Kosten," *loc. cit.*, pp. 357 ff.; *Der internationale Handel*, 1933, pp. 132 ff.; English ed., *The theory of international trade*, 1936, pp. 175 ff. It had been used, as a *supplement to* the doctrine of comparative real cost, by Pareto, in response to a suggestion from Barone. See *supra*, p. 509.

[6] A. Lerner, "The diagrammatical representation of cost conditions in international trade," *Economica*, XII (1932), 346-56.

[7] W. W. Leontief, "The use of indifference curves in the analysis of foreign trade," *Quarterly journal of economics*, XLVII (1933), 493-503.

that it avoids the difficulties involved in real-cost analysis for the most part only by ignoring the existence of some of the considerations which real-cost analysis takes into account.

The theory is presented in chart XI[8] in terms of so-called indifference curves. Any point on the curve *AB* represents by its

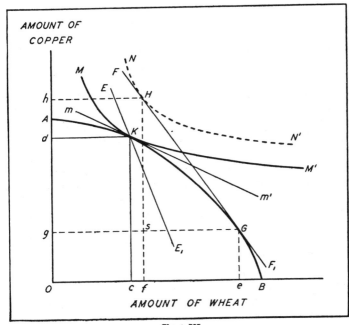

Chart XI

distance from the horizontal axis the maximum amount of copper and by its distance from the vertical axis the maximum amount of wheat which can simultaneously be produced by the country in question with its existing stocks of the productive factors. The slope of the tangent to the *AB* curve at any point represents the

[8] Chart XI was originally prepared for and presented in a lecture given by me at the London School of Economics in January, 1931. It is in its essentials similar to the later and more elaborate constructions of Lerner and Leontief. For my present purpose, which is to stress the limitations rather than the possibilities of this approach, my simpler diagram suffices, but as exhibitions of geometrical ingenuity their constructions are far superior. No use is made here of the *EE₁* line in chart XI.

alternative product cost of copper in terms of wheat, or the number of units copper which must be sacrificed to obtain an additional unit of wheat. In the absence of foreign trade, the relative exchange values of the two commodities must correspond to their alternative product costs, so that, e.g., if at the margin two units of copper must be sacrificed to obtain an additional unit of wheat, then under equilibrium two units of copper must exchange for one unit of wheat. The curve MM' is supposed to be a "consumption-indifference curve" for this country, tangent at some point, K, to the production curve AB, and points on it represent combinations of copper and wheat which would be equally "valued" by the community. At point K, where the two curves have a common tangent, mm', the alternative costs and the relative values of the two commodities would correspond. The point K is therefore the equilibrium point, in the absence of foreign trade, and od units of copper and oc units of wheat will be produced and consumed.

Suppose that if trade is opened with the outside world copper will be imported from abroad in exchange for wheat on the terms indicated by the slope of the FF' line, which is tangent at G to the production curve, AB, and at H to another consumption indifference curve of our country, NN', which is higher than MM', and is therefore taken to represent a greater total utility than MM'. If the slope of FF' is taken to represent the equilibrium terms of exchange of copper for wheat under foreign trade, our country will under equilibrium produce og copper and oe wheat; will consume oh copper and of wheat; and will import gh copper and export fe wheat. The amount of copper and of wheat available to it for consumption will therefore both be greater under foreign trade than in the absence of such trade. Whatever the slope or the point of tangency with the production curve AB of the FF' line, provided it is not the same as the mm' line, foreign trade will result in our country having available for consumption a combination of copper and wheat which will be on a higher consumption-indifference curve than MM' and therefore will indicate a greater total utility than MM', although less may be consumed of *one* of the commodities under foreign trade than in the absence of such trade. Foreign trade, therefore, necessarily results in gain. Such is the opportunity-cost theory as applied to the problem of gain from trade.

It is first to be noted that a true "consumption-indifference curve" must refer to a single valuing individual, and that the MM' curve, representing as it does a country as a whole, can be given meaning only if it is understood as representing the various combinations of copper and wheat which would have equal market value when the distribution of income was such as was consistent with the production of *od* copper and *oc* wheat. For every other productive combination, there would be another and different family of equal-value-combination curves, some of which would intersect the MM' curve—an impossibility if these were genuine consumption-indifference curves, independent of the actual allocation of production. Similar qualifications must be made with reference to the NN' curve. The NN' curve cannot, therefore, be accepted as necessarily representing a higher total utility, i.e., a higher "real income," than MM'.

The opportunity-cost approach encounters, therefore, on the income side, the same type of difficulty of weighting in the absence of knowledge of the proper weights as does the real-cost approach on the cost side. It remains to be demonstrated that the opportunity-cost approach avoids the difficulties on the cost side only by avoiding recognition of the considerations which give rise to these difficulties. Let us return to the production or AB curve, and examine its implications. On a true production-indifference curve, any two points would represent the product-combinations resulting from two allocations of productive activity equally attractive to the choosing agent after due consideration had been given to everything associated with such activity except the product outcome. As presented, the AB curve constitutes merely a series of maximum-possible combinations of product when a given stock of productive factors is employed, presumably to its physical maximum. In an actual situation, the actual product-combination would not be on this curve, but would be somewhere below it, if the amounts of the factors, or the extent to which they prefer leisure to employment, were dependent on the rates of remuneration and if the equilibrium rates of remuneration were lower (or higher) than those rates which would induce each factor to render the maximum amount of productive service of which it was physically capable. Even if the extent of employment of the factors was fixed, their allocation as between copper and wheat would be dependent, not only, as is assumed in the diagram and in the opportunity-cost theory, by the relative demands for copper and wheat and the productivity functions of the factors with respect to copper and wheat, but also by the relative preferences of the factors as between employment in copper production and in wheat production. Given the existence of such preferences, then even for a single individual the true production-indifference curve would not be *AB*, but some other curve lower than *AB* at some points at least, and higher at none. The opportunity-cost theory thus escapes the difficulties connected with preferences for leisure as compared to employment, preferences as between employments and variability of the supplies of the factor, only by ignoring them.

Haberler, in his later and more qualified exposition of the opportunity-cost theory as a substitute for the doctrine of comparative real costs, does take up the case of equalizing differences in wages, which I claim presents a difficulty for the opportunity-cost theory but not for the doctrine of comparative costs. He confines himself, however, to saying that "obviously the correct procedure" is "to take into account the advantages and disadvantages of different occupations other than the money wages"[9] which appears to me like an abandonment of the opportunity-cost doctrine as an alternative *product-cost* doctrine. He gives a reference, however, to an article by Lionel Robbins, "where it is shown how this and similar cases can be dealt with by the opportunity-cost doctrine." The only relevant material I can find in this article is the following passage :[10]

All economic changes are capable of being exhibited as forms of exchange. And hence, as Wicksteed has shown, they can be exhibited further as the resultant of demand operating within a given technical environment. It has been said that this becomes impossible if account be taken of the so-called other advantages and disadvantages of different occupations. Professor Viner . . . has urged this particular objection. The difficulty, however, seems to be capable of a simple

---

[9] *Theory of international trade*, p. 197.

[10] Lionel Robbins, "Remarks upon certain aspects of the theory of costs," *Economic journal*, XLIV (1934), 2, note 5. If "forms of exchange" means "results of choices between alternatives of all kinds" and if "demand" is read to mean "preferences between alternatives of all kinds" instead of what it usually means in economic theory, I would not think of objecting to what is claimed, except for the references to the Wicksteed constructions, which, however reinterpreted, are either wrong or useless.

solution. If the other advantages and disadvantages are treated as joint products, the Wicksteed constructions can still be maintained.

In this passage, and elsewhere in the same article, except for the suggestion he makes that, in effect, "value of alternative product" be substituted for "alternative product" in the formula, Robbins is *verbally* adhering to the original opportunity-cost doctrine, the doctrine that the cost of production of product A is the alternative product, B, whose production is forgone if A is produced. But the doctrine which he here expounds has no point of conflict with analysis in terms of real costs except in choice of terminology and in its implied suggestions that its emphasis upon choice between alternatives is novel and that, even in this vale of tears, man is required to choose only between *attractive* alternatives. By calling the excess of pleasurableness of occupation A over occupation B a "joint product" of A—and presumably by calling the excess of irksomeness of occupation C over occupation D a subtraction from the product of C, or, perhaps, by denying that occupations can be irksome—the "product" terminology is retained while proper account is taken of the significance for prices of choices between other alternatives than products. By the same terminological procedure, I suppose, if the alternative to producing E were producing F plus increased leisure, the increased leisure would also be termed a product, of "not-working," I take it. If a smaller product *now* should be chosen in preference to a larger product of the same kind *in the future*, such terminological virtuosity would not be overtaxed if required to find some way of expressing this preference as a preference for a larger "product" over a smaller one. But if the opportunity-cost theorists are now prepared to admit that all of the factors regarded by the real-cost theorists as influencing the determination of prices should be taken into account in explaining their determination and in appraising their significance, their insistence upon calling all of these factors "products" and their imputation of serious error to those of us who persist in regarding "real costs" as a better term for some of them, will not dampen the ardor of my welcome to them as belated converts to analysis in terms of *real* costs. Even with the aid, however, of the genuine contribution which the opportunity-cost technique can make to the treatment of land-use costs, the doctrine of comparative costs succeeds in demonstrating the profitability of trade only subject to the fairly important assumptions and qualifications examined above. In the next chapter I will endeavor to show that analysis of the strictly income aspects of foreign trade adds strength in certain respects to, but reveals additional weaknesses in other respects in, the case for free trade, and leaves it in that state of persuasiveness associated with incomplete demonstration which seems to be a universal characteristic of propositions of economic theory relating to questions involving human welfare.

Chapter IX

GAINS FROM TRADE: THE MAXIMIZATION
OF REAL INCOME

It is the mark of an educated man to look for precision in each class of things just so far as the nature of the subject admits; it is evidently equally foolish to accept probable reasoning from a mathematician and to demand from a rhetorician scientific proofs.—Aristotle, Ethica Nichomachea, 1094 b, as cited by T. V. Smith, International Journal of Ethics, XLVI (1936), 385.

1. "Mass of Commodities" and "Sum of Enjoyments": Ricardo and Malthus

In the comparative-cost approach to the problem of gain from foreign trade, the stress is put on the possibility of minimizing the aggregate real costs at which a given amount of real income can be obtained if those commodities which can be produced at home only at high comparative costs are procured through import, in exchange for exports, instead of being produced at home. In the later development of the theory of international trade, several methods of dealing with the income aspects of foreign trade are introduced, and in the exposition of Marshall and Edgeworth, though the comparative costs are still a factor in the situation,[1] they appear in the analysis only implicitly through their influence on the reciprocal-demand functions, which, in so far as they are

---

[1] The tendency on the part of Marshall and Edgeworth to allow cost analysis to recede into the background, and to deal with the question of gain or loss from trade primarily in terms of income analysis is in sharp contrast with Allyn Young's contention that the treatment of the problem should be solely in terms of costs: "Here again the study of costs affords the only practicable road to conclusions respecting net gains or losses. Gains come from *economies*. The economies of international trade are by no means an exact measure of its net benefits. But that net benefits are more or less according as the economies secured are more or less, is a justifiable assumption."—"Marshall on consumer's surplus in international trade," *Quarterly journal of economics*, XXXIX (1924), 150. (Italics in the original.)

welfare functions, represent "net" income or income-minus-cost quantities.

Ricardo and Malthus, in the course of a discussion of concrete problems of trade policy, offered some indication of the nature of the "welfare" presuppositions of their gain analysis. In Mill, Marshall, and Edgeworth these presuppositions are left unexpressed, as far as their international-trade analysis is concerned, and must be inferred from their other writings. As will perhaps be made evident, it is a question whether Marshall and Edgeworth, notwithstanding their more elaborate techniques of analysis, improved substantially upon what Ricardo and Malthus said, scanty though that was, with respect to the criteria of gain or loss from foreign trade.

Malthus attributed to Ricardo—whether rightly or wrongly is open to argument—the position that the saving in cost under free trade resulting from obtaining the imported commodities in exchange for exports instead of by domestic production not only demonstrated the existence of gain from trade but measured the extent of the gain. To this proposition Malthus objected that the excess in the cost of domestic production of the imported commodities over the cost of obtaining them in exchange for exports provided a grossly exaggerated measure of the gain from trade where the imported commodities could not be produced at home at all or could be produced only at extremely high costs :[2]

Mr. Ricardo always views foreign trade in the light of means of obtaining *cheaper* commodities. But this is only looking to one half of its advantages, and I am strongly disposed to think, not the larger half. In our own commerce at least, this part of the trade is comparatively inconsiderable. The great mass of our imports consists of articles as to which there can be no kind of question about their comparative cheapness, as raised abroad or at home. If we could not import from foreign countries our silk, cotton and indigo . . . with many other articles peculiar to foreign climates, it is quite certain that we should not have them at all. To estimate the advantage derived from their importation by their cheapness, compared with the quantity of labor and capital which they would have cost if we had attempted to raise them at home, would be perfectly preposterous. In reality no such attempt would have been thought of. If we could

---

[2] Malthus, *Principles of political economy*, 1st ed., 1820, pp. 461-62. (Italics in the original text.)

by possibility have made fine claret at ten pounds a bottle, few or none would have drunk it: and the actual quantity of labor and capital employed in obtaining these foreign commodities is at present beyond comparison greater than it would have been if we had not imported them.

Malthus held that the gain from trade consisted of "the increased value which results from exchanging what is wanted less for what is wanted more"; foreign trade, "by giving us commodities much better suited to our wants and tastes than those which had been sent away, had decidedly increased the exchangeable value of our possessions, our means of enjoyment, and our wealth."[3] Malthus, here as elsewhere, meant by "value" or "exchangeable value" not value in terms of money but purchasing power over labor or "labor command." He reached the conclusion that foreign trade increases the sum of "labor command" in the following fashion: foreign trade, when it results in a new assortment of commodities available for use which is "better suited to the wants of society" than the pre-trade one, increases income in the form of profits without a proportionate decrease in other forms of income, and therefore increases the amount of money available for payment as wages, or the demand for labor; wages do not rise in proportion to the rise in total money income; therefore the new income constitutes a greater sum of "labor command" than the old one.[4] Malthus would, therefore, presumably deny that there was gain from foreign trade if money wage rates rose relatively as much as total monetary income, so that there was no increase in "labor command." To measure gain by the increase in "labor command" without reference to the terms on which labor can be commanded is a fantastic procedure if laborers are recognized as constituting part of the population.

Malthus would have done much better if he had stopped with the exchange of "what is wanted less for what is wanted more" as constituting the content of the gain from foreign trade. He got into this muddle in an attempt to rebut the proposition with which Ricardo's famous chapter on foreign trade opens: "No extension of foreign trade will immediately increase the amount of value in a country."[5] Malthus regarded this as an absurd prop-

---

[3] *Ibid.*, p. 462.
[4] Cf. *ibid.*, p. 460.
[5] Ricardo, *Principles of political economy*, 1st ed., 1817, p. 107.

osition, whereas if he had ever succeeded in mastering Ricardo's peculiar use of terms he would have seen that it was a sterile truism. Ricardo's proposition rests upon his use of the quantity-of-labor cost as the measure of value and upon his tacit assumption that foreign trade influences what labor shall produce but does not affect immediately how much labor shall be engaged in production.

Ricardo, however, did not measure gain by changes in "value" as defined by him, and therefore did not deny that foreign trade resulted in gain. After laying down his proposition that foreign trade will not immediately increase the amount of value in a country, Ricardo went on to say that "it will very powerfully contribute to increase the mass of commodities, and therefore, the sum of enjoyments."[6] What was intended by Ricardo as the main proposition was, at least for our present purposes, of no importance. The incidental comment, on the other hand, was of great importance. It suggests two income tests of the existence, and perhaps also two income measures of the extent, of gain from trade, namely, an increase in the "mass of commodities" and an increase in the "sum of enjoyments." Ricardo did not expand these suggestions, but in his *Notes on Malthus* he repeated them : if two regions engage in trade with each other "the advantage . . . to both places is not [that] they have any increase of value, but with the same amount of value they are both able to consume and enjoy an increased quantity of commodities," adding, however, that "if they should have no inclination to indulge themselves in the purchase of an additional quantity, they will have an increased means of making savings from their expenditure."[7]

Both types of test, needless to say, involve in their application serious logical or practical difficulties. The "mass of commodities" is significant only as it is accepted as a measure or index of the "sum of enjoyments" and the "sum of enjoyments" is not itself directly measurable. The use of "mass of commodities" as a measure of gain from trade, or even as an index of the direction of change, would involve in practice the use of an index number of national real income. As in the case of the measurement of real

---

[6] *Ibid.*

[7] *Notes on Malthus* [1820], p. 215. Ricardo means presumably that the increased income can be saved and invested instead of being immediately consumed.

costs, the determination of the proper weights for the quantities of different commodities presents serious, and in strict theory insoluble, problems. There is no evidence that Ricardo gave any thought to these problems. Malthus, however, in defending his own "labor command" test, succeeded in locating the most vulnerable point in the "mass of commodities" test. Where the commodities imported were such as in the absence of foreign trade could not have been produced at home, or could be produced only at prohibitively high costs, Malthus objected, "we might be very much puzzled to say whether we had increased or decreased the quantity of our commodities,"[8] presumably because after trade the country would have more of the imported but less of the native commodities than before trade with no means available of comparing *exactly* the amount of increase in the one with the amount of decrease in the other.

Malthus could have gone further: even if there were more of *every* commodity after trade as compared to before trade, the removal of the duties would certainly have resulted in an increase in the quantity of commodities in any physical sense, but there would not necessarily have been an increase in real income or in "sum of enjoyments." The argument should scarcely call for elaboration. The removal of duties tends to alter the distribution of the national money income unfavorably for the owners of the services entering relatively more heavily into the production of the hitherto protected commodities than into the production of the export commodities. The removal of duties tends also to raise to domestic consumers the prices of the export commodities relative to the prices of the hitherto protected commodities. Suppose that labor enters relatively more heavily into the production of the protected commodities than into the production of the export commodities, and that labor is a heavy consumer of the export commodities but a light consumer of the protected commodities. The removal of the duties, therefore, operates injuriously to labor in two ways: it lowers the relative share of labor in the national *money* income, and it raises the prices, relative to other commodities, of the things on which labor spends its wages. It is still

---

[8] *Principles*, 1st ed., p. 462. Ricardo would not have disputed this. Cf. *Principles, Works*, 260: "One set of necessaries and conveniences admits of no comparison with another set; value in use cannot be measured by any known standard; it is differently estimated by different persons."

possible that labor may gain from the removal of the duties, for under the conditions given it is still possible for the buying power of money wages over the things laborers buy to be greater after the removal of the duties than before. Even if labor does lose, other classes will necessarily gain more than labor loses in physical income, if in measuring physical income the quantities of particular commodities are weighted for purposes of summation by their prices under free trade, or their prices under protection, or any *intermediate* scale of prices, and if the import duties were not merely nominal but were actually restrictive of import of the dutiable commodities.[9] But if labor is relatively a low-income class, the removal of import duties might result in a loss of physical income to labor which, weighted by its utility coefficient, might conceivably be greater than the gain in the physical income of the other classes, similarly weighted by its utility coefficient. It is possible, therefore, that even with the usual abstractions from short-run immobilities and rigidities, from monopoly conditions, and from changes in aggregate real cost on the production side, free trade may result in an impairment of psychic income. But the combination of adverse circumstances necessary to produce this result is so formidable as to justify the conclusion that there is ordinarily a strong presumption that free trade—given the usual long-run assumptions—will increase the national real income. Economic analysis can here at best yield only strong presumptions, but this limit in the power of economic analysis extends to the entire field of welfare analysis.

Haberler, on the basis of a combination of *a priori* and empirical considerations, claims that in the long run the functional distribution of real income is unlikely to be appreciably different under free trade than under protection, and that in so far as it would change with the adoption of free trade the change would more probably be favorable than unfavorable to labor. Free trade, he argues, will result in a rise in the real prices of those factors which are "specific to" the export industries; it will result also in a rise, though a lesser one, in the real prices of non-specific

---

[9] In a limiting case, where under constant cost conditions the relative prices of all the various commodities would be the same under free trade as their relative costs of production at home, import duties could still be restrictive of import without affecting the amount of the national real income, the distribution of the national money income, or the relative prices of different commodities.

factors; and it will result in a fall in the real prices of those factors which are specific to the protected industries which must reduce their operations or disappear under free trade. Labor is in the long run the least specific of all factors. It will therefore be in the intermediate position, and will gain from the general increase in productivity.[10]

While Haberler's conclusions may be sound, this reasoning seems inadequate justification for them. Haberler uses "specific" to mean occupational immobility, whether due to technical or to other causes. He compares the mobility of only labor and "material means of production," which latter is scarcely an elementary factor of production. Natural resources of the agricultural or mining type are no doubt the most specific of the factors, but in the long run it would seem to be free capital and not labor which is the least specific. In any case, it would seem to be not occupational mobility in general, but occupational mobility as between the tariff-sheltered and the unsheltered industries which would be of primary significance for this problem. If labor was used relatively heavily by the protected industries, relatively lightly by the unsheltered industries, and if its marginal productivity decreased slowly in the former and rapidly in the latter as more labor was employed while the other factors were held constant, the removal of tariff protection would lessen the relative share of labor in the national money income. I see no *a priori* or empirical grounds for holding this to be an improbable case. But even if labor on the average had low occupational mobility and were employed relatively heavily in the protected industries, its real income might still rise with a removal of tariff protection even though its money income and its relative share in the national money income and the national real income all fell, if it was an important consumer of the hitherto protected commodities, and if the prices of these commodities fell sufficiently as a result of free trade to offset the reduction in money wages in the new situation.

The concessions made above to the protectionist case do not qualify the conclusion that free trade—given the usual assumptions—necessarily makes *available* to the community *as a whole* a greater physical real income in the form of more of *all* commodities, and that the state, if it chooses, can, by appropriate

---

[10] *The theory of international trade,* 1936, pp. 193-95.

supplementary legislation, make certain that the removal of duties shall result in more of *every* commodity for *every* class of the community. When the Cobden Treaty was negotiated, Proudhon complained that while it admittedly made cottons cheaper and more abundant in France, it made wine dearer and scarcer, and that the French masses lost more from the latter consequence of the treaty than they gained from the former. It cannot be said with confidence, on *a priori* grounds alone, that Proudhon was mistaken. But the French government could have brought it about that the Cobden Treaty should not result in a reduction in wine consumption in France—or by any stratum of the French population—by levying special income taxes on the class which consumed cotton goods relatively most heavily and using the proceeds to subsidize the class which consumed wine relatively more heavily, or by levying *internal* consumption taxes on cottons (at lower rates than the effective amount of the import duties which had been removed) and using the proceeds as a subsidy to domestic wine consumption, or by some other stratagem of this general character, designed to offset an undesired effect of the reduction of duties on the distribution of the national income.

Free trade, therefore, always makes more commodities available, and, unless it results in an impairment of the distribution of real income substantial enough to offset the increase in quantity of goods available, free trade always operates, therefore, to increase the national real income. That the available gain is ordinarily substantial there is abundant reason to believe, but the extent of the gain cannot in practice be measured in any concrete way. These conclusions, which are little more than a paraphrase of some words of Cairnes's,[11] are, in my opinion, very nearly as far as the argument can with advantage be carried. The remainder of the chapter is devoted to an examination—as sympathetic as I can make it—of the more elaborate methods of analysis by which J. S. Mill, Marshall, Edgeworth, and others obtained results which were, seemingly at least, more precise and conclusive, with respect to the income gains from trade.

---

[11] "We know the nature of the gain [from trade] : it consists in extending the range of our satisfactions, and in cheapening the cost at which such as in its absence would not be beyond our reach are obtained; and we know that the amount which it brings to us under each of these categories cannot but be very great; but beyond this indefinite and vague result our data do not enable us to pass." (*Some leading principles of political economy*, 1874, p. 421.)

II. RECIPROCAL DEMAND AND THE TERMS OF TRADE

From the time of Ricardo on, the commodity terms of trade have been widely accepted as an index of the trend of gain from trade. Some writers have also derived a measure of the ratio in which the gains from trade were divided between two trading areas from their commodity terms of trade taken in relation to the comparative costs of production of the two areas. In earlier chapters the terms of trade have been dealt with merely as manifestations of certain objective price relations, without reference to their gain significance. Before proceeding to an examination of the validity of the use of the terms of trade as an index of gain, it is necessary to consider further the objective relationship of the terms of trade to other international trade phenomena, and especially the connection between the "reciprocal demands" and the commodity terms of trade. Analysis of this connection begins with Torrens and John Stuart Mill. Marshall and Edgeworth later made it a field for the exercise of their geometrical skill, but admittedly without departing substantially from J. S. Mill's mode of approach or conclusions. While a number of writers have reproduced their analysis in sympathetic fashion, Graham alone has subjected it to really severe criticism. This section, therefore, will be confined to an examination of the contributions of Mill, Marshall, and Edgeworth, with reference at appropriate points to Graham's criticisms. Since the original sources are all readily available, the summaries presented here will be restricted to the minimum necessary to afford a sufficient basis for appraisal of their techniques of analysis and their most general conclusions.

John Stuart Mill.—Mill's discussion of the relationship between reciprocal demand and the commodity terms of trade was in the main a pioneer achievement, and probably constitutes his chief claim to originality in the field of economics.[1] The problem

---

[1] Mill first presented his analysis in Essay I of his *Essays on some unsettled questions of political economy*, written in 1829-30, when he was twenty-three years of age, but not published until 1844. He reproduced it, with extensions, but also with important omissions, in the first edition (1848) of his *Principles of political economy*, bk. iii, chap. xviii, "Of international values." Edgeworth could not find terms of praise too high for this chapter; it was a "great chapter" (*Papers relating to political economy*, 1925, II, 7), a "stupendous chapter" (*ibid.*, II, 10, 20), and an exposition of the general theory which was

for which Mill seeks an answer is the mode of determination of the commodity terms of trade. He first simplifies the problem by assuming only two countries and only two commodities.[2] Mill held that the equilibrium terms of trade must be within the upper and lower limits set by the ratios in the respective countries of the costs at which the two commodities could be produced at home, but that the exact location of the terms of trade would be determined by the demands of the two countries for each other's products in terms of their own products, or the "reciprocal demands."[3] Equilibrium would be established at that ratio of exchange between the two commodities at which the quantities demanded by each country of the commodities which it imports from the other should be exactly sufficient to pay for one another, a rule which Mill labels the "equation of international demand" or "law of international values."[4]

Shadwell later objected that Mill had not really solved the problem by his "equation" or "law," but had merely stated the truism that "the ratio of exchange is such that the exports pay for the imports,"[5] and Graham makes substantially the same criticism.[6] Except for the case of pure barter, however, there is nothing "truistic" about the equality in value of imports and exports, and in fact they would ordinarily not be equal even after allowance for "invisible" items if, as is proper for present purposes, money and the money metals were not counted as exports or imports. It

"still unsurpassed" (*ibid.*, II, 20). Graham, on the other hand, declares that it presents doctrine which is "in its essence fallacious and should be discarded."—"The theory of international values," *Quarterly journal of economics,* XLVI (1932), 581.

[2] Graham's heaviest criticisms are directed against Mill's alleged error in assuming that the conclusions derived from this simplified case had general validity. Cf. *supra*, pp. 453-54.

[3] Mill does not seem to have used this term, whose first use is commonly attributed to Torrens.

[4] Cf. Mill, *Principles,* Ashley ed., p. 592:

The law . . . may be appropriately named the equation of international demand. It may be concisely stated as follows. The produce of a country exchanges for the produce of other countries at such values as are required in order that the whole of her exports may exactly pay for the whole of her imports. This law of international values is but an extension of the more general law of value, which we called the equation of supply and demand.

[5] J. L. Shadwell, *A system of political economy,* 1877, p. 406.

[6] "Theory of international values," *Quarterly journal of economics,* XLVI (1932), 606.

would be true, however, that Mill would not have accomplished very much if he had merely established the necessity under equilibrium of equality in value between imports and exports. But as Bastable pointed out in reply to Shadwell, "Mill's theory does not consist merely in the statement of the equation of reciprocal demand, but [also] in the indication of the forces which are in operation to produce that equation."[7] The terms of trade, according to Mill, are determined by the reciprocal demands, conceived in the schedule or function sense, subject to the condition that imports shall equal exports in value. A fair reading of Mill's chapter warrants no other interpretation. There is, moreover, supporting evidence for this interpretation. Mill, as we have seen, stated that "This law of international values is but an extension of the more general law of value, which we called the equation of supply and demand." To what appears to have been a criticism similar to Shadwell's made by Cairnes against Mill's use of the analogous "equation of supply and demand" in his general value theory, Mill replied:[8]

I think that the proposition as laid down [i.e., "the equation of supply and demand"] is something more than an identical proposition. It does not define—nor did it, as I stated it, affect to define—the causes of variations in value. But it declares the *condition* of all such variations and the necessary *modus operandi* of their causes, viz., that they operate by moving the supply to equality with the demand or the demand to equality with the supply.

To explain the determination of the terms of trade by reciprocal demand and the "equation of international demand" Mill used arithmetical illustrations. It is not surprising, therefore, that his results had sometimes a more restricted range of validity than he appeared to recognize. But the following summary and graphical illustration of his results in one of his hypothetical

---

[7] Bastable, *Theory of international trade,* 4th ed., 1903, p. 180.

[8] J. S. Mill to Cairnes, June 23, 1869, *The letters of John Stuart Mill,* H. S. R. Elliot ed., 1910, II, 207. (Italics in the original text.) Mill's reasoning here is clear enough, and sound enough, if it is remembered that, like all the earlier English economists, Mill distinguished in his thinking, even if not in his terminology, between "demand" as a quantity actually taken at a particular price and "demand" as a schedule of quantities which would be taken at different prices.

cases[9] may serve, nevertheless, to reveal the pioneer character of his analysis.

There are two countries, Germany and England, two commodities, cloth and linen, and production is tacitly assumed to be under conditions of constant real cost. In England 10 yards of cloth cost as much to produce as 15 yards of linen, while in Germany 10 yards of cloth cost as much to produce as 20 yards of linen. England will therefore be an importer of linen and an exporter of cloth, and the possible range of the terms at which cloth will be exchanged for linen is between 10 of cloth for 15 linen and 10 of cloth for 20 linen. Mill assumes that the reciprocal demands are such that equilibrium will be established at 10 of cloth for 17 linen.

Mill now assumes that an improvement is introduced in the method of production of linen in Germany, so that it now costs per unit only two-thirds as much as before. This will increase the German demand for cloth in terms of linen, and will cause 10 yards of cloth to exchange for more than 17 linen. Mill tacitly assumes here that the German demand for cloth *in terms of units of German effort of production* will remain unchanged, so that the German demand for cloth *in terms of linen* will at all points be 50 per cent higher than before. He concludes that the degree in which the amount of linen exchanging for 10 of cloth rises above 17 depends on the character of the English demand for linen in terms of cloth. When the German offering price of linen in terms of cloth is lowered: (a) if the quantity of linen England will take increases "in the same proportion with the cheapness" of the linen, i.e., if the English demand for linen in terms of cloth prices has unit elasticity, the new equilibrium terms of trade will be 10 cloth for 25½ linen; (b) if the quantity of linen England will take increases "in a greater proportion than the cheapness" of the linen, i.e., if the English demand for linen in terms of cloth prices has an elasticity greater than unity, the new equilibrium terms of trade will be 10 cloth for 25½ — linen; (c) finally, if the quantity of linen England will take increases "in a less proportion than the cheapness" of the linen, i.e., if the English demand for linen in terms of cloth prices has an elasticity less than unity, the new equilibrium terms of trade will be 10 cloth for 25½ + linen.

---

[9] *Principles,* Ashley ed., pp. 585-88, 594-95.

Chart XII, a modification of the Marshallian foreign-trade diagrams so as to make the vertical axis represent the linen-cloth terms of trade instead of the total quantity of linen, shows that Mill's conclusions, given his assumptions, are correct.[10] The reduction in the cost of producing linen in Germany results in the

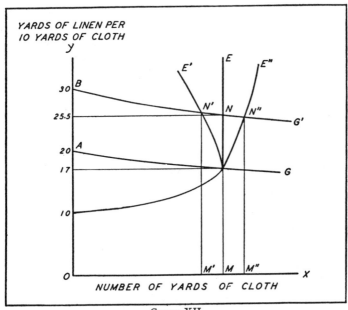

CHART XII

terms of trade moving against linen. Given the effect of the reduction in the German cost of producing linen on the German demand for cloth in terms of linen, the degree of this movement of the terms of trade against linen is smaller, the greater is the elasticity of the English demand for linen in terms of cloth.[11]

[10] Cf. Edgeworth, "On the application of mathematics to political economy," *Journal of the Royal Statistical Society*, LII (1889), 557, fig. 3, for a similar demonstration by means of a Marshallian diagram.

[11] The differences in the methods of constructing Marshall's and my curves do not call for differences in the elasticity formulae, if the same symbols are used to represent the same variables in the two diagrams. In both diagrams each curve can be regarded either as a demand curve or as a supply curve, each with a distinct elasticity coefficient. There will thus be a total of four elasticities. Write X for the total amount of E-goods, Y for the total amount

When the elasticity of the English demand for linen in terms of cloth (the E curve) is unity, the new terms of trade are 10 cloth for $25\frac{1}{2}$ linen. When the elasticity of the English demand for linen

---

of G-goods, the subscripts E and G for the countries England and Germany respectively, $y = \frac{Y}{X}$, for the price of E-goods in G-goods, and $\frac{1}{y} = \frac{X}{Y}$ for the price of G-goods in E-goods. Then if e_E^D is the elasticity of English "demand" or willingness to buy German goods, e_E^S is the elasticity of English willingness to sell English goods, e_G^D is the elasticity of German willingness to buy English goods, and e_G^S is the elasticity of German willingness to sell German goods, then:

$$e_E^D = \frac{dY_E}{d\left(\frac{1}{y_E}\right)} \cdot \frac{\frac{1}{y_E}}{Y_E} .$$

$$e_E^S = \frac{dX_E}{dy_E} \cdot \frac{y_E}{X_E} .$$

$$e_G^D = \frac{dX_G}{dy_G} \cdot \frac{y_G}{X_G} .$$

$$e_G^S = \frac{dY_G}{d\left(\frac{1}{y_G}\right)} \cdot \frac{\frac{1}{y_G}}{Y_G} .$$

The demand elasticity and the supply elasticity of each country are of course closely related to each other, as they are but different aspects of the same phenomenon. The relationship between the two elasticities for England can readily be shown:

$$e_E^D = \frac{dY_E}{d\left(\frac{1}{y_E}\right)} \cdot \frac{\frac{1}{y_E}}{Y_E}$$

$$= \frac{d(X_E y_E)}{-\left(\frac{dy_E}{y_E^2}\right)} \cdot \frac{\frac{1}{y_E}}{X_E y_E}$$

$$= -\left(\frac{X_E dy_E + y_E dX_E}{X dy_E}\right)$$

$$= -\left(\frac{dX_E}{dy_E} \cdot \frac{y_E}{X_E} + 1\right)$$

$$= -(e_E^S + 1)$$

Similarly,

$$e_G^D = -(e_G^S + 1)$$

When the coefficient of demand elasticity of a country is unity, therefore, the

in terms of cloth (the E'' curve) is greater than unity, the new terms of trade are 10 cloth for $25\frac{1}{2}$ — linen. When the elasticity of the English demand for linen in terms of cloth (the E' curve) is less than unity, the new terms of trade are 10 cloth for $25\frac{1}{2}$ $+$ linen. All these results are in conformity with Mill's findings.

As the result of criticisms from W. T. Thornton, and others, Mill, in the third edition (1852) of his *Principles*, introduced new matter intended to meet the objection that he had failed to demonstrate that, given the reciprocal demands, there was a unique rate of exchange between cloth and linen at which the condition of equilibrium that the value of imports should equal the value of exports would be met.[12] There has been general agreement that this additional material was unsatisfactory and unnecessary. Where at least one of the reciprocal demands is inelastic there may be more than one equilibrium set of terms of trade, and the problem is then indeterminate.[13] Where both the reciprocal demands are elastic, there must be a unique equilibrium set of terms of trade, which is adequately determined by Mill's original procedure.

Marshall.—Marshall's treatment of the relation of reciprocal demand to terms of trade is in the main an exposition and elaboration in geometrical form of Mill's analysis.[14] Marshall invented for this purpose a new type of supply-and-demand diagram, in which the vertical and the horizontal axes each represent the total quantity of one of the two commodities, thus differing from his domestic-trade diagrams, where only one commodity, and money prices, are involved, and where the vertical axis represents price per unit.[15] As against the alternative procedure followed here in

coefficient of its supply elasticity is zero. In the text, reciprocal-demand curves are referred to as "elastic" if the coefficient of their demand elasticity is numerically greater than unity and of their supply elasticity is algebraically greater than zero and as "inelastic" if the coefficient of their demand elasticity is numerically smaller than unity and of their supply elasticity is algebraically smaller than zero.

Although expressed in different terms, this usage corresponds to Marshall's use of the terms "elastic" and "inelastic" in connection with his reciprocal demand curves. (Cf. Marshall, *Money credit & commerce*, pp. 337-38, note.)

[12] Mill, *Principles*, Ashley ed., pp. 596-604.

[13] Cf. Marshall, *Money credit & commerce*, p. 354, note 3.

[14] Cf. letter from Marshall to Cunynghame, June 28, 1904; "As to international trade curves:—mine were set to a definite tune, that called by Mill." (*Memorials of Alfred Marshall*, A. C. Pigou ed., 1925, p. 451.)

[15] Marshall's analysis is available in his *The pure theory of foreign trade*

charts VII, X, and XII, of making the vertical axis in the international-trade diagrams represent the terms of trade, equivalent
to price, Marshall claims for his own procedure: first, that it
makes the curves of the two countries "symmetrical" and, second,
that the alternative procedure would have some (unspecified)
advantages, but "this want of symmetry would have marred,
though it would not have rendered impracticable, the application
of the method of diagrams to the more elementary portions of
the theory; but in other portions it would have led to unmanageable complications."[16]

The issue is merely one of comparative convenience, and has no
other significance. I have found it much more convenient as a rule
to follow the procedure which Marshall rejects, i.e., to make the
vertical axis represent terms of trade rather than the total quantity of one of the commodities. Aside from whatever aesthetic
value may attach to the "symmetry" which is abandoned when
this alternative procedure is followed, the only disadvantage in
substituting the "terms-of-trade diagrams" for Marshall's diagrams is that whereas in Marshall's diagrams it can readily be
determined by inspection, for *both* of the curves, whether their
demand elasticity is greater, less, or equal to unity, and for *both*
of the commodities, what will be the total amounts exchanged
under equilibrium, in my diagrams, to which I will henceforth
refer as "terms-of-trade diagrams," this information is directly
available only for one of the curves and one of the commodities.
But my diagram has the advantage that on it the commodity
terms of trade can be read off directly from the vertical axis,
whereas on Marshall's diagram they can be found only by determining the rate of slope of the vector from the *o* point to the point
of equilibrium.

The general nature of Marshall's analysis of the relationship
between the reciprocal demands and the terms of trade can conveniently be illustrated by means of one of Marshall's propositions
which Graham has criticized. That the use of terms-of-trade diagrams has some practical advantages over Marshall's procedure
will become evident, I believe, if the simplicity of the diagrams

(printed for private circulation in 1879, reprinted in 1930), and his *Money
credit & commerce* (published in 1923, though in the main written much
earlier), bk. III, and appendices H and J.

[16] *The pure theory of foreign trade*, p. 2.

presented here is compared with the complexity of those used by Marshall in the same connection. Marshall claims that if the English demand for German goods undergoes a given percentage increase the following rule holds:

The more elastic the demand of either country, the elasticity of the demand of the other being given, the larger will be the volume of her exports and of her imports; but the more also will her exports be enlarged relatively to her imports; or, in other words, the less favorable to her will be the terms of trade.[17]

Graham objects that the rule holds for Germany, but not for England, where "the more elastic the demand of E, the demand of G being given, the *smaller* will be the volume of E's imports and exports, and the less will her exports be enlarged relatively to her imports."[18] Marshall applies his conclusions only to curves of the "normal" type, i.e., curves whose "demand elasticities" in my terminology are greater than unity,[19] while Graham makes no qualification whatsoever with respect to the nature of the curves. Since the results in some respects vary *in direction* according to whether the elasticities are greater or less than unity, it will be assumed that Graham also intended to restrict his conclusions to cases where the elasticities are greater than unity. Since "increase" of demand can be given a variety of meanings, and the results obtained will depend on what meaning is chosen, I will assume, as does Marshall, that when a reciprocal demand "increases" it shifts *to the right* by a uniform *percentage* at all points of the original curve.

Marshall's proposition is tested with reference to the influence of the elasticity of *Germany's* curve in chart XIII, where EE is the original English supply curve (equivalent to Marshall's original English curve), $E'E'$ is the increased English supply curve, GG is the less elastic and $G'G'$ is the more elastic German demand curve. The more elastic the German demand curve: (1) the greater is the increase in the German exports (i.e., the rectangle $a'om't' > aomt$); (2) the greater is the increase in German imports (i.e., $om' > om$); and (3) the smaller is the amount of

---

[17] Marshall, *Money credit & commerce,* p. 178.

[18] Graham, "The theory of international values," *Quarterly journal of economics,* XLVI (1932), 601.

[19] Cf., *supra,* p. 539, note 11, and Marshall, *loc. cit.,* p. 342.

movement favorable to Germany in the terms of trade (i.e., $Aa' < Aa$). These results are all in conformity with Marshall's —and Graham's—findings.

The divergent propositions of Marshall and Graham with respect to the influence of the elasticity of *England's* curve are tested in chart XIV, where GG is the German reciprocal-demand curve, EE and $E'E'$ represent the less elastic English reciprocal-demand curve before and after its increase, and ee and $e'e'$ repre-

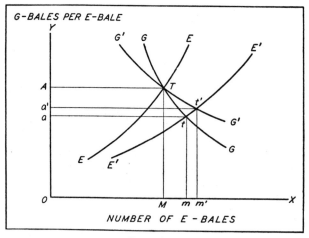

CHART XIII

sent the more elastic English reciprocal-demand curve before and after its increase. The more elastic the English reciprocal demand, then when the English demand increases: (1) the *smaller* is the increase in the English exports (i.e., $om < om'$); and (2), the *smaller* is the movement of the terms of trade against England (i.e., $Aa < Aa'$). Both these results confirm Graham's rather than Marshall's findings.

There remains to be considered Marshall's finding that the greater the elasticity of the English curve the greater will be the increase in the English imports when the English reciprocal demand increases, and Graham's contrary finding that the increase in the amount of English imports will be negatively correlated with the elasticity of the English curve. Marshall says, in effect, that in chart XIV *aomt* > *a'om't'*, while Graham contends that *aomt* < *a'om't'*. Their conclusions, it is to be remembered, are here being checked only for the cases where all the curves have demand elasticities greater than unity. Since the less elastic the original English supply curve, the further to the right from *T* along the *GG* curve is the intersection of the increased English supply curve with the German curve (i.e., *t'* is to the right of *t*), and since, because *GG* has an elasticity of demand greater than

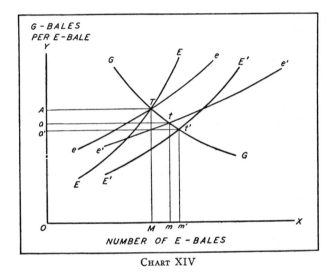

CHART XIV

unity, the further from the zero vertical axis is the point of intersection of the increased English curve with the German curve the greater must be the size of the rectangle bounded by the perpendiculars dropped from that point to the zero axes, therefore, *a'om't'* > *aomt*. Graham, therefore, is here again right, and Marshall wrong. The unnecessary complexity of Marshall's diagram seems to have concealed from him the fact that it provided no answers to the questions which he was putting, for the diagram by which he attempts to demonstrate the nature of the dependence of the results of an increase in the English reciprocal demand on the degree of elasticity of that curve shows three *original* English curves, different in locus as well as elasticity, and fails to present a comparison of the effects of an *increase* in an original English curve according as that original curve has high or low elasticity.[20]

Edgeworth.—In Edgeworth's treatment of the relation of reciprocal demand to the terms of trade the Marshallian graphical technique is still further elaborated, with conclusions similar in their general tenor, but with more detailed differentiation of the

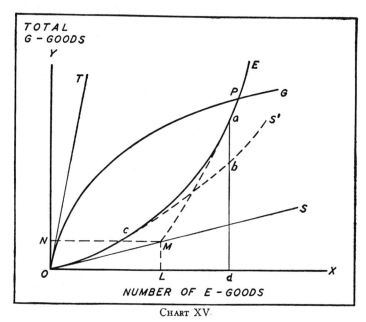

CHART XV.

various possible types of cases.[21] Of special interest is his diagram[22] reproduced above (chart XV), intended to show the nature of the relationship between the comparative costs and the reciprocal demands.

Chart XV is constructed on the Marshallian model, where the total amount of German linen is measured on the *Y* axis and the

[20] Cf. *Money credit & commerce*, p. 343, fig. 12.

[21] F. Y. Edgeworth, "The pure theory of international trade," in *Papers relating to political economy*, 1925, II, 31-40 (first published in *Economic journal*, 1894, in substantially the same form).

[22] *Papers*, II, 32.

total amount of English cloth on the X axis. The lines OS and OT are added, however, their slopes representing, on the assumption of constant costs of production, the (constant) ratio of the cost of production of a unit of linen to that of a unit of cloth, for England and Germany respectively. These lines therefore represent, respectively, the terms on which England could obtain linen and Germany could obtain cloth in the absence of foreign trade, and the equilibrium terms of trade must fall between these two lines. As Edgeworth draws the diagram, however, it is open to a criticism to which all the Marshallian diagrams as usually drawn are equally open, if they are supposed to represent two commodities or classes of commodities both of which are producible at home at constant costs (or at constant relative costs). In Edgeworth's diagram the OE curve begins immediately at its origin at O to rise above the OS line, and the OG curve to fall below the OT line.[23] But the OE curve will not diverge from the OS line until the point on OS is reached which corresponds by its vertical distance from the X axis to the amount of linen which England would consume and produce in the absence of foreign trade. Let us suppose that the amount of linen which would be produced and consumed in England in the absence of foreign trade is equal to ON. England would therefore be willing to export, at the limiting ratio of linen to cloth set by its home costs, any quantity of cloth not exceeding NM, or OL. The English export supply curve of cloth, in terms of linen, therefore, instead of being OE, would be identical with OS until the point M was reached, and would diverge from OS away from the OX axis only beyond M, the entire curve having somewhat the appearance of OME. Similar reasoning applies to the relationship of the OG curve to the OT line.[24]

---

[23] His diagram is drawn on too small a scale to make this certain, but the absence of any statement to the contrary in his text and the fact that in all his other diagrams his reciprocal demands are drawn curvilinear from their point of origin warrants this interpretation.

[24] Cf. *supra*, chart X, p. 468, for a terms-of-trade diagram drawn with reference to these considerations.

Edgeworth states that if production is not under conditions of constant cost, "there should be substituted for the straight line OS (and *mutatis mutandis* for OT) a curve of constant advantage, or indifference-curve (not shown in the figure) representing states for which the advantage to England is no greater than if there had been no trade." (*Papers*, II, 33.) He must mean a curve representing states for which the importation of an additional unit of

Graham.—Graham has criticized the reciprocal-demand aspects of the theory of international value as presented by J. S. Mill and Marshall as being fallacious in their essence.[25] Some of his criticisms have already been examined.[26] Still others, of greater consequence if valid, are here taken up for scrutiny.

Graham claims that where there are more than two commodities and more than two countries (all of them able to produce all or most of the commodities) fluctuations in the rate of interchange between the various commodities must be confined within a rather narrow range.

---

the G-good by country E would be no more advantageous than its production at home, if this curve is to be the analogue for variable costs of his OS line. In chart XV, OS is *not* a "no-gain from trade" curve, but is a curve of "no-gain from import as compared to domestic production of the G-good." If country E were to export more than OL units of E-goods at the $\frac{ML}{OL}$ terms— or even on terms more favorable to itself—it might be incurring a loss from undue specialization of the sort discussed in the preceding chapter. (See *supra*, p. 451.) The location in the chart of a "no-gain from trade" curve requires knowledge of the utility functions as well as of the cost conditions. It would never fall below the OS line (or, in the case of variable costs, the OS' curve) and would never rise as high as the OE curve. (See *infra*, p. 572.) I have inserted in chart XV a "no-gain from import as compared to domestic production of the G-good" curve, OS', applicable to conditions of increasing costs. At any point, b, on OS', the slope with respect to OX of a tangent to OS' at that point represents the number of units of G-goods which could be produced at home by country E at a cost equal to the cost of producing a unit of E-goods in addition to what would be its output of E-goods if it was exporting Od E-goods in exchange for db G-goods. (The slope with respect to OX of the tangent to OE at a represents the number of units of G-goods per unit of E-goods at which country E would be willing to export Od units of E-goods.) Since production is under conditions of increasing cost, the number of units of the G-good which country E could produce at the same cost as an additional unit of the E-good will be greater, the greater its output of E-goods. As OS' is drawn concave upward in chart XV, it is implicitly assumed that increased export of E-goods involves increased output of E-goods, i.e., that as more E-goods are exported, the domestic consumption of E-goods decreases, if at all, by a smaller amount than the increase in exports. The OS' curve must be drawn below the OE curve at all points, and the identity of the two curves from O to C in chart XV is an error. Since in country E, for each output of E-goods corresponding to a given export by it of E-goods, its relative marginal costs of production of E-goods and G-goods must correspond to its supply-price of E-goods in terms of G-goods, a tangent to the OS' curve at any point must be parallel to a vector drawn from O to the vertically corresponding point on the OE curve. This excludes the possibility of identity of the two curves for any part of their course.

[25] "The theory of international values re-examined," *Quarterly journal of economics*, XXXVIII (1923), and "The theory of international values," *ibid.*, XLVI (1932).

[26] *Supra*, pp. 453 ff. and 536 ff.

This is due to the fact that any alteration in the rate of interchange will affect the margin of comparative advantage of some country in the production of some one of the commodities concerned, will bring that country in as an exporter where formerly it was an importer, or as an importer where formerly it was an exporter, according as the terms of interchange move one way or the other, and, by the affected country's addition to the supply or demand side, will keep the terms of interchange from moving far from their original position.[27]

Graham claims that Mill, Marshall, and their school grossly exaggerated the importance of reciprocal demands in determining the terms of trade and correspondingly minimized the importance of comparative-cost conditions in the determination of the terms of trade, and he attributes this error mainly to their assumptions of only two countries and of only two commodities, or of fixed physical compositions of each country's exports and imports. He claims to demonstrate that "the character (urgency, elasticity, and the like) of reciprocal national demand schedules for foreign products is . . . of almost no importance in determining long-run ratios of interchange of products. . . ."[28]

Graham here does point to a defect in the exposition of Mill and his followers, but he exaggerates its prevalence, misinterprets the exact nature of the defect, and errs himself in the opposite direction. In the exposition of Mill and his followers, the defect is not that they exaggerated the importance of reciprocal demand in the determination of the terms of trade, which is logically impossible, but that, whatever they may have known, they did not sufficiently emphasize the influence of cost conditions on reciprocal demand. The terms of trade can be directly influenced by the reciprocal demands *and by nothing else*. The reciprocal demands in turn are ultimately determined by the cost conditions together with the basic utility functions.[29]

What Mill and his followers overemphasized was the impor-

---

[27] "Theory of international values re-examined," *loc. cit.*, p. 86.

[28] "Theory of international values," *loc. cit.*, pp. 583-84.

[29] The nearest approach to this proposition that I have found in the literature is the following, by Haberler: "Marshall employs . . . so-called reciprocal supply-and-demand curves. This theory forms an essential supplement to the theory of comparative costs; indeed, the latter, if carried through to its logical conclusion, merges into the former." (*The theory of international trade*, 1936, p. 123.)

tance of the basic utility functions in determining the terms of trade. This defect in the exposition of Mill and his followers was undoubtedly promoted by the practice of confining the analysis to two countries and to two commodities, or to exports and imports of a fixed composition as far as the range of commodities was concerned, and to the assumption of constant costs, for under these conditions the cost conditions exhaust their influence in setting fixed maximum and minimum limits to the range of variation of the terms of trade.

Whatever may have been true of Mill, however, Marshall, Edgeworth, and other followers of Mill were aware of the fact that the greater the number of countries and the greater the number of commodities, the greater is the influence of cost conditions on the reciprocal demands and therefore on the terms of trade, and the smaller, therefore, given the cost conditions, the range of possible variation in the terms of trade as the result of given changes in the basic utility conditions. The first quotation following shows that Marshall appreciated the importance of multiplicity of commodities and of countries in causing the reciprocal demands to be elastic and therefore in restricting the range of variation of the terms of trade, and the second quotation, from Edgeworth, shows that Bastable and Edgeworth both recognized the similar effect of multiplication of countries.

It is practically certain that the demands of each of Ricardo's two countries for the goods in general of the other would have considerable elasticity under modern industrial conditions, even if E and G were single countries whose sole trade was with one another. And if we take E to be a large and rich commercial country, while G stands for all foreign countries, this certainly becomes absolute. For E is quite sure to export a great many things which some at least of the other countries could forego without much inconvenience: and which would be promptly refused if offered by her only on terms considerably less favorable to purchasers. And, on the other hand, E is quite sure to have exports which can find increased sales in some countries, at least, if she offers them on more favorable terms to purchasers. Therefore the world's demand for E's goods . . . is sure to rise largely if E offers her goods generally on terms more advantageous to purchasers; and to shrink largely if E endeavors to insist on terms more favorable to herself. And E, on her part, is sure on the one hand to import many things from various parts of the world, which she can easily forego, if the terms on which they are sold are raised against her; and on the other to be capable of turning to fairly good use many things which are offered to her from various parts of the world, if they were offered on terms rather more favorable to her than at present.[30]

The theory of comparative costs is not very prominent from the mathematical point of view. . . . That the point of equilibrium [terms of trade] falls between the respective [trade] indifference-curves is the geometrical version of comparative costs. The expression which occurs in some of the best writers, that international value "depends on" comparative cost, is seen from this point of view to be a very loose expression. (No doubt, as Professor Bastable has pointed out, when there are numerous competing nations, the limits fixed by the principle of comparative cost are much narrowed and accordingly it becomes less incorrect to regard the principle as sufficient to determine international value).[31]

Graham's own error lies in his failure to distinguish between the reciprocal demands and the basic internal utility functions and to see that the cost conditions can operate on the terms of trade only intermediately through their influence on the reciprocal demands. Graham fails, apparently, to see that in the elaborate arithmetical illustrations which he presents as demonstrations that the terms of trade are fixed within narrow limits by the cost conditions irrespective of the state of the reciprocal demands, there are present, explicitly or implicitly, rigorous utility and demand assumptions, and that, consequently, his illustrations really show that it is the cost conditions *plus the utility conditions* which determine the reciprocal demands, and that it is only indirectly, through their influence on the reciprocal demands, that the cost conditions exercise any influence at all on the terms of trade.[32]

---

[30] Marshall, *Money credit & commerce*, p. 171.

[31] Edgeworth, *Papers*, II, 33. The sentence placed in parentheses appears in the original as a footnote.

[32] Cf., for instance, Graham's illustration ("Theory of international values re-examined," *loc. cit.*, p. 76) and the accompanying text, where it is assumed "that before international trade is opened up, each country devotes one third of its resources to each of the three products, and that each increases its consumption of the three products proportionately as it secures gains from international trade" (p. 70) even though important changes in relative prices are assumed to take place. With the additional information given as to the economic size of the countries, their cost conditions, and the prices within each country before trade, Graham is justified in his claim that the data given suffice to determine within narrow limits the equilibrium terms of trade when foreign trade is opened up. But he fails to substantiate his claim that it is the

Even if the reciprocal demands were highly elastic, moreover, while substantial movements in the commodity terms of trade would thereby be rendered less probable, they would not, as Graham contends, become impossible.[33] Let the original reciprocal-demand schedules be as elastic as one pleases, short of infinite elasticity, if they undergo pronounced shifts in position in opposite directions there will result a substantial change in the commodity terms of trade, as experiment with a Marshallian diagram will readily confirm.

Graham points out that in their explanation of the determination of the terms of trade by reciprocal demands the neo-classical writers from J. S. Mill to Edgeworth assume a fixed composition, as far as the list of commodities is concerned, of the exports and imports of each country. He claims, however, that commodities may shift from the export to the import status, or may cease to be exported or imported, and that the terms of trade determine (or are a factor in the determination of) the line of comparative advantage and, therefore, the composition of the export and import lists of any country.

It is, in consequence, impossible to determine international values on the premise of a fixed composition of export and import schedules of the several countries reciprocally concerned. In taking this premise the neo-classical writers are, in fact, implicitly assuming the very ratio of interchange of products which they are trying to discover, since the premise can be valid only on the supposition of *some* definite ratio of interchange. This defect in logic not only completely vitiates the general theory of international values which they set up, but it

cost conditions alone which determine the terms of trade. If the cost conditions are left unchanged but his utility assumptions altered, the equilibrium terms of trade can be changed, within broad limits, in whatever degree and direction is desired.

The same criticism applies to the interpretation given by C. F. Whittlesey —"Foreign investment and the terms of trade," *Quarterly journal of economics,* XLVI (1932), 449, 459—of results similar to Graham's obtained from arithmetical illustrations involving similar assumptions.

Whereas Graham criticizes the writers in the classical tradition for minimizing the influence of comparative costs on the terms of trade, Angell criticizes them for their alleged belief that comparative costs *"in themselves alone,* provide a sufficient *a priori* explanation of the course and terms of trade." (Angell, *Theory of international prices,* 1926, pp. 371-73.)

[33] Cf. "Theory of international values," *loc. cit.,* p. 604: "If both demand schedules were elastic, movements in the terms of trade must necessarily be small."

also renders useless for this, though not for another, purpose, the whole geometrical and algebraic supplement to the theory which reached its apogee, perhaps, in the work of Marshall.[34]

Graham rejects Marshall's suggestion of a "representative bale" and Edgeworth's suggestion of an "ideal" export or import commodity as solutions of the problem:

> It must be obvious that reciprocal demand is for individual commodities and not for any such uniform aggregate of labor and capital as a unit of the consolidated commodities concerned may incorporate, and that to construct demand schedules for representative bales the physical composition of which is inevitably changing as we move along the schedules, with commodities even shifting from one demand schedule to its reciprocal, is not only to build imaginary bricks with imaginary clay but also to commit the worse fault of assuming a homogeneity in the bricks which, though a logical necessity for the construction of the demand schedules in question, is at the same time a logical impossibility.[35]

I understand Graham's argument to be that the theory of international values, as presented, say, by Marshall, is completely vitiated by its use of reciprocal-demand and terms-of-trade concepts requiring for their logical validity a non-existent fixity in the physical composition of the exports and imports of each region, and that the remedy lies in carrying on the analysis in terms of reciprocal demands for and ratios of interchange between individual commodities.

In trying to express in terms of averages the changes in relative prices of groups of export and import commodities where the physical constituents of the groups change we encounter the insoluble problem of economic index numbers.[36] Marshall and Edgeworth probably gave inadequate attention to this problem, though it is impossible to conceive of their not being aware of it. Their "representative bale" concepts are obviously but euphemisms for "averages," although where constant costs are assumed

---

[34] Graham, "Theory of international values," *loc. cit.*, pp. 582-83. (Italics are in the original.)

[35] *Ibid.*, p. 583.

[36] Cf. A. C. Pigou, *Essays in applied economics,* 1930, p. 150:

The value of imports in general in terms of exports in general is a notion of exactly the same sort as the value of things in general in terms of money. No precise significance can be given to this notion, and no completely satisfactory measure of changes in it can be devised.

weighting of export commodities by relative prices does give an unambiguous and precise index of the terms of trade as a ratio between the quantities of productive services whose products have equal value.[37] It is a far cry, however, from conceding that precise and unambiguous measurement of the changes in the aggregate terms of trade is impossible where, as is always the case, the physical constituents of the exports and the imports are undergoing relative changes to conceding that analysis resting upon averages computed in the usual or "standard" ways is thereby rendered worthless. If that were true, then economics would indeed be in a hopeless plight. Graham's objection would then serve to condemn every economic concept involving a sum or an average, including his own concept of single "commodities," as he would soon discover if he were to attempt to define a "commodity," say wheat, so that it did not involve a medley of different things constantly undergoing relative changes in quantity, quality, and price. The use of such concepts, in spite of their admitted imperfections, can be defended only because superior alternatives are unavailable, and because their imperfections are believed—or hoped—not to involve a range of probable error in the results obtained by their use sufficiently great, or uncertain, to deprive these results of significance for the purpose on hand.

What Graham offers as an alternative for the use of imperfect "average" concepts, namely analysis in terms of pairs of single commodities, is not a satisfactory one. The significance of the results obtained when *expressed* in terms of a pair of single commodities depends upon whether the commodities singled out are "representative" or not of broad classes of commodities, and the problem of finding proper criteria of "representativeness" is essentially but another manifestation of the "averaging" problem. *Analysis* of the determination of the terms of trade cannot itself be carried on in terms of pairs of single commodities, except on the assumption that these are the only commodities entering into trade, or are "representative" of trade as a whole. "Reciprocal demand" is not only an aggregative concept, but it designates an economic force which operates as an indivisible entity. "Each transaction in international trade is an individual transaction," but the terms on which it is conducted are set for it by the market

---

[37] I.e., of what I call the "double factoral terms of trade." See *infra*, p. 561.

complex as a whole. The prices of any particular export commodity and any particular import commodity are functionally related to each other, react upon each other, not directly (except to an insignificant degree) but through their membership in the price and utility and cost systems of the trading world, taken as a whole. In the case of foreign trade, changes in the desires for or costs of particular commodities operate to change the ratios of interchange between these commodities and other commodities only indirectly through their influence on money flows and on aggregate demands and supplies of commodities in terms of money. The reciprocal-demand analysis is an attempt, imperfect but superior to available substitutes, to describe the aggregate or average results of such changes in desires or costs when they affect appreciably a wide range of commodities.

III. TERMS OF TRADE AND THE AMOUNT OF GAIN FROM TRADE

Terms of Trade as an Index of Gain from Trade.— From the beginning of the classical period, if not earlier, the trend of the commodity terms of trade has been accepted as an index of the direction of change of the amount of gain from trade, and it is therefore an old doctrine that a rise in export prices relative to import prices represents a "favorable" movement of the terms of trade. It has been recognized at times that the proposition is valid subject only to important qualifications, but systematic discussion of the qualifications which are necessary, or of the nature of the connection between the commodity terms of trade and the amount of gain from trade, seems to be almost totally lacking in the literature.

Ricardo had little to say of the terms of trade as related to the gain from trade, perhaps because the question then came up only in connection with the unwelcome arguments that by monetary expansion, or by protective duties, the commodity terms of trade of a country could be made more favorable. While Ricardo did not deny that, of itself, an increase in the amount of foreign goods obtained in return for a unit of native goods was a favorable development, he was careful to point out that whether or not it reflected a genuine improvement in the position of the country depended on how it came, or was brought, about. He was, in general, skeptical of the possibility of bringing it about deliberately, through governmental action,[1] but conceded, reluctantly, that the levy of import duties might have such a result, accompanied, however, by offsetting disadvantages:

We shall sell our goods at a high money price, and buy foreign ones at a low money price,—but it may well be doubted whether this advantage will not be purchased at many times its value, for to obtain it we must be content with a diminished production of home commodities; with a high price of labor, and a low rate of profits.[2]

Although J. S. Mill laid much greater emphasis than did Ricardo on the connection between the terms of trade and the amount of gain from trade, he also did not accept a favorable movement of the commodity terms of trade as necessarily indicating a favorable movement of the amount of gain from trade. Thus, while he conceded that the imposition of protective import duties operated to change in a favorable direction the terms on which the remaining imports were obtained, he claimed that this advantage was more than offset by the loss of the benefit which had previously accrued from the trade in the commodities now produced at home under tariff protection.[3] Similarly, when he showed that a reduction in the real cost of production of Germany's export products would operate to turn the terms of trade against Germany, he refrained from drawing the conclusion therefrom that the reduction in cost would be injurious to Germany even in the least favorable case where the commodity whose cost of production had been reduced was not consumed at all within Germany itself.[4]

As we shall see later, Marshall and Edgeworth both adopted changes in "consumer's surplus," or its supposed equivalent, as a better index of change in the amount of gain from foreign trade than the movement in the commodity terms of trade. Taussig pointed out specific circumstances under which the commodity terms of trade would be a misleading index of gain from trade.[5] The general position of the major writers in this field

---

[1] Cf. Ricardo, *Notes on Malthus,* pp. 70 ff.

[2] *Ibid.,* p. 76.

[3] *Essays on some unsettled questions,* 1844, p. 27.

[4] See *supra,* pp. 537 ff.

[5] Cf. Taussig, *International trade,* 1927, pp. 117-18.

was, it seems, therefore, that an increase in the amount of imports obtained per unit of exports was presumptive evidence of an increase in the amount of gain from trade, but that the validity of the presumption was subject to the absence of countervailing factors. As examples of such countervailing factors, Marshall took account of increases in the cost of the export commodities and Taussig referred to a decrease in the desire for the import commodities. But systematic inquiry into the relationship between the commodity terms of trade and the amount of gain from trade is not, I believe, to be found in the literature.

Jevons criticized Mill's use of the commodity terms of trade as a measure of the gain from trade on the ground that the total amount of gain from trade depended on total utility, whereas the commodity terms of trade were related to "final degree of utility": "in estimating the benefit a consumer derives from a commodity it is the total utility which must be taken as the measure, not the final degree of utility on which the terms of exchange depend."[6] In utility terms, the total amount of gain from trade can be defined as the excess of the total utility accruing from the imports over the total sacrifice of utility involved in the surrender of the exports. If it be permitted to waive the difficulty of applying utility theory to a group of persons or a "country," the commodity terms of trade will at any moment always equal the ratio of the marginal disutility of surrendering exports to the marginal utility of imports. Disturbances will change the terms of this ratio, but not the ratio itself. The marginal unit of trade, therefore, will never, under equilibrium conditions, yield any gain, and whether or not a "favorable" movement of the commodity terms of trade will represent an increase in net[7] total utility will depend on what, if any, changes occur (1) in the

---

[6] W. S. Jevons, *The theory of political economy,* 1871, p. 136. Cf. Edgeworth, *Papers,* II, 22: "It is a more serious complaint that Mill takes as the measure of the advantage which a country derives from trade, the increase in the rate of exchange of its exports against its imports. He thus confounds 'final' with 'integral' utility; ignoring the principle of 'consumer's rent.'" Cf. also *ibid.,* "On the application of mathematics to political economy," *Journal of the Royal Statistical Society,* LII (1889), 558: "To measure the variations in the advantage accruing from trade by the variations of price—or more generally rate of exchange—is a confusion which could hardly have occurred to the mathematical economist."

[7] I.e., the excess of the total utility accruing from imports over the total sacrifice of utility involved in the surrender of exports.

utility function for imports, (2) in the disutility function for exports, (3) in the volume of trade. Reasoning such as this was presumably the basis of Jevons's comment. As will appear from the subsequent analysis, however, Jevons went further than this reasoning would justify, when he suggested that Mill's argument that the gain from trade increased with the relative cheapening of imports as compared to exports was less likely to be true than its converse, on the ground that "he who pays a high price must either have a very great need of that which he buys, or very little of that which he pays for it,"[8] a proposition whose plausibility derives from the very defect of analysis which he had charged against Mill, namely, disregard of the total utility aspects of the problem.

There follows an examination of the possibility of so modifying the concept of terms of trade as to make it less open to Jevons's criticism that it rests on a confusion of final degree of utility with total utility, although this examination is for the most part only implicitly in terms of utility analysis.

Different Concepts of Terms of Trade.—We will write e to represent the export commodities, i to represent the import commodities, P for the price index number, o for the initial year, and 1 for the given year. An index of the *commodity terms of trade* can then be represented symbolically as

$$T_c = \frac{\dfrac{{}^eP_1}{{}^eP_o}}{\dfrac{{}^iP_1}{{}^iP_o}},$$

where the index measures the trend of the "physical" amount of foreign goods received in exchange for one "physical" unit of the export goods, with a *rise* in the index indicating a *favorable* trend, and vice versa.[9]

The case cited by J. S. Mill, where a reduction in the real cost to Germany of producing her export commodities would result

---

[8] Jevons, *op. cit.*, p. 138.

[9] This reverses Taussig's procedure, where a rise in the index indicates an *unfavorable* movement of the terms of trade. No question of principle is involved, but it seems to me to be more convenient to represent favorable movements of the indices by rising indices. The formulae which follow are so constructed that a movement of any element in the formula favorable to the country in question operates to raise the index, and vice versa.

in a movement unfavorable to Germany of the commodity terms of trade but might nevertheless not involve a reduction in the amount of gain derived by her from her foreign trade, suffices to demonstrate that the commodity terms of trade may fail to provide a satisfactory guide even of the direction of the trend of gain from trade if, when the commodity terms of trade are changing, changes *in the same direction* are occurring in the costs of production of the export commodities. If it were possible to construct an index of the cost of production in terms of the average technical coefficients of production of the export commodities, and if the commodity terms of trade index was multiplied by the reciprocal of the export commodity technical coefficients index, the resultant index would provide a better guide to the trend of gain from trade than the commodity terms of trade index by itself. This modified terms of trade index, which for lack of a better name I designate as the *single factoral terms of trade index*, can be represented symbolically as:

$$T_{c,f} = \frac{\dfrac{{}_{\bullet}P_{1}}{{}_{\bullet}P_{o}}}{\dfrac{{}_{i}P_{1}}{{}_{i}P_{o}}} \cdot \frac{{}_{\bullet}F_{o}}{{}_{\bullet}F_{1}} = T_{c} \cdot \frac{{}_{\bullet}F_{o}}{{}_{\bullet}F_{1}}$$

where $\dfrac{{}_{\bullet}F_{o}}{{}_{\bullet}F_{1}}$ represents the reciprocal of the index of cost in terms of quantity of factors of production used per unit of export, and $T_{c,f}$ represents the index of the physical amounts of foreign goods obtained per unit of cost in terms of quantity of factors of production.[10]

A still closer approach to an index of real gain from trade would be achieved if the single factoral terms of trade index were multiplied by the reciprocal of an index of the "disutility coefficients" of the technical coefficients of the export commodities. The resultant index would be a *real cost terms of trade index*, which could be represented symbolically as:

---

[10] If, when the technical coefficients of production of the exports were falling, a fall was also occurring in the actual or potential technical coefficients of *home production* of the import commodities, the single factoral terms of trade would tend to exaggerate the trend of gain *from trade* by treating as a gain from trade a gain from improvement in productivity which was not dependent upon foreign trade for its realization.

$$T_{c,f,r} = \frac{\dfrac{{}^{e}P_{1}}{{}^{e}P_{o}}}{\dfrac{{}^{i}P_{1}}{{}^{i}P_{o}}} \cdot \frac{{}^{e}F_{o}}{{}^{e}F_{1}} \cdot \frac{{}^{e}R_{o}}{{}^{e}R_{1}} = T_{c,f} \cdot \frac{{}^{e}R_{o}}{{}^{e}R_{1}},$$

where $\dfrac{{}^{e}R_{o}}{{}^{e}R_{1}}$ represents the index of amount of disutility (amount of irksomeness) per unit of the technical coefficients, and $T_{c,f,r}$ represents the index of the physical amount of foreign goods obtained per unit of real cost.

The amount of gain from trade depends, however, not only on the amount of foreign goods obtained per unit of real cost involved in the production of the export commodities, but also on the relative desirability of the import commodities as compared to the commodities which could have been produced for home consumption with the productive resources now devoted to production for export. To take account of changes in the relative desirability of the import commodities and of the native commodities whose internal consumption is precluded by the allocation of productive resources to production for export when such changes in relative desirability are due to changes in tastes, it would be necessary to incorporate in the "real cost of trade index" an index of the relative average[11] utility per unit of imported commodities and of native commodities whose internal consumption is precluded by allocation of resources to production for export. If we write U for average desirability or "utility" and a to designate the commodities whose production for domestic consumption is forgone as the result of resort to production for export, then $\dfrac{\dfrac{{}^{i}U_{1}}{{}^{a}U_{1}}}{\dfrac{{}^{i}U_{o}}{{}^{a}U_{o}}}$ represents the index of relative desirability of import and forgone commodities, respectively, and the new terms of trade index, in which the index of relative desirability

---

[11] "Average" and not "marginal" because, whatever changes occur, in each equilibrium situation the utility of the marginal unit of what is surrendered through export will tend to be equal, on the usual "representative individual" assumptions, to the utility of what is obtained in exchange for that marginal unit. What is really significant is the effect on *total utility* of foreign trade, and the terms of trade index is brought closer to a total utility index if provision is made in it for changes in *average* relative desirability.

is incorporated, can be designated as the *utility terms of trade index*, and represented symbolically as

$$T_{c,f,ru} = \frac{\dfrac{\cdot P_t}{\cdot P_o}}{\dfrac{\cdot P_t}{\cdot P_o}} \cdot \frac{\cdot F_o}{\cdot F_t} \cdot \frac{\cdot R_o}{\cdot R_t} \cdot \frac{\dfrac{\cdot U_t}{\cdot U_t}}{\dfrac{\cdot U_o}{\cdot U_o}} \,.^{12}$$

Still another terms-of-trade concept was used by the older writers, namely, the number of units of the productive services of the foreign country whose product exchanged for the product of one unit of the productive services of your own country. This concept might be designated as the *double factoral terms of trade*, and its index could be represented symbolically as

$$T_{c,ff} = \frac{\dfrac{\cdot P_t}{\cdot P_o}}{\dfrac{\cdot P_t}{\cdot P_o}} \cdot \frac{\dfrac{\cdot F_t}{\cdot F_o}}{\dfrac{\cdot F_t}{\cdot F_o}}$$

The older writers usually accepted the double factoral terms of trade as identical in their trend with the commodity terms of trade, which would be correct under their assumptions of production under conditions of constant costs and historically stable costs.[13] But with costs variable, whether with respect to output or to time, the trends of the two indices could be substantially divergent. The double factoral terms of trade index would ap-

---

[12] The commodities whose domestic production is forgone as the result of the allocation of productive resources to production for export may be (1) the same in kind as those exported, or (2) the same as those imported, or (3) different from both. In the second case, the ratio of relative desirability of import and "forgone" commodities will, of course, always be unity, and the incorporation of a relative desirability index in the terms-of-trade index will then have no effect on the latter.

[13] Cf. N. W. Senior, *Three lectures on the value of money,* 1840, p. 66: "the demand in Europe and Asia for thè produce of Mexican labor having increased, the results of a given quantity of Mexican labor would command in exchange the results of a larger quantity of European and Asiatic labor than before." Cf. also R. Torrens, *The budget,* 1841-44, p. 28: "Where any particular country imposes import duties upon the productions of other countries, while those other countries continue to receive her products duty free, then such particular country draws to herself a larger proportion of the precious metals, maintains a higher range of general prices than her neighbors, and obtains, in exchange for the produce of a given quantity of her labor, the produce of a greater quantity of foreign labor."

proach more closely to an index of the international *division* of gain than to an index of the absolute amount of gain for either country. If the commodity terms of trade and the index of export costs of a given country, A, remained the same, so that its single factoral terms of trade index remained unaltered, its double factoral terms of trade index would rise or fall according as the cost in the other country, B, of producing its exports rose or fell. But such divergence of the double factoral from the single factoral terms of trade index would have no welfare significance for country A, and, under the conditions stated, would merely indicate an impairment or improvement of productivity in country B.

Taussig has introduced still another concept of terms of trade, the *gross barter terms of trade*, or the ratio of the physical quantity of imports to the physical quantity of exports, the greater this ratio the more favorable being the gross barter terms of trade.[14] His purpose in introducing this concept is to correct the commodity, or "net barter," terms of trade for unilateral transactions, or exports or imports which are surrendered without compensation or received without counterpayment, such as tributes and immigrants' remittances. He gives an illustration where the price of wheat exported from the United States to Germany is 80 cents a bushel, and the price of linen imported into the United States from Germany is 76 2/3 cents a yard, so that the commodity terms of trade are 10 wheat for 10.4 linen. But of the 10,250,000 bushels wheat exported by the United States only 9,000,000 bushels are exchanged for German linen and the remaining 1,250,000 bushels are sent to Germany as the commodity equivalent of a compulsory tribute of $1,000,000. The United States thus surrenders 10,250,000 bushels wheat and receives 9,400,000 yards linen, with the ratio therefore, approximately 10 bushels wheat for 9.2 yards linen. This last ratio is Taussig's gross barter terms of trade.

It is appropriate, perhaps, to make allowance in an index of gain from trade for unilateral transactions, or transactions without offsets on the other side, if such gains or losses can be properly attributed—which for most cases of unilateral transactions seems doubtful—to *foreign trade* as their source or occa-

---

[14] Cf. F. W. Taussig, *International trade*, pp. 113-14.

sion.[15] But to use the statistics of commodity exports and imports as the basis for calculating the gross barter terms of trade would in practice be liable to lead to seriously misleading results. Such procedure would lead to treatment as unilateral transactions of commodity exports or imports whose compensating import or export had taken place in the past—as in the case of exports whose cash proceeds are used to liquidate old indebtedness—or would take place in the future—as in the case of import surpluses constituting an import of borrowed capital—or took the form of an "invisible" import or export of services not recorded in the commodity trade statistics.[16] It would seem, therefore, that, as Haberler suggests, allowance should be made separately for unilateral transactions, instead of incorporating them in the terms of trade index.

A further limitation of the terms of trade as an index of the amount of gain from trade, to which all the concepts of terms of trade differentiated above are subject, is that the terms of trade indices relate to a *unit* of trade and therefore fail to reflect whatever relationship there may be between the *total* gain from trade and the total volume of trade. But if whatever concept of terms of trade is used is accepted as a satisfactory index of the trend of gain from trade per unit of trade, multiplication of the terms of trade index by a physical index of the volume of trade will give an index of the total amount of gain from trade. For example, if we accept the commodity terms of trade as an index of amount of gain per unit of trade, and write Q for volume of trade, our *index of total gain from trade* would be

$$T_{c,q} = \frac{\dfrac{{}^cP_1}{{}^cP_0}}{\dfrac{{}^iP_1}{{}^iP_0}} \cdot \frac{Q_1}{Q_0} \; .$$

One advantage of a *total* gain index over a *unit* gain index

---

[15] The only clear-cut cases would be losses through defaults on trade debts, through shipwreck, or through seizure of goods by a belligerent in time of war.

[16] Taussig points out some of these limitations in the gross barter terms of trade index when computed from statistics of commodity trade alone. Cf. *ibid.*, pp. 119, 254. Cf. also Viner, "Die Theorie des auswärtigen Handel" in *Die Wirtschaftstheorie der Gegenwart*, II (1928), 121ff.; White, *The French international accounts*, 1933, pp. 238-41; Haberler, *Theory of international trade*, 1936, pp. 161 ff.

would be that it would clearly show that an increase in the total amount of gain from trade was consistent with an unfavorable movement in the index of unit gain from trade if the unfavorable change in the latter was associated with an increase in the volume of trade.[17]

Terms of Trade and the International Division of Gain from Trade.—J. S. Mill seems to have believed that the commodity terms of trade, taken in conjunction with its comparative costs, provided a criterion of the proportions in which the total gain from the trade of a particular country with the outside world was divided between that country and the rest of the world. He did not state clearly how he would determine the proportions in any particular case, given the actual terms of trade and the two limiting sets of cost ratios, but in one illustrative case, where costs of producing cloth and linen were in the ratio of 15 : 10 in England and of 20 : 10 in Germany, and where the actual terms of trade were 10 English cloth for 18 German linen, Mill says that "England will gain an advantage of 3 yards on every 15, Germany will save 2 out of every 20."[18] Cournot interprets this passage as postulating that England has a gain of 20 per cent and Germany a gain (or economy) of 10 per cent, although no percentages appear in Mill's text. He points out, first, as ground for rejecting this mode of measuring the comparative gain from trade of two countries, that if one of the commodities could not be produced in England at any cost the English percentage of gain from trade would be infinite. He proceeds to a further criticism on mathematical grounds, which seems to me both unimportant of itself and irrelevant to Mill's position unless it can be shown that Mill thought that England and Germany would, in his illustration, divide the gains from trade in the proportions of 20 and 10. Cournot says that it would be equally legitimate to hold that England as the result of trade gets 15 yards of linen for 8 1/3 yards of cloth instead of for 10 yards of cloth, a saving of 16 2/3 per cent, while Germany obtains, as the result of trade, 11 1/9 yards of cloth instead of 10 yards of cloth, for 20 yards of linen, a gain of 11 1/9 per cent. Measured this way, the ratio of the English to the German gain is 16 2/3 :

[17] Cf. R. F. Harrod, *International economics*, 1933, pp. 32 ff., where this point is emphasized.
[18] *Principles*, Ashley ed., p. 585.

11 1/3, instead of 20 : 10. "Or, les questions de calcul n'admettent pas de telles ambiguités. C'est qu'à vrai dire l'une et l'autre manière de compter sont purement arbitraires."[19]

The real difficulty lies, however, in the inadequacy of the commodity terms of trade as a criterion of amount or division of gain from trade. The fact that, given the amount of gain, it will be expressed in different *percentages* of gain according to what commodity is used as the base, seems to me to present a problem which is insoluble but of no consequence.[20] It can be questioned also whether the proportions in which the total gains from trade are divided between two areas should be regarded as of much importance to either country, especially if the only procedures by which a country could divert to itself an increased proportion of the total gain should be such as would operate to reduce the absolute amount of gain it derives from trade—a not unlikely situation. If production is under conditions of varying costs, moreover, or if more than two commodities are involved, there will not be a single pair of comparative-cost ratios from which to compute the division of gain from trade. In the case of production under conditions of increasing cost, a situation is quite conceivable in which all the commodities which the respective countries import are also produced at home and in which, therefore, there are no comparative differences in *marginal* costs under equilibrium, but where a substantial gain from trade nevertheless accrues from all the infra-marginal units of trade.[21] In such a case, the method of computing the division of the gain from trade by comparison of the commodity terms of trade with the comparative marginal-cost ratios would be patently absurd.

Statistical Measurement of the Trend of the Terms of Trade.—Statistical attempts to measure the trend of terms of trade for actual countries and periods have been restricted to measurements of the commodity or of the gross barter terms of trade, and chiefly to measurements of the former. The problem of statistical measurement is obviously a less formidable one for these two concepts of terms of trade than for the more complex

---

[19] Cournot, *Revue sommaire des doctrines économiques,* 1877, pp. 210 ff.

[20] Cf., however, the comments of Edgeworth (*Papers relating to political economy,* 1925, II, 22, note) and Bastable (*Theory of international trade,* 4th ed., 1903, p. 44, note) on Cournot's criticism of Mill.

[21] Cf. *supra,* p. 472.

and less objective ones examined above, but even if these simpler concepts are used the necessity of choice of index number formula to be used in computing the terms of trade index presents some difficult and in some respects insoluble problems.

The writers who have constructed statistical indices of the commodity terms of trade for particular countries and periods have made use of a wide variety of index number formulae, but have as a rule either offered no explanation of their particular choice of formula or have defended it on purely statistical grounds, such as simplicity, "reversibility," or availability of data.[22] Here, as elsewhere, it would appear that the choice of a formula should be made to depend on economic as well as on purely statistical considerations.

Let us suppose that an original static equilibrium in a particular country is disturbed by capital borrowings, that no changes occur except those resulting from the borrowings, and that the question asked is: what is the effect of the borrowings on the relative prices in the borrowing country of its export and its import commodities? Let us suppose also that the type of index number of export and of import prices which should be used in constructing the terms of trade index is a weighted aggregate index. Should the quantity weights to be used in comparing the terms of trade of a pre-borrowing with a borrowing year be those of the base, or pre-borrowing, year or those of the end, or borrowing, year?[23]

The proper answer depends on whether the question is asked as a question in the theory of the mechanism of international trade or as a question in the "theory of international values" or the theory of gain (and loss) from foreign trade. If the familiar proposition of the theory of the *mechanism* of international trade that capital borrowings tend to raise export prices relative to import prices is to be tested statistically in terms of weighted index numbers, the weights used must be the quantities exported

---

[22] See, however, Roland Wilson, *Capital imports and the terms of trade,* 1931, Chap. V, for a discussion of this problem.

[23] I.e., should the formula used in constructing the index of the commodity terms of trade of the borrowing country be

$$\frac{\dfrac{\Sigma^e p_1 \, {}^e q_0}{\Sigma^e p_0 \, {}^e q_0}}{\dfrac{\Sigma^i p_1 \, {}^i q_0}{\Sigma^i p_0 \, {}^i q_0}} \quad \text{or} \quad \frac{\dfrac{\Sigma^e p_1 \, {}^e q_1}{\Sigma^e p_0 \, {}^e q_1}}{\dfrac{\Sigma^i p_1 \, {}^i q_1}{\Sigma^i p_0 \, {}^i q_1}} \quad ?$$

and imported prior to the borrowings, since it is with the effect of borrowings on the relative prices of those commodities exported and imported before the borrowings that this proposition is concerned.

If what is to be tested, however, is the proposition that capital borrowings tend to improve the terms on which the borrowing country exchanges its exports for imports, the question of what type of weighting to use cannot be so readily answered. Gains to the borrowing country from the more favorable terms on which its exports are exchanged for imports can accrue only to the extent that such exchanges actually take place.[24] In computing the export and import price indices for this purpose, should the prices therefore be weighted by the quantities exported or imported when the borrowings are under way, rather than by the pre-borrowing quantities?

In a closed economy, abstracting from sampling errors, the operation of the (ordinary Marshallian) elasticities of demand will tend to cause negative correlation between the relative changes in the p's and the relative changes in the q's, if the changes in the relative prices of particular commodities are due to changes in their relative costs of production, and to cause positive correlation if the changes in the relative prices are due to relative changes in demands for particular commodities. Similarly, in foreign trade, if the changes in the export prices of our country result from changes in the relative *world* demands for its various export commodities, then the relative changes in the export p's and the relative changes in the export q's will tend to be positively correlated, whereas if the changes in the export prices are due to changes in the internal cost conditions, the relative changes in the p's and q's will tend to be negatively correlated. Similarly, the relative changes in the import p's and the import q's will tend to be positively correlated if they result from changes in the import demands for the various import commodities, and will tend to be negatively correlated if they result from changes in the foreign costs of production of these commodities.

But price indices based on end-year weights tend to have an upward bias as compared to price indices based on beginning-year weights if the changes in the p's and the changes in the q's are

---

[24] Cf. Roland Wilson, *op. cit.*, p. 53, note.

positively correlated, and a downward bias if the changes in the p's and the changes in the q's are negatively correlated. In the choice of formulae to be used in constructing the price indices on which the terms of trade index as an index of gain is to be based, there is no obvious principle to follow in choosing between beginning-year and end-year weights, since neither procedure permits a wholly satisfactory comparison of the terms on which the actual exports and imports of the two years are exchanged. If the correlation between the changes in the p's and the changes in the q's has the same sign for both exports and imports, and if the same type of weighting is used for both price indices, the terms of trade index will tend to be unaffected by the choice made between weighting methods. But if the sign of the correlation between the changes in the p's and the changes in the q's is not the same for both exports and imports, or if different methods of weighting are used for the two price indices, the terms of trade index obtained for the end-year may differ substantially with differences in the choice of weighting-method.

There may be no rational basis for choice between beginning-year weights and end-year weights in constructing an index number of terms of trade where the problem consists of determining the effect of a particular disturbance on terms of trade in the "gain" sense. Comparison of the results obtained by the alternative methods of weighting in particular cases may be made, however, to serve as a check on the conclusions otherwise reached as to the nature of the disturbance. The type of correlation between the changes in the p's and the changes in the q's for the exports and the imports, respectively, and, therefore, the direction of the biases in the two price indices when based on end-year as compared to when based on beginning-year weights, should depend on the nature of the disturbance.

This reasoning can be illustrated by reference to the problem of the influence of capital borrowings on the terms of trade of the borrowing country. It has been argued above that capital borrowings tend to result in a rise in export prices and a fall in import prices in the borrowing country, not because of a relative shift in tastes whether in the world as a whole or within the borrowing country in favor of the export commodities of the borrowing country, but because of a relative rise in the money costs of production of the products of the borrowing country as compared to the commodities it imports. If this reasoning is correct, we should expect to find the changes in the export p's and q's of the borrowing country to be negatively correlated, and its export-price index number for the end-year should be higher, therefore, if beginning-year weights are used than if end-year weights are used. If the export prices had risen primarily because of a rise in the world demand for the export commodities, the reverse results should be expected. Similarly, in the case of the import commodities, we should expect capital borrowings to result in negative correlation between the changes in the p's and the changes in the q's, and the import price index number, to be higher, therefore, for the end-year when beginning-year weights are used than when end-year weights are used; whereas if the changes in the import prices had resulted primarily from changes in the tastes of the population of the capital-borrowing country, the reverse result should be expected.

In my study of the Canadian experience under heavy capital borrowings, 1900 to 1913, I found that an export price index based on beginning-year weights rose to 135.6 in the end-year, as compared to 120.2 for an export-price index based on end-year weights, and that almost without exception the commodities whose exports constituted an increased proportion of the total Canadian export trade at the end as compared to the beginning of the period were commodities whose prices had risen by less than the average rise in export prices as a whole. These results are hard to explain for a small country, which would naturally tend to push most vigorously its exports of those commodities which had risen most in price, except on the theory that the rise in Canadian export prices relative to world price levels was the result primarily of a rise in Canadian production costs. I found confirmation of this theory in the fact that in general the commodities which did not clearly reveal the restrictive effect on Canadian exports of the general upward trend of money costs in Canada were commodities whose costs, because of conditions special to these commodities such as production from newly-discovered or newly-developed natural resources, escaped in part at least the general upward trend. Lack of necessary information prevented similar analysis of the import price trends for Canada. Studies by other writers of the effect of capital borrowings or other disturbances on relative prices have not treated these problems[25] and as a rule have dealt with cases where the disturbance was too small to be expected to have a clearly traceable effect on the price trends. The problem deserves further investigation, especially by the experts in index-number technique.

IV. "NET BENEFIT" IN INTERNATIONAL TRADE: MARSHALL

In what is in substance an attempt to find an objective counterpart for total utility analysis, Marshall applied to the problem of gain from trade a concept analogous to his concept of consumer's surplus.[1] Marshall here uses the terms "surplus" or "net benefit" instead of "consumer's surplus," perhaps because his procedure in his international trade analysis is supposed to account for "producer's surplus" as well as for "consumer's surplus." In chart XVI,[2] OG is country G's reciprocal-demand curve, and under equilibrium OH units of G's commodity are exchanged for OB units of the commodity of the other country, E. OR is the tangent to OG at O, intersecting BA produced at R. Through P, any point on OG, draw OPp to cut BR in p; and produce MP to P^1, so that, M^1 being the point at which it cuts HA, M^1P^1 may be equal to Ap. Then G is willing to pay for the OMth E-bale at the rate of PM G-bales for OM E-bales: i.e., at the rate of pB G-bales for OB E-bales. Country G therefore obtains a surplus on the OMth bale at a rate which if applied to OB bales would make an *aggregate* surplus of Ap G-bales, or M^1P^1 G-bales. Thus

---

[25] Roland Wilson (*Capital imports and the terms of trade,* 1931, pp. 98-100) discusses the type of index number to be used, but without reference to the influence of capital borrowings on the nature of the bias to be expected in the price indices according to the method of weighting used. He argues that when the world prices of Australia's imports are rising, Australians will tend to increase in relatively greatest degree their imports of those commodities which rise least in price. (*Ibid.*) This would be a valid presumption if the changes in relative prices were due primarily to the indirect effects on money costs abroad of capital movements or were due to relative changes in the world demands for the different commodities in which changes Australia did not participate, but it would not be a valid presumption if the relative changes in import prices were due primarily to relative changes in world demands in which changes Australia did participate.

[1] Marshall, *Money credit & commerce,* 1923, pp. 162-63, 338-40.

[2] Chart XVI is a slightly simplified reproduction of Marshall's fig. 9, *ibid.*, p. 339.

her surplus on that OMth E-bale is equal to $\dfrac{M^1P^1}{OB}$. If P, starting from O, is made to move along OG, then P^1 will start from U, the foot of the perpendicular drawn from R on OY; and it will trace out a curve $UP'A$ ending at A. Then the aggregate surplus or net benefit which G derives from her trade will be an OBth part of the aggregate of the lines M^1P^1 as P^1 passes from U to A : that is, it

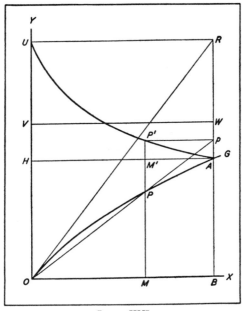

CHART XVI

will be an OBth part of the area UHA. Draw VW parallel to OX, so that the rectangle $VHAW$ is equal to the area UHA. Then $\dfrac{VHAW}{OB}, = VH$, will be country G's net benefit from trade, measured in G-bales.[3]

Marshall reaches these results by virtue of an interpretation of the reciprocal-demand curves which seems to me invalid. He

---

[3] The above is Marshall's exposition (*ibid.*, p. 339) reproduced verbatim except for the modifications made necessary by my modification of his chart and except for a few minor verbal changes in the interest of clarity.

assumes that since country G would have been willing to take an OMth E-bale at the rate of Bp G-bales for OB E-bales, but actually gets the OMth bale—as all the other bales—at the rate of AB G-bales for OB E-bales, $\dfrac{Ap}{OB}$ G-bales represents the surplus on the OMth E-bale. But this assumes that country G would have been willing to take an OMth E-bale at the $\dfrac{Bp}{OB}$ terms even if she had already purchased $(OM-1)$ E-bales at terms less favorable than $\dfrac{Bp}{OB}$, and it assumes similarly that country G would be willing to take an OBth bale at the $\dfrac{AB}{OB}$ terms if she had already purchased $(OB-1)$ E-bales at terms less favorable than $\dfrac{AB}{OB}$; i.e., it assumes that the rate at which earlier E-bales were actually obtained will not affect the rate at which country G would be willing to buy additional E-bales. The marginal utility to G of the G-bales she still retains will, however, be greater the greater the number of G-bales she has already surrendered, and, therefore, the amount country G would be willing to pay for an OBth E-bale, when all the OB bales are procured at the same price in G-bales, $\dfrac{AB}{OB}$, must be greater than the price she would be willing to pay for an OBth E-bale, when all the preceding $(OB-1)$ E-bales had been paid for at prices in G-bales higher than $\dfrac{AB}{OB}$. All of Marshall's M^1P^1's, therefore, except the initial one UH, and consequently also the aggregate surplus for country G, are made by Marshall to appear greater than they would be if correctly computed. This exaggeration of the amount of surplus is inherent in Marshall's method of computing it, which is capable of producing such improbable results as a surplus, measured in G-bales, many times greater than the total amount of G-bales actually exported, and—if the OG curve is inelastic—may produce such meaningless results as a surplus, measured in G-bales, greater than the total amount of G-bales which G can produce.

Correctly to determine the consumer's surplus measured in G-bales, it is necessary to go behind G's reciprocal-demand curve to her utility functions with respect to the G- and the E-com-

modities. Assuming this information to be available, we can proceed as in chart XVII, where the dotted lines and curves are a
reproduction of chart XVI, included for comparative purposes

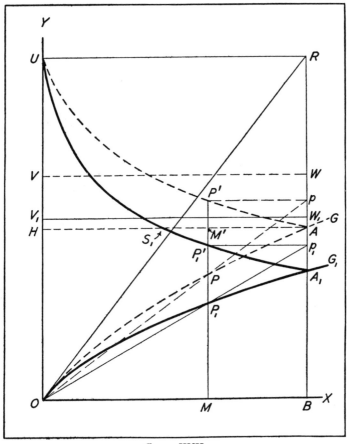

CHART XVII

only. By a procedure analogous to Marshall's, we can draw the
curve OG_1, such that at any point on it, P_1, $\dfrac{P_1M}{OM}$ or $\dfrac{p_1B}{OB}$ represents the number of G-bales which country G would be willing
to give for an OMth E-bale, when it had already bought ($OM-1$)
E-bales at the maximum prices in G-bales for each successive

E-bale which it would have been willing to pay, if necessary, given the prices at which the preceding purchases had been made. Except for the common point of origin, O, the OG_1 curve would be lower at every point, with respect to the OX axis, than the reciprocal-demand curve, OG, at the corresponding points. On MP^1 mark off, from M^1, $M^1P_1{}^1 = Ap_1$, where $\dfrac{Ap_1}{OB}$ equals the excess *or deficiency* in G-bales of what country G would be willing to pay for an OMth E-bale if all the preceding E-bales had already been purchased at the maximum prices country G was willing to pay, over the price actually paid, or $\dfrac{AB}{OB}$. If P_1, starting from O, is made to move along OG_1, then $P_1{}^1$ will start from U and trace out a curve ending at A_1, the point at which the OG_1 curve cuts BR. The aggregate surplus will then be $\dfrac{UHS - SAA_1}{OB}$, $\dfrac{SAA_1}{OB}$ representing what the sum of the deficits on the purchases beyond the S_1 point would have amounted to if each unit of E-bales in turn were assumed to have been paid for at the $\dfrac{AB}{OB}$ terms after each preceding E-bale had been paid for at the maximum price in G-bales which E would have been willing to pay, if necessary, given the prices at which the preceding purchases had been made. If V_1W_1 is drawn so as to make the rectangle $V_1HAW_1 = $ the area $UHS - SAA_1$, then the aggregate surplus of country G, measured in G-bales, will be V_1H, which is necessarily less than VH.

While the amount of surplus for country G will, therefore, necessarily be smaller than VH in chart XVI, it will increase with any decrease in the price of E-bales in terms of G-bales, provided this decrease in price is not the result of a change in country G's utility curves for G-goods or for E-goods—provided, that is, that it is not the result of a change in the OG curve—and if the OG_1 curve is known it will be possible to determine the amount of change in surplus. Changes in VH will normally be in the same direction, though not in the same degree, as changes in V_1H when the changes in the commodity terms of trade are not the result of changes in *OG*. For such changes, therefore, the effects on the surplus of country G, measured in G-bales, would be the same in direction, but would be smaller in degree, if determined by the method here presented than if determined by Marshall's method. If Marshall's "surplus" is accepted as a measure of gain, Marshall's method will therefore produce results which for such changes are qualitatively right though quantitatively wrong.

Allyn Young,[4] however, claimed that Marshall's consumer's surplus was a wholly unusable concept in international-trade theory: "consumer's surplus, as Marshall measures it, is not additive. Its sum, for any one consumer, comes precisely to zero";[5] the objections against use of the concept are even stronger in the field of international trade theory than in the field of domestic trade theory.[6]

It is a familiar objection against Marshall's concept of consumer's surplus as used by him in domestic-trade theory, and an objection whose validity he conceded, that it is not "additive"; i.e., that the surpluses as computed by him for separate commodities cannot simultaneously exist. But in international-trade theory, Marshall posits only one surplus, that associated with the foreign trade *as a whole*.[7] The surplus, moreover, is in international-trade theory measured in commodities having a direct utility of their own—or representing primary disutility—so that it cannot be said of G-bales, as it can of money, that their utility is merely a reflection of the utility of what can be obtained in exchange for them, and that the two utilities must therefore be equal.[8]

---

[4] Allyn Young, "Marshall on consumer's surplus in international trade," *Quarterly journal of economics,* XXXIX (1924), 144-50. The main theme of this article, however, was not the validity of the consumer's-surplus notion, which was discussed only incidentally, but some apparent errors in computation in Marshall's arithmetical illustration.

[5] *Ibid.,* p. 149.

[6] *Ibid.,* p. 150.

[7] And, it should be noted, taking account simultaneously of "producer's rent," which the domestic-trade theory concept does not do.

[8] In the consumer's-surplus concept, as modified here, it is true, however, that with every change in the amount of surplus measured in G-bales as we move along the *OG* curve from *O*, there occurs a change in the average utility significance of a G-bale if no change has meanwhile occurred in G's utility functions. What the direction of this change will be will depend on the elasticity of the *OG* curve, i.e., on whether a movement along the *OG* curve from *O* (and therefore an increase of surplus) is associated with an increase or a decrease in the amount of G-bales exported.

V. TOTAL NET UTILITY DERIVED FROM INTERNATIONAL TRADE: EDGEWORTH

Edgeworth's analysis of the problem of gain from trade,[1] the most elaborate and perhaps the least questioned in the literature, is both in method and in its conclusions in some important respects similar to, and in others different from, Marshall's analysis. Edgeworth's exposition is elliptical and cryptical, and is in part expressed in mathematical terms which I can follow only imperfectly. It is, therefore, with considerable trepidation that I present the following interpretation and criticism of his analysis.

Edgeworth uses reciprocal-demand curves of the Marshallian type to examine the direction of the effect on the amount of gain from foreign trade of disturbances of various kinds. He assumes tacitly that the curves in his diagrams represent the situation of typical individuals in the two areas, and bases his conclusions as to the direction of change in the amount of gain from trade on the proposition that movement from the point of origin of a given reciprocal-demand curve along the curve is always movement toward a position of greater total net utility ($=$ consumer's surplus) and therefore of greater advantage, a proposition which he had earlier demonstrated, given his assumptions, for domestic-trade demand curves in terms of money,[2] and which he here transfers to reciprocal-demand curves without further argument. Edgeworth does not here attempt to deal graphically with the *amount* of change in gain from trade resulting from particular disturbances, but only with the *direction* of the change in the amount of gain.[3]

---

[1] "The pure theory of international values," in *Papers relating to political economy,* 1925, II, 31-47 (first published in *Economic journal,* 1894).

[2] Edgeworth, *Mathematical psychics,* 1881, pp. 115-16.

[3] In an earlier essay, Edgeworth had dealt graphically with the determination of the amount of gain or consumer's surplus accruing from trade before and after a disturbance (in this case an import duty, presumably a revenue duty, levied by the country, Germany, whose gain is being measured). He uses for Germany not only its reciprocal-demand curve, but also a "no-gain from trade" curve, which he calls a "collective utility curve," and measures the gain from trade for Germany by the distance at the equilibrium point between the German "no-gain from trade" curve and the German reciprocal-demand curve. His construction is free, therefore, from the objection made above against Marshall's procedure of identifying the reciprocal-demand curve with a total-utility curve. I believe that Edgeworth's procedure here and mine in chart

The proposition that movement along a Marshallian reciprocal-demand curve from its point of origin tends on ordinarily reasonable assumptions to be movement towards a position of greater advantage can be accepted. But Edgeworth derives from it conclusions which differ substantially from those reached in the preceding two sections. These differences in conclusions can be summarized in the proposition that (with the exception of one special case, to be examined later) in Edgeworth's results the direction of change in the amount of gain from trade and the direction of change in the commodity terms of trade always correspond,[4] whereas it has here been argued that in many types of situations the commodity terms of trade and the amount of gain from trade may move in opposite directions. Edgeworth's failure to find any cases (except the special one to be examined later) where gain from trade and commodity terms of trade would move in opposite directions was due to his failure, in his interpretation of his diagrams, to distinguish between disturbances involving movement along a *given* reciprocal-demand curve and disturbances involving movement to a *new* reciprocal-demand curve. One of Edgeworth's diagrams, reproduced here as chart XVIII,[5] is supposed to cover all cases where (1) the gain consequences for country E are alone being considered, (2) the disturbance originates in country E, and (3) the specific nature of the disturbance can be described as "H, where the change originates on the side of supply: such as increased facility of producing or exporting native commodities; [or] h, on the side of demand: such as an increased desire for, or facility in admitting foreign commodities."[6] OE is E's reciprocal-demand curve and OG is G's reciprocal-demand curve, and under the original equilibrium conditions OM of E-goods is given by E in exchange for ON of G-goods. A disturbance ensues, which is assumed to

---

XVII, p. 573, *supra,* amount to the same thing.—Edgeworth, "On the application of mathematics to political economy," *Journal of the Royal Statistical Society,* LII (1889), 555-60.

[4] Edgeworth does not himself direct attention to this aspect of his results. Cf., however, *infra,* pp. 580-81.

[5] This is diagram 1 in Edgeworth's fig. 4, *Papers,* II, 37.

[6] *Ibid.,* p. 34. Edgeworth points out that disturbances of the type labeled H by him and disturbances of the type h require a different graphical procedure where OE, or country E's reciprocal-demand curve, is inelastic, but not when OE is elastic. In chart XVIII, OE is elastic, so that this chart is according to Edgeworth applicable to both types of disturbances. (*Ibid.,* p. 38.)

be an impediment rather than an encouragement to trade, and to result in the *OE* curve becoming "transformed" (the term is Edgeworth's) to *OE'*. Edgeworth traces the effects of the disturbance as follows:

In the new equilibrium indicated by the point Q, RQ of X is given in exchange for QS of Y. But Q cannot be a position of greater advantage than P', where the horizontal through Q cuts the original curve. For, on the most favorable supposition that the impediment

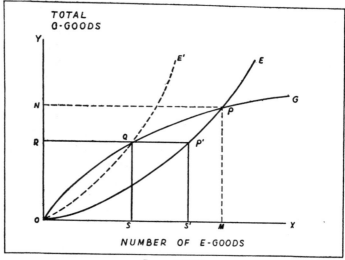

CHART XVIII

affects only exportation, not production for internal consumption, (for instance, a transit duty imposed by a third country) England's offer in exchange for OR would be reduced by the impediment from OS' to OS, so that Q would be a position of just equal advantage as P'. But P' is a position of less advantage than P (being nearer the origin as you move along the curve). Thus the native country is prejudiced by the change.[7]

The mistake in this analysis is the identification, from the point of view of gain significance, of point P' with point Q for all cases, including cases where there is no direct utility relationship be-

---

[7] *Ibid.*, p. 36.

tween the OE and the OE' curves. In the case of a transit tax on
country E's exports, levied by a third country, where the horizontal distance between the OE' and the OE curves represents
the total amount of tax, OE is still the real reciprocal-demand
curve for country E, as seen by its inhabitants, while OE' is the
same curve after the tax has been subtracted in E-bales, i.e., is
E's curve as seen by importers in country G. Under the new
equilibrium, therefore, country E gives up OS' units of E-commodities in exchange for OR units of G-commodities, while
country G receives only OS units of E-commodities in exchange
for OR units of its own commodities. The point P', therefore,
represents the new equilibrium point on country E's *unchanged*
reciprocal-demand curve, and because P' is nearer to O than is P
as we move along the curve OE, the new situation is less advantageous to country E than the old. The change in the gain from
trade for country E corresponds in direction to the change in the
commodity terms of trade for country E, since because P' is
nearer to O along the OE curve than is P, and the OE curve is
concave upward with respect to OX, the slope of the OP' vector
with respect to OX, which equals the new ratio in which G-commodities are obtained by country E in exchange for E-commodities, is smaller than the slope of the OP vector, which equals the
old ratio in which G-commodities were obtained by country E in
exchange for E-commodities.

But let us suppose that the disturbance which results in the
OE curve being transformed to OE' consists of (1) a reduction
in the desire of country E for G-commodities, or (2) an increase
in the real cost of producing E-commodities, or (3) an increase
in the desire of country E itself for E-commodities, all types of
disturbances which Edgeworth believes to be covered by the diagram reproduced here as chart XVIII. The OE curve, as the
result of any one of these types of disturbances, now has nothing
but historical significance, is a quondam curve of reciprocal demand, and OE' becomes the real reciprocal-demand curve for
country E. The utility significance of two points cannot be compared unless both points relate to the same set of utility and
disutility functions, whereas, under any of the three assumptions
listed above, the change from the OE to the OE' reciprocal-
demand curves is associated with a change in these basic utility
functions. It is therefore no longer possible to determine from

the position of Q with reference to P whether or not the new equilibrium situation is more advantageous to country E than was the equilibrium situation prior to the disturbance, since these are points on different reciprocal-demand curves whose utility relationship to each other cannot be known without more information than the diagram affords.

Note, however, the different effect on the commodity terms of trade of an impediment to E's trade which involves no change in E's real reciprocal-demand curve as compared to one which does involve such a change. The original commodity terms of trade were $\frac{ON}{OM}$, they become $\frac{OR}{OS'}$ for country E in the case of the transit tax, but become $\frac{OR}{OS}$ in the case of a disturbance involving a real change in E's reciprocal-demand curve. But $\frac{OR}{OS'} < \frac{ON}{OM}$, whereas $\frac{OR}{OS} > \frac{ON}{OM}$ i.e., the commodity terms of trade change in different directions in the two cases. In the transit tax case, the change in commodity terms of trade and the change in the amount of gain from trade are necessarily in the same direction; in the other type of case the diagram does not afford sufficient information to determine what is the direction of the change in the amount of gain from trade.

Except for one special case, still to be dealt with here, Edgeworth's failure to discriminate in his interpretation of his diagrams between disturbances which result in the movement of the equilibrium point along the *given* reciprocal-demand curve of the country under consideration and disturbances which result in that country acquiring a *new* reciprocal-demand curve pervades his entire analysis, and suffices to account for the differences between the conclusions with reference to the relationship between changes in the commodity terms of trade and changes in the amount of gain from trade reached by him, and those presented above. That Edgeworth had noticed the correspondence between his results with respect to the direction of the changes in the amount of gain from trade and his results with respect to the direction of the changes in the terms of trade is indicated by the fact that when he criticized Mill's procedure in accepting the trend of the commodity terms of trade as a criterion of the trend of gain from trade, he added:

However, it may be admitted that his definition is adequate to the purposes for which it is used. Where he says that the whole or none, or more or less, of the advantage will accrue to a certain country, it is generally true, I think, not only in his sense, but in the more correct sense.[8]

In the special case to which reference was made above, Edgeworth does deal with a disturbance which causes a displacement

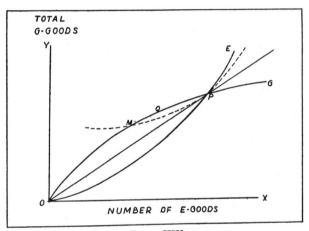

CHART XIX

of the equilibrium point off country E's reciprocal-demand curve. But in this case, for special reasons, the original reciprocal-demand curve does not lose any of its utility significance, and Edgeworth provides the additional information necessary to make utility comparisons between the new equilibrium point and the original one. The diagram which Edgeworth uses to present this case is reproduced here as chart XIX.[9] Country E levies a tax in kind on its exports, the proceeds, by exception, being distributed in such a manner as to offset any influence which the tax would otherwise have on the relative desires of the inhabitants of coun-

[8] Edgeworth, *Papers*, II, 22.
[9] Cf. *ibid.*, p. 39, fig. 6.

try E for the export and the import commodities.[10] *OE* and *OG* are the reciprocal-demand curves of country E and country G, respectively, and the dotted curve is an indifference curve or locus of positions of trade which are of equal advantage to country E as position *P*. We may call this dotted curve the trade-indifference curve. As Edgeworth says, this trade-indifference curve must touch the *OP* vector at *P*. If *Q*, which by assumption is the new position of equilibrium on the curve *OG*, is above *M*, and inside the trade-indifference curve, the inhabitants of country E are benefited by the tax; if *Q* is below *M* they are prejudiced by the tax.

Edgeworth is able here to use the position of the new equilibrium point with reference to the trade-indifference curve as a test of whether the new trading position is superior or inferior to the old for country E because *OE* continues to be the reciprocal-demand curve of E as seen by its inhabitants—though not as seen by country G—and therefore the trade-indifference curve on which *P* is located retains the same significance for the inhabitants of E after the tax as before. This special case, therefore, also fails to deal with a situation where a disturbance takes the form of a change in E's basic utility functions, but while the commodity terms of trade necessarily move in favor of E, it is nevertheless possible for the new trade position to be less advantageous to E than the old one.

VI. THE GAIN FROM TRADE MEASURED IN MONEY

Marshall's Curves and Monetary Curves.—In the theory of international value as expounded by Mill and his followers the analysis is conducted in terms of exchange ratios between certain broad groups or classes of commodities which together include all of the commodities existing in the two regions, or if the analysis is presented in terms of the exchange ratios between a few particular commodities, then these are assumed to be representative of the broad groups of commodities whose price interrelationships are the special subject of interest of the theory. In their general-value theory, on the other hand, the same writers dealt mainly with the prices in terms of money of single commodities taken one at a time and selected for examination from a universe in

---

[10] Cf. *ibid.*, pp. 38, 71-72. Edgeworth remarks: "It is not contended that the exception is of any practical importance." (*Ibid.*, p. 72.)

which there was presumed to exist an indefinitely large number of kinds of commodities. In their handling of the theory of international value, therefore, the English school made two important changes from their procedure in the field of general-value theory: (1) instead of dealing with money prices, they abstracted from money and dealt with exchange ratios between commodities; (2) instead of dealing with the variations in value of particular commodities taken one at a time on the assumption that the remainder of the system of values remained unchanged, they dealt with the internal variations occurring in the system of values as a whole. In their international-value theorizing, therefore, the English school, from the time of Mill on, made a substantial approach to the general-equilibrium method, although adhering, without important exceptions, to a strictly partial-equilibrium approach in the field of general-value theory.

This difference in method of analysis was not a historical accident but was a natural response to the difference in the nature of the problems which presented themselves most urgently for examination in the two fields. It is evident, however, that the earlier writers gave little thought to this divergence of procedure. Even in the case of Marshall, who is almost alone in drawing attention to the variation in his technique of analysis in the two fields, the explanation which he gives of the nature of the variation and of the considerations which make it desirable can scarcely be regarded as adequate. Marshall states that his reasons for dealing with international-value problems in non-monetary terms, as distinguished from the monetary approach of his general-value theory, are that any disturbance in international equilibrium will result in a change in the value of money in the two areas, or in "the standards of prices," that if the analysis is in monetary terms allowance must be made for this change in value, but that attempt to make such allowance results in wholly unmanageable complications if one proceeds far into the pure theory of foreign trade.[1]

---

[1] Alfred Marshall, *The pure theory of foreign trade* [1879], reprint 1930, p. 1; cf. also *ibid., Money credit & commerce*, p. 157:

Thus money, even when firmly based on gold, does not afford a good measure of international values, and it does not help to explain the changes in those values, which are caused by broad variations in international demand; but on the contrary it disguises and conceals them. For it measures changes in values by standards which are *automatically modified by the very variations in international demand, the effects of which are to be measured*. (Italics are in original.)

But the same objections, *in kind,* can be made to the use of money prices as a measure of value in domestic-trade theory, and it is a difference in the nature of the questions examined in the two bodies of theory, involving a difference in the degree of error resulting from abstraction from the variations in the value of money, which provides any basis for tolerating this error in domestic-value theory in the interest of simplicity while refusing to tolerate it in the field of international values. The substitution for the price-quantity demand and supply functions for single commodities used in domestic-trade theory of some such concept as reciprocal demand becomes almost inevitable if what is being studied is the value relationships between all the elements of the economy, grouped into broad classes, instead of the relative variations in value of money and one single presumably minor commodity.[2]

It is a misconception, however, to regard the theory of international value, because it abstracts from absolute money prices, as a theory of barter applied to foreign trade. The theory of barter, strictly speaking, is not applicable to an economy in which money serves as a medium of exchange and as a common measure of relative values. The theory of international value takes for granted the existence of money and its execution of its respective functions, but confines its analysis to the non-monetary manifestations of the equilibrium process.

Marshall, who wrote during a period when the exponents of the substitution throughout the field of value theory of general-for partial-equilibrium analysis were carrying on vigorous propaganda for their cause, cannot be supposed to have been unaware of the full significance of his departure in the field of the theory of international value from the partial-equilibrium method which otherwise he uniformly followed. It is regrettable, therefore, that he not only failed to emphasize the differences between his meth-

---

[2] Cf. the excellent statement by Haberler, *Theory of international trade,* 1936, p. 154:

> The *material* difference between the two types of curves is that the Marshallian [foreign-trade] curves give a *complete* picture, showing the final result of the whole international trade mechanism, and relate to *representative bales,* while the ordinary [domestic-trade] curves relate to the *money prices* of an *individual* commodity, upon the assumption that other things remain equal and in particular that all other prices remain the same, so that they can give only a partial picture . . ." (Italics are in original.)

ods of analysis in the two fields, but that he expounded the two types of theory in such closely similar terminology as to lead some students to postulate a closer resemblance between the two bodies of analysis than could rightly be attributed to them. He must be held largely to blame, therefore, for the fact that able writers have supposed that his reciprocal-demand or foreign-trade curves and his domestic demand and supply curves in terms of money were so closely related that the former were simple derivatives of the latter.[3] The two types of curves rest on radically different and irreconcilable sets of assumptions, so that it is impossible to derive one set from the other or to trace a definite relationship between them.[4]

---

[3] See H. Cunynghame, *A geometrical political economy*, 1904, p. 97. (But cf. *ibid.*, pp. 114 ff.)

See also T. O. Yntema, *A mathematical reformulation of the general theory of international trade*, 1932, pp. 47-50. In a footnote (*ibid.*, p. 48) Yntema concedes that the foreign trade curves which he derives from domestic demand and supply curves in terms of money may not be equivalent to Marshall's reciprocal demand curves:

> This derivation is based on the assumption that the import demand price on its fixed-height schedule is a function only of quantity imported and that the export supply price on its fixed height schedule is a function only of quantity exported. Marshall's comments on the interdependence of import demand and export supply seem to refer not to a functional interrelation of fixed-height schedules but to the interdependence which arises out of the necessity of balancing international debits and credits. Where a functional relation between fixed-height schedules does exist, Marshall's curves are still applicable, but they cannot be derived from their component elements by two-dimensional graphs.

The "fixed-height schedules" referred to here are supply and demand schedules of two commodities in terms of adjusted money prices. Marshall nowhere explains the derivation of his reciprocal-demand curves from the complex factors operating within each economy. As Edgeworth comments: "A movement along a supply-and-demand curve of international trade should be considered as attended with rearrangements of internal trade; as the movement of the hand of a clock corresponds to considerable unseen movements of the machinery" (*Papers*, II, 32). Marshall allowed the operations of the internal machinery to remain unseen, but since his reciprocal-demand curves relate to two "commodities" taken as constituting the entire range of commodities, it seems necessary to assume that Marshall would not have regarded the demand functions and the supply functions of these respective commodities within each country as independent functions.

[4] Cf., however, J. W. Angell, *The theory of international prices*, 1926, p. 454: "First, the assumptions on which the [Marshallian foreign-trade] curves are based, and the limitations to which they are subject, are precisely the same as for composite demand and supply curves of the more familiar sort [i.e., the ordinary domestic-trade theory curves?]. The preference for them is based simply on their greater advantage, for certain purposes, as a graphic device."

The substitution in the theory of international values of analysis in terms of reciprocal demands for analysis in terms of demands and supplies of particular commodities with respect to money prices marks, therefore, a distinct improvement in method of analysis. For introducing this improvement the credit belongs mainly to John Stuart Mill, and when Marshall and Edgeworth later elaborated and refined upon it, and invented a graphical technique for its application, they freely acknowledged their indebtedness to Mill.

There exists, however, a considerable literature, mainly of Continental origin, and still being added to, in which the problems of international value are analyzed in terms of absolute money prices and of independence of particular demand or supply curves in terms of money prices from each other. Of the many variants of the monetary approach to the problem of international value there will be selected for comment here the three types which appear to have had the greatest influence on later writers.

Cournot's Theory.—Cournot presents an argument for the profitability of import duties so obscurely stated and falling so far short of establishing its conclusions that it scarcely deserves attention on its own account. But his general authority as an economist is so high, and he is so often appealed to by protectionists as having successfully refuted the doctrine of comparative costs, that his argument cannot be wholly ignored. In spite of the fact that he stated his thesis at some length in all his economic works,[5] it is by no means easy to determine just what he was trying to prove, and almost every commentator has given a different interpretation of his argument. I will attempt to reproduce his argument essentially in the form in which he first stated it.[6]

Country B removes a restriction on the import of a commodity M. Let p_b be respectively the price and D_b the consumption of M in B before the removal of the restriction, p'_b the (lower) price and D'_b the (smaller) domestic production and E the quantity

---

Cf. also, *ibid.*, pp. 456-57: "The curves also permit an easy measurement of the direct benefits from trade. . . ."

[5] A. Cournot, *Recherches sur les principes mathématiques de la théorie des richesses*, 1838, pp. 173-81; *Principes de la théorie des richesses*, 1863, pp. 316-24; *Revue sommaire des doctrines économiques*, 1877, pp. 196-213.

[6] Cournot, *Recherches*, 1838. My subsequent references are to the translation by N. T. Bacon: *Researches into the mathematical principles of the theory of wealth*, 1927, pp. 150-57.

imported of M in B after the removal of the restriction. Then producers of M in B will lose

$$p_b D_b - p'_b D'_b \tag{1}$$

But for the consumers of M before the removal of the restriction there will be a saving of money available for the purchase of other commodities than M of

$$(p_b - p'_b) D_b \tag{2}$$

Since the import E must be paid for in other commodities, a foreign sum is added to the funds previously available for the purchase of other commodities than M, equal to

$$p'_b E \tag{3}$$

On the other hand, the increase in the purchases of M resulting from the decrease in the price of M will reduce the amount otherwise available for the purchase of other commodities than M by the amount of

$$p'_b (D'_b + E - D_b) \tag{4}$$

But $(2)+(3)-(4)$, or the additional funds available for the purchase of other commodities than M, equals (1) or $p_b D_b - p'_b D'_b$, i.e., equals the loss to producers of M in B. It would seem that so far there is no net change in the national money income, since the loss to producers of M is offset by a corresponding gain to the rest of the community. But Cournot, by virtue of a process of reasoning which no one has so far satisfactorily explained, calls this sum, $p_b D_b - p'_b D'_b$, the "nominal reduction" in the national income.[7]

---

[7] Attempts have been made to explain this by the argument that Cournot is assuming that no increase takes place in the production of other commodities, i.e., that the values (2) and (4) above are therefore eliminated, and the gain (3) is offset by a corresponding reduction in the domestic consumption of other commodities than M. This interpretation has been made, by Hagen and by others, the basis for a rejection of Cournot's argument on the ground that it makes an unwarranted assumption that the productive resources released from the production of M will find no other employment. By Angell (*Theory of international prices,* p. 245), the only writer who finds sense and significance in Cournot's thesis, it is made the basis for a defense of the validity of Cournot's argument within the limits of his assumptions. But Cournot, in reply to Hagen, expressly rejects this interpretation and claims that his method of computation gives full consideration to any income resulting from a transfer to other employments of the resources released from the production of M. (Cour-

Cournot concedes that the original consumers of M, as a result of its fall in price, are in the same position as if their income had increased by

$$(p_b - p'_b)D_b \qquad\qquad (2) = (5)$$

what we would call a consumer's surplus item if this were an acceptable way of measuring it. There is also a possible additional gain to consumers of M, because at its reduced price the additional purchases thereof may yield more satisfaction than the commodities which they replace. But since Cournot regards this gain as not measurable, he excludes it from his computation. He concludes that there is a "real reduction" in the national income of B equal to the excess of the "nominal reduction" (1) over the gain (5), or

$$(p_b D_b - p'_b D'_b) - (p_b - p'_b)D_b = p'_b (D_b - D'_b) \qquad (6)$$

It is impossible to find any significance either in Cournot's mode of computation of the benefits and losses from the removal of a restriction on import, or in the "nominal" or "real" results of his computations. The correctness of the general verdict that the technique which he used at this point was inadequate for the purpose and his conclusions of no value seems indisputable.[8]

In his final exposition of his thesis, Cournot concedes that if the removal of the restriction on import resulted in an outflow of money followed by a general fall in the prices of commodities, the problem would completely alter in character, and his conclu-

not, *Principes,* 1863, pp. 329-30; *Revue sommaire,* 1877, pp. 193-95, 205.) The only explanation I can offer, for which there seems some warrant in Cournot's exposition, is that Cournot held that since the change in the price of M and in the money income of producers of M would affect the price and the incomes of the producers of any other one commodity only to a negligible extent, it was permissible to assume that the prices and the incomes of producers in country B of other commodities than M would remain unaltered, it was permissible to ignore items (3), and (4) above. (See Cournot, *Researches,* pp. 130-32.) But this would be equivalent to saying that if the contents of a large tank of water were allowed to spread thinly over a great area, because at any one point the amount of water would be negligible, therefore the amount of water over the entire area could reasonably be regarded as negligible as compared to the amount of water originally in the tank.

[8] Cf. Edgeworth, *Papers relating to political economy,* 1925, II, 47-51; Bastable, *Theory of international trade,* 4th ed., 1903, pp. 173-75; A. Landry, *Manuel d'économique,* 1908, pp. 838-39; Irving Fisher, "Cournot and mathematical economics," *Quarterly journal of economics,* XII (1898), 130-32.

sions would not apply. This is an important concession, since the classical economists would have argued that a unilateral reduction in duties would have just these effects, and would have regarded as meaningless analysis of the effects of a reduction of duties which did not take these effects into account. Cournot also defends his technique of analysis in terms of money values by appealing to Mill's doctrine that the introduction of money would not alter the results of trade as compared to what they would be under barter. If this was correct, Cournot asserts, there could be no objection to the presentation of the theory of international trade in wholly pecuniary terms.[9] This is, of course, an extraordinary *non sequitur*. Because analysis in terms of real costs, on the one hand, and analysis in terms of real costs *and* money values, on the other hand, would produce identical results, it does not follow that the same results can be produced by analysis in terms of money values alone. In any case, Cournot's analysis fails to deal intelligibly even with the pecuniary aspects of the problem.

Barone's Graphical Technique.—Cunynghame, in 1904, expounded the theory of international value with the aid of a type of graphical illustration related to the ordinary Marshallian domestic-trade demand and supply diagrams in terms of money prices and derivable from them.[10] In Cunynghame's diagrams, as in Marshall's domestic-trade diagrams, only one commodity at a time is under consideration, and the diagrams relating to the two regions are set back to back for purposes of comparison and analysis. Cunynghame did not draw any conclusions with respect to gain from trade from his diagrams, but Barone, in 1908, used the Cunynghame back-to-back diagram to reach such conclusions.[11]

Chart XX is a reproduction of Barone's basic diagram.[12] The demand and supply curves of the particular commodity under consideration, expressed in terms of money in a currency common to both countries, are given separately for each country, with the

---

[9] *Revue sommaire*, 1877, p. 209.

[10] H. Cunynghame, *A geometrical political economy*, 1904, pp. 48 ff. See especially his fig. 51, *ibid.*, p. 98, and compare it with the Barone diagrams referred to later in the text.

[11] Enrico Barone, *Grundzüge der theoretischen Nationalökonomie* (German translation by Hans Staehle of the original Italian edition of 1908), 1927, pp. 101 ff. Barone does not refer to Cunynghame.

[12] Cf. Barone, *Grundzüge*, fig. 30, p. 102, and fig. 32, p. 105.

two diagrams set back to back. In the absence of international trade in this commodity, its price would be P_1N in England and PM in Germany. If trade is opened, England will therefore be the importer of the commodity and Germany the exporter. The cost of transportation per unit is assumed to be OO_1, and after trade, therefore, the price in England must be the price in Germany plus OO_1. Equilibrium will be established at the price, f.o.b. Germany, at which the quantity England would import,

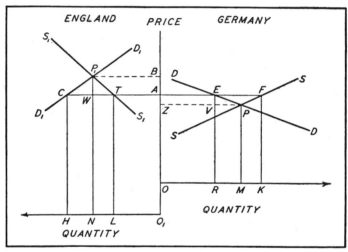

CHART XX

CT,[13] is equal to the quantity Germany would export, EF.[14] The price, therefore, will be RE in Germany and HC ($= RE + OO_1$) in England. Each country, says Barone, will gain as the result of the trade. In England the gain to consumers will be P_1CAB monetary units, which is greater than the loss to producers, P_1TAB. In Germany the gain to producers will be $AZPF$, which is greater than the loss to consumers, $AZPE$.

The grounds on which this reasoning must be regarded as inconclusive are many and formidable. First, it ignores the effect

---

[13] England at this price would consume CA, but would supply TA from her own production.

[14] Germany at this price would produce AF, but would consume AE herself.

which the removal of barriers to trade would have on gold movements and therefore on the heights of the demand-and-supply schedules and the prices in the two countries. Second, the area CP_1W included by Barone in the gain to English consumers is not homogeneous with the area BP_1WA, the latter being an actual saving in money (waiving the first objection), whereas the former is a "consumer's surplus" of indefinable meaning as compared to the area BP_1WA. A similar objection applies to the inclusion of the area EVP in the loss accruing to German consumers. These areas are akin to a portion of Marshall's consumer's surpluses in his domestic-trade theory, and are subject to the same criticisms. Third, the calculation of gain or loss to producers from changes in price and output assumes that the "producer's rent" areas represent net real income to producers without involving real costs to anyone else in the community, an assumption inconsistent with normal reality in the one respect or in the other, or partly in both. Fourth, the supply and demand curves in terms of money for each country are assumed to be independent of each other, and of the amount of national real income, an assumption always logically invalid, but seriously in conflict with the realities if the commodity under consideration represents, or is taken as representative of, a large fraction of the total national output or consumption, as is always the case in the theory of international value proper, as distinguished from the theory of domestic value. Barone's technique of analysis is invalid, therefore, even if what is in issue is the gain or loss resulting from the removal of a single minor import duty, although the results which he obtains are for most situations probably the same *in direction* as those which would be obtainable by more acceptable methods. But Barone claimed that his conclusions are "manifestly" applicable, without need of additional qualification, to the case of the removal of an entire tariff.[15]

---

[15] *Ibid.*, p. 105. Barone, however, had earlier stated that his diagrams deal with the problem "nicht in endgültig korrekter Weise" (*ibid.*, p. 102), but without indicating the nature of their shortcomings.

An algebraic formula introduced in 1904 by A. C. Pigou, applied statistically by Henry Schultz in 1928, and receiving authoritative acceptance today as the "correct method" of determining the effect of duties on prices and domestic output, is essentially an algebraic application of the Cunynghame-Barone graphical analysis. Provided the method is used only to trace the effect on the price of a particular commodity of a change in the duty on that commodity, all other related circumstances meanwhile remaining substantially unchanged, it prob-

Auspitz and Lieben.—Auspitz and Lieben attempt to trace the gain or loss effects of trade and of the imposition or removal of single duties by means of graphical constructions, independently devised by them, which are in some respects intermediate between the Marshallian domestic-trade diagrams and the Marshall-Edgeworth foreign-trade diagrams.[16] In their diagrams only a single commodity and money are represented, as in the Marshallian domestic-trade diagrams, but the vertical axis represents total amount of money instead of price per unit, and for each country the demand or supply situation is represented by two curves. In the case of the exporting country, one of these curves represents the total amounts of money in return for which the country would carry its export to the volumes indicated by the horizontal axis, while the other represents the total amounts of money which the country could accept for the indicated volumes of export without losing from the trade as a whole. This last curve, therefore, is a species of indifference curve corresponding to one of Edgeworth's "no-gain from trade" curves. It is assumed throughout that the money has constant marginal utility, and the effects of trade, or of duties, on the amount of gain from trade are measured by the vertical distances between the two curves. The restriction to single commodities makes the Auspitz and Lieben constructions akin to Barone's as far as the objective effects of trade and of duties are concerned, and open to the same

---

ably produces fairly reliable results, and does seem to me to be superior to other methods commonly used. The method would become seriously questionable, however, if applied to trace the effect on price of a substantial change in duty on a major commodity or group of commodities, since some of the factors supposed to be remaining unchanged in the *cæteris paribus* pound would then actually be undergoing substantial change and these changes would react on the price of the commodity in question. The method would be even more suspect if it purported to serve as a means of measuring the amount of gain or loss to a country resulting from a tariff change, whether the change was a major or a minor one. For the nature of the formula, and an account of the literature relating to it, see Henry Schultz, "Correct and incorrect methods of determining the effectiveness of the tariff," *Journal of farm economics,* XVII (1935), 625-41. Schultz makes clear that the results of the use of this formula become questionable if "the effect of the tariff on the prices of other commodities and on the balance of international payments [are] too great to be neglected" (*ibid.,* p. 641), which is certain to be the case when the tariff changes are major ones.

[16] R. Auspitz and R. Lieben, *Untersuchungen über die Theorie des Preises,* 1889, pp. 408-29. Cf. the comments of Edgeworth, *Papers relating to political economy,* II, 58-60.

objections, but their method of measuring gain, while not satisfactory because of the assumption of constant marginal utility of one of the constituent items in the trade, is superior to Marshall's because of its use of the indifference curve as an element in the measurement.

This book may appropriately end on a note which has been repeatedly struck before. The theory of international trade, at its best, can provide only presumptions, not demonstrations, as to the benefit or injury to be expected from a particular disturbance in foreign trade, for it deliberately abstracts from some of the considerations which can rationally be taken into account in the appraisal of policy and it never takes into account all the variables which it recognizes as significant and within its scope either because they are out of its reach or because to take them all into account would make the problem too complex for neat solution. The presumptions which the theory does provide, however, are important both because neglect of them in the formation of decisions as to policy would lead to wrong decisions in many, perhaps most, cases, and because these presumptions are not likely to be hit upon except by means of the rather arduous procedures of the theory of international trade in its more or less traditional form. Greater claims than this have been made for the utility of theory in the field of commercial policy, but their justification must await, I fear, an advance in power of economic analysis which is not yet in sight.

Appendix

A NOTE ON THE SCOPE AND METHOD OF
THE THEORY OF INTERNATIONAL TRADE

Since the comparative absence of methodological discussion in the literature of the theory of international trade is a condition whose persistence need not, in my opinion, be deplored, this methodological note is presented in the spirit of Henry Sidgwick's famous lecture on the futility of lectures. One of the methodological criticisms which has occasionally been made against the theory of international trade is that its exponents have not formulated an adequate definition of its scope and objectives, so that it fails to deal with matters properly within its range and perhaps concerns itself with questions which do not fall within its legitimate boundaries. I find it difficult to conceive what useful purposes the formal definition of the scope of a discipline can serve, except the purposes of editors of encyclopedias and administrators of educational institutions, whose responsibility it may be to prevent overlapping, to obtain full coverage, and to arbitrate jurisdictional disputes. No damage is likely to be incurred by economics if serious consideration of these jurisdictional questions is confined to those for whom it is an unavoidable occupational responsibility.

It is indeed arguable that energy spent in trying to define the proper limits of disciplines is often worse than energy wasted, since preoccupation with such definition often arises from an inadequately suppressed desire to confine analysis to one's own private set of assumptions and concepts. In the absence of precise delimitation of the scope of a field there will, it is true, tend to be much overlapping and much raggedness of boundaries. Overlapping, however, is, outside of encyclopedias with crowded pages and the curricula of universities with strained budgets, an evil of a minor order. The waste of effort which may result from it is more than counterbalanced by the mutual stimulation of the overlapping disciplines which it tends to provide, and by the safe-

594

guards which it sets up against degeneration of the individual disciplines into formal and lifeless academic systems whose original organs of contact with the problems of real life and with the development of thought in other fields have become atrophied through more or less deliberate disuse. The opposite evil, too restricted a scope, with consequent neglect of promising areas of investigation, is a more genuine one, and definition may conceivably serve to expose its existence and to indicate its specific nature, but a sample demonstration of how the discipline would be improved by an extension of its scope would seem to be a much more effective means of securing such extension. It is surely reasonable to expect the economist who urges a novel program of investigation upon his fellows to demonstrate his own faith in its possibilities and to give some concrete evidence that this faith is not misplaced by himself executing some portion at least of his program.

The discussion, however, often turns not on the propriety of the existing limits of the theory of international trade, but on the appropriateness of the doctrine's label to its contents. It has been repeatedly objected that the term "international trade" or "foreign trade" in the label is misleading, on the ground that the theory deals with trade between *regions*, irrespective of whether or not these regions are "nations" or "countries." Edgeworth remarked that: "International trade meaning in plain English trade between nations, it is not surprising that the term should mean something else in political economy."[1] That the theory was not concerned solely, or was not applicable solely, to trade between sovereign nations was recognized from the start. The writers, from Hume on, when expounding some doctrine in this field in terms of trade between countries would stop to point out that it was applicable also to trade between regions or provinces within a country. John Stuart Mill, when asked whether Ricardo was correct in stating that the same rule which regulates the relative value of native commodities does not regulate the value of the products of different countries, replied in the affirmative, but said that he would substitute "places" for "countries" in the proposition.[2] Bastable toyed with the idea of substituting "interregional" for "international," but concluded that: " 'interregional' would prove

---

[1] *Papers relating to political economy,* II, 5.
[2] Political Economy Club, *Minutes of proceedings,* VI (1921), 291.

a troublesome word; it is better therefore to adhere to the old term."[3] Ohlin adopted this "troublesome word," but in giving to his important book the title "Interregional *and* International Trade" he seems to imply that even for him the former term does not fully embrace the latter.

Finding flaws in labels is much easier than finding patently superior substitutes. If what has gone under the label of the theory of international trade was simply an investigation of the spatial aspects of trade, "interregional trade" would be a highly appropriate label. It would have the merit that it stressed the main methodological difference between the theory of domestic (or "closed economy") trade, as ordinarily formulated, and the "theory of international trade," namely, the assumption by the former of a single market without spatial dimensions and the assumption by the latter of at least two spatially distinct markets, each without internal spatial dimensions, but with substantial obstacles to the movements of factors of production and, in some cases, of commodities across the frontiers. But if the theory of international trade were distinguishable from the theory of domestic trade only by the recognition by the former, and the exclusion by the latter, of the existence of space in some abstract sense, it would have been surprising if someone had not long ago offered a demonstration that the theory of international trade could be absorbed into the theory of trade in general with gain to the latter and without loss from the abandonment of the former by introducing into the equations of the theory of trade in general additional s (for "space") terms in the manner in which the complex economic problems arising out of the temporal flux of phenomena have recently been solved for us by the introduction into the equations of general equilibrium theory of magical t (for "time") terms. Examination of the actual assumptions, explicit and implicit, of the theory of international trade reveals, however, that the role of "space" in the theory of international trade is too varied and elastic to be adequately disposed of by any such simple stratagem.

It has been alleged that what differentiates the theory of international trade from domestic-trade theory is solely the assumption in the former that there are transportation costs for commodities

---

[3] *Theory of international trade,* 4th ed., 1903, p. 12, note.

or factors and abstraction from transportation costs in the latter. Objection is then made to the differentiation of the two *theories* on the grounds that: there is no such difference in the *facts*; that if any differences exist in fact between internal and international transportation costs the differences are relative rather than absolute; and, finally, that transportation costs are often in fact greater between regions within a country than between countries. If these considerations are well-founded and relevant, there would nevertheless still be room for two theories, one abstracting from transportation costs while the other makes them its special concern. There would be no point, however, in labeling the latter the theory of "international" trade, and "interregional" would seem a highly appropriate substitute. But transportation costs are commonly abstracted from in *both* theories, and while spatial obstacles to movement are a special concern of the theory of international trade, these spatial obstacles do not, or need not, consist of transportation costs.

In their rare methodological dicta, the classical exponents of the theory of international trade explained that they were assuming international immobility and complete internal mobility of the productive factors. Mobility assumptions were important for part of their theorizing, but the mobility which they assumed to be absent internationally was a different kind of mobility from that which they assumed to be present internally. What underlay their analysis was the assumption of international *place* immobility of the factors of production, irrespective of occupation, and the assumption of internal *occupational* mobility of the factors of production, irrespective of location, and for a large part of their analysis only the former assumption was significant. Much of the criticism of the mobility assumptions of the classical theory of international trade as unrealistic is irrelevant because it fails to note this distinction between types of mobility.

It will be conceded at once that contrast between an international immobility and an internal mobility, if valid at all, is valid only as a relative and not as an absolute contrast. But a relative difference in mobility, provided it is a substantial difference, suffices as a foundation for a separate theory of international trade. The differences in degrees of mobility of the factors of production, moreover, seem obviously to be great when *countries* are being considered and to be minor, or non-existent, or in the reverse direction, when neighboring regions within a country are being considered, if the mobilities being compared are place mobility between areas, on the one hand, and occupational mobility within areas, on the other.

There is from the entrepreneurs' point of view perfect occupational mobility of a factor of production within a country if any desired quantities of its services can be hired or purchased by any industry at the same terms as by any other industry. In the long run, occupational mobility of "disposable capital" and of natural resources must approach closely to perfection. Because of occupational preferences on the part of labor and because of noncompeting occupational labor groups, there appears to be, however, a substantial departure from perfect occupational mobility of labor, whether from the entrepreneurs' or the laborers'[4] point of view, even in the long run.

An appropriate criterion of perfect long-run international mobility of the factors is the existence of sufficient place mobility to prevent persistent international differences in their money rates of return in similar occupations. There is obviously, in this sense of the term, zero mobility of natural resources: existing immigration restrictions suffice, today at least, to guarantee almost zero international mobility of labor; but in normal times at least there is a high mobility of capital and of entrepreneurial skill. These international immobilities of labor and natural resources are all that is needed as a basis for a separate theory of *international* trade even if there were perfect international mobility of capital and imperfect internal occupational mobility of all the factors, although any variation in the mobility assumptions as a matter of course makes necessary a variation of some portion of the analysis and conclusions of the theory.

There are additional reasons why "international" is a more appropriate term than "interregional" for the theory of international trade, given its traditional range of interests. In the development of the monetary aspects of the theory of the mechanism of international trade, the classical economists had generally

---

[4] The ability of labor freely to choose its occupation and the ability of entrepreneurs, whatever their occupation, to hire labor at uniform rates are, of course, different, though related, concepts. Both are significant for the doctrine of comparative real costs, but only the latter is relevant for the theory of mechanism.

in mind a particular area, England, partly because it had a single monetary and credit system and partly because it was for them an area of special interest. "Countries" fit these two considerations much more generally than do regions within a country. In the analysis of gain from trade, attention was definitely centered upon particular boundaries, enclosing areas of community of interest, and these areas were also generally countries or nations. As Sidgwick remarked: "it is only in the case of foreign trade that the investigation of the conditions of favorable interchange excite practical interest; because it is only in this case that there has ever been a serious question of governmental interference with a view of making the interchange more favorable."[5] In inductive investigations within the field of the theory of international trade, the unit of investigation has almost invariably been a "country," partly because this was an area of special interest to the investigator, and partly because the concentration of public interest on country units has resulted in a relatively much greater supply of statistical information for such units than for "regions." The subsidiary field of study of international economic policies confines its attention to the obstacles to economic intercourse, natural, institutional, statutory, administrative, which are associated with or correspond to national frontiers: import duties, immigration restrictions, differences in commercial law and commercial practices, differences in language, tastes, customs, etc. The theory of international trade is therefore to a large extent a genuine theory of trade between nations. Both by design and as an incidental by-product, it is also in large part an economic theory of regionalism. It is often something in between these two. Except for zealots in definition, this flexibility in its boundaries has not been a source of difficulty or confusion.

Williams has complained, however, that the assumption in the theory of international trade of international immobility of the factors prevents it from taking into account the important economic consequences of the substantial international migration of the factors which have actually occurred throughout the past.[6]

---

[5] *The principles of political economy*, 2d ed., 1887, p. 216.

[6] J. H. Williams, "The theory of international trade reconsidered," *Economic journal*, XXXIX (1929), especially pp. 205-09. It has conspicuously failed to do so in his own case. Cf. his *Argentine international trade under inconvertible paper money 1880-1900*, 1920.

It must be admitted that a theory which always assumes complete international immobility of the factors would be as inappropriate by itself for the economic analysis of the effects of migration of these factors as a theory of trade in general resting on strictly static assumptions has proved to be as an instrument for the analysis of business fluctuations. But this would constitute a valid criticism of the theory of international trade only if the latter professed to answer questions relating to the effects of international migration of the factors of production. The theory of international trade has departed sufficiently from its usual adherence to the assumption of international immobility of the factors of production to provide us with the only body of analysis of any pretensions relating to the mechanism of transfer of capital. But with the myriad long-run economic effects of the international migration of capital, or of labor, the theory of international trade has not dealt nor pretended to deal. While there is no doubt a valuable contribution still to be made by the theory of international trade in this connection, it seems to me that it is to the economic theorist, the economic historian, and other specialists, that we must mainly look for significant results in this field. Particularly in the field of immigration of labor, to whose vast specialized literature, as far as I know, no international trade theorist except Ohlin has made any contribution of consequence, it would probably sound like passing strange doctrine to the specialists in the field that they really were encroaching all the time on the legitimate boundaries of the theory of international trade. But it may be taken for granted that the specialists in industrial history or in immigration would welcome with open arms any genuine contribution to the analysis and solution of their problems which any specialist in international-trade theory has it within his power to make.

Williams makes another, and to me a completely novel, criticism of the theory of international trade, on the ground that, as a theory of benefits from territorial division of labor, its conclusions contradict its premises of internal mobility of the factors. Trade means national specialization for the world market. "Specialization is thus the characteristic feature and the root idea of international trade. But specialization is the antithesis of mobility, in this case of domestic movement of productive factors."[7] What

I understand him to mean is that national specialization, by leading to greater population and greater accumulation of capital within a country than could be productively employed within that country if access to foreign markets were cut off, brings into being (presumably by domestic growth as well as by immigration, since England is used as an illustration) such great increases in the amounts of the factors of production that the factors in large part have no satisfactory alternative to production for export, would with the cessation of foreign trade have either to starve or emigrate, and therefore have no internal occupational mobility. The effects of foreign trade on the amounts and rewards of the factors postulated by Williams are in kind quite in keeping with the expectations of the classical writers, though I cannot recall any instance of forecasts on their part so optimistic in degree. In default of careful investigation, I have no reason to doubt that the classical economists in general, and not only John Stuart Mill, whom Williams cites, overlooked the adverse effect on *average* occupational mobility of a great expansion in capital and population dependent on foreign trade for their employment. The alleged contradiction between the mobility assumptions and the conclusions of the theory of international trade, nevertheless, seems to me to be spurious. The relevant mobility assumption of the theory is not that occupational mobility is a *consequence* of national specialization, but that it is a prerequisite thereof, which instead of being a questionable proposition approaches closely to being a truism. Notwithstanding the passage cited by Williams from Mill, which seems to deny the possibility that foreign trade may result in a loss of average occupational mobility by the factors of production, I feel certain that Mill—or Ricardo, or Cairnes, or Marshall, or Taussig—would gladly have given assent to the proposition that a country can profitably employ more capital and can support a larger population at a given standard of living under trade than with foreign trade cut off, which seems to be the gist of Williams's argument.

---

[7] "The theory of international trade reconsidered," *loc. cit.* p. 203.

BIBLIOGRAPHY[1]

I. Works Cited in Chapters I and II

(a) PRIMARY SOURCES OF KNOWN AUTHORSHIP, BY AUTHORS

[ARMSTRONG, CLEMENT], Three memoranda, [ms. *ca.* 1530], first printed in Reinhold Pauli, Drei volkswirthschaftliche Denkschriften aus der Zeit Heinrichs VIII von England, Gottingen, 1878.

ASGILL, JOHN, Several assertions proved, in order to create another species of money than gold and silver, [1696], J. H. Hollander ed., Baltimore, 1906.

———— [————], A brief answer to a brief state of the question between the printed and painted callicoes, and the woollen and silk manufactures, 1719.

BACON, SIR FRANCIS, "Advice to Sir George Villiers," [ms. 1616], in Works of Francis Bacon, Basil Montagu ed., Philadelphia, 1852, II, 375-88.

B[ARBON], N[ICHOLAS], A discourse of trade, [1690], J. H. Hollander ed., Baltimore, 1905.

————, A discourse concerning coining the new money lighter, 1696.

BELLERS, JOHN, An essay for imploying the poor to profit, 1723.

BERKELEY, GEORGE, The querist, [1735], in The works of George Berkeley, A. C. Fraser ed., Oxford, 1871, III, 351-405.

BIESTON, ROGER, The bayte and snare of fortune, [*ca.* 1550], Glasgow, 1894.

[BINDON, DAVID], A letter from a merchant who has left off trade, 1738.

[BLEWITT, GEORGE], An inquiry whether a general practice of virtue

---

[1] This is a list of titles of works cited in the text (including the footnotes). In order to save space, a number of titles to which references of minor importance only are made are here omitted, and where a number of different items in the collected works of an author have been used, the items contained in such works are not listed here separately. Where a date is enclosed in square brackets, it represents, unless otherwise indicated, the date of first publication. Place of publication is not given for periodicals, and for other works is given only if it is not London. Since there is little overlapping between the two lists, separate listing is given for the titles cited in the first two chapters and for those cited in the remainder of the book.

tends to the wealth or poverty, benefit or disadvantage of a people? 1725.

BREWSTER, FRANCIS, New essays on trade, 1702.

[BRISCOE, JOHN], A discourse of money, 1696.

[BROWNE, JOHN], An essay on trade in general; and, that of Ireland in particular, Dublin, 1728.

CANTILLON, RICHARD, Essai sur la nature du commerce en général, [written *ca.* 1730, 1st ed., 1755], Henry Higgs ed., 1931.

CARY, JOHN, An essay on the state of England in relation to its trade, its poor, and its taxes, Bristol, 1695.

————, An essay on the coyn and credit of England: as they stand with respect to its trade, Bristol, 1696.

CHAMBERLAIN, DR. HUGH, A collection of some papers writ upon several occasions, 1696.

[CHILD, SIR JOSIAH], A treatise wherein is demonstrated, that the East-India trade is the most national of all foreign trades, 1681.

[————], A discourse about trade, 1690.

[————], The humble answer of the governor . . . of the East-India Company, [1692], in Somers' tracts, 2d ed., X (1813), 620-26.

CHOLMELEY, WILLIAM, The request and suite of a true-hearted Englishman, [ms. 1553], in The Camden Society, The Camden miscellany, II, 1853.

[CLEMENT, SIMON], A discourse of the general notions of money, trade, & exchanges, 1695.

[————], The interest of England, as it stands with relation to the trade of Ireland, considered, 1698.

COKE, ROGER, A discourse of trade, 1670.

————, A treatise wherein is demonstrated, that the church and state of England, are in equal danger with the trade of it, 1671.

————, Reflections upon the East-Indy and Royal African companies, 1695.

C[————], R[————], A treatise concerning the regulation of the coyn of England, 1696.

COLLINS, JOHN, A plea for the bringing in of Irish cattel, and keeping out of fish caught by foreigners, 1680.

COTTON, SIR ROBERT, *Cottoni posthuma,* James Howell ed., 1672.

DAVANZATI, BERNARDO, A discourse upon coins, [original Italian edition, 1588], 1696.

DAVENANT, CHARLES, The political and commercial works, Charles Whitworth ed., 1771.

[DECKER, MATHEW], Serious considerations on the several high duties, [1743], 3d ed., 1744.

[DECKER, MATHEW], An essay on the causes of the decline of the foreign trade, [1744], Edinburgh, 1756.

[DEFOE, DANIEL], An essay upon loans, 1710.

————, An humble proposal to the people of England for the increase of their trade, [1729], in The novels and miscellaneous works of Daniel Defoe, 1841, XVIII (separate pagination).

DOBBS, ARTHUR, An essay on the trade and improvement of Ireland, Dublin, 1729.

[ELIBANK, PATRICK MURRAY, LORD], Essays, I on the public debt. II on paper-money, banking, &c. III on frugality, 1755.

FORDE, SIR EDWARD, Experimented proposals, [1666], in The Harleian miscellany, VII (1810), 341-43.

[FORSTER, NATHANIEL], An enquiry into the causes of the present high price of provisions, 1767.

FORTREY, SAMUEL, England's interest and improvement, [1663], J. H. Hollander ed., Baltimore, 1907.

FULLER, THOMAS, The holy state, and the profane state, [1642], James Nichols ed., 1841.

[GARDNER], Some reflections on a pamphlet, intituled, England and East India inconsistent in their manufactures, 1696.

GEE, JOSHUA, The trade and navigation of Great-Britain considered, [1729], 1767.

GERVAISE, ISAAC, The system or theory of the trade of the world, 1720.

HAINES, RICHARD, The prevention of poverty, 1674.

————, England's weal and prosperity proposed: or, reasons for erecting publick workhouses in every county, 1681.

[HALES, JOHN], A discourse of the common weal of this realm of England, [ms. 1550, 1st ed., 1581], Elizabeth Lamond ed., Cambridge, Eng., 1893.

[HARRIS, JOSEPH], An essay upon money and coins, 1757-58.

[HAY, WILLIAM], Remarks on the laws relating to the poor, [1735], 1751.

HOBBES, THOMAS, Leviathan, [1651], Everyman's library ed., 1928.

HODGES, JAMES, The present state of England as to coin and publick charges, 1697.

HOME, HENRY, Sketches of the history of man, Edinburgh, 1774.

HORSLEY, WILLIAM, A treatise on maritime affairs, 1744.

[HOUGHTON, JOHN], England's great happiness, [1677], in J. R. McCulloch ed., A select collection of early English tracts on commerce, 1856, pp. 251-74.

————, A collection of letters for the improvement of husbandry & trade, 1681-83.

HOUGHTON, THOMAS, The alteration of the coyn, 1695.

HUME, DAVID, Political discourses, [1752], in Essays moral, political and literary, T. H. Green and T. H. Grose ed., 1875.

———, The letters of David Hume, J. Y. T. Greig ed., Oxford, 1932.

JAMES I, *Basilikon doron*, in The workes of the most high and mightie Prince, James, 1616, pp. 148-89.

[JOCELYN], An essay on money & bullion, 1718.

J[USTICE], A[LEXANDER], A general treatise of monies and exchanges, 1707.

[KEALE, ROBERT], The trade's increase, [1615], in The Harleian miscellany, III (1809), 289-315.

LAMB, SAMUEL, Seasonal observations, [1659], in Somers' tracts, 2d ed., VI (1811), 446-65.

LAW, JOHN, Money and trade considered, [1705], Glasgow, 1750.

LAWRENCE, RICHARD, The interest of Ireland in its trade and wealth stated, Dublin, 1682.

LEWIS, M[ARK], Proposals to the King and Parliament, or a large model of a bank, 1678.

[LINDSAY, PATRICK], The interest of Scotland considered, Edinburgh, 1733.

[LLOYD, HENRY], An essay on the theory of money, 1771.

LOCKE, JOHN, Two treatises of civil government, [1690], in The works of John Locke, 1823, V, 287-485.

———, Some considerations on the lowering of interest, [1691], in The works of John Locke, 1823, V, 1-116.

LONDON, JOHN, Some considerations on the importance of the woollen manufactures, 1740.

MACKWORTH, SIR HUMPHREY, A proposal for payment of the publick debts, 2d ed., n.d. (*ca.* 1720).

MADDISON, RALPH, Great Britains remembrancer, looking in and out, [1640], 1655.

M[AGENS], N[ICHOLAS], Farther explanations of some particular subjects . . . . contained in the universal merchant, 1756.

MALYNES, GERARD, A treatise of the canker of England's common wealth, [1601], in Tawney and Power, Tudor economic documents, 1924, III, 386-404.

———, The center of the circle of commerce, 1623.

MANDEVILLE, BERNARD, The fable of the bees: or, private vices, public benefits, [1st ed., 1714], reprint of 6th ed. [1732], F. B. Kaye ed., Oxford, 1924.

MANLEY, THOMAS, Usury at six per cent. examined, 1669.

MASSIE, JOSEPH, An essay on the governing causes of the natural rate of interest, [1750], J. H. Hollander ed., Baltimore, 1912.

MASSIE, JOSEPH, The proposal, commonly called Sir Mathew Decker's scheme, for one general tax upon houses, laid open, 1757.

[MILDMAY, SIR WILLIAM], The laws and policy of England, relating to trade, 1765.

MILLES, THOMAS, The customers replie, or second apologie, 1604.

MISSELDEN, EDWARD, Free trade or, the meanes to make trade florish, 2d ed., 1622.

M[————], E[————], The circle of commerce, or the ballance of trade, 1623.

MOLLOY, CHARLES, *De jure maritimo et navali*: or a treatise of affairs maritime, and of commerce, [1st ed., 1676], 9th ed., 1769.

MORE, SIR THOMAS, Utopia, [1516], reprint of 1556 ed., A. W. Reed ed., Waltham St. Lawrence, 1929.

M[UN], T[HOMAS], A discourse of trade, from England unto the East-Indies, [1621], Facsimile Text Society reprint, New York, 1930.

————, England's treasure by forraign trade, [written *ca.* 1630, 1st ed., 1664], W. J. Ashley ed., New York, 1895.

[NORTH, SIR DUDLEY], Discourses upon trade, [1691], J. H. Hollander ed., Baltimore, 1907.

PAPILLON, THOMAS, A treatise concerning the East India trade, [1st ed., 1677], reprint of 1680 ed., 1696.

PATERSON, WILLIAM, The writings of ————, 2d ed., Saxe Bannister ed., 1859.

PETTY, SIR WILLIAM, The economic writings of ————, C. H. Hull ed., Cambridge, Eng., 1899.

[PETYT, WILLIAM?], *Britannia languens,* or a discourse of trade, [1680], in J. R. McCulloch ed., A select collection of early English tracts on commerce, 1856, pp. 275-504.

PHILIPS, ERASMUS, An appeal to common sense: or, some considerations offer'd to restore publick credit, 1720.

[————], the state of the nation, in respect to her commerce, debts, and money, 1725.

[POLLEXFEN, JOHN], A discourse of trade, coyn, and paper credit, 1697.

[————], England and East-India inconsistent in their manufactures, 1697.

[————], A vindication of some assertions relating to coin and trade, 1699.

POSTLETHWAYT, MALACHY, Great-Britain's true system, 1757.

————, The universal dictionary of trade and commerce, 4th ed., 1774.

POTTER, WILLIAM, The key of wealth, 1650.

[PRATT, SAMUEL], The regulating silver coin, made practicable and easie, 1696.

[PRIOR, THOMAS], Observations on coin in general, [Dublin, 1730?], London reprint, 1730.

REYNEL, CAREW, The True English interests, 1679.

ROBERTS, LEWES, The treasure of traffike or a discourse of forraigne trade, [1641], in J. R. McCulloch ed., A select collection of early English tracts on commerce, 1856, pp. 49-113.

ROBINSON, HENRY, Englands safety; in trades encrease, 1641.

————, Certain proposalls in order to the peoples freedome, 1652.

[SHERIDAN, THOMAS], A discourse on the rise and power of parliaments, [1677], reprinted in Saxe Bannister, Some revelations in Irish history, 1870.

SMITH, ADAM, Lectures on justice, police, revenue and arms, [ms. 1763], Edwin Cannan ed., Oxford, 1896.

————, An inquiry into the nature and causes of the wealth of nations, [1776], Edwin Cannan ed., 1904.

[SMITH, CHARLES], Three tracts on the corn-trade and corn-laws, 2d ed., 1766.

SMITH, JOHN, *Chronicon rusticum-commerciale*; or, memoirs of wool, 1747.

STARKEY, THOMAS, England in the reign of King Henry the Eighth, [ms. *ante* 1538], Early English Text Society, 1871-78.

STEUART, SIR JAMES, An inquiry into the principles of political œconomy, 1767.

STOW, JOHN, "An apologie of the cittie of London," [1598], in A survey of London, reprint of 1603 ed., C. L. Kingsford ed., Oxford, 1908, II, 195-217.

TEMPLE, SIR WILLIAM, Observations on the United Provinces, [1668], in The works of Sir William Temple, Edinburgh, 1754, I, 1-157.

[TEMPLE, WILLIAM, OF TROWBRIDGE], A vindication of commerce and the arts, [1758], in J. R. McCulloch ed., A select collection of scarce and valuable tracts on commerce, 1859, pp. 481-561.

TUCKER, JOSIAH, Reflections on the expediency of a law for the naturalization of foreign protestants, 1751-52.

————, A brief essay on the advantages and disadvantages which respectively attend France and Great Britain, with regard to trade, 3d ed. [1753], in J. R. McCulloch ed., A select collection of scarce and valuable tracts on commerce, 1859, pp. 309-425.

————, The elements of commerce, and theory of taxes (privately printed, no title page), [Bristol, 1755].

————, Instructions for travellers, 1757.

[Tucker, Josiah], The causes of the dearness of provisions assigned, Gloucester, 1766.

[————], Considerations on the policy, commerce and circumstance of the kingdom, 1771.

————, Four tracts on political and commercial subjects, 2d ed., Gloucester, 1774.

Vanderlint, Jacob, Money answers all things, [1734], J. H. Hollander ed., Baltimore, 1914.

Vaughan, Rice, A discourse of coin and coinage, 1675.

V[ickaris], A., An essay for regulating of the coyn, 1696.

Violet, Thomas, An humble declaration . . . touching the transportation of gold and silver, 1643.

————, A true discoverie to the commons of England, [1651], 1653.

————, Mysteries and secrets of trade and mint-affairs, 1653.

[Wallace, Robert], A view of the internal policy of Great Britain, 1764.

[————], Characteristics of the present political state of Great Britain, 1758.

[Walpole, Robert], A letter from a member of parliament to his friends in the country, concerning the duties on wine and tobacco, 1733.

[Whatley, George], Principles of trade, 2d ed., 1774.

Whiston, James, A discourse of the decay of trade, 1693.

Wood, William, A letter to a member of parliament: shewing the justice of a more equal and impartial assessment on land, 1717.

————, A survey of trade, 1718.

[Young, Arthur], Political essays concerning the present state of the British Empire, 1772.

————, Political arithmetic, containing observations on the present state of Great Britain, 1774.

[————], The farmer's letters to the people of England, 2d ed., 1768.

(b) primary sources of unknown authorship

The libelle of Englyshe polycye, [ms. 1436], Sir George Warner ed., Oxford, 1926.

"Considerations for the restraynte of transportinge gould out of the realme," [ms. reign of Elizabeth], in Georg Schanz, Englische Handelspolitik gegen Ende des Mittelalters, Leipzig, 1881, II, 648-49.

"Polices to reduce this realme of Englande unto a prosperus wealthe and estate," [ms. 1549], in R. H. Tawney and Eileen Power, Tudor economic documents, 1924, III, 311-45.

"Memorandum prepared for the royal commission on the exchanges," [ms. 1564], in R. H. Tawney and Eileen Power, Tudor economic documents, 1924, III, 346-59.

"A discourse of corporations," [ms. ca. 1587], in R. H. Tawney and Eileen Power, Tudor economic documents, 1924, III, 265-76.

Decay of trade. A treatise against the abating of interest, 1641.

A discourse consisting of motives for the enlargement and freedome of trade, 1645.

Omnia comesta a bello. Or, an answer out of the west to a question out of the north, n.p., 1667.

Et à dracone: or, some reflections upon a discourse called Omnia à belo comesta, 1668.

Interest of money mistaken, 1668.

A treatise of wool and cattel, 1677.

Reasons for a limited exportation of wooll, n.p., 1677.

The ancient trades decayed, repaired again, 1678.

Englands interest or the great benefit to trade by banks or offices of credit, 1682.

Several objections sometimes made against the office of credit, fully answered, n.p., n.d., (ca. 1682).

Taxes no charge: in a letter from a gentleman, to a person of quality, 1690.

The linen and woollen manufactory discoursed, [1691], in John Smith, Chronicon rusticum-commerciale, 1747, I, 383-88.

A discourse concerning the East-India trade, [ca. 1692], in Somers' tracts, 2d ed., X (1813), 634-47.

A discourse of the nature, use and advantages of trade, 1693.

The interest of England considered: in an essay upon wooll, 1694.

An essay towards carrying on the present war against France, [ca. 1697], in The Harleian miscellany, X (1810), 371-89.

N., A., England's advocate, Europe's monitor, 1699.

Considerations on the East-India trade, [1701], in J. R. McCulloch ed., A select collection of early English tracts on commerce, 1856, pp. 541-629.

The circumstances of Scotland consider'd, with respect to the present scarcity of money, Edinburgh, 1705.

Remarks upon the Bank of England, with regard more especially to our trade and government, 1705.

Reasons offer'd against the continuance of the Bank, 1707.

Some queries, humbly offer'd to the consideration of both houses of parliament relating to the Bank of England, 1707.

A short view of the apparent dangers and mischiefs from the Bank of England, 1707.

The vindication and advancement of our national constitution and credit, 1710.

A vindication of the faults on both sides, [1710], in Somers' tracts, 2d ed., XIII (1815), 3-24.

The taxes not grievous, and therefore not a reason for an unsafe peace, 1712.

Torism and trade can never agree, n.d. (*ca.* 1713).

The British merchant, [1713], 3d ed., 1748.

A brief state of the question between the printed and painted callicoes, and the woollen and silk manufacture, 2d ed., 1719.

Considerations occasioned by the bill for enabling the South Sea Company to increase their capital stock, 1720.

Some thoughts on the interest of money in general, and particularly in the publick funds, n.d. (*ca.* 1720).

Proposals for restoring credit; for making the Bank of England more useful and profitable, 1721.

Some considerations on the nature and importance of the East-India trade, 1728.

An enquiry into the melancholy circumstances of Great Britain, n.d. (*ca.* 1730).

The present state of Ireland consider'd, London reprint, 1730.

Reflections and considerations occasioned by the petition . . . for taking off the drawback on foreign linens, &c., 1738.

"On the neglect of trade and manufactures," Scots magazine, II (1740), 475-77.

A letter to the . . . Lords Commissioners of trade and plantations, wherein the grand concern of trade is asserted, 1747.

The manufacturer's plea for the bounty on corn at exportation, 1754.

An inquiry concerning the trade, commerce, and policy of Jamaica, relative to the scarcity of money, Jamaica, 1759.

"Impartial essay concerning the nature and use of specie and paper-credit in any country," Scots magazine, XXIV (1762), 133-35.

"Considerations relating to the late order of the two banks," Scots magazine, XXIV (1762), 39-41, 89-94.

(c) SECONDARY SOURCES

ANGELL, J. W., The theory of international prices history, criticism and restatement, Cambridge, Mass., 1926.

BARNES, D. G., A history of the English corn laws from 1660-1846, New York, 1930.

BRENTANO, LUJO, Hours and wages in relation to production (transl. from the original German ed.), 1894.

CUNNINGHAM, WILLIAM, "Adam Smith und die Mercantilisten," Zeitschrift für die gesammte Staatswissenschaft, XL (1884), 41-64.

DIETZEL, HEINRICH, Weltwirtschaft und Volkswirtschaft, Dresden, 1900.

DOVE, PATRICK E., "An account of Andrew Yarranton," in The elements of political science, Edinburgh, 1844, 402-70.

DUBOIS, A., Précis de l'histoire des doctrines économiques, Paris, 1903.

FETTER, F. W., "The term 'favorable' balance of trade,'" Quarterly journal of economics, XLIX (1935), 621-45.

FRIIS, ASTRID, Alderman Cockayne's project and the cloth trade, 1927.

FURNISS, E. S., The position of the laborer in a system of nationalism, Boston, 1920.

GREGORY, T. E., "The economics of employment in England, 1660-1713," Economica, I (1921), 37-51.

HECKSCHER, E. F., Mercantilism (transl. from the original Swedish edition of 1931), 1935.

HELANDER, SVEN, "Sir Josiah Child," Weltwirtschaftliches Archiv, XIX (1923), 233-49.

JOHNSON, E. A. J., "The mercantilist concept of 'art' and 'ingenious labour,'" Economic history, II (1931), 234-53.

———, "Unemployment and consumption: the mercantilist view," Quarterly journal of economics, XLVI (1932), 698-719.

JONES, RICHARD, "Primitive political economy of England," [1847], in Literary remains, consisting of lectures and tracts on political economy, Wm. Whewell ed., 1859, pp. 291-335.

LIPSON, EPHRAIM, The economic history of England, 1929-31.

MAINTRIEU, JEHAN, Le traité d'Utrecht et les polémiques du commerce anglais, Paris, 1909.

MONROE, A. E., Monetary theory before Adam Smith, Cambridge, Mass., 1923.

PRICE, W. H., "The origin of the phrase 'balance of trade,'" Quarterly journal of economics, XX (1905), 157-67.

SELIGMAN, E. R. A., "Bullionists," Encyclopaedia of the social sciences, III (1930), 60-64.

STEPHEN, SIR LESLIE, History of English thought in the eighteenth century, 3d ed., 1902.

SUVIRANTA, BR., The theory of the balance of trade in England, Helsingfors, 1923.

TAWNEY, R. H., "Religious thought on social and economic questions in the sixteenth and seventeenth centuries," Journal of political economy, XXXI (1923), 461-93, 637-74, 804-25.

————, Introduction to Thomas Wilson, A discourse upon usury, [1572], New York, n.d., (ca. 1924).

VINER, JACOB, "English theories of foreign trade before Adam Smith," Journal of political economy, XXXVIII (1930), 249-301, 404-57.

————, "Balance of trade," Encyclopaedia of the social sciences, II (1930), 399-406.

II. Works Cited in Remainder of Book

(a) WORKS OF KNOWN AUTHORSHIP

ACWORTH, A. W., Financial reconstruction in England 1815-1822, 1925.

ADAMSON, ROBERT, "Some considerations on the theory of money," Transactions of the Manchester Statistical Society, 1884-85, 31-58.

ADDINGTON, BARON, *see* J. G. HUBBARD.

ANGELL, J. W., review of Jacob Viner, Canada's balance of international indebtedness, Political science quarterly, XL (1925), 320-22.

————, "The effects of international payments in the past," in National Industrial Conference Board, The inter-ally debts and the United States, New York, 1925, 138-89.

————, The theory of international prices—history, criticism and restatement, Cambridge, Mass., 1926.

ARBUTHNOT, G., Sir Robert Peel's Act of 1844, regulating the issue of bank notes, vindicated, 1857.

ASHBURTON, LORD, The financial and commercial crisis considered, 4th ed., 1847.

[ATTWOOD, MATHIAS], A letter to Lord Archibald Hamilton, on alterations in the value of money, 1823.

ATTWOOD, THOMAS, A letter to . . . Nicholas Vansittart, on the creation of money, and on its action upon national prosperity, Birmingham, 1817.

[————], Prosperity restored; or, reflections on the cause of the public distresses, and on the only means of relieving them, 1817.

————, Observations on currency, population, and pauperism, in two letters to Arthur Young, Esq., Birmingham, 1818.

————, A letter to the Earl of Liverpool, on the reports of the committees of the two Houses of Parliament, on the question of the Bank restriction act, Birmingham, 1819.

ATTWOOD, THOMAS, A second letter to the Earl of Liverpool, on the Bank reports, as occasioning the national dangers and distresses, Birmingham, 1819.

———— (AND SIR JOHN SINCLAIR), The late prosperity, and the present adversity of the country, explained; . . . in a correspondence between Sir John Sinclair and Mr. Thomas Attwood, 1826.

————, The Scotch banker, 1st ed., 1828; 2d ed., 1832.

AUSPITZ, RUDOLF, AND LIEBEN, RICHARD, Untersuchungen über die Theorie des Preises, Leipzig, 1889.

BACALAN, ISAAC DE, see SAUVAIRE-JOURDAN.

[BAILEY, SAMUEL], Money and its vicissitudes in value, 1837.

BARING, ALEXANDER, see ASHBURTON, LORD.

BARONE, ENRICO, Grundzüge der theoretischen Nationalökonomie (transl. from original Italian ed. of 1908), Bonn, 1927.

BASTABLE, C. F., "Economic notes," Hermathena, VII (1889), 109-25.

————, "On some applications of the theory of international trade," Quarterly journal of economics, IV (1889), 1-17.

————, The theory of international trade, 2d ed., 1897; 4th ed., 1903.

BEACH, W. E., British international gold movements and banking policy, 1881-1913, Cambridge, Mass., 1935.

BENTHAM, JEREMY, A manual of political economy, [ms. 1797-1803), in The works of Jeremy Bentham, John Bowring ed., Edinburgh, III (1843), 33-84.

————, The rationale of reward, 1825.

BICKERDIKE, C. F., "International comparisons of labour conditions," Transactions of the Manchester Statistical Society, 1911-12, 61-83.

BLACKER, WILLIAM, The evils inseparable from a mixed currency, and the advantages to be secured by introducing an inconvertible national paper currency, 3d ed., 1847.

BLAKE, WILLIAM, Observations on the effects produced by the expenditure of government during the restriction of cash payments, 1823.

BOASE, HENRY, A letter to . . . Lord King, in defence of the conduct of the directors of the Banks of England and Ireland, 1804.

BOLLMAN, ERICK, A letter to Thomas Brand . . . on the practicability and propriety of a resumption of specie payments, 1819.

BOLLMAN, ERICK, A second letter . . . on the practicability of the new system of bullion-payments, 1819.

BONAR, JAMES, "Ricardo's ingot plan," Economic journal, XXXIII (1923), 281-304.

BOOTH, GEORGE, Observations on paper currency, the Bank of England notes, and on the principles of coinage, and a metallic circulating medium, Liverpool, 1815.

BOSANQUET, CHARLES, Practical observations on the report of the bullion-committee, 2d ed., 1810.

BOSANQUET, J. W., Metallic, paper, and credit currency, and the means of regulating their quantity and value, 1842.

BOWEN, FRANCIS, American political economy, New York, 1861.

BOYD, WALTER, A letter to . . . William Pitt, on the influence of the stoppage of issues in specie at the Bank of England, on the prices of provisions, and other commodities, 1st ed., 1801 ; 2d ed., 1801.

BRESCIANI-TURRONI, C., Inductive verification of the theory of international payments, Cairo, n.d. (1932?).

———, "The 'purchasing power parity' doctrine," L'Égypte contemporaine, XXV (1934), 433-64.

BUCHANAN, DAVID, Observations on the subjects treated of in Dr. Smith's . . . Wealth of nations, Edinburgh, 1814.

———, Inquiry into the taxation and commercial policy of Great Britain, Edinburgh, 1844.

BURGESS, HENRY, A letter to the Right Hon. George Canning, 1826.

BURNS, A. F., "A note on comparative costs," Quarterly journal of economics, XLII (1928), 495-500.

BUTT, ISAAC, Protection to home industry, Dublin, 1846.

CAIRNES, J. E., An examination into the principles of currency involved in the Bank charter act of 1844, 1854.

———, Essays in political economy, 1873.

———, Some leading principles of political economy newly expounded, New York, 1874.

CANNAN, EDWIN, The paper pound of 1797-1821, 1919.

CARR, ROBERT M., "The rôle of price in the international trade mechanism," Quarterly journal of economics, XLV (1931), 710-19.

CARVER, T. N., "Some theoretical possibilities of a protective tariff," Publications of the American Economic Association, 3d series, III (1902), 167-82.

CASSEL, GUSTAV, "Memorandum on the world's monetary problems," International Financial Conference, Brussels, 1920, Documents of the conference, V, 29-77.

———, Post-war monetary stabilization, New York, 1928.

CASSEL, GUSTAV, The theory of social economy, new ed., (transl. from 5th German ed.), New York, 1932.

CASTLEREAGH, LORD VISCOUNT, The substance of a speech delivered . . . in the House of Commons, July 15, 1811, 1811.

CAYLEY, A. S., Agricultural distress—silver standard, 1835.

CHERBULIEZ, A. E., Précis de la science économique et de ses principales applications, Paris, 1862.

CLAY, SIR WILLIAM, Remarks on the expediency of restricting the issue of promissory notes to a single issuing body, 1844.

[COCKBURN, R.], Remarks on prevailing errors respecting currency and banking, 1842.

COCKBURN, W., Commercial œconomy; or the evils of a metallic currency, 2d ed., 1819.

COMBER, W. T., A view of the nature and operation of bank currency; as connected with the distresses of the country, 1817.

COURNOT, A., Researches into the mathematical principles of the theory of wealth (transl. from the original French [1838] by N. T. Bacon), New York, 1927.

————, Principes de la théorie des richesses, Paris, 1863.

————, Revue sommaire des doctrines économiques, Paris, 1877.

COWELL, J. W., Letters . . . on the institution of a safe and profitable paper currency, 1843.

CRAIG, JOHN, Remarks on some fundamental doctrines in political economy, Edinburgh, 1821.

CROSS, WILLIAM, A standard pound versus the pound sterling, Edinburgh, 1856.

CUNYNGHAME, H., A geometrical political economy, Oxford, 1904.

[DICKSON, ADAM], An essay on the causes of the present high price of provisions, 1773.

DOUBLEDAY, THOMAS, Remarks on some points of the currency question, 1826.

DOUGLAS, R. K., Brief considerations on the income tax and tariff reform, in connection with the present state of the currency, Birmingham, 1842.

DRUMMOND, HENRY, Elementary propositions on the currency, 4th ed., 1826.

DUNCAN, JONATHAN, The national anti-gold law league. The principles of the league explained, 1847.

————, The mystery of money explained, 2d ed., 1863.

DUNLOP, ANTHONY, "Sketches on political economy," Pamphleteer, XI, (1818), 403-41.

EDGEWORTH, F. Y., "On the application of mathematics to political economy," Journal of the Royal Statistical Society, LII (1889), 538-76.

EDGEWORTH, F. Y., Review of Bastable, The theory of international trade, 2d ed., Economic journal, VII (1897), 397-403.

————, Papers relating to political economy, 1925.

EINAUDI, LUIGI, "James Pennington or James Mill: an early correction of Ricardo," Quarterly journal of economics, XLIV (1929), 164-71, 544-45.

EISDELL, J. S., A treatise on the industry of nations, 1839.

ELLIOTT, G. A., "Transfer of means-of-payment and the terms of international trade," Canadian journal of economics and political science, II (1936), 481-92.

ELLIS, HOWARD S., German monetary theory 1905-1933, Cambridge, Mass., 1934.

[ELLIS, WILLIAM], "Exportation of machinery," Westminster review, III (1825), 386-94.

[————], "Effect of employment of machinery," Westminster review, V (1826), 101-36.

EVELYN, SIR GEORGE SHUCKBURGH, "An account of some endeavors to ascertain a standard of weight and measure," Philosophical transactions of the Royal Society of London, 1798, part I, 133-82.

FANNO, MARCO, "Credit expansion, savings and gold export," Economic journal, XXXVIII (1928), 126-31.

FEAVEARYEAR, A. E., The pound sterling a history of English money, Oxford, 1931.

FEIS, HERBERT, "The mechanism of adjustment of international trade balances," American economic review, XVI (1926), 593-609.

FISHER, IRVING, "Cournot and mathematical economics," Quarterly journal of economics, XII (1898), 119-38.

FOSTER, JOHN LESLIE, An essay on the principle of commercial exchanges, 1804.

FOWLER, WILLIAM, The crisis of 1866: a financial essay, 1867.

FOXWELL, H. S., Preface to A. Andréadès, History of the Bank of England, 2d ed., 1924.

FRANCIS, SIR PHILIP, Reflections on the abundance of paper in circulation, and the scarcity of specie, 2d ed., 1810.

FULLARTON, JOHN, On the regulation of currencies, 2d ed., 1845.

GIBSON, A. H., Bank rate; the banker's *vade mecum*, 1910.

G[ILBART], J. W., "The currency: banking," Westminster review, XXXV (1841), 89-131.

————, A practical treatise on banking, 1st American, from 5th London ed., New York, 1851.

[GOSCHEN, G. J.], The theory of the foreign exchanges, 1861.

GRAHAM, F. D., "International trade under depreciated paper. The United States, 1862-79," Quarterly journal of economics. XXXVI (1922), 220-73.

————, "Some aspects of protection further considered," Quarterly journal of economics, XXXVII (1923), 199-227.

————, "The theory of international values re-examined," Quarterly journal of economics, XXXVIII (1923), 54-86.

————, review of Viner, Canada's balance of international indebtedness, American economic review, XV (1925), 106-109.

————, "The theory of international values," Quarterly journal of economics, XLVI (1932), 581-616.

GRAHAM, SIR JAMES, Corn and currency; in an address to the land owners, 4th ed., 1827.

GRAY, JOHN, An efficient remedy for the distress of nations, Edinburgh, 1842.

GREAT BRITAIN, PARLIAMENT, HOUSE OF COMMONS, Report from the Committee on the circulating paper, the specie, and the current coin of Ireland, [1804], 1826 reprint.

————, Report, together with minutes of evidence, and accounts, from the Select Committee on the high price of gold bullion, [1810], octavo reprint, 1810.

————, Report from the Select Committee on the usury laws, 1818.

————, Reports from the Secret Committee on the expediency of the Bank resuming cash payments, 1819.

————, Report from the Committee on Secrecy on the Bank of England charter; with the minutes of evidence, 1832.

————, Report from Select Committee on banks of issue; with the minutes of evidence, 1840.

————, First report from the Secret Committee on commercial distress; with the minutes of evidence, 1848.

————, Report from the Select Committee on bank acts; together with the proceedings of the Committee, Parts I and II, 1857.

GREAT BRITAIN, PARLIAMENT, HOUSE OF LORDS, Report of the Committee of Secrecy, 1797.

————, Reports by the . . . Secret Committee to enquire into the state of the Bank of England; with reference to the expediency of the resumption of cash payments, 1819.

————, Report from the Secret Committee . . . appointed to enquire into the causes of the distress . . . among the commercial classes, 1848.

GREGORY, T. E., An introduction to Tooke and Newmarch's, A history of prices, 1928.

GREGORY, T. E., Select statutes, documents and reports relating to British banking, 1832-1928, 1929.

HABERLER, GOTTFRIED, "The theory of comparative cost once more," Quarterly journal of economics, XLIII (1929), 376-81.

————, "Die Theorie der komparativen Kosten und ihre Auswertung für die Begründung des Freihandels," Weltwirtschaftliches Archiv, XXXII (1930, II), 349-70.

————, Der internationale Handel, Berlin, 1933.

————, The theory of international trade, (transl. from the original German ed.), 1936.

[HALL, JOHN], A letter to . . . Thomas Spring Rice, containing a new principle of currency, 1837.

HALL, WALTER, A view of our late and of our future currency, 1819.

HANKEY, THOMSON, The principles of banking, 1867.

"HARDCASTLE, DANIEL," pseud., *see* RICHARD PAGE.

HARROD, R. F., Review of Roland Wilson, Capital imports and the terms of trade, 1931, Economic journal, XLII (1932), 427-31.

————, International economics, 1933.

HASLAM, JOHN, The paper currency of England, 1856.

HAWTREY, R. G., Trade and credit, 1928.

————, Currency and credit, 3d ed., 1928.

————, The art of central banking, 1932.

HAYEK, F. A. VON, Prices and production, 1931.

————, "A note on the development of the doctrine of 'forced saving,'" Quarterly journal of economics, XLVII (1932), 123-33.

HECKSCHER, E. F. (and others), Sweden, Norway, Denmark and Iceland in the world war, New Haven, 1930.

[HERRIES, J. C.], A review of the controversy respecting the high price of bullion, and the state of our currency, 1811.

HILGERDT, FOLKE, "Foreign trade and the short business cycle," Economic essays in honour of Gustav Cassel, 1933, 273-91.

HILL, EDWIN, Principles of currency, 1856.

HILL, JOHN, An inquiry into the causes of the present high price of gold bullion in England, 1810.

HODGSON, ADAM, Letter . . . to Peel on the currency, 1848.

HOLLANDER, JACOB H., David Ricardo a centenary estimate, Baltimore, 1910.

————, "The development of the theory of money from Adam Smith to David Ricardo," Quarterly journal of economics, XXV (1911), 429-70.

————, "International trade under depreciated paper; a criticism," Quarterly journal of economics, XXXII (1918), 674-90.

HOLLANDER, JACOB H., "Ricardo and Torrens," Economic journal, XXI (1911), 455-68.

HOOLEY, WILLIAM, "On the bullion reserve of the Bank of England," Transactions of the Manchester Statistical Society, 1859-60, 82-96.

HOPKINS, THOMAS, Economical enquiries relative to the laws which regulate rent, profit, wages, and the value of money,1822.

[HORNER, FRANCIS], Review of Thornton, Paper credit of Great Britain, Edinburgh review, I (1802), 172-201.

[————], Review of Lord King, On the effects of the Bank restrictions, Edinburgh review, II (1803), 402-21.

[————], Review of John Wheatley, Remarks on currency and commerce, Edinburgh review, III (1803), 231-52.

HUBBARD, J. G. The currency and the country, 1843.

HUME, DAVID, Political discourses, [1752], in Essays moral, political, and literary, T. H. Green and T. H. Grose ed., 1875.

HUSKISSON, W., The question concerning the depreciation of our currency stated and examined, 1810.

ISLES, K. S., "Australian monetary policy," Economic record, VII (1931), 1-17.

IVERSEN, CARL, Aspects of the theory of international capital movements, Copenhagen, 1935.

JACKSON, RANDLE, The speech of Randle Jackson, Esq., . . . respecting the report of the Bullion Committee, n.d. (1810?).

JACOB, WILLIAM, An historical inquiry into the production and consumption of the precious metals, 1831.

JAMES HENRY, Considerations on the policy or impolicy of the further continuance of the Bank restriction act, 1818.

————, Essays on money, exchanges, and political economy, 1820.

————, State of the nation, 1835.

JOPLIN, THOMAS, Outlines of a system of political economy, 1823.

————, An illustration of Mr. Joplin's views on currency, and plan for its improvement, 1825.

————, Views on the subject of corn and currency, 1826.

————, Views on the currency, 1828.

————, An analysis and history of the currency question, 1832.

————, Currency reform: improvement not depreciation, 1844.

KEYNES, J. M., "The German transfer problem," Economic journal, XXXIX (1929), 1-7, 179-82, 404-408.

————, A treatise on money, 1930.

————, "The commemoration of Thomas Robert Malthus," Economic journal, XLV (1935), 230-34.

KING, LORD, Thoughts on the effects of the Bank restrictions, 2d ed., 1804.

KNIGHT, F. H. "Some fallacies in the interpretation of social cost," Quarterly journal of economics, XXXVIII (1924), 582-606.

——, "On decreasing cost and comparative cost. A rejoinder," Quarterly journal of economics, XXXIX (1925), 331-33.

KREPS, THEODORE J., "Export, import, and domestic prices in the United States, 1926-1930," Quarterly journal of economics, XLVI (1932), 195-207.

LANDRY, A., Manuel d'économique, Paris, 1908.

LAUDERDALE, LORD, A letter on the present measures of finance, 1798.

——, Thoughts on the alarming state of the circulation, Edinburgh, 1805.

——, The depreciation of the paper currency of Great Britain proved, 1812.

——, Further considerations on the state of the currency, Edinburgh, 1813.

——, Sketch of a petition to the Commons House of Parliament, Edinburgh, 1822.

LAUGHLIN, J. LAURENCE, The principles of money, New York, 1903.

LEAGUE OF NATIONS, Report of the Gold Delegation of the Financial Committee, Geneva, 1932.

LEONTIEF, W. W., "The use of indifference curves in the analysis of foreign trade," Quarterly journal of economics, XLVII (1933), 493-503.

LERNER, A., "The diagrammatical representation of cost conditions in international trade," Economica, XII (1932), 346-56.

LESER, EMANUEL, Untersuchungen zur Geschichte der Nationalökonomie, I, 1881.

LEXIS, W., "Handel," Handbuch der politischen Oekonomie, Gustav Schönberg ed., 3d ed., 1891, II, 811-938.

LIVERPOOL, FIRST EARL OF, A treatise on the coins of the realm, [1805], 1880.

[LLOYD, HENRY], An essay on the theory of money, 1771.

LONGFIELD, MOUNTIFORT, Lectures on political economy, Dublin, 1834.

——, Three lectures on commerce and one on absenteeism, Dublin, 1835.

[——], "Banking and currency," Dublin University magazine, XV (1840), 3-15, 218-33; XVI (1840), 371-89, 611-20.

LOWE, JOSEPH, The present state of England in regard to agriculture, trade, and finance, 2d ed., 1823.

[LUBBOCK, J. W.], On currency, 1840.

LUZZATI, LUIGI, "Une conférence internationale pour la paix monétaire," Séances et travaux de l'académie des sciences morales et politiques, new series, LXIX (1908), 358-68.

[McCULLOCH, J. R.], Review of David Ricardo, Proposals for an economical and secure currency, Edinburgh review, XXXI (1818), 53-80.

[————], "Mr. Owen's plans for relieving the national distress," Edinburgh review, XXXII (1819), 453-77.

————, "An essay showing the erroneousness of the prevailing opinions in regard to absenteeism," [1825], reprinted in Treatises and essays on money, exchange, interest, 2d ed., Edinburgh, 1859.

[————], "Fluctuations in the supply and value of money," Edinburgh review, XLIII (1826), 263-98.

————, The principles of political economy, 2d ed., Edinburgh, 1830; 4th ed., Edinburgh, 1849.

[————], Historical sketch of the Bank of England, 1831.

MACLAREN, JAMES, The effect of a small fall in the value of gold upon money, 1853.

[MALTHUS, T. R.], "Depreciation of paper currency," Edinburgh review, XVII (1811), 339-72.

[————], "Review of the controversy respecting the high price of bullion," Edinburgh review, XVIII (1811), 448-70.

————, An inquiry into the nature and progress of rent, 1815.

[————], "Tooke—On high and low prices," Quarterly review, XXIX (1823), 214-39.

————, Principles of political economy, 1st ed., 1820; 2d ed., 1836.

————, The measure of value stated and illustrated, 1823.

MANGOLDT, H. VON, Grundriss der Volkswirthschaftslehre, 2d ed., Stuttgart, 1871.

MANOÏLESCO, MIHAÏL, The theory of protection and international trade, 1931.

————, "Arbeitsproduktivität und Aussenhandel," Weltwirtschaftliches Archiv, XLII (1935, I), 13-43.

MARSHALL, ALFRED, The pure theory of foreign trade, [1879], London School reprint, 1930.

————, Money Credit & Commerce, 1923.

————, Memorials of Alfred Marshall, A. C. Pigou ed., 1925.

————, Official papers by Alfred Marshall, 1926.

MASON, EDWARD S., "The doctrine of comparative cost," Quarterly journal of economics, XLI (1926), 63-93.

MERING, O. F. VON, "Ist die Theorie der internationalen Werte widerlegt?" Archiv für Sozialwissenschaft und Sozialpolitik, LXV (1931), 251-68.

MERING, O. F. VON, Theorie des Aussenhandels, Jena, 1933.

MERIVALE, HERMAN, Lectures on colonization and colonies, 1841-42.

MILL, JAMES, Commerce defended, 1808.

[————], Review of Smith, Essay on the theory of money and exchange, Edinburgh review, XIII (1808), 35-68.

————, Elements of political economy, 1st ed., 1821; 3d ed., 1826.

[MILL, J. S.], "Review of Blake's Observations," Westminster review, II (1824), 27-48.

————, Essays on some unsettled questions of political economy, 1844.

[————], "The currency question," Westminster review, XLI (1844), 579-98.

————, Principles of political economy, 1st ed., 1848; reprint of 7th ed., [1871], Sir W. J. Ashley ed., 1909.

————, Testimony, in Ministère des finances, Enquête sur les principes et les faits généraux qui régissent la circulation monétaire et fiduciaire, Paris, 1867, V, 589-96.

————, Autobiography, 1873.

MILLER, WILLIAM, A plan for a national currency, Glasgow, 1866.

MILLS, R. H., The principles of currency and banking, [1st ed., 1853], 2d ed., 1857.

MILNER, T. H., On the regulation of floating capital, and freedom of currency, 1848.

————, Some remarks on the Bank of England, 1849.

MUSHET, ROBERT, An inquiry into the effects produced on the national currency and rates of exchange, by the Bank restriction bill, 3d ed., 1811.

NEWMARCH, WILLIAM, "An attempt to ascertain the magnitude and fluctuations of the amount of bills of exchange," Journal of the Royal Statistical Society, XIV (1851), 143-83.

NICHOLSON, J. S., Principles of political economy, 1893-97.

NORMAN, G. W., Remarks upon some prevalent errors, with respect to currency and banking, 1838.

————, Letter . . . on money, and the means of economizing the use of it, 1841.

————, Papers on various subjects, 1869.

NORTON, EDWARD, The Bank charter act of 1844 and how to remedy its evils, 3d ed., 1857.

————, National finance and currency, 3d ed., 1873.

OHLIN, BERTIL, "Ist eine Modernisierung der Aussenhandelstheorie erforderlich?" Weltwirtschaftliches Archiv, XXVI (1927, II), 97-115.

————, "The reparations problem," Index, no. 28 (1928), 2-33.

OHLIN, BERTIL, "The reparation problem: a discussion," Economic journal, XXXIX (1929), 172-78, 400-404.

————, "Protection and non-competing groups," Weltwirtschaft-liches Archiv, XXIII (1931, I), 30-45.

————, Interregional and international trade, Cambridge, Mass., 1933.

OPIE, REDVERS, "A neglected English economist: George Poulett Scrope," Quarterly journal of economics, XLIV (1929), 101-37.

OVERSTONE, LORD (SAMUEL JONES LOYD), Further reflections on the state of the currency and the action of the Bank of England, 1837.

————, Tracts and other publications on metallic and paper currency, J. R. McCulloch ed., 1857.

[————], Letters of Mercator on the Bank charter act of 1844, and the state of the currency, n.p., n.d. (*ca.* 1857).

————, The evidence, given by Lord Overstone, before the select committee of the House of Commons of 1857, on Bank acts, with additions, 1858.

————, Correspondence between . . . Lord Overstone, and Henry Brookes, 1862.

[PAGE, RICHARD], Banks and bankers, 1842 (by "Daniel Hardcastle," pseud.).

PAGET, THOMAS, A letter . . . on the true principle of estimating the extent of the late depreciation in the currency, 1822.

PALMER, J. HORSLEY, The causes and consequences of the pressure upon the money-market, 1837.

————, Reply to the reflections . . . of Mr. Samuel Jones Loyd, on the pamphlet entitled "Causes and consequences of the pressure upon the money market," 1837.

PARETO, VILFREDO, Cours d'économie politique, Lausanne, 1896-97.

————, Manuel d'économie politique (transl. from the original Italian), 2d ed., Paris, 1927.

PARNELL, SIR HENRY, Observations upon the state of currency in Ireland, Dublin, 1804.

————, Observations on paper money, banking, and overtrading, 2d ed., 1829.

————, A plain statement of the power of the Bank of England and of the use it has made of it, 2d ed., 1833.

PATTERSON, R. H., "On the rate of interest—and the effects of a high bank-rate during commercial and monetary crises," Journal of the Statistical Society of London, XXXIV (1871), 334-56.

PAYNE, DANIEL BEAUMONT, "An address to the proprietors of bank stock," Pamphleteer, VII (1816), 375-406.

PELL, GEORGE H., Outline of a plan of a national currency, not liable to fluctuations in value, 1841.

[PENNINGTON, JAMES], Memorandum (not published), 1827.

———, "Paper communicated by Mr. Pennington," in Thomas Tooke, A letter to Lord Grenville, on the effects ascribed to the resumption of cash payments on the value of the currency, 1829, Appendix I, pp. 117-27.

———, "Paper communicated by Mr. Pennington," in Robert Torrens, A letter to . . . Melbourne on the causes of the recent derangement in the money market, 2d ed., 1837, pp. 76-80.

———, "Letter addressed to the author by James Pennington, Esq.," in Thomas Tooke, A history of prices, II (1838), 369-78.

———, A letter to Kirkman Finlay, Esq., on the importation of foreign coin, and the value of the precious metals in different countries, 1840.

———, "Letter from Mr. Pennington on the London banking system," in John Cazenove, Supplement to thoughts on a few subjects of political economy, 1861, pp. 48-54.

PHILLIPS, C. A., Bank credit, New York, 1920.

PIERSON, N. G., Principles of economics (transl. from the Dutch), 1902-12.

PIGOU, A. C., "The effect of reparations on the ratio of international interchange," Economic journal, XLII (1932), 532-43.

PLANT, ARNOLD, "Introductory note" to reprint of A letter on the true principles of advantageous exportation, [1818], Economica, XIII (1933), 40-41.

PORTER, G. R., The progress of the nation, new ed., 1851.

PRENTICE, DAVID, Thoughts on the repeal of the Bank restriction law, 1811.

RAITHBY, JOHN, The law and principle of money considered, 1811.

RAVENSTONE, PIERCY, A few doubts as to the correctness of some opinions generally entertained on the subjects of population and political economy, 1821.

READ, SAMUEL, An inquiry concerning the nature and use of money, Edinburgh, 1816.

RICARDO, DAVID, Three letters on the price of gold, [1809], J. H. Hollander ed., Baltimore, 1903.

———, Notes on Malthus' "Principles of political economy," [ms. 1820], Jacob H. Hollander and T. E. Gregory ed., Baltimore, 1928.

———, The works of David Ricardo, J. R. McCulloch ed., 1852.

———, Minor papers on the currency question 1809-1823, Jacob H. Hollander ed., Baltimore, 1932.